LETTERS OF

Archibald MacLeish

1907 *to* 1982

LETTERS OF

Archibald
MacLeish

1907 to 1982

EDITED BY

R. H. Winnick

HOUGHTON MIFFLIN COMPANY
BOSTON
1983

Library of Congress Cataloging in Publication Data

MacLeish, Archibald, 1892–1982
    Letters of Archibald MacLeish, 1907 to 1982.

    Includes index.
    1. MacLeish, Archibald, 1892–1982 — Correspondence.
2. Poets, American — 20th century — Correspondence.
I. Winnick, R. H. II. Title.
PS3525.A27Z48 1983   811'.52   82–11945
ISBN 0–395–32159–X

Printed in the United States of America

V   10 9 8 7 6 5 4 3 2 1

The letter to Elia Kazan was first published in *Esquire* (May 1959). The letters to Alexis Saint-Léger Léger are published here with the authorization of the Fondation Saint-John Perse (Aix-en-Provence, France), proprietor of the manuscripts. All letters with the credit line JFK are from the Ernest Hemingway Collection at the John F. Kennedy Library. All letters with the credit line NN are from the Henry W. and Albert A. Berg Collection, The New York Public Library, Astor, Lenox and Tilden Foundations. Letters with the credit line NYT are copyright © 1925, 1933 by The New York Times Company. Reprinted by permission. Letters with the credit line NJP are published here with the permission of Princeton University Library; with the exception of letters marked NJP to Adlai E. Stevenson (which are located in the Adlai E. Stevenson Papers in Princeton's Seeley G. Mudd Manuscript Library), all letters marked NJP are located in the Rare Book and Manuscript Room of Firestone Library. Letters with the credit line SIU-C are from Special Collections, Morris Library,

Southern Illinois University at Carbondale. Letters with the credit line SUL to Bernard De Voto are from the Bernard De Voto Papers, Stanford University Libraries. Letters with the credit line CLU are from the Department of Special Collections, Research Library, University of California, Los Angeles. Letters with the credit line ICU are located as follows: the letter of 5 June 1919 to Harry P. Judson is from the Presidents' Papers, 1889–1925, Box 47, Folder 32, University of Chicago Archives; letters to Harriet Monroe dated 29 November 1930, c. 5 May 1931, and c. 4 June 1931 are from the *Poetry* Papers, 1912–1936, Box 35, Folder 20, in the Department of Special Collections, University of Chicago Library; the letter dated c. September 1938 is from the *Poetry* Papers, 1936–1953, Series I, Box 15, Folder 13, in the Department of Special Collections, University of Chicago Library. Letters to John Dos Passos, though owned by Mrs. Dos Passos, are located in the John Dos Passos Archives (accession no. 5950ae), Manuscripts Department, University of Virginia Library. The letter to Arthur T. Hadley is from the Records of President Hadley in the Yale University Archives; the letter to Anson P. Stokes is from the Records of Secretary Stokes in the Yale University Archives; letters to Dean Acheson are from the Dean Acheson Papers, Yale University Library; letters to Francis H. Bangs, Stephen Vincent Benét, F. O. Matthiessen, Marianne Moore, Samuel B. Hemingway, Ezra Pound, and H. Phelps Putnam, marked with the credit line YCAL, are from the Collection of American Literature, Beinecke Rare Book and Manuscript Library, Yale University; the letters to Edwin Oviatt and Albert Beecher Crawford, marked with the credit line YARO, are from the Yale University Alumni Records Office, Yale University.

Acknowledgments

I AM PLEASED to extend heartfelt thanks to several persons and institutions whose cooperation and assistance made possible the preparation of this volume.

The following people generously permitted me to examine, make copies of, and publish herein letters from Archibald MacLeish in their personal possession: Alice S. (Mrs. Dean) Acheson, Alexander and Ishbel MacLeish Campbell, Alfred de Liagre, Jr. (photocopy of original document), Honoria Murphy (Mrs. William P.) Donnelly, Elizabeth H. (Mrs. John) Dos Passos, Valerie (Mrs. T. S.) Eliot, Helen E. Ellis, Robert Fitzgerald, Donald Hall, William Heyen, Edward Hoagland, Ilona Karmel, Eliza Howe (Mrs. William Scott) Keith, Harry Levin, Anne T. (Mrs. Ranald H.) Macdonald, Anthony Piccione, Alfred A. Poulin, Jr., May Sarton, Barbara W. Tuchman, Dorothy G. (Mrs. Mark) Van Doren, and Richard Wilbur.

The following people provided copies of letters in their archives and special collections and generously extended permission to publish them in this volume: Dolores Altemus, University of Delaware; Khani Begum and Mary E. Janzen, Southern Illinois University at Carbondale; Edmund Berkeley, Jr., and Joan Echtenkamp, University of Virginia; William H. Bond, Houghton Library, Harvard University; Nancy Bressler and Jean Preston, Princeton University; Timothy C. Callard and Albert W. Olsen, Jr., The Hotchkiss School; Mary Ceibert, University of Illinois at Urbana-Champaign; Erika (Mrs. James H.) Chadbourne, Harvard Law School; Philip N. Cronenwett, Dartmouth College; Lawrence Dowler, Judith A. Schiff, David E. Schoonover, and Patricia Bodak Stark, Yale University; Donald D. Eddy, Cornell University; Clark A. Elliott, Harvard University; Elaine Felsher and Lillian Owens, Time Inc. Archives; John Ferris, Franklin D. Roosevelt Library; Paul T. Heffron, The Library of Congress; Jo August Hills, John F. Kennedy Library (Boston); Margaret E. C. Howland, Greenfield (Massachusetts) Community College; Kenneth A. Lohf, Columbia University; Frank Paluka, University of Iowa; Wesley H. Poling, Alumni Records Office, Yale University; André Rousseau, Fondation Saint-John Perse

(Aix-en-Provence, France); Sem C. Sutter and Elizabeth S. Teleky, University of Chicago; Lola L. Szladits, New York Public Library; Sara Timby, Stanford University; Neda M. Westlake, University of Pennsylvania; Brooke Whiting, University of California, Los Angeles.

The following people allowed me to examine letters in their personal or archival collections, provided information that was useful in the preparation of the notes, or helped (as did many of those mentioned above) in other important ways: David C. Acheson; Carlos Baker; Dr. Francis Hyde Bangs; Ellen (Mrs. Philip) Barry; W. Jackson Bate; Daniel J. Boorstin; Frances M. Brennan; Katharine P. (Mrs. Harvey H.) Bundy; McGeorge Bundy; Stanley Burnshaw; Malcolm Cowley; Robert Cowley; Dorothy (Mrs. Giorgio) de Santillana; Richard Eberhart; Sarah Flynn; Kristin Fossum; Martha MacLeish Fuller; R. H. Ives Gammell; Judith Gleason; Allen Grover; Gerald Gunther; Robert Hawkins; Samuel Hazo; John Houseman; John D. Kendall, University of Massachusetts, Amherst; Arthur Knodel; Edward C. Lathem; James Laughlin; Dorothy M. (Mrs. Alexis) Léger; Mr. and Mrs. Robert A. Lovett; William Hitchcock MacLeish; Robie Macauley; Carolyn de C. MacLeish; Elena (Mrs. J. Noel) Macy; David C. Mearns; William Meredith; Honor Moore; Kathleen J. and Theodore Morrison; Alice-Lee Myers; Stuart Ostrow; Hester (Mrs. Edward M.) Pickman; James B. Reston; Daniel Sargent; Nicholas B. Scheetz, Georgetown University; Arthur Schlesinger, Jr.; William Schuman; Austin W. Scott, Esq.; Carolyn A. Sheehy, The Newberry Library; John D. Stinson, New York Public Library; Joan B. Surrey, Rockford College; Robert Penn Warren; Edward Weeks, Jr.

I gratefully acknowledge the support of the John Simon Guggenheim Memorial Foundation for a Fellowship in 1979–80 that enabled me to gather many of the letters, and much of the information, appearing in this volume. Richard B. McAdoo, formerly director of the Trade Group of Houghton Mifflin Company and now literary executor of the Estate of Archibald MacLeish, has been an intelligent and sympathetic editor and friend. My wife, Catherine R. Harper, applied her skills as a reference librarian to the solution of several thorny problems, and helped in a variety of other ways. Finally, and most important, I thank Archibald and Ada MacLeish for permitting me to embark on the biographical journey of which this volume is the first milestone, for extending to me their famous hospitality on several occasions during the past five years, and for allowing me access to the papers, recollections, and memorabilia of their extraordinary lives.

R. H. Winnick
Princeton, New Jersey

Contents

Introduction

ARCHIBALD MACLEISH, who died on 20 April 1982 just short of his ninetieth birthday, was a playwright, a lawyer, a teacher, a journalist, a Librarian of Congress, an assistant secretary of state, and, above all, a poet. The author of more than forty books of poems, plays, essays, and speeches, he won the Pulitzer Prize three times and received numerous other awards, including the National Medal for Literature and the Presidential Medal of Freedom. Amy Lowell was for a time his mentor; Ernest Hemingway and Dean Acheson were among his closest friends. He worked for publisher Henry Luce and for President Franklin Roosevelt. Adlai Stevenson once worked for *him*. He was called a fascist by communists and a communist by Senator Joseph McCarthy. Though Ezra Pound disdained his poetry, MacLeish was responsible, as much as anyone else, for Pound's release from long confinement in St. Elizabeths Hospital. The letters in this volume, nearly four hundred in all, seem to me to say best, among the many I have seen, what MacLeish did and who he was. They are, in a sense, the autobiography of one of the most remarkable men of our time.

Archibald MacLeish was born in Glencoe, Illinois, on 7 May 1892, the second son of Andrew MacLeish and his third wife, Martha Hillard. Born in Glasgow, Scotland, in 1838, Andrew came to America at the age of eighteen to seek the hand of a Scottish woman, Lilias Young, who had emigrated with her family from Glasgow, and to pursue his career as a merchant in the Far West frontier town, called Chicago, where the Youngs had settled. Andrew and Lilias were married in 1858 and had two daughters, Lily and Blanche, before Lilias died in 1878. In 1881, by now a partner in the wholesale dry-goods firm Carson, Pirie, Scott & Company, of whose Chicago retail store he was founder and manager, Andrew married M. Louise Little of that city, who bore a son, Bruce, in 1882, a year before she, too, died. In 1888, at the age of fifty, Andrew married Martha, eighteen years his junior.

A Connecticut Yankee one of whose ancestors was the Pilgrim leader William Brewster and whose father was a Congregational minister, Martha was a Vassar graduate, a teacher, and, until her marriage, principal of Rockford Seminary, soon to become Rockford College. After her marriage Martha devoted herself mainly to the raising of her stepson Bruce and of her own four children (a fifth, her first child, died in infancy), whose early instruction she managed herself with lesson plans borrowed from John Dewey's School of Education and with stories from the Bible and readings aloud from works of literature. While Andrew occupied himself, when not at "the Store," with the affairs of the University of Chicago, which he had helped to found, and of Chicago's Fourth Baptist Church, where he was the leading layman, Martha also took an active interest in the work of the Visiting Nurse Association, of Chicago's Hull House settlement (founded by Rockford College's first alumna, Jane Addams), and of the National Woman's Foreign Mission Society and Home Mission Society, in which she served terms as vice president and president, respectively. A founder, late in her long life, of the Chicago Round Table of Christians and Jews, Martha was a leading member of several other educational, religious, and civic organizations.

The first of Martha's four children to survive infancy was Norman, born in 1890, a sensitive, sweet-natured child who showed early signs of being an intellectual prodigy. Archie, two years Norman's junior — and older by two and five years, respectively, than his brother Kenneth and sister Ishbel — was also bright, but was high-strung and often combative. The enlightened theories of parenting that Martha practiced on all her children seemed to work least well on him.

At Hotchkiss and then at Yale, MacLeish distinguished himself by his academic and literary efforts, and was Class Poet and editor of the literary magazine at both schools. At Yale, where he was a member of the Class of 1915, his service on the *Lit*, as captain of the water polo team, and as a second-string member of the football squad led to his being tapped for Skull & Bones, the most highly esteemed of Yale's secret societies.

By his graduation from Hotchkiss, MacLeish had met his future wife, Ada Taylor Hitchcock, the gay and witty only child of a prosperous hardware merchant in Farmington, Connecticut. Well before his graduation from Yale, and Ada's from Westover School, they considered themselves engaged. But when he left New Haven with degree in hand in June 1915, MacLeish had no clear idea of what he would do with his life, or which of the several possibilities would permit, at the earliest date, his marriage to Ada.

After considering and then rejecting both a mercantile career with his father's firm and graduate study in literature, MacLeish entered, almost by default, Harvard Law School, with the understanding that his father would increase his allowance after one year by an amount sufficient to permit his marriage at that time. MacLeish made the *Law Review* at the end of his first law school year, married Ada in June 1916, and graduated in 1919 with the Fay Diploma, awarded by the law school faculty to the member of the graduating class who ranked highest in scholarship, conduct, and character, and who gave evidence of the greatest promise. After completing the second of his three years of law school, he had served eighteen months in the army, sailing to France with a hospital unit, transferring to the field artillery, and taking part in the second battle of the Marne. Kenneth, MacLeish's younger brother and a navy flier, was killed in action a month before the armistice.

After graduating from law school, MacLeish lectured in constitutional law at Harvard, spent the summer of 1920 as an editor *pro tem* of *The New Republic*, and then, while continuing to teach, joined Choate, Hall & Stewart, a leading Boston law firm. He excelled as a lawyer, and soon established himself as a protégé of the firm's senior partner, Charles F. Choate, Jr. But the law failed, as had commerce, teaching, and journalism, to capture his imagination, and he was increasingly convinced that his true calling lay in another direction: poetry. In 1923, after much soul-searching, MacLeish took the most daring gamble of his life. Declining the offer of a partnership in Choate, Hall & Stewart (an act many colleagues and friends regarded as perfect folly), he resigned from the firm, sold his house on Coolidge Hill Road in Cambridge, and set sail for France with his wife, six-year-old son, and infant daughter. That, he knew, was where the allowance his father had generously agreed to renew would go the farthest; that was where Ada could do the most with her natural, and considerable, talent as a concert soprano; that, above all, was where one went in 1923 if, as did MacLeish, one aspired to the life of a practicing poet.

For the next five years, with the exception of several visits home, MacLeish lived — and worked — abroad, mostly in France, but with trips to Belgium, Switzerland, Spain, Italy, Austria, Germany, and even Persia. Along the way he met, and saw much of, several of the leading young writers of his generation. With the publication of several poems and books of poems while he was abroad and immediately thereafter, he began to be regarded by many as belonging to that select group himself.

Never an expatriate though living abroad, MacLeish returned with his family to the States in 1928 and settled, as he and Ada had long planned to do, on a New England farm, the place they chose being the home in Conway, Massachusetts, where Ada continues to live. Enjoying an income from a stock settlement that was part of his father's estate (Andrew having died, at age eighty-nine, in the year of their return), MacLeish planned to lead, if on a modest scale, the life of a gentleman farmer–poet.

In the fall of 1929, however, Henry R. Luce, the dynamic young cofounder of *Time* magazine, completed plans for a new magazine of business to be called *Fortune*, and invited MacLeish, who had edited the Education section of *Time* in 1923, to join its editorial staff. The offer, which included a handsome salary and an arrangement whereby MacLeish could take periodic extended leaves to work on his own writing, was too attractive to refuse. It permitted him to complete his most ambitious poem to date, *Conquistador* (1932), which he had begun to work on in France and for which he would win, in 1933, his first Pulitzer Prize.

Despite the generosity of the arrangement, which also enabled him to write three plays and numerous other poems during leaves from the magazine, MacLeish became increasingly disturbed by *Time*'s coverage of the world political situation, and particularly of the Spanish civil war. He was no less disturbed, perhaps, by his lack of upward mobility in a growing journalistic empire that seemed to reward managerial and financial skills more than the ability to write a good story. In 1938, having written more than a hundred *Fortune* articles over eight years, MacLeish resigned.

President James B. Conant of Harvard had tried and failed to recruit MacLeish for a position at Harvard University Press in the mid-1930s. After learning that MacLeish was available, Conant approached him again, this time offering to name him the first curator of the Nieman Foundation at Harvard. MacLeish accepted the appointment and served for a year, launching a program under which young but tested journalists spend time at Harvard doing, essentially, whatever they like. MacLeish might have stayed longer, but in the spring of 1939 President Roosevelt, aware of MacLeish's pro–New Deal articles in *Fortune* and of his impressively varied credentials, asked him to accept appointment as Librarian of Congress, to succeed the retiring Herbert Putnam. If giving up the law was MacLeish's most daring decision, this was his most difficult.

A frequent — and valid — criticism of MacLeish's early poetry was that it was excessively derivative, particularly of Eliot but also of other poets of the time. In *Conquistador* MacLeish had emerged into his own more clearly than ever, and the poems of the 1930s — collected in *Frescoes for Mr. Rockefeller's City* (1933), in *Poems, 1924–1933*, and in *Public Speech* (1936), marked further progress toward a distinctive MacLeish poetic idiom. The job of Librarian of Congress, he knew, might — indeed would — occupy so much of his time and energy that significant advances in his art might be thwarted, perhaps forever. He was strongly inclined to refuse the appointment.

But President Roosevelt was not an easy person to say no to, and the President was convinced — as was his close friend and adviser Felix Frankfurter — that MacLeish was just the person for the job. MacLeish's nomination was announced in June 1939 and he took office the following October.

The reorganization over which MacLeish presided transformed the Library of Congress from a nineteenth- into a twentieth-century institution. The Library's administrative and fiscal procedures were brought up to date, its holdings were examined systematically for the first time, and its policies, purposes, and priorities were subjected to a thorough review. Before congressional budget committees MacLeish fought for, and won, significant increases in Library salaries, the effect of which was felt through the entire profession. In the Library, he inaugurated new cultural programs and revitalized existing ones. In speaking engagements around the country he helped to redefine the librarian's profession by urging librarians to see that their proper place in the modern world was as champions of a cause: freedom of speech, freedom of thought, and, ultimately, human liberty.

In one of his more controversial public pronouncements, MacLeish had argued, in *The Irresponsibles* (1940), that the scholars and writers of his generation had abdicated their responsibility to fight fascism and thus had unwittingly helped to disarm and demoralize the Western democracies. The piece caused a furor when it appeared, but it, as much as anything, probably accounted for MacLeish's appointment in December 1941 as director of the new Office of Facts and Figures — while he continued to serve as Librarian of Congress. Intended by the President to serve as a clearinghouse of information about the war effort, the OFF lasted only six months, was embattled from the start (and MacLeish with it), but did its job and was eventually replaced by the Office of War Information, in which MacLeish served as associate director under Elmer Davis. In December 1944, the reorganization of the Library of Congress completed, MacLeish resigned as Librarian, hoping to return to private life. But the government still had need of him. Shortly after Edward R. Stettinius, Jr., succeeded Cordell Hull as secretary of state, MacLeish was appointed assistant secretary of state for public and cultural relations, a post he held until the end of the war.

After World War II MacLeish served as chairman of the American delegation to the UNESCO organizing conference in London and was urged by several foreign delegates to consider serving as the organization's first secretary-general. But having spent nearly a decade in public life, and despite his hope that UNESCO might bring about "the republic of letters" in his time, MacLeish decided that the time had come when he must once again serve his art. In 1947 he returned to Conway and, except for one or two goodwill trips, he remained a private citizen.

The first major work MacLeish produced after the war was a long poem, *Actfive* (1948), that sought to interpret the events of the war as an expression of the heroic struggle of humanity to "endure and love." Received by critics with tepid interest when it was received at all, the poem, coming as it did after a poetic hiatus of so many years, signaled a decline in MacLeish's critical reputation from which, with the notable exception of the response to *J.B.*, it has never fully recovered.

J.B. (1958), for which he won his third Pulitzer Prize (the second was for *Collected Poems, 1917–1952*), was a verse drama based on the Book of Job. Thematically similar to *Actfive*, it took five years to complete and was MacLeish's most resounding critical and popular success; neither the response to the plays immediately preceding it — *The Trojan Horse* (1952) and *This Music Crept by Me upon the Waters* (1954) — nor to those immediately after — *Herakles* (1965) and *Scratch* (1970) — even remotely approached it. Many playgoers found Elia Kazan's Broadway production, starring Pat Hingle, Christopher Plummer, and Raymond Massey, a most powerful theatrical experience.

In 1949 MacLeish had rejoined the Harvard faculty as Boylston Professor of Rhetoric and Oratory, one of the oldest and most distinguished Harvard chairs. His thirteen years of incumbency, ending in 1962, gave him an opportunity to meet, and in part to create, the next generation of young writers. Among those who gained admission to his advanced writing course were William Alfred, Ilona Karmel, Edward Hoagland, Donald Hall, and George Plimpton; they, like many others of MacLeish's English S students, came to regard their professor as a friend. MacLeish's popular lecture course, which he called An Approach to Poetry, paid dividends of another kind: out of it came, by way of a series of public lectures, his first (and only) book of literary criticism, *Poetry and Experience* (1960).

A year or two into the Boylston professorship, MacLeish decided that one semester a year of teaching was enough. Thanks to Dean McGeorge Bundy and Provost Paul H. Buck, a one-semester-per-year teaching load was arranged, giving MacLeish free time that resulted, in conjunction with Harvard's congenial atmosphere, in some of his best work. *Collected Poems, 1917–1952* and *Songs for Eve* (1954) contained many of these new poems; in 1953 the former book was awarded (in addition to the Pulitzer Prize) a National Book Award and the Bollingen Prize for Poetry.

xvi

In 1952 the MacLeishes joined, and had a house built at, the Mill Reef Club, Antigua, and for many years thereafter La Désirade, as they called the place, was their winter home. There, at Conway, and in Cambridge, they led their lives, did their work, and enjoyed the company of their family (including their children, Kenneth, Mary Hillard, and William Hitchcock, and *their* families) and of their many devoted friends. After his retirement from Harvard in 1962 MacLeish published several books of poetry and prose, lectured and traveled widely, and continued to be what Homer said a poet was: "a man who knows the world." In the opinion of many of his friends, colleagues, and associates, few in his age knew the world as well.

* * *

Archibald MacLeish gave me access to all the letters in his personal possession (with the understandable exception of his letters to and from his wife), and to the letters among his papers at the Library of Congress and at all other repositories. He was also thoughtful in encouraging his friends, relatives, former colleagues, and other associates to help me in my work, and he and Mrs. MacLeish were extraordinarily generous with their time and their hospitality on numerous occasions over the past five years. Thanks to the many others helpful in the preparation of this book are offered in the Acknowledgments.

The letters in this volume may be divided into three general categories: those handwritten by MacLeish, those typed by him, and those typed by another from his dictation. With handwritten (autograph) letters, I have preserved unchanged all instances of idiosyncratic spelling, punctuation, and grammar, so that such letters duplicate typographically the way they were written. With letters MacLeish typed himself, I have preserved only such departures from standard form as appear to me to have been deliberate; I have silently corrected, however, such errors as are clearly mere mis-strikes of the typewriter keyboard. With letters typed by another for MacLeish, I have silently corrected both mis-strikes and such aural or orthographic errors as the spelling *Pappie* for *Pappy* (Hemingway) or the spelling *ferver* for *fervor*.

Dates that stand alone were given by MacLeish in the original document. Dates or portions of dates enclosed in square brackets were established on the basis of a postmark or internal references; since the date given in a postmark may or may not correspond to the actual date of a letter's composition, readers concerned with accuracy should take such dates as approximate. Dates in brackets and also preceded by *c.* (for *circa*) were established by such circumstantial evidence as the dates of letters to which they replied or that replied to them, or, more commonly, by internal references. Dates followed by a question mark and enclosed in brackets are still more open to question.

To avoid freighting the text with a profusion of changing street addresses (the MacLeishes having lived in some dozens of places over the years), I have recorded town or city names but not street addresses even when such addresses occur in the original documents. Town or city names that stand alone were given by MacLeish as part of the letters in which they appear, or were supplied on the basis of a street address written in the original document. Town or city names in brackets were established on the basis of a printed letterhead or a postmark; since, however, a letter bearing a letterhead or a postmark that names one place may in fact have been written in another, readers concerned with accuracy should assume such bracketed places of origin to be merely probable. Places of origin followed by question marks and enclosed in brackets are, as with dates so marked, even less conclusively established.

Readers who wish to know the bibliographic sources of letters and their original form may refer to the abbreviated credit lines immediately following each letter, which credit lines are explained in the Key to Abbreviations.

Key to Abbreviations

EACH LETTER in this volume is followed immediately by an abbreviated two-part credit line that indicates the nature of the document from which the published version was derived and that document's location, private or archival. (See the Acknowledgments and the copyright page for additional information on private and archival sources.) The portion of each credit line to the left of the colon is explained as follows:

ALS	autograph letter, signed
FDr	first draft
P	printed version of letter
P-TEL	printed version of telegram
TCO	typewritten copy of original letter
TL-C	typewritten letter, carbon copy
TL-Dr	typewritten letter, draft
TLS	typewritten letter, signed
TL-U	typewritten letter, unsigned

The portion of each credit line to the right of the colon is explained as follows:

M	Papers of Archibald MacLeish
CLU	Research Library, University of California, Los Angeles
CtY	Yale University Library (*see also* YARO, YCAL)
DLC	Manuscript Division, The Library of Congress
DeU	University of Delaware Library
FSJP	Fondation Saint-John Perse
GCC	Greenfield (Massachusetts) Community College
HMCO	Houghton Mifflin Company
ICU	Regenstein Library, The University of Chicago
IU	The University of Illinois at Urbana-Champaign
IaU	The University of Iowa Libraries, Iowa City
InU	The University of Indiana Library, Bloomington
JFK	John F. Kennedy Library, Boston
MH	The Houghton Library, Harvard University

MH (ARCHIVES)	Harvard University Archives
NIC	Cornell University
NN	New York Public Library
NNC	Rare Book and Manuscript Library, Columbia University
NYT	The New York Times
NHpR	Franklin D. Roosevelt Library, Hyde Park, New York
NhD	Dartmouth College Library
NjP	Princeton University Library
PU	University of Pennsylvania Library
SIU-C	Morris Library, Southern Illinois University at Carbondale
SUL	Stanford University Libraries
ViU	University of Virginia Library
YARO	Yale University Alumni Records Office
YCAL	Collection of American Literature, Beinecke Library, Yale University

ACHESON	Papers of Alice S. (Mrs. Dean) Acheson
CAMPBELL	Papers of Alexander and Ishbel MacLeish Campbell
de LIAGRE	Papers of Alfred de Liagre, Jr.
DONNELLY	Papers of Honoria Murphy (Mrs. William P.) Donnelly
ELIOT	Papers of Valerie (Mrs. T. S.) Eliot
FITZGERALD	Papers of Robert Fitzgerald
HALL	Papers of Donald Hall
HEYEN	Papers of William Heyen
HOAGLAND	Papers of Edward Hoagland
HOTCHKISS	The Hotchkiss School, Lakeville, Connecticut
KARMEL	Papers of Ilona Karmel
KEITH	Papers of Eliza Howe (Mrs. William Scott) Keith
KNODEL	Papers of Arthur Knodel
LEVIN	Papers of Harry Levin
MACDONALD	Papers of Mr. and Mrs. Ranald H. Macdonald, Jr.
PICCIONE	Papers of Anthony Piccione
TIME	Time Inc. Archives
TUCHMAN	Papers of Barbara W. Tuchman
VAN DOREN	Papers of Dorothy G. (Mrs. Mark) Van Doren
WILBUR	Papers of Richard Wilbur
YALE D.N.	Yale Daily News

LETTERS OF

Archibald MacLeish

1907 *to* 1982

Martha Hillard MacLeish to Huber Gray Buehler[1]

My dear Mr. Buehler,   18 June 1907   [Glencoe, Illinois]

I have arranged to have Archie's examinations superintended by one of our High School teachers, Mr. B. E. Powell. He has History and Civics. Archie studied Greek and Roman History with him last year, but as he is not trying an examination in those subjects I think that this arrangement will meet with your approval.

I want to explain our seeming fickleness in this matter. My husband has never been so enthusiastic over sending the boys East to school as I, who am a Connecticut Yankee. It was with difficulty that I secured his consent to the application, and later when Archie became very much interested in a chicken business which he has been conducting for a year with real success, and wanted to stay at home one more year to watch the development of his fancy stock, and reap the benefit of his spring labors, his father thought that might be the best course for him. He has been doing well in the High School this past year which was another argument in his father's mind against change. With this situation I did not write for examination papers, though perhaps it would have been better if I had.

I make this full explanation that you may understand. I am very sure that Mr. MacLeish has only to see the results of life at the Hotchkiss to be very glad his boy is going early enough to have three years there.[2]

Archie would like, in case he passes the examinations for 1910, to try the Geometry and English of the Lower Middle year when he comes on in the fall. I suppose there is no harm in his doing so, though I think there is very little doubt that his English, which has been exceedingly easy for him in the High School, will prove defective by your standards.

I enclose the check for 5\underline{^{00}}$ for the special examination, and wish to send with it my apologies for the trouble which our lack of decision is causing you.

With sincere appreciation of the work which you are doing for boys, believe me   Yours very sincerely,

                    Martha Hillard MacLeish.

ALS: HOTCHKISS

1. Headmaster of The Hotchkiss School, Lakeville, Connecticut.   2. On July 5 Buehler informed Mrs. MacLeish that her son had not done well enough on his algebra and

Latin examinations to permit his admission to Hotchkiss as a member of the lower middle class. In September, Archibald MacLeish — hereinafter referred to as, simply, M — entered Hotchkiss as a so-called junior (that is, freshman), with four rather than three years of schooling to complete before graduation.

To Andrew MacLeish

Dear father:-   21 September 1907   [Lakeville, Connecticut]

School is pretty well started now, and I find that I like it pretty well. I haven't been homesick much, but last night I felt pretty blue. Can you write me and send me mothers address, by the next mail?[1] I forgot to get it. Evrybody is supposed to go out for the foot ball team, and they are supposed to get their stuff here at school in order that it may be uniform and of good material. The bill will be sent by a firm here in Conneticut and will amount to about $12.00[.] I know that this is a large sum but it was necessary for me to get them. The rooms here are very bare and cold, and some of the fellows have theirs papered. I don't want to do that as it will be too expensive but I would like to get things (school flags, pillows etc.) from old fellows, if you think best. of course I would have to pay for them, cash down. My 50¢ a week wouldn't do much good in this connection. How is evry one at home? I would like to hear from you all. It makes a fellow feel a lot better to get a few letters.   your loving son   Archie.

ALS: M

1. Mrs. MacLeish may have gone to visit her Hillard relatives in Connecticut after escorting her son to Hotchkiss. She may also have had business to attend to in the East connected with her work for the National Woman's Foreign Mission Society.

To Huber Gray Buehler

Dear Dr. Buehler:-   [c. October 1907]   [Lakeville]

I have heard that there is a vacant room in the third story of Dr. Robinsons[1] Cottage. Would it inconvenience you a great deal to let me have that room? I know I could study a great deal better over there, because it would be so much quieter than the main building room which I now occupy. I am pretty sure I would get along better in every way. I would have a little time to myself and have a chance to read a little from my Bible in the morning. A thing which, without exageration, I hardly dare do over in main unless I get up very early. I don't say this to try to have you pity me or anything like that. It is the honest truth. There are many other reasons also and I hope very much you will let me make this change. I know Mother would be only too glad to

have me get the room, and I hope you will at least speak to me about it.
I am   yours very respectfully   Archie MacLeish.
ALS: HOTCHKISS

1. James J. Robinson, a member of the Hotchkiss faculty.

To Andrew MacLeish

Dear Father:-   10 October 1907 [Lakeville]
   I have not sent a list of my expenditures for the last half month,
because it was only half a month. I will include them in my Oct.
account. I hope every-body and every-thing, not forgetting the chickens,
is getting along well at Craigie Lea. I am getting to like it here more and
more. Aunt Mary[1] has just been here, and will probably come up again
tomorrow morning. You will be interested to know that my particular
freind here is a grandson of the last Earl of Douglas. His father, who
married a classmate of mothers, has become an American and does not
care to go back and take up the succession. I am getting along finely in
my work here. At least I think I am. I will get my report card on
Saturday. Tell mother my new room is a dandy. It is in Meeker cottage,
just at the south end of Biscuit Hall, and has two windows, two glims, a
big closet and dandy wall paper. I will write her soon and send a sample
of H. blue.   your loving son

                  my new signature   *A H L e i s h*.

P. S.   Please excuse the scrawl. I haven't got a good pen.
ALS: M

1. Mary Robbins Hillard, a sister of M's mother and the founder and principal of
Westover School, Middlebury, Connecticut.

Martha Hillard MacLeish to Huber Gray Buehler

My dear Dr. Buehler,   18 October 1907 [Glencoe]
   The bill for Archie's half-yearly tuition was forwarded to me in New
England. I mailed it back to Mr. MacLeish, and he has in some way
mislaid it. Will you be kind enough to have another draft of it sent him?
   I am also enclosing Archie's application for violin lessons. As to the
time of practising, I think he should give one study period a day. That
will probably be as much as he can afford to give in general, without
cutting out more of his out-door life than I wish him to lose.
   I had a few moments' visit with Archie last Saturday, as I passed

5

through Lakeville, en route for Chicago. I thought he was looking in very fine condition, and he seemed very happy. He is greatly pleased with his new room, and I want to thank you for making the change for him.

His report, which came home last night, shows that he is taking hold of his work well, and altogether I feel very happy and safe about him. I feel sure that the experiences and environment of the next four years will go far toward helping him to become a worthy and useful man.

Please remember me to Mrs. Buehler and believe that Mr. MacLeish and I thoroughly appreciate what you are trying to do for all your boys, Archie among the rest.

Very cordially yours,   Martha H. MacLeish

ALS: HOTCHKISS

Martha Hillard MacLeish to Huber Gray Buehler

My dear Dr. Buehler,   26 October 1907   Glencoe

In view of our conversation concerning the hazing at Hotchkiss, I am sending you a part of a letter just received from Archie. He has been in a very homesick and low-spirited state for the past week, and this letter would seem to account for it. It will give you an inside view that I think you may be glad to get. Evidently some of the seniors are somewhat overwhelmed by a sense of their individual importance, and are forgetting the responsibilities of seniorhood.

Archie seems not to have made any friends yet among the older boys. He speaks only of one or two of the new boys. I tried to introduce him to Norman Donaldson,[1] who used to know Norman MacLeish, Archie's brother, at the Chicago University School of Education, but had no opportunity. I think that if Archie could know one or two of the old boys, and get their point of view, it would help him to adjust himself.

Please dont take too seriously his statements of his feeling toward Hotchkiss. He is in a desperate moment, and he is a very intense boy. He really appreciates the school, and will be as loyal as anyone could wish, when he gets adjusted.

Sunday night. I could not finish this yesterday. Since beginning it two more letters have come from Archie, all in the same vein, begging that he may go somewhere else next year. Of course we want him to stay at Hotchkiss, and I am sorry to see him show the white feather, but I know he is having a hard time of it. When I wrote you a few days since I thought he was over his homesickness. He is reserved and shy, and does not make friends as easily as some boys. Mr. Monahan[2] thinks he had better not play football just now, and he seems to have no athletics. He loves long tramps if he can find other boys to join him. If he can be put in touch with a few more boys it will help him.

Yours very sincerely,   Martha H. MacLeish

[*Enclosed with the above, in Mrs. MacLeish's hand, was the following:*]

copy

Still naked, while the fellows snapped him with wet towels. He was pretty sick I can tell you. It does no good to tell the faculty. The fellows are afraid to tell the truth. Now what do you think of that for a nice state of affairs? I simply hate it here. I hope you will consider sending me to some other school next year. I don't believe I could live here for four years. — — — — — — — — — — — —

I am getting along well in my work except when I am too homesick. This homesickness is usually brought on by fear of those bullying seniors. I hope you wont laugh at this. I am not talking for effect. It is the truth. One of them came up to me the other day and told me I was going to get it for not holding a door open for him. I just barely got off, but I can tell you I was most certainly homesick for a few days. — — — — — — — — — — — — — — —

Please dont laugh at this letter and say all this is for my good. It is very real to me. But I know you'll understand, wont you?

Your very loving son,   Archibōld MacLeish.

(His signature shows that there's a gleam of humor left in him. M.H. MacL.)

ALS: HOTCHKISS

1. Norman Vaux Donaldson, a classmate of M's at Hotchkiss and at Yale and later head of Yale University Press. 2. Otto F. Monahan, physical education director at Hotchkiss.

Martha Hillard MacLeish to Huber Gray Buehler

My dear Dr. Buehler,   14 February 1909 [Glencoe]

Thank you very much for your kind note regarding Archie. It is certainly gratifying to know that he is developing the ability to write well, but I am even more pleased to know that he is gaining the power, perhaps I should say the capacity, for honest, earnest, steady work. His marks would indicate that this latter is true, and it is a capacity that he lacked when he went to Hotchkiss. Mr. MacLeish and I both feel that Archie has gained very much in every way from his year and a half with you, and we look forward with pleasure to the two and a half years more of the same influences. I do not believe there is a school in the world that does more to produce moral earnestness and manly

7

self-reliance than Hotchkiss, and I am very glad that this particular boy has the good fortune to be there.

You will perhaps remember what a struggle he had with homesickness when he first went there. Now his loyalty and devotion to the school are in the same measure.

With full appreciation of what you are doing for your boys, and with kind regards for Mrs. Buehler, in both of which Mr. MacLeish joins, believe me   Yours most cordially,   Martha H. MacLeish

ALS: HOTCHKISS

Andrew MacLeish to Huber Gray Buehler

My dear Dr. Buehler: 22 April 1910   [Chicago]

Yours of 20th inst., concerning the escapade of Archie and his companions, reached me to-day.[1] We had previously heard from him by telegram and letter, both of which showed his realization of the folly and impropriety of his conduct.

The salutary feature of the affair is that Archie was thoroughly scared at the possibility of his being expelled from school, and expressed the deepest penitence to his parents for his disobedience and thoughtlessness, and his willingness to submit to any punishment that might follow. His expressions of love for Hotchkiss explained his fear lest his offense should prove unpardonable.

I think the whole episode will prove salutary in Archie's case, at least, and he has been admonished that his offense was unworthy of him and of his standing in the school; and that it involved violation of law, thoughtlessness, and a bad example to the younger students.

Mrs. MacLeish and myself feel that the action taken by the Faculty in this case is right and proper.[2] We are very thankful that Archie's honor and integrity were not involved in this affair and that it was only the thoughtlessness and impulsiveness of youth that produced his misconduct.   I am   Very truly yours,   Andrew MacLeish

TLS: HOTCHKISS

1. On Sunday, April 17, M and four other Hotchkiss students had left school, hired an automobile in town, and driven to Pittsfield, Massachusetts, some forty miles away. This was in clear violation of school rules, and could have resulted in their expulsion or suspension.   2. M and his companions were punished with an indefinite period of sequestration, which barred them from visiting all living quarters except their own, from participating in or observing any athletic or other school activities (except study, chapel, Bible-study society, and appointments with faculty), from visiting the village of Lakeville, and from "riding, driving, and motoring."

To Huber Gray Buehler

My dear Mr. Buehler.   12 August [1910]   Manchester [England]

I recieved the enclosed this evening, and I am rather worried about the English rateing. On the board examination I got a fairly high mark and I certainly took everything in the way of elementary English that was offered by the Examiners so you see I hardly understand the mark. Can you tell me if there is something I ought to take in the fall?

My chief reason in writing this is to unburden my mind of certain things that have been weighing on it rather heavily since my automobile escapade. I have felt at other times that any thing I might say on the subject would be taken as needless. By that I mean that, had I spoken of it before my term of sequestration was up, I might have been suspected of false motives.

Of course that was a foolish fear but it hindered me. All this explanation simply leads up to the statement that I am and have been heartily ashamed of myself for my part in the trip. Since then I have felt acutely that not only you but many members of the faculty had lost a good deal of what little faith they may have had in me before. Of course you have a right to expect that I should be ashamed and I'm afraid I have quite failed to make you understand just what I mean. I'd give anything to have the ability to undo what I did that day and regain your confidence.

I'm afraid I've made quite a bungle of the three years that I've had at school and I can tell you I am thankful that I have a fourth left me. I feel so because of somethings Mr. Buell[1] very kindly told me about the opinion held by the faculty about me. He said that I had a reputation for being very irresponsible and "kiddish", and even for not being straightforward. I was very much surprised, I'm afraid, and it made me feel kind of shaky for a while. I don't doubt but that I had been concieted before.

Please believe that I say these things knowing myself that they must be true if you believe them so, and hoping that you will believe me when I say that I want to try to live them down. I wish I could feel that you will understand as I know you will when I stop to consider. I love the school as much, I believe, as my own people, and I am very thankful that I shall have one more chance. If ever you can use me, and you feel that you can trust me, please do.

I'm afraid I've made a miserable botch of this letter

                    very respectfully yours   Archie MacLeish

ALS: HOTCHKISS

1. Walter H. Buell, a member of the Hotchkiss faculty.

Martha Hillard MacLeish to Huber Gray Buehler

My dear Mr. Buehler,   13 March 1911   [Asheville, North Carolina]

I was glad to note in your letter received yesterday that you have had a good talk with Archie. I was just on the point of writing to ask if you would try to do so, as his last letter to me indicates that he is having a difficult time in his religious experience. He is at sea in the matter of faith, and his spiritual life does not mean to him what it once did.

Archie's first religious experience came to him as a little child, when he was less than ten years old. It was very real, but it was a child's experience, and I think the time has come when he must face the question again, and from the young man's standpoint reconsecrate himself to Christ.

There are certain things in Archie's nature that make faith hard for him. He intellectually wants to see to the very bottom, the last end of everything. He takes nothing for granted, and he doesn't realize that spiritual truth is not to be discovered by the same logical processes as intellectual truth. Also I'm afraid he doesn't do the things that are necessary for the feeding of his spiritual life. He admitted to me last summer that he had not taken the place in St. Luke's[1] and in the religious life of the school that he ought to have taken. I'm afraid this may be true this year as well. It is so important that he puts himself right in these matters while he is still at Hotchkiss.

I cannot help fearing that Archie's success in his literary work has not been altogether good for him in point of character.[2] He needs to realize that any ability he may have is a gift to him, and that he is responsible for the use he makes of it.

Also he is selfish, with the selfishness of a strong nature. It means achievement and power, but it means limitation and emptyness of life unless he makes something far bigger than himself the object of his living. He hasn't had the big vision yet, or if he has he hasn't been obedient to it.

Forgive me for troubling you with so long a letter, but I am sure you who know boys so well, and who have his respect, can help him. If you have not covered the ground already I hope an opportunity to talk further may occur.

Yours very sincerely,   Martha H. MacLeish

ALS: HOTCHKISS

1. The Hotchkiss Bible-study society.   2. M's contributions to literary supplements of *The Hotchkiss Record*, of which he was editor in chief in his senior year, by March 1911 included a poem ("The Song of the Canoe"), a short story, and four essays. He had also been elected Class Poet, as he would be again four years later at Yale.

To the Editor of the Yale Daily News

Sir: [29 January 1913] [New Haven]

The most interesting part of the News communication to the casual reader is that untried space which lies "between the lines." "1914's" communication to yesterday's paper offered unexampled opportunities for such as cared to venture into that seductive field. The libel laws, however, block the way to a full exposition of the matters there unfolded, and I must confine myself to vague surprise at reading in such a communication that "in universities the stress is laid on the mental development."[1]

The charge that the Sophomore Class desires the abolition of the Rush because of cowardice is, of course, too true for rebuttal. But in spite of that shameful fact it rather sticks in my mind that the cause of the entire discussion is the fact that last year's Rush was a failure. And last year's Rush was a failure because last year's Sophomores — with the exception, of course, of "1914" — failed to put in their appearance.

But there are reasons for the abolition of the time-honored custom in addition to our own natural fear of the Freshmen. In the first place, the Rush originally existed merely as an opportunity for the conclusion of hostilities between two Classes which were drawn to each other by a pre-historic "hatred." That enmity has now passed and with it the excuse for the combat, except in so far as communications like yesterday's may arouse the old ire. As for its value in preparing the participants for fist fights in after life we can only express the belief that no member of the present Sophomore Class has pugilistic ambitions.

Personally even the fact that the Rush would enable me "to take care of myself" "outside of the campus" (Poli's[2] perhaps?) hardly lends charm to the prospect of smiting and being smitten by the Class of 1916 against which I can summon no wrath whatever.   A. MacL.

P: YALE D.N.

1. M's letter and the letter — signed "1914" — to which it replied represented opposing positions in a lively debate then taking place on the Yale campus over the future of the Fence Rush, an annual event held on Washington's Birthday and involving a symbolic — and sometimes violent — battle between the freshman and sophomore classes for possession of the so-called Sophomore Fence. 2. A popular local theater.

To Huber Gray Buehler

My dear Dr Buehler;   [17 February 1914] [New Haven]

Your very kind letter has left me as literally speechless as I remember to have been these several years.[1] Indeed dumbness is not usually my vice — rather its opposite — and for that reason I find the embarrassment of scriptoral stutterings rather painfully keen. You have been so good as to commend by word my poor strivings after such light as illumes these somber years. I can only say that your "well done" carries a full measure of content.

As regards my immediate plans upon graduation I am still characteristically hazy. Your suggestion is very welcome indeed and should I decide upon such a life work I could only hope that you would watch over my first feeble chippings at the shell.

Trusting to see you shortly I remain   yours sincerely

Archibald MacLeish

ALS: HOTCHKISS

1. Buehler, in a letter dated February 16, had complimented M on his fine academic record at Yale, and had invited M to let him know if he had any thought of taking up educational work after graduation, including, perhaps, at Hotchkiss.

To the Editor of the Yale Daily News

Sir: [17 November 1914] [New Haven]

Yale is not overwhelmed with icons. A few brilliant names, a score of memorable lives, and our idolatry is complete. For that reason the preservation of such shrines as we possess is doubly important. Man — even the Senior — cannot exist nobly without objects of veneration. When, therefore, we see in the latest number of our exceptionable humorous paper a reference to "Nathan's strangulation" we cannot help but feel a sense of loss. Hale is our chiefest hero. To mock his supreme sacrifice is to mock what most of us hold worthy of reverence. The phrase is probably the cheap coinage of a cheap mind which can no more conceive the grandeur of martyrdom than it can realize the delicacies of humor. But the editors are to be held responsible, and they must eventually shoulder the blame which such errors of taste will arouse.[1]   Archibald MacLeish

P: YALE D.N.

1. The offending phrase had occurred in a humorous editorial entitled "Unfair Distribution of Statues" in The Yale Record 43 (6 November 1914), 6.

To Francis Hyde Bangs[1]

My dear Bangs.   [c. 11 March 1915] [New Haven]

I feel as I sit here listening to Prof. Reed[2] immortalizing the career of the apostle of emotional intensities[3] that life is a matter of bland ironies. To what base uses are the symbols of passion put! Suppose I were the child of genius. Suppose a grain of sand were Blake's world to me and a wild flower heaven. Suppose I should create eternal glories from the web of a green field and the woof of a golden fancy. Suppose I should die and be gathered to the bosom of East Rock.[4] Would not I, even I, find new birth on the uninspired lips of a gentlemanly pedagogue whose understanding of my work was based upon a brief knowledge of my felonies? Would not I achieve a fame I never deserved and lose an understanding I have a right to claim? What, then, is the end, aim, object or use of life? If the world disowns me, the critics knife me and the professors of English defend me with the tongues of grocers whither shall I turn? Nay, let me rather find peace and sympathy in the nunnery of thy chaste breast and quiet mind, Oh Bangs, that I may go down into oblivion when your tongue is ashes and your magic dust.   your devoted friend,

                                                        Blifil[5]

ALS: YCAL

1. Bangs (1892–1964), son of the American humorist John Kendrick Bangs, was a member of the Class of 1915 and among the more important of M's undergraduate friends. His annotated collection of M's letters to him from the period 1914–1924, at Yale University, is an important source of information on that decade of M's life, and was the source of many notes in this volume. 2. Edward Bliss Reed, in whose course on English lyrical poetry M was then enrolled. 3. A reference either to Blake or to Shelley, who were the subjects of Reed's lectures on March 9 and 11, respectively. 4. A New Haven park. 5. M was reading *Tom Jones* for Chauncey B. Tinker's course on the Age of Johnson.

To Andrew MacLeish

Dearest Father:-   2 May 1915   [New Haven]

Your wonderfully kind letter of some ten days back has been lying on my desk unanswered because I have been literally unable to do anything aside from the immediate task before me. I am to compete for the De Forest prize — writing and speaking of an essay — next Wednesday and the task has proved greater than I imagined.

I am quite sure that the frame of mind in which I wrote you last was the result of a misunderstanding of your first reply, and I beg of you that you will apply the same theory to the feeling that made you write that you hoped I would try to think better of you than I do. I assure you there could not anywhere exist a deeper gratitude or warmer affection than I feel for your past kindnesses and your present love; and your offer for my immediate future and my marriage arouses my heartiest thanks.[1] You have been not only the opportunity for my education and happiness but the figure I have most respected and admired in life. If anything I have done has given you pleasure it is small payment for your great gifts to me. I *do* wish though that you knew more of this university and more of the relative importance of things here because I feel that I have been a little more worthy of your hopes for me than you realize in your unfamiliarity with the things esteemed at Yale.

After Wednesday I shall have more liberty both for my report to you and my letter to mother.   Your devoted son   Archie.

ALS: M

1. M was engaged to Ada Taylor Hitchcock, of Farmington, Connecticut, a Westover student he had met in December 1910 during a visit to that school. The offer to which M refers was probably one of employment in the Chicago retail store of Carson, Pirie, Scott & Company, of which store Mr. MacLeish was founder and manager; also, perhaps, of a continuation of M's undergraduate allowance so as to permit his marriage at an early date.

To Andrew MacLeish

Dearest Father: [*c.* 26 June 1915] [Deer Island, New York?]

Just a line to tell you that I am somewhat recovered out of the state of discouragement (wholly physical) in which you left me. I am purposely keeping my mind off the problem at hand till my brain gets clearer and my nerves are more rested. After my Canadian trip I hope to be in much better shape and I shall then go into the matter with all my heart and soul. Your wonderful, generous offer leaves me more than ever in your debt and spurs me on to a willingness for any service to the world whatsoever that will merit your approval.[1]

You will be glad to know that I have received the kindest words from people of all sorts and kinds as to my Class Poem.[2] It is a source of the deepest gratification to me that you & mother were there.

Yale won all three crew races on the river yesterday — a thing unprecedented in recent years. We are all very happy.

I shall not be able to send you my monthly statement till about the 8th of July because my books are in my trunk, but I am going to ask for money for my Canadian trip now if I may. Round trip ticket is $12.50, berths (both ways) $5.00, and the cost of residence on the Island is $2.50 a day. I plan to stay a week. The total is thus about $40.00. Can this be sent to me at Deer Island, Alexandria Bay, New York?[3]

With dearest love to you & mother
your devoted & grateful son   Archie

ALS: M

1. As the next letter indicates, Mr. MacLeish, after meeting with various Yale officials while attending his son's graduation exercises, had offered to support him for three years of graduate study, after one year of which he would increase M's allowance sufficiently to permit his marriage.   2. M's "Class Poem 1915" was delivered at class-

day exercises on 21 June 1915, on which occasion it was also distributed in leaflet form to those present. Of the poem's four parts only the first was subsequently collected, as "Baccalaureate." **3.** A retreat of Skull & Bones, the Yale secret society of which M was a member.

To Francis Hyde Bangs

Dear Frank;   9 July [1915]   [Farmington, Connecticut]

Since we went each our several way in June last a most surprising thing has happened to me. Father came on to Commencement, talked to Hadley, Jones etc.,[1] conversed at some length with myself, and ended by offering me three years of graduate school (with Ada). I am now to decide whether or not I want to accept the offer — i.e — whether or not I want to teach. At present I am drawn to & repelled from the profession of pedagogue somewhat as follows.

Alurements:-

① Literary activity & surroundings, & opportunity for writing

② Work along lines for which I am best fitted

③ Possibility for large service

④ Practice of Platonism

Disenchantments:-

① Sedentary life & retirement into intellect

② Teaching seems to kill creative impulse. "If your mind is critical, teach; otherwise keep out". C.B.T.[2]

③ Petty jealousies, slow prefermcnts, wealth of incompetents upon whose death the future would hang.

④ Small income & straightened circumstances

And lastly and most strong a prejudice against teaching as a profession and teachers as a class. This is unfounded, wrong, barbarian — and unalterable.

But there is nothing else I would rather do. And, again, I *could* not pass by the golden opportunity.

For the love of ourselves let me hear from you. You know my capabilities and my limitations. You are kind enough to be ambitious for me, and true enough to sit outside your roof of colored glass for my sake. Will you take an afternoon off and look Gorgon in the eyes?

Write me Box 2 Farmington till the 16th. Then c/o C.K.G. Billings,[3] Glen Cove, Long Island, New York.   yours always   AMacL

ALS: YCAL

1. President Arthur T. Hadley and Dean Frederick S. Jones, both of Yale and both of whom had testified to M's intellectual powers. **2.** Professor Chauncey B. Tinker. **3.** C.K.G. "Ben" Billings, a wealthy businessman and sportsman married to M's half sister Blanche.

To Francis Hyde Bangs

Dear Frank;   [*c.* July 1915] [Oyster Bay, New York]

It may be a matter of some gratification to you to know that you have thus early had part in the shaping of the ends of one human being — whether or no you can lay claims to divinity. Your letter — for which I rest indebted to all time — so crystallized and formulated those objections to teaching which had been ruminant in the angles of what I please to call my intellect that it left me on the verge of renunciation and ultimately projected me into that pleasing and ascetical state. What you say of professorialism has been continually existent in my mind ever since I considered the possibility of teaching and the unhappiness with which I finally accepted it, should have been proof to me of the error in my decision.

But although I have limited the field of choices I have not as yet made up my mind as to what I shall do. I don't want to go west and I dislike business. The alternative seems to be law. Of course I have no mortal idea of my adaptability or inclination in that direction but it would be valuable training, it would keep me East, it would allow me to make use of an offer which has all the insistency of fate — and it would have all the advantages you claim for business with a greater leisure. Lets hear on that score.   yours etc.   Archie

The sonnets are not yet arrived. You shall have one as specified. A.

ALS: YCAL

To Francis Hyde Bangs

Dear Frank;   30 July [1915] Farmington

Here at last the folio![1] You will note a certain careless fluidity i'the paper revocative of Mr. Hacket's best conversations,[2] and a certain je ne sais quoi de jeunesse in the printing which may or may not accord with the subtleties of soul we boast us of. However I enjoy a throb of pride in the pursuance of my evanescent self down the printed page, which the same achievement on J. Berdan's best fool's-cap never accorded.[3] We gain a certain self-respect by putting machinery between our thoughts and our thinking. Indeed even when we pay the printer's devil ourselves we are filled with wonderment that so ponderous a labor should be granted our fancies.

Myself I never see the word "immortality" in print without a shudder. Where shall we be when that same word leers in jaundiced solemnity at our grand-children?

For two months, dear Bang, I have rotted a dry rot. I have read nothing, writ nothing, dreamed nothing. I have stuffed my mind full of luxury as a pig's belly of chestnuts. I have shackled my soul with the "touched and seen". I long with a nostalgia of spirit for the revivifying atmosphere, stale with tobacco smoke and onions, of 123 College.[4] Briefly I miss you as I knew I should, and never till I find myself again in the atmosphere of reality will I be capable of anything beyond digestion and reproduction. God save us all, Bang! God save us all!

I go to interview Hadley this afternoon. My heart is in my boots. He awes me with vocabulary.

Write me again at "Craigie Lea", Glencoe, Ill.. And write me forthwith. My respectful regards to your father. To yourself the adoration of the thirsty soul.   A.Mac.L.

ALS: YCAL

1. M's "Yale University Prize Poem/1915/Songs for a Summer's Day/(A Sonnet-Cycle)," which had just been published (possibly at M's own expense) by Yale University Press. 2. E. Byrne Hackett, manager of Yale University Press. 3. Professor John M. Berdan, whose course on English literature of the sixteenth century M had taken in his senior year. 4. The address of the Elizabethan Club at Yale.

To Francis Hyde Bangs

Dear Bang;   [c. August 1915] Glencoe

Your letter at hand and infinitely appreciated. You have the revivifying qualities of Nietzsche with a certain superornamentation of the intellect which we are pleased to call the soul besides. And I am not the less appreciative because I dwell in a manner of Land of Cockaigne.[1] My roast pigs are indeed no roast pigs at all but rather tall hollyhocks a'nod over the garden hedge; and my delectable pies are rather in the form of gold sunlight on green lawns. But for all that it *is* a Land of Cockaigne for I am neither impelled from it nor into it but rather dwell on the surface with no inclination save to maintain an angle of 180° in relation to the perpendicular of gravity. I feel like the reaction to a gratifying sneeze.

I am going to take up your attention largely with myself for various reasons — chiefly because I am not a channel for greater minds at this present writing but rather a most muddy spring for the bubblings of my own consciousness. My future then! Having seen President Hadley, simpered into the ear of the Rev. Stokes,[2] and exchanged a moist handshake with the ubiquitous Treasurer of the University,[3] I returned to Farmington to read your letter again and soliloquize on the alurements of a merchant's life. For, in the interim, I had approached a lawyer of my acquaintance with a reprint of my problem and had been informed with all gravity that the law leaves no leisure for the art of the pen.

Behold then two of my three alternatives reduced to their native volcanic lava. Upon the scene so set enter Judge Jenks, father of Almet and presiding Justice of New York's superior court.[4] The Judge comes into the wind, receives my fretful remonstrances with sails a'shake, and eases off with a full aft-quarter gale into the circumscribed waters of my future. Briefly he holds that (a) there *is* possibility in the law for the exercise of the quill, (b) the law is the only profession which would permit the exercise of my favorite vices, (c) the law opens into the most brilliant of ultimate futures (d) the law is the best preparation for any future. All this is based on the Judges casual — and, at times, close — observation of myself at Hotchkiss and Yale.

With my mind thus in a tumult I approached the guardian spirit of Westover. Aunt Mary declared unreservedly for the law. Her chief arguments were, first, that it gave me a full, instead of a limited education, secondly that it was an intellectual occupation as opposed to business, therefore an occupation for which I would be more ambitious and perhaps better fitted. I have returned to find Father very much inclined toward business and therefore I have had to formulate my opinions pretty carefully. The conclusion I have reached is somewhat as follows. Business would be, to me, a necessary machinery, a forced application to a loathéd subject, whereof the only value lay in a certain leisure pursuant upon a day of advertisements and counters. The business itself — its experience — would be of no value in the sort of literature I intend to write, and it would not stimulate or develop the mind but rather crowd out the intellect. In all probability it would reduce me to such a state of nausea as to preclude the writing of anything save Calls of the Congo,[5] and the leisure it would offer would be nothing at all for the first 6 or 7 years and after that no very great amount. Its advantages are altogether those of expediency — for it would solve the difficulty of my life with Ada. And its happiness would depend not on what I accomplished in my chosen vocation but rather what I accomplished in the flow of a pen that goes too often dry.

Law is not ideal. In fact it involves very much of a compromise. But it would have manifold advantages over business. First of all it would not be a necessary evil. I think I should enjoy it; I know I should be ambitious in it. Furthermore it would give a certain leisure during the next three years in summer vacations. Yet further I believe that if the impulses were strong enough I would make time to write later on. Law need only be absorbing to him whose entire ambition is in the law. Finally an intellectual occupation should certainly be more inspiring to the uses of the mind than an occupation that puts keenness and "business instinct" ahead of thought.

Education is the only one of the three that would give unlimited opportunity for writing. But we will not exhume the dead & damned. I beg all manner of pardon for thus intruding myself on your mind. Tell me what you think. I append a rejuvenated verse.

yours etc.
Archie[6]

ALS: YCAL

1. A legendary country, the subject of several medieval English tales, in which idleness reigned supreme; *The Land of Cockaygne* was a thirteenth-century English poem satirizing monastic life. 2. Anson Phelps Stokes, secretary of Yale University. 3. George Parmly Day, who in addition to being treasurer of Yale was founder and head of Yale University Press. 4. Almet Francis Jenks, justice of the Supreme Court, Appellate Division, Brooklyn, New York. His son, Almet Jr., had been one year ahead of M at Hotchkiss and at Yale. 5. Vachel Lindsay's poem "The Congo: A Study of the Negro Race" had been published in 1914. 6. In September 1915, after much soul-searching, M enrolled at Harvard Law School, Cambridge, Massachusetts.

To Francis Hyde Bangs

My dear Frank: [7 October 1915]   [Cambridge, Massachusetts]

Of course everything mortal is in the lap of the gods. You seem particularly so situate. Macmillans meant, at the best, an acquaintance with the outsides of books and the insides of ledgers. Your present condition reverses somewhat the order, and though you may never be privileged to add more than six figures at a time you will at least so live that life will be eternally aluring.[1] For myself I imagine it may not always glint as it once glinted. Already I range Cambridge Streets alone in the short hour or so that the Law permits, and meditate upon Time and Eternity. And already it seems to me that time is a very little thing and that eternity is now, and that love and life and twilight sadness and the sound of violins and the curve of a girl's cheek, and thrilling rhythms and bits of color and glamours of music are only the flowers wherein eternity hides his awfulness. We hear a girl laugh and we think how that laugh would echo down eternity to the heart that loved it. We see a marble of old Greece and we dream how older than all old things is the shadow of the shadow of immortality. And yet these things are not of eternity any-more than the stroke of a clock is of time. They are the rhythm of his rhythmlessness. They are the flowers in which he bows his head. And these of course are thoughts dangerous to the law.

But for you — you are now free to do what your heart urges. You are saved out of the polluting mercilessness of Things, you are free to dream. Will you remember, my friend, that you have our dreams to dream as well as your dreams? Will you think, when some immortal phrase startles your soul, that we who have given up immortality for mortality, we who have shut our eyes to the vastnesses and chosen the hearthsides instead, that we too are dreamers of dreams, and that all the dreams we should have dreamed cry like lost children in the wind? Am I writing as the victim of my own sentimental patheticism? I do not believe so. No one could live in this atmosphere of scientific extinction of the spirit without a feeling as of the echoed clang of a shut door.

I wish I could see you. I don't perceive when our physical manifestations will be able to meet again short of Elysium. It is next to impossible to leave the school & I have no doubt your year at Columbia will be too full of Skelton & Berdanese to permit of any roamings. Tell Doc[2] that there is a line in Henley that runs — "Over the hills and far away".[3] Do you know any phrase in English that, robbed of its Tom-Tom vulgarity, bears more of pathos and alure? Write me at 38 Quincy St. Cambridge.   yours et,   AMacL

ALS: YCAL

1. After several weeks' employment in the advertising department of The Macmillan Company, publishers, Bangs had resigned and enrolled in a master's program at the School of Education, Columbia University. 2. Charles A. Merz (Yale '15), who in July 1915 had joined the editorial staff of *Harper's Weekly* and who became its managing editor in October, was then sharing an apartment with Bangs in Manhattan. 3. From William Ernest Henley's "To H.B.M.W."

To Francis Hyde Bangs

My dear Francis;   3 December 1915   Cambridge

My recent epistles, whatever they may have conveyed of moods, have conveyed nothing whatsoever of matter, and matter is, i'faith, what we live in, whether or no we live thereby. So I return to mere prose. Whatever its faults and difficulties it yet hath a certain kinship with sanity & goodsense — unless, of course, it is hitched, like the donkey of "The Bible in Spain",[1] to a mere flux of imagery. But I digress. I never agreed with Larry[2] on prose as a medium. Indeed I am not sure it is a medium at all. Verse, music, clay, oils — yes, but prose is a different matter. These other things are constructible, objective. We take them up and turn them about and admire them. We glaze them for their own sake, and carve them and tint them. But prose I reiterate is a different matter. Prose is a mere modus dicendi. It is the natural speech of the mind. It is the everyday garb of thought. It is a part of the speaker, a part of the writer, unseverable and dependent. And when we create prose for its own sake we bastardize it. Alice Meynell with her lapidary artistry in words and her painter-on-ivory art of tinting words. Francis Thompson with his vast sunsets of verbal imagery, his tinkling of phrases, his antiphony of sounds. — What have these created? Nothing! — or everything. Nothing if you seek to pick up the glass and admire it; Everything if you hold the wind *in* the glass against the light. What I mean is not altogether easy of expression. Perhaps I can touch it more nearly by using the adjective "universal". These other forms are universal. Teuton & Austrian, equally with the light-sailed ones of the Entente and the subtle-eyed oriental, can understand and love a bit of bronze, a phrase from Moore (D.S.),[3] a sky of Turner. They can even appreciate verse in a language they do not understand. (Try the "In Memoriam" on any Colles Coe.)[4] But prose will be a mere hash of sounds, a splintering explosion of unrelated sibilants and respiratories & gutterals. The first forms are universal; the last is for the eye (— and the soul too —) that can look on the carved lettering and understand that thereunder a thought is buried — ah so deep — poor thought!

I have come a long way from Babylon. But perhaps its just as well. There was not overmuch to say. Just that I have suffered a great relapse — a keen desire to turn to teaching & the world of ideas & dreams — and that I have returned de profundis to a keener zest for the coldly intellectual. I suppose it will be thus with me all through life. The rhythms of my heart are rather more pronounced than I should have wished.

Speaking of an old argument of literature versus life — is it not true that he who sees life through the glass of great art sees life in terms of the soul — terms the soul can understand, terms the soul can assimilate? While he who lives in life must first retire out of it & translate faces & battles & emotions & failures into ideas before he can own them as part of himself? Why cannot we two so share our few years that I, condemned to the world, shall send my cries up to you at rest on the edge of the pit under your eternal sycamore, and so that you shall weave out of these cries truth? But "alas for our poor songs" — you would neither believe my cries nor should I agree with your deductions. The soul, like the child, must burn its own fingers.

Don't forget to let me know at once if you have seen Mosher's last catalogue with its excerpt from W.P.[5]

Prunes with the milk? May the stars shine on thy loves.

AMacL

ALS: YCAL

1. George Borrow's classic travel book (1843). 2. Lawrence Mason, an instructor at Yale whose course in English prose of the nineteenth century was taken by M, by Bangs, and by other Yale students with a serious interest in literature. 3. Douglas

S. Moore, a Yale classmate of M's and later a prominent composer. **4.** Coe, a classmate of M's, was described by Bangs as being well bred but oblivious to intellectual matters. **5.** Thomas Bird Mosher's *The Mosher Books* (1915 edition) reprinted the conclusion of the first edition of Walter Pater's *Studies in the History of the Renaissance* (1873).

To Francis Hyde Bangs

Dear F.   11 January 1916   Cambridge

Aunt Mary writes me to go to New Haven next Friday (14th), meet Masefield[1] & drive him up to Westover, spending the night there. She wants me to bring some one. I hereby damn well order you to come. Do you think I want to be left alone with the old Lion? No! Can anyone subdue lions with your firm facility? No! Moreover I want to see you. Moreover it is a golden opportunity — golden. The greatest poet in England — & you and I on each side of him — touching his sacred joints — for an hour and a half. What won't we have to tell the world — & our dinner companions. Now will you come? Damme you've got to. Meet me at the Elizabethan Club at 4:30 — or between then and 5:00. You be there at 4:30. Masefield speaks in Osborne at 3:00 & I'm writing Larry to take him to the Lizz Club & there await us. Car will be there at five & we'll set out together — the three of us. Bangs, the future A. C. Benson of Clur.,[2] Masefield, our greatest living poet. MacLeish, God knows what strange hybred of law & love. Then an evening in the sacred haunts of W'over, a night in the country & away again in the morning. Will you come? I mean — dare you refuse?

Wire me at once, collect, on receipt of this saying you'll come, at what time etc.. Dress suit or Tuck (my Tuck's in hock)

Now Damn You Come!!!!

If you don't I'll never write a dedicatory stanza to your blasted reputation — Never   A.

ALS: YCAL

1. John Masefield (1878–1967), British poet laureate. 2. Arthur C. Benson (1862–1925), the English essayist, poet, and scholar, was a master at Eton and, at the time this letter was written, at Magdalene College, Cambridge.

To Francis Hyde Bangs

Dear F.:-   25 January 1916   Cambridge

I have you most tremendously to thank for your generous pilgrimage. I appreciate that it was no light thing to go so far for so slight a purpose and my gratitude is in proportion. J. his words on my verse were naturally heartening. He wrote me a wee bit note himself later but your letter gave a much clearer idea of what he really thought; — perhaps that is harsher than is altogether necessary: my mind is that Masefield, in common with most poets, needs to have his ideas drawn out of him whether he is dealt with in paper or in person, and that you had a rare opportunity to observe the heavens at play and diagnose accordingly.

I still hesitate sending my verse to the Atlantic but shall shortly have the Class Poem, Dusk, Immortality III, "A song between two silences ———" and "Maria Mea" under way. The rest are yours to do as you will with. Would you publish the class poem entire? — under a new name of course — or would you split PtI from the rest? I can't decide.

At present I am completely swallowed by Law and I perceive little enough respite between now and June. It is a perfect jungle — the farther in you go the deeper the tangle gets and the more lies out behind you to be kept in mind. I won't say that it has not its fascination for it has. But it also fills me with a very real rebellion. I had a bully idea too — the fondness of the poet's mind for the imagery of death — the only instance where the image, whether or no, ripened into reality.

Aunt Mary has given me a very beautiful 1698 ed. of Dryden's Vergil. It is the regular 17th Century size — a foot and a half long by a foot wide & five inches or more through, with innumerable copper plates & bound in heavy calf. I had thought of giving it to the Y. Eliz. Club but I am not sure of its actual worth. I think I'll drop Keough[1] a line and find out.

The touch of New Haven was wine to my blood. I love the place more than I knew, when, last spring, I used to sit on the fence late in the evening and agonize myself with the thought of Time so brief, and eternity so long. Images and memories tumble over themselves in my heart — West Rock of a sunny afternoon, Elm street at dusk with Christ's against the sunset, the campus late at night, the fire at the Club, "Tink" taut in panicy pedagogy, our morning walks down Hill House, the Shore, the drowsy chapel, pigeons, elm leaves, ivy, mustiness, damp winds, rain, sun, wind — oh some day I shall find time to put *that* into verse and then — why then I shall never die for these are things that each year buries deep in a thousand and one hearts.

I bore you. N'importe — you also forgive. And while we are on the subject of forgiveness — don't hold my ten day lapse against me. I depend on you for breath   yrs   A MacL

ALS: YCAL

1. Andrew Keogh, Librarian of Yale University.

To Francis Hyde Bangs

My dear F:-   15 March 1916   Cambridge

I don't know whether or not it is a bad attack of Alice Meynell's Rhythm of Life.[1] Perhaps I am merely the victim of my own resiliency, — for the deadest of us will rebound under pressure. At any rate something in my day at Westover — the CXXXXIV[th] (or VIth) sonnet,[2] or the touch of the Master,[3] or words of yours — something set strange echoes reverbrating down my body's allies and set my thoughts to running back over the old paths. The law has become — not loathly but rather faintly humorous. The urge of the pen point is on me again. And best — or worst — of all the old questions are afoot to be hounded to earth again. Honey once tasted cookery savors flat. The old questions — the things of the spirit or the ways of the world. It is no less a choice than that. Somehow I am not frightened that the choice I thought made is still to make again. I cannot regret my year here no matter what happens.

The trouble seems to be that it is New Haven & not the world of teaching in general that alures. And one cannot sit him down in the shade of a single oak if he will know the forest. I play with the idea as the wind with the dead leaves, — I am forever tossing it before me or letting it skirl underfoot delighting in the flame & lightness of it. — I never come at it clean, face it and say This is the better way. It is a habit of mind — & one that hardly fits for the law. All things are figures of themselves. Nothing is a square issue to meet & know & conquer, nothing ever makes itself *part* of my thought. I am always conscious that my thought and the symbols it strikes at are different and apart. And only when the symbol becomes a condition of my life & penetrates to thought through physical & mental contact does it become part of my thought. I am not expressing it well but perhaps you know what I mean. So I am always half fearful that the thing that attracts is the symbol & not the thing it symbolizes. I think of teaching as a series of pictures — New Haven, high converse with noble minds, long vacations for creation of dreams — & these are not what teaching will be. So I fear the very thing that alures. Also I fear my heart's charge of vacillation. I wonder! And between wonderments I kick the red leaves at my feet.

Thank you for your loan.

Let me hear from you soon.   yours ever   Arch

ALS: YCAL

1. Mrs. Meynell's book of that title was published in 1893. 2. Masefield, in a February 11 talk at Westover attended by M and Bangs, had read, in addition to works of his own composition, Shakespeare's Sonnets 66 and 146. 3. A reference to Masefield.

To Francis Hyde Bangs

Dear F.B.:-   [*c.* June 1916]   [At sea, en route to Bermuda]
"A rainbow and a cuckoo's song
May never come together again
May never come
This side the tomb".[1]

And so in all sweet things is sadness and in all happiness the bitter fragrance of burning leaves. I have not yet realized in consciousness what change it is that has struck across my life.[2] But my soul knew Wednesday afternoon that there *was* a change and, joyous as it was, I yet felt a certain ache of memory of dear days that are now dear shadows. It is not that my wedding makes them so, — but my wedding marks the passing of time & there is enough of Il Penseroso in me so that I sit here in mid-Atlantic on as fair a day as ever bloomed with my utterly adorable Proserpine asleep in a chair beside me and grieve somewhat that the old infidelities to life are over, the old will o' the wisps are caught, the old Jack o' dreams gone lame. It is as you have said mourningly — we are now men and the world expects grist of us. No longer may we lie in elm tops and nurture sweet fantasies of suicide, — we are now pebbles in the eternal sack set to polishing to the end of time. God 'ield us all say I.

But these are grey thoughts. And at present I have no thoughts — neither grey nor glistering. I sit here with the warm wind on my cheek and the soft blue of the Gulf Stream stretching out dazzlingly into the June sun and my body is as listless as the soft clouds that melt into mist at the horizons edge. I am empty of dreams for life is become a dream — a dream woven of soft laughter and softer lips and the still, wide-eyed wonder of a little child. But these things are esotery and you are not yet of the Eleusinian. Sky & sea and a soft wind following — lips and laughter and eternal eyes — Bangs, I am spume on a wind out of Cockaigne.

Write me at Farmington on peril of eternal damnation.

Yrs
AMacL

ALS: YCAL

1. From W. H. Davies's "A Great Time." 2. M and Ada Taylor Hitchcock had been married in Farmington, Connecticut, on 21 June 1916.

To Andrew MacLeish

Dearest Father: 13 August 1916   Fenwick, Connecticut

You will forgive, I am sure, my delay in acknowledging your check when I tell you that I have been tutoring ten hours a day since my arrival at Gale's Ferry[1] and have not been very well. The work is tedious but remunerative. I am making about $14 a day now and will be making twice that in a week. I should clear about $400[,] a sum which I shall probably be glad of next March.[2] You will not be surprised however to hear that I shall probably not take the job another year. Life is too short to do work which is as deadening as this. My two remaining free summers I intend to devote to the great mass of reading I have yet to do and for the doing of which my mind is so thirsty. Law and literature are, of course, incompatible, but I want to acquire a sufficient background so that if I am ever able to turn to the thing I most love I shall be able to undertake creative work at once — not have to stop for research and scholarship.

You will be glad to know that my law school mark for the first year which I received yesterday was 76. This is an "A" grade and will probably be among the first ten in the class of two hundred. The highest mark in a class is usually about 80 and any mark above 75 is an honor mark. Marking is thus on a rather different scale at "the school" than elsewhere where the 100% grading is used. For instance, in actual worth 76 is really five or ten points above 75. The mark should result in my election to the much coveted Harvard Law Review.[3] I am, of course, much gratified, but particularly so in that I feel that you will perhaps feel happier about the wonderful thing you are doing for me. (Please ask some Harv. Law School man you know what an "A" means — but dont say that I hope for the Review.)

Is Kenny going on the Cruise of the Land-lubbers? I am eager for news of home in any form. Please tell K. he has my full permission to do anything he thinks wise with the Mercer — but that if he sells it he must remember that the other half-owner is not only poor but a shyster lawyer to boot. Is Ishbel at home? And has Norman gotten his exams off? God bless you all. Dearest love from your devoted son & daughter

your son   Archie

ALS: M

1. Location of the summer department of the Roxbury Tutoring School of New Haven, "an institution of Yale men engaged in tutoring Yale men." 2. Ada was expecting her first child at that time. 3. It did.

To Francis Hyde Bangs

Dear Frank: 17 August 1916   [Fenwick?]

My long silence is, as you may have surmised, "The brood of Folly
without father bred"[1] — i.e. the offspring of tutoring. Its length is in
inverse ratio to the amount I have to talk to you about, for "my problem" has festered till my mind runs strange essences.

I presuppose your interest in the matter and if I bore you you may
damn my hypothesis

As I left you I was lying, as 'twere, somewhere in that Cimmerian
desert of doubt that lieth 'tween teaching and the law. I believe my
prow was toward the stars. Now I am in a better and a worse situation.
I feel as I felt about law; I feel not at all about teaching. More suc-
cinctly my position is that both law and teaching are untenable for my
purposes. Since I have been here I have had rare talks with ① an assistant in the Yale English Department, & ② a keen observor of things
Yalensian who, with a background of remarkable culture and education on his own part, has taken advantage of four years residence in
New Haven and close acquaintances with J. M. Berdan and Ch. Lewis,[2]
to draw certain general conclusions as to teaching in general and teaching in New Haven in particular. The conclusions I, in turn, have drawn
from the observations of both these gentlemen are, briefly, as follows:

Teaching requires concentrated scholarship after the acquisition of a
P.H.D. as well as before if one would go up in his profession. To refuse
to do the drudgery and thereby to remain in an assistant professorship
is to accept a secondary position in a profession in which secondary
positions are not beds of roses. Teaching requires that one place him-self
at the disposal of his students to a certain extent, ('To be a great
teacher you must be loved by your students')[3] and a married teacher
could not play L.M. and 'Let his lamp be seen at midnight hour'[4] in
seclusion only. Worst of all, or, perhaps, next most unsatisfactory after
the Teutonic demands, is the fact that a college professor lives in a
social order the most delightful and also the most exacting. The struggle
for preferment is carried over into bed and banquet and whatever free
time one has aside from teaching and scholarship must be sacrificed in
that Hecatomb.

You will say, and justly enough, that determination of will can fend
off student and social order and maintain a pale against intrusion. But
there still remains the bugaboo of scholarship which, though doomed,
is not yet dead, and which rides the young man in teaching like an
incubus. I could never contentedly remain an Eddie Reed[5] even though
I were writing verse and even having it published.

My feeling toward the law remains as it was despite the fact that I

27

got a good A for the first year's work. To my two anathemas I add a third — journalism. In other words you see I have come to the solution. There is only one way — the pure and undefiled service of the high gods. And since that way is closed I am not sure that it matters where I turn for the present. I am convinced now the star will never dim. It has changed from mood to passion and cannot dim. So I must e'en walk my way along the world — remembering — and when the day comes (and it *will* come) I shall make great songs.

This is unsatisfactory!

And oh but I hate tutoring — loath it. I've been on the 1st Act of Macbeth 56 times in the most detailed and painstaking fashion, and much as my respect for W.S. increases, my love for the exact words of Act I Sc.s 1–7 is a negative quantity.

You need not fear to answer my letter from a feeling that I may unburden myself again in this wise. "I am settled, and bind up each corporal agency"[6] to try to remain settled.

> yours as always in tempore
> et sub specie aeternitatis
> AMacL

ALS: YCAL

1. From Milton's "Il Penseroso." 2. Charlton M. Lewis, whose course in English poets of the nineteenth century M had taken in his junior year. 3. A remark probably made by Lawrence Mason, or perhaps by Bangs. 4. Compare "Il Penseroso," lines 85–86. 5. While teaching English at Yale, Reed had published a volume or two of indifferent verse. 6. Compare *Macbeth* I, vii, 79–80.

To Andrew MacLeish

Dearest Father: [*c.* Fall 1916] [Cambridge?]

But why *be* left alone? We have a guest room — an extra one — that aches for your presence. Don't you suppose you could come? We should so love to have you. Mother plans to be here off and on for a week — why couldn't you come with her? You would love our house.

Your quotation from Emerson[1] is peculiarly à propos and one I have always felt the truth of. I am reminded thereby that I did not know you read Emerson to any extent. I am so glad you do. Someday I hope we can find time to discuss certain things in the essays. He is to me the great figure of his century — greater even than Arnold or Wordsworth or Meredith, — & one of the great figures of history. He is a later Plato who has known Christianity; & the conception of divinity he creates is, to me, the most satisfying conception I know.

That we are all, in essence, god-head, that there is in each one of us that common soul which eternally IS, that the soul in me may know & touch the soul in Christ and Grotius[2] & Shakespeare if only the vague glass of my mind can be clear enough to comprehend all that they are — this is a conception to which I *can* subscribe. It does not yield me a comforting faith in an individual immortality — a continuance of the ego — but it does give me an unshakeable faith in God that exists, & eternity that is *now*.

I heard Dr. Gordon of the The Old South this morning.[3] His subject was the change in the tenets of the church since his Scotch youth. He introduced his idea by condemning utterly the "three disciplines" of his theological school days — the sovereignty of God, Ecclesiastical History & the Introduction to the Old & New Testaments, — as being defunct. The old idea of a Parmenidian and changeless God with his "predestination" & his condemnation of the world for its original sin, was, he said, held by no independently thinking man today. The old idea of ecclesiastical history flowing in one pure & unadulterated stream out of the past must be exchanged for a new figure — a manner of snowball rolling down out of antiquity picking up much that is pure & much that is folly, much truth & much evil. The old conception of a single Isiah and a single David who wrote all the psalms must fall before modern biblical criticism. *But,* though all these things are past, though we suffer today from an Heraclitean doctrine of flux & change & scorn of the stable & changeless, yet, underneath, it is one god — the Lord God of Our Fathers.

It was a sermon you would have enjoyed. My abstract of it is very incomplete & utterly fails to suggest Dr. Gordon's phraseology & personality. But I suppose you know him of old. The point I had in mind was that there really has occurred a gap between 1860 & 1916 in religious thought that it seems impossible for Dr. G's more ancient parishioners to bridge. It is altogether marvelous to me that you, raised in an atmosphere of Calvinism, have bridged that gap long before your sons ever reached it.

Mem. as regards note & stocks received & noted. Thank you for informing me thereon.

Dearest love to mother. Tell her the China, books & chairs together with the rug, have all arrived. Would you ask her again for me to look up the freight on the Davenport, chair & rug? She evidently forgot to. Everything else from the store came prepaid but these articles cost me about $9.00 with expressage at this end. I just wondered if the charges had been paid twice, — the Camb. Express Co. is capable of it.

Haven't you at home an extra dictionary that you could loan me?

That is a very abrupt question but it seems to me I remember something of the sort. I have a small one now but I am very anxious to get a large dictionary & some sort of an encyclopoedia. Since they are so expensive I thought I'd see if there were anything extra at Craigie Lea.

Also — would you prefer that I should transfer my Chicago Bank acc't to Cambridge & take care of my U. C. Co stock myself? It seems too bad to trouble you with it, and, while I am more than willing to leave it in your hands, I can relieve you of that care very easily.

your devoted son,   Archie

Tell mother we await her coming eagerly. Can't you possibly come with her? On acc't of the expected addition to our family we may not be able to get to Glencoe at Xmas. Please come.   AMacL.

ALS: M

1. The letter from Andrew MacLeish that would supply the reference to Emerson apparently has not survived. It may have been the passage from "Self-Reliance" quoted in M's letter to his father of 9 May 1917. 2. Hugo Grotius (1583–1645), Dutch jurist and humanist generally regarded as the founder of international law. 3. George Angier Gordon (1853–1929), the Scots-born Congregational pastor of the Old South Church, Boston.

To Francis Hyde Bangs

Dear F.B.:   11 November 1916 [Cambridge]

You will forgive a long silence if for no other reason because it has been. I am laboring in a cursory fashion at the law and revolving certain things in my mind. Have you noticed how every now and again the platitudes on which you have walked rise up and engulf your very life? It is so. For instance the platitude of God, which we played with and which became one day a reality — wind in the paleness of blown leaves; crickets in summer grasses. My particular engulfing universality is sincerety. I have played with sincerety — so have we all God forgive us. Usually we have spat upon it and preferred the taste of mood. Now suddenly it has swallowed me. Deep in my soul I have sworn a great oath that never again shall I put on paper verse for the sake of a twisted conceit or a sound of wings save that conceit & that sound of wings be of me & in me: — chiefly, that I shall never attempt poetry till there is in me a great truth crying to be *preached*. Yes — pedagogy in verse — even so! After all what excuse outside the realm of aesthetic philosophy can support the mere creation of prettiness for prettiness sake? If I am MacDowell[1] & charm you with a Wild Rose or a Waterlily what do I do but give you pleasant visceral sensations or stroke your epidermis? I say that Keats when he is lovely & no more is charlatan & quack. Grace and exquisiteness for their own sake I would damn eternally. Art that exists for its form merely is a painted harlot. And if "neo-platonism" is ever applied to that thing I avow myself Aristotelian eternally. What has your poet the power of verse *for*; *why* is he given the art wherewith he creates "Land" out of hawthorn flowers? Surely not to paint *himself* with! Great art that exists for *itself* only is a candle before a mirror. When there is *Beauty* to serve, & *God* to worship and *Thought* to weave with shall we go through the world painting mollusc shells with the irisation of dead fish? If I may sing I must teach — not by logic nor by law (God forefend) — by suggestion — perhaps even *by* prettiness & conceit. But I must teach or there is no health in me.

So much as to the health of my liver.

We had a delightful dinner with M'tt S'g't[2] in the course of which I told her I disagreed with your sketch of her — & must then (fool that I was) outline your most complimentary sketch. She now demands to know wherein I differ with you — & what shall I say? One doesn't tell a lady he admires that her personality is a brazen trumpet about Jericho — be Jericho a city walled or not.

N.B. a stanza dropped from an attempt to revise the Ode to Ships[3]

—————————(The sea which)
Stills the yelping words that hunt
Every shining thing the soul
Hunts in that dark land a'front
Death's encircling diastole.

I love it — but its too involved for the attempt at simplicity in the rest

I just saw Harvard & the referee beat Princeton 3–0. It was a marvelous game. How I hate a red sweater. Its a native ferocity bred in the bones by breaking them.

God shield you & your sheep.[4]   AMacL

ALS: YCAL

1. Edward A. MacDowell (1861–1908), an American composer whose works included the symphonic poems "To a Wild Rose" and "To a Water-lily," both of which appeared in MacDowell's *Woodland Sketches* (New York: P. L. Jung, 1896). 2. Margarett Sargent, of Boston and Ogunquit, Maine, to whom Bangs had introduced the MacLeishes on October 2. Strikingly beautiful and a talented painter and sculptor, Sargent, later Mrs. Quincy Adams Shaw McKean, was a source, or the source, of inspiration for several MacLeish poems including, in *Tower of Ivory* (1917), "The Showman (A Portrait)," "The 'Chantress," "Our Lady of Troy," and "Soul-Sight." 3. M published a revised version of his "Ode to Ships" as "Escape," in *Tower of Ivory*. 4. Bangs was teaching at St. Paul's School, Concord, New Hampshire.

To Francis Hyde Bangs

My dear F.B.   [*c*. Winter 1917?] [Cambridge?]

My silence is as the frogs — a continued din in your ears. Trés [*sic*]
bien! we must err on occasion or there were no virtue. Hence there is
much virtue in me. You see already the slimy mark of the legal mind
like snail or leaf. I will grow frog's legs & be altogether a subject for
Halieutics.[1]

We add W. W. Gibson to our list.[2] A charming, weak, unvisible
person, — the sort to whom labor is always glorious. Coleridge spoke
for the world when he said — "I always write best of what I know
nothing of." But I do the good man an injustice. He is poor as poverty
and right royally he pays for his fame such as it is. He has the innocence
& wonder-eye of childhood.

Did I tell you that I had had a most marvellous conversation with
de la Mare? He, with all his magics, is a tremendous lover of Donne and
a true metaphysician. We discussed *verities, death*[,] *life, art, reactions,
immortality, single, collective and seriatim.* I have seldom enjoyed a
conversation more — save when with thee, Oh Columbus, I whirled the
egg. I have summed it up in a brief 12 lines in d.L.M's favorite verse
form. And there is more real labor here than meets the eye. Frankly,
I love it myself:-

> There is no gone, — to be,
> There is no shall, or was, —
> Only there's Now and Now,
> And the wind in the grass.
>
> Days I remember of
> Now in my heart are now;
> Days that I dream will bloom
> White the peach bough.
>
> Dying shall never be
> Now in the windy grass:
> Now under shooken leaves
> Death never was.[3]

Dinner last night with Josephine Preston Peabody Marks, Mr. Josephine P. P. Marks[4] & W. W. Gibson. Much talk of W.V.M.[5] whom
she tremendously admires, & some verbiage on E. A. Robinson whom
she knows well. Indeed she knew W.V.M. too. She remembered you
very readily. Ah Francis! She is utterly charming I think but conversa-
tionally a bit given to Zeppelin work. Once she's up its forever & a day

before she lights on concluding punctuation again, and for all that her suspension is graceful & lovely its a bit wearing on the neck to watch her. Also she has a way of being very kind with one when one is in opposition that makes one feel the Christian religion has its drawbacks. I can't believe she is a great intellect or a great spirit. As for her verse I know it not. I must read it. She is so interested in mothers. And she urges them on you logically. Its unnerving.

Oh but I forgot. I took Willy Wilf. (Gibson) through New Haven & invited Larry to the Lizzy Club for tea. It was charming. Gibson says he never thinks & doesn't like poetry he can't understand. Hence the daggers. W.W. referred to E.A.R. as too intellectual. Larry said "a pleasant vice." Silence & coolness. Oh rare! Larry was trying so hard to realize that the bucolic is still a form of literary expression. But he can't do it. He is a brain and, shades of Ossian![6] he can't be flesh. This by the way:

Certain Poets

Words & words & words, a twittering blur
Of Sparrow wings that puff up from the rye
When something hidden stirs there, — up they fly
A wheeling, huddled, undecided whir,
And what it was aroused them, Pan or cur,
Appears not, save that 'twas a prodigy,
A portent sure, and, at its passing by,
A new world dawned, a grubs & rye-fields *were*.

And so their verses go, a clamorous blur
Of words unformed, unbeautiful, distraught,
That eddy in the mood like feathered stuff,
And underneath the sound of them a thought
Of something hidden stirring, like enough
Apocalypse, or miracle, — or naught.

"A portent then! a dumb and groping urge
Of something blind, like voices in a mist;
Lord but it 'wilders one! — to feel it twist
Old earth with iron, mutter in the forge,
Threaten in steel, — I tell you we're a'verge
Of worlds undreamt, and every silly fist
That curses God's a sign. There's wondrous grist
A'grinding, wondrous new-sown corn a'surge."

New worlds! These things were seedling in dead Cain!
But you! for you old magics yet remain

Of restless whispering winds that press along
Dark casements of the sense-enshuttered brain.
Beauty has called you, and the worlds that wain
From crescent into crescent of their song.[7]

ALS: YCAL

1. A word defined by the *Oxford English Dictionary* as "the art or practice of fishing."
M appears to have thought it had to do with frogs. 2. Gibson (1878–1962), the
English poet, was on an extended tour of the United States. 3. An early version of
"An Eternity," later published in *Tower of Ivory*. 4. Josephine Preston Peabody
(1874–1922), a well-known poet and dramatist, was the wife of Lionel S. Marks, a
professor of mechanical engineering at Harvard. 5. William Vaughan Moody (1869–
1910), American poet and dramatist best known for his play *The Great Divide* (1906).
M and Bangs were more interested in his poetry, which included *The Masque of
Judgment* (1900) and *The Fire Bringer* (1904). 6. A legendary Gaelic warrior and
poet, Ossian was alleged by James MacPherson (1736–1796) to have been the author
of various poems that MacPherson, in fact, had himself written. 7. A revised version
of this poem appeared under the same title in *Tower of Ivory*.

To Andrew MacLeish

Dearest Father: 4 February 1917   [Cambridge?]

Your most gratefully received draft arrived duly and I am fortified
for the next three months. That is, I believe I am. My Gales Ferry
money ought to see me through Doctors and nurses with a margin to
spare and I am trusting it complacently.

The events of the last two days are startling to say the least of them,
aren't they.[1] I don't suppose there is much room to doubt that we will
be actually at war before another fortnight is out. The only question
in my mind is as to the part we can play. If it is to be an expeditionary
force the issue isn't quite clear, but if the project will shape into the
building of a great American army to meet whatever may transpire I
shall feel obligated to get officer's training in some way or other —
always provided it will be possible for me to leave my "family". It
would seem to be the duty of well educated young men to put themselves into a situation to teach. However it is all so *very* nebulous at
present that its pretty hard to talk about it. I am glad with all my soul
that we have proved that we exist as something more than a commercial combination. And I think the alliance with England that will result
will be a consumation devoutly to be prayed for. Dearest love to you
both.   your devoted son   Archie

ALS: M

1. On February 3, President Wilson had broken diplomatic relations with Germany.

To Francis Hyde Bangs

Dear Bang: [*c.* 2 March 1917] [Farmington?]

It seems impossible that you should not have heard — but I suppose it may well be that you have not — that Ada & I have a son born a week ago.[1] He antedated the period of probable expectancies by three weeks or more & was thus unduly small but I haven't a shadow of a doubt but that this new edition of my ego in Old Rose Boards & brocade will eventually read as well as any folio. I have no intention of sending him to Hotchkiss but should like to enter him at S.P.S.[2] — provided S.P.S. doesn't charge a fee for entering boys. If it does I must just dree my wierd and hope.

This event — I speak as tho' I hadn't expected it — naturally makes any dream of Ogunquit[3] for this summer impossible. We shall go to a bit of a lake in the hills of Western Connecticut where father-in-law has a shack. But that doesn't terminate my plan for seeing some'at of you. What I should tremendously enjoy doing would be walking from the lake four or five days journey up into the lower Berkshires. It is unbelievably beautiful country & English in its flavor. Our goal could be a deserted & magical hill village just this side of the Mass. line where an ancient friend of mine would put us up.[4] I have already worked my plan out pretty well & I won't hear a no. Then if you wanted me I could spend a few days in Maine with you. We must plan it definitely before summer comes

Another plan I am nursing is a project for a dinner of L.M., D.S.M., C.A.M., F.H.B.[5] & AM^{ac}L in New Haven this spring. It must be done. Flint needs steel, & beach, ocean. It would please L.M. down to the ground & it would be quite feasible if you & C.A.M. could leave your opposite ends of creation contemporaneously. Let me know what you think.

I have been reading W.V.M's Fire-Bringer. I confess to an inability to comprehend the scheme back of it altogether. It is obviously symbolic but the symbols may be many things. I had thought Pandora must be soul till I discovered Prometheus was. Then what is Pandora — Hope? "Where thou goest I am; there even now I stand & cry thee to me". Woman? (Her last lyric) And what is the sum of Prometheus['] great excathedra on p 257.

But aside from all this I proclaim the poem as sheer poetry unutterably great. Few similes or metaphores but gorgeous, swooningly *beautiful* phrases, & epithets that mirror on eternity. Caesar! Saluto. I would be your debtor into eternity were W.V.M. all I owed you. Instead R.W.E[6] has always a connotation of yourself, & my own self-respect is in the same coin pretty largely.

I have seen M.S.[7] quite a bit of late. She is all you claim for her —
which is more than you say. These few lines which I dare not show her
for fear of annihilation may amuse you:-

Lo, the lady Margarett!
Cunningly her fingers fret
        Witcheries in clay.
She is Circe, sorceress.
Mulberries make red her press,
Moon-ripe poppy blooms confess
        Her way.

Lo, the lady Margarett!
Spreadeth beauty for a net,
        Springeth souls thereby;
Springeth souls to light her clay,
This for laughter, this to pray,
This to dance the spring away
        And die.

Lo, the lady Margarett!
Her dark hair is springes set,
        Her two hands, a spell.
Whom she tangles, him they bind,
Ariel in oak-tree rind,
In the dark clay, dumb & blind
        To dwell.

Lo, the lady Margarett!
All her dryad folk forget
        Bubbles in the bowl —
April & the running seas,
Stars & rainbows; what are these
So her clay have foam & lees
        Of soul.[8]

Your last letter much appreciated. Who is the "Bayard T —"
(Taylor?)? Of your translation of Faust?
    Ada is doing beautifully. She's a marvel — & there is now a marvel
set therein.   yrs   AMcL

ALS: YCAL

1. Archibald MacLeish, Jr., rechristened Kenneth after the death of M's younger
brother in combat in October 1918, was born on 24 February 1917. 2. St. Paul's
School. 3. The town in Maine where Bangs's family lived. 4. Unidentified; possibly
the friend in Winsted, Connecticut, referred to in M's letter to his family of c. August
1921 (see note 2 to that letter). 5. Lawrence Mason, Douglas S. Moore, Charles A.

Merz, and Bangs, respectively. **6.** Ralph Waldo Emerson. **7.** Margarett Sargent. **8.** A version of this poem with only minor revisions was published in *Tower of Ivory* as "The 'Chantress."

To Francis Hyde Bangs

Dear F. — 22 April [1917] Cambridge
 The enclosed will explain itself & my continued silence.[1]
 I plan to present this and such of my shorter verse as seems worth it to Hou. Miff. & Co with an eye to the ovulation of a volume.[2] Query as to the result. Continued failure to place my stuff in magazines & the continued success of persons of utter mediocrity to find place for theirs is slowly disgusting me and somewhat shaking my faith. I wish you would let me have such of your valued criticism of the within as you may have time for. Can you think of a title? "Faustus" in any form challenges confusion with Goethe, Marlowe, Vernon Lee et al.. This of mine is a newer — & an older — Faust. Indeed he is no Faust at all. He is your vices.
 Ad Astra!
 Nox venit!
 Well, so much. Please return the mss. with all due care at your early convenience. As for the care — it is the only one extant. As for the haste — I must remove or attempt to remove this cacodemon of continued failure from my chest. Shadows of Barneys & Bracketts & College Maidens who have been given to conceive certain vapidities *in print* ride me like blue demons.[3] Particularly Brackett, a mind of warm, wet, dough garnished with a female decorative instinct and blessed with a memory as plagiaristic as a poll parrots! I could write iambics in the original Greek sense about him
 Enough for such bile.
 I will come to St P's with all joy the moment I have been able to surmount a few Olympuses of Law
 Go' bless thee! AMacL

April 22 — and a fair fine day — devoted to the law of <u>Sales</u>.
Man! What a fool thou art!

ALS: YCAL

1. "The enclosed" was the manuscript of M's most ambitious work up to that time, a closet drama in iambic pentameter originally entitled "The Death of Faustus" and later published, in *Tower of Ivory*, as "Our Lady of Troy." **2.** M may or may not have submitted a manuscript to Houghton Mifflin Company about this time; in any case, a manuscript consisting of "Our Lady of Troy" and thirty-seven shorter pieces was accepted by Yale University Press and published under the title *Tower of Ivory* on 6 December 1917. Lawrence Mason contributed a foreword. **3.** Danford N. Barney, a year behind M at Yale, had in 1916 published through Yale University Press a collection of verse entitled *Dust of Stars*, also with a foreword by Mason. Charles Brackett was a Cambridge lawyer and writer of M's acquaintance. "College Maidens" refers, no doubt, to Edna St. Vincent Millay, whose *Renascence and Other Poems* was published in 1917, the year she graduated from Vassar.

To Andrew MacLeish

Dearest Father: 5 May 1917   [Cambridge]

Thank you so much for your letter. I realized of course that writing isn't a very useful way of spending a vacation. But I'm glad the small man had this salutation. After all he's the only MacLeish in the third generation save Jean,[1] whose offspring will probably be Guelphs or Romanoffs at the least. And in these troublous times a male heir is worth his dividends.

I have spent three or four very anxious weeks trying to decide where my duty lies. It seemed at first that I had no choice but to get training in one of the R.O.T.C.s at once. Great as the number of available men for enlisted positions may be, the number of men who by education and physique are fitted for officerships is limited. And I felt it incumbent on me at first to apply. Then when it appeared that the camps were going to be over-applied I decided to wait for the second series of camps which will start in August according to reliable information here. That will give me an opportunity to finish out my year here and to move my family away from Cambridge (— whither they shall move is yet nebulous. Farmington for a while certainly. And I had thought of Craigie Lea for next winter if you and mother are to be alone there & would want them. But all that can be decided later[.]) It will also give me an opportunity to put things in shape generally[.] Of course I run the risk of being drafted in the mean time — there is no exemption of married men. But I think that I will be able to fight clear till August. If I can I shall come west to see you if only for a brief visit. And I might be sent to Fort Sheridan for training in which case I would be very near you.

After a great deal of thought this seems the best plan open. I have got to go eventually. Something in me stronger than draft-laws makes that imperative. And if I am going to go I had better go in a trained position of leadership. The result is to leave my wife & baby dependent on you for a period perhaps longer than the one we had contemplated & to retard my advance to a position of self-support in a discouraging way. But all this is necessarily consequential on the terrific overturn of established order that Germany has wrought. At first I hated the thought of enlisting. Now I can contemplate it with a certain grim joy. It means doing my part against a nation of madmen. It means giving my strength to tramp down an Idea of government and society as abhorrent to me as are crawling lice or dead things. It means, also, a blow for world peace in order that this small son of mine, this grandson who will bear your name and carry on your mortality, may live his life in freedom of wars and lust and lies, and may realize all that I feel *I* might realize if the day were really as young as it should be.

When convenient for you will you send on our quarter's check?

Dearest love to you & mother from all of us here.

your devoted son   Archie.

ALS: M

1. The daughter of M's half brother Bruce MacLeish.

To Andrew MacLeish

Dearest Father: 9 May 1917   [Cambridge]

As I have thought back over the letter I sent you two days ago I have been wondering whether that letter might not have conveyed a false idea of my convictions & plans in the present situation. I spoke, as I remember, of my conviction that the only course open to me is training in the next Plattsburg Camp.[1] Subject to discussion with you that remains my purpose. The civilian jobs in Washington etc. that men have been going from the Law School to fill seem to be few, and of little value to the government, and primarily apt for men who are physically incapable for active service. I have gone carefully into this matter with Dean Pound[2] who has just returned from Washington & who has been intrusted by the administration with the task of procuring men for the openings now available. Of course the situation will change but the Dean is of opinion that the opportunities open on the Civil side will be of two sorts: ① those open to expert administrators, food specialists, [railway] men etc. ② ordinary clerical work that will be easily taken care of by the over-aged & physically unfit. Neither class includes myself. And on the other hand I am athletic, intelligent & accustomed to handling men and absolutely fitted for an officer's work[.] This brings me to the vital question in issue. What effect does my marriage have on this situation? I start out with the proposition, which you will heartily indorse, that I must serve my country in this present crisis at all sacrifice short of the actual physical want of my wife & son. Tho' there were a thousand others who *could* go nevertheless *I* must go. To requote a passage of Emerson you once quoted to me: "What *I* *must* do is all that concerns me, not what the people think."[3] Now what will be the effect of my going? First of all I will have two years of law well behind me. With that preparation I could get into any law office or the legal department of any business etc. This is particularly true in view of my standing here. The progress would be harder of course. But I want to emphasize the fact that the two years here are no less a gain because the third may not be added to them. So the result of my serving would very likely be (subject to the duration of the war) that I would get at the earning of my living — a consummation I long for as devoutly as you — about as soon as though I finished up here in ordinary course. I believe that almost all offices will make allowances in favor of men who have enlisted. Indeed I know that this will be done from the express words of the members of the best N.Y. & Boston firms. So my future will not be materially interfered with — or at least very slightly in comparison with the momentousness of the social upheaval and the necessity of my serving.

But there is an additional question — what will happen to my family in the immediate present? This is just where my Plattsburg idea becomes important. They would of course have to look to you in a measure. But since we had contemplated some such relation extending down to the time when I should be established this would not be a variation of your original intention in regard to me. But, as I have said, my Plattsburg idea changes this situation rather for the better. If I got my commission as a 2nd or 1st Lieutenant — as I probably should — my salary would be such as to keep Ada & the son alive, or at least materially to lessen their dependency on you — a dependency which, war or no war, you have been so good as to permit down to the time of my establishment in business.

I speak of all this because I am particularly anxious that you should not conclude that I intend to rush off in a blind way throwing all my obligations on your shoulders. I am too deeply sensible of my present obligation to you & too desirous of your good opinion to allow you to continue in such a conclusion if you have already drawn it. And it is really to free your mind of any such doubt of me that I write to such length. For, so far as the actual decision of the problem goes, I shall come west to see you before I take any step whatsoever. I have already held myself aloof from two opportunities to which I was strongly inclined because of my desire for your advice & you may trust me to so act until I see you in late June or early July.

I hope you will feel that I am acting in good faith & attempting honestly to meet the perplexing problem before me. And I also hope you will believe me when I tell you that the one unalterable fact that stands out in all this is my conviction that *I* must serve. Else I were not your son.

I congratulate you profoundly on the conclusion of your 50 yrs connection with C.P.S.. What a growth you have witnessed & guided! I should think the contemplation of that great industrial institution would make you very proud &, in a measure, atone for the hardships you must have gone through to accomplish it. I didn't know you were only 29 when you started to manage C.P&Co.

Love to mother   your devoted son   Archie

ALS: M

1. A military training camp in Plattsburg, New York. 2. Roscoe Pound, of Harvard Law School. 3. From "Self-Reliance," in *Essays, First Series* (1841).

To Samuel B. Hemingway[1]

Dear Mr. Hemingway: 15 June 1917   Cambridge

Tremendously obliged to you for your manifold blessings. It looks as though I might have an opportunity to buy copper wire after all. Have you any idea in what the examination consists? It would be a tragedy to be recommended and then display a lamentable ignorance of the aesthetics of book-keeping.

I shall be at 35 Bowdoin St Cambridge till Monday — then at Box 2, Farmington Connecticut.

Do you imagine that I would gain anything by going to Washington? My eagerness is somewhat increased by the fact that Dr. Streeter has offered me an alternative position of some sort (declension unknown) with the Yale Mobile Hospital,[2] & if I should be so unfortunate as to miss out with the aeroplanes, I should like to connect up there. Please don't trouble to write me in answer to all these questionings unless you feel there is some additional insurance I might take. You have put me so much in your debt as it is that I shall never regain a perfect equanimity. The Harvard Int. Int. Bureau man says he understands the examination is in the nature of a personal interview. If that is so a haircut may be a sufficient preparation. If that is not the case then I have a few tumultuous days ahead.

Please thank your mother for her Charity in putting me up. I'm afraid I was an Arabian guest.

very gratefully yours   Archie MacLeish

ALS: YARO

1. Assistant professor of English at Yale and head of the Yale branch of the Intercollegiate Intelligence Bureau. Hemingway had been trying, so far without success, to arrange a commission for M as a supply officer in the Army Aviation Corps. 2. The Yale Mobile Hospital Unit, organized by Dr. Joseph Marshall Flint, head of the Department of Surgery at Yale Medical School, Dr. Edward Streeter of Boston, and others. In June 1917, having failed to obtain a commission in the Aviation Corps, M enlisted as a private in the Yale Unit and was shipped with it to France. Some three

months later, the unit showing no sign of movement toward the front, M and three Yale — and Skull & Bones — comrades sought the aid of another Skull & Bones man, Major Hugh A. Bayne (Yale '92), a member of General Pershing's staff, and obtained transfers to — and officer's commissions in — the field artillery.

To Francis Hyde Bangs[1]

My dear Preterite:-   23 December 1917 [Saumur, France]

Heaven is our home! For that reason all heavenly spots upon earth merely remind us of the divine original and turn our thoughts toward death. This is no platonical doctrine of an obfuscated reminiscence. It is a matter of common experience. Lo! I am here in a city as much more beautiful than the fair town of patisseria[2] as that fair town is more beautiful than Erie Pa.. I am surrounded by a rolling valley land which bears, in season, the grape of the wine of sensory intoxication. I am surmounted by an ancient castle of extraordinary lovliness. And my mind, oh great Bang, knocks at the doors of death. I explore dynamite and chew upon the cud of salt peter. I engage my mind with destruction, and my soul I turn toward the obliteration of the enemies of the Lord

All this is in the way of saying that such an ugly business as death has no place in all this lovliness. Why, shades of Cadbury,[3] the very Y.M.C.A. is hewn out of an old mansion with open fire places; & the great buildings of the school are surrounded by mansions of white stone. Save for the cold that hath no termination it is all very wonderful. We are true soldiers & no longer members of a stinging, fussy, ill-ventilated houseparty made up of the dregs & the Keators[4] of American man-hood among whom you walk like a white god among toads. We are up & breakfasted & through an hour's lecture before the sun so much as hints at day. We are crowded to the last minute of a long afternoon with lectures & field work & gun-drills & horse-back riding. Its an almost ideal existence. The intellectual labor is hard & exacting, the exercise is keen & dangerous, the food is such as befits a son of Mars. Instead of six blankets on a feather bed one has two blankets of dubious weight on a cot. Instead of eight hours a day of idleness one has two hours a day for outside study. Instead of moping & fearing death one acquires the breach-end attitude — the attitude of dealing death like a swift avengor of beauty trampled on. I glorify God for his mysterious ways.

Last evening we dined & wined (oh sunny wine of France) with Bill Jessup & Henry Grey[5] both of whom will write letters for you before they leave — a matter of three days now. There is a rumor that no more commissions in F.A. will be given. But, at all events, they will always take properly accredited men into the school & commission them if they successfully complete the course. I will investigate the matter at once. You may rest assured that I will not give over the search till you are safely out of the Y.M.U.. The memory of it with the single burning exception of precious days & hours of you, is a foggy hot horror to me. To think that I breathed the same air Keator breathed for three long months. God!

Have any boxes come for us? They say the mail here goes swiftly to the devil & I want to be on the look-out. Please tell George S. or John Alsop[6] that our address is

> 2nd Lt. Archibald MacLeish, U.S.R.
> Field Artillery School of Instruction
> P.O. 718
> A.E.F.
> France

Let me hear from you soon   yours   AMacL.

My best to Lt's Smith & Streeter

ALS: YCAL

1. Bangs had joined the Yale Mobile Hospital Unit shortly after, and at the instigation of, M. When, however, M transferred with his three Skull & Bones friends to the field artillery, Bangs, who was not a member of that society, was left behind. 2. Limoges, where the Yale Unit had been stationed since its arrival in France. 3. The officer in charge of the YMCA at Limoges. 4. Samuel J. Keator (Yale '09), a member of the Yale Unit. 5. William H. Jessup and Henry B. Gray, Jr. (both Yale '15), were, like M, studying field artillery at Saumur. 6. Lieutenant George Smith, of Waterbury, Connecticut, and Alsop (Yale '10) were members of the Yale Unit.

To Andrew MacLeish

Dearest Father:-   30 January 1918 [Saumur]

I am going to write you again about a subject concerning which I troubled you some months ago and on which my mind is not yet altogether at rest. It is merely a matter of precaution against an altogether improbable contingency but I take occasion to discuss it again because, if the contingency should come to pass and the matter be undecided, it might be the cause of life long misery to my wife & son. I have in mind, then, the question of the disposition to be made in your will in case of my predeceasing you. You will remember that I wrote mother about this in the fall & that she spoke to you. Her reply to me was that it was "all right". And I have not a shadow of a doubt but that it is all right. But nevertheless I cannot feel at ease in my mind until I know *from you* that, in case of my predeceasing you, Ada shall have at least a life interest (& a full interest in case of little Archie's death) in that part of your estate which you have intended for me. I realize that in speaking thus freely I am contravening all laws, unwritten & implicit, of human relations. But you will forgive me because you will understand that under the circumstances I cannot but feel a tremendous anxiety for the wellfare of my wife & son. Unfortunately I have not myself anything to leave to them, should I fall in the war. I am taking out the maximum of $10 000 insurance in Ada's name, but this would not amount to much over a long extent of time. They must, therefore, look to you, & I know that it is your happiness that they should so look to you. I know that, generous as you are, you expect them to look to you. But I want to be sure for the peace of my very much troubled mind that a provision *has been* made for them which nothing can upset & which will, above all things, take care of Ada. I trust her entirely to use whatever is hers for the wise up-bringing of our son. My only fear is that, while little Archie may be well cared for, she may have to suffer.

You will forgive my importunate questioning I am sure. I have every certainty that I shall return safely. But the slight chance that I may not — a chance which attends every human act — leads me to beg this favor of you. You will see how much it means to me & will tell me exactly what provision has been made for Ada, I am sure. She knows, & shall know, nothing of all this, of course. But I would not be a good husband to her or father to my son if I let the whole matter go on faith, however well founded.

I have just received word tonight of your Christmas draft. Such things are slow in war but none the less grateful.

I am well & happy — & altogether ignorant as to my future course of service. I may be here a month or six weeks more.

Dearest love to you & mother[.] I am tremendously grateful to you for supporting me in my transfer here. You can't know what it has meant.   your devoted son   Archie

ALS: M

To Francis Hyde Bangs

Dear Frank: [*c.* March 1918?]   [French Tractor School]

Your various letters thankfully received. It regrets me that I have been so long about answering either your silence or your suggestions, but many pilgrimages make the heart weary. And I have had strange pilgrimages — not of the feet solely. Since I last wrote you I have heard death close overhead & have felt the swiftness of death & have seen the hand of death.[1] The thunderbolts of the King of Olympus were not more terrible. Out of the darkness a droning as of tremendous flies humming in the immensity of some mid-day of the moon. Then a louder

& more insistent sound of the whish of air between wooden blades. It draws near, it is overhead, it passes, circles — you can hear the engine falter as the wings bank, — it is overhead again: the heart numbs with elemental dread & there is a taste in the throat as of powder smoke: there is a lull that seems eternities long — then a leap of the earth underfoot & a shock of the air — then a dead, reëchoing roar that seems to come out of the center of the earth. Then silence blank as a white wall in the rain. Then the droning of diminishing exhausts. Then a sudden joyful music in the heart — joy of danger met & faced & trampled down.

The peace of the evening is now a portentious thing & the sound of birds singing an irony, & the look of stars in green water a threat.

But after all — what matters it at all? We know that the world liveth & that we are the life of the world & that such labor as we do, such beauty as we speak, such divinity as we perceive, enter into the life of the world. And we know that certain things there are which we *must* do for the yea-saying of our hearts. And if we do those things which are necessary for us to do, which we must do, then who are we to question in what coin we shall be paid? Surely the great stream of human life shall go on, & we in it, by the beauty which we have uttered & the labor which we have done. When I think of the generations of the dead who loved & desired & hoped, & all for naught, & are forgotten, and their bones dust, then I feel a certain great joy such as the leaf must feel in the swift water, that I am driven in this flood & that I am nothing, but only the work of my hands & the thought of my brain has meaning & intent & end. For surely this tide of life has somewhere its ending as the tide of love has ending in white arms & hair thrown wind-wise to the night, and a breast like summer's dusk for softness & sweet peace. Now it struggles against itself, stung somehow by the poison of old time, & why it struggles or whither no man knows, but only that out of the pain fire cometh. So then, if I fall in this moment or in that, what matters it since I shall have labored & dreamed & sung the labors & the dreams & the songs of *life*. Life is! Life is! — And life shall be; the poet singeth. Then I who am but a moment of life, & thou, who being stronger, are yet but an hour — *are* we not also — & *shall* we not be?

* * * * * * * * * * * * * * * * * * * *

Why do you ask me about Curtis?[2] How shall I tell? I do not understand grief that jests nor pain that makes sport of itself. That he was deeply hurt I know. That he faced his grief & won it to himself I do not know. Perhaps. Perhaps, again, he strove to forget. Surely he had soft hands to help him & a sweet mouth. Now he is torn many ways. That his wife is here & must return to the States again; that she must bear her child far from him; that his work here is distasteful to him — these things might embitter any man's heart, — even more so a heart which, like his, sees God jesting in the strange shape of man & roaring outright in a dull giraffe.

But why do you write me? I know nothing about men, — not even myself. You I know because you are the symbol of intellect & intellect I understand. Carter[3] I comprehend because he is the symbol of cell-life, & cell life I comprehend. But men wise in the world & scornful I do not understand. So I love Curtis but know him not at all.

Eyre is wonderful![4] Here she is *not* affected. Here she is woman. "I do wish it".[5] Oh Bang — look not upon the wine when it is dead but upon the grape when it is hot i' the sun. This is Wisdom!

Why in *God's* name did D.B. enter the Herald competition?[6] He should have *known* that they wanted claptrap. He's too good for that sort of thing. I am insulted in him.

Let me have a letter soon. My heart is grey. Eternity is not longer than the year.   yrs   Arch.

ALS: YCAL

1. M was now at a French tractor school where, nearer to the front, he had recently witnessed an aerial attack. 2. Curtis B. Munson (Yale '15), whose brother, a close friend of Bangs's, had recently committed suicide. 3. Lyon Carter (Yale '15) was one of those who had transferred with M from the Yale Unit to the field artillery. 4. Elizabeth Eyre, a friend of Bangs's to whom he would shortly, and unsuccessfully, propose marriage. 5. Compare *A Midsummer Night's Dream* IV, i, 179. 6. Danford Barney had entered a poetry contest sponsored by the Paris edition of the New York *Herald*.

To Arthur Twining Hadley

21 June 1918
My dear President Hadley:-   1st Battn, 146th F.A.   A.E.F.

You, engaged continuously in the warlike pursuits of peace, have little time to read, nor have I, occupied from reveille to taps in the peaceful pursuits of war, much time to write, of the world of sentiment. And yet I feel that I must tell you, while I still can, something of what Yale means to me throughout the hours and days of these long seasons of preparation and waiting. I have never been quite sane about Yale. I have done silly things. I have spent summer evenings perched like some night-blooming fowl on the fence of the College Campus, dreaming over the deserted walks and windows, and repeopling the worn triangles of green with a hundred generations of young Americans. I have sat an autumn night through in a window of the old college remembering things I never knew. I have travelled hundreds of miles when I could ill spare the time, to breathe the wind off the salt marshes again. I have done, I say, silly things. But nothing I have ever done could be compared for sheer sentimentality with the strange mental processes I have let myself go through in these last eleven months, almost, of France. I have let myself come to confound all America with Yale — to see in my memories of her keen swift hours, the keen young years of America, — to find in her standards of things good the ideas of liberty my country is fighting for, — to recognize in the ideals of beauty and intellectual strength & bodily fitness that inform so many Yale men of the decade past, the ideals for which an American ought gladly to lay down his life.

This is the sum of my offense against reason. And I hope I shall never acquire sanity again if utter sanity would drive me from these my symbols of our country's best purposes.

I have no words for the things Yale has given me. Friendships a man finds even in the armies of selfishness. Education — of sorts — a man acquires, I am informed, even at certain large universities of the far north.[1] But belief that life is worth all & more than it costs, that beauty is attainable, that the world of the mind is real, that men are in nature seekers of the true God — whatever the name they call him by — these things I have found only at Yale. And I am forever meeting in France young men of other universities who know these things to be true only of Yale.

Is all this to be true after the war? Pray God it may. If we shall have lost the ways we held, even though Germany is ten times destroyed, the war will have been unworth the winning.

Forgive me for boring you who have so much else to think of with all this. It would out.

Please give my love to Mrs Hadley & to Morris[2] when you write him. I hope I shall meet him in France if only for the pleasure of standing stiffly to attention   yours very sincerely   Archibald MacLeish

ALS: CtY

1. An oblique reference to Harvard University. 2. Morris Hadley (Yale '15), son of President and Mrs. Hadley, was a field artillery officer serving in France.

To Edwin Oviatt[1]

My dear Mr. Oviatt:-   1 November 1918   Camp Meade, Maryland

You might be interested in the following information relative to my brother and myself.

My brother went to France in October, 1917, and after a brief period of training in France and England, he joined a R.A.F. squadron at Dunkirk. He served with the British for about eight weeks, taking part in the Zeebruge show, and other similar bombing parties. He was then given a rest and promoted, and sent back to the front again. He has been missing in action since October 14th. When last seen he was in combat with a superior number of enemy planes above a small Belgian village. It seems to be a slight possibility that he may have been captured.[2]

I went to France in August 1917 with the Yale unit. Was commissioned in Field Artillery in November. Went to the front with the 146th Field Artillery in the spring of this year, and was ordered home in the middle of the Chateau-Thiery drive. Since arriving in the States, I have been promoted to 1st. Lieutenant, and assigned to the 33rd Field Artillery, where I am now Operations Officer.

Kindly renew my subscription to the weekly, and send me any back numbers since September.

Is it true that Henny Keep was killed in action?[3]

Very sincerely yours,   Archibald MacLeish

TLS: YARO

1. Editor of the *Yale Alumni Weekly*. 2. Confirmation of the death of Kenneth MacLeish (on 14 October 1918) was received by his family just after Christmas of that year. 3. Henry B. Keep (Yale '15) had died at the front on October 5.

To Albert Beecher Crawford[1]

My dear Crawford:-   10 March 1919   Cambridge

I don't know whether or not you care to be troubled by letters from those whom you are so generously interested to serve, but on the off-chance that it may be in line with your wishes I am hereby presenting my sad case.

I am looking for a chance to do editorial work with a political or political-literary magazine of the type presented by the Dial, New Republic, Nation etc.. By September of this year I shall have finished my work at the Harvard Law School and shall be most anxious to get located in some such work.

I have, of course, had no experience in work of the kind I suggest. At College I was chairman of the Lit [and I have] since perpetrated a volume of verse. I had a $\phi\beta\kappa$ stand there & have had an "A" stand at Harvard L. S.. This constitutes my entire claim to consideration. Recognizing its complete feebleness when applied to the mind of the modern Editor I hope for nothing but shall nevertheless be tremendously grateful to you for whatever you can do.

yours very sincerely   Archibald MacLeish (1915)

ALS: YARO

1. Acting director, Bureau of Appointments, Yale University. In February 1919, M had been mustered out of the army and had returned to Cambridge to complete law school in a special session for returning veterans.

To Francis Hyde Bangs

Bang:-   19 April 1919   Cambridge

Through half a circle of the careless sun
The world has wavered & our love has run
And only strangers tell me that you live;
Strange mouths & uncouth phrases give
The naked angles of your livlihood.
I'll not condemn your silence. In the blood
Strange alchemies occur that tinge the brain
With love & loathing — I'll no thing complain
If cognac intermixed with irony
Has wrought such change & carelessness in thee
That thou nor lovest nor remembrest me.

What change beside? Dost still with lordly mind
Bend every leap of intellect to bind
This apple-flavored life against thy will?
Dost see each girl mysteriously still?
And still dost read the all too towering script
Of this much written ball? Undiapered, stript
Of every woven counterfeit, dost charge
With heart heroical along the large
And misty horizons that cup us in
Crying "God's Evil & the Lords of Sin".?
Thou art not changed whatever else doth change.
Though many that were beautiful are strange
Stopped with the heavy earth; my brother's heart
Tho' clay indeed to that great Potter's art,
Thou art not changed. Still gracefully aloof
Thou laughest at the centaur's horsey hoof
Deridest still the paunch that mocks the brain
As granaries naysay the poppied plain.
Still dost'ou wonder (yet without amaze)

At woman's beauty & the sensual blaze.
Still dost believe that if we kiss her close
Earth will give answer & the summer's rose
Open her heart to us. Oh Bang! Oh Bang!
We are the damned in whose dull ears the clang
Of Heaven's overstanding gates still rings!
We hear not earth however sweet she sings;
We hear not life however clear he blows;
"This *is* the riddle read, the opened rose."

Damned! We're not damned! We're lady-bugs that crawl
A mighty printed page, and flop & fall
And blunder till at last the spirit's light
Discovers all: we cry: Life's black & white!
And if thereafter some uplifted fly
Drones us a sentence as he flickers by
Of all the sentences that life has writ,
We laugh & bid him come to us & sit
Close to the very fact; so shall he know
With fine assurance how the seasons go.

Sargent last evening on the city street!
A jar of brakes, a veering car, a fleet
Unlaughing smile behind the shining glass
And she descended: — winds that stirr the grass
Sunset on water, fanciful as these
And momentary, stabbed with the hot disease
Of beauty, & the deathless dream
That stone can prison the unprisoned gleam;
Mocking herself in mocking all she loves
Loving her mockery, — our lady moves
Forever westward, opposite the world,
Her eyes a jest, her hair a dream unfurl'd.

When do you come again — the earth is full
Of shadows & hobgoblin things — I pull
A worm occasional from withered sod
And dodge the acorns that a school-boy God
Throws at my peeking head. Art still in love?
I care not yet I crave a word thereof.

                                                        Arch

ALS: YCAL

To Anson Phelps Stokes[1]

Dear Mr. Stokes: 28 April 1919   Cambridge

Thank you very much for your letter about the few sentences of Kenny's. I don't know where the card could have come from but I do know the letter it must have quoted and I have always thought it very beautiful. Mother will be so happy to know of the use to which you put Kenny's words.[2]

I am taking advantage of your interest in my various attempts to get back to New Haven to lay before you my most recent and most serious attempt. Shortly after coming back to the Law School I made up my mind that my job in life was teaching — not English but Government. I was a little sceptical about my equipment but I was reassured by Dean Pound and Laski[3] and a few other people to whom I went. They all seemed to feel that a Harvard Law School training was almost an ideal preparation for teaching in the general field of government. As a result I went to New Haven two weeks ago to ask Max Farrand[4] for his advice. He was most cordial and told me that very possibly I might work in as an instructor in History for a year and then get over into the teaching of Government. This morning, however, I am in receipt of a letter from him to the effect that opinion in the Department seems to be against the making of an offer to me, — though final decision has not been made. In the meantime I have received an offer from the University of Chicago which would seem to require immediate action[. . .].[5]

My problem, briefly, is that there seems to be no opening whatever in the Government Department as it now exists (I have talked to Prof. Johnson),[6] that no one seems to know whether there will be an opening there or indeed whether there will be a Department, and that the History Department is naturally not over-eager to make a place for a man who wishes to work in another field — at least I presume that to be an item though there may be more personal objections. You will see where all this leaves me. I can't afford to put in further time in graduate work. I know I can teach Government. I want to work at Yale. And — there doesn't seem to be an answer.

I am troubling you with all this because you have been good enough to be interested in me and because you can tell me whether I am on a wild-goose chase. If there is to be increasing emphasis on the teaching of Government and Political Science at Yale I would do anything I could to put myself in a position to work in that field.

Please do not feel that I am writing with the hope that you will intercede in my behalf. I am troubling you simply because I cannot find out elsewhere what the situation is, or is going to be, at New Haven.[7]   Sincerely yours,

Archibald MacLeish

TCO: CtY

1. Secretary of Yale University.   2. Possibly a reference to a leaflet entitled *A Soldier's Version of the Easter Message*, which contained excerpts from a letter Kenneth MacLeish had written from the front in January 1918, and which had just been privately published, perhaps with Stokes's help.   3. Harold J. Laski, the British political scientist, then teaching at Harvard.   4. A member of the Yale history department.   5. This letter was transcribed from a typed copy of the original document, which I have not been able to locate. The bracketed ellipses indicate a point at which the text of the typed copy is garbled. *See* the following letter, note 1.   6. Allen Johnson, a professor of American history at Yale.   7. *See* M to Allen Johnson, 24 December 1920.

To Martha Hillard MacLeish

Dearest Mother:-   7 May 1919   Cambridge

Your very beautiful letter & the wonderful pictures of Kenny have come. For the latter I have no words of thanks. You know how glad I am to have them & how much everything connected with Kenny means to me. I think they are very, very wonderful. They show a great deal of Kenny that more formal pictures miss — his charm of expression & his beauty.

Your letter goes right to my heart. I cannot feel that I deserve your happiness in me but if you can have happiness in me then perhaps it doesn't matter whether I deserve it or not. I don't suppose that even now I understand in the slightest measure the full meaning of all you & father have given me and done for me. I suppose it is part of the ironical justice of this life that we only learn the full value of things by seeing them unvalued or lacking & I have not yet had that experience. I feel very keenly my own unworthiness just now. To be twenty-seven years old & to have accomplished no more than I have accomplished is not a matter for congratulation. And still less can I feel any complacence when I am not sure, even now, in what way to use my life. My various plans circle around me like moons, now in eclipse & now in a full & alluring light. Each one has its elements of attraction & each one its elements of repulsion. And the poor sea of my inclination has as many conflicting tides as there are rising & setting moons. I suppose I will find my decision made within a few days & shall then give over indecision for regret. Why is it so bitterly hard for me to choose?

I have written Dr. Judson[1] & forwarded the questionnaire to Mrs. Aldrich. I should use the same picture you used before. It is particularly good for that I think. It is dear of you to want to get the Flandin[2] a wrist-watch with Kenny's money. And in this I cannot feel any hesitancy. For you see she was very good to him too & oh so fond of him. I wrote her three weeks ago at Beaumont & should hear from her within a month. Then I think it would be best as you suggest to send the watch from C.P.S. direct to her.

Dearest love from all of us to all of you there at Craigie Lea   God bless you   your devoted son   Archie

ALS: CAMPBELL

1. Harry Pratt Judson, president of the University of Chicago, with whom M had been discussing his possible appointment as a member of the university's Department of Government. 2. An unidentified friend of Kenneth MacLeish's.

To Harry Pratt Judson[1]

Dear Dr. Judson:-   5 June 1919   Cambridge

Since the receipt of your letter I have been trying to find out what my status here at Harvard was — whether or not the position teaching Constitutional law, which I had said I would accept some weeks ago, was to be offered. I hoped very earnestly it would not be. Dean Pound was very frank in his advice to me to go to Chicago if I possibly could, & many other things drew me in the same direction. For one thing the work you describe sounds much more interesting, and for another the present reward & the future opportunity are very much greater. And since Kenneth's death I have been most anxious to be near father & mother.

It was only this afternoon that I was finally able to ascertain that my appointment here has already been voted & that I am bound by my promise to accept the position if it was offered. I have only myself to thank for the result, — but that doesn't make it any more pleasant. Please accept my most heartfelt gratitude for your interest & for all you have done for me. I would give a great deal to be able to unsay what I said in April to the head of the Government Dept here.[2] But unfortunately he is in France & I am tied hand & foot

very sincerely yours   Archie MacLeish

ALS: ICU

1. See the preceding letter, note 1. 2. George Grafton Wilson, with whom M worked closely during his two years as a Harvard lecturer, 1919–1921.

To A. Lawrence Lowell[1]

My dear President Lowell:-   7 September 1919   Farmington

Although I wired you yesterday setting forth my position in regard to President Judson's request for my release as well as the brevity of a telegram would permit, I should like to explain more in detail what the situation is — or was. It must seem to you that I have been engaged in very curious diplomacy. As a matter of fact I have made no motion since I accepted the appointment I now hold at Harvard. Just after I had accepted it I received an offer from Chicago carrying a larger salary & a more responsible position which I declined on the ground that Prof. Wilson had sailed for France & that I could not reopen the question at Cambridge. Very recently President Judson made inquiry of my mother as to the obstacles in the way of my accepting an appointment at Chicago if Harvard would consent to release me. I heard of this through my mother & thereupon wrote you. By that time I had made all my plans to remain at Harvard & had done a good bit of work on my course of Constitutional Law & desired very much to see it through.

If my efforts to escape a better paid & larger position in favor of a temporary appointment in a subsidiary capacity at Harvard seem curious they must be explained on the basis of another curiosity — that it is possible for Yale men, born & bred, to feel, after three years of Harvard Law School, a very persuasive affection for Harvard

I am sorry to have been, in any way, the cause of extra trouble to you.   sincerely yours   Archibald MacLeish

ALS: MH (ARCHIVES)

1. President of Harvard University.

To Martha Hillard MacLeish

Dearest Mother: 23 October 1919   Cambridge

I like your fore-word so much.[1] It seems to me you have perfectly caught the spirit of Kenny's boyhood and maturity — if it is not ironical to apply that word to one who had just arrived at a first perception of things. I can think of nothing to add unless it were possible in some way to give expression to some of the estimates of Kenny's work as a flier. Bob Lovett (Lt. Com. Robert Abercrombie Lovett, US.N.A.F.) told me last week that Kenny was the best shot in the Northern Bombing Group or in any one of the English schools he attended or in the 213 Squadron. He also said that not only in his opinion but in that of many of the English officers with whom he talked Kenny was the most beautiful flier along his part of the front — a flier whose work was never rough or rash but perfect in detail and in execution. Bob also says that Kenny's report on the training methods in use in the navy for training fliers was a subject of debate in naval aviation circles for a long time and finally brought about a complete revolution in the whole scheme.

As to the title of the book — I find there is very little that occurs to me along the lines you have laid down. "The Wings of the Morning" would well express what you have in mind but it has the vice of being trite. It would seem to me that the simplest title would be the most desirable. After all is said and done this is simply a book about Kenneth for Kenneth's lovers, and a title which might be very fitting and expressive for a book of fiction or for a book of letters that was to be put on the market for general sale might seem stilted and sentimental for such a book as you plan. I dont think your titles are subject to this objection but I feel we can get even closer to what we really want by calling the book just what it is. Why not name it "Kenneth". Or if that seems too informal then "Lieutenant Kenneth MacLeish, U. S. Naval Air Force"? I offer this because you ask for my opinion. I by no means feel that my suggestion is the better. It has always been hard for me to name my own things well.

I should suggest that you call my piece about the body "A Letter from Bruges"[2]

Ishbel's letter I fear is not available. We put it away for little K. in Farmington and there is no way of getting at it until one of us goes down there. Mrs. H. is congenitally incapable of finding anything — and we put these things away where we hoped she would not find them. I am so sorry.

My name might as well be signed Archibald. Leffinghe should be changed to Schoore.[3]

Of your titles I like best "They shall Mount Up with Wings"

The whole scheme sounds beautiful.

Very hurriedly your devoted son   Archie

TLS: M

1. Mrs. MacLeish had prepared an edition of Kenneth MacLeish's wartime letters home; entitled *Kenneth*, it was privately printed in 1919. 2. *Kenneth* contained four poems by M; the one here referred to was published as "A Belgian Letter." 3. Leffinghe was the Belgian town near which Kenneth was initially thought to have gone down; Schoore, some ten kilometers to the southwest, was where the body was found.

To Dean Acheson[1]

My dear Dean:- 17 November 1919 [Cambridge?]

It was tremendously thoughtful of you to let me have the typed sheets of O.W.H.'s dissent, and Pelion upon Ossa to let me have the printed report of the whole.[2] Holmes' test certainly goes the whole way — Zack[3] says it goes as far as *his* imagination is capable of pushing the thing. And if Clark's opinion displays anything it is that the principal crime of Abrams et al was not their pamphlet but their beliefs. I read Holmes' dissent to my Class with what I thought was a fairly tragic solemnity: then fought about it with Kimball[4] who thinks our obligations to Kolchak[5] foreclose us utterly & who seems to think that International Law permits intervention to prevent murders by proletarians though it presents a brass front to intervention to ameliorate the cruelty of Gordon.[6] We argued until I discovered that Day believed nations exist to support their foreign offices. Then I withdrew with heavy losses. Day's mind, set in the midst of Days social opinions, reminds one of a blazing electric incandescent fixed to the stem of some massive candelabra of old France.

The Russian meeting was a strange & wonderful thing.[7] Ada & I stood in a crowd of non-Anglo-Saxons in front of Faneuil Hall only to be shut out after an hour of jostling & shoving and swaying and swearing in an atmosphere of stinking breath, meat-market odors and a haze of garlic. We then made our way to an overflow meeting at Tremont Temple where we paid 25¢ for seats in the midst of a family of swarthy jews, & plotted pogroms.

Dr. Morison of H.U.[8] began the evenings vocal exercises with a very concise, clearly-put outline sketch of the history & development of European intervention in Russia, a summary of our part in it, a statement of the International Laws applicable, & a denunciation of the wholesale starvation planned. He supported Bullitt[9] at all turns and in general conducted himself very well. The only exciting incident during his speech was a reference to Lenine which his audience greeted with resounding cheers much to the poor lecturers discomfort.

Col. Robbins[10] followed him. His address is that of William Jennings Bryan leading a Sunday School Class in a negro settlement.[11] His substance is usually worth listening to. His point of attack was the policy of intervention as a policy. 'Lenine & Trotzky are anything but murderers and thieves (Roars of Applause)[.] Their theory of government & of society is economically & morally vicious & stupid (Applause by the other Anglo-Saxon present; followed by hisses from the representatives of Russian culinary labor, rear center)[.] If we would let them alone the extremists would be out of power in six months (Dead silence)[.]

As it is we are stamping Bolshevism in, not out. Blockade means that the Bourgeois who are the finest people in Russia (an obvious slip greeted by an astonished & unbelieving silence which melts into tolerant relief as R. recounts the evidences of their fineness — their culture & artistic taste & real education) will starve first. (Roars of laughter by thick-lipped, bull-necked men & women obviously well supplied with the comforts of life[.]) I thank God I am not one of those who believe that the great foundations of our government can be overturned by a Foreigner gesticulating on a street corner (Sharp intaking of breath)[.] My forefathers have fought for the Republic for 200 years. I never doubted its greatness until I saw it abolishing freedom of speech & of the press to secure its stability. (Applause) But it shall not be overturned (Groans) etc. etc. etc..'

It was a most interesting evening. Robbins wasn't very informing but his audience was as eloquent as the builders of Babel. They were all well-to-do, all alien — & almost all jews. They had come to weave red ribbons in their beards & shout Hallelujah. And here stood a man who had been in Russia at the head of the Red Cross for two years, who thought intervention was bad because it was an unAmerican policy — not because it was anti-Bolshevistic — & who believed in personal liberty of speech and opinion because these were Anglo-Saxon traditions — not because their negation stopped the mouth of alien propaganda. They simply couldn't believe their ears. At least they couldn't until Fisher[12] got up to make a request for funds. But when his voice cracked in an hysterical & ungrammatic sentence about the existing economic order they rose as one jew & rejoiced. They recognized their own kind & loosened their neck ties.

The gist of it all is, as Z.C. says, that the wrong people went. To an audience of granite-brained, Plymouth-Rock begotten Bostonians, the meeting would have been revolutionary, aggressive, unbelievable, but it would have set them thinking & Robbins words would have been forceful. To the amateur revolutionaries who did attend Robbins was as conservative as Pres. Taft and his arguments were incomprehensible.

My personal reaction was one that I'm not too proud of. I find race feeling runs pretty hot in my veins. If economic change & political advance mean unsaddling our vulgar, uneducated but nevertheless agreeable leisure class to seat the Jews of the Ghettoes of Russia in their places I'm a reactionary. God, how I wished for a pogrom in Tremont Temple.

But I wont bore you any longer with this. If you disapprove of my attitude attend the nearest "Red" debating center & react for yourself. Believing as you do in the solution of the problems of civilization by intellection you will be as disgusted as I was with people who mistake words for thoughts and a gesture for the millenium.[13]

I went to N.H. over the Princeton game & spent much time in conversation with Jenks about practice in New York.[14] Almet is thoroughly discouraged with routine & pay & prospect. Macdonald[15] hates the whole petty circle. I must say I can't work up any enthusiasm over John's[16] determination to go there. Laski seems to be creating the usual unusual stir at New Haven.[17] They all say they think he's clever but untrustworthy — & then they confess to no evidence of any kind on the latter charge. On his side he says Yale undergraduates are (a) more gentlemanly (b) more homogeneous (c) less mature by a year, than Harvard dittos. As to (a) — one trip across the Campus last Saturday convinced me that he is right

I must bring this Examination to a close before I consume too much of Wilson's paper & your patience. God bless you Sir.

yrs   Arch

ALS:CtY

1. Acheson (1893–1971) was a classmate of M's at Yale and at Harvard Law School and one of his closest lifelong friends. He was serving in Washington as law clerk to Justice Louis Brandeis. 2. Associate Justice Oliver Wendell Holmes of the U.S. Supreme Court had recently dissented in *Abrams et al.* v. *United States* (250 U.S. 616, 624), a case in which radical leader Jacob Abrams and others had been found guilty of violating the Espionage Act of 1917 by distributing leaflets that opposed the sending of American troops to Russia to support White Russian (anti-Bolshevist) forces there following the revolution of 1917. The majority opinion had been written, as M indicates, by Associate Justice John H. Clarke; Justice Brandeis had concurred with Holmes's dissent. *See* M to Arthur N. Holcombe, 29 May 1921. 3. Zechariah Chafee, Jr., a professor at Harvard Law School and a noted champion of freedom of speech. 4. Day Kimball, a law school classmate and friend of M's. They joined Choate, Hall & Stewart at about the same time (1920) and worked together on several cases. 5. Admiral Aleksandr V. Kolchak, leader of the White Russian forces that the American troops had been sent to support. 6. A reference to General Charles George Gordon (1833–1885), the British soldier whose exploits in China and the Sudan made him a symbol of British imperialism. Lytton Strachey wrote of him in *Eminent Victorians* (1918). 7. In November 1919 radicals and other interested persons held several mass meetings in Boston and elsewhere to mark the second anniversary of the Bolshevist regime in Russia. The meeting M attended, judging from the speakers present and M's account of their remarks, was a good deal less partisan than most — at least on the podium. 8. Samuel Eliot Morison of the Harvard history department. 9. William C. Bullitt, an American delegate to the Paris Peace Conference following World War I, leader of a secret, and ill-fated, diplomatic mission to Moscow during the conference, and an early defender of the Soviet regime in Russia. (*See also* M to Ernest and Pauline Hemingway, 19 June 1927.) 10. Colonel Raymond Robins, another American defender of the Soviet regime, had traveled widely in Russia (as an honored guest of the Soviet central committee) while a member of the Red Cross Mission to Russia, a relief group. 11. Bryan, three-time Democratic presidential nominee, was noted for his gifts of oratory. 12. Presumably Judge Harry M. Fisher of Chicago, head of a committee of the Jewish War Relief Fund of America that raised millions of dollars

for the starving Jews of Poland and the Ukraine. **13.** Compare M's poem "Background with Revolutionaries," in *Frescoes for Mr. Rockefeller's City* (1933). **14.** Almet F. Jenks, Jr. **15.** Ranald H. Macdonald, Jr., class- and club-mate of M's at Yale and later, as a member of the investment firm Dominick & Dominick, M's financial adviser. **16.** John H. Vincent, a Yale and Harvard Law School graduate friendly with both Acheson and M. **17.** Harold J. Laski was a professor at Harvard but, at the time this letter was written, a visiting lecturer at Yale.

To Dean Acheson

my dear Dean: 1 December 1919 [Cambridge]

Your letter arouses so many & such various emotions that, although I have but twelve minutes between me & my one:thirty I can't put off the beginning of a reply

① *Poetry*: If we are as nearly agreed about all things as we are about this let us hang out our shingle (of this more anon) where & when & as you will. Obscurantism — the attempt to use words by virtue of their sound in fact or their sound in fancy (i.e. their connotations) to convey a sort of overtone of emotional or imaginative excitement without the double bass of sense is to me the vainest of all vain things. The man who seeks that mode of expression is as clear a failure as the born mason who aspires to needle-work: he is a musician turned wordster — & no one is the richer. You remember that, in Plato's Apology for Socrates he has S. say that, in his search for one wiser than himself, he accosted the poets — that the poets did not understand themselves what their verse meant. This has been accepted by some fiddlers in poetry as a graceful statement of Plato's conviction that poets were above mere Aristotelian reason. But God save us! — Plato kept them out of the Republic. No — the truth is on the other horn of the moon. Poetry must not prove, must not explain, must not logically establish — but it must come, as you put it, to a "clear end". You must have an *expressible* idea of what the poet is after. If the idea is not expressible it shouldn't be attempted in words. Might as well go about from house to house stroking the genitalia of his readers[1] as attempt to convey some vague nebulous erotic conception that no crystallized idea has ever included. For words are simply the sign posts or indicca of mental apprehensions which have reached such a degree of clarity that they are capable of transmission. And to attempt to use words which have such clear meanings for things sensed or dreamed that have not yet emerged from the mist of mere subconsciousness is like using bricks to convey the idea of a dawning glow. But I must run to lecture on the Fed vs the State Jud. Power — Cohens v Va etc..

3:00 P.M — The philosophic advantage of poetry seems to me to

59

be merely this — that the poet is not restricted to logic & chronology to get his ideas across — he has also access to the emotional short cuts, to metaphors that prove themselves, & to a melodic form of expression that makes the reader anxious to believe. The practical benefits are that the poetic form offers a medium for short pieces, that the reader of poetry habitually expects non-logical forms, & that a certain poetic convention makes wild flares of highly figurative verbiage understandable & reasonable. Poetry made up of words so arranged as to give a certain beauty of sound and a certain aura of suggestion, with no attempt whatsoever to make use of their vital quality as expressions of ideas[,] is like a juggling feat performed with pianos — ludicrous because of the essential misuse.

But the difference between us is that, to my mind, the Masque[2] is perfectly clear — a work of intellection as well as a work of art — great not only for its subtle statement of the oneness of man & God but great as well for its perfection as sheer art, supreme beauty of form, depth of emotional feeling.

This is a long lecture but I am under compulsion to deliver it because your criticism comes so [close] to my state of mind. D. Barney attempting with Websters favorite children to unscrew the inscrutable is to me as pitiable & humorous a spectacle as ever was poor lunatic who went about the world playing Desdemona to his jack-knife's Othello.

Your suggestion as to practice is one that warms the cockles of my poor, throbbing, pedagogic pump. I think you have put your finger on a possible solution to the great problem: How can I avoid "SUCCESS" intelligently?. Working together with a common sense of the greatness of the law as a social instrument, the infinite capacity of the human brain to shape that instrument and with a very real opportunity to engage in an actual warfare with the stubborn Great Ones of our time to the end that the law may be justified — working so even practice might be delightful. The fields open to us would be varied &, if not over profitable, at least tremendously interesting. And I have a shrewd suspicion that we might be able, by dint of exceeding great labor, to insert a stealthy legal poiniard between the joints in the armour of Gary-ism.[3] At all events we must talk this over & see whether something can't be worked out. I suppose an apprenticeship w'd be necessary. But the geographical q. is one of the most vital.

I must get to work reading papers & so heap to myself my dull reactions to your exceedingly interesting states rights argument

yrs   Arch.

1. In a note above the salutation of this letter, M wrote, in reference to this passage, "*N.B.*:- Dont let Alice [Mrs. Acheson] see the unfortunate slip bottom p 2 for wh. I hereby apologize." 2. Probably a reference to Moody's *The Masque of Judgment*. 3. Gary, which was probably the surname of a lawyer of whom M disapproved, is unidentified.

To Francis Hyde Bangs

Dear Francis   26 December 1919   Glencoe

I cannot be sure whether it was the subtle flattery of your request or that sense of the coming on of the end of the world which approaching vacation gives in an academic surrounding. At all events I put off answering your letter in accord with its request so long as the material for so answering it was at hand. Now I must simply pound out certain fitting sentiments on this damn old wreck of a 1912 Remington — a machine which adapts itself to the expression of ideas about as well as the mind of the average Harvard undergraduate adapts itself to the absorption of them. As a matter of fact I am not at all sure the world is not better off for that. The imperviousness of the ordinary mind to liberal opinion is the best guarantee of clean hard thinking we have. Imagine a world in which people could be persuaded with a simile. Instead of Platos and Macchiavellis and Maitlands and Arnolds we should have had a full flood of lyric philosophers, gentlemen who interpret history in the light of burnished armor and the soul of man by its reflection in the moods of a country-side. Or worse, we should have had literary men who made no attempt to think a reaction through to its cause in action, gastric or psychic, but accepted the result as in some way complete and self-sufficing and worthy of expression. A stomach-ache in itself is of no importance — hitched up with its causes it may be the type of tragedy or a cosmic guffaw. Or worst of all we should have had poets who not only refused to rationalize what they did think but even went so far, or stopped so short, as not to express what they felt in terms of thought at all, using words for their effect on the drum of the ear or the saliva glands of the mouth, and succeeding only in giving the effect that one gets from a juggling feat in which the acrobat uses pianos instead of dishes. Fortunately the world is persuaded by none of these.

But we who believe in the efficacy of thought and thought and yet more thought have need nevertheless of the tempering winds of first perceptions and unrationalized impressions. If you act only upon that which grounds your philosophy and if you are honest you will never act. Extraordinary admission for a rationalist — it appears that one must take his most perilous steps in life on the imperfect evidence of faith. Yet this is the merest platitude. For every man who grows takes first of all the supreme act of faith — he agrees with himself to believe that the world and all that in it is is something more than the stuff of his own dreams; that life in it is worth while. And from that point on he continues to act on faith — he takes his freinds on faith, he marries on faith, he chooses his proffession and his religion on faith. Only after the preliminary act of belief has put him in motion does he, *can* he rationalize. Therein lies your greatest danger. You refuse to love with your eyes shut. Noblesse oblige — and you watch your freinds with every organ of intellect awake, ready and eager to laugh at their mistakes because the integrity of your mind seems to demand of you that you never blind yourself to the weak or the comic. And the extraordinary part of that attitude is that the very fact of your being here at all is evidence that you have been playing blind-mans buff for more years than I care to remember.

I give you my word I never intended this when I sat down to write.

yours always   Archie

TLS: YCAL

To Dean Acheson

My dear Dean:-   30 December 1919   Glencoe

Your telegram came this morning &, together with your letter of this morning, your letter of 10 days ago & the book I expect to find awaiting me in Cambridge, puts me in your debt beyond redemption. However, since all our intercourse has more' or less the same effect I am enured to the burden.

It was good of you to talk me over with the J.[1] & to notify me so expeditiously of his award — &, what I value much more, your own. But I think if you had seen me this morning tramping up and down the frozen beach in the snow you would have wondered whether I was inspired with gratitude or resentment. I haven't felt as much like the volitionless wind-buffeted creature of circumstance in all my life of opportunism before. I took out my three pitiful shadows of careers — teaching, practice, journalism[—]& examined them individually & serially & in patterns till I was dizzy. Then I became philosophical & examined myself. And finally I gave it up & came home with a sense of having occupied a morning in silly imitation of the Lake which, with each breaking wave, breaks down the ice-wall along the beach & builds, with the same motion, new barriers beyond. An endless battle of shadows — & I myself am the battlefield & the opposing armies. How can any thinking man imagine that there is any thing real outside his own mind? The reality is not the chair but the chair as he sees it. The reality is not the career but the career as we think of it. Well do we say that we "make up our minds". We do just that & therein do we erect, each one of us, the universe. The difference is that only one or two in a generation project themselves the plan upon which they shall build.

I took one step ahead. I discovered that my ambition to date has not been to *do* a certain work in the world but to *be* a certain person. When I think of practice I think of the great practitioners & wonder whether I really desire to be as they are. If I think of the work at all it is to query whether work of that kind will give me an opportunity to *be* a little broader (more "cultured" the phrase was once) than the ordinary lawyer. When I think of teaching I think of the men who are teachers — & shiver. When I think of journalism I imagine the life of the adequate journalist & hesitate a bit over the lack of "position". All this is perfectly healthy. It is the imitative instinct in full play. I dare say it represents the steps of the usual method of selection. A man decides that he would like to *be* a literary man, or a broker or a merchant — & embarks, as an incidental thing, upon the labor necessary to become such an one. Ask the ordinary business man what the significance of his work is sub specie aeternitatis & he will talk about you over the coffee as long as he lives. He's never thought. He isn't interested in his work as work; he's simply interested in the job that sets him off as a banker or a manufacturer. The reason why he wants to be banker or m'f'rer may simply be that he hopes thereby to achieve the greatest wealth. But that doesn't change the character of his choice. He has chosen to *be*, not to *do*.

Now I was at one time what we shall call, for lack of a better title, a Platonist. I nurtured what I thought to be the Greek ideal. Perhaps I was not altogether in error about it. At all events it came down to a matter of self-development. One was to choose that way of life & thought & faith which would give him most in body, & brain & soul. I am not prepared at this time to argue the rightness or wrongness of that theorem. But one thing *about* it is most assuredly true; that it leads a man to make his choice of a profession in life with an eye to the sort of man he'll be, & the sort of position he'll occupy when his profession gets through with him. He isn't to do things through his job. His job is to do things to him. And the ideal job is that job that gives you most & hurts you least.

If that is a perversion of the Greek ideal we can still save our gods. If it is the natural application of the Greek ideal we'll have to tear down the old meeting-house. For if this is anything it is the blind, sheep-like acceptance of the pattern of the world as it is; the thing we most want to avoid. God save us, if a man is anything more than a potential prize vegetable it must be his purpose to act upon the world, not to wait to see what the world will do to him. It should be his ideal to free the world not to fatten himself. And he should choose that way of living that gives him the greatest leverage on the world. Incidentally, as non-Christians you & I may guiltily acknowledge the profound wisdom of the remark that he who loseth his life shall find it. For I imagine that he who intelligently undertakes, & loses himself in, a conscious labor is infinitely more likely to realize the Platonic ideal than the man who pursues his own ideality through youth & middle-life to find himself a shell at sixty.

If you can bear with me for a page or two more I want to free my chest of the apparent application of all this to my alternatives. First practice. If you strip practice of law of its attributes of income & position & look at it as a means of effectuating a purpose, as changing the scope or direction of the growth of law, or redeeming a class from bondage through the decisions of the courts it at once becomes apparent that almost any purpose for which the law might be practiced except that of wealth & "honor" may be better accomplished in some other way. As to the latter two — complete demurrer.

Second teaching. The trouble here is that you work at second hand. You are training *other men* who will work in *another generation* to effectuate the ideas you have developed or acquired. It is arguable that teaching in the narrow sense of the term is the only method known to man of giving true currency to ideas. But I query that. If that were true compute the number of ideas that would spread in the United States. Not one B.A. in a hundred carries an idea out of College. I think it is that feeling of working at second hand that makes the public think of teaching as an inferior profession and makes teachers themselves share the opinion. I do not mean that a man is only a man when he is engaged in putting ideas into practical operation. It is not the practice of the idea but its expression in terms that will convince that produces change. Once an idea is accepted its effectuation is certain. But I do mean that a man who works, not upon those now in active control but upon those who may be in control in a generation & who may or may not remember his name & face & purpose in a generation — such a man is working at second hand. In the eye of an all-seeing divinity his merit may be great & his accomplishments tremendous. He himself will never know whether he won or lost. Of course this applies only to the actual teaching. As an essayist & scholar your teacher may exert a tremendous effect in his own time. But there you are trenching on the field of journalism, using journalism to mean the profession of purveying news

& molding opinion. The Teacher-scholar speaks with authority the journalist never borrows — but for all that he is a journalist.

Thirdly journalism. We've been over this field. God knows that from the side of *being* somebody one doesn't achieve much. But I believe that as a means of accomplishing in ones own time journalism — editorial journalism — is a most effective vehicle. The right sort of paper would give its editors sufficient leisure to do substantial work in the field they were to cover & to give fair expression to their conclusions. And though such a paper might not have great power it would have power. The rare thing about it is that journalism offers a chance for thought & study & for the attempt to make ones conclusions current in the world which we call influence.

So here we stand. Incidentally the N.R.[2] has just thrown me over & left me high on the beach. I don't know which way I shall jump. But damn me purple if I don't land, geographically at least, near your point of impact.

So much — & much it is — for me. Your problem is more interesting because you know what you want & less intricate for the same reason. I think teaching is almost the perfect choice for you *because* the creative work you want to do lies in the field of legal philosophy, your teaching will give you material for that & your summers will give you the opportunity to do your writing. And once you have begun to get your ideas before the world the sense of working at second hand will never trouble you. Add to this the fact that you have a genius for teaching (witness all you've done to me) & the answer is simple. I want very much to see you at Harvard if you do teach & to that end I have talked to £ & written F.F..[3] If someone is going to get a job at the L.S. next year it ought to be you. If there is a chance of that you should know at once for £ has demanded my answer by Jan 7. Please wait, if possible, till I get back before you decide to stay in Washington. If nothing opens at Harvard this year why don't you stay with Brandeis another year? You lose nothing & you gain what a law teacher needs — outside experience. Then next summer you can write here. It seems almost certain that we can have the place. And it will be almost ideal for what we want to do.

Is there the remotest chance, think you?, that we might both go to the L.S. next year? I'd take it like a shot. Keep me informed won't you.

yrs   Arch.

I leave here for Conn. Jan. 5..

ALS: CtY

1. Supreme Court Justice Louis Brandeis. The awards to which M refers are unidentified. **2.** *The New Republic* magazine. **3.** Dean Roscoe Pound and Professor Felix Frankfurter, both of Harvard Law School.

To Dean Acheson

Dear Dean:- 12 January 1920 Cambridge

Shame & no other emotion or circumstance has imposed so durable a silence upon me. Henry Adams says that the distrust of ones own judgment & a total repudiation of that of the world is characteristic of the New Englander. Add a liberal supply of Scotch hopelessness & you have the man who can never reach a conclusion. On Friday last I told £ I wouldn't teach in his Law School. That was eleven A.M.. At two P.M. I rushed in to ask him to hold it open till Tuesday. That's tomorrow. In the mean time I've been twice around R. Hood's barn. No sooner do I determine upon one course than the other beckons like the cults of Artemis. The result is that I have lost belief in myself & interest in my destiny. I hope I become a shyster practitioner with an eye to fees & a habit of reading Mr. Hearst. I refuse to play Jean Jacques & lay my secret shamefulness open before you.[1] Anyway you're not an XVIIIth Century Catholic God & you might be bored. After I've seen Croly[2] tomorrow night & talked with a rich lawyer or so I shall flip a coin and decide my fate. (I shall see the rich lawyer merely in order to borrow the coin) Then I shall write an ode to departed opportunity & blow my brains out. I'd rather be in love with two girls than to find myself in my present predicament. A man's other career will live to haunt him: the girl he decides not to marry will develop uninherited characteristics about 40 & bother him no more.

The whole trouble is that you & I have permitted ourselves to become interested in the game for the candle's sake. The great & happy majority never sees the candle & usually doesn't know there's anything more to the game than left tackle. I'd lay you our perambulator against the surrender value of your Life Insurance Policy that the average adult male of our acquaintance never once doubts but that the motions he goes through from breakfast to bed are *Life*. Get any banker to confess & he'll assure you that banking is living. Of course there are men of other trades but they are either debtors or creditors or mortgagees or sureties. Get any lawyer to pray aloud & he'll divulge to Almighty God his conviction that lawyering is living & that the potential clients or possible malefactors he sees about him were put into the world by a forethoughtful god who would have been a lawyer himself if he had had better instruction. The point is that they've all swallowed the pattern — or let it swallow them. Since the breakdown of religion destroyed mankind's common sense of a common goal — eternal salvation — we none of us know where we're going or why. But having once started in the persons of our great-great grandfathers we keep going like mad. When my great-great-grandfather Brewster[3] became a divine on the ground that it was a respectable profession he made his choice because such a way of life was admittedly a direct road to salvation — & so reputed. The same thing was true of the Law. It was a dignified profession because it enabled a man to be godly without too much humility. E contra acting was disreputable because actors, as everyone knew, committed adultery. And now god's gone & we choose because of the desirability of the profession per se caring not one whit where it leaves us as long as we're rich & notorious when its through with us. So I say that when you & I look for a profession because of its value as a means for operating upon the world — when we postulate a Life around & above & beneath the rut we intend to get wedged in we're all wrong. We might as well choose a profession on the basis of our maternal great-grandmother's maiden predelictions. Damn the Irish!

This started out to be a paean of praise on Livingstone.[4] I've gone a very slight way but the book is utterly delightful. The Introduction promises heaven on earth. I think I'll not try to do him injustice by indiscriminate enthusiasm till I've read him. I'm not a Frankfurter (Bless him!)[.] But you've saved my life (as usual) with the Introduction alone.

Yours in the Hope of Heaven   Arch

My love to Alice & Jane.[5]

ALS: CtY

1. A reference to Jean Jacques Rousseau (1712–1778) and to his *Confessions* (1781, 1788). 2. Herbert Croly (1869–1930), cofounder of *The New Republic*, best known as the author of *The Promise of American Life* (1909). 3. Elder William Brewster (1567–1644), English separatist, Pilgrim printer, and spiritual leader of the Plymouth Colony. 4. Acheson had given M a copy of Richard Winn Livingstone's *The Greek Genius and Its Meaning to Us* (Oxford: Clarendon Press, 1912). 5. Jane Acheson, daughter of Dean and Alice Acheson.

To Martha Hillard MacLeish

The worst blizzard of years —
3 & 4 ft of snow in places
5 February 1920   Cambridge

Dearest Mother: (Read this to yourself first)

Forgive the use of type. I'm trying to keep my hand in all I can.

Its a long time since you've heard from me and I shouldn't blame you in the least if you gave me up. I don't know why it is that I find such difficulty in arranging my time so as to give me an opportunity to write the necessary letters.

A good deal has happened in some ways in the last few days. I've been struggling manfully as you know to come to a decent conclusion as to the thing I ought to do in this world and I've not found that it was any easier as time passed. I threw over the chance to teach at the Law School first. It wasn't easy to do but it was easier than the other decisions and it had to be attended to first. Then I spent some of Sister Blanche's check in a trip to New York where I talked to cousin Russell Hillard Loines[1] about practicing with him, and to members of Mr. Root's[2] firm about practicing there. Then I went down to see Mr. Croly at the New Republic. The first two offered me jobs. Croly said there was nothing there just now but that he would make a place for me if he could — and I now learn indirectly that he has.[3] I came home to fight it over. After a great deal of thinking I had about decided in favor of journalism. I recognized the obvious drawbacks. I saw that journalists were not as a class very highly respected and I saw that people are not as deeply affected by what they read in the papers as once they were perhaps. I was also doubtful about the future in such work. That is, if I found I didn't like it I would be in a difficult position. It would be very hard to get back into the practice of law and it would be impossible to get into the teaching of law again. But it seemed to me that the advantages outweighed the disadvantages. I would at least have plenty of opportunity to write and I would be very much in touch with the affairs of the world and possibly I might be able to make whatever small influence I have count. I say I had about decided — but I reckoned without my host. A week afterwards I was laid up with a cold. Under those auspicious circumstances Aunt Mary appeared. We talked: at least she did; at first I was too tired and done in to talk back. Then I got angry and we went at it. We argued general industrial conditions and politics and Wilson: she thought I was a bolshevik, and I thought she was a reactionary. Then we got down to my case and the fur flew. She told me journalists were of no influence, that even if they were I didn't know enough to influence anybody, that men of position, men of affairs were the really influential members of society, that I would be bitterly disappointed if I tried it and that my bridges would then be burned, and finally that life in New York on the amount of money we would have would be terrible for Ada and for Kenny and for me etc.etc.etc.ad inf.. I replied in kind as to the practice of law and we reached no conclusion. That lasted all evening until I was ready to cry. Then we started it again in the morning. When we parted we were hardly on speaking terms. But the result of it all was that I sat down to my thoughts again. It is certainly true that we could live delightfully in Boston for an amount that wouldn't pay present rents in New York. It is also true that we like Boston exceedingly whereas we both dislike New York and I go so far as to hate it. But it was hard to give up the idea of writing for which I have always lived. Finally I decided that perhaps by rigorously holding to my purpose of writing and rigorously sacrificing the ambition to be the greatest lawyer in Boston to the ambition to write I might be able to write about as much after a year or two in practice here as I would in the mills of New York journalism. The chances are against it. But I believe it is possible. And if it is I think I ought to practice. For the probability, if it is a probability, that I will realize my other ambitions is greater in the practice of law than it is in other things. What do you think?

I am still balking at the inevitable but I must soon reach a conclusion. Just at present we are troubled by the chances of finding a desirable place to live in Boston if we do stay. Rents are simply prohibitive and are scarce as hens teeth. We think that it might be a wise thing to buy a house. This must sound almost funny to you; it certainly does to us. But in talking to our friends we find that in the end it is much cheaper. We have been looking at old houses on Beacon Hill and they seem much more possible than anything that we have seen yet. Do you know Beacon Hill at all? It is the most fascinating part of Boston. A hundred or more years ago it was the fashionable quarter of Boston, but fashion began to move into the Back Bay and for a time most of the hill was given over to boarding houses of the shabby gentile order. Now people are beginning to buy back these old houses at a very reasonable figure and fix them over. The houses are all made of brick with the most marvellous doorways. Like most city houses they go up and up and up, but they get lots of sun and have little yards and even trees.

Of course there is so much to be said for and against the city. If we could not be perfectly sure of having our summers in the country we could not consider it for a moment. On the other hand, if we decide to live in Boston it will be with the understanding that we will be there for some time to come, and the sooner we can make a place for ourselves in the community and among the people we like, the better it will be for all of us. If we should start out in a suburb we should have to give up all hope of really knowing the people in Boston, a few of whom we already know slightly and like immensely. In another year we shall have to confront the school question and that fairly solves itself in the city.

We very much need the advice of wise persons like yourself and please let us hear just what you think of our scheme of buying a house. We find that we could buy and restore a house for an amount, the interest on which would come to much less than the smallest rent we have heard of. When taxes are added to this and a sufficient amount for upkeep, it amounts to about $78.00 a month rent. Of course we should not even mention this to father for it would be sure to worry him. Mr. Hitchcock[4] is coming home from the south in a week or ten days and we are going to talk it over with him. He could get the money for us without any trouble if he thinks we would be wise to buy.

Dearest love to you all — or both.

We are all well and happy.   your devoted son   Archie

TLS: M

1. Loines (1874–1922), a member of the firm of Johnson & Higgins, wrote poetry and was deeply involved in the world of letters. 2. Elihu Root (1845–1937), the American statesman, diplomat, politician, and lawyer, was head of an eminent New York firm specializing in corporate law. 3. M worked at the magazine in the summer of 1920 as an associate editor *pro tem.* 4. William Hitchcock, M's father-in-law.

To Dean Acheson

My dear Dean:-   20 February 1920   [Cambridge]

Not altogether as a mark of esteem, nor yet altogether to make amends for a long and clumsy silence do I thus address thee in this cardiac fluid, this bitter carmen ooze, such as one time did throb within the veins of Gary. Rather because the old pen is dry. Enough for verbiage.

Did I write an article about L. Wood in the Boston Transcript? I did.[1] Am I the president of the Hoover League of Harvard?[2] God wot I be. May these exhibits be reconciled by other consideration than the fact that I received $30.[00] for copying down General Wood's opinion of himself & submitting it in proper typewritten form to the editor of the Transcript? I confess I don't know. I wish I might lay claim to a glorious inconsistency but I'm afraid I can't. I acted in the first instance as a boughten journalist; in the latter as an undergraduate orator. Heaven may comprehend. As Brackett puts it — it must be sad to be like God — understand everything & so have no one to hate. Did you see his story in the Sat. Eve. Post? It purported to embalm the memory of Francis Bergen:[3] to my mind it owed whatever success it had to the verbatim rendition of certain of F.B.'s remarks. For the rest the F.B. of the story was as much like the F.B. we rejoyced in as a man's letters from France are like his deeds there. He writes home about the nearness of God & the stickiness of the mud and he actually adds tremendously to the color of Prunier's.

I have decided to practice law in Boston. If you care to refer to mountains & mice you are welcome. God knows I do. I have persuaded myself to believe that I can practice (at least to an extent) and find some opportunity within five years say, to write. I admit it is a myth — the sort of thing one loves to believe in when ones windows open over clothes lines & ash barrels rather than the "foam Of perilous seas".[4] Perhaps it is because my alternatives do not convince me. Perhaps it is because I'm getting on. Perhaps it is only that I want to live on the crown of Beacon Hill & so tempt you by my front door & attic study that you will come back to Boston too. I don't know. But I'm sure its not a willingness to let the world have its way with me — to let my generation move through me. I'm essentially a Carlylian for all your brilliance & John's doggedness. I have not given up the dream of setting my seal on the brow of the world: I've simply given up the hope of it.

The N.R. wants me to come down there this summer to fill in in Hackett's (!!!) absence.[5] I am so enamoured of our summer at Craigie Lea that I don't believe I shall go. I am tempted by the thought of a summer just before a great political campaign with them but I am infinitely more tempted by the four of us at Craigie Lea. So it depends somewhat on whether you can come in certainty. Can you tell at this date? Please don't think I really want to go to N.Y. & am simply being dull. My words are as true as the dicta of Holmes. It rests with you — & also, of course, with father's final decision about Europe but I understand that he intends to go now. Move Heaven to decide to come & write me about it when you can. Forgive an utterly stupid note. Our love to you all   Arch

ALS: CtY

1. Major General Leonard Wood, United States Army, a founder and veteran of the Rough Riders and in 1920, after a thirty-year military career, a candidate for the Republican nomination for President. M's article on Wood, entitled " 'Steady!' Is the Watchword Says Leonard Wood," appeared in the *Boston Evening Transcript*, 17 January 1920, Part II, page 6.   2. A club whose purpose was to encourage the presidential candidacy of Herbert Hoover, whose war relief work during and after World War I had brought him national prominence.   3. Charles Brackett, "The Counsel of the Ungodly," in *The Saturday Evening Post* 192 (14 February 1920), 26ff. Francis Bergen (Yale '14) had been killed in an automobile accident in May 1917.   4. From Keats's "Ode to a Nightingale."   5. Francis Hackett, an associate editor of *The New Republic*.

To Dean Acheson

Dear Dean:-   27 March 1920   Cambridge

I am but newly returned from an invasion of the 19th Century, following in your foot steps, & I am moved to wonder. Allowing for the wit, the queer intimacy-in-aloofness of Mr. Strachey, allowing for the literary quality of his book[1] — allowing for all the queer refractions & blendings of light that play about the dead, there is left an impression of men & women intensely, painfully, concerned with problems that concern us not at all. Neither you nor I nor anyone we know well enough to wish to know better spends hours & days demanding of immensity whether we have been truly called to that life we have adopted. Yet Florence Nightingale was alive ten years ago! These men spoke our language, they were sustained by the literature that sustains us, they endured similar traditions of propriety & of achievement. Think of the difference in the motive forces that drove their lives & that now drive ours. They were not interested in a solution of the universe; they were interested in an explanation, a rationalization of preconceived formula, that should please God. They were not interested in success; they were concerned with the Voice that urged them toward success. They believed in God & they believed in the Church of God & their whole concern was to reconcile themselves to the Spirit & his mundane expression. They found themselves in the world & their problem was to keep free of it. We find ourselves in the world & our problem is to remould it nearer to our heart's desire. We admit God — somewhere — somehow — & we wonder how we can fit him into our world. And this is within a generation or at best two. Are we the miserable creatures born into the lull after the great storm of faith had broken, or were they the blind victims of a city of thought built to such heights of intricacy — such towers of definition — that it could not but fall to earth? The book has had a profound affect on me. I cannot be scornful of the anguish of Newman however much his refinements of dogma & his lives of saints move my mirth. It has suddenly occurred to me to wonder where you & I are if our grandfathers were right! Lakes of Brimstone. My God! Let's go fishing! But is it not true that our equanimity as regards the problem of religion is due altogether to our ignorance of its premises? It requires no courage to whistle in a morgue if you think it a drawing room. Has it ever occurred to you as odd that we, indwellers in a communistic world & true children of its processes, should have lost altogether the communistic, organic idea of religion? We are intense individualists. God in my own heart means my particular concept of God shaped for my needs — perhaps myself in its purest aspects — it does not mean a universal divinity of whom the whole world is shadow — in whose image we are. What do you say?

No word from the N.R.. I hope now that they have forgotten me. Then we could find some place here in the East & have our summer anyway.   Love to you all   Arch

P. S. — Yale Review has taken an article of mine (& yours) on Education.[2]

P. P. S. — Tell me about Child Labor Case & other recent decisions.

ALS: CtY

1. Lytton Strachey's *Eminent Victorians* (1918).   2. M's "Professional Schools of Liberal Education," *The Yale Review* (new series) 10 (January 1921), 362–372.

To Martha Hillard MacLeish

Dearest Mother:-   18 April 1920   Farmington

It is an age since I've written you isn't it? So much has happened. I've decided on a life-work, bought a house[1] and found some Hillards. And that is as much as I've done in all my life before. Ada has written you that I have decided to go into Choate, Hall & Stuart [*sic*] in Boston & become a barrister. I am also going to teach my course in Constitutional Law at Harvard for one year more. After that I am going to apply myself altogether to the law & try to arrange to have time enough to write on occasion. Its an uninteresting outlook isn't it? Most high hopes boil down to that at last.

The house we have you to thank for. The seller was so anxious to break his contract & sell to someone else for $3000 more that we never should have gotten it if father's draft had not come when it did. I think you will like the house. It has at least the advantage of modernity & high ground & that means sun & air for Kenny. And it is attractive if not beautiful. I can tell you I thank the Lord for its possession. Rents are going up 50 to 100% & there are no rents to be had. Houses worth 8 & 10 thousand are selling at 20 & 25 — & there aren't any at any price. Most of our friends who are not settled are in despair. But its a general situation with which you must be familiar.

As for the Hillards. Mr William Emerson a great grandnephew of R.W.E. & the head of the school of Architecture at Technology[2] married some years ago a Mrs. Moffett of N.Y. whose mother was a Hillard, a neice of George S. Hillard. Mrs Emerson is a perfect delight & her husband is charming. They are very much of the grande monde having lived a long time in France (He is a chevalier of the Legion d'Honneur) and are very cultivated and charming people. Her mother is Mrs. White of Brooklyn, a delightful little old lady whose husband is the great American collector of Shakespeariana.[3] We had all three — the Emersons & Mrs. White — to dinner on Friday — & had a lovely time. I think you would fall in love with them. Mrs. White is very much of a Hillard. Mrs. $\left(\begin{array}{c}\text{Emerson}\\\text{Moffett}\end{array}\right)$ isn't. And her son & daughter (Moffetts) who are my age, not at all. You must come on & meet them all very soon.

I have sold an essay to the Yale Review for publication some time next year — subject Education. It will probably amuse you but its a serious matter to me.

I am going to work with the New Republic from the day I leave Havard [*sic*] in June till the middle of August when I shall start in practice. I'm taking no vacation at all. But I am taking a few days now. I have been here since last night & tomorrow my friend Day Kimball

& I motor down to Westover, then up to Lakeville for two days & then home. A bit of golf & a bit of law on the way.

Do you know whether Ishbel ever received two books I sent her at Tryon[4] in March?

I think your little Easter editorial in the Baptist paper very lovely. Prof. Wilson showed it to me. I cant tell you how wonderful & beautiful your faith is to me.

Give my dearest love to father & thank him again for his manifold kindnesses.

I am enclosing the first draft of something I did lying in bed this morning. If I wait to finish it it may never reach you.[5]

Ada & Kenny send their dear love as does   your devoted son
                                                                                Archie

ALS: M

1. Forty-four Coolidge Hill Road, Cambridge. The MacLeishes had been renting since the fall of 1919 at 10 Mason Street; prior to that they had lived at 9 Phillips Place. 2. Massachusetts Institute of Technology. 3. William Augustus White. 4. Fort Tryon, site of the Manhattan estate of the C.K.G. Billingses. 5. M enclosed an early version of "Sonnet" ("O too dull brain, O unperceiving nerves"), first published in *Parabalou No. 2* (1920) and later in *The Happy Marriage and Other Poems* (1924).

To Stephen Vincent Benét[1]

My dear Steve: 16 July 1920 [New York]

I am returning you the manuscripts you submitted in reply to my letter of last week.[2] I need not say, of course, that I like them all and particularly the first five as I have them now arranged. It would have been possible to have gotten *July Night on Spring Street* past the board but one or two of them were rather negatively interested and Charlie[3] and I thought it wiser in view of the hopes we have of you in the future, not to start you off with a piece which did not appeal very strongly to the whole editorial staff.

You can appreciate my emotion in appearing to be one to pass in judgment on your things. At least I feel it very keenly. But it is precisely because your general work is so very fine that I feel justified in taking the step I have mentioned. Please believe that Charlie and I are absolutely sincere in our hope that you will continue to submit things to the New Republic. Personally, of course, my connection with the paper being temporary, my interest is rather more in you than in the literary department of the New Republic and I really feel that you will reach a public here and reach it in a way that would be impossible in any other magazine I know of.

I rather gather from your letter that you did not think too highly of these pieces and that is my only consolation in being a party to their return. Certainly your work in Parabalou[4] was beyond criticism and up to the highest mark achieved in American letters, or English for that matter, in the last decade. John Gould Fletcher[5] told me very flattering things of your reputation in England. Please don't construe this letter as bunk. I mean it thoroughly and I do feel that I am in a very curious position.   Very cordially yours,   Arch

TLS: YCAL

1. Benét (1898–1943), the American poet and playwright, was a member of the Yale Class of 1919. 2. M was writing from the offices of *The New Republic*. 3. Charles A. Merz, formerly of *Harper's Weekly*, was now an associate editor of *The New Republic*. 4. A magazine of verse by recent Yale graduates, including M and Benét; three issues were published in 1920 and 1921. 5. American poet (1886–1950), then living in London.

To Martha Hillard MacLeish

Dearest Mother: 12 October 1920   Cambridge

This should come to you on the second anniversary of Kenneth's death. As time goes by I have a strange impression that it is we who are leaving Kenny, rather than Kenny who has left us. Two years ago only the reported fact that he had been killed altered the situation for us. We really had him still as much as though he had been alive. He was no farther removed from us in our last impression of him then than he would have been had he lived and remained in France. But now days & weeks & months have passed & we must, if we would touch the living Kenny, retrace all that length of time and labor to relimn the images time has been so busy effacing. We dont feel, at least I dont, that Kenny has gone farther from us. But I feel as each period of time goes by that the current of time & change is bearing me away from the things he & I knew together, & gradually wearing out my memory of the tone of his voice & the way he had of laughing as though he were really glad & the carriage of his head & his smile. I can still feel the grip at my heart when I write of these things because they still have a vitality & existence. But I know that in a few years I shall not be able truly to feel them. And when I have been so far carried away from the Kenny who was my brother that I cannot reconstitute any single quality or characteristic of him with such certainty as to make the nerves respond as though he had been really there — why, what will Kenny be to me then? I think perhaps he will have a truer because a more idealized existence. Men become the symbols of ideas by losing their familiar & personal qualities. And Kenny as the symbol of brave youth content to die for the battle's sake will really exist when the Kenny who so nearly

& intimately touches my heart has a little paled & faded into oblivion. For Kenny is the only one of us all whose immortality is provably sure. He belongs now & will belong more & more as time passes to the immortality of great ideas. He is one of the innumerable points of star fire that make up together man's great conception of the capacity for splendid and generous daring of the human heart. Whether he will live in his own proper person with his own lovliness & gentleness & timbre we cannot know. I, for one, cannot believe he, or any of us, will. But he has immortality nevertheless for his death flung him at one stroke into the heaven of man's deepest faith. Kenny cannot die so long as men believe in youth and the beauty of youth and the perfect generosity of youth's sacrifice.

I don't believe I gave you a little verse I wrote at Craigie Lea this summer. You will think of the days when there is a strong East Wind & the gulls hang in the sun motionless between heaven & earth, or slide gently against the wind, just over the lip of the bluff. On those windy days the garden is always very still where the trees & the hedges shield it —

> Here in this inland garden
>   Unrumorous of surf,
> Here where the larches warden
>   Only the sunny turf,
>
> Here in the windy weather,
>   Here where the lake wind lulls,
> Slowly on silver feather
>   Drift overhead the gulls.
>
> O heart estranged of grieving,
>   What is a sea bird's wing?
> What beauty past believing
>   Are you remembering?[1]

Dearest love to you all   Archie.

ALS: M

1. A revised version of this poem was first published as "Alien" in *Parabalou No. 3* (1921) and later in M's *The Happy Marriage and Other Poems*.

To Dean Acheson

Dear Dean: 5 December [1920?]   Cambridge

There must be something beside delay to constitute lackers — & that something more is here lacking.

I shant observe the usual historical tradition and bring myself down to date — largely because your challenge is dateless & has nothing whatever to do with time. You allege in effect, & by artful innuendo & colloquium, that, if the law is an excellent game it is therein & thereby justified, and that it is mere surplusage & impertinence to say of it that it has no meaning. And you enlarge this allegation by your second Count which deals abruptly with the claims of poetry. I have no time to demur knowing the inevitable consequence. So defend you upon the merits — if you have any.

I take it that we would both agree that the one common quality of all games is the incidental quality of the objective. Even in sports it is no object to win the particular match. Save to the Johnny Macks of this world[1] the purpose of all intelligent men in opening their pores is exercise & physical well-being. And in the less violent games like chess and gambling the purpose is variously excitement, distraction, release, nepenthe — results equally well obtained by winning and losing. No man plays a game to acquire skill unless it be by way of insuring his power to distract himself in future. Now if the law is a great & thrilling game & if it is professed by intelligent men for that reason it must be because it offers an eminently practical means of escape from self. And that is what I intended to suggest when I said the law had no relation to reality. And that I suppose is what you assumed when you said that even so it was as good a way to spend ones life as any other.

My disagreement is based upon my conviction that the high function of the human mind is not such activity & interests as will best blind it to its own existence in the universe, but rather its own expression. And its own expression must mean the expression of its ideal of life — usually in terms of its ideal conception of this world, for it has no other tools and symbols. That expression is not important as a reforming agency or indeed as an active & effective agency of any sort but is vitally important in & of itself. It is an act of creation, and creation justifies itself in its proper person. It is an exercise pro sese of the powers we attribute to God — to our highest ideal of ourselves. It may be answered that it is an ephemeral creation for it is destroyed with the mind that dwelt in it. But longevity is no test of the sufficiency of work. Consider the pebbles of the Azilians[2] and the civilization of Palaeolithic man. All we can ask of time is a glimpse of a possible perfect world to make our defeat in this present world endurable. And who knows but that the pictures painted on air are eternal being of a different pigment and a different use.

Dec. 9 At which point I stopped & gave you time to slip in your letter of last week condemning utterly the vain & airy idea, & longing for the tangible original. You will confess it may well have silenced me.

Still I think you answer yourself. I think your attempt to find the reality "whereof all living is the shadow cast" is simply a further wandering into the wilderness of ideas. You call the reality "food" & "grain" and "trade". Was there ever a more perfect example of the idea disassociated from its representations than the general & generic noun? I wish I had time to labor the point simply to bore you. I must run. Thank you infinitely (if you will admit the adverb to your society of notions) for your two life-saving letters. Our love to Alice & the lady Jane. Ada is very well & so, of course[,] is K. When do we meet?

yrs   Arch

ALS: CtY

1. Mack was a well-known Yale football trainer and track coach. 2. An early Mesolithic culture.

To Allen Johnson[1]

My dear Professor Johnson: 24 December 1920 [Boston?]

I have your letter of December 20th and I appreciate very deeply the fact that you thought of me in connection with the project you have in mind.

It is rather difficult for me to answer your letter in a way that would present a clear issue. You may remember that some two years ago I attempted to get a position teaching at New Haven with eventual Government work in mind. I saw both Mr. Farrand and yourself and I understood from both of you that there would very probably be an opening in the Fall of 1919.

I continued to correspond with Mr. Farrand on the subject for two or three months and finally, as it was necessary for me to reach a conclusion in order to make my own plans[,] I asked him for a definite decision. He replied in a very curious letter, in which he intimated that it would be very unwise for me to return to Yale as an instructor because of probable opposition to my advancement on the part of some persons unnamed. Mr. Farrand's letter was not calculated to create any amount of enthusiasm on my part.

I wrote Mr. Stokes (and I must ask you to consider this communication as extremely confidential) and asked him whether he knew what the opposition that Mr. Farrand had in mind might be or what its source was. Mr. Stokes's reply was highly diplomatic and not particularly enlightening. I, of course, had no knowledge of any such attitude of mind.

The immediate result of all this was that I applied for a position as an instructor in Harvard College where I was altogether unknown and had no reason to expect generous treatment, and was immediately given a Lectureship in constitutional law. I could not help, at that time, comparing the treatment I received in Cambridge with the treatment I received in New Haven.

However, your appeal to me, if I may so describe what is in reality a very generous offer, is made upon the basis of love for Yale and willingness to sacrifice pride and more material things for the good of the University. I certainly have no intention to cultivate a grudge on the basis of the experience I have referred to, but I am left with the feeling that it would be hardly wise for me to go to New Haven as an instructor or as an assistant and throw myself altogether upon the mercy of a group of people who seemed to have an interest of some sort in frustrating my advancement. I think you will see what I mean.

I have an assured future at Harvard if I decide to teach there, and I suppose I may safely say that I could have an assistant professorship almost at once. I am moreover devoted to the law, and very much interested in practise, and I doubt very much whether it would be wise for me to give up the practise of law and to give up the very delightful associations in the practise that I now have for anything as indefinite as the thing you suggest.

I realize that it is apparently a closed circle unless you can get a man to take a chance that a Department of Government will be organized, and I realize too that so long as Yale has not a Department of Government she is woefully behind Harvard and other institutions with which she is naturally in competition.

I wish that I felt at liberty to run the risk which you will agree with me is a very real risk in my case of coming to New Haven, and attend the decision of the gods, but with the obligations I am under to the members of my family and with the very real sacrifice of very real opportunity it entails, I do not feel that I would be justified in giving up my life here for a chance in New Haven.

I have attempted to consider this problem without any bitterness or feeling of unfair treatment, and I think I have considered it in that way, but you will perhaps permit me to say that in my humble opinion, so long as Yale University persists in taking the position that her younger graduates ought to be so willing to sacrifice everything for her sake that they will endure any slight or inconvenience she may care to impose, for the sake of becoming members of her faculty, she will not get men of any self-respect or men of the type she needs.

I am thinking in this connection not only of my previous experience with the Department of History, but of an invitation from Dean Swan[2] to teach at the Law School which was so conditioned and so hedged about with qualifications that I should not have thought of accepting it even if I had not had, at that time, an offer to teach at Harvard University Law School in an infinitely more favorable atmosphere and with infinitely greater opportunity.

I do not know why I should take this out on you. I am with you heart and soul in the thing you want to do. I will do anything in my power to help you, but I should not myself consider going to Yale to teach until a definite offer carrying with it a definite position was made formally by the University.

Very gratefully and sincerely yours,   [Archibald MacLeish]

TL-C: DLC

1. *See* M to Anson Phelps Stokes, 28 April 1919.   2. Thomas Walter Swan, dean of Yale Law School.

To Martha Hillard MacLeish

Dearest Mother:-   11 May 1921   [Cambridge]

Thank you a thousand times for your wonderful letter with its enclosure.[1] And thank you for transmitting the very flattering invitation of the Fortnightly.[2] Indeed I shant say no. I should be tremendously pleased to accept & so far as I can see there is no reason why I shouldn't. I think as you do — that father would probably pay Ada's way out. And I think it would be lovely to have her sing some of the songs. She would be the best part of the program. Will you tell the proper persons that I shall be very happy & proud to come & that I shall do my best by J.K..[3]

I always look forward to your birthday letters because you always sound as though you were glad I occurred & I like to think that someone beside myself feels that way. I have never regretted it. First of all there were you & father & then there was Craigie Lea which was almost personified & then there were Kennie & Norman & Ishbel, and then there was school — which wasn't too good — & New Haven & Cambridge. I have had a most wonderful, full & happy life. And Ada & my two small sons[4] are the mark of the miracle. But you are the beginning of it & you have always been the quality & texture of my life & I rather imagine that you will be the end of it — something like you. God bless you both & give my dearest love to Ishbel. We are looking forward to seeing you all in a little while & it will be great fun to go west next Christmas.

Tell Ishbel that I have a place to keep a car but that I don't think she should drive it on unless Bruce comes with her when they come East.

your devoted son   Archie

ALS: M

1. The enclosure was presumably a gift occasioned by M's twenty-eighth birthday on May 7.   2. The Fortnightly of Chicago, that city's first women's club, of which Martha

MacLeish was a member. **3.** M and his wife did visit the Fortnightly later in the year, M lecturing on the poetry of Keats and Ada, a gifted concert soprano, singing some of M's poems that had been set to music. **4.** *See* M to Martha Hillard and Andrew MacLeish, 21 June 1921, note 1.

To Arthur N. Holcombe[1]

My dear Professor Holcombe: 29 May 1921   Boston

I have been informed that certain charges have been brought against Professor Chafee relating to his Harvard Law Review articles and his book on the general question of freedom of speech and I understand that the charges relate in part to the propriety of teaching the theories of free speech set forth in those articles and in that book.

I think it proper to state to you as my superior in the Department of Government that I have used the material and theory of law set forth in those publications in my course in constitutional law. My use of them is due in part to the fact that no other adequate treatment of the subject is known to me, but more particularly to the fact that I agree with Professor Chafee in his theory of the meaning of the guaranty of the First Amendment and in his treatment of the Espionage Act[2] and cases decided under the Espionage Act insofar as the published reports of those cases properly present the facts. I have not hesitated to express my opinion of the constitutionality of the Espionage Act and the observance of constitutional guaranties in the trial of cases under that statute.

I make no excuse for my conduct in this regard and I believe that you will feel no excuse is necessary. It is impossible to teach a case method of constitutional law without treating cases and where the question of law involved is largely a question of political policy it is impossible to avoid the discussion of questions of political policy. But if it is improper to teach the theory of freedom of speech which Professor Chafee has adopted and to my mind established, and if it is improper to comment upon decisions and cases involving the application of the constitutional guaranty, and if it is improper to use a chair in Harvard University for the purpose of discussion of controversial questions, then it seems to me that I deserve censure from you and from your superiors in the University. The fact that my connection with the University unfortunately terminates at the close of this year renders my present confession of conduct rather vain, but I am now and shall be until next fall subject to the jurisdiction of the authorities of the University and their decision upon my conduct would certainly be effective to a material extent.

I request that unless you feel the step to be improper you will submit this letter to the officers of the University who are concerned with the charges against Professor Chafee. I need scarcely add that Professor Chafee has no knowledge of the writing of this letter or knowledge that I am cognizant of the charges brought against him.[3]

Very respectfully yours,   [Archibald MacLeish]

TL-C: DLC

1. Chairman of the Department of Government, Harvard University. 2. The Espionage Act of 1917 mandated a fine and up to twenty years of imprisonment for persons found guilty of interfering with the draft or of encouraging disloyalty to the United States. Extended by the passage of the Sedition Act of 1918, it led to the arrest of more than fifteen hundred persons. *See* M to Dean Acheson, 17 November 1919, note 2. 3. In a May 30 reply to M's letter, Holcombe assured him that neither he nor Chafee was in any danger of being censured.

To Martha Hillard and Andrew MacLeish

Dearest Mother & Father   21 June 1921   [Cambridge]

Bruce's message will have reached you before this. You will wish to know more about what happened.[1] There is so little to tell. Ada put Brudy down herself at noon on Saturday, as well & as lovely as he had been all his little life. At three O'Lasha[2] went to pick him up, Ada being just behind her, & he was dead. He was lying on his face & he had been very sick. His body was all discolored. Ada hadn't been out of the room next to the porch where he was sleeping except to bathe Kenny & there had been no outcry. The doctor came at once but it was too late. He could only guess at the cause but his guess was that a thyroid or thymus gland had suddenly swelled. He said it was impossible that a strong little baby like Brudy should have suffocated. And I feel sure of that.

It was very terrible for Ada. I had gone down to New York on the noon train to the dinner of Kenny's old unit of which I wrote you, & Ada had to face it all alone — the doctor, the undertaker, the medical examiner. Then for a long time she sat with the poor little body. I couldn't get back that night & Pauline Jones[3] stayed with her. Bob Lovett met me at the train when I arrived & told me, after a while, what had happened. There was no train back until the midnight. Bob had taken a room for me at the Yale Club & I stayed there until the train went.

Sunday morning Mr. Hitchcock came up & Ada & Kenny & he & I went down, the undertaker having taken the little body. Ada was simply wonderful — I learned in those hours how much I love her. Then Monday — yesterday — my friend Stewart Rand[4] brought the little body down, Ishbel & O'Lasha coming on the same train. O'Lasha has been simply wonderful. She loved Brudy with all her heart.

I met them at the station in the car & we had a little service here at the house. Henry Hobson[5] came up with Aunt Mary from Waterbury & read the service & Aunt Emily & Phyllis & the Misses Taylor[6] & Stewart Rand were there. It was a beautiful service & the room was filled with pink roses. Then we buried the little body in Unionville.

There is nothing else to say. Everyone has been wonderfully kind & Ada & I have won to a very real peace & understanding.

I am so sorry father never saw the little lad. I don't think that a more beautiful baby ever lived. He was perfect.

You mustn't feel badly because you couldn't be here or get word to us. We understand   Dearest love to you both   Archie

Post-script:- Mother:- In reference to my letter about the Inst Dinner — if you could help me it would be a blessing now. I have had such heavy demands these few days. A.

ALS: M

1. The MacLeishes' second child, born on 4 January 1921 and christened Brewster Hitchcock MacLeish, had succumbed to sudden infant death syndrome on June 18. 2. The family nurse. 3. Presumably a family friend. 4. Stuart C. Rand (Yale '08) was one of the younger partners in Choate, Hall & Stewart. 5. Henry Wise Hobson (Yale '14), an Episcopal clergyman, later bishop of southern Ohio. 6. Emily Fenn, a younger sister of Martha MacLeish; Phyllis Fenn, Emily's daughter; the Misses Taylor, friends of Ada's mother.

To Francis Hyde Bangs

Dear Frank: 3 July [1921]   [Cambridge]

Thank you for your letter. I missed seeing you too & it was something more than a pleasant incident to get your letter. It is strange, but in my desperate search for a sufficient faith to carry me through the first bitter suffering I have ever felt, I have turned back to our talks & wonderings & discovered hints of divinity. We did then truly & earnestly, though with a half satiric interest, search our souls & our brains & the universe around us, for the answer to our passionate Why. And we loved L.M. then first because he offered to us a method of search, a key to tangled roads, a light illuminating our minds. That we formulated no sufficient answer is nothing. That we sought is everything. The hunger for god is god in us.

Since that time, that golden, golden time, when tragedy was a stage-trick and sorrow but a quieter happiness, I have lived otherwise —

forgetfully — uninquiringly. And it is for that reason that, to search my experience now for the mark of divinity upon it is to turn back to New Haven roads & twilight times at the Club, & late afternoons in L.M's class room. We judged rightly when we judged that he offered us more than books & men.

I want to come up tremendously. Early August is my earliest hope. May I come then?   yrs   Arch.

ALS: YCAL

To the MacLeish family

Dearest Family:-   17 July 1921   [Cambridge]

We are doing splendidly. As time goes by the thought of cruelty, wantonness, chance, becomes more & more shadowy in the light of our memory of his lovliness & our assurance of God's reality. I could not now — I am sure I never shall be able to — codify my ideas of divinity. Most of them are not reasonable. But I feel that there is a will, a hope, an intelligence laboring in the universe & subject[,] as we are, to the laws & limitations of the universe, which hates cruelty & wantonness as we hate them, & which in us labors on toward some unseen & happier destiny. To know — to experience — the power & nature of that force is to know God, to see the world as the spirit sees it, & to endure the loss of this world's companionships hopefully knowing that the spirit never dies.

— — — — —

The Buick came yesterday & we offer up thankful sacrifices to all of you for bringing it about. Bruce has been wonderful in attending to everything in connection with sending it. At present I am keeping it in Cousin Frances's[1] garage & you may be sure that it will have excellent care.

Please tell Norman that I spent Thursday of this week in his delightful city of Philadelphia & spent part of the time with Fred Ballard[2] who wished to be remembered to him.

Your books have all come mother & I expect to get through them within the week. I have already read a good bit of The Spirit[3] which I found very happy in spots & a bit sermonistic in other spots

Kenny & Ada are very well. I expect to send them to Farmington in two or three weeks & to vacate myself late in August. We all send our love. You must be having the nicest kind of a time now that you are all old enough to enjoy cathedrals!!   Affectionately   Archie.

ALS: M

1. Frances Emerson, the Mrs. Emerson mentioned in M to Martha Hillard MacLeish, 18 April 1920. 2. Frederic L. Ballard, a Philadelphia attorney. 3. Probably B. H. Streeter, ed., *The Spirit: The Relation of God and Man, Considered from the Standpoint of Recent Philosophy and Science* (New York: Macmillan, 1920).

To the MacLeish family

Dear Family:-   [c. August 1921]   [Cambridge]

A long letter from Mother, a long letter from Ishbel & a long letter from Norman — I feel as though I had been gossiping with you all. Apparently this is *not* like the European trips of our teens when regularity, impulse & truancy pulled three ways at our time. Father in Paris, Norman & Mother in Autun & Ishbel in the fifth dimension sounds much more entertaining than six of us corporeally in Llandudno with our souls variously wandering — mother's in a groined cathedral, father's in a stretch of heather, Norman's in a questionable adventure, Kenny's & mine in the nearest swimming hole & Ishbel's — but Ishbel didn't have any until she learned to swear.

We do as we may. We have the Buick & thanks to Ishbel's check (God bless you my dear: passing on the generosity of our billings is harder than giving away our most cherished possessions) we run it. At present Ada is at the Lake with Kenny & I am keeping delightful solitude with two maids & the finest house in Cambridge to observe its rites. At the end of the week, God willing & Mr. Choate[1] remaining absent, I take a week or so off. And that week or so we plan to spend almost all over the East. Ashfield Mass., Winsted Conn & Locust Valley N.Y.[2] are the mere perimeters of our adventurousness. Ada isn't well a bit. After being wonderfully brave for a month or so she had a rather bad let down. I think she was trying to carry us both & it was too much for her. But I hope to get her away and make her think about temporality again. She is such a wonderful, wonderful woman. Father is the only one of the four of you who will ever have so wonderful a wife.

The law is crowded — interesting — & full of despair. It offers its own rewards but none other. Nothing that I would gladly be or have promises through its devolvement. As a game there is nothing to match it. Even living is a poor second. But as a philosophy, as a training for such eternity as the next hour offers it is nowhere — a mockery of human ambition for reality.

Our dear love to you all. It delights my heart to hear that father is so well. You must all remember to come home again

                         your devoted _____ (Fill in to suit)
                               Archie.

ALS: M

1. Charles F. Choate, Jr., senior partner in Choate, Hall & Stewart, with whom M worked closely during his employment by the firm. 2. Mary R. Hillard had a home in Ashfield where the MacLeish family frequently stayed; Robert A. Lovett and his wife, Adèle, lived in Locust Valley. The reason for the visit to Winsted is unknown; possibly M went to see the friend referred to in his letter to Francis Hyde Bangs of c. 2 March 1917 (see note 4 to that letter).

To Dean Acheson

Dean: 18 September [1921]   [Cambridge]

I have felt too badly about the miscarriage of our plans to do more than mope. So far as I know Madison offered the only real chance of seeing you between now & senility & I have needed to see you tremendously. There is primarily this matter of teaching to which you refer.

I am afraid I am persuaded by my disinclinations. My renewed interest in teaching results from no new enchantment with that profession but from a profound suspicion of the practice of law. If I correctly analyze my emotions I am attracted to the law by considerations the most superficial imaginable. I am attracted by the general approval accorded to lawyers in an industrial society which is not sufficiently cognizant of its own interests to damn them; I am attracted by the game with its immediate success or failure — &, I suppose, by the fact that I have had some success; I am attracted by my chief[1] & his occasional approbation; I am attracted by the possibilities of money-making. None of these considerations seem to me of weight in a world which is at best an opportunity for life & at worst a mystery of living.

Teaching on the other hand has all my reasoning allegiance. Theoretically it is almost the only thing worth doing. The drawbacks are either superficial — the reverse of the arguments pro the practice of law — or such as a man with ambition cannot fail to overcome. The argument of limited income is not serious. Why then, in heaven's name not teach, is the question with which my vacation posed me. I confess there is no answer.

Just at present I am working up my course on Civil Procedure.[2] It involves numerous fascinating imaginary foxes for hunting — as this: apparently at first (Middle Ages in Eng.) there was no *trier* of fact *or* law. The defendant waged his law or offered battle or went through the ordeal. Witnesses were mere compurgators — co-adjutors. The whole theory of the thing was that one man was right & the other wrong & the way to find out which was which was to throw the accused upon God's temper. If you swore falsely God would strike you dead etc.. Does this mean that English law was then at the stage which Maine[3] says all societies pass through — the stage in which rules of law are not distinguished from divine precepts? And does the development of the jury as a finder of fact mark the beginning of true law? What do you say?

John [Vincent] is up here at his Uncle Bradley's living luxuriously, surrounded by admiring women (always his seniors) & impressionable youths. Much as I love John I must yield to your dictum that John is terrible when he is liking something. Just now its a lady of 39. This is given under pledge of secrecy which I now exact.

affectionately   Archie

ALS: CtY

1. Charles F. Choate, Jr. 2. M was to teach a course on this subject at Northeastern College School of Law, an evening school affiliated with the Boston Young Men's Christian Association. 3. Sir Henry James Sumner Maine (1822–1888), English jurist and historian.

To A. Lawrence Lowell

My dear President Lowell: 4 January 1922   [Boston]

I should greatly appreciate an opportunity to see you in reference to one aspect of the work in the Department of Government which Mr. Holcombe and I have discussed, and concerning which you were so good as to advise with me two weeks ago. In order that I may not trespass upon your time with matters which you may well feel to be of insufficient importance to deserve discussion I should like to state briefly the point in issue.

You may remember that, during our recent conversation, you told me of the improbability of an increase in courses taught in the Department of Government, and described the movement away from course instruction toward tutoring. Mr. Holcombe's suggestion had been that I teach one course my first year and take a half assignment of tutoring, with a view to increasing my course instruction in later years. He had not, of course, made any definite statement as to such a development, and I realize that I should not expect a definite statement upon a matter which cannot now be known. But at the same time, I am somewhat perplexed as to the conception of the future in teaching which I should permit myself to hold. A decision to give up a trial practise in which the future is reasonably sure and to which I am fairly well enured, is sufficiently difficult in itself. If there is added the possibility that I may find myself committed to a kind of teaching which, in forethought at least, I should not choose to do, it becomes almost impossible.

I trust that this extension of our recent conversation will not seem to you to be improper. The question involved, though it cannot possibly be of any importance to the University, is of the first importance to me, and I should deeply appreciate any help you can give me in the solution of a very difficult problem.

Very respectfully yours,   Archibald MacLeish

TLS: MH (ARCHIVES)

To Francis Hyde Bangs

Dear Francis:-   22 February 1922   Cambridge

I had expected to see you today and seeing you to tell you how much Ada & I have been thinking of you since we heard of your father's death.[1] I have no means of knowing how sudden or how unexpected it may have been. And though I have means of guessing how you would face such a thing I cannot do more than guess. Please believe that I wish you peace and understanding. And yet you must laugh at such a wish for peace you will never have so long as eagles can out-soar you and understanding such as you can have will never convince you. Death is so great a marvel that we choose not to think of it until we must. Either we laugh, or we ignore it because it is common to all men, or we fear its silences. But when it stands opposite to our thoughts, when we can neither laugh, nor look aside, and when we have no need to fear, then we see how strange a thing it is. And then in a measure we understand it. But why we should think then of God I cannot say unless it is because one marvel invites us powerfully to another. Surely there is no necessary connection between the God of life and living thought and living inspiration, and this death, which is none of these things. Please write me when you can and tell me how the world goes with you and what you are thinking of and what you are going to do. It troubles me to be out of touch with you for though I never doubt but that you & I are sufficiently implicated so as never to become strange to each other I depend upon a more living contact with you than that. The failure of correspondence as an art is a subject of wonder and grief.

I am now in the throes of deciding whether to stay on in the practice of law or chuck it & take an assistant professorship at the H. Law School. My ancient and misplaced ambition to write lies dreadfully at the bottom of it for the whole purpose of the change would be more time for the concoction of words into verses. I wonder why I cling to that ambition so tenaciously. Once, in the faith created by you and L.M. I had no doubt but that I could justify you. Now I wonder. I teem with purposes. I am beset with the passion to bring forth. But the process of begetting is tasteless to me. A lusus naturae you admit. It is partly the product of my timeless days. But it is also in part the product of advancing years. God rest us, Bangs, we are no longer lusty beggars to lie endlessly under the lip of a haymow & work miracles in the patterns of the flesh. To teach or not to teach! I mistrust my worldliness. But if a man must ride two horses does it much matter whether the beast that bears his weight goes at a gallop or a canter? I might as well break my neck riding Old Dobbin, the law, at a full clatter as suffer sea-sickness on the back of Old Pansy, the pedagogy. I don't know. I shrewdly suspect my worldliness. And as for the service of God & my fellow men I'm not sure that I think twice about it. That's what they taught us at Yale, Bangs. Service! Service be damned! You do or you don't and little enough you have to say about it. I might go as a missionary to Papua & serve no man. And again I might grind the faces of the poor and serve them well enough. Let me hear from you on this service.   yrs.   A.

ALS: YCAL

1. John Kendrick Bangs had died on January 21.

To Dean Acheson

Dear Dean: 4 June 1922   Cambridge

I endure the dissatisfaction of silence so long as I may & then I write you. Having no other calendar but that to move me the results are what you have experienced — three months or so of empty skies & then a bit of a flurry of yellow sheets.

And then too I have the spur of my difficulties. Just at present I am on the horns again. I have been offered membership in the firm of C.H&S, I have declined on the ground that Day [Kimball] & I have long planned an office of our own dedicated to the practice of litigation, & I have been asked to reconsider. And of course as soon as I reconsider — I reconsider. Now I don't know what to say or do. The personal element plays so large a part & my determinative powers are so frail that I despair of ever being satisfied on heaven or earth.

I suppose you are at the Hague by now representing to the permanent court of international arbitration the substantial merits of the Norwegian race and the legal merits of the claims of that seafarious government.[1] I shouldn't be surprised to learn of your appointment as ambassador to these United States as a result — one result. And of course you would refuse & dedicate yourself to the further multiplication of economic theories in Washington. I consider at mute length (when occasion offers) the probable direction of your future. And I divide my suffrages between two resultant pictures: one of yourself at the top of your profession in Washington, retired from the exertions of active liberalism to the sheltered lee of a slightly ironical humanism & largely engaged in teaching so much of the world as lends itself to instruction the vital but much obscured truth that words are short hand signs, that conclusions are at most two bar rests, that you can only balance an egg by spinning it, that the purpose of life is consciousness: the other of yourself seduced by one of your own enthusiasms to leave the law & the practice thereof & to engage in the actual administration of doubt at the expense of most that you delight in, to an end that only the twenty-first century will evaluate. You are so perfectly fitted for life that you will never find a satisfactory way of living. And you will continue to waste upon such sandy vessels as myself water that the dry world requires.

Is there a scientific approach to the problems of society? If there is you should profess it. You should observe, induce, hypothesize. You should write at last a newer Novum Organum.[2] But I wonder if there is. I feel within my darkest interior the beginnings of an anti-scientific qualm. After you have observed all the facts that are observable, after you have applied your enlarging prisms and your spectroscopes, after you have set your observations & your complementary deductions in order & numbered them & indexed them where are you but where you were before — save that you see ten thousand objects where before you saw one? No doubt but we are primates & mammals; no doubt but our skeletons correspond bone for bone with the skeletons of chimpanzees & siamangs & gorillas & horses & whales & whatever else suckles its young. And no doubt but we have vestigial ear points & gills & notochords & vermiform appendices. No doubt therefore but we are not now what once we were. But as one bewildered adult to another, I ask you how on earth all those facts or fancies aid us in determining what we *are!* James Harvey Robinson[3] tells me I have a savage mind & an infant mind as well as a human mind, & mediaeval thoughts as well as modern thoughts. And I am ready to believe that I have. But except insofar as I am made more distrustful of my mental processes than I was I am not aided by that information to live more wisely nor to think more justly.

I say we need poets & not scientists. We need another Lucretius or a wiser Dante. We need to dream what we think we know in order that all we know may *mean* something.

Forgive this chatter.

Our love to you & Alice & the Lady J & the unknown but much admired D. Campion.[4]   yrs   Archie

ALS: CtY

1. A member of the Washington law firm of Covington and Burling, Acheson was serving as counsel to the Norwegian government in a suit against the U.S. government for damages and claims arising from the American requisition of Norwegian ships during the world war. 2. A philosophical treatise (1620) by Francis Bacon. 3. American intellectual historian (1863–1936), author of *The Mind in the Making* (1921). 4. Jane and David Campion Acheson, Dean Acheson's children.

To Francis Hyde Bangs

Dear Frank:-   24 August [1922]   Boston

Your whimsical adventure in ink has given me a great deal to think about. But particularly plans. I think you are right about Maine vs New Haven (I assume of course that we are to spend the time together somewhere). The question is where & how we can live in Maine. I expect to be able to get away sometime around Sept. 7. Say Sept 7–10. And from then on I have no plans. My fishing trip has collapsed. I suppose we could have a week to ten days in Ogunquit. But what about finances. I am impoverished by doctors & nurses & I can't afford to spend much. But then neither can you. When you decide where we are to put up drop me a line about budgetary items. If we could secure lodgings that promised reasonable quiet for writing during part of the day it would be grand. What are the chances?

Ada was delivered of a female child this morning. If her debut is an index of her career she will be inconsiderate & impulsive. And she *wont* be beautiful. But these things change. No doubt you & I were no[t] exactly decorative at the age of 1 hr 50 min. She is to be called Mary Hillard (elide). Imagine the situation if she proves a rake! Ada is feeling very well considering & she is quite happy.

Drop me a line as to programs at your earliest.   yrs   A.
ALS: YCAL

To Dean Acheson

Dear Dean:-   12 September 1922   Ogunquit, Maine

Mary Hillard MacLeish launched herself somewhat precipitately upon this earthly tide on the 24th August & has since continued to drift in the proper direction. So far as physiognomy goes she is without character except for a certain femininity of head. But her hands & feet are delicate & she has a forgiving nature. So I dare hope that she will be all woman in her time. Though the God of Elder Brewster alone knows what it will mean to be all woman in the year 1940 or there-abouts. And I am doubtful about his influence. You remember that the greatest of the Puritans declared he could not "praise a fugitive & cloistered virtue that will not sally forth to meet her adversary but slinks from ~~that~~ the (?) race where that immortal garland is to be run for, not without dust & heat."[1] Not without dust & heat! Well, there will be dust & heat & plenty of it. Queen Cleopatra said she could make neither head nor tails of it: it always came out tails. And I suppose it always will. Tails is the natural state of society.

I envy you your Hagues & your arras-backed tribunals & your Swedish & Norwegian fare. I envy you the romance of the task & the delight of charicaturing with your nimble wit & etcher's burin the gyrations of the father of all the Fishers. But chiefly I envy you the feeling of operating upon the body of the earth. My discontent rises from my increasing conviction that I am working in thin air, or in blown dust — at all events to one side of the object. The only subject of importance is my relation to mortal earth & human-kind & spiritual divinity. Nothing else is worth working at. Any other labor is a mere manufacture of new dirt to cloud the issue. The purpose of our profession is even poorer for we merely stir up the dust that others have made. The question is how to work at reality. We can't be scientists & so we miss the pulse of modern thought. We can be amateur philosophers in the intervals & lacunes of our busy-ness. But that won't do. What you & I are fitted for is the serious & healthy-minded study of political & social science considered not as an academic "subject" but as the means of salvation. Political science & such poetry as I really wish to write will fuse. Law & such poetry are eternal irritants.

This is an ancient whine of which you have long been weary. The practical solution or half solution is clear — a job at the Law School. And I have refused that. I have also refused a partnership with C.H&S.. My present plan is to go out with Day next spring. Its a bad plan. What must I do to be saved?

"The Lord Chanceller" came out in the No. Am. Rev. in August.[2] In the mean time I have sold a poem to the Atlantic which you will like.[3]

Ada is well but is being kept in bed in Camb. I started a vacation last Thursday which I expect to continue until October 1. I wonder when you are coming back & where you will be. I am writing this to Washington in the hope of catching you.

You will forgive me for repeating what I have said before — that the more I see of the world the more I cling to you. Love to you all from all the four of us   Archie.

ALS: CtY

1. An approximation of a passage in John Milton's *Areopagitica* (1644). **2.** M's poem "The Lord Chancellor Prepares His Opinion" appeared in *The North American Review* 216 (August 1922), 209–211. **3.** "Hands," *The Atlantic Monthly* 131 (May 1923), 643.

To Dean Acheson

Dear Dean:-   10 October 1922   Cambridge

State Department or practice? You & I seem to be forever choosing between utterly indistinguishable ways of achieving distinction. Our real trouble is that we don't want anything in particular: we just want the world. If we wished for wealth or political prestige or social priority (ISCC Rates) I have no doubt but we could achieve. There are ways into banks and cabinets and teas which may be ascertained by a little thinking. And if worst came to worst courageous and ambitious young men like ourselves might attempt the front doors. But we want none of these things — as such. No good fairies, each with a labelled and wrapped wish in her hand, surrounded the couches of our first ineffectiveness. And, so far as I know, no bad fairy applied a poisoned pin to our posteriors injecting pestilential possibilities. Like Blake's sunflower we counted the steps of the sun seeking after that sweet golden clime where the traveller's journey is done — done in the sense of performed. We haven't started to march. We are merely drilling in barracks with a vague suspicion in the back of our minds that there may never be a war.

Its stupid for moralists to remark that one can achieve anything he chooses to achieve. Its the labor of a lifetime to make a choice of an achievement. Particularly if you happen to be conscious of the fact that you are not a Yale graduate, class of —— of whom Something Is Expected, but a colony of cells inexplicably related to electrons you cannot sense and suns you cannot see, living in more or less antagonism to other similar colonies on a spinning shell which is occupied in moving as rapidly as possible in as many simultaneous directions as possible, the whole picture complicated and de-focused by the peculiar power of the colony of cells to see anything in the universe from above or below or near or far or inside or outside and to imagine things that don't exist in heaven or earth and generally to act as though it had made creation over night. In which case, I repeat, it is very hard to decide on anything to achieve. It is rather ridiculous to decide on anything. If you do nothing at all you will last just as long in the Record

Of The Rocks. And after all the point is to know, to learn, to touch, to feel. We can't "be" anything. Or rather we are everything in the world to start out with. The problem is to know what that is.

One thing is clear & that is that you can't trust reason to decide anything of any importance about yourself. Reason is an excellent pander. It ferrets around among the hormones to find what complexion you desire for the moment & at once it has the very damsel of delight in hand. When I went up into Maine in September I went out onto the cliffs above the sea & watched the moon rise alone. (We were both alone). There was a land breeze blowing over moors covered with sweet fern & bayberry which had been cooking all day in the sun. The sea broke the rhythm of time. The moon devolved out of a rosy mist over the horizon. I began to think of myself — humanity's one release from great beauty, unbearable lovliness. I began to think what I must do. I knew at once. Only one thing is important — which is life — which is no living thing but a process, a progress, a wind out of eternity, a wind which tossed that icy frozen moon like a crystal bubble on its breath & would break it at last, & all moons & all suns & planets of suns at last. And life as we see it was not a progress, for we die too soon, but a relationship. Some things are older, more complicated, nearer death, than others. We see something of the progress if we cut across life living. The important thing for a man is to have a sense of it — to see it — to see himself in it. Beauty is the means & the end. Beauty is what a man *sees*. Anything that he *sees* is beautiful which means merely that he sees it. For when our minds comprehend a thing, they love it, they *see* it; it is beautiful and they see it & it is beautiful. This is the function of art — to see first, then so to represent in terms of *other* beauty already known that the thing which the artist has seen is made to appear beautiful to other minds. (And art which does not translate but attempts to reproduce as nearly as may be the thing seen thus avoids that which is the true labor & all the justification of all art). Well, I saw all this. I saw what I must do. I must go about looking at things, laboring to see them. If I could understand them too then so much the better. But first I must see what they were — not to a chemist, or a biologist, or a sociologist, but to so much conscious life as was in me to see them with. Then I must think about them & I must find words for them. Then I must write poetry of these words. Reason was ready with every argument. Nothing but the attempt to write with almost certain failure ahead mattered.

Well, I am back at C.H&S & reason says — Solid lad!

I have beggared reason. But perhaps you serve yourself better. By the way Conrad Aiken sometimes sees. This from "Senlin".[1]

"It is morning. I stand by the mirror / And tie my tie once more. /

While waves far off in a pale rose twilight / Crash on a white sand shore. / I stand by a mirror & comb my hair; / How small & white my face! — / The green Earth tilts through a sphere of air / And bathes in a flame of space. / There are houses hanging above the stars / And stars hung under a sea —— / And a sun far off in a shell of silence / Dapples my walls for me —— / "

So with much of myself & a little of you I have put off the really important matter of David. I cannot tell you in what way I am touched to be thus connected in some way with his life.[2] Even to be appended upon the end of a swinging cobweb of decalogues & credos is a great deal. And being myself of a spiritual turn of mind I may be able to save him in some measure from the dangers of an intellectualizing father. That is all in the future. For the present I am very happy & very proud that you should want me to stand between God & yourself when David's sins of ignorance ecclesiastical are charged against you. I think Alice is a saint and a lady of as much generosity as lovliness to permit it. (And he may go Bones if I evangelize hard enough.)

We carry on. Ada is tired but well & Mary Hillard blooms. Love to you all.   yrs affectionately   Archie

ALS: CtY

1. From "Senlin," II, ii, first published in Aiken's *The Charnel Rose; Senlin: A Biography; and Other Poems* (Boston: Four Seas, 1918).   2. Acheson had invited M to serve as his son's godfather.

To Dean Acheson

Dear Dean: 8 January 1923   [Cambridge?]

Of course you have me there. I can't put this last away in my pile of cherished envelopes with a few notes for the perfectly whopping epistle I plan someday to write you. And so you must simply take the uninspired & accidental present — though not utterly uninspired. I feel considerably beyond the power of any words of mine the curious singularity in our acquaintance. There never was another D.G.A.. And for the matter of that there never was another remotely approaching the formula; I have given up the attempt to establish by elaborate explanations the clumsiest kind of a working basis for such conversations with other human beings as I may have with you without so much as an i.e.. And there is another curiosity here. In spite of some hundreds of miles of the Atlantic sea-board intervening & in spite of the rigors of the written word I am convinced of an increasing comprehension. I have no doubt that ten years from now meeting you again for the next time (which God forbid) we might perfectly well pick up with an "As I was saying yesterday", such as the Spanish professor made use of after five years in prison. For all these reasons it gives me more happiness than I care to express to such an ironical poet as yourself to know that you appreciate the existence of this not-to-be-valued phenomenon.

I can't seem to work out a Washington trip to save me. Baltimore was all set for three weeks ago — but they settled. South Carolina is a February possibility but via what I can't even guess. Curiously enough I have all Mr. Choate's New York work & that apotheosis of the reasonably prudent man, J. Garfield,[1] has all the Washington work albeit quite incapable of comprehending the values of Washington from the only intelligent point of view. I name no names. Ada & I promise ourselves a Washington trip "sometime" but railway fares stay up & salaries stay down & "sometime" is a long way away. And next summer Ada [and] the children plan to go West for the summer! I merely mention obstacles that we may the more magnificently overcome them. I must see David & determine whether or not you are dealing intelligently with him, to say nothing of suggesting a little outside reading in those Echt-Keltic fields which neither of you with your delicate accuracies of mind would think of prescribing for him in course.

Ada is going great guns this winter. At present she is coaching with Povla Frizsh[2] who is enamored of her voice & would like to see me buried. If only she could get started! If only! She is singing now & her voice is as newly wonderful, as clear, as excellently musical as it was when we first heard it after the war at Phillips Place & knew the damn business was over. In addition she has an increased power of expression which lifts you out of today into the time that never was. I still believe she will get her chance. But it will be a miracle

I'm delighted about the New Republic articles. They need a little of the white light you can turn on their paragraphs. Felix is oriental to the fullest refracting power of the maniest-colored dome of glass that ever Shelley imagined. I wish you would tell me when you are to have a run — I presume they will be unsigned.

You shall have the L.C.[3] — thank you for wanting it. I am hard on a new volume of verse — & I'm getting queer. Not unrhymed or unrhythmed but rather undressed mentally. I wish I dared send you some to see. Our love to you all   Archie

ALS: CtY

1. James Garfield, a member of Choate, Hall & Stewart. 2. Povla Frijsh, a Danish-born concert soprano who specialized in modern vocal music and who introduced Negro spirituals to Paris and Copenhagen. 3. *See* M to Dean Acheson, 12 September 1922, note 2.

To Dean Acheson

Dear Dean: [*c.* 25 March 1923?]   [Boston]

Its a mark of my quality that I allow myself to lag so far in punctuality that my delight in getting one of your always delightful letters is tempered with shame.

It is practice.

At the precise moment of decision I was thrown into the Warner Fuller libel case,[1] the political case of which I have told you, and in the excitement & anguish of that trial everything else faded into insignificance. I decided to stay. Even the elements of decision have faded out of my mind now & I can only remember that it was a sense of my pitiful incompleteness as a practitioner which kept me here. Perhaps I am missing the boat. I don't know. But I have a tremendous sense of relief in having made a decision & perhaps that is the only reward I can expect.

The trial was tremendous. We tried down in Bristol County, commuting ordinarily but staying the night sometimes. The court room was packed. The personages ranged from the Lieut. Gov. who was dfdt, through the Atty. Gen'l. as a witness for us, through our client, the Speaker of the House, to petty pols & newspaper men. It was beautifully tried. Our opponent was the President of the Mass. Bar Ass'n., a grand old Victorian Irishman named Cummings, a grand pleader, a shrewd lawyer & an actor of parts. He had with him his brother (a jesuit priest gone wrong) & two others. Mr. Hall[2] of our office, D.K.[3] & myself tried for the plaintiff. And you may be sure that the examination throughout & the arguments were brilliant. There was a great deal of law from beginning to end of the case & we were uniformly successful. But our great triumph came in defeat. After a 3 hr. charge the jury went out at 4:00 Thursday afternoon. Mr. Hall went home. Day & I stayed. We stayed in the bleak smoky old Court House until 2:30 A.M., went home, slept till 8:00[,] came back, & found the jury still in disagreement. Finally at 10:00 we went to the judge & asked him to direct a verdict for nominal damages. And after a long fight he agreed. The poor old jury was called in and a verdict directed for Warner for $1 & the case reported. I almost died. And the newspapers have been trying ever since to find out who won. But it was a famous victory.

Your Sundays sound delightful. Would to God the accidents of location had befallen differently. But there you are & here we are & I suppose that, barring a miracle, we shall never really be in reach of each other unless, when we can afford it, we agree on a summer place along the coast somewhere. When the time comes I shall fight for that.

I am delighted about the house. It sounds attractive — your word Georgian — & I can see your books & Alice's ascetic, intellectual & exquisite living room with its meditative colors & its two pictures & its cool light, & I can see Jane & D. Campion in the green yard — & I would to God I could see us in it for a day or two before we die

yrs affec.   Arch

ALS: CtY

1. Joseph E. Warner had sued Alvan T. Fuller for libel for remarks made when both had been candidates for nomination for lieutenant governor of Massachusetts on the Republican ticket. The case had been argued in January 1923. **2.** John L. Hall, a senior partner of Choate, Hall & Stewart. **3.** Day Kimball.

To Martha Hillard MacLeish[1]

Dearest Mother   2 May 1923   Boston

If you havent been suffering from fever of the ears these last few days it is because your receiving set is too small for the distance intervening between Boston & Chicago. The way in which you ignore yourself & assume all the burdens of your entire family is beyond my poor powers of expression to appreciate in words. And your capacity for sympathizing with aspirations & plans & purposes which most people would think rash is one of the saving graces of life for me. You need no assurance of my love for you but it wont hurt you at all to know that my admiration for you is as great & that I am completely unable to tell you how great that appreciation is. You are mature enough to be praised without ill effects: it is only my capacity for praise which is restricted.

Well, it's done. I've sold my house for $1000 more than I paid for it & we are going to vacate early in June. As Ada sadly puts it 'We got no home'. I have not yet talked to Mr. Choate but I am going to do that within 48 minutes so that by the time you read this you will know that I have been well spanked. I plan to leave the office October first.

In the mean time we are to be at Ashfield where, as I understand your letter, you have promised to visit us. We can talk all about it then. For the present however we take what courage we can from the fact that Ada sang professionally for a Mrs. Brooks here in Boston last night & made a tremendous hit & that I have recently sold two poems to the New Republic & one to the Yale Review.[2] With time & leisure we shall do better.

I haven't heard a word from Bruce. I don't want him to be agin me if it can be helped but if it can't he'll just have to forgive my follies. Try to persuade him that I'm not mad if you can will you?

Ishbel has arrived in apparently excellent spirits & has started to work. She is to live with us for a month of course & at the end of that time we'll try to find rooms for her. I am going to live this summer with a chap named Firuski[3] from July to the end of August. After that I'll probably use the Tavern Club in town.

God bless you my dear. I wish you could be here just now to talk plans with us. But since you can't we'll just have to wait till you can. Mary Hillard sends you her sweetest love — which is very sweet indeed.

devotedly your son   Archie

Oh! About the "Chronicles". You're very generous indeed. But really I cancelled my subscription because I didn't want 'em at the price. And I don't think you should pay it. The chap who is selling them is a perfect divil to get away from. If you want to celebrate my 31st (!!) birthday with something nice give me a good clean-faced copy of Sir. Thos. Mallory of any edition or period, 1st or 2nd hand

yrs   A.

ALS: CAMPBELL
1. M had recently decided to leave the law, move his family to France, and there practice — or attempt to practice — the art of poetry. 2. "High Road" and "Impulse" appeared in *The New Republic* on, respectively, 16 May and 29 August 1923, "Captured" in *The Yale Review* in January 1924. 3. Maurice Firuski (Yale '16) was proprietor of the Dunster House Book Shop in Cambridge.

To Martha Hillard MacLeish

Dearest Mother:-   4 July 1923   [Cambridge]

I *hope* it was as nice for you as it was for me. I don't know when I have felt as close to you & father & Bruce as I did last week. It was so easy not only to feel but to express our affection. And Craigie Lea was a sublimation of all my memories of it. It is filled with ghosts which make me sad because they are themselves so happy. Somehow or other memories of childhood are more poignant than they are sweet and my memories of the garden & the beach & the ravines, memories which the smell of the earth and the lake & the green weeds brought back, are of the sort to bring tears to my eyes because of their happiness. I have been puzzled ever since I spoke to you of it to account for the curious power that a bit of the surface of the earth possesses over a man's brain and soul so that he seems to find something there which no beauty of oceans or hills or mountains can ever have for him. I do not see why it should be true. But somehow it is true. We had vegetable ancestors of course (no reflexions on you, my dear) but I doubt if we remember their sensations.

This was my toast for father as nearly as I can remember it: "I give you one of the bravest toasts you will ever drink — even the youngest of you. I give you the 85ᵗʰ birthday of one of the last of that great generation which built the West — one whose courage & generosity & justice we all know — one whose blood we are very proud to claim — my father". Something like that.

Ada & the babies are settled at Ashfield whither I go in two days & glad I will be to go. They seem to be comfortable & I hope they are happy.

My dear love to you & to father. It would make you both so uncomfortable if I should tell you how wonderful — how true & generous and fine — I think you two are. You have all the love of your children of whom I am so proud to be one   Archie

ALS: M

To Maurice Firuski

Chere Maurice: 21 August 1923   Cambridge

Your letter came too late to answer to you in France for which reason I sit writing to you in your own house in which same place you will read what here I write — which makes abundantly clear the insignificance of geography in the affairs of such great spirits as ourselves who follow each other through the stopping places of the flesh as souls follow each other in the bodies of women or worms in the carcasses of men.

It is blowing great guns from the southwest, a sweet soft wind such as would appeal to your oriental sensuality but making a tremendous and altogether unwarranted racket among the doors and windows. John, that most perfect companion and most thoughtful gentleman, is down at the shop trying to recover Roy's review of the Academic Politician,[1] or rather he left for that ostensible purpose about two hours ago. Undoubtedly he is now reclining in Roy's best leather chair drinking Scotch and discoursing on Titian with Apphia or his ancestor Socrates with Roy. That is, John's ancestor. Titian, qua Titian, had none.

I dont suppose you can possibly begin to understand what you have done for me this summer. First of all, you have given me peace and occasion to finish up my sequence — which is a damn good sequence and worthy of your hospitality.[2] Secondly you have given me books and comfort. Next to your shower in point of luxury comes the Petit Trianon. Thirdly you have given me no small measure of yourself. I find you in your books and in your pictures (it is not as yet perfectly established that it *is* Potiphar's wife) and in the whole air and meaning of your house. And I am very much moved by what I find. When you write me that you have made a mess of things you betray ignorance upon that point on which, according to Plato, ignorance is most shameful. I told Walker[3] that you had written me in the vein of the quarterback who dropped the ball and he replied properly enough that you were cucu (to use the well known French spelling without however suggesting a French meaning) — that you were one of the wisest people he knew. And I invite your attention to that dictum. You are engaged in the only artistic labor worth doing in the world which is the labor of making of your own life a work of art. And you have had as full a measure of success in that undertaking as is good for you. You have health and beauty of body. You have a living and sensitive mind. You are able to meet and converse with the great minds of another age. And you have friends in this among whom I am proud to number myself. So go to Hell with your vainglorious protestations of failure.

I shant attempt to thank you for what is beyond thanks but I want you to understand that in no polite nor courteous sense — O surely in neither of these — do I consider myself

your humble and ob'd't serv't
and your devoted friend
Archie

TLS: NjP

1. John, Roy, and the Academic Politician are unidentified. 2. M was then working on "The Happy Marriage," collected in *The Happy Marriage and Other Poems* and published by Houghton Mifflin Company on 1 March 1924. 3. Charles R. Walker, Jr. (Yale '16), then an assistant editor with *The Atlantic Monthly*, later associated with *The Independent* and *The Bookman*.

To Dean Acheson

Dear Dean: 3 September 1923   Paquebot Lafayette, Third Day
    Whatever a Paquebot is.

We liked your letter much more than we can expect you to like anything we can write you by way [of] rejoinder, and we were able to understand you which is more than we dare to hope, with the combination of ourselves and a portable typewriter between you and the light, upon your heart. Jamesian, I call that effort — the sandwich in literature.

You accuse us of knowing what we want and being therein blessed as compared with your own unhappy state of being utterly without objective. The slander is obvious. There are three reasonable ways to live and a fourth which is unreasonable. The fourth is to believe in heaven — any heaven — any where — in this world or out of it. The third is to believe that heaven is impossible (!) but nevertheless keep shooting at it upon the theory of the rule of irony which is the rule expressive of the observation that it is in sailing for the Indies that mankind finds its Pittsburgs. The second is to believe that all human heavens are vain and wicked creations of the soul of man but that the effort of trying to get there is in and of itself somehow efficacious. This is, of course, Puritanism. In its refined form it is the doctrine that the effort of trying not to get anywhere is itself the good life. This doctrine is properly stifled in its own thistles. It produced us and we use it as the stuff it is. If burdocks produced donkeys the sequence would be the same. The first is to believe that nothing is worth believing. In its bald terms it is of course the negation of all action and the end of all hope. But it has implicit in it a conception tremendously dynamic. It rests upon the assumption that it is worth while retaining openness of mind for some future seeding of possible truth. If we believe that there is a demonstrable truth and that it is possible for us to recognize its demonstration then we are already half aware of truth and we need only cultivate the sense to secure it. We suppose there is a possible fifth classification of belief in nothing because nothing seems believable but this class can contain only the insane and the overeducated, — who are in the last analysis the same.

We are either in the unreasonable fourth class or the consciously self-hypnotized third. You are in the first. You know from experience that there are truths capable of arousing your entire loyalty and you are too sensitive to the world to. fail of finding them again. We are not sure but that Alice already has found them. We wont worry about you.

You may be amused to know that Houghton Mifflin have taken the book subject to final executive committee say-so. It will be published next spring.

Ashfield was all that the heart could wish — with you there. One of our dearest hopes is now to go back and buy the nearest farm to yours. Preserve yourselves from the devil.   affectionately   Archie

TLS: CtY

To Martha Hillard MacLeish

Dearest Mother   4 September 1923   SS Lafayette, Fourth Day

Here we go over the grand banks in the middle of a raw fog tooting away like an enraged cow at the pasture bars. For three days the weather has been heavenly but this morning it changed and now it gives no sign of changing back. However it continues smooth and everyone, including Mrs. Hitchcock, is well and cheerful so that we have no cause for repining as yet. Mary Hillard gets rosier with each breath of air and Kenny, in the company of the tom-boy daughter of a professor of French at Chicago is, of course, in Heaven itself.

Your letters were delightful. I too am glad that we had you by yourself for a while at Ashfield. It was great fun. I am only sorry that a concentration of Achesons made it so hard for us to really see much of you except in disconnected bits. When we get back we will all buy a farm at Ashfield wont we. Then we can live like the gods who forget time.

You will be interested to know that the editorial department of Houghton Mifflin accepted my book of poems for spring publication before I left Boston. It remains only to secure the approbation of the business end which is almost always forthcoming. I am delighted of course. They are good people for verse and their appreciation is heartening. I read the book to Amy Lowell before I came away and she also professed to find it interesting. In fact it was largely due to her backing that I succeeded in interesting H.M. at all.

I appreciate tremendously your observations upon my religious development. To a certain extent I think you are right. That is, I quite agree that I have been remiss in the practice and discipline of religion. But I dont think I am lacking in that gravitation of the spirit which is properly called faith. With Havelock Ellis, it seems to me to be a matter of indifference what name we apply to our sense of the *not-self* so long as we have that sense. And I think I have that sense in a measure at least. In any event you mustn't think of me as being merely lazy in that regard, — I dont think I am that. It is partly to find myself in that direction that I want this time for real work.

Please write me more about Ishbel when you reply to this.[1] I am extremely anxious to know exactly how she is and how much difference it is going to make to her to spend her winters in a different climate. And tell me all about father and yourself. We shall be hungry for news.

Dearest love to you all. Think of us often and remember that we are always thinking of you.   your devoted son   A

TLS: M

1. M's sister Ishbel had recently been found to have tuberculosis. About the time this letter was written she entered a sanatorium in Colorado Springs, Colorado, where she remained, largely bedridden, for the next three years. She eventually recovered, with the only lingering effect of her illness being a partial loss of sight.

To Martha Hillard MacLeish

Dearest Mother: 29 September 1923   Paris

Is this one chain in the account of our wanderings or have you failed to receive our steamer letters and Ada's more recent accounts? Since it is better to be credulous than redundant I shall proceed upon the simple theory that you know all about our history at least to the point of our first stop at the hospitable pension of the meddlesome Montagnes in Neuilly. We had our rooms and our gardens and our "C" bus to Paris and if it hadn't been for the cooking which was often intricate and sometimes rancid we should have had nothing to complain of but the fact that our hosts were set upon palming off upon us in one capacity or another all their more indigent friends and relatives. We did pick up quite a bit of French and no doubt but we tremendously improved our accent but for all that I have a fixed aversion to pensions from this day forth. Partly for that reason and partly for other reasons to be set forth in due course I am simply delighted to be here at long last. "Here" is the little apartment on the rive gauche formerly occupied by the Emersons.[1] It is small enough. It has a little salon adequate for about four people at one time, a dining room only slightly larger than the ordinary stomach, one decent sized bed-room, two small ones, a tiny bath-room, a cell-like "horror" and a bit of a hall. But it has nice furniture, most of it old, and it is decidedly comfortable. That's the inside of it. But the best of this apartment is its outside. It is right beside and under the walls of St. Clothilde and about ten metres from a little green square with beautiful big trees which it overlooks. One block to the south is the rue de Grenclle with its auto-buses. One block east and west are the rues de Burgogne and Bellechase with their dittos. North is the beginning of the busy Boulevard St. Germaine. Ten minutes walk away is the Place de la Concorde and the rue de Rivoli. But here in the center of the world, here in the midst of Paris, all is peace and sweet quietude. The bell of St. Clothilde rings its patient quarter hours and tolls at dawn and dusk for mass. A few stray heels click along the streets at irregular intervals. Once in a great while a car goes past. For the rest all is silence punctuated by the horns of distant taxi-cabs and the cries of singing street vendors. And here we are.

It must be admitted that we are here — some of us — under objection and complaint. Frankly Ada didn't like it too well at first. It was dirty before our able bodied Josephine got to work. And it was old and small. But she liked the quarter and now that she has persuaded herself that the children can keep well here she has had a change of heart. She has a studio two hours a day over in Passy and next week she is going in search of Clement[2] who has returned to town. Kenny is to go to the

Ecole Alsacienne on the rue Assas, a famous French school with a kindergarten equipped with English speaking mistresses. We thought it best to put him back into kindergarten since the real purpose of the year for him is to teach him French. There will be at least one other American boy in his class, the son of a friend of mine,[3] and after the first shyness wears off we expect him to be very happy. I was very much impressed with the directeur and I feel as does Ada that the school is well run from top to bottom.

Needless to say, with the labor of getting settled I have not had much time for work but I intend to start at all costs Monday morning. I have several extensive pieces in the back of my head and I expect to get somewhere with them. My plan is to write for about three hours in the morning, and use the afternoon in part — about two hours — for writing and the rest for work at the bibliotheque national or for walks in or out of Paris. This schedule may not work out at all but it will at least serve as a temporary model. I have planned to do so much that I may end by getting nothing done at all.

Our budget seems to be well within our means at present. We pay eleven hundred francs a month for the apartment, we expect to pay about seventeen hundred a month for food and the rest in proportion. So long as the franc stays down we shall be all right. But if it takes another plunge upward I shall begin to worry a bit. It is a help to know that in case France grows too prosperous we can look to you for a bit of help.

So far we have had no word from home. How is young Andrew MacLeish?[4] And how is his mother? And where is Ishbel and how long is she going to be there? And how are you and father? We long to know. I think you had best write us here or in care of the Bankers Trust. And by the way, I wish you would take out administration papers for Kenny's estate together with the other papers called for in the letter you showed me and send them all here to me with a power of attorney to me to receive the amount standing in Kenny's name at the Guaranty Trust. I think I can get the French inheritance tax claim withdrawn. I will of course remit to you in dollars at the then rate. Will you also send me when next you write a full description, — name of cemetary and number of grave — of Kenny's present grave? I want very much to go up there as soon as I can.[5]

Our best of love to all of you. We miss you very much more than you could get us to admit and we think of you far too often.

You might send this wretched letter along to Norman as I shant be able to write him at any length for some little time and I should like him to know where we are and roughly at least how we are getting on.

devotely your son   Archie

1. At 23, rue Las Cases, Paris. 2. A reference, presumably, to Edmond Clément, a French tenor associated with the Opéra-Comique. 3. The friend was Richard Myers, who, with his wife, Alice-Lee, had known the MacLeishes in the States. 4. Son of M's brother Norman. 5. *See* M to Ishbel MacLeish, 31 May 1924.

To Martha Hillard MacLeish

Dearest Mother:- 14 October 1923 [Paris]

Perhaps it was a day like this — six years ago.[1] There was a bright sun in the morning with clouds nacreous & shining & clear lakes of blue. There was a wind from the west & it was cold. We drove out with the Baynes[2] to Dourdans where we had lunch and walked around the walls of the château. Coming home the ash trees along the road were in silver leaf like apple blossoms but dead & hanging stiffly from the tree. There were woods just tarnished with winter. The little villages were like islands in yellow fields. I saw an aeroplane flying low with the wind like a wasp and I did not follow it with my eyes. We remember that the world loses its most beautiful, but we forget that beauty is revenged by its own completeness upon such a world. Only it is true that a man is something more than a representation. He is a combination of a great many vitalities held in a momentary restraint. It takes hundreds of years to produce balance & harmony. But war takes one with another — Frenchmen & Italians & Belgians & young Americans. They are killed by the emotions of other men. They run to kill themselves for the emotions of other men. And when it is all over the emotions evaporate like a rotten vapor & a flat and weary sunlight shows the thing as it is. Dreary. Only the dead do not see that. They do not see the sun come back. And those who peopled the mist with giants & dragons & the beautiful princess never knew that it was a mist they died in. They only were happy. They only lived.

At St. Cyr the military school was full of young men. At the château at Rambouillet young lads of twelve & fourteen walked the streets in uniform. Paris is crowded with youngsters doing their term. What else can we do. We are only men. We are not gods. No, but we can become gods.

This morning Kenny with Kathy[3] went to Mass at St. Etienne du Mont back of the Pantheon. Kenny lighted a candle for Uncle Kenny & said a prayer for his soul. There is beautiful glass there and stone carved with reverence, and rich music. A child lighting a candle for the rest of a soldier's soul — that at least is simple & true & pure. I cannot think simply about it & my thoughts are not pure. I would be cynical if I were not afraid & angry if all my attitudes were not ineffectual. I have only words. And those wordy.

We keep cheerful in this apartment & well. The baby is disgusted with her teeth but otherwise happy. Ada works regularly & I long & aimlessly. Some day the wind will blow again.

Love to you all — we love you   yours   Archie

ALS: M

1. The letter was written on the fifth anniversary of Kenneth MacLeish's death. **2.** *See* M to Samuel B. Hemingway, 15 June 1917, note 2. Bayne had remained in Paris after the war, and was now serving as counsel in Paris of the Reparation Commission. **3.** A governess employed by the MacLeishes.

To Maurice Firuski

My dear Maurice: 20 October 1923   Paris

What to say to you! It is of course your emotion that I am concerned to meet & not a Fact. There are properly no facts of life — merely feelings about appearances — or absences of appearances. And I can only guess the outline of your emotion — that you were shocked — brought up short — that you were thrown back upon a thousand memories, a thousand pictures, which produced finally the one picture of what you had lost — that in your concern with that picture you relived all your relations to it & realized that you had lost not only your father but part of your childhood. We are so much a part of those who reflect us — or they are so much a part of us — that when they go they leave us very different from what we have ever been before. As a house is different standing alone.

I think you are wise to stay in Cambridge at almost any cost to *yourself*. Because you will not be happy elsewhere &, much as you have always doubted it, you are happy there. The rest of your problems I can only guess at. I wish for your sake I were at hand — & for my own that I could see you

---

I too am sorry about the book. I wanted you to have the sequence.[1] But you see the mote clearly enough.

I am doing something now which you might like to do. You will like it yourself. But perhaps no one else would. You shall see it.

My love to John & Isabel & to yourself, Sir, my love

Archie

ALS: NN

1. Firuski published a limited number of books with the Dunster House imprint, and had expressed an interest in publishing M's *The Happy Marriage and Other Poems*. He later did publish M's *Nobodaddy* (1926) after Houghton Mifflin declined to do so.

To Martha Hillard MacLeish

Dearest Mother: 12 November 1923   Paris

I live on your letters for the only thoroughly unprejudiced news which comes to me. Norman says that he has Lenore's beautiful deep blue eyes. And of course Norman is an incorrigible romanticist. A baby of two months never yet had anyone's eyes of any colour whatever.

It is just like you to revel in our good fortune. And it is good fortune. It is the wisest thing we have ever or will ever do because it is going to make not merely a singer but an artist out of Ada. Even Madame Frijsh now says that Ada is straight on the road to success as a singer of concert songs — and that is more than a compliment, it is a diploma. Aunt Mary to the contrary notwithstanding she is going to go through with it if I live and keep my strength. I believe in her absolutely and I am willing to risk all the possible home-wrecking which Aunt Mary's excited imagination can conceive. As for myself things are going about as I thought they might. I have just finished one fairly long piece in a manner fairly new for me[1] and I have other more or less experimental things in mind to try. I don't feel that my last Atlantic poem[2] is as revolutionary as you seem to think it. But then it isn't a political poem as you have apparently read it. It is a poem about marriage, and the impossibility of communication in marriage as elsewhere in this inarticulate earth. Do please read it again giving the first line all emphasis you can and see if you dont like it better.

We keep well and exceedingly happy. Kenny learns no French but does like his school and the Luxembourg and Mary Hillard blossoms like the apocryphal green bay tree. In spite of our lack of central heating we expect to keep warm and unless the cost of living climbs with the exchange we shall keep alive. So that is that. If we could only have an occasional dearly desired visit from those at Craigie Lea we should have nothing left to wish. Catherine[3] is trying to go to sleep in the next room and I must stop my racket. Our love and all our love to father and yourself. I am writing Ishbel at the same time but I suppose she has already gone west.   your devoted and grateful son   Archie

TLS: M

1. Possibly a reference to M's poem "Biography of Mr. Beck the Suicide." Later retitled and published as "Einstein," it first appeared in *Streets in the Moon* (1926) and was later published separately by the Black Sun Press (1929). 2. "Separate," *The Atlantic Monthly* 132 (November 1923), 628. It was a section of "The Happy Marriage." 3. The governess elsewhere referred to as Kathy.

To Charles R. Walker, Jr.

Dear Charlie: 13 November 1923   Paris

Efficient be damned. It was a perfectly expressive letter carrying all the news of a not too virtuous city which it is good for a young man in your position to hear. Suppose you had been told that it is a habitude of the people of these parts to void their bladders in all places and directions or that it is not at all uncommon for citizens of opposite sexes to kiss upon the public ways? What, I put it to you, could you have done about it? No my poor young friend the Paris which you knew is no more, and worse than that, it never was. No more or never will you see little groups of revolutionaries arguing about l'esprit des lois on the trottoir of the deux magots. They prefer fornication inside. And as for those beautiful and passionate youths who used to dance through the gardens of the Luxembourg to the long roll of the hexameters, they now do the rolling themselves and let dance who will. Who rarely will. It is a degenerate metropolis. I saw enough of middle class French apartments in our search to be sure of that. They have come to baths and steam radiators and there is too much health in them. Imagine a man in health loving the arts. Why should he? They say Joyce enjoys the worst of all possible bad stomachs with eyes to match. The countess de Chambrun, born sister to our own irrepressible Nich. Longworth,[1] whom we had the ineffable pleasure of meeting, says Joyce is an Austrian Jew. It later transpired that he had insulted her at dinner by asking to be allowed to sit elsewhere than at her side. Also she hasn't read Ulysses but thinks nevertheless that J. is obscene. She does know what obscenety is. She says so. But query.

So much for matters of importance. Betty[2] dropped down upon us from London the other day on her way to Italy. You won't mind if I say that Betty isn't getting ahead. I mean you won't think I'm depreciating beauty for motives of Christian charity. Or something. The shoe is on the other foot. Anyway. She just doesn't *know* anything. And though I don't believe in erudition as the necessary basis for literature, I do feel that one ought to have some sense of movements past and present in his own language. WHY not give her a course of reading yourself. She might do it for you and get something out of it. She has honesty and intelligence but neither one is in the final pinch a substitute for a certain modicum of education. Let the rebels rant. And I think you will agree with me.

I'm glad the book is coming on so well.[3] What after that? I should advise a novel. Cover the world with the awning of your spirit and see where the shadow falls most gracefully.

Speaking of efficiency, will you bear it in mind that Nettleton mustn't print the poem about K. until after H.M. do the book and with their consent?[4] If you don't think that is understood do let me know and I'll write him.

Phelps was grand.[5] While he was here I missed no one but you. Now I have to miss you both. But you were duly celebrated at diverse places of resort and I can meet your ghost with ease. May the goddess love you. Yrs A.

TLS: M

1. Nicholas Longworth, a U.S. congressman (later Speaker of the House). He was married to Alice Lee Roosevelt, daughter of the former President. 2. Elizabeth Choate, daughter of M's former employer Charles F. Choate, Jr., and one of the MacLeishes' Boston friends. 3. Walker was then working on a novel, published in 1927 as *Bread and Fire*. 4. George H. Nettleton, professor of English at Yale, planned to include M's poem "Kenneth" in his *Yale in the World War* (1925). 5. H. Phelps Putnam (Yale '16), a poet with whom M spent much time in his first months abroad.

To Francis Hyde Bangs

Beloved Bang: 15 November 1923 Paris

If you do not recognize this combination of paper & ink it is only because you have forgotten the Central at Limoges & your therein adventures epistolary & other. But now you must substitute for the Central the little Café Maturin & for the rather urinary rues of Limoges the Carrefour de Medici with the Luxembourg on the other side. The pen I should say was the same.

This is not altogether a letter of love in spite of the fact that I have seen Eyre & her de Lanuxated husband[1] & might very well occupy my paper & your patience with the labors of a new Saint-Simon. The truth is that I want to get at a certain angle or possibility of truth & that I think to do it between you & myself by some possible & not too angular reaction of one of us upon the other. I appeal to you then not in your capacity of Bang nor in your office of apostle of the flesh to all not too desiccated damsels but to you in your proper person of Doctor Litterorum et Legorum. That is as author of Bangs on the Theory of Poetry.[2] After a summer of T. S. Eliot I feel the need of a theory.[3]

Which is to be approached as follows. Poetry is, properly speaking, an art of words. That is, its medium is words as the medium of sculpture is stone. A word is not a thing but the Name for a thing. Which is to say that it is a means of directing attention toward the thing for which it stands. At best it is never quite successful. (A small white dog has just urinated within a yard of my foot) I write "tree" & you think of a perpendicular object floriated above & fixed below in the common earth. But you do not think of the precise tree I have in mind. Above all you do not *think tree*. Something must happen to resolve tree to an idea capable of thought before that can happen. And the metamorphosis is impossible. In other words there will always be a discrepancy, a gap & fissure, between any word or group of possible words, & the thing meant. So that actual realism, i.e. actual reconstruction of the object, is impossible. At best one has a choice between an inadequate description of the object and an artificial creation within the mind of the reader of the mental state which the object itself would create.

But these names of objects are not used in poetry for the mere purpose of directing attention to the object. They are used to direct attention toward the object in such a way as to present some phase of the human significance of the object with the purpose eventually of inspiring an emotion intellectual or sentimental. And between the object & the emotion there is no more necessary coincidence than between the object & the word, for although there is a general human experience of certain objects it is limited & not universal. Nevertheless it is necessary to work by the direction of attention to objects (I use the word to include also actions in the objective world) for it is not possible to act directly by the mere look or sound of a word upon the emotion. I say not possible. I realize that poets have attempted it, that some as A.C.S.[4] have had a measure of success & that it is possible to choose & arrange words in such a way that the sound (for even when *read* we get a sense of the sound of poetry) will have the desired effect. But intellectual emotions are not reached in this way & the emotions which may be created are vague & fleeting. However it must be admitted that the result of literary history has been to give to certain words the very character & quality of the emotion with which they are usually associated. These are "poetical" words & their very power so limits them & associates them with such restricted operations as to make them rather a burden than a benefit in the language.

To create an emotion by the imperfect representation in words of objects which are imperfectly associated with the emotion desired. That is, I take it, the problem. To succeed requires the description of the object not in terms of objective truth but in terms of the emotion desired. The pathetic fallacy. But the opposite method leaves a too restricted field of possible objects & too wide a fissure between object & emotion.

So far as the lyric is concerned grammatical construction beyond the absolute minimum is not desirable. The effect desired is the direction of attention. It may best be done by breaking the mould & leaving the lines bare & angular. But beauty of rhythm & sound are tremendously desirable because they are the greatest possible aids *in the creation of the emotion desired.*

Well, there is an utterly unsuccessful attempt. Have at it & tell me where I have gone off. You might come over for a glass of beer & have it out.

Also give me some news of yourself   yrs   Archie

ALS: YCAL

1. Elizabeth Eyre, to whom Bangs had once proposed marriage, had married Pierre de Lanux and was living in Paris. 2. Bangs had sent M a copy of a paper he had written on this subject for a graduate course he was taking at Yale. 3. M's reading notes indicate that he had been reading *The Sacred Wood* (1920), along with other works including Santayana's *Little Essays* (1920), Croce's *The Essence of Aesthetic* (1921), and the *Cambridge History of English Literature*. 4. Algernon Charles Swinburne.

To Harvey Hollister Bundy[1]

Dear Harvey: [c. December 1923]   [Paris]

A letter from your all too perfect wife plus the progress of the calendar precipitates this — done into English on rough paper with Chinese Ink & a Hell of a pen. The importance of the calendar first. For Kay is of an importance in our universe altogether unique. Should I or should I not send the within to the Court of Internal Taxation? And if I do should I make out a return? And if so what kind. To be more courageous with my secret — I don't think I'm going to get away with my request. But if I file a return with my letter — or thereafter — I surely won't get away with it. Whereas if I don't file a return & I am turned down — well I never could compute interest. I don't need to send the letter until Jan. 1 so don't bother your head about this until you have reorganized the Union Pacific & proved to the satisfaction of Judge Anderson that chocolate is — or isn't — edible when inhaled under another name. But when that is all finished & done with please drop me a line at your usual mail-order rates — payable on the maturity of Mary-Hillard MacLeish.

Now the urgent question — *Are* you really coming next Spring or is Kay merely attempting to keep our courage up through a Labrador winter? I can't tell you what a help it would be — equivalent of two suits of red flannels per adult at least. But I doubt the so-great kindness of the divinities. You would no more leave your entrancing & rollicing practise during term time than you would leave a bottle of ∴ in the Ford. Do assure me that the S.J.C.[2] has taken a vacation of two months in April-May next. It would be educative you know. I expect to have a considerable list of places you ought to see (between midnight & 2 A.M.) by April. And the price of gasoline is going down.

There is only one way to assure me of your sincerety. Instruct me to buy francs for you at 17.55 or better. Then you will have no choice but to use them. You can't sell them. And they should hit 17:55 before April 1 — even the French newspapers allow one to see that.

Ada has written Kay all the news so you & I can coast. We approximate the GOOD LIFE (don't tell Kay) in most ways. Ada works two hours a morning in a studio — which with going & coming makes about 4 hours: she won't use the Metro & the Trams just dont go. Besides which her studio is in Passy whereas we are — obviously — in the Luxembourg. I write about two or three hours here — I find it is all I can get done at a time — in the mornings & then go for Kenny at his school. Then dejeuner. By the way — petit dej in bed after a cold bath while the maid polishes your shoes has an *effect* on the sternest disposition as, for instance, mine. At dejeuner (12:30) I *try* not to drink wine. I may say in my own defense that I am still trying. Then I dig off to the Bib. National where you can't possibly find the book you want & they have *no* artificial lighting, & stay until about sunset (3:45 at this season — or say 4:10 on a bright day[.] That leaves 3½ hrs by actual computation before dinner. With Putnam in town I usually spend those precious jewels from the necklace of God in going to & from the Crillon Bar; to say nothing of a stop between journeys. Two afternoons a week I devote to exercise — pulling weights in French & being sprayed with a fire hose afterwards. Our evenings — when not in company — we spend alone — as this evening. It nets about three to four hours of writing & the same amount of reading (I am trying to find out *who* wrote English LITERATURE) which with some slight drinking & an occasional meal satisfies my daemon. What I miss most is such conversation as we occasionally scared up between 373 Marl, 6 West Hill Pl. & 44 C.H.Rd..[3] Or rather what I miss most — & with a surprising intensity in view of the fact that I have no right to claim it — is Boston. Meaning by Boston K&H, & I.G. & CPCJr & E.R.C & their moons & satellites.[4]

When you write me please give me Chaucerian pen pictures of ① Charlie ② Edith ③ Curtis CP & Curtis R.,[5] Advocates ④ George Denny[6] ⑤ Ives ⑥ Charlie Coolidge[7] — & above all the Bundies. My love to 'em   Archie

ALS: M

1. Bundy, an attorney with the firm of Putnam, Bell, Dutch & Santry (and later with Choate, Hall & Stewart, where he was M's attorney), was married to a niece of Amy Lowell's, the former Katharine Lawrence Putnam. The Bundys were among the MacLeishes' closest Boston friends. 2. The Supreme Judicial Court of Massachusetts. 3. Abbreviations for the residences of, respectively, the Harvey H. Bundys, Mr. and Mrs. Charles P. Curtis, Jr., and the MacLeishes. 4. Respectively, Kay and Harvey (Bundy); Ives Gammell, a Boston painter; Charles P. Curtis, Jr.; and his wife, Edith

R. Curtis. **5.** Richard Curtis, brother of Charles P. Curtis, Jr.; both formerly of Choate, Hall & Stewart, they were practicing law together in Boston. **6.** A Boston doctor and member of Boston's Tavern Club. **7.** A lawyer with the Boston firm of Ropes & Gray; like Bundy and the other men M names, he was a member of the Tavern Club.

To Martha Hillard and Andrew MacLeish

Dearest Mother & Father: 8 December 1923   Paris

This ought to reach you about Christmas. Whether it does or not it must stand for my share of Christmas at Craigie Lea where I wish with all my heart I might be. It will be a little lonely for you wont it — with Ishbel in Colorado, Norman in Philadelphia & all of us here. But Bruce & Elizabeth are a whole set of brothers & sisters & cousins & aunts in themselves and you are so marvellously brave & generous, you two, that you will remember what Christmases we have had & what Christmases we are to have again & be very happy as we intend to be happy here with a Christmas tree & a Christmas dinner & a considerable amount of reminiscence. It is poor Ishbel out in Colorado who will have twinges of homesickness. She is just as fine as she can possibly be. But you can't be cheerful on Christmas day in a sanitarium — can you? At least not altogether cheerful. I do so hope she is going to get the whole miserable business cleared up this winter & be able to go about her work next year. One year out is enough Heaven knows.

Marion Cleveland Dell who is here in Paris & who had a year or so of Colorado Springs with her husband who was laid up has promised to write a friend of hers there — one of the few, she says, who would talk Ishbel's language — & put him into touch with Ishbel. I begged her to do it. It would mean so much for Ishbel to have some one like that.

Our work goes on a pace. The proof of my next book is here for correction & I am working along on another which will be a verse play in more or less blank verse.[1] Ada makes perfect strides. She sang last week for Mlle Boulangier,[2] who is probably the leading musical figure in Paris so far as her contacts with the world go. The purpose of the singing was to be advised as to a teacher. B. told Ada that she was much too modest, that she mustn't go around looking for teachers like a green girl, & that she ought to be doing concert work. Something may come out of it but in any event it shows the way of the wind. She is working famously & she is now told that she sings French better than most French singers & practically without accent. I am alternating my writing with work in the Bibliotheque Ste Geneviève & with some study of Aesthetics. I've just finished Croce's Aesthetic translated by

Douglas Ainslee (Macmillan) which is a fine piece of work. I am unfortunately so constructed that I need to know where I am going. I am not sufficiently intuitive just simply to go.

The children keep well although the usual small things happen. Kenny has had a cough he found it hard to get rid of & the baby had a bit of a cold yesterday. But really they are as well or better than they were in Boston in spite of the fact that the sun just never does shine. We have had one glimpse of it since before Thanksgiving. However it is not very cold & one doesn't mind. The spring will be enchanting!!

How good you are to be glad that we are here & to praise us for coming! In the ordinary family your attitude would have been that of Aunt Mary.[3] Thank Heaven I had you for parents. I think of you a great deal & I love you with all my heart   Archie

ALS: M

1. M was reading the proofs of *The Happy Marriage* and working on the play published, in May 1926, as *Nobodaddy*. 2. Nadia Boulanger. 3. Mary R. Hillard had taken violent exception to M's decision to leave the law; she continued for some time to exert pressures aimed at making him reverse it.

To Amy Lowell[1]

Dear Miss Lowell:-   8 December 1923   Paris

December eight is sufficiently far from that late day in August when I saw you last & when you told me that if I wrote to you you would read my letters. But I haven't dared permit myself the sea-room you offered because I haven't been sure, until recently, that I could write from any eminence of justification whatever. Now I am getting my feet a bit nearer together & a few things have succeeded in writing themselves & I am satisfied that the adventure was at least worth undertaking. For myself, that is. For Ada there was never any question. She found herself at once & she got just what she most needed & I have no doubt at all but that she will be doing beautiful work when she comes home. Of course you will say — or at least I hope you will say — that my chief trouble was Paris. And I think that would be a fair diagnosis. After seeing three or four people of the American literary group I concluded that my alternatives were two — to see nothing but American poets or to see none of them. I decided to see none of them. And I have been living since in an isolation that isn't enviable & doesn't work out too well. The trouble is, saving your ears, that they are such damn fools — the ones I met at least. I have even seen your long library in my dreams, & in my so-called waking hours I spend hours there. I think it would be worth two hundred & eighteen lines to me to talk with you for ten minutes. But then it would probably cost you as many. But there is so much I want to know. What happened to "Which Being Interpreted —"? I want to see it in form readable whenever it is published. I don't suppose you even considered sending it to Harpers. I told Freddy Allen[2] that there was a one in a million chance of his landing it but I then regretted my folly because I was quite sure you wouldn't hear to the match. You know I have never gotten over it — hearing it. And I never will.

Littell[3] has told me that there is to be a N.R. Literary Supplement in Nov. or Dec. with a theoretical article of yours on poetry (if you will permit me the adjective theoretical — I like it)[.] I have been watching the stands for it but the N.R. doesn't seem to reach Paris. Please save me a copy to read next year. These papers of yours are much too rare.

Please give our love to Mrs. Russell[4] & tell her that in spite of a lack of central heat we have all kept warm so far. The children seem to thrive — though Kenny complains that the French talk very peculiarly — they hardly make sense at all. Don't forget us, will you?

Affectionately yours (— you will
allow a homesick soul so much?)
Archie MacLeish

ALS: MH

1. Lowell (1874–1925), the American poet and critic, had befriended the MacLeishes and seen them with some regularity at her home in Brookline, Massachusetts. 2. Frederick L. Allen, an editor at *Harper's Magazine* and the former secretary to the corporation at Harvard University. 3. Robert Littell, associate editor of *The New Republic*. 4. Ada Russell, companion of Amy Lowell.

To Charles R. Walker, Jr.

Charlie, me pink: 11 December 1923 Paris

Bless you for the suggestion. Like Leonardo before the Last Supper (not his own) I am engaged in conceiving the matter in silence. And I agree that the idea is a good one. Consider it my copy until I prove I can't do it will you?

The North American Review (9E37NYC) per one E. B. Cutting wrote for some mss. a bit ago and I sent them an essay and a longish poem with instructions to return to you.[1] As I had no American stamps I said you would refund them their postage — if they are cheap enough to ask it. To defray such items I am sending you a check in some elegant sum or other as soon as I have a balance. I hope there wont be much mailing to bother you anyway. As for the enclosed, they too are intended for the N.A. unless you think it worth while to submit them to E.S..[2] I hardly suppose you will but they go to you on the chance. If the N.A. sends back the essay will you try the Forum and the Bookman or anything else you may have in mind. The New Rep. accepted it and then sent it back on the ground that they couldn't get around to printing it — thereby causing a scandal. Any verse sent back you might try on the N.R.. Except the long poem*. [*MacLeish wrote in the margin*: *I.E. "The Biography Of Mr. Beck The Suicide" which the N.A. now has] I am very much interested in that although you may very well not like it. Unless you think it too bad will you shoot Harriet Munroe with it?

All this is an outrage to load onto you. But there you have it. You are simply too damned nice. I want to write you my reactions to Croce's Aesthetic. After I've abstracted it and am sure of my ground I think I'll go after you. I think you will want to read it if you haven't already. All well here. Love from the tribe.   Hurriedly   Archie

TLS: M

1. The former was, presumably, "The Beginning of Things," an informal essay on narrative technique in the short story and the novel, among other subjects, published by *The North American Review* in March 1924; the latter, which *The North American Review* bought but did not publish, was "Einstein," about which *see* M to Martha Hillard MacLeish, 12 November 1923, note 1. 2. Walker had agreed to help M by submitting his poems and articles to American periodicals. He was later superseded in this undertaking by Maurice Firuski. "E.S." was Ellery Sedgwick, editor of *The Atlantic Monthly*.

To Andrew and Martha Hillard MacLeish

Dearest Father and Mother: 26 December [1923]   Paris

Thank you with all my heart for your Christmas presents. Shall I tell you what they are going to be when they alter from the potential to the actual? Well I think they will probably take the form of a bit of a trip down into the Tourraine come spring or a jaunt to Bruges or perhaps farther. We have only taken one trip so far because we want to save everything of that nature for the pleasanter months when in all probability Ada's father and mother will be here to keep an eye on the children while we amuse ourselves. Besides which we are too busy now to get away. If I hadn't been so canny and far-sighted a few months ago we should be rich enough in the spring to take quite extensive jaunts. But when the franc got to seventeen I was so sure that it wouldn't go any higher that I bought our requirements for the spring as well as for the winter at that rate. The result is that the franc at twenty means nothing to us but a lost opportunity. However unless the cost of living takes a bounce we shall be well enough, and in April the franc may well be higher. French policy with Poincare running it doesn't tend in the opposite direction. As a matter of fact I know less about politics now than I have known for years. Most of my reading is in the fifteenth century and although French imperialism is old it isn't that old. As I am sure Ada has written you we had as nice a Christmas as we had any right to expect this far from you. Kenny was delighted with his toys and we blew ourselves to a bangup dinner with turkey and a liquid comestible which I am led to believe you cant get at home. We had Frijsh in for dinner and afterwards she and Ada and I walked as far as the Place de la Concorde which we reached in time to see the winter sun going down over the water in a cold rose sky the reflection of which in the stream was mauve and opalescent and changeable as the throat of a pigeon. One appreciates winter sunsets in Paris. There are about two to the month. In the evening we dined with the Myers who seem to be the people we like best here. Mrs. Myers was Alice Lee Herrick whose father was a lawyer in Chicago and whose uncle was a professor at the University. Did you ever hear of either?

I think so often of your understanding and generosity of mind in making it possible for us to have this year. How you could have had enough faith in us to see our point of view I can't understand. But I think you will be justified. Not that I expect recognition for myself — Ada may well have it. But I think we are both going to do a great deal more this way than we ever should have done as a lawyer and his wife in Boston or anywhere else. Which inevitably and by a process of opposites puts me in mind of aunt Mary. Ada, after writing her five times[,] has just had an endless letter filled with minute accounts of everything aunt Mary has been doing in the last month and making no sense at all. Do you suppose she feels the termination of the old relationship? Or what is her trouble? Anyway thank god for you two. Her defalcation only throws into relief your altogether inexplicable constancy. Merely being a parent doesn't explain it.

I wish you could see your darling granddaughter. She is simply too wonderful. I am mad about her — absolutely.

with all my love your devoted son   A.

TLS: M

To Amy Lowell

Dear Miss Lowell: 31 December 1923   Paris

I simply can't think how you happened to remember us in the middle of one of your Christmases with so many other and more important people to remember. I take it kindly. At the time I took it so kindly that I all but wept. And I continue to have what the anatomical sentimentalists used to call a warm feeling around the heart. Thank you a thousand times.

We hear about you at second hand and rather indefinitely, chiefly through your delicious neice[1] whom we more and more cherish as we more and more anticipate her letters. But she throws out the most perplexing intimations that never quite achieve three dimensional reality. Aunt Amy and the Dusa.[2] The Dusa and a bottle of Champaigne. All more or less mixed up together — not the first and the last but all the others. I suppose tours of the great west start about this season with faithful servitors breaking their shoulders and I suppose some other strangers in Boston are sitting around your fire feeling as though they had never been strange in their lives. But I am sentimental enough by inclination without giving way to such recollections. I prefer to observe — as for instance the touch of your fine Italian in the forthcoming publication by J. Farrar, rest him, of Hervey's Saga.[3] The part of it he read me sounded grand. A letter from Fred Allen of Harper's thanks me for putting him in the way of getting North, South, East and West of a Man.[4] I was puzzled but no less amused. I am no more than the least of those who know why they admire Miss Lowell's poetry. And Miss Lowell had heard of Harper's. So it goes. Please remember that we think of you very often.   Archie MacLeish

TLS: MH

1. Katharine (Kay) Bundy. 2. Eleanora Duse (1859–1924), the Italian actress, had been visiting Sevenels, the Lowell estate in Brookline, Massachusetts. 3. Hervey Allen's "The Blindman: A Ballad of Nogent L'Artaud," first published in his *Wampum and Old Gold* (New Haven: Yale University Press, 1921), a volume in the Yale Series of Younger Poets, of which John C. Farrar was editor. The poem was reprinted separately by the press in 1923. 4. Lowell's "East, West, North, and South of a Man" appeared in her *What's O'Clock* (1925).

To Robert N. Linscott[1]

Dear Linscott: [c. January 1924] [Paris]

There are one or two things about my book I want to talk about and because you have been decent to me in the past I propose to show my gratitude by loading them onto you. The first is the name. Certain cryptic indications in the proof suggested an ironic purpose to call the book Many Marriages either in a spirit of Elizabethanism which might be lost on the world — or such part of the said sphere as shall rush to read — or in unhappy emulation of Mr. Sherwood Andersons washable multiplicity of consumations.² I feel quite clear that what little restraint the title may hold inheres in the singular and is lost in the plural. So I attempted to make clear on the proof that I preferred The Happy Marriage. Would you mind seeing that we hold to that?

Secondly, is it necessary to acknowledge previous magazine publication? If so the list is as I recall it (practical certainty) Atl., Yale Rev., New Rep., No. Am., with others in now defunct magazines of verse.

Thirdly, you once suggested that I give you the names of any critics or mag. people who might have some reason for treating me without malice — or anyway treating me. I give you for what they are worth J. Farrar of the Bookman, Bob Littell of the New Rep., Frederick Allen of Harpers, E. B. Cutting of the No. Am., Helen McAfee of the Yale Rev.. If a copy could reach the Boston Herald through O'Brien with an intimation that it was by his late adviser in Libel he would see to a notice. As a lawyer he almost liked me. Other suggestions may occur to me later. For one thing I shall attempt to locate a little journalistic sympathy in my native Chicago. Oh, Canby, or better Bill Benet on the N. Y. Evening Post would help. And Elinor Wylie on Vanity Fair owes me a word good bad or indifferent.³ Although Edmund Wilson Jr. there is the bird to feed I suppose. And he might come through.

I am just finishing a verse play which I am going to send you with this question. Shall I hold it as the core for another book or had I better send it elsewhere than H.M. for immediate publication? The answer depends I suppose upon your opinion as to whether H.M. might look kindly upon it in connection with a possible second book. It is merely your personal opinion I ask and I apologize for asking you. But you will see why I think when you look at the poem.

I have just sold to the No. Am. a poem which I wish you might see. I had you in mind — you and your John de Boresch no Boschere or whatever — when I wrote it.⁴ But it is too long to appear before you forget this suggestion that you read it. So let it go.

I wish I might drop in on one of your Greek lunches with a bottle of Napoleon Brandy.

My best to Don. And please tell Whitney⁵ that I duly got his very nice note when Walker got around to forwarding it which was about two months afterwards.   faithfully yours   Archie MacLeish

TLS: MH

1. M's editor at Houghton Mifflin Company. 2. Anderson had published, in 1922, a collection of short stories entitled *Many Marriages*. 3. M had favorably reviewed Wylie's *Black Armour* in the 5 December 1923 issue of *The New Republic*. 4. The poem to which M refers was "Biography of Mr. Beck the Suicide," later published as "Einstein." Jean de Bosschère was a French poet and book illustrator. 5. Don and Whitney were, presumably, colleagues of Linscott's at Houghton Mifflin Company.

To Francis Hyde Bangs

Cher François   10 January 1924   Paris

This, your last, I may confess grieves me. You are like a sweet water poured upon the sands of the desert. And why you continue to be poured I don't understand. I wish with all my heart you were out of New Haven & using yourself somewhere in a less arid world. I don't for a moment suggest that you owe any duty to anyone not yourself to make use of the very rare faculties you have produced in yourself. I merely mean that in some not altogether to be explained manner, it is only by making use of oneself that one maintains that balance called happiness. Like riders upon bicycles we must move to remain mounted. And you are unhappy because you do not move. It is not possible indefinitely to write your poems in the dramatic actions of your own person. You must, sooner or later, find the verse tedious. And the number of possible solutions is limited. As Sczornik would say, no tragedy was ever successful beyond five acts.[1] And we all know what the acts must be in a world in which we act only débout or in bed. For God's sake, if you will permit the apostrophe & the preaching, get out of New Haven & use your brain & body in pursuit. A new world in criticism, in letters, opens. Whatever you may think of the poems of T. S. Eliot there is no doubt about The Sacred Wood. And you are by mind & by training the proper inventor of that grandeur.

Between you & your writing stands only the pride which will not permit you the second rate performance in which I indulge. But only by being amenable to the second rate can you ever get at the first. If you wait for an a priori perfection you will wait forever.

So much for AMacL upon F.H.B. for whom he has perhaps too much affection to be wise & in whose happiness of mind he sees perhaps too much mental happiness for himself.

As for F.H.B. upon AMacL — I admit the charge. The lack I feel is a lack of salt — of directness — of prosiness. Believe that I war against it. But I suffer from inhibitions too strong for me. I cannot write save at two removes from the fact it seems. Nevertheless I essay. I have about decided to give up writing for the present with any view to publication & instead to experiment & educate myself. What a hell of a waste I made of four years at Yale! $\phi\beta\kappa$ & a major in English taught me nothing of what I ought to know. I am now going over the period of Barclay & Skelton. Is John Berdan arid? Or did I merely throw away hope & heritage by paying no attention to him?[2] How *shall* we be saved anyway? I now regret bitterly every hour but the few, the golden few which in your company & that of L.M. taught me the little I learned of that priceless thing which at Yale is bottled & corked & called "English

Literature." Why didn't somebody tell me that the roots of English lay through France & Italy? Why didn't I learn to read Dante? Why didn't I — do the million things which would have saved me. I don't unduly blame Yale. I rather blame it on my own vanity, conceit, obsequiousness, folly. But is Jutte[3] who resented the system better off? You only of all of us secured the shadow of an education. And now you pour back your clear water into the sink. Write! Write! Write!

Well, something too much of this. I have been as pedagogical as E. B. Reed. Forgive me & — consider what I say.

If you see Peabo[4] give her my love. How go your own? Are you yet mounted upon that glory which beneath the face of Venus shadows a Gorgon?   yrs   A.

ALS: YCAL

1. M and Lawrence Mason had published, in the May 1923 issue of *The North American Review*, an article entitled "The Next Philosophy," purporting to be a review of *The Lyric Tense, a Grammar of Life* by a Czech philosopher named Peter Sczornik. As M admitted publicly in *Poetry* magazine in October 1948 — and as Bangs knew — the Sczornik article was a hoax. 2. Alexander Barclay (1475?–1552), author of *The Ship of Fools* (1509), and the poet John Skelton (*c.* 1460–1529) were among the writers M studied in Berdan's course on English literature of the sixteenth century. 3. William R. Jutte (Yale '15). 4. Grace Allen Peabody, later Mrs. Bangs.

To Amy Lowell

My dear Miss Lowell:-   31 January 1924   Paris

You won't mind my addressing you on the paper & — what is worse — with the pen — of the Café des deux Magots? I understand now the well known Gallic affectation of writing in cafés. Its too cold to write at home. And if you aren't enjoying your bok at least I am.

I wrote you at some length exactly a week ago but it all came to nothing. I had something very definite to say & it didn't get said. I succeeded in thanking you for your letter which overwhelmed me with its mere presence & ravished me with its material. But beyond that nothing. In the mean time arrives the N.R. with your fine historical review.[1] I would give eighteen months & three days off my life for your sense of fairness & justice & a year more for your way of expressing it. Curious that I should have echoed your theory of the feminine quality of the new Lyricists — as you well call them. I'm tremendously obliged to you for letting me see the magazine.

Now for the thing that doth devour me. (Can you still read this pen? I can just make the thing out) I suppose the short way to describe the issue is to say that my creative & critical intelligences (or lack thereof) are engaged in bitter war. More briefly I don't like what I do. In fact I dislike it very strongly. And I don't seem to be able to do anything about it. It comes to this. Algernon Charles was my boyhood idol. What I wanted was mellifluousness — unbroken curves. I developed the very ordinary youthful style for which one, whoever she is, Louise Bogin offers the word 'adverbial'.[2] I was adverbial as Hell — which I believe to be mosaiced with adverbs. As I went along I dropped my thees & thous & checked my more Tennysonian decorations but I still wrote "musical" verse. I use the word with emphasis. During this time — the time when most people are all mixed up with the activities of their contemporaries — I wrote in a shell. I knew nothing of them. Even Amy Lowell I came to late — say 1915. And in her I saw what I now see in the Cezannes in the Salle Camodo — a development of the tradition. It was all I had eyes to see. For the rest I was too busy with the War & the Law School & the practice of law to do more than write myself. Then I met you. Then I got away from the law. And then I began to see. What I saw was of course the possibilities of a poetry with salt in it — with precision — with a rhythm of ideas. I reread Miss Lowell. I reread "Tears" Eliot (as that curiously unsuccessfully successful young man, Mr. Cummings[,][3] calls him)[.] I read for the first time Mr. Pound's critical exuberances. I read Yeats' explanations of himself. I even read Marianne Moore whom I can't pretend to admire. And it became perfectly clear to me that there was a kind of poetry possible in this day, a compact, precise edged poetry which could be terribly poignant, exquisitely moving. But in my own writing it was impossible. I would compact a line. I would look at it & leave it. And the next day I would strike it out & change it for a line having the rhythm which to my hand seems to be the only one possible but to my brain is unendurable. And then words. My words are all ships which have carried ivory & peacocks between England & the Levant for two hundred years. They have ceased to evoke images. They are coins. But what can replace them? Surely not the commercial-jargon impersonalities of Miss Moore. Surely not Eliots multisyllabilities. What?

Well, there you are. I have written a rather curious, contracted, longish poem which the No. Amer. has taken, a lyric for Sedgwick, & a long verse play which I am too discouraged to type. I have practically decided now to stop writing for a number of months & read — learn Italian & read Dant', read Laforgue & de Gourmont, read the English fellows who can help. But I am more than haunted with the fear that it is too late. That this rhythm & vocabulary which my intelligence knows for second rate are me, my "style", all that I have.

I'm glad that's done. I think you will understand & its good to get it off my chest.

gratefully & affectionately yours   Archie MacLeish.

ALS: MH

1. "Two Generations in American Poetry," *The New Republic* 37 (5 December 1923), Part II, pages 1–3. 2. Louise Bogan applied the phrase to M's style in "The Springs of Poetry," *The New Republic* 37 (5 December 1923), Part II, page 9. 3. E. E. Cummings, then studying art in Paris.

To Dean Acheson

Dear Dean: 5 February 1924   Paris

I don't know why you shouldn't think me the world's greatest and most convincing washout. Perhaps you do. And I have nothing to say for myself but to make the obvious observation that I haven't written at all except to perpetrate more or less unsatisfactory verse in the seclusion of my not at all theoretical attic. To complete my sense of my unworthiness to further address you arrived a few days ago your much appreciated Christmas package which had got itself tied up in the Parisian douaine in some way known only to the dieties who shape the ends and middles of French imports. We hadn't seen E.W.'s novel[1] (though that hadn't prevented our talking about it) and we thoroughly enjoyed it. She has a mastery of a small perfection which is simply amazing whatever one may think of it as a literary symbol. Thank you a thousand times to which add the innumerable gratitudes of Kenny and mary Hillard for constructive toys and wonderful talking dolls.

I am overwhelmed with your new grandeur. It is not at all remarkable that they should have admitted you to a place on the letter head and a share in the firm debts but it is simply amazing that they should have further increased your already Tommy Tompkinsesque remuneration.[2] I do not mean to suggest that you are now paid or ever will be paid within reach of your value but I do intend most earnestly to remark that you are now the highest paid lawyer of your age in the field of my knowledge — which, if not large, is certainly deep. I congratulate you with just the proper emphasis of envy to make the acknowledgement real.

As for myself I have little that is interesting to write though a good deal that would be important in conversation. I have been brought up standing. Or perhaps spinning is the word I want. When I arrived I set to work to write with a little polite reading in the background. I did a verse play which I am holding for future decision and several other pieces, one of them quite long, all of which I have sold to the Atl. and The No.Am.Rev.. Then suddenly I had a thought — an event rare enough to be important. It suddenly occurred to me that I was definitely embarked upon a literary existence, that literature was at least as much of a science as an art and that in either case I was thoroughly without knowledge. I had nothing but that most inadequate of all possible preparations for anything, a college education, — and a college education in which I had succeeded in wasting four years in the most successful possible manner. I decided almost over night to stop writing for the present at least and go to work upon my education. As a result I am now at the labor of learning Italian with a view to reading Dante while at the same time reading Laforgue in French (a terribly difficult task) and working over such pre-Chaucerian stuff as I can unearth in this world capital. That for pure letters. My theory is to follow the trend from Anglo-Saxon and Provencal (if I can get at them) sources through Dante and thence through Petrarch and the Pleiade into Chaucer (pre-Pleiade of course) and Surrey and then down. It means a reading knowledge of four languages counting O.E. and Prov. as two. At the same time I want to do the Golden Bough and follow that line. Eliot uncovered something when he did the Waste Land and it would be the purest folly not to pursue it.

All that means of course a very long time and the question is whether I am wise, even admitting the work is necessary, to attempt it as late as this. At twenty I could start with some hope of getting through. But one only has a certain number of years with the fires going underneath and you cant throw them away. Is it bunk to blame the American system of so-called education now? Have I a right to ask that a university which gave me a major in English Literature with a P.B.K. stand should at least have given me some sense of what English literature was and should have forced me to learn to read Italian and French at the very least? I don't know. The complaint sounds sort of inadequate. I suppose the truth is that you can't educate other people. You can only educate yourself and perhaps intimate to others what you have done and what the problems were in relation to which you did it. But that last requires more honesty and courage than most teachers are capable of. But if you are going to have schools at all you ought at the least to teach people who want to know, what there is to know and what things are conditions precedent to what other things and in what order. That is my kick. No one ever so much as suggested the existence of a tradition of English literature. I was left to make that vital discovery at the pages of a mere poet turned critic.[3] Of course one trouble in the field of English is that the people who teach it are unsuccessful writers who have never been seriously faced with the problems that they teach as practical problems applicable in their solution to the difficulties of making more literature.

We are now trying to decide whether to come back next fall. If we stay we burn our bridges because I will never be able to get back into the law. I don't want to but at the same time we can't live in America upon our income. Thats the rub. And it will be some time before Ada will be earning anything. By the way she appears in public here to-morrow night in one song on a program of modern music. She is scared to death of the song but I have no worries for her. It may possibly bring her some work. But she still feels that she has a lot to do which needs doing at home. Write me what you think. If my facts offer any data sufficient.

They are burying Woodrow today.[4] Does it strike you as whimsical that a man who spent most of his public life, all his popularity and the greater part of his health in the fight for peace should be loaded onto a gun carriage as soon as he is past resistance and put away to a tune of gun fire and brass? But they can't get rid of him that way. Hot air through a bugle will do for H. C. Lodge[5] when he goes down to his last constituents but Woodrow wont squeeze through a horn.

Love to Alice. What we wouldn't give to have you both here for about eight hours of an evening doesn't exist.

affectionately yours   Archie

TLS: CtY

1. Edith Wharton's novel *Son at the Front* had been published in September 1923. 2. A reference to a Yale classmate of Acheson and MacLeish's. 3. Probably T. S. Eliot, whose *The Sacred Wood* (1920), containing the essay "Tradition and the Individual Talent," M had recently read. 4. Former President Wilson had died on February 3. 5. Senator Henry Cabot Lodge, a conservative Republican opponent of President Wilson's, was ailing, and died on November 9.

To Andrew and Martha Hillard MacLeish

Dearest Father and Mother: 10 February 1924   Paris

I have just written Ishbel[.] It is impossible to put into words one's feeling about her courage or one's sense of the tragedy of her illness.[1] She of all people. It is only within the last month that I have had any idea as to the seriousness of the situation and this most recent news that she will be out of the world for at least a year or two more is almost unbelievable. But her letters are so cheerful that she shames me. I wish I could make her know how I feel about her. It seems as though I had had all the luck in the world and she had had none. I feel like a cheat. I am so glad you are there with her and so glad that you have been able to do it without too much suffering from cold and height. Father's lovely letter to Kenny which came this morning sounds as though he were finding Colorado almost a possible substitute for Florida.

There is at once a great deal and very little to say about us. Since Madame Frijsh left Ada has been working through programs with Mlle. Boulangier who though in her thirties is one of the musical powers of Paris. As a result of that work she sang last Wednesday night in the Salle Pleyel doing a song upon a program of modern music. The song as you will see from the program was a modern piece [by Aaron Copland] with flute and clarinet accompaniment — no piano. It wasn't too good qua song but Ada did it beautifully and it was the success of the evening. We hope that she is going to be able to get other work of the same sort to do. As for myself I find the future rather doubtful. That is I have piled up so much work ahead of myself that I have no idea when I shall get to writing again. When I first got here I set to work at once to write and I finished six or seven pieces of varying length all of which I have sold to the No. Am. Rev. or the Atl. without having anything refused. I have also done a long verse play which I am uncertain about publishing. But all the time that I was working on these things I was more and more conscious that if I ever hoped to succeed with poetry as a definite profession I would have to educate myself first. Outside of the law I know nothing. I can't read Dante, I can't read the Greeks, I can't really read the Frenchmen and as for English poetry I have a college graduates misinformation and nothing more. So I decided about a month ago to stop writing altogether until I had learned enough Italian to read the Div. Com. and enough French to make sense out of Rimbaud and LaForgue. In addition to that I am working over the foundations of English again. So that you can see the basis for my uncertainty about the future. And this all bears upon the question of our staying for another year about which mother was kind enough to express her confidance in our judgment. I can do this work here. I am not able to see how I could do it *and* write *and* do whatever is necessary from a financial point of view at home. But the difficulties are not easily brushed aside. Ada can do comparatively little with her music here. [A]nd the essential job will be harder to find at the end of a year than this next fall. We are trying to be quite honest with ourselves in facing the problem and I think we will be able to work it all out in some way.

Kenny must be put to bed and I must tend to our twenty fires so I must rest the Underwood for the evening. Dearest love to you both from all of us.   Your affectionate son   Archie

TLS: M

1. *See* M to Martha Hillard MacLeish, 4 September 1923, note 1.

To Amy Lowell

Dear Miss Lowell: 3 March 1924   Paris

    It is simply ridiculous for me to try to thank you. From the time that I posted my letter to you I lived in hope and fear that you would do precisely what you did — hope because I knew you could help me more than anyone else and fear because I knew I had no right to ask you to do it. If I had known that it would mean a hand-written letter on the eve of one of those trying trips of yours I should have felt even more fearful. But no amount of foresight would have prepared me for the letter itself. Of course, as you realize, must realize, the thing in your life which would give even a stone courage is that you were willing to put in ten years of silent work with no encouragement and with no help but your own conviction of what you wanted to do. That without the event ought to cure the whimpers in anyone. The event is a different thing. It is of course not the ten years that explains you.

Your suggestion that I do critical work to get into step with myself is a very keen bit of analysis. I have a perfectly clear cut dissatisfaction with what I have already done but no more than a sort of sense of gravitation toward the thing that would give me satisfaction to do. Of course I have been trying to get my ideas into shape but they remain pretty nebulous so far. The rhythmic problem troubles me for one thing. I suppose the truth is that old brother Algernon made deeper ruts in my brain than I had supposed. Diluted Algernon of course. I find that under the pressure of any sort of emotion I fall back into cadences which I know to be stale before I use them. Working with deliberation I can get effects that don't disgust me on rereading but only then. That's one thing. The other is the equally basic problem of verbiage. Where are the living waters of the word? As I tried to say before I don't think Miss Moore's attempt to give poetic edge to words already stale in academic or commercial conversation gets by. Neither do I feel that the extensive usage of words generally omitted from polite conversation is enough, though one must admit that it appears to give reality. Neither again does it seem enough to twist the order of words inter sese for the purpose of directing attention. The dodge is too obvious. And yet some such thing seems necessary — not for a carefully planned novelty but in order [to] secure any sort of intensity. The trouble is that you people who made poetry of natural diction, who threw the poetic vocabulary so-called into the ashes where it belonged, have left little for the bottom layer but extremities. I don't mean that I sympathasize with the position which you so effactually squash — the position of those who apparently put idiosyncrasy above poetry. But I do mean that one must get hold of a speech which seems to him fresh — as you did — with the additional factor that you carried over the impression to the rest of the world. I suppose one answer to my difficulty is the perfectly tenable theory that you can only get a certain amount of poetry out of the speech of any particular age anyway. But one doesn't believe that sort of thing until one has to.

I have just come, late as to all things other, to Fenellosa's essay on the Chinese Written Character in the back of Pound's Instigations. As a theory (I admit your charge that I'm susceptible to 'em) I can't help being impressed by his amorous attachment to the verb and his contention that it is possible to feel backalong the stems of language to the acting and active sense of particular words. But the philological erudition required leaves Mr. Fenellosa in the theoretical stage so far as I'm concerned. Well, enough of that. I have no right to inflict my half baked notions on you. It is enough that you give me the necessary nudge to slide me into a period of thrashing these things out for myself. To what end I'm sure I don't know.

I should love to see your paper on the relation of poetry and music and I shall work along the lines of your suggestions about modern music. Ada is working out a suite of Milhaud's now which is intriguing precisely in that way. She will have quite a bit of stuff when she gets back which will interest you. From her one public appearance in Paris so far it is perfectly clear that her voice with its extraordinary precision, clarity and tone is fitted for such songs as Stravinsky is now writing and Sati has been writing. There is another thing I am bold enough to ask you for and that is news as to where and when I can see Which-being-interpreted[1] in print. I should rather leave everything else of current production unread than that — even including, — well all of them, male and female.

As I say it is ridiculous for me to try to thank you. But its all I can do. Please believe that you have done one of the kindest and most generous things on record in the elaborate books. Only the suspicion that I wasn't worth saving can possibly detract from your peace of mind.

Ada sends you her love and I that and all my gratitude.

Archie MacLeish

TLS: MH

1. "Which, Being Interpreted, Is as May Be, or Otherwise," a long poem collected in Lowell's *What's O'Clock* (1925).

To Martha Hillard MacLeish

Dearest mother: 12 March [1924]   Paris

I've already written you about Ada. By the time we get home we'll have all the facts on that. She is giving her first real concert the 9 May with Champy, the pianist, whom we hire for the occasion, at the Conservatoire. Watch the stars and pray she doesn't have a sore throat.

Ishbel's letter about Kenny is fine. I'm delighted that she loves him so much and it will be a wonderful thing for him to have her friendship.

And I understand what she has to say about my relation to him although I quarrel with her words. The truth is that Kenny irritates me when we are together and I often bully him. I don't think I try to impress my will upon his to any appreciable extent — no more than one must to force a child to do such things as eat, wash, behave etc — and as for Kenny's sacred personality or anyone's sacred personality, well there aint no such animal. Meaning that there is no RIGHT constitutional, natural or aesthetical not to be invaded by others, and that those humans who have the largest vacuum around them in which to flower and expand are usually the feeblest. All we can hope for in that direction is, in the words of one of our most significant younger poets,

> Standing between the sun and moon preserve
> A certain secrecy or seem to keep
> Something inviolate[1]

I hope I quote him accurately. All we can hope for is to establish a kind of integrity, a kind of probity while still alive such as the dead preserve. And we have got to fight for it or we cant possess it. Strange law but true.

I'm not arguing that I treat Kenny well. God and I know I don't and Ishbel has guessed it. I'm just blowing off steam about sacred personalities. Neither do I believe that I am divinely sent to present that necessary friction against which Kenny can build his leaning walls. I think I should respect him and advise him and let who will (and lots of them will) toughen him. All that education can do is to try to replace, under the weight of self-consciousness, that absolute sincerity which civilization takes away. To have that and to savoir choisir. And its because education is at present merely an adjunct to civilization and not a kind of contra-ceptive assuring the soul its if not virginity at least lonliness that I hate education. What I should like to give Kenny is himself. Not being able to give him that what I should do is to prevent others from taking it away from him. And others will take it away from him not by opposition but by help. It is the easy tangents we slide off by. It is the friend who slightly diverts you in the direction of your own genius who betrays you. It is those who go before and beat down the grass who lose you the way. I speak of myself, of us all. The sin I cannot forgive aunt Mary is not her sin of disloyalty in opposing me when I made my own decision but her sin of friendship in leading me into the road of my talents and out of the road of my life. *I am not warning* Ishbel about Kenny. She is forewarned and also generous. I suppose what it all comes down to is the fact that you can't do much for a child. Anymore than you can for an artist. State aid and rich men's prizes ruin. And too much fingering of children doth rot them young. Feed em, keep em alive, respect em and teach them to ask.

Although that's all and perhaps more than I have a right to say I am going farther. I don't think you are right about Norman. It was not father's lack of sympathy — which of us in childhood had his sympathy? (Instead a cold clean-cut relationship which remains in our memories like the lake and the stars) It was no one's fault. Norman was a child prodigy. His senses were delicate, his reactions delicate, his powers of expression with words or paint or music facile and marked. He was the artist. So much so that when I began to write and indeed until I had written a considerable amount and began to have a reputation I was not seriously considered as an artist at home. (This is *not* complaint. I thank God for it) The reason was simply that that was Norman's prerogative. You were wise and Norman did not become self conscious. But he was given all the encouragement the son of cultivated and well to do parents could be given. The result was that his artistic mechanism developed rapidly but he himself did not develop. He became a misfit. And he suffered enormously. By the time (at Williams) he found himself he had come to associate his artistic impulses with his unhappiness and he turned from them. Also they were no longer fresh to him but stale and used. I may be following the wrong line but the result was about that. It was no one's fault. It was the inevitable history of the talented child. Once in a million times the talented child arrives. The rest of the time his talents remain unrooted because they devour his life as fast as he lives it. The very fact that he can express himself as he goes along prevents his having a life rich enough to express importantly.

I wish I knew where the American picture of the artist came from. The type — the ultra-sensitive, inefficient, dreaming type [—] has nothing to do with art except the relation of amateur to thing loved. (Again — I am not describing Norman) Art is a hard thing. It comes out of much living. It requires the highest and most efficient intelligence. It requires toughness and strength. The great artists have always been the best men. I suppose the only explanation for the American attitude is the fact that to the artist the things with which the so-called practical men concern their minds are fundamentally impractical, inefficient and frivolous. Sub specie aeternitatis what on earth is sillier than the spectacle of a rich man spending his time manufacturing automobiles.

Well, assez. Send this on to Squish.[2] I love her and you and I like bickering with you. I don't expect you to agree. By the way — do you believe . . . ? Well let that go.

All my love to you two and father   My best to Miss T.[3]

A.

TLS: M
1. An approximation of the opening lines of "Einstein." 2. A nickname for Ishbel MacLeish. 3. Miss Tillinghast, a retired trained nurse then serving as nurse-companion to M's father.

To Amy Lowell

Dear Miss Lowell:-   4 May 1924   [Salisbury, England]

This is from the middle of a tour of poets & Downs. I have been thinking of you more even than I usually do. Every new poet I meet makes me realize the blessedness of having one poet for friend who not only will but can discuss the art of poetry. May all the gods in the Golden Bough preserve you.

I am trying to meet Eliot but so far in vain. He gets ill when I enter the same country with him. I understand he is an affable & rather slick young man. I can't believe it of the author of the Sacred Wood & editor of the Criterion. I find no one (!) (of course) in Oxford has heard of him. Masefield is guarded — guarded. He likes the poetry of power!

I've told H.M. to send you a copy of my book. You may use it between those slender split logs of yours if it pleases you to do so. But be as kind as you can.

Forgive this interruption of wise peace.

Affectionately yours   Archie

ALS: MH

To Ishbel MacLeish[1]

My dearest Ishbel:-   31 May 1924

Here begins my performance of what is at once an obligation and a free act. I know all too clearly what it will mean to come to that place on the earth where the body of Kenny lies. Try as we may — try as I have — to reduce my life to those intangible conceptions of things which cannot be hurt & which we imagine cannot be destroyed I have only to open my eyes to realize that these intangible things are not real. It is only when an idea resumes the form from which it was at first distracted that it exists. The conception of beauty is only the memory of beauty seen & the expectation of the recurrence of the seen thing. That is why the mere soil of the earth so powerfully affects us. That is why the idea of death taking form in shapes & outlines of soil & stone is only then poignant again. I dimly foresee what it will mean to stand beside Kenny's grave. There are reasons why I should be glad not to go

*   *   *

We are standing now indefinitely in the Gare du Nord — I in a first class carriage forced upon me by the extreme popularity of the second class. It is hot as Skokie on the bright side of a July morning & the ornate & highly perfumed French lady opposite insists on walking back & forth over my feet. If I live I shall reach Brussels at six o'clock odd & the Daniels may or may not meet me. This evening I expect to dine with them & in the morning we are all to go out to the Cemetary, where there will be a Memorial Service attended, as I understand it, by all the village. I hope to come back to Paris in the evening.

Mimie[2] is so wise. She fathomed the fact that I was leaving & permitted me to hold her on my la' twice in succession. When she hears the pedlars calling their singsong calls in the street she puts up her left forefinger slightly crooked & hisses like a little snake. The cracked piano banging in the court produces the same effect. Celestial movement. Celestial music. More than celestial child.

Kenny wanted to come the worst way. After all he argues he's seven years old & he's never been anywhere but Granny Patty's[3] & Paris. Well, yes, Farmington & Camp Meade. But those places are all in America! He is now tremendously excited about gravity. If it pulls you down why doesn't it pull you in? And why if iron goes down does wood stay up? To which one replies by choking over a chop. Then too there is this curious business of love which is not the love we have for Momie nor the love we have for Daddy. For instance why did Dame Liones want to get into Gareth's bed?[4] Why, why indeed. But our descriptive powers wax. A strange gentleman called yesterday leaving no name. After meticulous inventory of complexion & personal effects which brought no light to a stupid parent he concluded with this: "He looked as though his name was Tom". Roars of laughter at my expense.

Ada still in England touring at large with her family — off we go —

* * *

Frances Daniels was Frances Hancock of Evanston. Tom was a Bones Man a year ahead of me & is now second secretary at Brussels. On the platform Tom. In a car outside Frances & the nurse & two grand-looking little boys. The Daniels live in a grand house with a liveried butler and a beautiful salon on the first floor (2nd American style). I am to put up at a charming little pension around the corner which, after a scotch & soda, I examine. Then Tom & I go down to the florists to see what kind of a wreathe the good lady is making. Walking to my pension alone I have a sudden sense of the strangeness of this country. The air is very soft with a curious fragrance I cannot quite designate. I feel that Kenny & I are both in a strange land & that he is waiting for me. My sense that he is waiting for me out there beyond the city somewhere is terribly poignant.

I bathe in the hottest bath in Europe & get into a crumpled dinner coat. Fifteen butlers let me into the Daniels & fourteen people come for dinner. One or two nice Americans — mostly men if you stress the adjective — both sexes if you sit on the noun. After dinner I am made to sit on the hearth rug & expound Joyce to my own disgust & the even more obvious meprise of the entire male population. Then the rest play Mah Jonggggggggg and bridge & I am left with a lady from Kansas & a lady from Kansas City to continue Joyce (who gets badly frazzled) & stir about in the Education of Children. At one thirty they go & I. The night is softer than the afternoon. The smell is a smell of hay blown in over the city. The stars move under vague clouds. I feel Kenny's body under the earth in this land so strangely soft and fragrant & far away.

* * *

In the morning I am called at nine thirty & presented with the best hard rolls & coffee I have ever eaten. The sun is pouring down into the court & I shave with equanimity. Even the razor works. At ten fifteen I enter the Daniels' front door again & am face to face with the largest wreathe I have ever seen. But marvellously beautiful. It is all made of pansy things that are small & purple & look like violets. At the top are long roses — white, & cream & yellow, with sweet peas among them. Frances is alarmed at the size, & so, in spite of myself[,] am I. Little John is amazed & delighted. Little Forrest who wants to go too grieves silently on the bottom step. At half past ten we start off with my wreathe & a great bunch of iris — we call them flags at Craigie Lea — & white stock, tied to the front of the inside of the car.

The country is green mixing into blue & vague greys. The clouds are low & unbelievably bright. The light seems suffused in the air like golden dust. A little before twelve we come to Ghent where the campanile is tolling a hundred bells at once & the inside of the cathedral is packed. Here we lunch at the hotel with about twenty people who have come in various cars — the Ambassador (Billy Phillips of Boston) the British, French & Polish military attachées. Some stray British officers & a group of five or ten Americans who have resumed their uniforms & medals for the occasion. It is a long & effective lunch. I talk about divorce with the wife of the British military attaché. The Ambassador looks pleasant. Frances glowers at the uniforms. At one it is over & we go out & get into our cars again. The Ambassador leads off.

As we ride along we talk of everything in the world. The country is still flat with only the gentlest roll. Village after village, the faces of the houses scarred with mitrailleuse bullets. The trees are rich and green & the wheat is almost as high as it was six years ago in the valley of the

Marne. Larger & larger silver clouds pile up behind silver clouds. The gorse is yellow as pollen and the rhododendrons are red and mauve and dark green. I feel more than ever the unendurable tension of that waiting silence, that dead body that waits. The living Kenny is gone from my mind & I can only feel his bones in the earth listening for me.

At last Waereghem. The houses are draped with the rich Spanish folds of the Belgian flag. On the Mairie is the drapeau étoilé. Tom gets out to perform his proper Diplomatic devoirs & Frances & I drive out through a side street of the village over a cobble stone road winding between houses until we come to open fields again. There are clusters of deep red roofs and occasional trees. The houses are banked in gorse. The wheat waves. A stray, steady wind from the south west blows the dust in dragging puffs out over the grain fields. After a ten minute drive we are in front of the gate of the cemetary. To the left of the gate, inside the low red brick wall[,] is a little guest house built in the manner of the farm houses of the country-side. Ahead, in the center of the plot[,] is a flag pole bearing the two flags stiff & struggling in the wind. On the three far sides are the three blocks of white crosses, perhaps four hundred in all. With my wreathe I go alone to the last grave at the far corner of the middle block. The cemetary is shaped like this

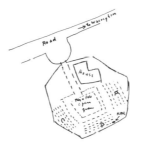

Behind the last rows of graves & inside the walls trees & rhododendrons have been planted but most of them have died because of the sandyness of the soil. The grass in the middle is sparse & light. But Frances says that you would scarcely know it for the same place it was last year. I hardly hear her. Kennys name on the grave is like the cry of a hurt child. There are little faded wreathes & a few flowers on each grave. I move them from Kenny's grave & put the wreathe there with the little wreathe inside it. Touching the sandy earth above him I suddenly knew — it seemed for the first time — that he was dead. I cried so that I could not stop.

Over the wall back of his grave — north, for he faces the sun, — the earth slopes slowly away. The wheat is thick & high. People are coming through the paths toward the cemetary. Beyond there are a few houses & on top of the hill, the gentle rise, soft, tender trees. Over my head a lark sings & sings, dropping and flinging itself up again, flickering & falling. There is a tinkling of leaves in the little poplar trees that still live in the cemetary. After a time I go back & Frances takes a few pictures of the grave. Then we get into the car & drive back to the village. I feel the most withering bitterness. It seems to me grotesque, absurd, silly that that beautiful boy should be lying under the sand in a field he never saw — for nothing — for nothing. It is no longer even sad. It is horrible. Absurd. The lynx face & the grey beau-brummel hair of Senator Lodge[5] dance in front of my eyes. He suddenly becomes — what I suppose he is — the type, the epitome, of the cowardly, selfish, cold-blooded stupidity of the old men who make wars. His face crinkles. It crumbles. He stinks.

Then we are back in the village. A little procession has formed in the Place. A band, two lines of young men & boys in white with the banner of their running club. Long lines of little girls in white with flowers. A few militia. Various clubs & banners. At the end the Mayor & the Ambassador followed by military attachees & women. Two American soldiers carry a wreathe to the foot of the village statue to its village dead — a dapper little bronze Belgian with a twirled mustache. Then we march out over the cobbles in the hot sun. As we approach a ditch full of dead water traversed by a little bridge someone back of me explains in laborious English that it was here the Germans retreating made a stand in the face of French & American troops. Most of the Americans out at the cemetary were killed here. There is slime on the water. "Unknown U.S. Soldier." "Unknown U.S. Soldier." Kenny's neighbor on his left is Private Tio. At his feet is a boy of Germanic blood. There are no Yankee names near him.

The sun is hot but the clouds are piling into the corners of the sky. A few drops of rain fall. Then we are at the cemetary gate. The boys in white clothes have formed in two long lines. The band is playing a dead march. Down there under the sand you can just [hear] it, a buzzing, a squeaking. The crickets make a sleepier noise.

The mayor mounts the little stand. He reads a graceful address in Flemish with a Flemish poem. Then he reads a graceful address in French with a French poem. Our little country — your sons, our comrades — lesson to these little ones. Under the sand you cannot hear that. Then the American Ambassador gravely in a tail coat gravely ascends the rostrum gravely. He has just come from Holland & he reads French very badly. Vous Belge — notre grand pays — vous Belge —. He pleads for closer relations with the American Ambassador. He reminds himself gravely of the dead — but they were not Ambassadors. And he — at forty-five — it is a record in the service. He looks so young!

A priest climbs up the steps. A storm is sweeping up from the south. Over the flag pole one bright cloud, bright as the peaks of the moon, towers. The priest asks very simply that all people there present will bow their heads & silently pray. I edge out through the crowd & go past to Kenny's grave. It is very still. The sky has become black & threatening. I feel nothing except the numbness of the earth, its silentness. The earth seems waiting, the whole earth as before.

Is it absurd? It is absurd to die anyhow. What difference does it make when you die. It is ridiculous to lie quite still.

The earth seems to be waiting. Suddenly the band plays lugubriously the Star Splangled Blanner with variations. Then it stops. Then — "(What's he to Hecuba or Hecuba to him That he should weep —".[6] All those children singing all together sing together the same song in English. Their voices go up & up. At one place they leap an octave. And yet — it is beautiful. It is the most beautiful thing I have ever heard. It is beautiful. I wonder if you can hear that singing under the weight of sand.

It has begun to rain — splashes of water. I tear some flowers out of the wreathe & walk back. The rain soaks me. I feel like a stone or a tree.

And then the heavens break. Everyone scurries for cover — & there is very little. The girls in their white dresses & their flowers, the boys in their white suits, are soaked, dripping. Women are draggled and soured. Inside the car I do not think about that, I think about the flood of cool clean water beating onto the sand, sluicing onto the sand, clogging the sand with wet & slowly, slowly, seeping down into the dust, down past the roots of grass, past the roots of the dead rhododendrons, down between cracked dry boards to the beautiful clean bones that lie there.

The earth relaxes, the dead relax, sleep. They are no longer waiting. They listen no longer. They are one with the strange earth of a strange land. They are quiet. They rest.

* * *

I have just read this over. It sounds literary. Forgive it that. If you feel it is nothing more then I can say nothing.

I don't know that I should send this on to mother. I intended when I began that it should be for both of you. You must decide. I think perhaps you will understand the feeling about the war that creates my feeling about Kenny. It was an awful, awful, failure. A hideous joke.

* * *

I am going to find out if father can give money to the upkeep of the Waereghem cemetary without having to run the risk of having his money spent elsewhere or in other ways. A little money would insure trees & flowers there. I shall see.

Dearest love to you dear girl. I am very proud of you.

Archie

ALS: CAMPBELL

1. Compare to this letter M's poem "Memorial Rain," first published in *The Yale Review* in October 1925 and based closely on the experience here described. 2. Mary Hillard MacLeish. 3. Martha Hillard MacLeish. 4. Characters in Malory's *Morte d'Arthur* and in *Gareth and Lynette*, Book Two of Tennyson's *Idylls of the King*, the latter of which, presumably, M had been reading to his son. 5. Henry Cabot Lodge. 6. An approximation of *Hamlet* II, ii, 569–570.

To Martha Hillard and Andrew MacLeish

Dearest Mother & Father: 24 June 1924   Granville

If I can find one I am going to enclose a post-card to show you the magnificent mansion your impoverished son is able to afford in the present state of the franc. To be sure we have come to a town of no pretensions as a summer place where only the cheap French & the cheaper English foregather but for all that we have done well as I trust you will see. We are perched up on the top ledge of a cliff about one hundred & fifty feet high facing the Atlantic with the Isle of Jersey just visible on clear days straight out to the North-west and the Brittany coast beyond Mt. St. Michel clearly visible to the south west. To the north the coast arches away in a long sand line toward Cherbourg and just south of us the old town of Granville built on its all but isolated rock juts out into the sea, a sky line of old roofs & queer chimneys terminating in a Second Empire Barracks and a wind-mill. Back of us is a high stone wall, a narrow path and the higher wooded Garden of our proprietaire cutting us off from the new town which is, simply & literally, a horror. The house itself is beautifully built if not beautiful. All the walls & partitions are of stone about a foot through & it is bare & clean with the sound of the sea always running through it. There is a funny little salon, a big dining room & a beautiful big kitchen on the rez de chausée. On the next floor is a large bath room with all necessaries (which, due to lack of water[,] we use only in part) a maid's room & two big bed-rooms occupied, the largest by Katherine & Mimi & the smaller by Kenny. Upstairs is a smaller bedroom which Ada & I use & a slightly larger but less attractive room occupied by the chamber maid. I use our bed-room to write in. The whole face of the cliff in front of the house has been gardened & pathed & planted with flowers down to the place where the rocks fall sheer & your hearts would gladden at the amazing combinations of color the gardener has produced. For the children it is ideal. Kenny is already fatter & eating like a horse & Mimi loves it. At low tide they can play on the beach. And at other times they have yards & yards of sand paths between the pines. For us it is almost equally nice. It isn't as quiet or as secluded as I could wish but writing is certainly possible. And Ada's only want at present is a piano. A considerable want. But all this I secure for 8000 francs a quarter of which I bought at 24 and the other three quarters at the horrible price of 14. It makes the house come to about $500 or a little less for 3 months. Which is enough obviously. But I can swing it and it is more than worth it for the children alone.

I am also enclosing two pictures which I took in Belgium. One is of Kenny's final grave & the other of the cemetary. Neither is good but they will give you some idea of things. I have written Ishbel at length about my trip & I think she may have shown you the letter. If she hasn't tell me & I will write you in full. Let me say now however that while the cemetary is not yet in shape it looks much better than the picture. It needs trees badly & I am making inquiries now to see if we can do anything about it by private gift.

I wish so much I might be in Glencoe about now. Ada & I have talked of father's birthday often & I should like nothing better than the power to present myself with Ada & the two sprouts miraculously before you that day. Mimi does look like me. I have to admit it. She is Hillardy to the last inch & as stand-offish and independent as the hardiest Scot that ever drew breath. Kenny looks more & more like Ada. But he has father's hands & a good bit of father in his disposition. I think you two have K & M between you.

Ishbel is a grand girl. I tell you I admire her. Her courage is away beyond me. Curiously enough I find it impossible even to feel very sorry about it now. She seems to be turning even her captivity to use.

Curiously enough both you & she were moved to send checks for $50 to straighten Kenny's legs at the same time.[1] We have decided to take the liberty of applying one of the checks to a different use. We had intended to have a Mlle Charbonnet here for the summer to teach Kenny French & to tutor him in reading & writing etc.. She is a wonderful teacher of small children as proved by her labors with little Ed. Whitney this winter. But we found when we got here that there was no room for her in the house. Now, with your check, we can take a room in the town & have her. It will make all the difference in the

world to Kenny who really has learned very little French in school &
I feel sure you will approve. We can pay her wages all right but we
couldn't have done the other.

Our plans are all in a haze. When, what & why we don't know, but
I imagine we will be here another year. It depends on lots of things.
God bless you both my dears   your devoted son   Archie

ALS: M

1. Kenneth MacLeish had suffered a mild case of polio, which had caused the slight
deformity to which M refers.

To Amy Lowell

Dear Miss Lowell: 21 July [1924]   Granville

This is not to be even an attempt at an adequate reply to your
generous letter to me. Not that I think I can express my gratitude
except by appealing to your power of faith. But even that I must put
off. The point is to get a letter into the mails on the matter of the
essay for the N.A.. It goes without saying that I am proud to think you
should be willing to entrust me with a job which if well done should
be of the first importance. Nothing that I have in mind in my own
work could possibly take precedence over a study of yours. And so far
as I am concerned — though I have not yet heard from the N.A. — I
shall be delighted to do my best to put into order my at present none
too orderly because too immediately felt reactions to the poetry of
A.L..[1] But there are several things to say first which I feel may affect
your desire to have me undertake the work. The chief of these is the
fact that I know nothing about, and am, unhappily not interested to
know very much about, H.D., John Gould Fletcher, Aldington and
other members of the Imagist Group. I should want to do a portrait
rather than a group picture. And that fact bearing as it may upon
your *external* history may change your feeling as to my qualifications
for the post. Secondly I am not a convert to imagism as a theory although admiring the theory as a critical weapon and the thing itself
when it is alive as you give it life. What I mean is that the still-lifes
of [Joseph] Auslander who fancies himself as an imagist seem to me
of no value off the dining-room wall, proverbial hanging place for such
products. What I am trying to get at is the fact that I should want to
treat you as a poet and not as a regimental commander — even granted
that many of your soldiers joined up without your consent. The important thing is that you are that rarest of spiritual phenomena, a poet,
and the reasons why you are, if capable of statement at all, are probably not those which in your critical writing or the critical writing of

others about you, have been assigned. I don't mean that I can assign them. But I want a free hand to try. The same thing is true of your verse forms. Clearly they do not establish the fact of your poetry; they are merely its faces. Is all this a bit over wise for one in my position? Perhaps so but I trust you not to think so. I am purposely overstating my position because I want you to have every opportunity to reconsider beforehand and myself to have the illusion of freedom of mind when I go to work. If you still want so speckled a rooster to interpret you to mankind there remains the question of books. Houghton Mifflin owe me something in morals if not in law and they should be willing to let me have your books complete — not otherwise available to me in Granville. Will you try to persuade them? And please give me any facts of chronology not apparent from title pages. I would like to include "Which Being —" etc. which seems to me to mark a change in method of the greatest interest. Can that possibly be arranged?

Please don't kill yourself over Keats.[2] Even he isn't worth that. We are all well and happy here and rejoiced over the expected arrival tomorrow of G. and K. Putnam[3] for a week.

Hurriedly and affectionately yours   Archie MacLeish

TLS: MH

1. See M's "Amy Lowell and the Art of Poetry," *The North American Review* 221 (March 1925), 508–521. 2. Lowell was working on a major biography of John Keats. It was published by Houghton Mifflin Company in February 1925, three months before Lowell's death. 3. George and Katharine Putnam, Lowell's nephew and his wife.

To John Peale Bishop[1]

Dear John: 30 July 1924 [Granville]

The problem before me is not where I'm going to live but how I'm going to replace you. Here I am only about two months removed from our last talk & already all balled up again. The symptoms are bad.

You'll have to forgive a calligraphy worse than usual. I made the initial mistake of going swimming in what they please to call the middle of summer & I followed that with the second principal error of coming down here & drinking two demis. Which have the cardiac effect of making me think of you & M. with an unsteady emphasis on the down beat of the organ concerned but can't be said to be warming. In general Granville does well enough. We have the sound of the sea in our house all day (except when, at low tides, the water retires to Jersey to recollect itself) & if we have not you at least we have the happy alternative of having nobody else. I work & work & crumple & crumple but do get on & Ada does her regular two hours & the children prosper in spite of the cold. We have been here of course almost since you left. I count out the two weeks after that event which were spent in getting over it. We went back to town once to hear the Strawinsky festival which was not up to the Sacre without ballet which you took us to at the Opera. Don Stewart[2] was there with the Murphys[3] & proudly retired at the beginning of the second part of the program to miss Pachinella (?) & came back later for Noces. And of course it was Noces he retired from. Newly married Gallantieres[4] held reception in front lobby & Seldes's,[5] equally newly married, circulated throughout. There is something queer about Seldes. I fancy its the fact that, in spite of erudition & surprising power of evoking affection, he *is* a kike (how does that write itself) and a pithy one. Don showed me parts of his new humorous book (to appear this fall).[6] I must admit that it *is* funny. He told me that he had just gotten himself going & for the first time had been utterly at ease. What he has done is to employ the rudiments of Joycian technique — idea suggesting idea without logical or reasonable sequence. The technique is, of course, a god-send for Don. Hasn't the time almost arrived to admit that Ulysses is a method which, qua method, is too easy, & a result which, as result, is too hard?

We are not going to Egypt. I found upon interchange of letters with Judge Brinton[7] that the court was at Alexandria, that it was overloaded with work (& unless you have seen it in operation you can't imagine what an appalling thing an overworked court is) and that living was so high that your salary just about covered items A7 to C32 in the family budget. But neither are we going home. I'm perfectly honest in saying that I can't imagine Paris without you two but I imagine that Paris it will be. Ada had a real triumph in singing for Sczymenowski (?) just before we left & will probably do some singing for him or one of his group (for whose songs her voice was made) in the fall. So that we've got to be there then. I imagine it will be a house in Passy. I'll never live under anyone in an Aptment House again. As for you — you live on top of the world. Properly enough.

I can't help feeling your reactions to Cleveland & they make me ill in the tummy. Wasn't it enough for you to be born two centuries late without the added indignity of dumping you in America? Why don't we form a Colony of four at some point East & by all means South of Granville, Manche? And I don't like Vanity Fair for you though that can't be helped. And I don't like your getting no time to finish your novel. And all of this is not my business at all.

The tree I am up now is the tree labelled emotion. Since I give considerable weight to your opinions even recollected in tranquillity, I am perpetually reminded of your insistence upon the element of emotion. But that word may mean any one of a number of things. And the more I think about it the more I am driven to a position that, while having foundations in common with The Sacred Wood, differs even from Eliots. It seems to me clear that a poem is not to be called good or bad because of its power to stimulate emotion. It is rather the power of the poem to *withstand* emotion that is important. It is the beauty of the poem as a poem, as a form, which is significant, & not its power to act as an agent toward any indirect goal. And as for the emotion of the poet, granted that that must exist to fuse the materials used, to give vitality to the form, nevertheless the great poem should *contain* rather than transmit that emotion. To praise a poem because it was written with sincere emotion is as foolish as the musical criticism of Paul Rosenberg[8] (to take the worst writer in the world). The poem must stand or fall without relation to the poet. Well what then? I can't get around these conclusions. And I can hear you agreeing with them. But they seem to me cold & dead. And I can hear your voice telling me why. But I can't hear your words. You are so damn far off.

Our love to both of you. Do write us (here until Sept 15; then Bankers Trust 3 Pl. Vendome) & tell us all about plans & places. We miss you like the devil.   yrs   Archie

ALS: NjP

1. American poet and critic (1892–1944). Bishop and his wife, Margaret, had met the MacLeishes soon after the latters' arrival in France and had quickly become their close friends. Much to the MacLeishes' disappointment, they had returned permanently to the United States in the spring of 1924. 2. Donald Ogden Stewart (1894–1980), American parodist and, later, playwright and screenwriter. A member of Yale's Class of 1916, he was living abroad. 3. Gerald and Sara Murphy, a wealthy American couple who, with their three children — Baoth, Patrick, and Honoria — lived in Paris and Antibes. Murphy (Yale '11, Skull & Bones) was a gifted painter. 4. Lewis Galantière, of Chicago, was Paris secretary for the International Chamber of Commerce. 5. Gilbert Seldes, American critic and, from 1920 to 1923, managing editor of *The Dial*. His examination of popular culture, *The Seven Lively Arts* (1924), attracted widespread attention. 6. *Mr. and Mrs. Haddock Abroad* (1924). 7. Judge Jasper Yeates Brinton, justice, Court of Appeals, Mixed Courts of Egypt. 8. American proprietor of a leading modernist art gallery in Paris.

To Martha Hillard MacLeish

Dearest Mother: 3 August [1924]   Granville

Age does not seem to medecine my habits as a writer of epistles inter or intra familia. But its no use apologizing to you. You know perfectly well that I'll go and do it again. Please extend your already well practiced foregivness as much farther as you can.

I am sorry about my letter to Ishbel on the subject of my visit to Kenny's grave. If I had had your reading it more in mind I should never have written as I did. Not that I should have tried to disguise my emotions but that I think I should have had rather different emotions. I find it harder and harder all the time not to see life as a professional literary man. And in my letter to Ishbel I let myself work out the metaphor which the experience assumed for me with my attention directed more to the complete expression of that metaphor than to a searching of my mind to find the basis for my experience. The experience was perfectly real. And the statement was as complete as I could make it. But I have observed that emotions, mine at least, have a way of crystallizing around some sensuous object or group of objects which absorb all the life of the emotion and compel my mind to see them rather than the real origin of the state of mind. As in this case the devil wind which was blowing. So that you see my mind was not directed to Kenny so much as to [the] way I felt going to see for the first time the grave where Kenny is buried. I agree absolutely with you that Kenny's life was a wonderful and beautiful thing and that it reached a great moment and ended on that moment. And I agree that there was no mockery about the affair for him. Nor was there for any of us then. My feeling that Kenny is there in that earth is one that I cannot avoid but which cannot touch him. Nor you with your marvellous faith that it is not so. The point is that if I think about Kenny and not about my feelings about Kenny I feel happy for him and proud and not bitter. Please believe that I know how my letter must have hurt you and that I would not for the world have added even that much weight to your grief which you have born so beautifully and so altogether yourself.

I wish when you write me next you would give me a sort of brief resume of Ishbel's case. There is still part of it I don't understand. I am so dreadfully sorry for these upsets she has been having. She is a marvel. But how long can even Ishbel keep happy with so little encouragement. It makes me feel very guilty to have so much when things are so rotten for her.

Ada and I have now about decided to go back to Paris for six months, October through March, and then move to Florence for three months where we will be able to live more cheaply and where we can go on with what has been for us the grandest experience of our year extending the pages of our Italian note-book to Sienna and the rest of Tuscany and perhaps to Venice and Rome. Then we will either go up into the Tyrol for the summer coming home in the fall or go home from Genoa in June depending on what we can find and how we are and how things are going at home and how much money we have and so forth and so on. You get to Florence by a night train from Paris and the trip would really not be bad at all. I am really excited about the project as I am firmly convinced that, for me at least, France holds nothing except Chartres to compare with Florence.

Aunt Mary is still apparently tremendously disturbed about our staying over. Or perhaps I should say that she is now at the height of her disappointment since she was apparently reconciled to our coming for a year as a sort of vacation (she never admitted that there was any use my trying to write) but a second year, she saw only too clearly, would be fatal. She had me buy francs with the idea of coming to France for the summer but later she changed her mind and turned her francs into dollars again. I understand now that [she] has gone to England feeling that it would disturb her too much to see us under the circumstances. I am really sorry that she is so disturbed although I have not, and I am afraid cannot, forgive her for what she did last year. Or rather I can forgive her but I cannot trust her as I did before and I have an altogether different picture of her which it is difficult to feel affection for. But I have tried hard for my own sake to see her point of view. She is obviously disinterested, she desires my good, she has considerable knowledge of human character, and she is, if not as cultivated as I thought her, nevertheless a cultivated woman. And she feels very strongly that it is a mistake for me to try to write and that I ought to go back to the law. Two things are immediately clear. She is convinced that I would have a brilliant career at the law and she is convinced that I am not really a poet in the narrow sense of that term. I have differences with her on both heads. I doubt very much whether I would go as far in the law as she expects and I think there is a chance, quite small but still existant, that I am a poet. But those aren't arguable matters. So I assume Aunt Mary's premises. Assume that I would win great success at the bar and that I will never write a line of true poetry. But agree also that my one desire is to write poetry, that I feel the practice of law to be a waste of time, an unreality of unrealities, — and where are you? Aunt Mary has got to make one of two points. She must either argue that success in and of itself, success in a matter which one finds lifeless and vain, is valuable, or she must argue that the successful doing of anything is preferable to the unsuccessful doing of anything else. I do not think even she would argue that the law as a career is more desirable than letters. In either case she is left balanced on that word success. Now I don't pretend to despise success. But in trying to make a decision according to my best ability, in looking at things at a little distance, I cannot feel that the hope of success is of sufficient importance to determine the decision. I cant help thinking that the way a man must live is dictated not by the accidental fact that some of his abilities coincide with the requirements of some artificial profession or business but rather by the whole of himself, by precisely his desire, his longing, as to which he may be destined to be fooled and cheated but which is at least himself speaking and not society speaking at him. As for Aunt Mary's "duties" owed to a society one did not create and does not love, I count them not a fig. And as a postscript to all this I may add that it is really my belief (often clouded) that I can write which drives me on and that I think Aunt Mary has about as much appreciation of art as of billiards. Witness her ineffable remark that I should first make a success of the practice of law in order to have an eminence from which to write poetry. If you heard that Mr. Hughes[1] had accomplished a volume of verse, what, barring a desire to laugh, would you do about it? I beg pardon for all this. But it is much on my mind. Do write me what you think about it all.   Dearest love to you   Archie

TLS: M

1. Charles Evans Hughes, then U.S. secretary of state and formerly an associate justice of the U.S. Supreme Court.

To Andrew MacLeish

Dearest Father: 3 August [1924]   Granville

Having written mother a long resume of my intricate feelings about a lot of things of more or less importance it seems only fair to myself to tell you something about what we are doing. As you probably know we came down here from Paris in the middle of June, "here" being the little city of Granville in southern Normandy on the shores of the Manche as the French so inadequately call the Channel. I had come down in March on the advise of some friends who said that Granville was a nice spot for a quiet summer and although I wasn't much taken with the city itself I did find a really nice little villa on the top of a cliff overlooking the sea with a terraced path down to a little beach and enough ground for the children to turn around in. Its chief attraction for me was the fact that you would hear the sound of the surf in it all night, something I have always missed since I left that northeast room at Craigie Lea where Kenny and I used to sleep. And although I had forgotten to take the tides into account it has worked out much that way. At low tide I must admit that one doesn't hear much. The tide retires almost to Jersey when it gets going. All in all however we are very happy. The children live much as we lived at Craigie Lea. They are on the beach almost all the time and they are healthy and cheerful. My only real objection is that it is cold almost all the time.

And although that is very conducive to work it does leave something to be desired when it comes to swimming.

You would simply love the baby who has christened herself Mimi. She is not exactly beautiful. That would be difficult in view of the fact that she looks an extraordinary lot like my baby pictures. But she is as distinct a person as you could very well imagine with a delicious sense of humor, a way of her own with her nurse and a perfect passion for that epic John Smith A Fellow Fine which I am afraid I execute very badly. I have promised her that she shall have it rendered by its most perfect performer as soon as we get home. Kenny is of course all boy and no baby. He talks French much better than I do and has the livliest interest in everything which goes on under his nose. He has a fine head and fine clear features and I think he is going to be a credit to us all.

I have thought so often in Paris this 1st winter about your visit there with Sister Lily[1] years ago. That is the Paris I should have loved to know. It has become too much like other large cities recently. But the flavor that still hangs around the grand Boulevards is a flavor of the eighties. I wish I might have known it then.

And another thing I think about as often as we make a move into an unknown town is the courage involved in your going out to America when you went as a boy. I can never get used to it. I should no more have had the courage to go out to New Zealand when I was that age or indeed any age than I should have gone to the Pole with Peary. Men in your generation had something which we didn't inherit. But I'm proud to remember that you had it.

We talk of you a great deal and I am looking forward to bringing Kenny and Mary Hillard out to Glencoe to see you as soon as we get back. I think you will approve of them.

With much love from all of us   your devoted son   Archie

TLS: M

1. Lily MacLeish Day, M's half sister.

To Martha Hillard MacLeish

Dearest Mother: 21 September [1924]   Granville

This can only be a note — though you deserve a book — because we are en train to pack up for a few days in Brittany. I don't want to cut the strings without thanking you for your letters which are continual joys. It gives one a very pleasant not-cut-off feeling to think of you thinking about me still. The sort of satisfactory emotion I used to let myself taste when I was about half-way over the ravine bridge on a dark winter's night (half-past five p.m.) and I could see the warm light in the sewing room window and no one had caught me yet. Not that there is anything parallel to the terror of those days in my present situation. I am sitting in our little green-walled salon with the door open to let in the warm sweet foreign-smelling air after an all day drizzle and nothing more dangerous glares at me than the light over on Chausey which opens a languid eye erey so aften and then looks away again as though it had known all along I would still be here. And as for sounds no terrifying crunch of unknown boots on the wooden planking but only the sea telling the rocks over and over how tired it is. But all the same it is good not to be alone. I wonder how I should feel if those three people upstairs had no one in the world but me to look to and I engaged in the economically unsound practice of cutting sentences up into lines. As it is I still rest in your arms. I still feel not quite grown up, not quite responsible, not quite alone. Which is no doubt a very wicked way to feel. I'll go up stairs and think about you my dear.

Oh — *will* you be sure and ask Bruce if he got my draft to the order of the Income Tax Director? I haven't heard from him and the tax people are threatening with penalties. It is more than two months since I wrote him first. Don't scold him. Just ask him. And get him to write me care Bankers Trust Paris.   love to you both   Archie

TLS: M

To Robert N. Linscott

Dear Bob: 31 October 1924   Saint-Cloud, France

Here is the opus[1] which I have been threatening to send you. It is as you see not long — about six hundred lines — but I send it in this way because I should like to publish it alone and because I find myself increasingly taken with small books of verse. A fat book of verse is either treated as an anthology or as a task. However I am perfectly willing to provide other MSS if you want 'em. I have on hand quite a bit of stuff which has appeared or is about to appear in the No. Am., the Atl., the N.R. etc. together with some lyric pieces which I have not as yet peddled — enough to make a book as big as the H.M.. That is for you to say.

But the main point is this poem. I don't believe in the prevailing custom of introducing oneself to the world. But I think I can properly tell you how I feel about something that means as much to me as this does. As you know, I was not without misgivings as to the H.M., misgivings which the event has removed but which were real enough. Likewise I was sufficiently doubtful of Nobodaddy to ask for a special consultation. But somehow this is different. I have at last hit upon a loosening of blank verse which lets me move around a little more freely than Coleridge's fly in a glue bottle. Also I have been able to use what one must call for lack of a better name the Joycian method of presentation of action to my own (if to no one else's) satisfaction. I mean nothing grandiose. I merely mean that I have solved the problem I posed myself of employing that method in verse. But since it has permitted me to move in action as well as in words I feel it a first rate victory over myself. But chiefly I have been able at last to achieve a sense of reality of the thing said. That is it continues to be mine after it gets onto paper. Which, I suppose, is only a manner of saying that I have found a form which will hold and continue to hold a certain amount at least of water. Is there water in this particular cast? To me, yes. Because to me it is not the conflict between the spiritual and the animal in us that is tragic but the conflict between the spiritual and the vegetable, or better, between our mis-conscious selves and a vegetable universe.

But that is all by the way. I am sorry for the sake of my agreement with Whitney — or his with me — that I am as far today from believing in the sovereign power of the visual image in English poetry as I was a year ago, — farther, for in the mean time have appeared the calculated little still-lifes of Auslander which were obviously constructed upon the theory that poetry was a fabric of visual images — and which no omnipotent divinity could ever turn into anything but the dining-room scenes they are. The theory neither explains Shakespeare nor Cummings. And I find Coleridge extremely helpful:

> "It has been observed before that images, however beautiful, though faithfully copied from nature and as accurately represented in words, do not of themselves characterize the poet. They become proofs of original genius only as far as they are modified by a predominant passion; or by associated thoughts or images awakened by that passion; or when they have the effect of reducing multitude to unity, or succession to an instant; or lastly, when a human and intellectual life is transferred to them from the poet's own spirit, —"[2]

which is all very erudite but none the less true to my ear. However I make no attempt to claim as a virtue a characteristic I can't control. It happens that I cannot express myself in vignettes. And all I ask is that

my stuff be criticized for what it is, not for what it is not. A consideration you generously give.

I need hardly add that this is for your particular and pvt ear.

faithfully yours   Archie MacLeish

TLS: DLC

1. The manuscript of M's poem *The Pot of Earth*, published by Houghton Mifflin
Company on 1 May 1925. 2. From *Biographia Literaria*, Chapter XV.

To Martha Hillard, Andrew, and Ishbel MacLeish

Dearest Mother & Father & Ishbel: 23 November 1924   Saint-Cloud

This is my first letter to you from St-Cloud — a sad & shameful confession for which I have no excuse but merely explanations. For one
thing I have finished the MS for a new book which I hope — but more
or less against hope — H.M. are going to take. For another I have done
a long critical article on Amy Lowell for the No. Am.[1] — a job which
involved reading & rereading all her stuff, published & unpublished, &
more thinking about my theories of poetry than I have put in for a
long, long time. It was a hard &, I think, a foolish job but I undertook
it for her & at her request & at least it served to familiarize me with
her poetry & to shake down my own ideas. It is to appear, I believe, in
the March (April) number. I don't know if Amy will like it. But at
least its done & my problem now is to get back into a condition in which
I can write my own stuff again. Nothing is harder on poetry than an
excursion into criticism.

I am publishing a verse play with the Dunster Press in Cambridge
next year. It is a reworking of Adam & Eve & the Garden which H.M.
refused on account of the subject but which Maurice Firuski liked. I
like it myself better than the Happy Marriage. But this last book (The
Pot of Earth) carries all my hopes. It is all I have to say & I'd like to
get it said.

I am planning to spend most of this winter studying French Poetry
with a chap in Paris named Pierre Garanger who teaches philosophy
in the Lyçees & knows French Literature in & out. The result ought to
be to help my French & to teach me something about French verse.
How long I can fight off the restlessness of not writing dayly I don't
know. Not long from present appearances.

Ada has probably told you that I had — or rather she had — a very
frank letter from Aunt Mary in which she said that she didn't believe
in my verse, that it didn't give her the "Bread Of Life", that she knew
no one (& she had been asking for years) who had ever found anything

I had ever written either beautiful *or* true & that I had better go into active affairs (whatever they are) & become a leader & an example to the young, very affectionately yours, Aunt Mary. I replied *as* frankly that I would never give up the profession of letters while I could afford to stick at it, that I didn't believe in her world of active affairs, & that poetry is an art & not a means of purveying bread of any variety. I added gratuitously that she had no understanding nor appreciation of poetry & that all I asked of her was to leave me alone. She has not offered us the Ashfield House & I don't believe she will & if she did I shouldn't accept it. Aunt Mary & I have nothing in common & although I shall never forget her kindnesses to us in the past I shan't allow her interference in the future.

I am simply delighted that Ishbel is so much better. I was very much worried when Alice Cowles returned with gloomy reports in October. Is there any chance she will be at Craigie Lea next summer — or fall?

Mother's remark about C.P.S. stock is exciting. The present arrangement does seem to me inequitable but of course I am too happy to be free for writing to question it. I should however feel freeer in my mind if I could put by from year to year enough to cover the childrens' schooling. They are so grand, those children.

Paul & Isabel Harper[2] have been here for the day. Paul is as nice as ever — perfectly charming. Isabel has a mind like a biscuit tin — all full of square white objects in rows — & no sense of humor. She & I do *not* agree.

Please write me more about Ishbel & take my dearest love for you, all three   Archie

Yale 19 — Harvard 6 !!!

ALS: M

1. *See* M to Amy Lowell, 21 July 1924, note 1. 2. Paul Harper was the son of William Rainey Harper, first president of the University of Chicago.

To Amy Lowell

Dear Miss Lowell: 24 November [1924]   Saint-Cloud

Four days ago I sent Miss Cutting the result of my months work and six weeks reading. I am not satisfied with it but at the same time I am satisfied that I have sketched an outline roughly corresponding to the planet observed. The difficulty was to get thirty or forty thousand words into six thousand — Miss Cutting's limit. I soon saw, as you suggested, that there would be no room for biographical information so that the stuff you sent me in reply to my frenzied appeal had to go out. The problem was to state a critical position and from that critical position explore six volumes of poetry all in about sixteen pages of mss. As I wrote Miss Cutting, it seemed to me idle for any one at my level to offer a solution of any one at yours without first naming the factors of the equation and his understanding of their meaning. Well, on the third draft I got down to six thousand and a few odd words. I consider that I have at least shown great powers of restraint.

The question remains whether you will like the article. You will disagree violently with my fundamental thesis about you. But as to that all I can say is that my guess is as good as yours just as Paul Rosenburg's — to take an unlikely person — would be as good as either. Nobody knows. The fact remains.

Lunched with Cummings today — just arrived. Has two books coming out this fall, one of which he believes and hopes will be suppressed.[1] He's a great spirit but he always depresses me horridly. He's so excessively good. I wonder why I keep on trying.

On which note   affectionately yours   Archie

TLS: MH

1. Cummings's *XLI Poems* and his *&*.

To John Peale Bishop

Dear John: 7 December 1924   Saint-Cloud

I hereby make formal demand upon you to send me the pages from the N.R. containing your Wallace Stevens[1] — either that or a copy of the MSS. You are the only living mortal or immortal (you may be both) whose theories of aesthetic give me hope. And God knows I need hope. I have just arrived (properly enough, because I trail you by two years in everything) at the point you arrived at as regards your own poetry, viz. that after Eliot nothing except more Eliot. I have come to the point of complete anarchy. Critically I admire the work of Cummings, Stevens, Moore enormously — a kind of taste for anchovies, celestial anchovies but still anchovies, which formed spoils all victuals else. But creatively, if I can still use the word, I realize that the only thing I want to do, the only thing I take delight in doing, the only thing the doing of which rests upon an impulse in any way poetic, is at the other end of the spectrum. I want to work in Fugue-like melodies, but above all in melodies — De la musique encore et toujours. I want to arrive at a direct statement. I can't use, and don't want to use[,] the exciting and difficult and suggestive circumlocutions of Stevens, the sustained and inverted suspensions of Cummings. I want lucidity and concreteness. And there I am. Critically I have lost the taste for the thing that sensitively I alone desire. I need not attempt a more accurate statement. You understand more completely than I what it is I am suffering from.

And it is not a subjective state only. I am just now awaiting the return from Houghton Mifflin of the poem I wrote this summer. I can't imagine their taking it. And yet it is all and everything I have to say and its refusal will be a defeat for which I cannot prepare myself in advance. The trouble is that the thing is impregnated with something that is not Eliot only because it is me. Though one would have to assume much in my favor to agree to that conclusion. The fact is that Eliot has opened to a few people like you and myself a world which we recognize at once as our own and from which we can no more retire than we can go back to the nursing size. And why should we? But what can we do while we are there? Recognize the great man's prior claims and shut up? And what if we can't shut up? Talk about the tragedy of the man who is ahead of his age: it is nothing to the tragedy of the man who comes after the man who is. The man who suffers is the man who can only live by expression and who finds himself already expressed. Or something like that.

I think I told you that I was doing at Amy's request an article on her for the No. Am. Rev.. I finished it about two weeks ago and have been recovering since. I used it pretty largely as a cover for the development of the ideas about form in poetry which I broached to you and which you haven't yet anatomized. But I began it with a statement of our joint faith in the objective nature of The Poem. It will appear in March if they take it and though it will probably not evoke much comment elsewhere it may induce you to tackle the problem you have so far shamefully neglected.

By the way, you saw of course a wretched review of Harmonium in a recent Broom.[2] The "cultured hand" of Wallace Stevens! Resembling the "cultured hands" of, respectively, Cummings and that baudy fraud w. carlos williams! The same number containing some rehashes by Cummings and a new edition of Euphues His England by your friend Malcolm Cowley. What has happened to that once interesting sheet? They should rename it Duster.

Have you seen Reverdy's Epaves du Ciel? Answer. Because if you haven't I want to send it to you. And may I ask you to do a job for me? When Cummings two new books come out will you get some book shop to send them to me with the bill on your assurance that I am good for the amount? Also M. Moore's. Brentano's have no sense about these things.

Saw Cummings at lunch. Where, think you? At Gladys Saltonstall's on the rue l'Elysee![3] What has happened to him? Gladys asked him to come and he came. He spent most of the period damning art and artists to Ada in the corner. But he was charming and sociable and extremely nice to Faÿ[4] who had just informed France through the columns of some one of his journals that Cummings is a genius. The aloof and retired poet has vanished and though I am enormously attracted by the charming young man who has appeared back of that smouldering face I must admit the loss of a cherished illusion.

Paris simply isn't the same. There are none to take your places and the result is that the entire city looks different. I cling to Lewis[5] whom I momentarily expect for lunch, and we both like the Murphies though talk with Gerald is a charming promenade the object of which is to get back in time for tea. For the rest there are a lot of new rich Bostonians (female) who, to use Gerald's phrase, have recently gone intellectual and some richer people of the genus Ritz who have been sicced on us by well meaning friends and who have been mislead by the appearance of our house. We have adopted the bye-law that we can only go out one night a week. Ada is teaching a little and working hard. Last week she sang at the Revue Musicale where the managers and directors foregather and we watch the postman with interest. But she too is discouraged. Only the certainty that nothing else is worth doing keeps us both from — I don't know.

Enough of that. The Swedish Ballet is as bad as ever. The new Picabia-Satie Ballet[6] was a combination of bad Musical Comedy and second rate movies to an accompaniement of pleasant music. These people have their tongues so far in their cheeks that they can't chew. Tell Margaret anything that will make her feel worst about her corspdnce.   yrs   Archie

TLS: NjP

1. The piece to which M refers, presumably a review of Wallace Stevens's *Harmonium* (1924), is unidentified, and may not have been published. 2. Matthew Josephson had reviewed Stevens's *Harmonium* in *Broom* 5 (November 1923), 236–237. 3. Mrs. John L. Saltonstall, of Boston and Paris. 4. Bernard Faÿ, French historian, journalist, and translator (b. 1893). 5. Lewis Galantière. 6. *Relâche* (1924).

To Maurice Firuski

Dear Maurice: 29 December [1924]   Saint-Cloud

I hope you will believe that I never dreamed it would be so bad or I shouldn't have sent the stuff to you in the first place.[1] Sig. For Tempo[2] seems to me the best poem I have written and all the others I like. I thought there would be no difficulty about getting rid of them even among the expensive magazines. I should say I would have to change my objectives and find a magazine of poetry which one could respect and which would accept verse in metrical forms. Its not as easy as it sounds. But at any rate let me apologize with all my heart to you. You have been a saint to trouble about it. When you have a moment just ship my children home and I'll try to work out a happier future for them.

It is ages since I've had a letter from you. What do you plan to do — if anything — about Nobodaddy? H.M. have taken the long poem I was writing this summer for spring pblctn. Does that make any difference to you?

I hope you have received or will receive a book I sent off to you about a month too late for the Christmas mails. It is something I want you to have for all too obvious reasons.

Do write me when you have time and accept in the interim all my thanks for your kindnesses. My love to John and Jimmy.[3]

yrs affec'ly   Archie.

TLS: NjP

1. Firuski had agreed to act as M's agent, without compensation, in the submission of his poems to American periodicals. **2.** "Signature for Tempo," first published in *The Yale Review* in October 1925 and later collected in *Streets in the Moon* (1926). **3.** Employees, presumably, of Firuski's Dunster House Book Shop.

To John Peale Bishop

[*no salutation*]   28 January 1925   [Arles-sur-Rhone, France]

I might perhaps have written you from Avignon where in the gardens of the Popes small blasphemous birds made history and a man with solemn plop of laborious and worldly spade removed the rich bone of Clement VI from beneath the fatted ducks that might have pertained to Pius — however many.[1] Instead from Arle in whose amphitheatre the doves are an old man sawing wood, and the Fines are Grand Marniers. But qu'importe. From either locus I should have assailed you with

Paterne Berrichon
Jean-Arthur Rimbaud
Le Poète
(1854–1873)

with whom, alone, I travel.[2]

Let us a moment conceive Puritanism turned catholic. Let us add thereto Bourgeois-ism turned inward. And let us from the apex of that pile of merde attempt to explain the poetry of *Jean*-Arthur Rimbaud. I tell you, my young & promising Stravinsky, there are worse books in French than ever were written — in English.

Here, for instance. Rimbaud "inventor" of vers libre. Rimbaud poet of Christianism. Rimbaud pure, well-mannered, respectable Bourgeois youth. Rimbaud incapable of homosexuality because so different from Verlaine — "Car s'il est vrai que les impressions, chez Verlaine (!), montaient par les sens au cerveau pour redescendre aussitôt au coeur et, par le sang, se reponde furieusement dans toute la chair, il n'est pas moins vrai que, chez Rimbaud, elles arrivaient au cerveau pour s'y embraser et s'y consumer sur place." God! God! God!

I began the book in love of Rimbaud. I end it in contempt of any man who could inspire in another, even his brother-in-law, such twaddle as here suspires. Ah the Shelleys, the Shelleys, the Shelleys of this world. What has poetry to do with them! Dante knew the taste of other men's bread and the steps of other men's stairs. But he never, in his poetry, ceased to be a poet. Rimbaud wrote an anonymous letter to his mother advising her that her son was going to Hell in Paris & advising that he be returned to the foyer!

What has the French critic of XIXth Cent. poetry to go on anyway? Villon, a great & greatly l't'd poet. Marots & Charles d'Orleans. Malherbe and the graceful Ronsards by Malherbe overturned. A gentile & perspicuous Racine utterly guiltless of anything that we, of the English tradition, could honestly call poetry. (Read, drunk, the great scene from Bajazet!) Moliere — no poet at all. La Fontaine of great power of concentration. André Chenier. What else? Du Bellay of the *Regrets* was a poet. Agrippa d'Aubigné, Protestantly excited in a Catholic age was a poet. Corneille of the Cid was a poet. But Jesus H. Cheerist not one of them was fit to tie old John Donne's nether laces. No wonder V. Hugo called Racine a second rate poet. He was. And Hugo none the less one for calling him names.

You have to come to Beaudelaire to find the first & to Rimbaud & Laforgue & Verlaine to find the second & third & fourth competent of consideration from the Insular point of view. Deny it if you can. You wont be drunk as you read this & I am drunk — drunk alone in the Grand Café Des Negociants without a speaking acquaintance within 500 K. more or less. But still I defy you. I have devoted a year to the proof in French letters of Eliot's assumptions as to English ditto & I conclude halfway through that Eliot is the patent dupe of his own wishes or his own snobbism. Fr. poetry, frankly (my opinions may be given Frankly since there is nothing to concede) does not exist. There are merely a few exceptions to the prose rule. And they are all, Rimbaud included, second-rate as Hell. And their influence in America is all bad. (I speak thus, I need hardly add, in utter bravado, since I know you will brilliantly refute me. But before you do, read, as you would read an offering of mine, Rimbaud's *Voyelles*. Even J. G. Fletcher (Even!!!) has done better.)

From which I pass with suspicious ease to Eliots three poems in the last Criterion.[3] And of these I can only say — *Are* there any better poems of their kind in English? If there are — well, name seven.

Thence to M. Moore's *Observations* for which many thanks. You know how I admire M.M.. But really — one must keep a sense of humor. Simply because T.S.E. adds to the obfuscation of the W.L. by adding legendic notes need this lady librarian add similar puerilities to prove that it was Philip Littell & not herself who wrote "something feline, something colubrine"?[4] I here prophecy that the *Mosaic school* with fat appendices will long flourish. All one needs (they will say) is a public library & a pair of scissors. And they won't be as wrong as we think. M.M. has written a few poems & a number of lines. But she is a victim of daily journalism. And her preferment over E.E.C. by the Dial adds the final straw to the back of that double humped elephant.

Sometime I must *tell* you about Cummings' Sunday at St-Cloud. I have no pen to silhouette it.

And I am too — as I have said before — to fight you over the field of your last brilliant letter. Your analysis of Eliot is a work of genius. But your assumption that there is a "modern conscience" which must find its own instruments of expression is not sound. Within the limits of so called historical knowledge human consciousness has changed not at all. It has merely satisfied alternately unsatisfied instincts alternately. Ultimately the pendulum may crack the side of the clock. But it will be the same pendulum. The whole damn question is one of being in fashion — in the *gout contemporain* — not someone else's fashion but your own. But we aren't "new men". And a sonnet will do it as well as one of M.M.'s Sunday Tribune ¶s. Only no one has yet written the sonnet. The point is, there is no substitute for discipline. Not even invention. But anon.

We will *not* adopt your scheme of paying for books. I pay 7.50 frs for P. Reverdy & you pay $2.00 for M.M (who is really not worth that much more). No. When E.E.C. arrives I pay you in $. And if you can ever add the books I send you up to 1$ you can do likewise. But not until.

Will you understand an intoxicated inflection if I say that I am
Most affectionately & respectfully & eternally & humbly
Your friend in esperance   A.

(My next appears with H. Mifflin in April-May etc)   A.

Dante did here walk in the *Alys camp* of famous tombs as you will remember. If I am not too enthusiastic, he had from these graves his scene with Cavalcanti's father. Wh. canto?[5] But you know all this.

God — how it can rain en Provence!

ALS: NjP

1. Clement VI was a French fourteenth-century pope whose court was at Avignon. Pius XI was the current pope. 2. Paterne Berrichon, *Jean-Arthur Rimbaud, Le Poète (1854–1873)* (Paris, 1912). Berrichon was Rimbaud's brother-in-law. 3. "Three Poems" ["Eyes I dare not meet in dreams," "Eyes that last I saw in tears," and "The eyes are not here"], *The Criterion* 3 (January 1925), 170–171. 4. A footnote to that effect accompanied the poem "Marriage" in Moore's *Observations* (New York: Dial, 1924). 5. The Alyscamps of Arles, ancient above-ground tombs dating back to the city's Roman origins, are mentioned in *Inferno* IX. Cavalcante Cavalcanti, a Florentine Guelph, was the father of Dante's close friend Guido Cavalcanti; see *Inferno* X.

To John Peale Bishop

Dear John: [*c.* March 1925]   Saint-Cloud

Which all comes down to the question I suppose whether what's goose for the gland is gland for the gooser. And I doubt whether it will ever have a more telling discussion than your quatrains give it.[1] I must say that your effortless mastery of that form makes me grudge your novel your time — much as I admire your novel. If these are the rhythms which your over-secst critical instinct informs you are Eliotic I can only say that you are, for the first time in my experience of you, guilty of a first rank critical error. Eliot's four beat lines are characterized by the fall of the stress in the exact center of each accented syllable. Whence their poetic parsimony. The amazing Three Poems in the last Criterion are a happy exception but still farther from your lines which, casual as they may be, are most decidedly your own.

What is the connection between the stirring of the subsoil and the renewal of poetic self-respect? You are back on your feet; Cummings (you write Lewis) believes again in the respectability of art; and last and least, I have suddenly discovered for the first time in my life and long, long after your kind assurances on the score that I am a poet. I don't know to what the change is to be attributed. I have just read the proof for my spring book which I find less like the W.L. than I had feared and better than I had hoped but not good enough to justify my state of mind. And I have done some short pieces which I know are poems — but just barely. And I have a grand idea for a new book — but only an idea. And yet my old agonies of legal doubt are gone and I believe in myself — so much so that I can loaf for a day without suffering for four. Marvels. How do you explain me?

But the best news is that you have become habituated to New York. So long as there is no hope of your returning to the native land of your soul you might as well acclimate your soul in your native land. Our plans are nebulous. I have a little more money and we can now afford to live at home if we have to. At present we are both strongly disinclined thereto. Partly for reasons — partly because the mist over the Place de la Concorde is rose colored at five o'clock in the afternoon — partly because the brioches at the Deux Magots are not only stale but still stale. Ada's chance is much better here. She is singing more movingly than ever before and the kind of stuff she, as a first-rate musician blessed with a voice, can do will be listened to here whereas one understands that even Stravinsky reputation and all was a failure in New York. All we know for certain is that we have taken a house for the summer at Antibes and that we must go home for two or three months in the fall to see our families. After that I think we shall return to Paris — say for two years. Which probably means for good. Though I agree with that coffee-house critic Chris Morley that one needs to live at home — for some things — perhaps to share the opinions of Canby.[2] God! What a sheet he runs. I find it a bit stiff and unyielding even for its proper — its only proper — purpose.

Speaking of which — will you, when you see Wilson, tell him for me that his review of Gorman's book on Joyce[3] was one of the high points of my winter? Contrast that with the burblings of Burton Rascoe[4] (who came to call one afternoon while Cummings was at the house — an amazing afternoon which fixed E.E.C. forever in my affections — and discouraged me by his lumpiness and lack of sensibility to such a point that I all but had him shovelled out) if you would have the high and low of American culture. Rascoe: 'Conrad Aiken who has written the best long poem except the Waste Land yet written by an American.' or 'E. E. Cummings who has written the best poem of seven and one half lines with no punctuation yet written by a left handed Anglo-American under thirty seven years two inches' or 'A. MacLeish who has written the worst serious poem yet written between Kalamazoo and a line drawn horizontally from Greenwich to half-past four P.M.' etc. etc. the whole interlarded with personal observations dealing with his own obviously opaque experience of living and the equally — to him — opaque experiences of his poet friends. You will reply that he has to live somehow. But I respond that I doubt it.

Did you receive a copy of the new anthology of French verse which, together with a Surrealist Manifesto[,] I had sent you?[5] The Anthology though obviously inadequate in choice represents a laudable effort at intelligent criticism of the moderns in the light of those who were but aren't. The omission of Verlaine will be painful to the gentlemen who write book reviews with an air of international culture — if they ever see the book — and I must say I think the gesture is a little forced. As for the youngsters — well I would be willing to be matched with them myself — and I can say no more to prove my belief in the superiority of the young Americans. What a rotten poet our friend La Rochelle is.[6] Saw him the other day chez Paul Rosenberg — looks badly — asked for you with what, in him, is taken for warmth. And so intended.

As for Surrealism — what continually gets me about the French is the way in which they will seize and elevate to a theory a practice which has always been common in English poetry and which in a way constitutes English poetry. They have to be convinced before they can feel. They have to be made to see first. Their emotional experiences in art are the consequences of their intellectual experiences. You or I will feel a poem sensuously: your Frenchman will receive sensuous pleasure from the fact that he has comprehended a poem intellectually. Hence the success of Surrealism. It is significant that they describe all the great English poets as charter members of their group. But pour moi we have no need of the point of view in America. Your theories of poetry and mine are much more necessary.

You once offered to send some stuff to the S_4N[7] for me. Can you still conveniently do that?

I have ordered your books and will have them shipped Tuesday.

Please tell Margaret that failing to hear from her by April 1 current I shall be forced to conclude

(1) That you have done away with her depositing the pieces in a small paper parcel in the Wall Street subway station.

(2) That I have in some way altogether unknown to myself alienated her affection.

(3) That I never succeeded in alienating her affections in the first place.

(4) That she is just plumb lazy and indifferent and generally too happy in New York.

Your letters are eternal joys. I hate to rush a reply at you like this — and I shouldn't: I owe letters all over the exposed surface of my family. But it is forced from me.   affectionately yours   Archie

Gerald's new picture is a marvel — the inside of a watch — grand idea and beautifully carried out.[8]

All the Mallarmé — all but one Appolinaire & some others are épuisé!!! Sorry. Sending the rest

TLS: NjP

1. Probably a reference to Bishop's "Speaking of Poetry," in *The Measure* No. 48 (February 1925), 6–7; collected in Bishop's *Selected Poems* (New York: Charles Scribner's Sons, 1941), 3–4. 2. Henry Seidel Canby, editor of *The Saturday Review*

of *Literature*. **3.** Herbert S. Gorman's *James Joyce: His First Forty Years* had been reviewed by Edmund Wilson in *The Dial* 77 (November 1924), 430–435. **4.** Literary editor of the *New-York Tribune*. **5.** The former work was the most recent edition of the *Anthologie de la Nouvelle Poésie Française*; the latter, André Breton's *Manifeste du Surréalisme*, both published in Paris by Simon Kra. **6.** Presumably Pierre Drieu La Rochelle (1893–1945). **7.** A literary periodical that ceased publication with the July 1925 number. **8.** The MacLeishes purchased the painting from Murphy and owned it for several years. They later exchanged it for a smaller Murphy painting, *Wasp and Pear* (1927), which fit better in the music room of the MacLeish home in Conway, Massachusetts. *See* M to Gerald Murphy, 29 September 1964.

To Amy Lowell

Dear Miss Lowell: 1 March [1925]   Saint-Cloud

You must, if you've thought about it at all, have decided that I was either dead or indifferent. Which would come to the same thing because I will be when I am. The truth is however that I didn't dare write you until I had read J.K.[1] which you so generously ordered sent us. And the further truth is that I am writing you now — although J.K. has not as yet arrived — because I don't dare permit you to continue in the assumption that I am an ungrateful wretch. In other words I write you as much out of fright as affection no matter which end you take it by. And that, my dear, is quite as it should be whether you see it that way or not. When I stop being afraid of you may the harpies harry me for I shall be carrion for them.

I wonder a great many things the first and last of which is what you will think of my article on Amy Lowell and The Art of Poetry when it appears. That however is a question which will doubtless be answered all in good time and the answer to which I may well be willing to forego when it comes. Also I wonder about J.K.. Tinker's constipated review in Canby's ridiculous sheet was only spared from the ignominy which should have been its lot by the fact that it found itself set up beside a poem I have admired since first I saw it in MS.[2] But he whetted my curiosity. In spite of himself he left me on pins and needles of attent.

I gather from Kay Putnam's[3] last letter that your departure for England is imminent and I wish I might feel that the same thing was true of a possible meeting with you. But I fear you have no intention of coming to the Continent. And even your presence could not lure me to England again. A digestive and ruminating race incapable of sole Meunier! A contented people! I am afraid there is nothing you can do for them just as I am sure there is nothing they can do to you. Have they not tried? England is the place for Eliot — you couldn't run the

Criterion, which is certainly the foremost literary review du monde, in America, and anyway Eliot's peculiar genius, like certain beetles, feeds on death and makes life out of it. But England for Aiken who needs to reside on a rotating planet if he is to rotate!! I don't think it matters in the case of Fletcher as to whom I can in no way agree with you. I don't believe he would have been a poet anywhere. But for Aiken it is a great mistake.[4] And I am not sure but that life in France or America might just have made the difference for H.D..[5]

My ideas are so valuable. . . . helpful even. . . .

affectionately yours   Archie

TLS: MH

1. *John Keats*, Lowell's monumental biography, which had just been published by Houghton Mifflin Company. 2. Chauncey B. Tinker's review, "The New Life of Keats," had appeared in *The Saturday Review of Literature* 1 (14 February 1925), 521, beside Lowell's poem "The On-Looker." 3. Probably a reference to Katharine (Kay) Bundy, whose maiden name was Putnam. 4. Conrad Aiken had recently gone to live in England, partly to be near his friend John Gould Fletcher. 5. Hilda Doolittle (1886–1961), the Imagist poet, had lived in England for several years with her husband, Richard Aldington (1892–1962), the English novelist and poet.

To Amy Lowell

Dear Miss Lowell: 10 May [1925]   Saint-Cloud

I was shocked to hear from your secretary that you had been forced by illness to give up your trip to England.[1] I know how much you had wanted to go and I know further how much your going would have meant in the process of British civilization (that tardy process) and I know further still how much I had counted on the slight chance of seeing you either here or there. But of course I don't know how much your illness adds in unhappiness to your disappointment. Please believe that Ada and I think of you often and with deep affection and with the hope that you will be well and yourself again soon — O soon.

I wont pile the events of my own history upon you now. They aren't particularly enlivening even at best and as aids in convalescence of no value. My "Pot Of Earth" has reached me in advance copy and I am pleased with it. The first time I have had such an experience. I think you will agree that the attribution of a predominant Eliotic influence is superficial to say the least of it. I do admire Eliot. But not in that way. The only similarity between this poem and the Waste Land which presents itself to me is an approximate equality of length and a common debt to Frazier.[2] But you may see more. At any rate that is all past history. I have been working out an idiom which I feel to be very completely my own this winter and though I have not written much —

I have spent a great deal of time reading French verse, particularly Rimbaud, Laforgue and Baudelaire — I like some of the things I have written.

Our plans are in a state on the other side of nebulosity. We have taken passage for home for the fifteenth of August intending a visit of two or three months but the more we consider that step the less we think of it. Ada who is going great guns is to start giving concerts in the provinces and in Paris next winter and it seems almost suicidal for her to lose the entire autumn. Also it seems ridiculous to take the children home for so short a visit. And the expense is enormous. But my father is an old man and my mother is unable to leave him to come abroad and the resultant feeling of moral obligation is, as you can understand, very strong. There is the further fact that I feel more and more strongly that I should go home for good after another year. It is not that I find it hard to work in Paris. But these continual moves from house to house and from place to place are upsetting and I am most anxious to avoid them. If we decide to do that we shall not make the trip now.

The summer we are to spend at Antibes on the Mediterranean. Sun and sea and a cruise to Greece. I expect to be able to work there but the time is brief. I should like to be able to forget time for a while.

I am glad you did not except to the article. I had expected you to dislike my insistance on the conscious quality of your poetry. It delights me that you understood what I was trying to say. As for Which Being etc. I had to cut all that on my second draft. I found I had written a book on your as yet unpublished verse! But to say I like it ——

Don't think of writing to me. Dont dare to. Until you are quite well again. And then (with equal insistance) please do.

affectionately yours   Archie

TLS: MH

1. Amy Lowell died on May 12, two days after this letter was written and thus before she could have seen it. 2. Sir James George Frazer (1854–1941), Scottish anthropologist best known for *The Golden Bough* (1890).

To Katharine Putnam Bundy

Dear Kay: 19 May [1925]   Antibes, France

Will you let me write you about Amy? There is no one else I know. And I know how much you loved her although I am not sure you know how much I did nor how close she and I really were to each other.

Curiously enough I have no feeling of loss for Amy Lowell the poet. She had done a full life's work, one that, to have done, most of us would be willing to take her place now. "Legends"[1] alone would be enough for any life. And her later verse, all of which I have in MSS, will only broaden her fame, not deepen it. She had books enough left to write — it isn't that — but her great book, I believe, she had written. I miss *her*. And beside herself all her books, all her battles, become insignificant. Beside the stillness that fills now that long room of hers all the noise she made in the world is nothing, not a whisper even, nothing —. The night that must have been her first night in the earth I came from Paris to Antibes and the only thing I could think of was the beautiful, ridiculous, tragic question, the old, old asking, the unfulfilled desire of her body. There was a thing she had wanted to know as there is a thing we all ask, only she had hidden it beneath her pride, her intelligence, her business, her skill and only now, only now that she is dead, only now that she lies still could her soul hear it. Something that isn't a poem at all began making itself in my mind, something that goes

> Do you think
> Death is an answer then?
> Ah, to the How, the When,
> Ah, to the longest word.[2]

TL[S]: M

1. Verse collection (1921). 2. The opening lines of "Interrogate the Stones," first published in *Streets in the Moon* (1926), where the word "longest" in line four is replaced by "hardest." The rest of the letter has been lost.

To Robert N. Linscott

Dear Bob: 5 June [1925]   [Antibes?]

It sounds silly but the truth is that I am really almost content to have your good opinion for the play.[1] I know you for an honest man. And one writes for about eight people anyway. But I do regret the outcome naturally. I suppose from the point of view of the public a publisher is bound to consider the play is "about" the garden of Eden. As a matter of fact however it is as complete an expression of the modern consciousness as I can at this time realize. As J. Middleton Murry[2] put it in one of his few lucid utterances, the modern consciousness rests, or fails to rest, upon the paradox of the two knowledges: the irrational and inspirational knowledge of self and the rational and hence logical knowledge of the external world. Add to that the vital element ignored by Murry that our rational knowledge of the external world is merely science, i.e. merely convention, and that true knowledge of the external world can only be had as inspirationally (but through media clogged for us who have attained self-consciousness) as true knowledge of self and you have my play. Except that my play tries to state emotionally the evolution of the event. I merely used the garden because it offered a metaphor which required no elucidation.

As to its fate — I can't imagine anyone connected in any way with the Dial liking it. But if they should, why tant mieux. I'd like to leave it to you, Maurice and Charley to decide. If they agree with you that it is *really* good then lets send it to the Dial people or anywhere else. If they have reservations lets let it sit a while. And thank you with all my heart for being so damn nice about helping me. I tell you I do appreciate it.   yrs   Archie

TLS: DLC

1. *Nobodaddy*, rejected by Houghton Mifflin and published by Dunster House in May 1926. 2. English literary critic and editor (1889–1957).

To John Peale Bishop[1]

Dear John: 26 June [1925]   Antibes

Unless you can imagine the anxiety with which I attended your letter you cannot possibly estimate my delight in it. It is practically your judgment alone upon which the Pot Of Earth stands or falls because you are the only one of the three living critical intelligences which will be called upon by the accidents of personal acquaintance etc. to pass upon its merits. Consequently your praise leaves me feeling as though I had received the larger part of the universe. And your dispraise only serves to set off your praise. I quite agree with you about the blatant evidence of my admiration for Eliot. All I can say about it — and you already understand better than I can explain — is that I had no choice. But since that time I think I have come through it to an idiom more nearly my own. You can judge for yourself. I am having a group of poems published in *Commerce* (Valery Larbaud etc.) this October and I shall see that you have a copy.

I shall cherish your letter as long as I have a box left to cherish anything in. I owe you the beginnings of confidence.

Your suggestions as to the next step interest me enormously. Firuski is publishing for me this summer a verse play which is not the play you have in mind and of which nothing further need be said. And since the Pot Of Earth I have been doing stray verse and reading — principally Rimbaud. But in March I started to frame and I am now working on a book which will lie much nearer the roman than the theater. I intend taking the next year to it and I hope much from it. It will be made up of short poems but in a manner — i.e. the combination — which has not yet been used so far as I know in English. Jacob's Room offers in part the plan.[2] After that I had vaguely thought of a play and I now think definitely of one. But the old problem arises, the problem of the afternoon we walked to the Jardin des Plantes. What is the field for the verse play written to be acted? Must it not perforce be large, gross, melodramatic? Can the peculiar sensibility which we recognize as modern find expression in it? To me it seems that Cocteau's poetry of the theatre — largely a poetry of production — is the modern replication to the 17th century's poetry for the theatre. And a Romeo and Juliet, much as I admired it, I have neither envy nor equipment to do. Apparently you have something approximating an answer. Do write me about it when you can.

Antibes is crowded and noisy but really beautiful and for six weeks more it will be tolerable. We leave the eighteenth of August reaching New York (Fabre Line) September 4. You will probably be out of town then but I shall see you when I come east on our way back to France late in October. If there is any chance of your coming back do come with us. But don't tell me that there is unless there really is. The disappointment would be enormous, unbearable. Talking last night with Charlie Walker about the difficulties of getting oriented in France and of all you did for me in that regard I became all but maudlin and the mood is still upon me.

You do not speak of the novel. I hope to have definite news of it in August when Esther Murphy[3] comes down but I should appreciate word from you. Are you working on it? Or does the delicate and unresurrectable slaughtering of Ben Hechts, Chicago, Semite, Venalese, leave no time for it?[4] *Don't* let it go. The memory of it in my mind is clean and hard and sharp as the sky in the mistral — no mist can endure the pressure of that wind.

Did you say you had ordered E.E.C's Forty Poems for me? It hasn't come. Never mind about it unless the book seller has slipped up. I am picking up your books as I can. Love to Margaret.

affec yrs — and gratefully   Archie

If it ever crosses your path to move for a decent consideration of the P. of E. in the Dial will you shove a bit?   AMacL

TLS: NjP

1. The MacLeishes were spending the summer at Antibes with the Murphys and several mutual friends. 2. A novel by Virginia Woolf (1922). M's projected work, which he first planned to call *The Intimate Poems of L. T. Carnavel*, was published by Houghton Mifflin as *The Hamlet of A. MacLeish* in October 1928. 3. Gerald Murphy's sister. 4. Bishop had reviewed Ben Hecht's novels *Humpty Dumpty* and *The Kingdom of Evil* in *The Saturday Review of Literature* 1 (6 June 1925), 803.

To Andrew and Martha Hillard MacLeish

Dearest Father and Mother: 19 July 1925 Antibes

I have treated you shamefully — it does me some little good to confess it even if it is small consolation to you to have me. The trouble is that I have gotten into the habit of spending all the time I can each day writing and though that time is not long — from three to six hours — it always manages to consume all my ink expending energy and I feel as though the last thing I could do was the construction of a letter. I keep wondering how Emily Bronte managed to write such long and beautiful letters. To take only one example. As to my writing itself, I am now in the precarious position of starting work on a book — a long poem — which I have been working over in my mind since March and which, in idea, fascinates me but in cold fact proves elusive. In the course of my attempt to plot its movement I have been sponge-diving in the seas of my own infancy and though I have not brought much up I have uncovered the most amazing depths. I don't quite know how to put it but in moods of waywardness when I felt great fatigue I have suddenly, myself, in this thirty fourth (!) year of mine age walked out of the sitting room at Craigie Lea into the hall, touching the curtain with my left hand, feeling the cool smooth boards under bare feet, and wondering, *with the mind of twelve years,* what to do with the interminable rest of a long summer afternoon. I am trying to get that part finished before I return this fall because the actuality completely smothers the memory. But it is a most difficult and delicate task and lately I have been completely discouraged. For the rest, the Pot Of Earth seems to be getting good reviews, barring the New York Times and the Lexington Herald, and at least two reviewers have miraculously understood it. My verse play Nobodaddy should appear early in the fall, and in October I am having the best poem I have yet written published in the Yale Review (Signature For Tempo) and seven poems published in a French Quarterly — the best in France — called Commerce, a new review edited by Valery Larbaud and Leon Paul Fargue etc.. I plan to put the next year or year and a half on the book I am now working on and after that I vaguely contemplate a verse play written to be acted and unlike anything ever etc. etc. — you know the phrases. In the mean time I know I am a poet and the rest can wait. Your appreciation of The Pot Of Earth meant more to me than I can say. You now take my work seriously and that is all I ask. That you also like it is an added and unearned increment.

As a place to work in Antibes is, I think, a success. You can't fool the climate. That is, you do fall asleep after lunch if you try to work after lunch instead of yielding to the siesta habit. And the dry sun and blue water is a temptation toward noon not to be denied. But by starting early you can get everything done that is in you to do. I have made several breaks of two to three days in connection with the various short cruises of the Picaflor — Gerald Murphy's boat — from Marseilles down the coast to Antibes and just now back along the coast — with Ada and Sara Murphy aboard — to St. Tropez, a little fishing port west of St. Raphael with the usual corsair-Roman-Greek-Phoenician history but with much more than the usual charm and individuality. We went over with a head wind in the Mistral quarter which blew up to half a gale and gave us a lively two hours working into the gulf: we came back with a light head wind which pulled around behind us in the afternoon and finally, toward four, left us slapping and rolling in a ground swell off the enormous red headland of Cap Roux where we stayed till an evening breeze pushed us to within a mile and a half of the mole at Cannes from which point we pulled ourselves in in the dingy shadowing into the harbor just as the Saturday evening band concert under the plane trees trumpeted itself out, and dropped anchor in the sliding long reflections of the quay-side lights through a blur of hand accordions and overshot tenor voices and merry-go-rounds. I don't think we shall go to Greece. For one thing the boat is too small. For another Dos Passos[1] is sick and can't come abroad. And for another we don't much want to be gone a month. Gerald and I and Geralds Russian studio hand[2] may slide down the Italian coast and across to Corsica but I am fighting it. I have too much to do and only four weeks left to do it in.

I have definitely, and, I am afraid, not very regretfully, broken with Aunt Mary. She wrote Ada a long rambling letter filled with everything which she thought would most hurt both of us — Ada's mother was fatally ill — Bruce thought Ishbel would not get well — she had had my book for some weeks but had not had time to read it — and so forth. I replied that Ada and I were too busy to give up two or three days to the pain of her letters and that I should have to ask her not to write us again and not to attempt to see us. I went on to say that I could not permit her to go on revenging on Ada as well as on myself my refusal to live her life instead of mine etc.. I am sorry to say that I have no love left for her and that I do not wish to see her again. She seems to feel that her kindnesses to me in my childhood and youth give her power over my adult life and I cannot endure that attitude. And I feel that she is a malevolent and rather hypocritical old maid with all the qualities that go with that state in New England. I tell you all this frankly begging your forgiveness for hurting you. But I think you understand the history of our relationship and I feel that you should know its end.

Alors — early in September we meet again. Mimi and Katherine and

I will come straight out and Ada and Kenny in two weeks. I should overlap Norman a week at least. Isn't it great luck that they are to have a new baby. If only Ishbel could be there. But we mustn't even suggest it. Couldn't Norman delay his vacation a week so that he and I could go out to Colorado together? I wonder.

My dearest love to you both. I'm mad to see you.

your devoted son   Archie

TLS: M

1. John Dos Passos (1896–1970), American novelist, was a close friend of the Murphys and the MacLeishes. 2. Vladimir Orloff, a set designer with Diaghilev in Paris and a naval architect.

To John Peale Bishop

My dear John: 8 August 1925   Antibes

I keep asking myself what I have done to deserve you.

Gerald and I have spent the last five days cruising down the coast into Italy and discussing backward and forward two of your remarks on the subject of tragedy — remarks which you throw off as casually as though they had occurred to you over the wash basin. And last night in the Murphy's garden we went on with it with Esther and the Barrys[1] and Ada and Sara. I quote you to yourself: "Terror for us cannot be drawn from any such paraphernalia as Webster used: it is the horror of evil, of unexpected, sharply contrasted depravity, of helplessness before one's own nature — *not death, but life and its terrible possibilities.*" So completely obvious! — like all profound observations. We are afraid of our own lives — and beside that fear, death, which is at least a fact, is a small matter. Witness the sophisticated reaction to the slaughter of the Romanoffs. Your modern is Hamlet — but Hamlet without the ghost, without even the dead father, with nothing but the soliloquies — which are not overheard. Gerald would have it that you dissect particularly the American mind but to me your remark goes to the bottom of much more than that. And then: "I need hardly say that it must be derived from something mysterious, not fully explained, sagely removed, but from something which the audience knows does exist." Need you not? I think even Yeats could ponder that statement. But these things need talking and it is the fact that they can soon have it which makes me write you now when a letter is an impossibility.

First — of our arrival. It is good to know that you will be in New York even then. We get in the fourth and I am to go right on out to Chicago with the children which means that I shall not have more than a half day in New York. But that will suffice to at least see you and make plans for later on. You are good to want to feast us. I want enormously to meet M. Moore and Bunny Wilson[2] and beyond that any one you like. If Cummings can be found I should be delighted to see him again. But chiefly I want to see you and as much of you as possible. I have lagged this summer and I need tightening up.

You mustn't think of dropping your own work to do a review of the Pot of Earth. But if you could get M. Moore to look at it with an interested eye I should be eternally grateful. It sounds as though the novel might be done by the time I get there. At least you will let me see what there is. I believe in that book more and more and I shant be able to get it out of my mind until I can feel it whole.

My seven poems for Commerce have dropped to two but Valery Larbaud is to translate them and that more than makes up. You shall have a copy of the Octobre number as soon as I get hold of it.[3]

We are now in the middle of getting away and time presses. Forgive my so feeble response to your so otherwise letter

affec. yrs   Archie

TLS: NjP

1. Philip Barry (1896–1949), American playwright, and his wife Ellen, a painter. 2. Edmund Wilson, a close friend of Bishop's, was associated with *The Dial*, as was Marianne Moore. 3. The autumn 1925 issue of *Commerce* contained M's "Train-stop: Night" and "Pastoral," accompanied by translations into French by Valéry Larbaud.

To the Editor of The New York Times

29 September 1925   Paris

In your issue of Sept. 20 you devote editorial attention to a poem of mine in the current number of The Yale Review.[1] The contention of your editorial, which is brightly satiric in tone, is the perfectly lawful if somewhat unflattering contention that my poem doesn't mean anything.

The poem in question is a poem of about thirty-five lines printed in three movements. To prove your contention you selected from the middle of the poem a group of nine lines, which constituted neither in sense, rhythm nor phrase a unit, and offered them as evidence. The result was what might have been expected — what, perhaps, was intended. I need hardly point out to you that the same thing could be done with the work of better poets than I am with equal effect.

To prove in good faith that the poem was incomprehensible it was only necessary to reprint the poem with such comment as you saw fit. Unhappily, the poem as it stands in The Yale Review proves rather the opposite. And the writer of your editorial, who however uninformed he may be in some ways is a gentleman of obvious wit, must have observed that fact. Which leaves me to assume that he did not altogether by accident fall upon the nine lines he chose to amputate and misprint.

Archibald MacLeish

P: NYT

1. The *Times* editorial, entitled "Poetry, New Style," was a comment on M's poem "Signature for Tempo" in the October 1925 issue of *The Yale Review*. M's letter, dated as above, was published in the *Times* on October 6.

To Martha Hillard MacLeish

Dearest Mother: [*c.* October 1925] [Farmington?]

Having completed the grand tour of Boston and assured myself anew that they all love us very much and that we can't possibly live there I find myself returned to these dying hills over which a faint and momentary sun suggestive. Small green apples rotten in the road-side grass, leaves fallen or falling, horizons and perspectives opening, closing — the distance coming nearer and near things moving into the beginnings of distance, two black horses in a brown pasture, small rolling hills of middle Connecticut and shallow valleys and the old New Britain road up over the Mountain where nothing ever passes now. I should be happy in it if like you I could call it my own country. To me it remains scenery.

It was a wonderful visit at home, a wonderful visit with you and with father and with Ishbel and with all of you. Craigie Lea is neither in time nor space for me. It hangs at the edge of both and the roads that lead to it stop, all of them, before they reach its bounds. And for the first time I got a sense of Chicago. I liked it. And I loved our afternoon. And never so long as I live shall I forget the Cathedral of Chartres or the Kwan Yin at Chicago.[1] When you are sad go to her. She knows. And not as woman, not as goddess, but as labor of art.

Any news of my five dollar shirt? I left a lot of things I didn't want in our room and one thing I did want — my sponge. Will you send it to reach here before the 22nd if possible? And will you do one thing else for me? Will you get someone to buy at the Evening Post offices five or ten copies of the Literary Review for Friday August 28th with the criticism of the Pot Of Earth in it? And send them to me here or send them to Firuski, Dunster House Book Shop, Cambridge if they can't get here in time? I'll send you my check.

Do get a rest this fall. And do go to see some absolutely first class doctor for a general examination just to reassure yourself and to reassure us and to regulate your goings and comings in the interest of science. Did Hasbrouck tell you what his specialists thought of my plate?[2]

My love to father and do give my warmest regards to Miss Tillinghast and tell her again how glad I am she is there.

your devoted son: Archie

TLS: M

1. M had presumably viewed the monumental Chinese Buddhist religious icon that was on display at the University of Chicago's Oriental Institute Museum. Another such figure was located at Chicago's Art Institute. 2. A principal reason for M's trip to the States was to have his back, which he had injured diving off Eden Roc at Antibes, examined by medical experts. *See* M to Martha Hillard MacLeish, 22 December 1925.

To Maurice Firuski

Dear Maurice: 28 October [1925]   Aboard S.S. *Leviathan*

Thanks for your cable. It was nice to hear from you just at that minute. Ada regrets so much not having seen you to talk to. Why not drop over for a few hours — or weeks?

About Nobodaddy. The story is this. Aiken, Linscott and I talking together. Poem mentioned. Slight tenseness. Ask why. Well, frankly, they don't think it good enough — at least not good enough to follow the Pot Of Earth. I query. Haven't seen it for a year and a half. Don't remember. But the suspicion of Aiken is as good as another man's veto. Hence deep concern. Leave them to read proof. Read first Act. Fine. Read second Act. Bunk. Read third Act. Fine. There you are. The question was, could it be revamped? And around that question revolved a lot of considerations as that the poem was already set up and a considerable amount of money involved. As that the destiny of the poem lies properly not in my hands at all but in yours. And so forth.

As I see it there are three things that can be done and the decision is for you to make. The poem can be printed as it stands. It might or might not be a flop: but it will not be a success. The poem can be suppressed (on condition that I bear the financial loss and not you.) That would seem to me unfortunate because the play has some excellent things in it and because the psychological effect of suppression is not good. The poem can (perhaps) be revamped. By that I mean the second act may perhaps be rewritten in such a way as to give the third act a raison d'etre without committing the grossities it now commits. I confess that at the moment I don't see it and it may be many a long month before I do. On the other hand I may perhaps be able to see the light at once. The trouble is that the story of the Garden and the story of Cain are separate stories having only a moral unity in common and the attempt to make the second the essential dramatic resolution of the first is an attempt only a sophomore like myself would have exercised.

Well, there you are. And you can imagine the emotions with which I present this situation to you. In effect I have put you to expense and trouble over the publication of a poem which, now, at the last moment I skittishly find unworthy to print. I am ashamed. I can only say in extenuation that a considerable period has elapsed since the winter of '23–'24 and I am not the guy I was.

Please write me fully and without sparing my feelings. Tell me what you think of the poem, what you think of me, what you want done.

In the mean time I have held the proof and I have written Canby to go ahead on a review of the Pot Of Earth.

With all my gratitude and affection the poor thing I call me 'eart.

Archie.

TLS: NjP

To Maurice Firuski

Dear Maurice: 1 December 1925   Paris

I send you today under highly separate cover the proof, somewhat revised, of Acts 1 and 3 and a completely rewritten Act 2. As regards its idea I am now completely satisfied with the new act. The play is now so changed as to become what it was always intended to be, a play built upon the beginnings of human self-consciousness in a universe in which self-consciousness is an anomaly. In the old second act Adam and Eve become at once rivals of god. They are terribly taken up with the cruelty of the universe. They plan to remake the world. And they are physically kicked out of Eden. Here they merely become human. And they are driven out of Eden by their own sense — it comes down to that — of the impossibility of communication between themselves and the world that they have previously inhabited. The result is that Cain's revolt in the last act with its tragic denouement in nothingness has some meaning. As a play the play now hangs together. My question is as to the verse of the new act. Am too close to it myself to have any opinion but think it not bad. You must be absolutely frank. One thing you must also bear in mind is that the expenses of setting up the new act are to be born altogether and separately by me. It is very decidedly my funeral. There is no argument about that. None.

I enclose a foreword which I think must be printed. As a rule I detest them but the play of Nobodaddy needs some explanation on the point I try to give it on. The material in the foreword, i.e. the things I there say I do not pretend to find in the bible, is the best statement

I could give for your blurb. At some point in his history man became self-conscious — accidentally I should say — whence all his ills but chiefly his exclusion from the earth and from the only god worth calling such. He attempted to build his own world outside the physical world. And that's where we all are today right there. In other words god's greatest work of man is ant. Brother ant was made to live in the world and does it. See on another side of this a bum poem of Hardy's in Human Shows, page 145[,] called the Aerolite which I have just read this afternoon.

That's that. As for the books you are sending me — two small pckgs have come in. Are the rest coming in one big box? And to what address?

As you saw I hit the Dial. It also looks as though I *might* hit the Criterion.[1] Eliot writes that he has found my last batch interesting and wants to keep them a while. He has had them since August already so he may just be — but I don't believe it.

    My best to John   aff'ly yrs   Archie

TLS: NjP

1. M's poem "Nocturne" was published in *The Dial* 81 (July 1926), 65. His "Poem" ("No lamp has ever shown us where to look") and "Land's End" were published in *The Criterion* of April 1926 and July 1927, respectively.

To Martha Hillard MacLeish

Dearest Mother: 22 December 1925   Paris

For me after all these years as they say to apologize to you for the state of my correspondence would be merely ridiculous. But that doesn't mean I am not heartily ashamed of myself. I am. And when toward two and three of the morning the nights I can't sleep my childhood comes back over me as it does at those times — as though by not sleeping when one should sleep one had broken through time itself — as though, that is, time were not a length but a repetition and can be rescinded by a movement opposite the pattern — at such times I have a sense of guilt, of failure which fairly, I can assure you, punishes me. I don't know why I am so bad at it. Perhaps its because I get so fed up with the tricks of reproducing words on paper that the thought of trying to communicate in that way repels me. Or perhaps I am merely selfish and lazy. I am prepared to believe the latter. Forgive me if you can. And believe that its not for lack of thinking of you that I am silent.

I have done no real work since I returned. The first month went to the rewriting of the second act of the verse play Maurice is publishing for me this winter. When I read proof on it in New York the day before sailing I saw suddenly that it was just simply rotten. There was nothing to do about it. Proof had been set up and Maurice had incurred expenses and there was no help but to go on. The second act being the worst I attacked that and ended by completely rewriting it. It is now better. But I am still very far from taking any pride in it. After that I started getting together my short stuff for another volume with H.M. and I have just this windy afternoon finished that task. Most of the pieces required some redoing and the work was a bore. I am now ready to go at the book I have had in mind ever since last April but I really doubt if I can write it now. These breaks in existence are terribly serious for me and they may prove fatal. We'll see.

In the mean time my back has been laid to rest. I felt it a good deal and finally decided to go and see Calvé. I had X-rays taken which made the X-ray man look very grave and I took them to Calvé's office with a sinking heart. He looked at them, told me I was one of the most interesting cases he had ever seen, examined me in all positions and finally said there was nothing at all the matter with me, that the irregularity in my back bone was probably congenital, like a crooked nose, and that there was no reason why I shouldn't do anything I wanted. I told him about our friend S----. To which he replied in the most suave French imaginable that it probably wouldn't have done me any harm to have a piece of my shin in my back. My feelings about S---- are not mixed. And they carry with them feelings about the osteopath in Glencoe which are not altogether friendly. He ought to know more about a man whom he recommends. Apparently S---- is the rankest kind of quack. Three excellent doctors have now by implication said as much. I think the sound of the name MacLeish was too much for him. But don't get into a libel suit by repeating this.

By the by — where is the bill for the flowers I sent Ada? Did you pay it? If you did you will please don't. How much was it? You can't do that you know. You are altogether too generous.

Which brings me to the checks which came today and were explained by your dear letter. You are too good. Please thank father and yourself formally. I hope father's scarf got there in time. And that you liked your pendant. Best to Miss. Tilly.   your devoted son   Archie

TLS: M

To John Peale Bishop

Dear John:-   3 February 1926   Paris

Just when I was most wondering what the everlasting had happened to you lo & behold out of the clear blue of a month after Christmas your amazing aquarelle. For God's sake! Tell me about it? I've rarely been so sharply kicked by anything. Who is Mr. Pî? And whence? & when? And thank you a thousand times. It shall most deliciously grace our already by André Masson, Juan Gris & Gerald Murphy bedecked attelier. Mes homages à Madame votre charmante femme et baisers de ma femme pour tous.

Little news. Almost none. Back three months & seven lines of bum verse to show for it — not including a 2nd Act to Nobodaddy & a month of typing Mss for a book of short stuff which H.M. seem to be having a Hell of a time accepting & even may not. But aside from that — nothing — nothing. What in Hell is the matter I simply don't know.

A letter from Phelps Putnam just arrived informs me that E. Wilson had been "most flattering" about a certain ballad of the said Putnam which I saw last summer & thought, frankly, was so much tripe. That news leaves me gasping. As I told you — in spite of his adverse opinions of my stuff — I am bound to say that Wilson is the American authority (you refusing to exercise your genius). But how to get around this! One or the other of us is simply mad. It isn't a close case. It is a case of grand or rank. And if Wilson is right, then I am a very bad poet and also a very ignorant & insensitive reader of poetry. If I were contemplating suicide I should jump from that eminence.

Seldes is in town though I haven't seen him. Some remark about a contribution of yours to the 7 Lively Arts controversy.[1] Can this be the celebrated essay on murder? Where can it be found?

Also Hemingway has just gone through on his way home to murder Messers Boni & Liveright. It seems they have turned down a satire of his on Anderson[2] & there is a great to do. I was out of town when he went through but found bear claw marks all over the front door.

Dos is in Africa & refuses to come back. What do you say to Manhattan Transfer? I thought the method extremely interesting but the book as a whole unsuccessful. As Gerald puts it, you keep expecting that all this scattered disparate energy is going to gather itself up at the end & blow New York off the map. And it never does. It just runs down. Or doesn't even run down — just stops. Dos seems to me to be a man who can't write a novel, looking for an excuse for not writing one. And yet there is grand stuff in the book & the tempo is amazing. Give me your theories.

I may be leaving the end of this month for Persia for 3 months. A League of Nations opium commission is going down & I have been asked to go as Secy to the head.[3] You go into parts of Persia no European ever sees. It sounds exciting. But the work is dull & dangerous. And I hate to be away so long. Also I hate the thought of a desert grave.

Do you know how hippopotamuses copulate?   yrs,   Archie

ALS: NjP

1. The essay in question is unidentified, and may not have been published. 2. Hemingway's *The Torrents of Spring*. 3. Colonel Frederic A. Delano, formerly president of the Wabash Railroad.

To T. S. Eliot

Dear Mr. Eliot: 21 February [1926]   [Paris?]

I can imagine no good reason why you should publish a poem of mine of this length.[1] But I send it nevertheless in the hope that you may unreasonably like it enough to excuse its bulk.

I was disappointed to miss you last spring when (I believe) you lunched with Mme de Bassiano.[2] It isn't because I think that I could tell you better verbally than I have already done in ink how much I owe you (indeed you must be only too painfully conscious of it if you ever happen on my *Pot Of Earth*). It's simply that you're becoming legendary and I have a very human desire to look at you. Seriously I'd take it most kindly if you would let me know when next you pass through Paris. It will save you a lot of importuning and give me the greatest pleasure   faithfully yours   Archibald MacLeish

TLS: ELIOT

1. M may have sent Eliot the manuscript of "Einstein," for possible publication by *The New Criterion* (of which Eliot was editor). 2. Princess Bassiano was the former Marguerite Chapin, sister of Katherine Garrison Chapin; also known as Marguerite Caetani, she was the owner of the French literary journal *Commerce*, which was edited by Paul Valéry, Valéry Larbaud, and Léon-Paul Fargue.

To Maurice Firuski

Dear Maurice: 27 February [1926]   Paris

On the eve of leaving for Persia I endite thee this. I have just had a cable from H.M. saying that they have written me offering one hundred dollars for the rights to the collection of short stuff I sent them in December.[1] The letter has not as yet arrived and I am therefore in doubt as to the date of publication but I assume the spring. Would you call Bob and ask him? And if it is to be spring would you do a very necessary and bothersome job for me? Would you write Canby, Munroe[2] and anyone else who has accepted stuff and tell them that I should like to include the pieces in question in my book if their convenience made it possible for them to publish before the date of the volume? I hate putting this on you but I don't know who the people are and the job has to be done. I have myself already written the Dial and I shall tell Bob to include Nocturne if Marianne publishes it before his date. I think she will. Eliot has taken one for the Criterion but that is to appear in April.

As to Nobodaddy — I assume that is to appear in the spring as well. I trust you to see that no one with an alleged ear changes my rhythms as they were changed in the first proof. It is criminal to put things on you as I do. It is only because I am so sure of your affection that I can. Which means so sure of my own.

I wrote Conrad [Aiken] a while ago asking him to visit me at Antibes this summer. He replied that he couldn't afford it. I then wrote him and told him my father was a rich man and that he was an animal of a Puritan if he wouldn't let me pay the P.L.M. his fare. To which no reply. Do you think I have hurt his feelings? If you do please tell him when you next write him that I was troubled about it. It never crossed my mind he might take what was so simply meant in any other sense.

I look forward to a grand three months la-bas. But God how I hate leaving Ada and the children for so long a time. Why do we inflict such voluntary sufferings upon ourselves? Take care of yourself and remember to send me the bill for the second act proof which is mine a moi.   my love to you   Archie

TLS: NjP

1. *Streets in the Moon,* published by Houghton Mifflin on 12 November 1926. 2. Harriet Monroe, the founder and editor of *Poetry: A Magazine of Verse.*

To Ernest Hemingway [1]

Dear Ernest: [*c.* June 1926] [Antibes]

For it is Ernest isn't it? How is your life? Have any sweet and deep things been happening to you? Have you plunged into any wells of living water? And in general how do you? I feel very sad. Miss Simpsin is playing old English airs — I think they are airs — on the piano below stairs and it has been raining all day and the sea isn't what you took it for and I have thought of a new way to represent the process of dying — or is it dieing? Dye if you would be with Adonais. Also my testicles give me no end of trouble at these interseasonal periods. I'm one of your late generators. Of all times of the year save me the necessity of procreation in the spring. Sheep breed in the spring. But come at me with your dreaming Aphrodites of an off winter evening or just as summer putting back her drawers draws down the hither hand of autumn or about the holy solstice whenas old earth doth turn her other rump and I can get you cabbages upon the very body of corrupted death.

178

Or thereabouts. Nothing other works for me at all. I have been seven days over a thirty line soliloquy for my redraft of 'amlet. And last night Scott[2] told me he was thinking of selling the serial rights to the World's Fair to some magazine or other for thirty-five thousand deollars! I know I can't write fiction now. How is the escaped convict getting on? Jake stays with me. So does Ashby. So do bulls. So do fish and fern leaves. A lot of stuff like the memories you bring back for yourself from a week like that. As they go farther back they don't lose vitality. My one criticism is the one I gave you — and from me worth nothing — that the novel is less of a block than your best stories are.[3] But I don't see how it can help but be a success, both d'estime and d'argent. It has got the one rare thing — common life. And so much more. Thanks so much for the books for K. When I get where I can find out the price of an Everyman ed. I'll reimb.. Till when my secret thanks. I've made a list of all the good people in the world. There are nineteen of which you are seven.

Why not meet again   yrs aff'ly Archie

TLS: JFK

1. M had met Hemingway (1899–1961) at the Closerie des Lilas in Paris in the summer of 1924, and the MacLeishes saw much of him in Paris, Antibes, and elsewhere until their return from abroad. Thereafter, M and Hemingway saw one another less frequently, and the MacLeish-Hemingway friendship was punctuated by a number of unpleasant episodes that led, eventually, to almost complete estrangement. 2. F. Scott Fitzgerald. *See* M to Fitzgerald, 15 September 1930, note 1. 3. Hemingway had brought with him to the Riviera the carbon copy of the manuscript for *The Sun Also Rises*, which M (as well as Fitzgerald and, perhaps, others) had immediately read.

To Lewis Galantière

Dear Louis: 8 July [1926] [Antibes]

Back from Persia & already asking favors again — And how are you anyway?

Your ever loyal Kenny has run out of books & there's nothing to be had here at all & no one in Paris who could & would but you. What I have in mind is this. When you pass, one day, Galliani's on your regular Sunday afternoon rue de Rivoli ramble would you see if there are any titles in the publications of the Hakluyt Society which you think he could go? (He's reading Treasure Isl & Tom Brown etc.) I fancy there are some. If not in that series perhaps under the general head of voyages — Mexico & Peru above all. And only not Marco Polo. Will you see? And if you find anything tell 'em to send it down here (counter reimb.) as fast as they damn well can: we're going crazy. Spend what you please — or rather order.

How I long to talk to thee, incredible man, of Persia! Where have you not been, what have you not read (La vie est triste, Hélas —), not suffered? Forgive me for asking this present favor of you. I know you will understand why I beg so apparently trifling a matter of you.

Affec'ly yrs   Archie

ALS: NNC

To Martha Hillard MacLeish

Dearest Mother:-   25 July [1926]   [Antibes]

It has been a long time since & but for the loving labor of Ada it would have been a longer. Persia was — I now but only now see — worth doing. I shall increasingly feel that way. But at the time I found three months away from Ada too much. I seem to be increasingly unable to be happy away from her. I'm not sure its the best thing in the world. But I wouldn't trade my captivity. Mrs. Hitchcock wrote Ada à propos of our 10th anniversary that at least we'd had those ten years: she is always expecting that I am going to leave my family — a touching tribute to her conviction that I am a poet & a balm to my maleness but not altogether a profound attitude of mind.

How are you both? Please tell father that I love him very deeply — that I think of him a great deal. I hope he has not suffered too much in the terrific heat you have been having. And I do hope you are not too worn out with it. Your news of Ishbel is reassuring but as always puzzling. *Is* there a connection between her tummy & her T.B.? *Could* she leave now if she wanted to? And when does she really expect to be free? Is she really well but just staying there to be sure? Or is she still sick? I don't quite understand. She *never* writes.

We are all blessedly well. Kenny is long & thin & restless & happy. I'm afraid his mind is going to cause him trouble. He can't concentrate & yet he does so much speculating that it seems cruel to make him. Mimi is simply a gift from heaven. She is the lovliest child I have ever seen — like a fairy physically & as sweet and charming mentally as an angel. I can hardly keep my hands off her

Ada is working hard with an accompanist & I am trying to work. I have a grand idea for a book but I find I am prosy as a horse-dealer's almanac. *Nobodaddy* seems to get on. I expected the critics to assassinate it. The few reviews I have seen were quite the opposite. My fall book is however the best book I have yet done. I stand or fall by that — probably fall — no pun intended.

You will be glad to know that we are decided to come home in the

Spring & settle down (for a year — or more?). Where or how we don't know. But at least there won't be an ocean between.

Dearest love to you. Take care of yourself & be happy.

Your devoted son   Archie

I was shocked by June's death.[1] His life was so meager — so truly tragic.

Please ask poor overworked Bruce to tell you (so that you can tell me) how & *when* I pay my income tax? I've paid nothing yet. And give him my love & thanks —   A.

ALS: M

1. Albert ("June," for Junior) Billings, son of M's half sister Blanche, had died of typhoid fever.

To Allen Tate[1]

Dear Mr. Tate: 26 July [1926] [Antibes]

I don't see what use it can be to receive the applause, as you hereby do, of someone of whom you have never heard. But it relieves me somewhat to tell you that I am lost in admiration of your New Republic review of Eliot's Poems.[2] Particularly your examination of French influences (with which I don't altogether agree) which is by all odds the most illuminating thing that has yet been said of Eliot's background. You get, in general, what Wilson's too instructed mind missed.[3] But I understand you are a poet — which explains. Forgive this intrusion.   very sincerely yours   Archibald MacLeish

ALS: NjP

1. American poet, critic, novelist, and biographer (1899–1979). 2. Tate's review of Eliot's *Poems: 1909–1925* had appeared in *The New Republic* 47 (30 June 1926), 172–173. 3. Edmund Wilson had reviewed the same work in "The School of Strachey," *Vanity Fair* 19 (January 1923), 92.

To Robert N. Linscott

Dear Bob: 1 September 1926 Antibes

You are probably right. Anyway there's nothing to do about it.[1] And your report of the looks of the book excites me. Want to hear a good title? Scott is publishing a novel next spring to be yclept The World's Fair! Try that over on your mouth organ.

Are we getting older? Time is a smooth wind on the lip at twenty but it will wear the iron knees of the gods upon the tomb of Cyrus.

I saw it. And its such damn small consolation to know that several billion have done it before us and all the goddam young will do it after us. The one relief I know is Montrachet, 1915. I wish to god you could come over here for a bit and crack a few bottles with me. I plan to go home for good (?) in the spring. Which means that I must travel a lot this winter. Why not break away and do some of it with me? I'll put you up in Paris or anywhere else I may be. You'll have an ocean passage and very little more. And you'll be a new man. Not that the travel will do a hard-boiled poet like you any good but the wine will and I'll furnish all you can drink. We might even investigate the lesser German beers. Lesser! Than what? The trouble is you wont face the fact. Just say, By God I'll Go. And you will. I've got two projects — over and above the thing I'm now at work on to talk over with you. Not that *that's* an inducement.[2]

I'll send along the critic list and directions for my copies in a day or two. Somebody sent me a copy of the Sat. Rev. with a pat for Pot of Earth in it.[3] So we aren't dead yet.

Write me the date of your boat.   yrs affly   Archie

TLS: DLC

1. M had written to Houghton Mifflin on August 5 requesting that the title of his fall book be restored to what he had originally planned to call it: *Under the Sun.* Linscott had replied on August 20, defending the choice of *Streets in the Moon* and saying that in any case it was too late to make the change. 2. Linscott accepted M's invitation and sailed for France on November 7. 3. Stephen Vincent Benét had reviewed *Nobodaddy* and *The Pot of Earth* in *The Saturday Review of Literature* 2 (17 July 1926), 934.

To Louis Untermeyer[1]

Dear Mr. Untermeyer: 9 September [1926]   [Antibes]

I found your letter this morning lying on top of a pile of lingerie which my wife brought down from Paris a week ago. I shall be continuously grateful to the now forgotten impulse which led me to stick my head into that particular armoire. But I regret even more warmly the delay in answering it. It was uncommonly nice of you to write me. You know by now what a word from you means to any of the rest of us — & particularly to one like myself who has been desperately fighting down an amateur pseudo-reputation for these three years. May your beer be Pilsener! Nothing else could reward you.

As to your questions. I should of course be happy & proud to be included in the Miscellany.[2] I am publishing almost all my recent short pieces in a book which appears this fall & am now at work on another long one. So that I might need some time. But you can trust me to move heaven & earth to meet your calendular requirements. Please tell me what kind of stuff is in order, & when, & whether heretofore unpublished (as I assume) etc..

As to your questions of place — I go to Paris next Thursday (16) & expect to be there the rest of the month. My address there is 44 rue du Bac (Fleurus 62–20) or, if not there, under the name of P. M. Hamilton somewhere in the Ave. du Bois — I don't know where but see P. M. Hamilton in phone book.[3] Please come & dine with me. Drop me a note at 44 or telephone me at Hamiltons on arrival & give me some of your however brief it may be time. England I hope to make in October. It is good of you to like the pieces in Poetry & the Sat. Rev..[4] Your review of the Pot of Earth I haven't seen.[5] I must. Indeed I await that as an event of major if not conclusive importance. Was it in the Yale Rev.? Or where? Thank you again for writing me & do let me know where & when I can see you either in Paris or London

faithfully yours   Archibald MacLeish

ALS: INU

1. American anthologist, critic, and poet (1885–1977). 2. *American Poetry 1927: A Miscellany*, published in August 1927 by Harcourt, Brace & Company, included six poems by M: "Bleheris," "Revelation," "You, Andrew Marvell," "Weather," "Poem" ("On the beaches of the moon"), and "Anniversary." 3. Pierpont Morgan ("Peter") Hamilton, a great-great-grandson of Alexander Hamilton and a nephew of J. P. Morgan, the banker. He and his wife, Marie Louise ("Marise"), had separated, and Hamilton had offered the MacLeishes the use of his residence at 41, avenue du Bois de Boulogne, rent free, requiring them to pay only the wages of the household staff. 4. "Ars Poetica," published in *Poetry* in June 1926, and "In My Thirtieth Year," in the 3 July 1926 issue of *The Saturday Review of Literature*. 5. Unidentified.

To Louis Untermeyer

Dear Untermeyer: [20 September 1926] [Paris]

Since I find this gorgeous object on Mr. Hamilton's mahogony writing (or is it filing) desk I am forced to assume that this is where I am. Though I am still giddy from yesterday's violent exchange of Riviera Indian (c'est à dire indo-chine-ian) summer for Paris autumn. (Do you know anything more obscene than the effort of a horse chestnut to flower in Sept. when all its leaves are dead?)

First about your coming to Paris. I wish to point out that there is not only chocolate but a Monrachet 1915 which has never crossed the Manche — not even in a bathing suit.

If that doesn't move you the thought of chocolate is in vain.

For us it lies something as follows. We have been ordered to put our small boy on a Swiss mountain for the winter & there we are to go as soon as we can buy him everything a French doctor's ingenuity can conceive. Then we go to England. That would be around the 1 October. At which date, I understand[,] you will still be in London. But I also want to see your Paris extension. Why not try to do it? As for our return from Suisse — certainly the 27ᵗʰ or 28ᵗʰ of Sept.

Failing formal declarations of intention to visit these shores, however, I shall, D.V., call upon you at 65 Curzon St W 1 London about the 1 Oct.. — & bring you back with me.

yrs. faithfully.   Archibald MacLeish

ALS: DeU

To Martha Hillard MacLeish

Dearest Mother: 7 October 1926   Paris

Ada has written you all about our new and sumptuous apartment, property of Pierepont Morgan Hamilton & wife on beautiful Bois de Boulogne Paris France with maître d'hôtel chef & five maids & a governess. You should see us! Three baths! And a mechanical piano. And me with a valet!!!

Do write Norman: "Ada & Archie seem to be doing very well for themselves. They have a beautiful twelve room apartment with three baths and a salon sixty by thirty on the Avenue du Bois de Boulogne. They have a butler, a chef, a governess and five maids. They have a handsome Renault car with a liveried chauffeur. They give dinner parties for the Conte de Beaumont[1] (*surely* you know about Conte Etienne de Beaumont, Norman) and the Prince & Princess de Caraman-Chimay (the oldest aristocracy of Belgium, as Norman knows, don't you?) and Picasso, who is the greatest living painter (as of course no one in Philadelphia would know but we in Chicago admire his work very much) & Ambassador & Mrs. Philips[2] & a host of other celebrities. Their most intimate friend is the famous Baron d'Almeida of the house of d'Almeida da Gama. They have their oldest son (I think his name is Kenneth) in a fashionable Swiss School[3] and they are planning to spend the winter travelling in Germany, Austria & Russia. I believe they finance all this by their income plus Archies sales of poetry for which he now receives prices commensurate with his great reputation & Ada's income from the Opéra Comique. We are quite proud of them" —— and see what he says. Oh Lord — I'd love to hear it.

But don't tell him ① that the apartment is a gift & that the cost of upkeep even without rent is almost breaking us ② that the Renault is the French equivalent of a second hand Ford & the chauffeur gets $30 a month ③ That we hate the Prince & Princess Caraman Chimay & won't have 'em again — even if they'd come. ④ that Picasso is a great pal of Adas ⑤ that Ambassador & Mrs Philips think we are such a sweet, simple little artistic couple, ⑥ that Tony d'Almeida is going to marry a girl in Highland Park named Taffer who wants to be a Baronness (But she's in love with him too) ⑦ that Kenny's school is a medical prescription ⑧ that if we travel we travel 2nd Cl. Kl. Qul.. ⑨ that I still get $10 a poem — when they sell. ⑩ that Ada will be in the Comique as soon as Caré[4] hears her — but he hasn't yet ⑪ that we are bust! But what of it.

Streets In the Moon should be out about now. Do make your intelligent friends buy it. Its a good book.

Nobodaddy does pretty well. It gets fair reviews & staggers along. Not so badly as I expected.

Working hard on another long poem.

Mimi is your most adorable grandchild & some day you're going to know it.

Dearest love to father. We talk of him so much. Mimi asks about him every day.

Our love to Miss Tilly

And to you all our love   Archie

I can't answer your questions about politics. I have thought so little about it. I do think that, right or wrong, we have been about as clumsy over the debts as a nation could be. We have lost more here than we can ever repay ourselves for the loss of. I suppose the reason is that our statesmen are so just. Just that.

ALS: M

1. Étienne de Beaumont, an art connoisseur and patron; he had been the model for the title character in Raymond Radiguet's *Le Bal du Comte d'Orgel* (1924). 2. William Phillips, the American ambassador to Belgium mentioned by M in his letter to Ishbel MacLeish of 31 May 1924. 3. Chalet Marie José, in Gstaad, Switzerland. 4. Albert Carré, honorary director of the Opéra-Comique.

To Maurice Firuski

Dear Maurice: 29 October [1926] [Paris]

Well — are you coming? Bob Linscott is. Why not Maurice? I was almost knocked over by Bob's decision. I never thought he'd do it. And pleased to death. I'll try to make it worth his while. Last letter I wrote him I asked him if he wouldn't make you come along. He's only going to be here 3 wks & you & he & I could see quite a bit of the world. Then too you could come with your beloved Conrad. They sail the 10th of

November. Just time to pack your bag. Why not? I couldn't put you up here but that wouldn't disturb your Hamletic soul. Think of it!

H.M. agree with you about my keeping a two years tryst with silence. You don't need to worry — I write slower & slower every page. Pretty soon I'll be a week to a comma.

When are you going to send me my bill for Nobodaddy? Damn your eyes — I *know* I owe you a lot. *Please come across.*

By the bye — will you send a copy & a copy of the Pot of Earth to the Bones Library? Address Hugh S. Knox, Librarian, 309 St. Ronan St. New Haven. The boys are all crazy to read me in the original. Charge me.

Will you do me a job? Will you see what you can find in the way of early English (O.E.) poetry published with translations but giving some idea of O.E. verse forms? I mean really early — time of Layamon's Brut etc.. I doubt if there is much but I want to get at the swing of Anglo Saxon rhythms — Saintsbury[1] ought to have a bibliography. Don't go out of your way. It isn't pressing. Also will you get your girl to give me a list of the more literary or more interesting folk lore stuff — Golden Bough sort of thing. And something on the distribution of races — general.

I'm sorry about John. I hadn't known that sweet marriage could ever dissolve. I hope it wasn't too much of a wrench for you.

And how about coming to France   yrs affecly   Archie

(Do the Independent People ever pay their bills? They owe me for stuff published this year early or last fall. Keep whatever you can get out of them to cr. of my acct)   AMacl

ALS: NN

1. George E. B. Saintsbury (1845–1933), English literary critic.

To Ezra Pound[1]

Dear Pound: 16 November [1926]   Paris

Hemingway brought your letter around yesterday. Hence delay.

So far as I am concerned Old Problem resolves itself affirmatively or in the yes.

That is to say unless you object very strongly to seeing your own face in muddy water — this piece[2] being one which owes much — if not all — to a certain rhythm in your IInd Canto which said rhythm saved my for the time being life. It would run to 150 ll.. Also some shorter pieces if you wish.

Hemingway very uneloquent about purposes, that is to say limits, of proposed review. Except as to women which pleases me. Otherwise he is silent.

As to $ or Fr or L — if you need any for the printer I should be pleased to do what I can (Above address is misleading³ but I could at least aid)

If you decide to go on will you drop me a line with any commands pertinent?   yrs faithfully   Archie MacLeish

ALS: YCAL

1. American poet and expatriate (1885–1972). M did not meet Pound until 1939 and their correspondence was strained both by Pound's disdain for M's poetry and, later, by their mutual disdain for each other's political beliefs. Yet, as several letters in this volume indicate, M played a central role in the efforts, eventually successful, to bring about Pound's release from a lengthy incarceration in a mental institution following World War II.   2. The third, or "Bleheris," section of M's work in progress, *The Hamlet of A. MacLeish*, which section M had sent to Pound for possible publication in Pound's new review, *The Exile*.   3. The letter was sent from the Hamilton residence.

To Ezra Pound

Dear Pound   22 November [1926]   Paris

Variously and touching the mute keys.

Hemingway errs — thou also — as to the writers. There are millions of them. And they *all* write well. That isn't whats wrong. And you need a different word than Writer to club them with. The trouble is that they cannot speak, they cannot speak, they cannot speak. There is no intonation. There is no utterance. (Art thou there, truepenny?) As you yourself have ere these drabber days so pertinently remarked. The reason, if I may truthsay without unction of flattery, why I turn to your stuff when my blood changes to sand and the dry grains grate in the heart tubes, is that I do there *hear*. Speech beautifully. Lang-uage. Put it better. And if I steal, as I swear I never till this time did, a rhythm from your lines it is half willfully as knowing wherein excellence, and half unwilled as after long talk the voice fall.

I can name you ten thousand who can write. Do you want their names?

As to the others — of the four you name I know nothing save of Auslander and of him I know nothing good. He is a word fellow. With the labial not to say digital dexterity of a masturbating monkey and as little fecundity. Ernest likes the stuff of a young man named Shipman.¹ Shall we get some together?

As for my own stuff. Detailed situation is this. I have agreed at point of publisher's (Houghton Mifflin) gun to accept the invitation of one L. Untermeyer to send some stuff to his American Miscellany. I have also just published (first copy yesterday) a volume containing all my short stuff for the last couple of years. And I am now working on a longish sequence. So that I find myself with little short work on hand and what there is already committed to the Miscellany. That means that I can at the present time send you (a) either certain longish but self-supporting sections of my sequence, one of which seems to me to show signs and traces of the excessive admiration in which I hold your cantos, but is nevertheless, I believe, my own, or (b) the batch of short pieces intended for the Miscellany if and provided they could appear here in whole or in part before the appearance of that monumental work. If neither appeals to you I shall have to wait until I can send you some short bits with no strings attached. I shall begin to prepare the long pieces in attending a word from you.

If I seem to you too much the eager contributor and not enough the pote seeking a refuge from the stupid editors I can only reply that such is indeed the case. Not that the stupid eds have been any kinder to me than they have been to anyone else. But that I should rather appear under your editorial and poetic sig. than under any other in any case. Which is, I fear, all too clear.

Question demanding answer: When did you ever write like W.B.Y.?[2] Name seven.

Financial. You can rely on me for 100 of your 400 bucks the first year. And if the franc's recovery doesn't bust me for more.

As a reply to your magnificence this is indeed a hell of a letter. I can only say that the insomnia has got me and that every four words I put my foot through the mud. I'll see Ernest about TransMITTING at once.   yrs   AMacL

TLS: YCAL

1. Evan Biddle Shipman (1904–1957), a young poet and horse fancier then living in Paris. 2. William Butler Yeats.

To Ezra Pound

Ezrascibilissimus the Precise: 3 December [1926]   Paris

Regret long delay amounting some fraction of week between receipt of and reply to your most informative of twenty oddth ult.. Will say in extenuation that we were obliged by unforeseen contingencies to send ourself to Rouen for the wk nd and that, as we work more or less directly into a note book we have had to type out the accompanying. We send you the carbons because this goddam ribbon dont write for about two yards in the middle.

I have taken your orders literally. That is I have raped and ravished my note books and have included pieces that except for your instructions I should have kept to myself. I have entitled the unities "poems" not because I necessarily think so but to give you some idea where one leaves off and the next begins.

Certain of these go to Untermeyer Dec. 30 for publication as aforesaid in month of Feb.. If you will tell me which if any you could use I will at once reply whether or not the jew is underneath the lot. Also one long one goes to the American Caravan or whatever but that is later. Please don't consider my drivel about Wilson as a submission for publcn.[1] I wouldn't have you think me as thus far imposing upon your widely reported kindness to young authors. For purposes of communication I am Numbering the various pieces.

And very seriously. Please believe that you can count on me for any help within my power altogether aside from your decision about my stuff. My interest — and I am in no wise vending soft soap — is to see more Cantos.

yrs briefly but not briefly faithfully
Archie MacLeish

I am sending you one more piece – but anon.

TLS: YCAL

1. Along with copies of several poems intended for publication, M had enclosed (or perhaps sent separately at about the same time) a satiric twelve-line poem attacking Edmund Wilson as a sort of intellectual pervert. Though it was clearly not meant for publication, Pound compared it favorably to the other poems M sent, saying that in it M was more intent on his subject matter than on being poetic.

To Maurice Firuski

Dear Maurice: 18 December [1926] Paris

For the books a thousand thanks. I have enjoyed Bridges no end. The British laureate is so British. He fairly reeks of mashed potatoes. God what a race they are. When I hear Aiken — at second hand — praise 'em my mouth falls open with astonishmint. He even likes their goddam cooking. Now I admire their navy and the way they put in baths on the Persian Gulf and the way they polish leather and the remnants of their tailoring ability but I detest their cooking. And I don't like their cute little countryside. And as for the islanders themselves — well they're too red and too big and though they may be the only elocutioners of the langwidge once spoken by let us suppose Shakespeare who can get all around their consonants they are simply murderous to vowels. Put an "o" into an Englishman's mouth and it wont know whether it is an e or a u or just dust on the intake. Also consider the state of litritchure in that country. There are from three to eight great poems per week all announced in full in the critical columns of the London Weekly Times Literary Supplement. And there isn't a poet in the blinking isle if you exclude the Americans, the Irish and the very old. Who belong as it were to another country. Or try to. Not later than last night a brilliant young Englishman who writes for the New Statesman told me that Joyce had the dullest and emptiest mind that ever existed! I never should have guessed it! But that all goes to prove — something or other. And the women. The great open faces where teeth are teeth as Ada has it. There are French-men who deny that the islanders have women. But aside from miraculous parthenogenesis how do they explain Masefield? There he is. And he wasn't born at sea. He must have had a mother be she never so what do you call it. And anyway we've all seen them.

I have almost despaired over the book I am sending you.[1] It was to have been done a month ago and is still on the wheys. It is a volume by that eminent horse doctor G. Stein illustrated by probably the best living painter if you feel as I do about it. It ought to be a swell looking book from the time they're taking to [do] it. Oh, the painter is Juan Gris.

I am delighted you liked Streets In the Moon. I think myself it has my so far best stuff in it although there are inclusions I can't under-stand myself having made. I haven't yet seen a review of any kind but I am hoping the boys will be kind to it. My next will be different and I am taking your advise to take my time.

Bob was grand. The ideal guest. Never in the way and liked his breakfasts. It was fun batting around with him and seeing everything for the first time again. Particularly Chartres. I think I persuaded him about the English so called Cathedrals. At least he looks honest when he says things.

I am so sorry you have been at the bottom of the run again. I know vaguely what you mean though you may think I don't. This thing called time that is working in us always is a strange poison. It has its crises and it has its intervals. But it is only because we have always had it before our eyes that we are not continuously shocked by it. We soothe ourselves by calling it a river which bears us all along. But it is no such thing. It is an always changing in us which makes things different to us. As though we all carried the eternal dying in us which shall at last be our death. You can Billy Phelps[2] it or you can face it. Or, as Ada says, you can live day by day and die astonished. Which is a great saying but no comfort to you or to me. People like ourselves can only win through by biting on the nail. But there is a joy in that too. Come, isn't there?   affectionately yours   Archie

TLS: NN

1. Gertrude Stein's *A Book Concluding with As A Wife Has A Cow. A Love Story*, a deluxe limited edition with lithographs by Juan Gris, privately printed by D. H. Kahnweiler. 2. Professor William Lyons Phelps of Yale University.

To Ezra Pound

Dear Ezra: 29 December [1926]   Gstaad, Switzerland

Yours of the 5 Dec. here yesterday. I am enormously in your debt. I suppose nothing on earth is as difficult as to get oneself *criticised*. You can get reviewed by any ninny who can borrow a typewriter. The point is that criticism presupposes knowledge and of the two or three now living who *know* none but yourself, so far as I am informed, would take five minutes off for the purging of the contemporary what you call it.

The fundamental point of your criticism in my case is that I have not found my own speech. The negative of which is that you discover traces not only of E.P. but of T.S.E., G.S. & J.J..[1] As to these derivations — I am not particularly concerned. You can find any derivations you look for and if the stuff is good it doesn't matter. As here — I have never read G.S. except in advertised patches. But that doesn't touch your real point. And there I am forced — with considerably more pain than you might imagine — to agree that you are right. The situation, as nearly as I understand it, is this. I started to learn to write pretty late, having played with verse through a couple of years of the War and a law practise of three years. In the mean time I had gotten myself "educated". So that when I finally started I found myself with a lot of accepted ideas which tied me hand & foot. Then I began to discover that there were some who had been that way before me and who had gotten out. Chiefly you. Later Eliot. (This was about 1923) That was, I suppose, the most exciting thing that ever happened to me. And the result was that I accepted your road & your way of going it completely and altogether. I couldn't even imagine an alternative. With the consequence that you observe. Everywhere I arrived I arrived at your pace and everything I found out for myself I immediately found out more or less as you would have seen it. Nothing seemed fresh or real to me, nothing seemed my own, which didn't come that way. All of which is shameful. I admit it here to myself for the first time. But I must also add somewhat in self defense and somewhat in the interest of truth, that I have always felt (even in a poem like Bleheris, & even facing the patent debtorship) that the stuff *was* my own. Paradox if you will —. I have also felt that I was going along the way I had to go. That is, I preferred to do what I was doing rather than to choose one of the so easy recipes for novelty such as Mr. Cummings (rest his ashes) so deliberately chose. Please whatever gods are concerned you may be right in your "And that with one heave more, one crunch of the teeth, you ought to get through to your OWN". I wish I believed it. If you can kick, beat or lead the donkey on for Christ's sake do. Or is it worth the heave?

Forgive the tone of the confessional. And remind yourself that I know you much better than you do me & since long time.

As for more specific remarks.

Mode of Bleheris. I have not adopted this mode. I should never write another poem in that manner. The reasons why I adopted it here are stated in the foregoing read in the light of the subject matter of the piece. (And there's an odd thing. I know the sea & sailing extremely well. But when I tried to make it as real in words as it was to me in fact I *could* only use the mode which had before made it *verbally* real to me, viz. yours. I imagine — but without data — that I know sailing better than you do.)

Which brings me to

Ecbatan. And Herodotus. And your preëmption. I used Ecbatan (Hammadan=) because I have twice lived in the city and carry certain sensations which seem to me related to it. Herodotus yourself.

And lastly the question of *Subject. Content. Matter.* I have reservations. I think you are confusing something actual with a word which comes perilous near to being a prescription. Your war on "literature", your clean, hard, *real* poetry, is the most important cerebral [*MacLeish wrote in the margin:* no limitations to "cerebral" implied] activity of our time. But I think you are wrong in taking insistence on Subject as the affirmative of your negative. Rhetoric is bad. And one way of avoiding rhetoric is not to use it. And one way not to use it is to be in earnest. And one way to be in earnest is write what you're writing and not something else. But it doesn't follow that the mere and absolute (or whatever) presentation of subject is good writing. As your own stuff so damn well shows. Your Cantos (appropriate ones) aren't poems because of Malatesta's vitality. Why not admit that it is neither manner nor subject we're after but poems? May be true, as reverend and sagacious little Mr. Cocteau says, that to epauler gracefully doesn't make good shooting. But neither is the precisely pierced and subsequently exposed target good shooting. Good shooting is good shooting. And it helps to think what the target is going to look like after you've hit it. But it helps more to have a good gun rest & to know the wind.

I'm a fine one to be saying this to you. And don't think that I altogether misunderstand you. And don't think that I think (if it matters to you) that you run an exhibition of bull's eyes. I believe you are right in recommending to me that I write about the things I'm writing about. But pushed farther — I think Content is a theory like another. And I think you are a poet because you know how to make poems. And I think I'm not because I don't — yet.

But all this is beside the point. Which is that you have perfectly exposed my malady. And that your suggestion for a cure is, I know, sound. The trouble is that its you I've got to get over.

I can't thank you for what you've done for me. I merely hope to God I'm worth the trouble.

If I have anything in Feb. which I think has enough life in it to stand the trip to Rapallo I'll send it. As to the rest — let me know when you need cash moneys for the Review.

Wish I could make Rapallo now. Thanks for asking me to come. I'll do it in the spring if humanly possible.

Forgive the script.   yrs   Archie MacLeish

Have sent all of Mss transmitted to you which seemed passable to Untermeyer & the Caravan   A.MacL.

ALS: YCAL

1. That is, Pound, Eliot, Gertrude Stein, and James Joyce.

To Princess Bassiano (Marguerite Caetani)

Dear Princess Bassiano   1 January 1927   Gstaad

Forgive my delay in answering your two letters. My attempts to learn skiing have had a fairly disastrous effect on my thumb-joint and I have had to *forego* the making of small curves for almost a week. I can hardly claim to have learned to ski either. Which deprives me of whatever consolation.

About American contributions to Commerce. I am always glad to be of any service I can. I believe in Commerce and that would be quite enough even if there were not more. I wrote Wylie,[1] Cummings and Dos Passos before I left Paris (Dec. 20). We should hear from Wylie at once, from Cummings shortly if ever, and from Dos Passos when he gets back from Mexico. I have also been after Hemingway (the success of whose last novel is spectacular and will shortly put him in that category of the contemporary great where he least desires to see himself). Hemingway promises a good story for February first if not before. As to myself, if I can *break* through certain difficulties that are now besetting me, I shall have something for you in February or March. It is hard going just now because I have come to the end of *one run* and have got to turn. And these turns are hard. Particularly on a stiff slope. And with rutted snow. O — Aiken. I have asked him. As yet nothing has come. I think it will.

And I'm glad about Beaulieu.[2] I hope you won't feel the Mistral.

And that brings me to what I want to say to you about Perse.[3] I had no idea where the books came from. But I had long heard of Leger Leger and I wanted to read him under any name. So I started *Anabase*. There are three or four books in a writer's life which are like the changes of direction in a long valley — the cols where the world opens up again and you take a breath and go on. *Anabase* is such a book to me. I believe it is very great poetry. But I cannot tell. It is too close to me. Perse — let him deny it — is my blood brother. Infinitely wiser and infinitely better. But mine. You will see that I cannot thank you for that gift. But that I am grateful with all my heart please believe.

More when I hear from America.   yours   Archie MacLeish

TCO: KNODEL

1. Elinor Wylie (1885–1928), the American poet then married to William Rose Benét. 2. A seacoast town in the south of France. 3. Alexis Saint-Léger Léger (1889–1975), the French poet and diplomat who wrote under the pseudonym St.-John Perse, later became a close friend of M's.

To Robert N. Linscott

Dear Bob: 5 January 1927   [Paris]

Thanks awfully for your note. Missed you like a hell for a week & miss you still. It was grand of you to come. Kwan Yin looks down on your bed & my back in helpless pity.

Had a good 2 wks in Suisse with Ernest. Ginnie[1] there too. Ginnie very funny at high altitudes.

Pound liked the Bleheris fragment & crapped on the rest. Pound has too many rules. The rules of revolution are as revolting as the rules of reaction. And there are more of them.

Glad Streets in The Moon is selling. Never yet have received my copies. Will you have 'em sent?

No reviews yet. Untermeyer is doing it for Canby[2] & Tate for the Nation.[3] Somebody named Winter for Poetry tells me via Tate it is a "great book".[4] He ought to read more. Thanks for Priapus.[5] Write when you can.   yrs affecly   Archie

ALS: MH

1. Virginia Pfeiffer, sister of Hemingway's future wife Pauline Pfeiffer. 2. "MacLeish Emerges," *The Saturday Review of Literature* 3 (12 February 1927), 578–579. 3.

"Toward Objectivity," *The Nation* 124 (16 February 1927), 185–186. **4.** Yvor Winters, in a review of *Streets in the Moon* in *Poetry* 29 (February 1927), 278–281, praised the book for its "remarkably high percentage of completely and beautifully achieved poems." **5.** Presumably Conrad Aiken's *Priapus and the Pool*, published by Dunster House in 1922, or perhaps Aiken's *Priapus and the Pool and Other Poems* (New York: Boni & Liveright, 1925).

To Robert N. Linscott

Dear Bob: 25 January [1927]   [Paris]

Tanks for yr 2 jolly ltrs (as Pound w'd put it)[.] Must tell you about Pound. Pound wrote me that he would have thought that I would have known better than to mention Ecbatan in a ms intended for his eye: why didn't I open my Herodotus & find another that hadn't been preëmpted by him. I replied that it had taken me four weeks to get to Ecbatan — that as a result I had paid some attention to the city — & that I named it because I had been taken by it. And as for Herodotus — he had mentioned Herodotus not I. He wasn't a bit happy about that. The old turd!

As for the Anthology.[1] Coincident with yr letter comes letter from Tate saying he's going ahead & would love to sign up with H.M. if they'd have him. My function is editorial — suggestion — veto — criticism. He writes the introd., makes the selection & is responsible for the book. If he can't be less academic in tone than he was in the introd. to a book by one Hart Crane[2] God help us. But I'll keep after him. His address is 27 Bank St. N. Y.. Why not write him & tell him to send you his prospectus? Remember that my name doesn't appear — if that makes any difference. I think it ought to be a damn fine book. And I think you people would put yourselves at the front of the modern stuff by publishing it — if you care for that. Reference my remark above — Tate *is* academic in tone. But only in tone. He's intelligent as Hell. And if necessary I'll rewrite parts of the introd.. I've saved all my rights.

He may ask for an adv. on royalties! Never mind that. He's sane.

Thanks for the Atl. Rev.. Untermeyer, Aiken, Tate, Winter et al ought to be appearing soon. And here Ernest has had 1000 clippings to date. The lot of the bard is hard.

My best to Greenslet   Affec. yrs   AMacL.

ALS: MH

1. M and Allen Tate had been corresponding for some months about an anthology of modern poetry to be partially subsidized by M. Plans for the project collapsed some time after this letter was written. 2. Tate had written a foreword to *White Buildings: Poems by Hart Crane* (New York: Boni & Liveright, 1926).

To Ernest Hemingway

Dear Pappy: [14 February 1927] [Paris?]

Just to ack. receipt of *Pursuit Race*

All I am, in this business, is a gadget for receiving & forwarding. As I told you before in re *Alpine Idyll* I do *no editorial work* for any man including Barsiano. Anything you want to publish I receive & send on. And I say nothing to nobody*. [*MacLeish wrote in the margin:* *no expressions of opinion. I can't do it without being either your agent or a lady editor. And I don't want to be either.] B. understands that perfectly. You'll hear from her direct. If she takes the story let me know at once & I'll write her for the money.[1]

Nothing to thank me for. I didn't suggest your name. All I did was talk up price.

Pound is crazy. Last letter he asked me to learn Arabic so as to write like myself. Also have something to talk to him about when we meet. I'm getting a bit fed up with the Ezraic assumption that he is a Great Man. Let the rest of us say so for a while. Nothing on earth is worse than a literary gent talking about his own stuff.

Had an idea about [Sherwood] Anderson the other day. Trouble with Anderson is he thinks naïveté & honesty are the same thing. Which they damn well aren't. Honesty is very hard. You may have to write like H. James to be honest. Or you may have to write like the primer to be honest. But to assume that because you sound childish you are therefore true is the real bunk. But I've met him since my last letter & I like him. He told me about your correspondence over the Torrents. Them letters ought to be published. They sound just grand. Love to Pfeif & Pfeiffer[2] & to Pappy   A.

ALS: JFK

1. *Commerce* did not publish either of Hemingway's stories. 2. Pauline and Virginia Pfeiffer.

To Allen Tate

Dear Tate: [*c.* 16 February 1927] Paris

Read your poems with interest and excitement. Sent 'em off to Pound. Don't know if they are Successful because don't know what word means. But you've got your own speech and you make it *say*. Which is the point. [*MacLeish wrote in the margin:* Also I like them. If that's permissible!] Do you want these copies back? Because you won't without a fight with Pound who never sends back anything.

Also read your review.[1] My quarrel with you is one of nomenclature

— like all good quarrels. Appreciate value of "success" and "failure" as substitutes for the old heavenly twins of criticism. They have a certain freshness. But [I] feel they are extremely dangerous. They carry with them a faint taint of their competitive and win or lose origin. To my mind it is only possible to say that a work of art is a success by assuming that the artist was trying to solve a given aesthetic or other problem and finding that he succeeds[.] Since the solution of such a problem is never explicit with a first rate artist the test becomes a very incidental test. To me the statement that the Pot Of Earth is a failure simply doesn't mean anything: because to me it contains a good deal of good poetry and is dramatically effective. To you the phrase means that you don't like the poem (i.e. very roughly — you understand). I.e. it is a paraphrase of your reaction. And I should say a confusing paraphrase. Also it tends to produce a kind of absoluteness which recalls — but vaguely I grant you — Wilson's "The Waste Land Is The Most Considerable Poem Yet Written By An American".[2] A statement which probably did more to destroy [*MacLeish wrote in the margin:* No. Because it exists toujours. But to crack it — to crack it.] Wilson's critical reputation than any ten others. Albeit the statement was true.

God knows I'm not advising you on Your Critical Vocabulary. And I'm all for courageous iteration. But I feel myself that the true post of criticism is not at the finish line to hand out the prizes but way back along the road. You can never say with any certitude who *has* won and the knowledge is only interesting to the papers. But you can say a lot about a man's running — particularly if, like yourself, the critic can run himself — and what you say about that will not only help the boys, it will be better commentary on the performance.

Please don't misunderstand me. My quarrel as I said at the beginning is abstract. I do happen to think you are wrong about the Pot Of Earth and I am quite sure you are wrong about Einstein. But that isn't the point. I am enormously flattered that you liked the later things. No. The point is verbal. Can you say a poem is a success or a failure? I say no. Either you assume that the artist was trying to do something other than write a good poem and say (as Eliot says of Hamlet) that he failed because the poem isn't something *more* (or *less*) — in which case you say — Eliot said — precisely nothing.[3] Or you say with a show of absolute rightness to which you are not entitled that the poem doesn't move you etc etc — the old problem. What do you say? I don't mean what do you say about my two poems. That isn't important and we're past that anyway. Neither do I mean what do you say in defense of your article. It needs none and for myself I'd never change a word of it. But what do you say for your gol-dinged *words?*

Don't expect anything of Pound. He's cucku. A foin pote but no critc. Thinks one Cheever Dunning our best yng pt!!!⁴

yrs AMacL

Have just reread your review. This is all cheese. You do a fine surgical job & you have a right to apply your epithets when you're through. I take it all back. Except that I *don't like them woids.*

TLS: NjP

1. *See* M to Robert N. Linscott, 5 January 1927, note 3. **2.** Wilson had made the statement in the essay cited in M to Allen Tate, 26 July 1926, note 3. **3.** A reference to the chapter entitled "Hamlet and His Problems" in Eliot's *The Sacred Wood* (1920). **4.** *The Exile*, No. 2 (Spring 1927), contained a poem and a short story by Dunning as well as a laudatory article about him by Pound.

To Ernest Hemingway

Dear Pappy: [20 February 1927] [Antibes]
  That's what comes of writing in the

margin¹ —

  your best friends mistake you & think that a guy who would
             between the lines.
  write in the margin would write   So you go
  & compose a long letter full of various ways of saying that
  I'm a turd & all filled with expert blocks for undelivered
  blows. What the Hell! I never meant none of them things
  you say I couldn't have meant. What I meant was that I
  wasn't going to get myself embroiled with either you or
  Bassiano by expressing any opinions either way since I was
  neither yr agt nor her MS reader but just a poor guy who had
  agreed to get a story from a promising young Author. And
  the result is that I'm embroiled with you up to the ears. (I
  haven't heard from the Prances.) Also you ask me point blank
  my opinion which one of the reasons why I refused to give
  it was that both you & I know its no good. Well I'll now
  provide it. Though why you want it I can't say. My opinion
  is that I don't like that story. I remember your telling me
  that there were six good poems in Streets In The Moon &
  that that was a high average. I can beat that. I have never
  before seen a single story of yours I didn't like. Of course I
  admit to degrees — degrees all the way from a great story
  like the Killers, which is still one of the swellest things that
  ever happened to me, down to Mr. & Mrs Elliot (which John
  [Bishop] incidentally thinks is very good too) & the Roman

Soldier story, which I like but with reservations. But the Pursuit Race took me all wrong. (I'll lay myself right open for you to stick pins in.) I thought the first paragraph sounded like a parody of your stuff & had nothing honest to do with the story. And I thought the story itself missed fire by that narrow fraction of an inch which is the difference between failure & success in work as close to the bone as yours. It will now transpire that *The Pursuit Race* is Mr. Hemingway's finest story!

That's all. Well, I take no pride in my opinions & I have offered this particular opinion to no man. I don't see why you want it.

After that do you want my opinion of *A Simple Enquiry*? Well, whether you do or not, I think its in your real manner, a fine, cool, clean piece of work, sure as leather, & hard and swell.* [*MacLeish wrote in the margin:* *Ten things "said" for every word written. Full of sound like a coiled shell. Overtones like the bells at Chartres. All that stuff you can't describe but only do — & only you can do it.] Can I send it to Bassiano? I can't quite read what you write about it in your letter. I'll just say that you sent it for me to see & that I'm sending it on too.

As for me — God I wisht I was wid you. I can't go through. We're having a terrible time finding a place to live. We've just about decided to give it up. Rents are awful (when you count in the tax) & I can't borrow money to buy without having a fight with my best brother. We may have to move into 44 rue du Bac when Peter [Hamilton] comes April 1. I'll tell you if we do. Its probable.

Reviews are coming along. Helpful review by Aiken in New Republic[2] & by one Ivor Winter in Poetry. Both guys discover that I'm the first important poet since the Vorticist-Imagist etc business. What do you think of that, Pappy? Pappy never guessed Archie was an important poet. Well, well. Neither did Ezra. Well, well, well. Archie must talk about his own WORKS more. Perhaps now Pappy wont publish article outlined in Zaragoza saying that The Pot of Earth is shit. Pappy wouldn't say that about an important poet. And anyway he'd have to read the book first & that would be a what you call it. But then there's a guy in the N.Y. Herald Tribune who would agree. Louis Bromfield carefully sent me the clipping.[3] Nice Louis. What does he think I live in Paris for?

As for Ezra — I'm getting more & more doubtful about that bird. You say he's one of the few who *know*. He may be but I like hell don't think so. Got a letter from him last night advising me if not to study Arabic at least to study Gaelic so as to develop an idiom of my own & warning me to choose between being a literary guy & being a poek [*sic*]. I replied that I'd choose the former — that the most literary thing known to me was the attempt to escape from literature — viz Da Da & Paul Eluard et al. — that after all we *were* writers, not happy children — that the trouble with a reformer is that he's always got to be against something — that this business of trying to learn to write like somebody nobody had imitated yet in order not to write like anybody else is crap — that why in hell should we let ourselves get chased up into the ravines just because other people had farmed the good land before us — that the really great boys have been interested in writing poems not in writing poems differently — that why are we so scared of a cliché anyway — & in conclusion that I was satisfied in advance he wouldn't like the pieces of literature I had produced & I wasn't sending them. Honest to God, Ernest, that guy is as full of fears as a maiden school teacher & as full of shit as a cess pool. You can see it in his stuff. When he forgets that he is a reformer with a mission, when he forgets that he hates literature & that he writes with the style of E. Pound, he's grand. And when he's putting over his theories of how a guy ought to write he stinks. We all owe him a lot. And he knows it. But he doesn't know why.

Also, rebellions are useful things — but no rebel was ever any good after peace was declared . . .

Forgive all this tripe. I've been taking advice from aged maidens too long & I was bound to blow up some time. My love to Pf. & Pfr   Yrs always   A

Yes G & S are here — Antibes

ALS: JFK

1. *See* the marginal comment in paragraph two of M to Ernest Hemingway, 14 February 1927. 2. "Another Murex," *The New Republic* 49 (9 February 1927), 337. Aiken also reviewed *Streets in the Moon* in *The Independent* 118 (26 February 1927), 246. 3. Louis Bromfield (1896–1956), an American novelist and journalist then living in New York, had presumably sent M Newton Arvin's review of *Streets in the Moon* entitled " 'Time — Is It Time Still?' " from *New York Herald Tribune Books*, 16 January 1927, page 4.

To Maurice Firuski[1]

Dear Maurice: 14 June [1927]   Ashfield, Massachusetts

Wot a guy you are. Cunningham Graham[2] is right of course. And those are just the three I want. But no more. Now can you get me the Bernal Diaz?[3] Better write me what Merriman[4] recommends before ordering as I am damn well broke at the moment. Wish you would also get me a book to teach myself Spanish or anyway the rudiments.

Also don't forget to write me if anyone else has ever used Cortes for a long poem — that is, if you know. And you would know. And keep it all under the hat as I wont be able to start for another half year anyway.

Sorry they're troubling you. I've said nothing and certainly shall not.

As for a chin — did you know the drive up here from Boston was one of the best in the world? I'd love to see you. When could you come? In another week or so I could put you up in the house. But even now I could put you up in a damn fine Inn in the Village. Write me.

Would it bother you if I sent down some law books to sell to the Coop? I suppose they still buy them. Say so if it would. I'll send them straight to the Coop if that will be easier and tell them to pay you.

                                      yrs very affec   Archie

TLS: NjP

1. The MacLeishes had returned from France in May. Having had a partial reconciliation with Aunt Mary Hillard, they were staying at her Ashfield home while M looked for a permanent home for his family and, at the same time, projected a long poem on the conquest of Mexico, published, in 1932, as *Conquistador*.   2. Robert Bontine Cunninghamc Graham (1852–1936), a British travel writer, had published biographies of Hernando de Soto (1903) and of Bernal Díaz del Castillo (1915), and *The Conquest of the River Plate* (1924).   3. A. P. Maudslay's 1908 Hakluyt Society translation of Bernal Díaz del Castillo's *True History of the Conquest of New Spain* (1632) was M's principal source in the writing of *Conquistador*.   4. Roger Bigelow Merriman, a professor of history at Harvard, was the author of the four-volume *Rise of the Spanish Empire* (1918, 1925, 1934).

To Ernest and Pauline Hemingway

Dear Pappy and paulinda: 19 June [1927]   Ashfield

(Here comes Louis with the Scotch. Pull in your legs you bloated week-ender)

How be you? My Gord (Scuse, pappy) but I'm homesick for you two and a nice nip of something out at Montsouris and the rain coming up back of the terrasse and the profound literary apothegms (look 'em up, pappy, look 'em up) which always grace our mutual conversations. I could write a sweel history of my life out of the things pappy and me have done together what with Bayonne and the smell of wet bark and the barges going by in the thin sunshine while we waited for it to be time to get into a garage and the flat light on the square at Tharagotha and the smell of melting snow on our pants at the station bar at Gstaad and all those swell talks we had with pappy up to his eyes in La Pedale and me trying to interest him in General Culture and that afternoon on the high land going out to Chartres with guys ploughing on the flat way off and the inside of my hip bones god only knows how sore and getting pleasantly stupified in front of the fire out on the Avenue du Bois in that blasted aptmt only pappy could take the curse off of. But who am I to do justice to these mutual I trust memories. My only hope is that Pappy will immortalize us all in five pages and couldn't he do it though or couldn't he if he remembered them the way I do right now with all this rain and the trees too green and a half furnished house cold as a deserted cellar and no one within twenty five miles to talk to but Bill Bullitt the American aristocrat who is so busy taking a view of America he has forgotten to see any thing for the last twelve years[1] and couldn't see me anyway — not if I saw him first. Not around here.

And what are you up to? Down at Antibes are you? And listening to the Murphys tell how they broke with the MacLeishes because they really couldn't let anyone act as though anyone could ever have responsibilities toward anyone? Or how? In Spain perhaps? Or spending the weekend with dear Bassiano out at Versailles? Write us.

This place isn't so bad. But the golf course (shut up) is worse than I dared to hope. The first green is beside the front porch so that three out of every seven players have a six to eleven chance of holing out in your iced tea and do. However this is all transient. We have just about bought the town farm down at Salisbury Conn[2] with a couple of hundred acres of wood land and a good ole house built for an Inn with rooms for Pappy and Pauline and Jinny and good lake swimming in summer and good skeeing in winter if ever and when we come back next summer we'll be there and will you? Expect to get to Paris about November. Tell you the date when we know. No litrry news. Aint seen nothing but Wilson's verdict that 'emotionally and intellectually Mr. MacLeish talks through his hat'.[3] And what does that leave of Archie? When is the Killers coming out? Or have I missed it?

all my love to you both and ditto for Ada.

It was grand of you to send us a wire. I am

by cricky   yours   Archie

TLS: JFK

1. William C. Bullitt (1891–1967), a member of the American delegation to the Paris Peace Conference following the world war, had bitterly repudiated the Treaty of

Versailles and retired to private life in Ashfield, Massachusetts. (*See also* M to Dean Acheson, 17 November 1919.) **2.** The MacLeishes did buy a property in Salisbury, but its former role as that town's poor farm so upset Ada that they quickly sold it and bought another, their long-time home, in Conway, Massachusetts. **3.** Edmund Wilson, "The Muses Out of Work," *The New Republic* 50 (11 May 1927), 319–321.

To Sylvia Beach[1]

Dear Sylvie: 23 June [1927]   Ashfield

You'd think I might have written before! Well — the first month in America is a wallop. I haven't done anything I should. And less I wanted to. Of which this was one.

Dubliners I brought home & gave to my friend Firuski, an excellent book dealer, who agreed to sell it with no charge to us. He is now trying Rosenbach[2] but as yet he has had no luck with him. Later he'll try his fancy list. I'm sure we'll put it over.

I get awful homesick for you & Adrienne.[3] Don't we have good times. Gosh, I like you two! There are so few *adults* in the world.

Has Bécat[4] come through with the photos? I'm waiting with anxious hope.

Ashamed to see I put your bill in my pocket & came home! Now I've got to buy some francs to pay off. Terribly sorry. Sending it as soon after July 1 as I can get to a bank. Love to you both from Ada & Mimi & yrs

                                                                    AMacL

ALS: NjP

1. Beach (1887–1962) was the proprietor of Shakespeare and Company, the Paris bookshop. **2.** A.S.W. Rosenbach, the American book collector and dealer. M refers to the proof copy of Joyce's *Dubliners* (Maunsel edition), which Joyce had asked M to sell for him in the United States. **3.** Adrienne Monnier, the owner of a Paris bookshop on the rue de l'Odéon and a close friend of Sylvia Beach's. **4.** Paul-Emile Bécat, an artist who was Adrienne Monnier's brother-in-law.

To Marianne Moore[1]

Dear Miss Moore: 27 June [1927]   Ashfield

I have just had forwarded to me from France the proof of Cowley's review of *Streets in the Moon*.[2] You must know, knowing my opinion of Cowley, how much I am pleased. He has picked out the thread that gives those pieces what unity of emotion they have with a delicacy and precision that is beautiful to watch, and he has given his excerpts from the poems a context in his own phrases which gives them an appearance of value I had not thought they possessed. I wish, when you see him, you would thank him for me as warmly as it is proper for one to thank one's judges.

It was most kind of you to let me see the article. Won't you add to that kindness the further act of sending something to the Princess Bassiano for *Commerce?* Her last request to me before I left was to try to get contributions from you. I have bothered you too often about this I know but I shant let you off until you have given her something. She will pay as the Dial would and she will assure you the very best translator.

I am also to try to get a shortish prose piece from work in progress from Glenway Wescott.[3] Can you help me to get in touch with him? And with Cowley from whom I am to ask a poem? May I write them both in your care?

Thanking you again for your kindness, I am

most sincerely yours
Archibald MacLeish

TLS: YCAL

1. American poet (1887–1972), then editor of *The Dial.* 2. Malcolm Cowley, "The Margins of Infinity," *The Dial* 82 (June 1927), 516–517. 3. American novelist and poet (b. 1901).

To Sylvia Beach

Dearest Sylvienne: 13 August [1927]   Ashfield

The doctor has my tonsils: who has yours?

Any way I have the three photos and I think I'm lovely and awfully poetic and kind of puzzled by life and I hope you both are too — I was going to say I hope you both are two but that would have been LITOTES because you both are TWO as all the world knows and there aren't any nouns good enough to fill that out — only I'm not really so bald though SUFFERING does ripen the sparse sheaves as someone must have said before me, and I haven't satyrs ears though passionate in a good cause or without one only too too often and I don't think I'm SLY that way though Scotch by trade and long bred to it. Anyway I'm lovely — and I think the salient, if I may say so Miss Beach and Miss Monnier, characteristic of my nature is innocence. A kind of innocence of the kidney. Congenital and proof against Mr. William Bullitt who is here taking an aristocrats view of America which is done by standing back to the object and leaning over so as to have one's own tenderloin in short perspective. But that is all beside the point. Mr Bullitt is a power in the world or was before he left and knew many important people by their last names first and has written a really significant novel[1] which is like Ulysses in that the text is read from the top of the page down — provided, of course, it *is* read.

Well, well — shall I tell you about my tonsils? And here is a check for ninety fran[c]s for Sylvia to give Adrienne and please order a dozen more pictures of Mr. MacLeish, the New England farmer poet and let me know the cost. And please keep the original SAFE chez vous. And please subscribe to all these Fargue N.R.F. reprints of poetry — poetry only — and give my love to EVERYBODY and tell Joyce — O tell Joyce he is a POET. God what a swell *book*.[2] Family album, says Pound! He'll eat that. And our love to thee both our love to thee both   A.

TLS: NjP

1. *It's Not Done* (1926).   2. Joyce's *Pomes Penyeach*, which had recently been published.

To Ernest and Pauline Hemingway

13 August [1927]

Dear Pappyline — or Paulypap — or Paupline —   Ashfield

When do we go to Switzerland? Kenny is going back to Gstaad. So that's a starter provided you want a starter. I don't. But I suppose nothing will satisfy you but a pair of Chinese Chippendale skees and the Elburz range. Myself nearer home will do. In fact you could skee right here if there were any reason for it and it weren't too cold. But I just LIVE for skeeing. And I want to get you all dated up so those clever Geoffrey Dodges wont ask you down to their private run in the Novgorod Alps and what would become of poor us? Fancy. I'm trying to learn to talk like Bill Bullitt who is up here taking his favorite view of the Republic through a shall we utter it pig's ear and who in turn talks like Sheean[1] who it appears was *not* educated for a priest as represented but is having trouble with his love life just the same and when he knew dear Mrs Bullitt was going to have a baby he just cried. Which brings me by a not too natural sequence to Mrs. Bullitt herself[2] who says she knows ALL about Pappy and I didn't press her because who am I to be told ALL about Pappy which I dare say he doesn't know himself but anyway she does and what I want to know is how does she? because I understood Pappy knew her very slightly and respected him for it and lets NAIL that lie. I wont have more than every other person I meet know ALL about Pappy. It gets monotonous. I know what fame is. I've read about it in Mr. Pages letters.[3] And I know Pappy must suffer. But has every goddam turtle eating rabbit scotcher in North-Eastern Mass have to know more about Pappy than I do which is what I want to know.

Nothing has happened since my last communication except that Fifty

Grand has come out in the Atlantic at #1 position with an explanatory note in The Contributors Column in which it appears that Pappy is still a bull-fighter in spite of frequent denials by the bulls and others and that Prize Fighting though immoral is a proper subject for tragic treatment and that a foul is a blow delivered you know where — try it on your self. Also Mr. MacLeish's epoch making perhaps poem has appeared in the Criterion[4] without comment except what I saw on the back of the Ms and I'm not boasting about that. Also Mr. MacLeish's truly lyric tonsils have come out in the Hartford Hospital and my throat feels like Hell and we'll be back in about three months and see that you're there when we do. Love to you both and Jinny who's in the country.   A.

P. S.   I think youre pretty damn magnificent about the Hearst business and wiser than Solomon and well — grand.

P. P. S.   I always knew and so told you that Gerald would get over whatever was eating him the moment he saw you. I didn't know for sure that you'd get over your irritation with Gerald ditto. These damn school girl quarrels of Geralds are the things that make it so hard for me to believe in his affection. Relationships built on your personality and my personality just aren't relationships. I may be vulgar and prep school and all that but I still want friendships and no whipped up substitutes. And in a friendship Mr. H. you pay for what you get.

P. P. S.   Solomon was a very wise man who lived a long time ago and wrote feelingly of LOVE.

P. P. S.   Which doesn't mean I'm not all for a Murphy-Hemingway revival. Nor that I shouldn't be sick if Gerald had decided our relationship must END. Simply that the whole business is on the plane Gerald has chosen to live on — viz, Amusement. Taint serious.

TLS: JFK

1. James Vincent Sheean (1899–1975), American journalist and novelist. 2. Mrs. Bullitt was the former Louise Bryant Reed, widow of John Reed. 3. Burton J. Hendrick, *The Life and Letters of Walter Hines Page* (Garden City, N.Y.: Doubleday, 3 volumes, 1922–1925). Page (1855–1918) had been literary adviser to Houghton Mifflin Company, editor of *The Atlantic Monthly*, and United States ambassador to Great Britain. 4. "Land's End/For Adrienne Monnier," *The Criterion* 6 (July 1927), 14.

To Harry and Caresse Crosby[1]

Dear Harry and Caresby Caross   [c. 13 August 1927] [Ashfield]
or Painted and red Skeleshores[2] (which by the way where are they?) or however: Are you actually going to Poisia? (I mean where are they to be had?) And if so are you going to stand vacant at 19 rue de Lille or are you filling yourself all three floors and lovely cellashoop with Boston

relatives? (Boston relatives to what?) Because if not we know two nice youngish though not so young as once Americans of mildly lit'ry tastes named MacLeish who would be so careful of your hearth and pay large rentals and add tone to the neighborhood. Write me at once that you wont do it or we shall die of longing. We'll take it for any combination of months you can mention. Kenny will be en Suisse again and Mimi is like feathers.

Utterly no news here except that they had rats at 44 rue du Bac and a doctor in Hartford has my tonsils and a lot of good may they do him.

We are addressable at ASHFIELD, MASS..

aff'ly   Archie MacLeish

TLS: SIU-C

1. Harry (1898–1929) and Caresse (1892–1970) Crosby were wealthy American expatriates from Boston who lived in Paris and ran the Black Sun Press. 2. M is playing with the names of three Crosby books: Caresse's *Crosses of Gold* (1925), her *Painted Shores* (1927), and Harry's *Red Skeletons* (1927), all collections of poetry.

To Ernest Hemingway

Dear Pappy: 18 September [1927]   Ashfield

That was damn fine of you and made me feel grand.[1] I don't expect our mutual affection to run to our works — though yours have always had mine — but it takes all the crums out of the bed to have your praise. And aside from all that it gives me a lot of confidence I need awful bad after a summer in this melon eating land where Millay is a great poet, Tate is a great man of letters and only man is vile.

Thank you.

We laughed ourselves sick over Pauline's epistle. The touch about Sara and the gypsy girl was — is — immortal. I hope you have had as good a time as it sounds. Though it doesn't seem humanly possible to have so good a time. We have been buying and selling houses and now that we have a fine one we spend all our time thinking about it which is all right but not productive of much. However when its done it will be worth the trouble. If you'll spend some time in it.

We'll be back in November and see that you're in Paris. And write once anyway before that.

The Bullitts are a pair of deuces. And not wild either. Bill has just discovered the Free Life — at fifty thousand a year. And Louise is always trying to play the Dowager Queen with a tin monocle and a pair of property tights. They make Archie ache.

Fifty Grand in French! It was fine. But the poor French will never know what they missed. French is a hell of a language. But it was a grand test of that story. To have it go over like that even in N.R.F.

language was a triumph. Your theory about the good stuff always translating is bunk. Nobody else can write your kind of stuff within twelve laps of you. And how in hell do you expect a hack translator to do it. A writer writes with words not plots like Bloofield.² And the words are different. They aint the same words. No, your theory is bunk. But your story is a knockout and no foul either. Even in French I got hollow in the solar plexus.

Take the history of the same piece in the Atlantic. Bob tells me the thing was full column news in every paper in the east. They reviewed it like a book. And old Sedgwick was as proud of himself as though he had had a baby. Went around telling the folks downtown how many cancellations he had had. It was the big event of the year in these parts.

Next to Sacco and Vanzetti.³ That was a stink. Nobody cared. The only decent fight was put up by the defenders of our ancient institutions. The communists used it for propaganda but the only birds to get in jail were the sons of Boston's oldest families and the New York Poets. They had the jail covered with machine guns the night of the execution but not a shot was fired. I'll enclose the story in the local paper. Now its all stale and no one will talk about it. Wash their hands. The only trouble is that it must have hurt Sacco and Vanzetti a little to be killed. The fight has gone out of these people. Me for instance. I was wild about it. So I argued a long time with some Boston lawyers and then changed the subject. A great race. Stink. Luke warm. Spew them out. And perhaps the boys were really guilty. O hell!

love to you both a[nd] Jinney who's in Portugal   A.

TLS: JFK

1. Probably a reference to Hemingway's praise of M's "Land's End/For Adrienne Monnier." 2. Louis Bromfield. 3. Italian-born anarchists whose execution on August 22, after repeated appeals of their 1921 conviction for robbery and murder, had been attended by intense international protest.

To Robert N. Linscott

Dear Bob: 18 September [1927]   Ashfield

You're a swell guy and I hope you go a long way and why not? Thanks for the book though I hate to take the young man's only copy. Please thank him too. Its a *damn fine* book.¹ I'm amazed at the way Conrad handles the conversation of his Social Inferiors. How did he get to know them? And there is some swell poetry in it. My only objection is filed to the use of psychological jargon. But I'm sure he had a good reason. And of course the book ought never to have been published. Its too damn painful. As [*several words lost, probably the follow-*

ing: for American Poetry 1927; A] Miscellany I agree with you with the exception of MacLeish. *Commerce* — its a shame. The goddam Boston public. *What* does it read besides Bromfield and Millay? And the suppressed books. Well, you did your best and thank you for it. Be gentle with Bassiano.[2] [Phelps] Putnam was here for a couple of days and showed me some of his new stuff. I'm probably insane but it seemed bad to me. It all runs to abstractions — Death and Fate and Chance and all that tripe. Even the bawdy side of it is abstracted. Bones are all right if they remind you of flesh. But synthetic bones wont fool anyone but Wilson. I dont mean that he wont have fine reviews and sell a lot. He will. That's the worst of it. But Mum!

God bless you   A

TLS: DLC

1. Probably Conrad Aiken's novel *Blue Voyage* (New York: Charles Scribner's Sons, 1927). 2. Linscott may have attempted to arrange for the distribution of *Commerce* in Boston.

To Wyndham Lewis[1]

My dear Lewis: [*c.* December 1927?]   Paris

Just ran into Hemingway with your address. Illegible but imagined[.]

I am making bold to send you a copy of a book I published last year.[2] *Not* to show you what a hell of a guy I am (irrelevant & conceivably I'm not). *Nor* to provide you (as you might think on perusal) with a little rough material for the crucifixion of another anonymous & deserving American in a foot note. *But* because I want you to read a poem in it called EINSTEIN. I don't think you will *learn* anything from reading it. But I think it would amuse you to see an attempt by an obviously not very well informed person to shoot the kind of mentality presented by you under the names Whitehead & Alexander.

I don't get your angle on Pound. Is obsession with *The Past* equivalent to Bergsonian-Whiteheadian-Alexandrian-Time-Durée obsession? If so every poet of any stature has been so obsessed. Never have met Pound but his poetry which I admire seems to me quite free of the taint. Mine — you will find — if you read it — reeks with Time-romanticism. Curious I should like your attacks so well!

Thanks for letting me have lunch with you. I enjoyed it enormously

Archibald MacLeish

ALS: NIC

1. Lewis (1886–1957) was a writer and painter who, with Ezra Pound, had founded and edited the vorticist magazine *Blast* (1914–1915). His *Time and Western Man*, an anti-Bergsonian, antiromantic treatise published in 1927 in London, is referred to in this and the following letter. 2. *Streets in the Moon.*

To Wyndham Lewis

Dear Lewis   8 December 1927   Paris

I didn't mean to force you into a correspondence which must certainly be an intrusion upon your time. But I'm deeply in your debt for your letter. My difficulty was to reconcile, not your attitude, but your specific criticisms, with the geography of your general position. I could see why you should attack Pound as a poet — though I myself should be rather inclined to praise him. But I did not altogether see why it was important to the war you were engaged in to get that name into the field of fire. I think your letter sets me straight. I have been considering you somewhat as a man engaged in writing a brief every ¶ of which is directed toward a petition for a specific ruling at the end. You are rather, I think you would say, occupied with the creation of a clean, new consciousness — to which, obviously, all phenomena whatever are material, as every tree in a field is pertinent to a man trying to really see a perspective. My image is not happy. And it is somewhat naive for me to write you about your purposes. But I am so deeply moved by your effects that your purpose becomes my concern also.

I continue to ponder a question I tried to raise at lunch that day — a question that carries me out of my swimming radius. Do you really believe that the peculiar willingness of intelligent people to yield themselves to Andersonism & Lawrenceism is due to the propoganda supporting those authors? And to go farther — even to the sill of your time problem — Why should the time conception so move our generation? Why do I for example respond to images of the turning world as to nothing else? There is, at least, a peculiar sensitiveness to the *fact* of time, coexistant with the school of thought which plays on that sensitiveness. I cannot myself believe that the school created the hunger that received it. Rather the other way about. But why? When the posts of religion are knocked out does the whole flood come down of necessity? And who will rebuild us these piers?

But I seem to be fishing for further letters. For God's sake pay no attention. You have enough to do.

As for Ernest — your criticism was just. His stuff has a sensationalist base which I think he would concede & support intellectually. For me he is a true stylist (taught, curiously enough, pretty largely by G. Stein (in conversation) if you will believe his assertion!!) whose future is only limited by his willingness to seize it, & his ability to understand the attitude of mind from which proceeds such criticism as was yours. The question is what is going to happen inside his head.

yrs   A. MacLeish

ALS: NIC

To Harry Crosby

Dear Harry: 24 December 1927 [Gstaad?]

I do not know how I can thank you. You are much too kind.

You once said you would like the ms of the enclosed poem — that is to say, the enclosed ms.[1] I hope you meant it. In any event I should like you to have it. I am sorry that the only copy should be a torn leaf out of a note book. The remarks on the reverse are notes for a poem I shall not write. I don't think I'd bother much about them. The point is that I had it in mind to write the intimate poems of an imaginative personage named L. T. Carnavel. This poem was one. The prologue to *Streets* was another. But Carnavel demised.

Are you coming to Gstaad? My best to Caresse   yrs   AMacL

ALS: SIU-C

1. "Carnavel's Poem About Illumination," first published in *The New Criterion* (April 1926) as "Poem," next in *Streets in the Moon* as "No Lamp Has Ever Shown Us Where to Look." The Crosbys had derived the name Black Sun Press from a phrase in the poem's last lines: "Still fixed upon impenetrable skies/The small, black circle of the sun."

To Ferris Greenslet

My dear Greenslet: 12 January 1928   Gstaad

I am very happy that you will publish my "Hamlet".[1] And I am grateful extremely for what you are kind enough to say about it & about my work. Your more than merely theoretical support has meant much to me these years.

The possible obscurity of the poem troubles me. It is a thing one cannot judge oneself. I used the frame of Hamlet in order not only to support but to explain the changing content. I can make the marginal notations much more full if you are of the opinion that that is necessary. Naturally I should prefer to leave them as they are.

As to publication — I long ago made up my mind that a serious poet must combat with all his resources the passion of the American public & of American critics to classify & group writers to the end that they may forget them. I therefore have made it a rule to belong to no group & never to contribute frequently to any one magazine. The result is obscurity with self-respect. But obscurity in an age of universal fame is something in itself; & self-respect is not too common a flower among the buds I see in Paris. You will understand, therefore, my feeling that I could not take membership for my book in a series or group.[2] I do not mean to even suggest a criticism of your project. What you did for the Imagists was well done. And you will undoubtedly do as much for your next fall's group. I merely mean that I prefer, to the obvious advantages of such a publication, the more questionable advantages of a publication apart. And I know that you will understand my feeling.

As to financial terms — I do not expect to make money out of my writing & I should much prefer to put any small margin that might be mine into the physical book. I wrote Bob about my ideal of a book of verse and though it may not be realizable at a comparatively low selling price I'd like to shoot toward it. What I have chiefly in mind is a fair page & margin, a title page without ornament, & a cover something like the Dublin ed. of Yeats' Oct. Blast concerning which I have written Bob. Also a shape generally like that. I think (though I am a fool about book selling) that we can expect to sell several times as many copies of this book if published at a middle or low price as of STREETS. In any event why not leave any royalties to me out of the first edition & provide for royalties only in case of a further printing — putting the first edition or printing at 500 or 750 or 1000 as you think best. These, you understand, are the suggestions of an ignoramus & subject to all & any kind of criticism from you.

I take it from what you say that you cannot publish till fall. Would it be possible in that event to announce the book by title in some good medium at once? I value the idea of the construction of the book so highly that I wish to preëmpt the ground & avoid any however remotely possible "coincidences". I have, as you know, published two parts of the poem in the Miscellany & in the - - - - Caravan.[3] And they bear the seeds of the idea.

I also gather that you do not object to the English edition — a matter I took up with Bob last summer

I too regret our frequent failures to meet. I hope for luck next summer.   faithfully yours,   Archibald MacLeish

P. S. — You don't happen to have heard whether or not the Caravan is paying its contributors? Neither Hemingway nor I have been paid & we have heard that others have. We want to make a stink if necessary.

 AMacL

ALS: MH

1. Greenslet, literary adviser to Houghton Mifflin Company (a title roughly equivalent to editor in chief), had conveyed the firm's willingness to publish *The Hamlet of A. MacLeish* in a letter to M dated 29 December 1927. It was published on 26 October 1928. 2. Reminding M that Houghton Mifflin had successfully published a "New Poetry Series" — including a number of imagist works — some years before, Greenslet had suggested the inclusion of *The Hamlet* in another such series being planned for the fall of 1928. 3. Van Wyck Brooks, Lewis Mumford, Alfred Kreymborg, Paul Rosenfeld, eds., *The American Caravan: A Yearbook of American Literature* (New York: Macaulay, 1927), contained M's "Fragment of a Biography," which, slightly revised, became section 4 of *The Hamlet of A. MacLeish.*

To Harry Crosby

Dear Harry: 20 May 1928   Conway, Massachusetts

Damn sorry to have missed you like that. Wondered where you were. Your concierge is a SPHynxxx. Eliot's Anabase I haven't seen.[1] But on unpacking here I find copies of yours & Caresse's for which ten thousand original thanks.[2] Most complimented by your printed attention to me at the end of your vol.

This was the world's worst winter. One month in Paris working. One month en Suisse swearing. Home for five weeks acct death father.[3] Back to find no aptmt to live in. Off for a cruise with Murphy which flopped. Back to work as an interior decorator (& then we sold the goddam aptmt)[.][4] And here now trying to settle a farm in process of reconstruction. Hell! Bile & Corruption!

Love to you both. Write me   Archie

ALS: SIU-C

1. Eliot had published a section of Perse's *Anabase* and his translation thereof in *The Criterion* 7 (February 1928), 137–138. 2. Probably a reference to Harry Crosby's *Chariot of the Sun* and Caresse Crosby's *Impossible Melodies*, both published under the Crosbys' Editions Narcisse imprint in 1928. 3. Andrew MacLeish had died, at the age of eighty-nine, on 14 January 1928. 4. At 44, rue du Bac, Paris.

To Ranald H. Macdonald, Jr.

Dear Ranald: 8 June 1928   Conway

The theory that poets live on pallets & pellets is exploded. Poets are rich & comfortable. Their verses are universally read & admired & they are excellently paid.

As for the apartment — it isn't mine.

The "Caravan" is sad trash — all except my poem which is a section of my "Hamlet of A. MacLeish" appearing next fall & most moving. I agree with you about the avant-garde view of the universe. It is almost as false and nearly half as silly as the American Business Man's (*and* I don't mean you) professional optimism. The former is due to festering introspection & the latter to the absence of thought, feeling & sense, inner & outer. Never to question cloud, earth or sea; never once to imagine darkness or death's self; never to poke a finger through the paper screen: but eternally from Sunday morning through to Saturday night to seriously & importantly act & move as though life were the inside of one's hand, and the operations of keeping alive important, is a condition as much worse than that of the young intellectuals of the Caravan as their condition is worse than that of the one or two wise men. Ourselves say. What New York bright-boy of your acquaintance would even understand the admonition of Melville: "For as this appalling ocean surrounds the verdant land so in the soul of man there lies one insular Tahiti, full of peace & joy, but encompassed by all the horrors of the half known life. God keep thee! Push not off from that isle, thou canst never return!"[1] Let alone need it.

As for Jenks — I hardly know him.[2] I mistrust people who wear the ironic mask:- they are usually trying to act a part out of an old number of the Century Magazine — the suave gent of the 90s who sees & laughs at his own weaknesses. We don't. Not honestly. I prefer carpenters who look what they mean. I prefer people without outsides. Occasionally you meet one. One with *insides* I mean.

What a lecture. Thanks for your letter. I thought you had forgotten your promise. I went to the Bank to find you after your first departure

yrs   A.

ALS: MACDONALD

1. From Melville's *Moby-Dick*, Chapter 58, "Brit." 2. Almet Francis Jenks, Jr.

To Ferris Greenslet

Dear Greenslet: 24 August 1928   Conway

I hope you won't think me unduly headish if I return to the charge.[1]

Bob tells me that H.M. would prefer not to alter the *Hamlet* even at my expense and would feel obliged, if the book were altered, to raise the price in order to protect other books of verse issued at a dollar and a half in the smaller format.

I wish to put the case to you as strongly as I am able. The book as it stands at present is really unsightly. The marginal notes, even on the right hand pages, will be so morticed into the text as to serve no purpose but to interrupt the reading of it. On the left hand pages they will be jammed into the space between the ends of the bruised lines and the central crack & sewing pit of the book. Neither there nor in the more fortunate pages will they stand free of the text in comment upon it.

Whose fault it is does not matter. Had the April proof reached me my objection would have come sooner. But the ill is obvious. I feel so strongly about it that I am willing to undertake to dig up the necessary two hundred dollars more or less although the matter properly falls not upon me but upon the publisher. And God in heaven knows that what with a new son[2] & an old house I shall have pain enough doing it.

If I am willing to do that for the sake of the salvaging of what is, after all, our common venture it seems to me H.M. should be willing to let the change be made & to let the price stand. Do you really believe anyone is going to measure the *Hamlet* of AMacL & the *Bitten Apple* of Horatio Parnassusschnippel & wonder why they get ⅞ of an inch more of the former for 1.50 than of the latter?

I get nothing out of my books but the looks of them. To which you may very well reply that all you get is the deficit. But for the hidden motives of God & the publishers I can't answer — I only assume they must exist or there would be no marriages & no poets. And in the present case it is not only the looks but a good part — say 20% — of the interior legibility of the poem.

One bar may be real. Viz. that to change would delay the book beyond Oct. 15. As to this I put myself passionately on your good will & sense of justice. You can, if you wish, beat me with that stick. You can also if you wish — I believe in your miracles — get the altered book out of the printer's hands by long before Christmas.

Won't you do what you can for me? I am willing to do all I can for the book with my pocket as I have already done all I can with my heart. Forgive me if I seem to weep. I am indeed deeply, deeply concerned & bitterly miserable about the whole affair. I think the poem is good. I cannot bear to have its chances of comprehension hurt. There are too many already [*sic*] to throw the foggy eye glass at my head

yrs　AMacLeish

ALS: MH

1. M had written to Linscott on August 15 about the same problem that is the subject of this letter. 2. Peter Hitchcock MacLeish, born 7 August 1928 and later, at the urging of his namesake-less maternal grandfather, rechristened William Hitchcock. He was, nevertheless, long known by family and friends as Peter.

To Robert N. Linscott

Excellence   [*c.* 27 September 1928]　[Conway]
　　You return my poem advising with exquisite skill
　　And the kindness of love delightful interior changes.
　　These are successfully made with a gum eraser.
　　You mention however a likeness to Li Tai-po:[1]
　　What will erase the sunward cant of the sunflower?
　　I have burned the goddam thing on the front of the fire.

Excellence
　　Since you express an interest in Li Tai-po I have made so bold as to copy out for you the verses he wrote for his friend Ro-li[2] at that epoch when Ro-li was Master of w'Hors to the Governor of Bos-tong and Li Tai-po, or po-po as he called himself in affection, was living alone with

his wife three children a governess a cook a waitress two carpenters a plumber and a mason in complete seclusion upon the north-east corner of the Ber'k'shi mountains looking toward the sky

> For the first time in many days I can see to the Mountain
> The cawing of crows is under the high sky
> By noon the last of the clouds will have blown over
> Now that the world is large again there is I
> And the blue hill and the high clouds and the cawing
> Before in the rain there were two of us You and I
> It is true there is one chair and no place at the table

As for Er-hem, he has promised to come in the tenth month to the Ber'k'shi mountains. And You?   [unsigned]

TL-U: DLC

1. An eighth-century Chinese poet of the T'ang dynasty; also known as Li Po. 2. A play on the name Robert Linscott, as "Er-hem," farther on, is a play on Ernest Hemingway.

To Robert N. Linscott

Dear Bob: 25 October [1928] Conway

Your observations on the story are, as one foreknew they would be, beautiful & precise. You are everywhere right. The persons are masks. The end is collapsed. And above all in your question of my native objectivity. Which isn't. My difficulty is to find in subjective prose any justification. I mean for myself. When I attempt it it seems fluid, unclothed & shamefully naked. I suppose I haven't really come to it yet.[1]

What concerns me more is your attitude to the Hamlet. I once forced you in conversation to admire it. I do not know whether you do. And now I never shall. As for the critics — it is only the personal pain one minds. Their opinions cannot touch the book. But you all seem agreed that they will crucify it. Young Kirstein[2] writes me a letter of personal praise & much premonition of disaster. I suppose I am stupid. Why should they hate it more than they hate any pure thing?

Thank you again for your care & thought of the story. Someday I'll have something better to throw at you.

When do you want me to bring out my next vol. of short things? Have wired Ernest for news   yrs gratefully yrs   Archie

ALS: DLC

1. Linscott's observations, and M's response in this letter, concern a story that was never published and the manuscript of which, apparently, does not survive. 2. Lincoln Kirstein (b. 1907), a cofounder of *Hound and Horn*, a modernist journal of literature and the arts.

To Harry Crosby

Dear Harry: 4 November 1928   Conway

Nice letter. Also containing excellent news. I am to be in Boston with Hemingway this week end (Nov. 10). Are you? Lunching Sat. with the Chris. Herters[1] & dining that night with the Curtises. (Chas. P. Jr.) Game in the afternoon. Where if ever will you be? Leave a call either house or call us Sat. morning at H. H. Bundy's 131 Beacon — or 133 or thereabouts.

As for Einstein — I'd be delighted to have C. do a ltd. ed. on any conditions she likes. I am sure H. M Co would not make difficulties[2]

Hoping to see you both   yrs hurriedly   Archie MacLeish

ALS: SIU-C

1. Christian A. Herter (1895–1967), editor of *The Independent* from 1924 to 1928; later a congressman and governor of Massachusetts, as well as undersecretary and secretary of state. 2. Black Sun Press published a limited edition of *Einstein* in 1929.

To Lewis Galantière

Dear Lewis: 18 November 1928   Conway

As though the rain had fallen after a year's drought.[1]

You work at a thing for a year — almost two years — your publisher is sceptical — the thing appears — days go by (mostly nights go by) — nothing happens. You don't know what you expect to have happen but anyway nothing does. And all the motion goes out of the world & you wish to Christ you had been dead a century & buried in quick lime. It seems incredible you should have made a gesture of complete sincerity & no one should have seen it. You become ashamed ——.

You can't know, my boy, what I'm trying to say because its never happened to you. You have never spoken into silence. You have always been heard. I don't mean that you can't sympathize with lonliness. You better than any man I know can do that. But you have never been made to feel ashamed.

Ecoute, mon ami. You alone — you only — have saved me from that. It seems to you a small thing to have done perhaps. It seems to me a great thing. I hold my lip in my teeth to keep from writing here the thanks — the more than thanks — I want to write. I have learned nothing. I have no discipline. I have no maturity. Otherwise I should not weep ——

I am in truth obliged to you pour toujours

I am as grateful to you as though you had given me Savoy. And indeed you have.   Archie

ALS: NNC

1. Galantière had presumably written a letter praising the recently published *Hamlet of A. MacLeish*. He reviewed the book favorably in "Hamlet for Our Time," *The Nation* 128 (17 April 1929), 471–472.

To John Peale Bishop

Dear John: [*c*. December 1928]   [Conway]

We drive down for the evening mail here. I read your letter in the car in front of the post office in a kind of hollow of silence that came up out of me. I have neither the sincerety nor the dignity to answer it.

What you say of my poem[1] is, as you know, one of the few tributes it is worth labor in our age to have. I mean that your praise is that. You yourself know that this is true. Of it I can only say that it alone changes what has been the most sour and hating experience of my life.

Nevertheless the rest that you say is of more importance to me. I am assuming, dangerous and naive as it is to do so, that when you speak of our friendship for each other as intolerable and tombed, you do not merely announce to me the alteration in yourself. If I am in error do me the last grace to read no more of this.

Truth between two is an almost imperceptible gesture, an inflection, an unexpected honesty of eye that changes all that has been said and done. Truth of that kind cannot be imitated in writing because its imitation is too easy. Truth of that kind is a sort of fault in the preparation which, written, is merely a fault. And yet what I have to say to you has no power but its truth. It is only this, that I did not know there was this change between us. I know that since that year we have seen less of each other — nothing for years together—few words. I know to what interpretation is open the reading of old letters in an empty room before morning. I know what relation our talk with each other of this time bears to the talk we had together five years ago in the Boulevard St. Michel, in the Jardin des Plantes, in the Square Alboni. And yet I know nothing of this. I will tell you why it is so. My relation with you has been from the beginning of it like the relations men have with places in the world — with Florence, first seen in one's youth, with the City of Paris. It was *there* that these things were first found — there that poetry existed — there that this kind of beauty was. The City is always there, seen or not seen, however visited. Will you try to understand what I mean? You were (and remain) the first, the only, adult poet I had ever met. You showed me poetry in a real world. (So far as poetry or the world go this is a very small matter for I have touched neither.) If the figure of you were taken out of my soul the whole thing would collapse like a blown cloth. Between you and me there can never be, so long as I live, this change you speak of, however change may be apparent to you.

I am aware that as a relation between living men this is a poor thing. I do not ask you to accept it. I ask you to believe in it whether you choose to accept it or not. Of the chronicle of our relation to each other in the world it is almost impossible, it is impossible, to speak. Too much is expected of us here. We are to move among the living filaments and break none of them. I am inexpert in this. My affection for you has never in any way changed. If yours for me is lost it is a great loss. If I have injured you I beg you to forgive me. If I have bored you as I have always feared to do, think the least ill of me you can.

Ghosts do not bury. The voice works under ground.   A.

TLS: NjP

1. *The Hamlet of A. MacLeish.*

To Sylvia Beach

Dearest Sylvia   9 December 1928   Conway

Acceptez chere Mademoiselle these unworthy enclosed

If you think them well will you submit them to Transition?

We think of you and Adrienne. And almost cable you out of mere pressure of affection.

I also enclose a check for cent frs.. Will you like an angel purchase therewith three or four bouteilles of Joyce's favorite white at the sign of the stork next to Pruniers and present with our love and wishes? I think you can get it for twenty five. But do as many as this princely sum permits. (And *no more*. I know you. Making up balances out of yr own poche)

And can it be that we have left with you or with Adrienne the original of Becat's of me? I find it nowhere. Can it be?

Do you like my Hamlet? The critics hate it. Ernest, whom I have never pleased before, says perhaps I'm a great poet. Which is a nice way of saying he likes it. He is almost alone. He and Galantiere. On that minority I stand and thumb my nose at the whole goddam lot of them. Please join up.

All our love to you and Adrienne. We miss you horrid. But we like this hill. Too.

And our best to les Becats and to the merchants as pappy puts it

                                        affly   Archie

TLS: NjP

To Ernest Hemingway

Dear Pappy: 14 December [1928]   Conway

There is nothing to say. There is never anything to say about death.[1]
Except that it made us know how much we love you to read those
words in the paper. Certainly beyond that anything is an impertinence.
I know how the death of your father changes him in your mind and
he becomes what he was when you were very young and your heart is
destroyed with tenderness for him. No one can talk to you then. You
are walking in your own boyhood and everyone is very far away.

But there is one thing I am going to say to you whether I should or
not. You must not let your mind work over and over the way it happened. I know how your mind works round and round your pain like
a dog in cover going over and over the same track and what a torment
it is to you. But now you must not. It is too serious. The consequences
to you are too grave. I don't know how you are going to help it. I know
that what I have written is just so much language. But I believe that
you can oppose that agony and end it. Somehow. I beg you to fight it
in every way you can. And to forgive me if what I have written is more
than I have a right to say.

This is not the time to thank you for your letter about my poem.
You must know how much I have always wanted to please you. But it
was more than that here. The book has been received with perfunctory
notices and tepid hostility. (Except for Kirstein's magazine where it
was violently attacked!)[2] I had hoped everything from it. Your letter
gave me a rock to stand on in the seas of shit — a rock I wouldn't
exchange for all their continents.

Sometime I will tell you what you did for me.

For now — there is nothing you can ask me to do for you in your
unhappiness I will not gladly do. Believe it.

My love to Pauline and Bumby and you   Archie

TLS: JFK

1. Dr. Clarence E. Hemingway, Ernest Hemingway's father, had shot and killed himself on December 6.   2. R. P. Blackmur, "Am Not Prince Hamlet Nor Was Meant to
Be," *Hound and Horn* 2 (Winter 1929), 167–169.

To Ernest Hemingway

Dear Pappy: 11 January [1929]   [Chicago?]

When you get bank accounts & hurt feelings mixed up together there
is nothing I know of to do about it. Everybody was fine. Everybody
acted for the best. There was nothing to complain of. And I might just

as well have been where Loeb & Leopold are so far as going south was concerned.[1]

The reason it got me so was that I had it all settled in my head. Ada had a trunk packed with my Antibes stuff & I was deciding whether or not to grow a beard & memorizing your letters & imagining what it would feel like to have it 90° on the back of the neck again & thinking about afternoons & a bottle of Fundador & the chances of getting you to go to Mexico & working mornings in a hotel room. And the day before I was going to sail on the Clyde liner for Miami I was on the Michigan Central bound for this ash can! And the winter seems longer & colder & dirtier than a winter ever seemed before & the people seem shittier —

There's no doubt about it, Kid, you have chosen what the bards call the better part. I was pretty sure of it when I found how right you were about the apartment in the rue Guynemer[2] & now I know it. You can't have it both ways & you & Pauline are honest enough with your-selves to see it. Well — there's no more to say, I suppose. Its like that. I'm a damn fool.

Anyway we're here for the rest of the winter & in the spring we're going back to Conway & next fall I am going to Europe again if I go alone. As to work — there's no such thing.

I wish to god I knew about your book.[3] I wish to god I was there with you two. As for next fall — try to hide your tracks!

I guess that's enough weeping for a while. Do you know any human beings in Chicago? The shells should reach you from N.Y. in a few days. Love to you all   yrs   Archie.

Never realized how deadly the *Torrents* were till I read a story of Sherwood's in a magazine coming out here. He doesn't believe in it himself anymore. He feels silly as he writes. You can't help but be sorry for him.

ALS: JFK

1. Hemingway had invited the MacLeishes to join him and Pauline at Key West, a trip M's shaky finances prevented him from making. Richard A. Loeb and Nathan Leopold, Jr., were serving life sentences for a widely publicized 1924 murder. 2. The MacLeishes had stayed at 14, rue Guynemer, Paris, in March and April 1928, their last two months of living abroad. 3. *A Farewell to Arms* (1929), which Hemingway was about to complete.

To Robert N. Linscott

Dear Bob: [*c.* 24 January 1929] [Chicago?]

Don't bother to answer my question about Conrad's review.[1] I have read it.

This is a stroke at the heart and the knife goes in. Conrad is entitled to hold opinions about poetry and he is my well-wisher. If my poem seems to him counterfeit then it is so. Whether or not his charges of derivation are strictly true. For instance, I have never read Stevens. But that is beside the point.

And yet I am deeply puzzled. When he writes about my technical excellence he means that my poetry is as such beautiful. When he goes on to say that nevertheless he cannot like it because it contains so many echoes of other men he means that he cannot allow himself to be moved by what would otherwise move him because his previous reading will not permit it. But when he goes on to say that therefore my poem is false I am bewildered. If the poem is false and affected it must be so altogether apart from its likenesses to others. And it must be this he means. If this is true it is a fatal ill. For I am not conscious of it. I am aware of the fact that I have been influenced (though not I think in this book) by Eliot and that this book is influenced by Pound and by Perse (and by Aiken himself) in four specific sections. But the experience I thought was mine, the emotion mine, the poetry mine. If this is not so, if the reason why Conrad can not give himself to what he feels to be beautiful is the reason I suggest — namely that he feels the counterfeit under the coin, then there is no health in me for this has happened without my knowledge and is therefore past my cure. I have written him to learn what I can.

There is another matter that is strange but without importance. Conrad's review, the N.R. review[2] as Ada describes it to me, and the Hound and Horn review, say much the same thing though in very different ways. I do not believe Conrad took his opinions from them. Did they take theirs from him? I do not believe for a moment that Conrad is responsible for or desired the attacks of the bright young men. Doubtless he merely expressed his opinion in their presence and they used it. I am too sick with it all to care.

When you can write me will you answer this question? Are any of our poets doing anything that you know of with the Conquest of Mexico — planning to or in process? Would it be a good idea to let it be known that I am engaged in a long poem on that subject? (*Not* need I add a counterfeit of Benet)[3] Or perhaps I do need.

And what are your plans? Are you going?   yrs aff'ly   Archie

TLS: DLC

1. "Unpacking Hearts with Words," a review by Aiken of several of M's works including *The Hamlet of A. MacLeish*, in *The Bookman* 68 (January 1929), 576–577.
2. Theodore Spencer, "Two Poets," *The New Republic* 57 (9 January 1929), 226–227.
3. Stephen Vincent Benét's verse epic of the American Civil War, *John Brown's Body*, had appeared in 1928.

To Waldo Peirce[1]

Dear Waldo: 25 January [1929] [Chicago?]

You are one of the people I'd like to see about now. Chicago needs
you Waldo. There are too many women and too many young theos-
ophists and not enough hair. Pubic or other. Why do our greatest
American cities, our toughest banlieus, breed the weakest knees? Talk
about the vigor and crude strength of America — its about as vigorous
as an exspensive motor car and as crude as Steinbloch clothes. Just
about. I suppose all the more sensitive guys are forced into the lily pen
by the vulgarity of the cigar chewers. Probably the only place where
you can get sensitive people with strong nerves is in a highly civilized
place like Paris where the tendency is to get away from elegance and
knowledge, instead of away from Kiwanis and the stock market. But
anyway you look at it there are too many women in it for any good
end. The only really good end of women is lacking with these.

To hell with all that. I liked your Maine poems fine. The trouble-
double poem is a grand one. Can't you get Canby to run them at the
top of his Yale Harvard literary review?

Hope you didn't go up to Conway to find us. We got frozen out and
had to come here for the winter. Are you going south? I tried to and
got bitched.

I think we had a pretty good time in Boston. We wouldn't have if
there hadn't have been three of us together. I understand some of
them thought we were just so interesting and nice and some of them
thought we were terrible and they haven't got over talking about it yet.

Ada sends you her best as do I.

We must meet agin   yrn   Archie

TLS: ViU

1. Peirce (1884–1970), from Bangor, Maine, was a painter, a dabbler in poetry, and
a close friend of Hemingway's.

To Ernest Hemingway

Dear Pappy: 4 February [1929] Glencoe

You are probably wondering what the hell I mean by breaking out
with this Mexican plan all of a sudden. And I don't wonder. Answer
is that I was talking to mother the other day about how much I wanted
to go to get a little dope in them parts on the conquistadors and she
offered to loan me the money. Result wires to you. I didn't dare even
hope you would go but it was worth the remote chance and I knew
you would want to if you could.

I'm going down alone leaving day after tomorrow. I think I'll go straight to M.C. [Mexico City] and find out there what I can do about going down over the Sierra to V.C. [Vera Cruz] on foot or mule. The Mexican RR bird here says there are bears in the hills but I doubt it. I'm not going to be brave about it but I am going to find out.

I will try to come back via Havana and K.W. [Key West]. Expect word anyway. Crazy for a sight of you birds. Will you be there all Feb.?

Grand news about the book.[1] I'd give my tweeds to see it. Financially I hope you serialize it. But if you don't I'll be happier. I hate to see your stuff go through the sausage mill with the other boys' stuff as though it were the same kind. Not that my emotions make any difference but I can't help having them. I'd like to see them set aside a special year for the book to come out in — no other novels to appear.

yrs   A.

TLS: JFK

1. *Scribner's Magazine* had just offered $16,000 for first serial rights to *A Farewell to Arms*.

To Harry Crosby

Dear Harry: 8 March [1929] [Glencoe]

About Einstein is fine and 200 is a fine lot of money. I hope you won't divide profits with me unless you have some.

Thank you for the many things — for Ozenfant[1] on photography & for the beautiful ms of Laforgue. You spoil me. How can I answer all your questions. Yes I think Kay Boyle is grand.[2] I like her prose especially but her verse more than any other woman's verse of our time & most mens. I think she is an even better writer than she lets herself be. I mean to say that the world is her oyster. All she has to do is open it. And she won't. She's afraid of not being modern. Well she doesn't need to think of modern or not modern or anything like that.

Hamlet is all right. Everybody crapped on it & now everybody is accusing everybody else of being unjust. It will still be there when they get through.

I have just gotten out of Mexico. I was down in the mountains back of Jalapa on a mule trip alone. I got out one day ahead of the revolution. It is a fine country. Better than Persia. I like plateau country.

Your farm sounds swell. You both sound swell. I wish I were where you are. Give my dear love to Caresse.

As for a frontispiece — why not use a copy of the drawing Bécat did of me. Sylvia has a copy & (I think) the original.

Thank you again for all your fine gifts   yrs   Archie.

ALS: SIU-C

1. Amedée-Julian Ozenfant (1886–1966), French painter and writer. 2. Kay Boyle's *Short Stories* was published by Black Sun Press in 1929.

To Ernest Hemingway

Dear Pappy: 11 March 1929   Glencoe

It all ended so differently from the way we expected. There was that General down in the lobby at Vera Cruz grabbing for his gun every time the door opened and there was the breeder of beef cattle on the road into Tlaxcala who had to see all my papers before he would let me through and there was the former Colonel under Obregon[1] who said he would go with me *if* I could get through in ten days because he had business in ten days of a (underlined) political nature. But I didnt pay any attention to any of them. I expected to take a vessel from Vera Cruz to Havana to Key West and drop in on you out of a southwest gale some evening. And the first thing I knew there were no trains down to Vera Cruz and they were tooting around the streets in Mexico city with their bayonets on and I took the rattler for Laredo. I wish I were a courageous guy like Charlie MacArthur[2] who stayed down there. My liver turns over at the thought of shooting.

Well, what happened was this. I wanted, I think I told you, to take a mule and go over the road between Vera Cruz and Mexico City that Cortes took going in because I want to write a poem about the Conquest and everything that Prescott[3] says about it is fine and rhetorical and obviously false as bloody hell and you once told me and I have never forgotten it, nor wont, never to write about anything I didn't know all about. I went to Mexico City first. You know about my Spanish. So I had to arrange for horses or mules and get somebody to go with me who spoke English or some American who spoke Spanish. I farted around Mexico City for a long time which is a fine city like a piece of Paris built in Spain on Sunday morning and the beer very good and the cocktails rotten and the wine too expensive for you and me and I saw two bull fights with nice little grey Mexican bulls and a Spaniard named Barrera who was fine with the cape but dying of consumption and couldn't kill bulls and got the rasberry from the brave Mexicanos who have a feeling about killing and don't know (not that I do) a cape from a saddle blanket, and a Mexican Indian named

Freg who could kill like a sledge boy at the Stockyards but just waved his shirt at the bulls when he was playing them and a clever Mexican named Ortiz who got it twenty-five centimeters into the bowel from a Spanish bull the next week because they have an inch or so more in the horns. The Pic-ing was rotten. That, and I went to see the Ambassador[4] to find out if he knew whether my trip was safe and he didn't know at all nor, may I say, give a good god dam, but I met Mrs. Morrow who is grand and a great admirer of pappy so I fixed myself up there too by talking about my old friend pappy and our days together. But all this wasn't getting me anywhere and all people gave me were a lot of letters to other people and all I could find out was that Mr. Richard Hollowbutton, the great Adventurer[5] who got himself photographed on the Acropolis with his neck out claimed to have made the trip with all its many dangers the year before but nobody at all believed him and as a matter of fact he made it as I later found out but in parts by train. So I went down to Vera Cruz and hired a car there and went up largely on my ass with the car vaguely in between to Jalapa and stayed there three days and finally found an American who found me a Mexican kid who spoke some English and set out. We put in two days going up over the Sierra on the old road which isn't one and saw two fine ruined cities and came out on the Mesa near a place called Limon and then went north and west to the pass into Tlaxcala by car and went through there in two more days travelling all night one night. We would get mules in one town and a guide and go to the next and change and so on. Then we went across Tlaxcala by car and climbed the old pass into Mexico on donkeys. It was really grand. By God I wished all the time you were there. It is fine country. Around Jalapa it is like The Riviera only with rain and the air soft all the time and on the Mesa it is like New Mexico but absolutely clean and hard and in the mountains of Tlaxcala it is cedar forests and upland grazing, and between the volcanos it is all pine and you come out on the top and look a thousand miles. And as for the bandits there weren't any and no one even thought of offering me a military escort. I was sick you weren't there. Then I had to get out. I feel rotten about not seeing you. I send you both my love. We are all well. We have straightened out a lot of things and I guess it is all all right now except about the money and we can arrange that I know. We probably go abroad next fall. Where and when will you be? And about the book? I am crazy to see it. Write me with news.

love   Archie

There is a fine painter there named Diego de Rivera[6]

TLS: JFK
1. Álvaro Obregón (1880–1928), Mexican general and president. 2. MacArthur (1895–1956) was an American journalist and playwright. 3. William H. Prescott (1796–1859), American historian, author of *History of the Conquest of Mexico* (1843). 4. Dwight Morrow, banker and diplomat, was then United States ambassador to Mexico. 5. Richard Halliburton (1900–1939), a popular American travel writer, had described a trip to Greece in *The Glorious Adventure* (1927) and had visited Mexico in 1928 in connection with his book *New Worlds To Conquer* (1929). 6. Diego Rivera (1886–1957), Mexican mural painter. M had probably seen Rivera's large murals in the Preparatory School and the Ministry of Education in Mexico City.

To Charles R. Walker, Jr.

Dear Charlie: [c. April 1929]   [Conway]

I noticed with pleasure my preferred position and do thank you.[1] As to your suggestion for the future, I answer it in two ways:

(1) I send you herewith a description of my Mexican trip.[2] I went down for material on an poem re Cortcz which I have had in mind for some years. This was a bye product. I did not send it to you at first because I didnt think there was a chance of your taking it. (Good way of selling it to you.) But it has just come back from Freddy Allen who says (usual compliments) Harpers aren't much on "travel with a literary background". If you could use it I would be delighted and would cut or alter to suit. If, as I guess, you can't I would be everlastingly in your debt if you would hand it on to somebody (*Not* the Atlantic) who might take it. I am hard up after that jaunt and I'd like to get some back.

(2) I am going to get together the stuff I read Linscott and which he told you of and for which you wrote me before. I will give you first crack at it.

Please show the enclosed clipping to the boy editor and tell him he certainly chose a good poem when he chose that one![3] And then return it to me.

I agree with all you say — not half loudly enough — about The Bookman. You are doing a swell job. Except for Mr. Wilson's unfortunate verses in the last number[4] there isn't a whiff of Farrar left. And as for the verses — they delight me. A bit more of that and Wilson's attacks on me will lose their venom. The man who wrote that has no right to an opinion about anyone's poetry.

(And a hundred dollar heifer calf died on me this afternoon. *On* me. The poor wet thing limp in the bloody straw with the cunt ooze over it and the awful dignity of death lolling its foetal head into grotesque majesty. Majesty of dead calf. The blue tongue and the lustrous eye majestical. Is it because we *know* what death is that we think these things? Or is there true change? Does the passage from mobility to immobility, from the quick levity of life to the rigid state of stars and winter, all unapparent in its stealing on, so terribly affect our there-too-I imaginations? Tell me this Oh thou blue eyes angelical)

As to Green.[5] Will write my friend Adrienne Monnier, 7 rue de l'Odeon. Do thou call on her in company with Sylvia whom I much affect. Adrienne will arrange everything. Drink you beer in the back room at Lipps in memory of me.   yrn   Archie

TLS: M

1. M's poem " 'American Letter': For G.M." had appeared in *The Bookman* 68 (January 1929), 509–511, immediately following Allen Tate's essay "American Poetry Since 1920." 2. The manuscript of this prose account of M's Mexican trip apparently has not survived. 3. Possibly a reference to Robert Linscott, and to a favorable review of M's *The Hamlet of A. MacLeish*. 4. Edmund Wilson's poem "Provincctown" appeared in *The Bookman* 69 (April 1929), 166. 5. Probably Paul Green (1894–1981), the playwright whose *In Abraham's Bosom* (1927) had won a Pulitzer Prize. He was then studying abroad.

To Harry Crosby

Dear Harry: [22 April 1929]   [Conway]

All any man can give another is his honesty. That is a difficult gift both because it may be distrustfully received and because it comes awkwardly out of the pocket. I think you have got hold of something valuable in Transit of Venus.[1] I think also that the valuable thing you have got hold of (and this is almost always the case) is a by-product of the thing you were most after. To be precise I am not convinced that your device of the incompleted phrase is what you want. It gives you some good effects but it is very voulu. On the other hand you hit upon a kind of true brevity in those and other poems. And that brevity is signed with your name. Thus in Nor Look Behind. And Last Contact regardless of anything is a good poem. I mean on any scale. And passages that I think beautiful are in the end of Eventuate, the fine Shakespeare run of Forecast, the magnificent second phrase of We are One. There are of course others. These most. I think you have learned the smell of your own flesh. I think you should be well satisfied with where you are going.

I don't know whether you have started Einstein. I am trying to get H.M. to let me have a de luxe edition of my new book myself. If they assent I should be glad to have you do it if you wish. But I think it unlikely.[2]

My congratulations to you and to Kay Boyle on her Short Stories. She has the power and the glory. I believe in her absolutely when she writes — even when I want not to. I talk of her everywhere — not that it can do her any good. Simply that I must. I am sending Charlie Walker, the managing editor of The Bookman to you. He is a strange being — more than half seraph — but awkward in his envelope of flesh. Please be nice to him and put him in touch with K.B.. They are trying to make a magazine out of The Bookman and it might be of use to her to know Charlie.

Love to you both.   Archie MacLeish

TLS: SIU-C

1. A collection of Crosby's verse first published by Black Sun Press in 1928. 2. Black Sun Press published a deluxe edition of M's *New Found Land: Fourteen Poems* in the spring of 1930, and printed the trade edition for Houghton Mifflin, which published it on 4 June 1930.

To Louis Untermeyer

Dear Louis: [24 June 1929]   [Conway]

Forgive my delay. I have been laying up a dam for the last 2 wks & only one finger on one hand still works. (Laying — not lying)

I never got the text book but should be pleased to give any biog data extant. (I believe I am still alive but you must ask Mr. Aiken & Mr. Wilson & yourself.)

I also gladly give any permissions for reprintings of any poems you choose.

As to your review of my "Hamlet"[1] — I was hurt at the time because I had believed you would understand what I was doing. But the hurt was lost in the larger bruise of practically universal disapproval. The bright boys saw it all as a translation of St. J. Perse or P. Valery or Hugo Stinnes or Little Bo Peep — I don't know. And the rest just plain hated it, with one or two valuable exceptions. I counted on you to hear the voice. If you didn't it was as much my fault as yours. And if I still believe in the poem it is because I know I shan't do better. And that's all there is of that.

Glad you are back in the sugar bush. Your plans sound like ours. Only ours hit the plumbers bill & we spent the first winter in Chicago. Run over in your flivver & I'll show you how to use Epple Jeck.

                             yrn   Archie MacLeish

ALS: InU

1. "Everyman's Soliloquy," *The Saturday Review of Literature* 5 (8 December 1928), 463.

To Ernest Hemingway

Dear Pappy: 1 September [1929]   [Conway]

I have just finished the Sept. instal..[1] I haven't anything to say. It is beautiful — beautiful beyond words. The seriousness & precision & candor of your writing makes you feel the way you feel after tears when everything is suddenly simple & profoundly clear & perfectly tender. I cannot think about Catherine without love for her nor of you without emotions which are simply not to be spoken. You see it is merely silly for me to attempt to talk of it. And yet I go on — there are two moments equal in tenor to the crisis of *The Killers*. And there is something you have never reached before — a deep & true pity with no irony & no self-consciousness. I was terribly moved by the lad under the canvas on the car. By Ferguson. By Catherine. By that night.

What has happened is that you have mastered the self-imposed problems of your technique. There was a time when I wondered whether the restrained & tense understatement of your prose would not limit you to a certain kind of material. Now no one can wonder that. The world of this book is a complete world, a world of emotion as well as of feeling. To subject the whole experience of a man's soul to the pure & perfect art of your prose is a great, a very great, achievement. I send you my complete praise & my profound respect. You become in one book the great novelist of our time. It is not for me to supply you with accolades & titles. But I *know*. And I am glad with all my heart. I think now you can forgive me my stupidity in Saragossa, for it was this achievement that I then wished for you.[2] And do always wish. And, because I feel as I do about you, with no envy but with pride.

When can we meet? We shall be here in the spring — winter in Chicago. This house is yours.

Give my love to Pauline & forgive my literaryisms about the book. I know no other way to write. I hear praise of you on all sides from all kinds of people. You should be completely happy. Of course you won't be. You have planned so long a journey for yourself. But, for the rest of us, it is accomplished in this book.   A.

ALS: JFK

1. Of *A Farewell to Arms*. 2. M and Hemingway had gone together to Saragossa (Zaragoza), Spain, in October 1926 to attend a late-season bullfight. At that time, M had apparently expressed only qualified praise for Hemingway's novel *The Sun Also Rises*, published during that month by Charles Scribner's Sons.

To Louis Untermeyer

Dear Louis: [4 October 1929] [Conway]

I can't write on *time*. I always write afterwards. Its hell.

Recall yrs of Sep. 9.. You recall it? Well what you said about Edna [Millay] was that she touched greatness. And I merely rose to remark with what does she. Because if she does then I'm a cracked thermometer. I can't understand why birds like you & Wilson (though he has his reasons hors de commerce) think Edna is a poetess. Let alone a poet. I never have understood. There are at least fifty (or say five) better she poets in America as of Oct. 4, 1929. (I say five merely because I won't name fifty people.)

That's all there ever was to our debate about the unknown. And I admit its mere muggery.

As for your additional request — I suppose I ought to be hurt that you won't mortgage the Adirondacks for a permission. But I'm not. How about the poem in the current Yale Review[1] or the poem in the Sept. Harpers[2] if you saw either. Both if you want them.

Love to Elizabethtown

(And don't quote me immortal lines from Edna. Quote me some *poetry* of your own)

(The natural consequence of Edna is Dotty Parker[3] — a comment on both) yrN AMacL

ALS: DeU

1. "Immortal Autumn," *The Yale Review* 19 (September 1929), 26. 2. "To Praisers of Women," *Harper's* 159 (September 1929), 485. 3. Dorothy Parker (1893–1967), Amercian writer of short stories, verse, and criticism, all of which were known for their sardonic wit.

To Henrietta Crosby[1]

Dear Mrs Crosby, 12 December 1929 New York

As one grows older and realizes what a lonely and uncertain place the world is one comes to value above everything else those evidences of human fortitude and dignity and virtue which it has, sometimes, to show. I hope I may never forget, in whatever I am given to endure, your courage.

Those of us who knew Harry know that he was always, however his desires may have realized themselves, on the side of the angels and against the authority and numbness and complacency of life. Recklessness and freedom of soul are dangerous things and those who condemn them condemn them with reason. As those who love them suffer for them. But without those fires lighted sometimes in the world it would be a dark and hopeless place. The pity is that you and Caresse must be so dreadfully, so deeply hurt. It seems that women must bear not once but till their lives end, the beauty and strangeness and passion they bring into the world, or nurture there. We others, we should kiss the earth at their feet.

Forgive me for writing you in this way, on this paper, at this time. I feel I must say this to you.

Will you give my deep love and sympathy to Caresse.

Archibald MacLeish

TL-C: SIU-C

1. The mother of Harry Crosby, who had killed his lover, Mrs. Josephine Rotch Bigelow, and then himself on December 10.

To Ernest Hemingway

Dear Pappy: [10 February 1930] [New York]

Thanks for the warning about the mosquitos. Its a damn shame. I had wanted Ada to be near you and Pauline. But I can still take advantage of her father's generous offer to put her up at Daytona and she'll have the sun if she doesn't have anything else.[1]

Met Dotty Parker Saturday night and think she's swell. I have always been afraid of her because I thought she was the kind who would be affectionate to you with her right hand and murder you with her left. But she was so fine in talking about the Murphys and you and all her friends and so damn wise and so intelligent about people that she took me in about eight minutes. She may be serving me up cold at this minute for all I know but I doubt it and if she is it doesn't matter. Hoyty Wiborg[2] had a big arty rout for her last night and I went and feel this morning as though I had a smirk tied back of my ears and oats in my collar. I ought to have known better.

Don [Stewart] was there and was nicer than I have ever seen him. I wanted to talk to you about Don when you were in New York but I simply didn't have the wits to talk about anything. I don't pretend to know what your state of mind is. I'm completely outside your relations to Don and Dotty and those people and I don't want to meddle with them. But I got the impression from something you said here that you thought I had. It isn't to defend myself against that, because I think you know that I don't go in for that kind of interference. But I do want to set the thing straight if I have set it crooked. So far as I know, and I think I know pretty well, Don is a very loyal and very true friend of yours and always has been. At least he talks as though he were and

232

acts as though he were. What he said about the Farewell made me sore because I thought it was bunk and I told him so. But what he said came out of his admiration for you as a writer and his belief in you. If my repetition of it to you gave you a different impression I am sorry as hell. I suppose I was an ass to get sore at Don's ideas about writing, few of which I share, and a worse one to write you about them and a consummate fool to think you would see them as I saw them. To me they seemed to be about as spontaneous a tribute as anyone could desire. Anyway I am sorry as hell if I seemed to you to be making a situation. There isn't any. I hate writing this kind of stuff. I wanted to tell it to you here. But I couldn't talk about anything.

I'm afraid your New York visit was a good deal of a flop and I'm sorry. I was more worried about Ada than I should have been and pretty sick about a lot of other things beside and I guess I let everybody see it. Dotty says everything you heard in New York was shit and I guess I told you most of it. Try to forget about it and to forgive me.

I haven't been able to work at my poem since I finished the prologue and I don't feel now as though I ever could again. You are right when you say I ought to get away. I can't. But when I leave this place in the spring I *leave* it.[3]

Write me sometime. And please count on a stay in Conway whenever you can and for as long as you can.

Love to Pauline.   yours   [unsigned]

TL-U: JFK

1. Ada MacLeish was recuperating from an operation. 2. Mary Hoyt Wiborg, a sister of Sara Murphy's. 3. On 10 October 1929 M had joined the staff of *Fortune*, a business magazine newly created by Henry R. Luce of Time Inc. Under the arrangement he worked out with Luce, M worked at *Fortune* for several months a year and then took several months off to pursue his own writing. He remained on the magazine until June 1938.

To Martha Hillard MacLeish

Dearest Mother: 12 February 1930   [New York]

I am so terribly sorry about John Hillard. Aunt Mary has just written me. To bear that name & die of Typhoid is dreadful.[1] You & she must both feel that. I did not know him. But I am shocked. Poor little Tom must be hurt so deeply. I cannot write to him about the death of a boy I did not know. I wish I could — or that it would matter. But I send you my love. It is dreadful for youth to die. Now that I feel as I do about dying — for it is nothing now — I wonder how you were able to endure Kenny's death. It is dreadful for the young to die. But when you are older & have learned that we die to ourselves alone —

that there is no one writing it down — that the only thing that matters is to be alive with all one's mind & soul & body so that for one moment at least this flowing away & away of still & stone may cease, & this flowing away of years & faces & words may cease — then death is a small thing & once one is ready for it one is ready for it always. But I do not recognize this world. I have never seen it. I have never been in this city before. What I must do is to step aside into the quiet & think. By thinking one begins to see. It is strange. Only by ceasing to see can I see. Myself I do not love but unless I behold myself once in these windows I am nothing & never lived & the roar of the wheels will roll over me. Over us all. Over us all. And all that was young & lovely in the world. I am not afraid of death. But I pity it. I pity its silence. I sat for a long time in the vault with the body of poor Harry Crosby. He had shot himself. He lay on a narrow couch under a dark red cloth. He had made a great noise with his death. But already I could hardly see his face. I had to turn back to see him.

I am hurting you with these words. Forgive me. Believe me. I am not what you think. I am an evil person. I take no happiness in anything on earth but the sonorousness of certain words. It is a very wrong thing. Poetry is not always in me & sometimes coming out. I go to it as a man goes to what he loves & is ashamed of. I go to it out of my life. I come back ashamed. You do not understand. Do not try to. "How do the winds follow unfortune"[2] — I write that & my heart is smooth. What at all have I written? Well, I am a poet. I do not describe myself by this word. I do not speak it. No one speaks it to me. But I am that thing. And it is an agony. It is not wisdom like a quiet light in the brain, nor wisdom in the ankles of the body. It is no wisdom. It is thirst. Only with this wine —— And only I can make this liquor. Out of what? Out of —— Oh be still, be still. I do not write such letters as this. I am not to speak so. Never answer it. Ishbel will speak kindly of it & that will be enough.

Ada is happy. She walks a little. Day after tomorrow she comes home. A week from that day she goes south. "And Christ receive thy soul". So it goes. Something & sleet & candle-light. Sleet means salt. This night & aye night & every night & all. This human time is deep enough & long enough for me. Deep enough. And long enough. And dark enough.

Forgive me. Forgive me. I love you. But to whom am I to speak? Let Ishbel speak for me to you   your son   Archie

ALS: M

1. A son of M's uncle Frederick Hillard, John had been the namesake of another of M's uncles who had also died of typhoid. 2. An approximation of a line from the Prologue of M's work in progress, *Conquistador*.

To Ernest Hemingway

Dear Pappy: [c. May 1930]   [New York]

This is a letter that by its nature simply can't be worth reading because you can't thank people for things and make any sense. You do it because you have to get it off your chest and when you do get it off its so much what do you call it. But you and Pauline were grand to me. And I left Key West Friday night a new boy. Every time I see you — which is so seldom and will probably continue to be so seldom that I wonder why I permit it to be so seldom — I get a new revelation from god about the whole business, — about why its worth while to play as well as you can play to an empty house and an old gentleman in the last row. Not that *you* have to do it any more. There are more people in the house than you would believe and more response of the kind you would like than you'll ever know. But somehow you make it all right for me to go on no matter how empty they make it on my side of the street. Also, goddam it, I like being with you.

Mike sure is a grand egg. And Charles.[1] I could have cried when he brought me that bottle down to the boat. Give them both my best wont you

I can't tell you what I think about Key West. As you saw I am no fisherman. But I got more out of those days on the water and my clumsy efforts at trolling than I've gotten out of anything in years. I can't get that day on the Gulf Stream out of my eyes.

I sent you yesterday a spool of fifteen thread line. Hope you got it[.] I am having the boy up in Conway send you and Charles each a ham if he has any good ones left. I think he has. Give my best love to Pauline and Patrick and the Kat Kat Kas (Bloom!)

No news. D. Parker is ill with silver-polish poisoning. (Vrai.) Mark Connolly's play[2] is such a big hit that people talk about it in a new voice. He is said to have written the American Divine Comedy.

Ada was much better and bored to death and Daytona is horrible. It was all I could do to persuade her to stay south another week.

yours   Archie

Clipping is a little piece out of a leading article in the London Times Lit. Supp Adèle [Lovett] gave me for you.[3] The article would bore you but they certainly put you right up with their best nature gods.

TLS: JFK

1. Henry "Mike" Strater and Charles Thompson, frequent companions of Hemingway's at Key West and elsewhere. 2. Marc Connelly's *The Green Pastures* (1930), a dramatic adaptation of Roark Bradford's *Ol' Man Adam and His Chillun*. 3. Probably a review of *A Farewell to Arms* that had appeared in *The Times Literary Supplement* of 28 November 1929, page 998.

To F. Scott Fitzgerald[1]

Dear Scott: 15 September [1930]   Conway

What a good guy you are! That letter gave me an amount of pleasure that I hope will pour back upon your head in sweet oil and excellent dreams. Or however you would like it to return upon you. How damn kind of you to write me. I can't get over it. I don't see why you should. And of course what really matters is your liking the book — really liking it.[2] It gives me the kind of feeling you have in surf when you get the good sand under your feet. Even your friend Bunny [Wilson] can't wash me out now.

I am coming abroad this winter for a week or two on a matter.[3] And this next summer Ernest and I go lion hunting in Africa by way of (I think) France.[4] Hope to see you one time or the other.

Gerald is here now but no one has seen him. Skulks like a shadow. Why I can't think. He likes us all. But he has deflated the world so flat he can't breathe in it. I'd love to see him.

My love to Zelda and all my thanks to you   yrs   Archie

TLS: NjP

1. Fitzgerald (1896–1940), the American novelist and short story writer, and his wife, Zelda Sayre, saw the MacLeishes on several occasions while visiting the Gerald Murphys at Antibes. The Fitzgeralds' erratic behavior prevented the development of a close friendship with the MacLeishes; this letter is one of only two or three MacLeish letters in the Fitzgerald papers at Princeton University. 2. *New Found Land*. 3. The "matter" was probably a trip by the MacLeishes to Montana-Vermala, Switzerland, where the Gerald Murphy family had been living for several months while Patrick Murphy was hospitalized there with tuberculosis. Several of the Murphys' friends made pilgrimages to Montana-Vermala to stay with them during their long and lonely ordeal. 4. For various personal and financial reasons, M canceled his plan to join Hemingway on his African trip, which was postponed in any case when, in an automobile accident in November, Hemingway suffered a severely broken arm.

To Harriet Monroe

Dear Miss Munroe: 29 November 1930   [New York]

What a lump you must think me! I was extremely grateful for the very fine copy of Poetry you were good enough to send me. And I read it with pleasure. My only regret was that you did not elaborate your French influence piece.[1] There is a great deal to be said on that subject and you are obviously the person to say it. Ezra is so completely out of touch with America that he recently wrote one of the boys he supposed he would be lynched if he set foot in New York. Poor devil, not more than ten people would know who he was. And they would be more apt to hang him with laurel than with feathers. I admire that man so much and hate things like his ridiculous Imaginary Letters[2] so thoroughly. Why can't he act like a poet? Why does he have to pamphleteer in the accents of an exasperated asp? I don't suppose you can answer that question any more than I can.

Congratulations on the award of the Poetry Prize. That may just succeed in indicating to the Pulitzer Committee their equal duty to Mr. Crane.[3]   yours faithfully   Archibald MacLeish

TLS: ICU

1. Harriet Monroe, "The French Influence," *Poetry* 37 (October 1930), 44–49. 2. Pound's *Imaginary Letters* had been published by the Black Sun Press in October 1930. 3. Hart Crane's *The Bridge* had just been awarded *Poetry*'s Helen Haire Levinson Prize.

To Sylvia Beach

Dear Sylvia: [*c.* January 1931] [Farmington]

Thank you so much for your lovely letter. Ada & I loved seeing you both. Ada is miserable about the dinner still. She can't forgive herself for being ill. When, I wonder, will it be again?

Hemingway's arm is much better & he will be able to write in a month or more. Just now he is at "Dry Tortugas" — the middle of the Gulf.

I carry such a delightful impression of Joyce. It is always the same thing. The same impression of beauty in him & out of him. He would laugh & be annoyed if he knew what I think. What I think is that he is like one of those violet-breathing incarnations of the god in that sea-coast morning of the world. Perhaps a heifer or a tree. It is ridiculous to think so.

I cannot possibly afford the Spanish book. Perhaps there is a newer edition of the Relación Anónima & the Andrés de Tapia?[1] But don't bother too much. Dear love to you both.   AMacL

ALS: NjP

1. Because of its potential value to his work on *Conquistador*, M may have been considering the purchase of Joaquín García Icazbalceta, ed., *Colección de documentos para la historia de México* (Mexico: J. M. Andrade, 1858–1866), in which appeared the two eyewitness accounts of the Spanish Conquest M mentions.

To Maxwell Perkins[1]

Dear Mr. Perkins: 4 January 1931 [Farmington]

Coming to Farmington today I found your very kind letter of the 30th which gave me a great deal of pleasure. I have not been within reach of New York since my return from Billings & I must make that my excuse for not having called you.

As to Ernest — he had (a few days before I arrived) a very bad time indeed. After apparently healing, the arm unexpectedly showed an infection which worried him a great deal. And he suffered very real & unrelenting pain over a long time. I went out because I know how his imagination works when his health is concerned & because I thought any normal event such as the arrival of a friend might give him some kind of a date to hold on to. When I got there the pain was largely over & the wound was beginning to heal. The question now, as you know, is the recovery of the nerve of the arm. The surgeon who has my entire confidence (though I am judging only on his manner & personality etc.) thinks there is a 90% chance of recovery. It will be slow & in the meantime Ernest must take it very easy in the head & not easy at all in the arm — i.e. he must exercise the arm as much as he can. If the nerve does not recover of itself an exploratory operation will be necessary. But Dr. Allard is quite confident that things will come along naturally. I think all his friends can do is to keep him cheerful in idleness — a hell of a job. Poor Pauline ——.

While I was in Billings I told Ernest that I had had a very sharp disagreement with Houghton Mifflin about *New Found Land* (my last book) & that when *Conquistador* was finished (one year or two) I would be looking for a publisher & that I liked most Scribners but doubted whether they would like me. He told me he would write you & I felt rather ill at ease because I did not want him to shoulder himself with me because I have no book ready & will have none for at least a year & it seemed rather theoretical for me to offer myself now. But I am very glad he did it if you would yourself be interested. You were very kind to write me and I appreciate it deeply & I will present myself to you when I have a manuscript ready for you to read.

faithfully yours   Archibald MacLeish

ALS: NjP

1. Ernest Hemingway's editor at Charles Scribner's Sons.

To Henry R. Luce[1]

Dear Harry: 16 March 1931 Farmington

Thank you for a very generous & kind note which I know how to value.

I shall wait, then, until I hear from Parker.[2] If it is of great importance to him I shall of course go down in June for a month. I am working very schön now & I am in hopes it will hold. But if he wants it very much I will go.

My idea for the fall was that I would work full time. If I understand your January letter you are doubtful whether you can better my former pay of $5000 a year for half time which was, as you note, *at the rate* of $10,000 a year. May I assume that this means that I would receive $10 000 a year for full time? Or don't you want me for full time? I bring this up now, not to bother you gratuitously, but because I should like to know what I can expect. Indeed I suppose I may say that I am obliged to know, for my position by fall will be pretty precarious. I don't mean that I want a contract or any such tripe. I have complete confidence in you. But I have got to do a certain amount of long division ahead of time. Hope you understand.

Thank you again for your letter. And please ask Parker to give me all the warning he can. yrs always Archie

ALS: TIME

1. Henry Robinson Luce (1898–1967), a member of Yale's Class of 1920 and of Skull & Bones, was cofounder and publisher of Time Inc. 2. Parker Lloyd-Smith, first managing editor of *Fortune;* he died, a suicide, in September 1931.

To Harriet Monroe

Dear Miss Monroe: [*c.* 5 May 1931] [Conway?]

Liberty nothing. I am proud and grateful that you cared enough about anything of mine to devote a piece of your time to it. Very proud.[1]

I'll send you the proof back at once as you ask. And as to the name — its just this. I found out a few years ago that writing prose about what I was also making poetry of, or trying to, had the effect of turning me around so that I got to looking at the outside of what I was doing instead of being inside it. Same thing that happens to me when I read reviews of my own stuff — I get to thinking about my Reputation and my Position and I get to thinking of my work from the audience point of view and that is absolutely fatal to sincere and innocent labor where nothing matters except the labor and what they think of you is utterly unreal. So that having written this piece you have to read and not to print and having been kindly flattered by you into printing it I thought I could short circuit the evil by not signing it. But I suppose that is very childish. Please do as you wish therefore.

Thank you so much for your kind letter and your kindness about this piece.

What a shame Crane didn't get the Pulitzer. Not that the prize would elevate him much. But the cash is still cash. I suppose old Frost ought to have a reward and he is certainly a very deserving and estimable writer. But a prize for a man's collected works is like an LLD at seventy-five.[2] Just a pat on the back. Whereas a prize to a single poem is a prize to a poem. Ah well. . . .   yrs always   AMacL

TLS: ICU

1. Monroe had commented, presumably, on M's essay "Nevertheless One Debt," published in *Poetry* 38 (July 1931), 208–216. 2. Robert Frost's *Collected Poems* had been chosen over Hart Crane's *The Bridge*.

To Harriet Monroe

Dear Miss Munro: [4 June 1931]   [Conway]
    Thanks for the Magazine & for your thought of me & for the nice things you say of my books & for bothering about me in any case.[1] Hadn't, perhaps, thought of my life as so exceptionally sheltered — although Papa Cezanne's was & Joyce's is & Strawinsky's is & it wouldn't so much bother me if I had thought so. Perhaps I was sheltered all that time in the Kotals & up in Tlaxcala & never knew it.[2]
    Prior to my "Fortune" experience I should have agreed with you about the robust demoniac laughter of American Industry. But I've seen more industrialists in the last year than I hope you ever have to look at. And a sadder, stubborner, more timorous, whistle-in-the-graveyard lot never before lived on earth. Ogden Nash — if you mean the New Yorker wise-cracker — is just the boy to do them.
                                    most cordially yrs   AMacL

ALS: ICU

1. Harriet Monroe, "Archibald MacLeish," *Poetry* 38 (June 1931), 150–155, a review of M's life and work. 2. M had journeyed through the Kotal-e Dokhtar Pass in Persia during his Opium Commission trip to that country in the spring of 1926; he had crossed Tlaxcala during his Mexican trip of February 1929.

To Robert N. Linscott

Dear Bob: 4 September [1931]   [Conway]
    We could go on with this forever. I may be wrong of course but it seems to me that you wrote me (sometime before the lump sum offer) that I was to have 10% straight. So that what I was given is really very much below what I would otherwise have had.
    However we won't go on with it. At least I won't. First of all because

I won't be argued into a quarrel with you over matters which have nothing to do with a friendship I very much value.

And secondly because these monetary details are altogether beside the point except in so far as they aggravate my state of mind in re Houghton Mifflin. The important point is that I am, & have been, against high-priced limited editions, that H.M. knew that fact, that H.M. knew that I expressly objected in this case, & that H.M. published & sold a high-priced limited edition without my consent — my *real* consent. You will say that I should have understood the word "limited" to mean high-priced. And of course I should. That is why I admit to having been stupid. But in view of my express rejection of the proposition when it was put to me before, H.M. might very well have been more explicit. It was because of that previous proposition & its rejection that it never occurred to me the book was to sell for more than a dollar & a half, whatever it was called.

As you see, I have no legal ground for complaint. Everything is ship-shape & in writing & duly signed. But that doesn't change my feelings which are pretty well defined.

But that doesn't, I sincerely hope, affect things between you & me. I want very much to see you & get things right with you. So far as H.M. are concerned, they will weep no tears over the loss of one un-profitable poet. But I should weep real ones over the loss of your affec-tion. Please write me a human letter when you can & let's forget all this.

I didn't see Blackbur's review.[1] I see no reviews & I could have spared the reminder that that bastard still breathes. You might have told me of some nice ones.

Mina[2] is sad you can't come. How about the next week end? Ada will be away but I'll be here with the applejack.

yours always   A.

ALS: DLC

1. As R. P. Blackmur does not appear to have reviewed M's *New Found Land*, M is presumably referring to the review of that work by Dudley Fitts in *Hound and Horn* 4 (July–September 1931), 637–641. Blackmur was the magazine's editor. 2. Mina (Kirstein) Curtiss, a friend of the MacLeishes' who had a home in Ashfield, Massa-chusetts, not far from the MacLeish home in Conway.

To Robert N. Linscott

Dear Bob: [*c.* 30 October 1931]   [Conway]

Thank you for a very kind letter. The chance of seeing you in Boston is so slight that I think I had best answer it. I'll try to be as compre-hensible as a very complicated mental state permits.

I realize that my books have cost H.M. money but grateful as I honestly am for their early aid & comfort I don't feel that that fact alone is conclusive. I *did* feel so before New Found Land. But I can't help feeling that had New Found Land appeared in a regular edition & had it been pushed it would have sold extremely well. What reviews I saw were favorable & the book was a book of short poems. As a matter of fact, if Hart Crane is not misleading me, the *Bridge* sold in the same year very very much better. Comparisons are ridiculous but what else is there in this world?

As to the misunderstanding about the format & price of N.F.L. — there is no use going into that. I am sure it was a misunderstanding. I regret it & that's all there is to it.

But the event, & the failure of N.F.L. to sell as it should, & the number of people who have told me or written me that they had no idea where to get my books, & the feeling I can't help having (as a result of the correspondence & interviews prior to the acceptance of N.F.L.) that H.M. were not really very much interested in the book & were rather loath to take it & took it only because of your influence on my behalf — all these things have made me wonder about the future. As some one said — there is only one good publisher & that is the publisher who is excited about your stuff. And I can't feel that H.M. (your kindness in person excepted from all this) is really very enthusiastic about me. After all, books of verse *have* been advertised in America — *have* been pushed. You know & God (if it isn't an anti-climax) knows that I loathe blurbs & have no desire to see my name like Edna Millays with "Immortal Poetry" over it. But there are things a publisher can decently do for a book which the poet can't do — unless the Poet is Amy Lowell & as rich as Amy & as gifted in self-publicizing. And those things H.M. have never done for my books. Because you lose money on a book of verse anyway, you will say. But isn't that a vicious circle?

But this is futile. I certainly can't, & don't wish to, teach H.M. their business. But I have worked on Conquistador for many years. I believe it is going to be a really good poem — but certainly not a popular one. And I want to see it well treated by the publisher — not just issued with an item in a trade paper & allowed to sell itself if it can. (I do not, in that sentence, describe H.M.'s method with verse: but what seems to me to be their method.) Therefore I am now strongly inclined to send it around among the publishers & see if I can find one house really enthusiastic about it — & enthusiastic in terms of those things which prove editorial enthusiasm — money & deeds. If you think I am doing a dishonorable or unwise thing I count on you to tell me. I am not acting in rankor but in pure selfishness. And also with a little feeling that the book is too good for tepid treatment.

Of course it may be that no one will want it. Harpers & Scribners have both written me as has Liveright — or B&L — I forget. But how much they want it I don't know. Perhaps H.M. will really want it. Perhaps they won't. In any event I hope to have a draft in two weeks — reserving the right to make (if necessary) considerable galley proof changes. (This writing in the recesses of hack work is Hell. But we are as poor as the rest of the world this year.)   affly yrs   A.

ALS: DLC

To Maxwell Perkins

Dear Mr. Perkins: 24 November 1931   [New York]

First of all, and more important than anything else (because nothing else is really important about a poem), I am grateful enormously for your understanding of the quality of the poem. I don't mean your liking it. I mean your reason.

As to the rest. . . . I appreciate and admire your scruples about dealing with me in the ambiguous position in which I am now presented to you. Until I have definitely terminated my relation (if so it may be called) with Houghton Mifflin, you do not wish to make an arrangement with me for Scribner's. That seems to me to be entirely right and proper. But at the same time it leaves me somewhat at a loss. I am under no illusions about the market for poetry and I loath the kind of advertising which announces books of Immortal Poetry seven times a year. But I have worked for the best part of three years on *Conquistador,* and with everything I possess, and I am determined that it shall not puddle into oblivion like the rest of my books. In other words I feel that before I definitely exclude one possible channel of publication, I ought to know what terms you would be willing to offer — whether, that is to say, you would be willing to undertake a guaranteed advertising program (or whatever it is called when you are dealing with those writers who are fortunate enough to write novels) etc., etc.

I hope you will not think that I am making an improper request. I am perfectly rotten at all aspects of business and part of my trouble in the past has come from the fact that I was unable to conceive as a matter of business what is clearly nothing else — that I let the whole question ride and that my books merely vanished. I hope that I do not now give the opposite impression. I am not, however it may appear, trying to play one publisher off against the other. I have received no offer from Houghton Mifflin. And I am writing you this letter so hurriedly in part for that reason and in part because, if the poem is to appear on anybody's spring list, it should, I suppose, be placed at once. May I hope to hear from you soon?

I have, unfortunately[,] a luncheon engagement for Friday which I am now trying to break. The lunchee is out of town but I am sure I shall succeed.   Yours faithfully,   Archie MacLeish

TLS: NjP

To Maxwell Perkins

Dear Mr. Perkins: 27 November 1931   [New York]

I have been back and forth over this business, sleeping and waking, ever since Wednesday noon. I am, perhaps unduly, affected by the personal aspects of it on both sides. And I am perhaps too fearful of the situation which might arise as to a selected edition. Realizing how slight a profit any publisher could look forward to making from such a book I cannot help but feel that no publisher could properly be expected to undertake it if he were obliged to pay a considerable sum of money for the doubtful privilege. I do not mean to say that I think Houghton Mifflin would be maliciously obstructive. But I am afraid I do think that they would not make it easy — human nature being no prerogative of poets. I have therefore decided that I ought to publish *Conquistador* through them.

My feeling that I have imposed on you and that my conduct has been lacking in the kind of consistency you have a right to expect from me is not lessened, but very much increased, by the extraordinary decency and consideration you have shown me. I value your letter about the poem more than you would believe. I am humiliated by the course of events and I can only hope that you will not think as ill of me as I think of myself. I can say only this as perhaps having some bearing on the matter — that I did not in any way use my negotiations with you as an instrument in my dealings with Houghton Mifflin. As a matter of fact I have accepted terms from them which are less generous than those you were kind enough to offer. Of your terms they know nothing.

I hope very much we may meet and see something of each other during this winter. Would you be able to get as far down as Sullivan Street[1] one of these evenings?

                    Always faithfully yours,   Archibald MacLeish

TLS: NjP

1. M had an apartment at 182 Sullivan Street, New York City.

To Robert N. Linscott

Dear Bob: [*c.* 14 December 1931]   [New York?]

Thanks for your letter. You should have mine backing water about the jacket by now. I think you are quite right.

I have just received the most curious document from Greenslet. He says that "in the event of a satisfactory success of Conquistador we are to give favorable consideration to your suggestion of a collected edition". Of course that won't do at all as I have just written him. And if he asks you I hope you will assure him that I mean it entirely. To be completely frank there were just two reasons why, having submitted the poem to Scribners[,] I withdrew it and went to HM. The first was Linscott. The second was the fear that if I changed publishers it might be so expensive to get the rights for a collected edition that a collected edition could not be brought out. (This suggestion, you will recall, you made to me.) Perkins felt that the objection was not vital and said Scribners would bring out a selected edition. But since the selected edition was the heart of the matter to me I felt I couldn't take a chance of any kind and I made my decision for that reason — you having told me over the phone that HM would bring out such an edition if Conquistador sold.

I am very much upset over the whole thing as you can well understand. It looks as though there had been no change of heart at all. And I think the only thing to do is to make a flat issue of it. If HM wont specifically agree to publish a selected or collected edition within eighteen months in the event that Conquistador has sold as many copies as some good long poem of the depression era (say Aiken's best sale or something of that sort) then I think we had better kiss and regretfully part.[1] Greenslet may object that that means taking too big a chance. But Scribners or somebody else may be willing to take it and I should be an ass to lose my one chance of making decent terms for the edition.

                                                              Yrs   A.

P. S.   If my state of mind is blind to you just imagine yourself having gone through one of the most difficult decisions conceivable and having made it for a specific reason and then getting that kind of an undertaking — a promise to think favorably in the event of an undefined "success" and at an unnamed date. No by God. You better hold the presses until we get this thing worked out. Jesus Christ. . . . .   A

TLS: DLC

1. *Poems, 1924–1933*, M's first collected edition, was published by Houghton Mifflin Company on 7 December 1933.

To Ernest Hemingway

Dear Ernest: [29 February 1932] [New York]

Forgive me for not writing. I was laid up for ten days & then when I got out there was so much stuff backed up at Fortune I was running around in circles. We seem to have fixed it up so that I can get down to Key West & I am leaving with Mike next Saturday evening. It was swell of you to offer to loan me the money but I have enough — but it was damn swell of you anyway. I am going up to Vassar(!) to lecture on Wednesday & that will pay my fare. God knows what I'll tell them.

I got your letter Saturday morning & went right over to the Empire Trust. They said the Power of Attorney wasn't any good because it didnt specify the Empire Trust. Then they called up the main office & they said the same thing. Then I got them to call up their lawyers & the lawyers said it was Jake. The damn fools! Max came over & identified me & I took out 5,000 out in his presence & bought a cashier's check which I mailed down registered mail to the Farmers Trust. It wouldnt have reached you in Key West by wire until after banking hours & it seemed foolish to spend the $7 on a telegram. I didn't count the balance but the envelope was sealed so I suppose it was all as you left it.

Dos wrote me that you were fine & had caught a sail fish while he was with you. "1919" is swell — much the best thing Dos has done. Have you seen it or shall I bring down the advance copy I have? Also do you want me to bring down any cartridges or fishing tackle or a cheese? I'll bring down a cheese anyway but wire me about the rest if there is anything you think of.

Pauline looked simply lovely when she came to see us. I've never seen her look so lovely. She gets better looking and more beautiful all the time. It was grand to see her.

I am looking forward more than you would ever guess to Key West & seeing you & Dry Tortugas. Thought I'd never get to that place.

Love to you all. Archie

ALS: JFK

To Ernest Hemingway

Dear Pappy: [7 April 1932] [New York]

[W]ell the stick has stuck. Please don't say anything about it because it might make an already bad situation worse but they have written me this morning to say that there will be no more [Carson, Pirie, Scott & Company] dividends. The result is a fact about as hard as any fact could be. Which is that Ada etc are dependent on what I can earn here and that my mother may be before the summer is over. So that my worst fears have been abundantly realized. I suppose I have known it all along. I suppose I have always known that I couldn't really go. But that doesn't make it any easier now that it has happened. Tortugas was just a taste of what Africa with you and Mike and Charles might have been and it makes it just that much harder.[1] Well. . . . what is there to say. You know or if you don't you ought to how much I appreciate your wanting me. And you ought to know too how much I want to see that country. Its true I am no great hunter. But it wasn't the hunting I thought of but the country and being there with you three.

Your letter has just come.[2] Which makes the above doubly hard to write. I didn't mean about the fire and the island when I wrote you. I meant the emotions I felt as I was trying to write you about Tortugas. But I understand what you mean. I suppose we don't see eye to eye about action. I hadn't thought of it before. It is true that I am not particularly adventurous and that the few dangerous things I have ever done like along the Marne and the trip alone up through Mexico I took very seriously even though I should have liked to take them in some other way and that I have always had to try very hard not to be afraid although it is not dying I have ever been afraid of. But I hadn't thought of that in connection with the fire because I thought the fire was accidental and that the obvious thing to do was to stop it and I knew from the bad grass fires up at Conway that they will burn back and around. The thing about the fire that troubled me was that you felt what I did was in some way a criticism and I hadn't meant it so in any way. Indeed the thing that troubled me always was that you seemed to be on the defensive against me and not to trust me. I know that you do not believe in trusting people but I thought I had given you about every proof a man could of the fact of my very deep and now long lasting affection and admiration for you and it puzzled me that you should be so ready to take offense at what I did. I think it is perhaps in the very fact of the relation between us that we do not see eye to eye. To me what we do together is only an excuse or an occasion for being together and it is the being together which is important. And this is all the more important to me because we see each other so seldom and because you are, as you know, one of two or three men whom I can now still count my friends. So that it is very hard for me to think of us as being competetive because there is nothing to compete for that begins to be as important as just being there. I know that I have a very strong competetive streak which I developed at Yale and which I dislike but it is true whether you will believe it or not that there is nothing we have ever done together (except perhaps rouleing to Chartres!) in which I have not implicitly in myself acknowledged your superiority. And that includes in addition to skeeing, shooting and fishing writing. I do not say this to humble myself or to make flattering statements but because it is true and because I think the competition you feel comes from something else — from some uneasiness between us which I would give a very great deal to know the source of and to remove.

This is not the kind of talk you like nor do I like it. But since you have spoken of it I feel I must tell you what I think. I won't refer to it again.

I understand absolutely about the Saturday Review and I'll tell Canby. The book[3] doesn't need friends and never will. I wanted to write about it because there was so much I wanted to say but no reviewer could fail to see how grand it is.

Stewart has gone to Hollywood for good — i.e. for several years or so I am told. And I haven't seen anyone. Not even Mike. We have missed each other about five times. Hope to see him tomorrow. Give my best love to Pauline.

Best to Charles   yours always   Archie

TLS: JFK

1. In late February 1932, M had joined Hemingway, Mike Strater, and Gus Pfeiffer — Pauline's uncle — on a fishing trip to Dry Tortugas, during which trip the fire to which M refers below occurred. 2. Hemingway's letter to M, and M's letter preceding it, do not appear to have survived. 3. *Death in the Afternoon*, published earlier in the year, about which M had planned to contribute an essay to *The Saturday Review of Literature*.

To Ezra Pound

Dear Pound: [*c.* 20 May 1932]   [New York?]

Farrar has just called up to say that your agent reached him and that the contract for the Cantos[1] has gone through as per cable plus an advance. I can't tell you how delighted I am about the whole thing. American publishers are such goddam fools in general. But Farrar and his man Nash saw the light at once and when I timidly said they ought at least to give you ten, twelve and a half and fifteen they replied they would give you straight fifteen and be proud to do it.

I was afraid you might think my wire officious as you had never authorized me to act for you. But when Abernethy came in and told me the situation I decided I'd take that risk. Its more important that the Cantos be published in a form we can afford to buy than that you think well of my intervention — and you will probably think the worst as usual.

I assume you will write me to give me hell when you get around to it but please don't make it too long. For one thing I am very anxious to get your cracks at Conquistador which I sent you a month or so ago. You once told me I couldn't take criticism. Well, I can take yours and like it.

You can take some comfort in the fact that you are making the reputation of a publishing house at the same time that you are making whatever small amt of dough a great poet gets while on this ball of whatever.   yrs   A.MacL

TLS: YCAL

1. Pound's *A Draft of XXX Cantos*, published by Farrar & Rinehart in March 1933.

To H. Phelps Putnam

Dear Phelps: [*c*. June 1932?]   [New York?]

[N]o I didn't ask you but I leap to find out. You are the only honest man I know who also knows poetry. Why didn't it [*Conquistador*] ring your bell? I have had plenty of cracks. Pound wrote me that it was damn bad and Tate informed the world that although I was skilful enough I was morally obsolete.[1] And neither comment disturbed me much because I know myself the poem isn't damn bad and I also know why Pound says (but does not think) it is. While as for Tate I simply have to confess that I don't understand his vocabulary. He apparently means that the poem is written in the past tense. But I'd like the truth out of you because I'd like to know how the mind of a man I respect reacts to the piece. I feel pretty sure about it myself. I have had to read it aloud a good deal and it stands up to that and the comment of the socialogues that it isn't about OUR TIME hasn't made much of a dent in my convictions because whether they know it or not it is a lot more about OUR TIME than most of the daily papers but your sayings about it would be treasured.   yrn   A.

TLS: YCAL

1. Allen Tate, "Not Fear of God," *The New Republic* 71 (1 June 1932), 77–78.

To Ezra Pound

Dear Pound: [*c*. June 1932]   Conway

Well, as you say, that's that and I'm sorry for it because there is no man living whose support I should rather have.

Naturally I don't see the surface traces of the Cantos on Conquistador as you see them. It would be odd if the author of the Cantos didn't see them, however. There never was an artist whose work did not show the marks of his deepest admirations. You for one. As you admit. I suppose the question is whether a work is bad so long as those marks are visible and only good when they have been suppressed or amputated or gelded (for unless the admiration ceases the force will be there.) You apparently would say Yes. I should say No on the basis of your own poetry. But I admit that the attempt must always be to work freer and freer of what one loves, and that much of your criticism of me I take to heart. Adding that Conquistador seems much freer to me than it apparently does to you. But that difference is natural.

You should be warned — I don't know that it will make any difference to you, but you should be warned that Farrar and R. have asked me to write something about the Cantos for their catalogue and that I have complied.[1] You would probably prefer the praise of someone whose work you respected. If so just instruct them. I shall thoroughly understand.

Thanks, and quite honestly, for the two pages.   A.MacL.

TLS: YCAL

1. M was one of fifteen authors who, at the invitation of Ford Madox Ford, contributed to a pamphlet entitled *The Cantos of Ezra Pound: Some Testimonies by Ernest Hemingway, Ford Madox Ford, T. S. Eliot, Hugh Walpole, Archibald MacLeish, James Joyce and Others.* It was issued by Farrar & Rinehart at the same time as *A Draft of XXX Cantos.*

To Ernest Hemingway

Dear Pappy   [*c.* 1 June 1932]   [New York]

[S]orry to be so long answering fine letter about magnificent fish also beautiful photographs of fish standing on heads and Charles's Wain[1] (or Charles's Wax or whatever we shall probably agree to call it) and Pappy in fine postures with and without fish but with Havana and water and ships and everything else very fine and useful. I have been dragging my ass around finishing up MacLeish on Housing[2] and finishing up MacLeish too for the matter of that and I haven't had much time for writing. I wish I could have gone down. I wish to God I could have.

I got the money out of the bank all kakie kakie. I don't know how much you are supposed to have in there. It looked to me like 7500 left after I took this last out but I didn't count it. Might be 7000. Will count if you wish.

What you say about Africa plans has all my interest. On the one hand, if you don't go this summer you may not go for a long time because it looks to us experts in the financial ass-hole of the goddam universe as though there were going to be financial piles for the next century. But on the other hand god only knows what is going to break this fall. Almost anything. Its going to be very very interesting to see and watch and perhaps a bit painful too. I wouldn't know what to say in your place. I think you would not enjoy it very much being out of touch with things just at that time. But then you don't worry the way I do and it might be all right. I am trying to be very noble and not let my judgment warp around the fact that I might be able to go another year. I guess I really think you ought to go now because it will certainly be a long time before everything will clear up.

Give my love to Paulinos and the babes. What are your plans? Max and I talked about the book and he thinks it is the best thing you have done. He is crazy about it. So is Dos. Dos is crazy about it. Fortune is running some bull-fight photos with dope provided largely by Franklin[3] and they are going to put in a reference [*MacLeish wrote in the margin:* Caption under picture says "A Three-Act Tragedy. . . . Ernest Hemingway calls it in his great forthcoming *Death in the Afternoon*" (Max says this is O.K.. They have already announced the title. This appears in July)] to the book. I haven't seen it but they say it will be good to stir up interest and may make a few sales that wouldn't know about the book anyway — if there are any such.   yrs   affly always   A.

TLS: JFK

1. A British term for the Big Dipper; possibly a play on the name of Hemingway's frequent hunting and fishing companion Charles Thompson. 2. M's six-part *Fortune* series on housing, published between February and July 1932, was republished by Harcourt, Brace & Company, on 27 October 1932, as *Housing America*, "by The Editors of 'Fortune.' " 3. Sidney Franklin, the American matador who had achieved success in the bullrings of Spain and who was the subject of an appendix to Hemingway's *Death in the Afternoon*.

To Louis Untermeyer

Dear L: [22 June 1932] [New York?]

Whathehell! Your taste has been through hell-water before and since, and you know and trust it. Why shouldn't you? It isn't the lyric as such I object to. Its just the synthetic lyric manufactured for the effect. Lets take O westron wynde for the true lyric. It is a once-and-for-ever utterance which is at one and the same time the true, the perfect vocable and the essential power of speech. It *says* entirely. It is a complete saying — as true poetry is always more complete saying than the most realistic prose. It does not seek to charm. It does not seek to delight. It does not seek to move. It is speech perfectly speaking with all the powers heard and imagined of speech — of speech bringing into one net all the memories of the senses. For the memories of the senses are caught in words. But what is Millay? Millay is prettiness conscious of its own prettiness being very, very pretty. I don't deny the prettiness.

I don't deny the lilt. I don't even deny the mist of emotion. What I do deny is the speech. Nothing she ever wrote or ever could write has the essential, vivid, for-itself-only power of speech. It isn't speech. It is poems. Made to be poems. And the same thing a thousand times more so is true of the little Hey-diddle-dillon-the-spirit-is-willin'.[1] He has arts but no art.

I suppose I could make more sense — and open myself to more dangerous attack — by quoting masters. I should have to admit that I don't much like Keats — that I think the quality of speech has been absent from English poetry (occasional exceptions) for three hundred years. Hopkins sometimes hit it. And so on. But there isn't time or chance by mail. As for Pound and his Dunning — Pound is a unicorn who turns into an ass every time you look at him too closely. He should never be approached except when he is being himself — that is to say when he is being a poet.

All the above is very cock-sure. I have to be to save space. Accept the humility herewith and the regards of   AMacL

TLS: InU

1. George Dillon (1906–1968), American poet and editor (1937–1950) of *Poetry: A Magazine of Verse*. His 1931 book *The Flowering Stone* had won the 1932 Pulitzer Prize for poetry.

To Allen Tate

Dear Tate: 9 July 1932   [New York]

I have read with admiration your *Comment* upon Crane in the last number of *Poetry*.[1] You have acquitted yourself there (and elsewhere) of a duty you had every reason to accept and you have acquitted yourself with an integrity and a devotion which we all must honor.

But it is not to approve what requires no approval from me or from any other that I write you. I ask elucidation.

You refer to the poet's "first problem, which is to define the limits of his personality and to discover its moral properties in an appropriate symbolism." I take it "first problem" here means "principle problem." And if I am right in so understanding, I ask you why this should be so — why it should be the principle problem of the poet to define the limits of his personality and to establish appropriate symbols for its moral properties? I do not ask this as a challenge or because I wish to precipitate a literary controversy illuminated by the publication of letters written for third persons to read. I ask it because you have lucidly and explicitly stated a position which has, I believe, the adherence of many intelligent and honest writers in our generation and because I believe you can answer my question.

For the sentence to me is dark. I do not understand why it should be true. I do not understand why the personality of the poet should be the arena in which he is to work nor why the establishment in appropriate symbols of its moral properties should be his first preoccupation. Indeed it seems to me that the personality of the poet is merely the instrument, the voice, and that its qualities will enough color his poetry without a conscious and introspective labor of self-exploration and self-definition. That is to say, I suppose, that I do not think of the poet's personality as the subject matter of his poetry, nor of the moral properties of his personality as having primary value. All that he is will color all that he does but what he does must be distinguishable from what he is. For otherwise there will result that confusion of workman and work which ends in the unachieving gesture of the mirror.

I do not wish to appear to you too naive. I have certainly considered this matter before. I once wrote a poem called *Einstein* which was a poem of the definition of the limits of a man's personality in its distinction from what was not himself, and his attempts to communicate beyond himself by revery and music and religion and analysis and his final failure, which threw back "Himself to answer him . . ." But I wrote it feeling that the peculiar consciousness of my hero was surely disastrous and that only the ecstasy which annulled him for himself could bring about the harmony he desired.

I suppose in a way the question reduces itself to one of those futile questions — futile because the vocabulary has been rendered ambiguous — of the function of the poet. People have always been puzzled by the poetic activity. It has seemed to them very strange that generation after generation of poets should make and leave their images of an earth, and a life in the earth, which earth and which life would long survive them. Why should they scratch upon the rocks: Here I saw rain; Here I loved; Here a child died? Why should they record such facts as the fact that tilled earth has a certain smell, that dark comes late in summer, that men at midnight think of such and such things? (I tried to write of this in *Epistle To Be Left In The Earth* in one of my books). There is no answer. The compulsion is strange. And the accomplishment is also strange, for the poignancy of a poem seems curiously to depend in very large part upon its faithfulness to the earth and to mortal life and not upon its faithfulness to the poet's personality. I say poignancy. I mean also beauty. "That the small rain down can rain . . ."[2]

But attempts have nevertheless been made to explain this activity of the poet. And one explanation has been that the poet's perceptions of the world had a value altogether beyond their power to delight or to move as the world itself clearly and purely seen delights or moves. And that that value came from their use by the poet as the alphabet of a kind of knowledge and wisdom he (and often he alone) possessed. Or, more obliquely, as the equivalent of his personal quality which personal quality, since he was a poet, must be both fine and desirable. From this attitude sprang Imagism which, with true Poundian muddle-headedness, had the cart not only before the horse but hind-side-to as well. To the Imagist the sensory world existed as a kind of water-color box for the poet's uses and the poet, having "something to express," expressed it in assorted images. The consequence, to Pound, was the mutilation of a great talent and to most of the rest of them an apt amateurishness which is now unreadable.

The evil, as I see it, lay not in the return to a sensory poetry (which was right) but in the attempt to graft that sensory poetry upon the Romantic verb. Byron (with help) rediscovered the individuality and the personality of the poet and, in the midst of the Bourgeois-individualist revolution, was carried thereby to glory. Pound, in revolt, saw the evils of the Romantic method as the XIXth Century had worked it out but was blind to the fundamental Romantic vice because he was himself at heart a strutting Romantic with an ego exaggerated to the Falstaffian proportions we now observe. (E.P. stands for English Poetry in London: for Ezra Pound in Rapallo.)

And even in the generation after Pound the ambiguity remains. And the confusion increases. Irony and satire are introduced and the anti-Romantic acidity of Mr. Eliot's early work. But the Romantic personality remains. Romanticism dissects itself with all the horrors of what has been called, I believe, Realism. But it dissects itself, anatomizes itself, before a mirror. Where its close-up agony produces a new and more Romantic Romanticism. For here the personality of the poet is the total arena and his subjective fears and deaths the rout. If I may again refer to my own work, I once wrote a much bespatten piece called the *Hamlet of A. MacLeish* by way of commentary. But it was not so taken.

The present task, therefore, seems to me to be the task of destroying the Romantic personality and reestablishing the distinction between the workman and his work. We are mortal. That is a fact. It is not a particularly sad fact. But we must be guided by it. We are mortal and we are poets. Which is to say that we perceive the world and that we have the power, according to our fortune, to fix momentarily or for many generations, the aspects of the world we see. It is enough to do that and to do it with self-forgetfulness and humility. Why should we assume other tasks not ours? Why should we regret the lack of an ordered society as Mr. Eliot regrets it and feel that we must string the fences before we climb the ground? Why must we wail, as Mr. Pound wails, that no one accepts responsibility for the literary (meaning the intellectual meaning the social) health of England? The literary health of England be damned. Pound would set up the statues and then instruct the people how they should feel about the statues. Eliot would delight an audience and also control the reactions of the audience in its delight. And the job is too much for any man and no part of the poet's task in any case. And the result is that Eliot writes despondent editorials in the *Criterion* instead of writing poems and Pound abuses editors and officials and younger poets and imaginary censors to give himself a frantic sense of notoriety in place of the fame he might have enjoyed.

So I return to my question. Why is the problem you name the poet's first problem? Why is it not the poet's first problem to learn his *metier* and his second to serve it? You are in a position to influence deeply the course of American poetry in our generation and thereby the course of English poetry, for the power is now here. I wish you might influence it away from the poet and toward his work.

May I congratulate you again upon your book.[3]

Yours faithfully,   Archibald MacLeish

TLS: NjP

1. Allen Tate, "Hart Crane and the American Mind," *Poetry* 40 (July 1932), 210–216.
2. A line from the anonymous English lyric "Western Wind." 3. Tate's *Poems: 1928–1931* (1932).

To John Peale Bishop

Dear John: [*c.* September 1932] [Conway]

There is some curious chronological connection between our lives. I came up here on the first September after ten months of solid Fortune work with a bad case of buck fever. I had no idea what would happen when I started to work again. I was moreover in receipt of a letter from Pound containing a savage attack on *Conquistador* & on my work in general. And I had not heard from you. I could only assume from your silence that you had nothing to say of the poem which you thought it desirable to tell me.

You can imagine, if you remember your letter — & I trust you do — what it meant under those circumstances to hear from you & to hear from you in such terms. As you well know I have thought of you as my poetic conscience for almost ten years. You have one of the surest ears

255

& certainly the purest sense of poetry itself — the thing poetry; not its contemporary mode — in our time. And you have the apparatus of criticism to make these things effective. In addition to which you are primarily the poet. It is impertinent of me — or would be — to suggest that I make use of you. You know that it is not that I suggest. But it is against your imagined attitude that I have long been accustomed to try what seemed to me doubtful & upon your imagined judgment to accept or reject. That is I have not made you as critic but you as poet serve me. This is unexpectedly difficult to express but I think you will understand what I mean. It is, after all, fairly Celtic I suppose. What I wish to say is this — that your letter constitutes an actual vindication of what, so far as certain matters of rhythm & line go, I had assumed you to feel during the three years the poem was in construction. And goes much beyond anything I had dared to hope. For your generosity in writing it I am eternally grateful.

The poem you send me has a new fine length of phrase which is distinctly your own & comparable to the nobility of phrase of your prose. It seems to me a severely just & truly eloquent expression. I took the liberty of sending it to the editors of the Hound & Horn (a sort of sequel to *The Dial* but more special) saying I had no right to submit it & they wrote me to say they wished you had submitted it to them.[1] Shall I do so?

I had hoped we should meet this fall & here. When?

yours always   A.

ALS: NjP

1. Bishop's poem "Perspectives Are Precipices" was published in *Hound and Horn* 6 (January–March 1933), 286–287.

To John Peale Bishop

Dear John: [*c.* April 1933]   [New York]

I have meant to write you all this month — indeed I have meant to write you for a longer time than that — about your dress-makers story.[1] I thought it was grand and never more so than in final dismemberment. For even after Ingersoll[2] had had it hacked to pieces and patched up fore and aft the vrai Bishop stood out like the bones of divinities among the disjecta membra of sheep on an Irish fell. Why he did not run it as was I shall never know. I have decided that there is some inherent blindness which prevents me from understanding the editorial function for Fortune seems to be well edited — at least it pleases its public which is I suppose the test — and yet most of its editing in process seems to me inanely dull.

256

However I imagine you have long since lost all interest in the piece — provided you have been paid which I assume you have. Were you not planning to come home this summer? Or where did I dig up that idea? The Murphies are here restoring a few of the geodetic points of our lost topography. But otherwise the scattering is still complete. Indeed I have given up all hope of time's ever bringing our other world together again. Time bringeth all things except its own patterns. I become more and more insocial. Seeing practically no one except the utter strangers of this office and the two quite unknown young men with whom I share a house up the Hudson. That is we share the rent. We rarely meet. Ada and the children are at Conway where I go as often as I can afford the trip. The smell of a Porto Rican cigarette brings back the plane tree leaves on the Avenue Malakoff. I remember standing with you on a grilled iron balcony outside the apartment in the Square Alboni. It is very distressing to find that all my nostalgia is for a few years and a foreign city. Well, I offer you gratuitously this: that however you may sometimes chafe — if you do — under the ropes which halter you to the Department of Seine and Oise you are nevertheless fortunate because if you were here you would have taken a journalistic job of some kind and you would have lost your freedom of mind as I have. Your poverty, if you suffer it, will fix your body but leave your pen free. Mine has taken both. However I suppose I am peevish to complain about it. We have absolutely nothing now but what I earn here and if we were now across the valley from you we should be seriously at a loss. But it has meant that I have written nothing for a year. Which I cannot endure.

When do your poems appear?[3] I remember them so gratefully — particularly the poems of the war. I do not mean that I think them better. But that they stand nearer somehow. I was told that they were appearing in an American magazine but I have been unable to find them.

I hope you will give my love to Margaret. I wish I might hear from you. The arid industrialism of American letters and American men of letters chaps my soul. Your friend Mr. Wilson has taken them through Humanism into Communism. Even Mr. Pound has written a short book on Economic theory[4] — of which he is as innocent as the well-beloved apostle. He is of course, as always, a voice crying in the wilderness. He has discovered the thirty-hour week. And of course no one in America understands him. Only the American Legion, the American Federation of Labor and the National Association of Advertising Men have thus far supported the thirty hour week and it is a very novel idea — certainly not over twenty years old. Pound is really such a bleeding fool when he is doing anything except writing verse. Have you by any chance read a little masterpiece called How To Read? It is Eliot's Five Foot Shelf⁵ cut down to Five Inches. Showing how much smarter Pound is. It is about great poets. There are practically no first rate poets in Pound's list but still that would seem to be a minor weakness. I expect his next will be How To Dance or How to Vote Republican. The man has sheep herder's madness. I wish he would stick to Cantos. I kidded Johnny Farrar into publishing the Cantos here. They are to come out this fall. Odd combination — Farrar and Pound. But Pound was very nice about it. He tells me I took Conquistador from him. I dare say the Cantos are all in terza rima with assonance instead of rima. They must be. After all. . . . .   yours always   A

TLS: NjP

1. "The Dressmakers of France," *Fortune* 6 (August 1932), 17–21ff. 2. Ralph McA. Ingersoll, managing editor of *Fortune*. 3. Bishop's *Now With His Love* (New York: Charles Scribner's Sons, 1933). 4. Pound's *ABC of Economics* (London: Faber & Faber, 1933). 5. The Harvard Classics series known as such was edited by Charles William Eliot (1834–1926), the long-time president of Harvard University.

To Ernest Hemingway

Dear Ambos Mundos:¹   [31 May 1933]   [New York]

I can only go backward by going forward and anyway what do you care about ten days in England² where there were if anything more English than I can conveniently remember and a hell of a lot of the island itself which I had the more or less bad fortune to see from the air over one whole Sunday when young bucko Selfridge³ without any previous warning that I can recall hoisted me into the sky on the rumble seat of a Puss Moth (imagine any other country calling a machine a Puss Moth) and set me down at Cambridge and then hopped me somewhere into the west counties and set me down for tea and then eventually hopped me back to London. Then after that I had the bad luck to go across to Paris on the train the day before Good Friday so that every other bleeding tripper on the tight little isle was eating buns in my face so as not to have to eat that horrible French food. I had enough. By Yee I had enough. And when I got to the Gare de Nord (North Station) I almost kissed the taxi driver but he thought I was an Englishman too and told me he had worked in England seven years and if I could have gotten out I would have. And then when we got down to the Riviera the goddam Malta fleet was lying off every port between Saint Tropez and Jooan the Pines and at San Raphael damn if a launch didn't pull along side and let off a smartly dressed naval aide who pulled himself to attention and saluted me and me in

258

a dirty blue set of dungarees with half my lunch in my cheek and he thought he was going to find a whole boat load of fine American girls and cocktails and I wasn't even polite to him and Ada gave me Hell but I had had enough of the English I had had enough. Of the English. Anyway Gerald's boat is fine.[4] It is built like a fishing boat with all the money in the hull where it belongs and in the decks and only light wood painted partitions inside except that Sara has had comfortable beds put in and there is a bathtub but you can't use that because it takes too much water. The only trouble is that with a crew of five you can't lift a finger and you just sit around and eat. But she sails fine and she is big enough to take anything and Vladimir much to my what do you call it was perfectly willing to go out in a Mistral and we did twice. His only trouble is that he keeps the motor going all the time to charge the battery because the frigidaire takes so much juice. Ada calls it a bateau à frigidaire. But it was a fine trip and we got a lot of rest and came back looking a little more like something you would choose than when we went away. When I got back I saw those stories in Scribners[5] and I will salute the orb and say that if old Pappy is going back then that is the way every young man on live would give his pants to be going. You are right about the Swiss stories. They are comprehensible. They are goddam comprehensible. And then too they are swell. They are very swell. Also they have the horsepower. They kept young man Kirstein awake all one night. He says so himself. You have no greater tribute than what poor Mr. Kirstein is forced to ejaculate. But I'll never convince you of that and I don't think I'll try. Mr. Kirstein is now writing about the ballet. Later on he will write about some other subject.

Mike [Strater] has moved out of his ten thousand dollar apartment and hopes to sublet for six. Next winter he is going to Arizona because of Maggie's sinus. Maggie and the children have been sick for the last three months straight and Mike has been playing nurse and he has had enough. He is going to Arizona.

Dos has sailed for the still vexed Antibbies. I saw him one evening. He looked like hell.[6] Very small in the face and with very big eyes and kind of yellow. Also Katie[7] not looking too well. They do need sun. Dos was sick about not getting down to Cuba but they told him at Johns Hopkins he couldn't lift a hand for a couple of months and he thought some of those fish mightnt get into the boat without a bit of a lift.

As for me — well its the same old hellofit. I am now doing a story on Morgan, a story on the Port of New York Authority and a story on Marshall Fields all for the August issue. And I can't even get to

Conway for every weekend. Its lousy luck. And we are all getting older. How is the novel?⁸ God I'd like to see a bit of it. Love to the beautiful Mrs. H. and to all your fine children and to you

Archie

TLS: JFK

1. The name of Hemingway's hotel in Havana, Cuba. 2. M had gone abroad to work on a *Fortune* story on the American-born Harry Gordon Selfridge, "the merchant prince of Oxford Street." 3. Presumably a son of Harry Gordon Selfridge. 4. *Weatherbird*, a hundred-foot schooner designed and built for the Murphys by Vladimir Orloff. 5. Hemingway's "A Clean, Well-Lighted Place," "Homage to Switzerland," and "Give Us a Prescription, Doctor" (the last later retitled "The Gambler, the Nun, and the Radio") had appeared in, respectively, the March, April, and May 1933 issues of *Scribner's Magazine*. 6. Dos Passos had suffered an attack of rheumatic fever. 7. Katharine "Katy" Smith, Mrs. Dos Passos. 8. Hemingway was in fact working on a new book of short stories, *Winner Take Nothing*, which was published in October 1933 and dedicated, with deliberate ambiguity, to "A. MacLeish."

To the Editor of The New Republic¹

Sir: [c. 8 June 1933]   Conway

Mr. Max Eastman's opinions about Mr. Hemingway's *Death In The Afternoon* are his own business. They follow logically from his admission that, for him, "confessions of honor" are the true poetry of this generation. At that price he has a right to them.

But Mr. Max Eastman's statements of fact about the author of the book in question are another matter. On two occasions in the course of his article, once when he chooses to contrast Mr. Hemingway with the ex-heavyweight champion and once when he resorts to the current literary gossip, he implies that Mr. Hemingway as a man is lacking in masculinity. His arch phrase is: "It is of course a commonplace that Hemingway lacks the serene confidence that he *is* a full-sized man."

If Mr. Max Eastman were the only critic to publish this scurrility — a scurrility which in another generation would have been reserved for the private and shame-faced snickers of literary envy — I should not write this letter. For certainly Mr. Hemingway needs no defense against Mr. Max Eastman at my hands. But unfortunately Mr. Max Eastman is not alone. His remark is quite accurate: his gossip *is* a commonplace — a commonplace among the young sensitives, the old humanitarians and all the rest of the literary impotent to whom Mr. Hemingway's style and Mr. Hemingway's vividness and Mr. Hemingway's vitality are an implicit reproach. Unable either to endure his prose or to disparage it (but only to imitate it) these persons have resorted to the one solace they could find — the whisper that Mr. Hemingway's artistic virility proceeds, by some psychoanalytic hocus-pocus, from the fact that Mr. Hemingway himself believes himself unvirile. Precisely why that unction should have flattered the critic soul I do not pretend to say: it is still Mr. Hemingway's books and not Mr. Hemingway's glands which condemn his critics. But the fact remains that the libel has been spread, that it is a libel of such sort that the victim cannot defend himself against it, and that its publication now and at length in the *New Republic* demands notice.

I therefore beg the privilege of your space for a statement which, one would have thought, neither your magazine nor any other magazine would ever need to carry. I have known Mr. Hemingway intimately for a great many years. I do not know what constitutes confidence of virility in Mr. Max Eastman's mind. I do know that I have seen Mr. Hemingway in positions of considerable danger once at sea, once in the mountains and once on a Spanish street. I have also seen other men in positions of danger both in war and out of it. Being myself in no way remarkable for courage I have had occasion painfully to regard their conduct. No other man has ever impressed me as strongly as has Mr. Hemingway with his complete confidence in his own courage, nor has any other man more completely justified that confidence in the event.

Of those more personal evidences of virility to which Mr. Eastman so daintily and indirectly refers I have no personal knowledge. I refer him however to the birth records of the cities of Paris and Kansas City where he can satisfy his curiosity in secret.

Archibald MacLeish

TL-Dr: JFK

1. This letter, which Bruce Bliven of *The New Republic* declined to print, was written in response to Max Eastman's "Bull in the Afternoon," *The New Republic* 75 (7 June 1933), 94–97, a review of *Death in the Afternoon*.

To Allen Tate

Dear Tate: [*c*. July 1933]   [New York]

Since there is nothing more shameful than ingratitude for excellence I am ashamed of my failure to write you about the Hound and Horn poem of last spring.[1] It is a noble piece of work and alive and moving and I do congratulate you on it. I saw it first after I got home from England in late May. I have written Bishop about it at length but that does not discharge the obligation. It seems to me much the best thing you have done of which I have any knowledge. It ought to make you very happy.

The enclosed of Ernest and his enormous feesh may please you. You need not send it back as I have several. Did you happen to see the shocking Eastman piece against Hem in the New Republic a month ago or so? Or did it not shock you? No one else seemed to read it as I read it. Perhaps there is something wrong with old Mac too. But it infuriated me to the point where I wrote Bliven a letter he refused to print. Some day I am going to run my neck away out and take a crack at the use of bogus psychology as an excuse for personal attacks on honest writers. Not however in the N.R.. Debates in the N.R. seem to run out to warm water. Although I must say Mr. Gold keeps the acid content up.[2] My Frescoes seem to have been successful at least in so far as the penetration of the Communist hide is concerned. Did you by any chance get a copy I told John Day to send you? If you didn't let me know and I'll send one along.

How is the Lee book going?[3] And when are you coming to New York? And are you going to let me know when you come? Or are you not? yrs etc. AMacL

Malcolm [Cowley] just called me up at this juncture to say he had another poem of yours he liked better. Please send it to me to read.

TLS: NjP

1. Tate's "Aeneas at Washington," *Hound and Horn* 6 (April–June 1933), 445–446. The poem was a companion piece to another poem by Tate, "Aeneas at New York: To Archibald MacLeish," which had appeared in *The New Republic* 73 (14 December 1932), 125. 2. Michael Gold's "Out of the Fascist Unconscious," a review of M's *Frescoes for Mr. Rockefeller's City* (New York: John Day Company, 1933), had appeared in *The New Republic* 75 (26 July 1933), 295–296. Gold, a communist, detected in *Frescoes* a "mystic nationalism" that was, he said, the "first stage of the true fascist mind" and reflective of M's "unconscious fascism." 3. Tate had been contemplating a biography of Robert E. Lee, but it was never published.

To the Editor of The New York Times

20 September 1933   Washington, D.C.

Regret to inform you I did not marry Miss Lofting in Vienna yesterday, having passed the day quite comfortably in New York and being, moreover, eminently satisfied with Miss Hitchcock, who, I hope, reciprocates. Miss Lofting was presumably married by a gifted young man who spells my name Archibald MacLiesh, instead of MacLeish, and who had the misfortune to break his or my back in Austria last Spring. Mr. MacLiesh also writes verse which, fortunately for me, promises to be good. He has also, fortunately for me, a middle name, which he will learn to use. It would be a kindness if you would restore me to my own wife, who is an excellent soprano and mother.[1]

Archibald MacLeish

P-TEL: NYT

1. This wire, published in *The New York Times* on September 21, was accompanied by a note correcting a story in the *Times* the day before. The person whose marriage to Miss Lofting had been reported was Archibald Fleming MacLiesh, who, as a student at Princeton University in 1931, had won an undergraduate playwriting prize for his comedy *Three Artists and a Lady*. MacLiesh's subsequent works were published under the name Archibald Fleming.

To Ezra Pound

Dear Ezra: [*c.* January 1934?] [New York]

Farrar: Says what is holding him up is working out terms of contract because book being smaller book for which he can only get smaller sum of money he can't make same terms as before.[1] Believe it or not. Anyway he is still alive and still intent on doing the cantos and I am the horse fly to sit on his arse until he does.

Yale: I shall immediately transmit your final instructions. They ought to jump at the Fenellosa volume.[2] If not I'll try on the others. Went up there and had a long talk with them. They then thought (before your letters) that How To Read was too light for them. I told them they were crazy. But you yourself prefer to use them if at all for something else. Anyway they are crazy to have you on their list. Which is another kind of insanity and a more useful one.[3]

Myself: For Christ's sake lay off the abuse when things go slow. I'll do everything I can regardless of your liver. But I don't like to be cursed and I have no intention whatever of holding onto the shitty end of one of your famous correspondences. I know what you think of me and frankly I don't give a good goddam. You have praised too many really rotten writers for your condemnations to go very deep. What I am interested in is your poetry and fixing things up so that you can go on writing it. And I want neither thanks nor the opposite for that. I merely want to be told as civilly as possible what I can do in your behalf and then I want a little patience while I try to do it — you remembering that I am earning my living eight and ten hours a day in this boiler factory and attempting to write my own rotten stuff on the side. If you don't like that you can go to Hell. But as long as you will let me and will make it in any way possible for me to do so I shall go ahead attempting to find you publishers.

The above does not of course refer to what you may say about me in print for the public. You may go on damning me there to your heart's content and I shall still be glad to do what I can. The above refers merely to private communication which I have to read because of your goddam system of mixing up valuable information with it.

Archie MacLeish

TLS: YCAL

1. Pound's *Eleven New Cantos*, published by Farrar & Rinehart in October 1934. 2. Probably a reference to Ernest Fenollosa's *The Chinese Written Character as a Medium for Poetry*, which, with a foreword and notes by Pound, was first published in London by S. Nott in 1936. 3. Pound's *ABC of Reading*, an expanded version of his *How to Read* (London: Desmond Harmsworth, 1931), was published by Yale University Press in September 1934.

To Robert N. Linscott

Dear Bob: [c. January 1934?]   [New Haven]

Good boy. Thanks for the dope.[1] But I don't see why you think its queer. Ever since the *Invocation To The Social Muse*[2] every social-conscience critic in America (& that's the fashionable school) has been after my heart. And ever since my piece on Spender in the *Hound & Horn*[3] every intellectual has been after my hide. And who else is there? Well there are the poets themselves. And you might expect love from them. But not from Aiken.[4] I was naive enough once to be hurt by Aiken's attack on the *Hamlet* after his earlier encouragement. But I'm not that naive any longer. I don't know *why* Aiken dislikes me. That's between him & his typewriter. But I know he does & bitterly. All I can say is that he is still a fine poet & that I'd like his good opinion & regret not having it.

The point is that the work is just as good or just as bad after an attack as it was before — even if the attack comes from Aiken. The only person who suffers is the poet himself. His *work* doesn't suffer. It doesn't change. The change takes place only in the poet's fame. Because I haven't read anything written about myself for five years (a few exceptions for the comments of people who knew what they were saying) I have no idea what my "fame" is. I don't know whether, Pulitzer Prizes altogether aside where they ought to be,[5] I am considered one of the good American poets or not — nor who so thinks me. But I am quite sure that if I have been so placed it lies in the power of the termite army of critics to bring me damn well down. And I am also quite certain they will do it if they can. *Which* they can. So that I must simply grin & go through with it. I won't pretend

I am superior to it for one minute. I have a passion for fame. And I am very doubtful as to the extent to which my work really deserves to enjoy it. So that I am directly in the line of fire & apt to be shot pretty full of very painful holes. But that is my affair & no one can do anything about it. Please don't worry about me. Just let me know who deliver the worst attacks & where & who, if anyone, stands by me. Has the Times *Book Review* (Sunday) cut me down yet? And by whom? And how about Cowley's sheet? Thanks for your letter. Anyway if it gets bad enough you can make publicity out of the hatred. (Only you wont)   yrs affly   A.

ALS: DLC

1. Linscott had reported on the reviews of M's *Poems, 1924–1933*. 2. Poem by M published in *The New Republic* 72 (26 October 1932), 296. 3. "Stephen Spender and the Critics," *Hound and Horn* 7 (October–December 1933), 145–147. 4. Aiken reviewed M's book in "Development of a Poet," *The New Republic* 77 (17 January 1934), 287–288. M must be referring, however, to comments made by Aiken to Linscott, as M asks, farther on, if "Cowley's sheet" — i.e., *The New Republic* — had been heard from. 5. In May 1933, M had won a Pulitzer Prize for *Conquistador*.

To Robert N. Linscott

Dear Bob: [*c.* January 1934?]   [Conway?]

Thanks for your trouble about the ballet.[1] I think your copyright man is wise. There is sufficient protection at common law & no reason to try to copyright now. Will you please thank him for me for his trouble.

I don't quite understand your addendum on the jealousy point. You don't accuse a man of nostalgia & a flight from life because you think he has more money than you have. Did you feel you had said something unfair to Conrad or what the Hell? I realize of course that affluence is a social sin & therefore welcome to some degree my present state of grace & indebtedness. But the explanation doesn't seem to me quite to carry. There are plenty of gents known to be better off than I.

However any light is helpful. Or is it? The whole subject is becoming a bit unpleasant. There is nothing we can do about it & the work will answer for itself. It will at least survive its current critics. The only point of any merit seems to me to be this: that the attacks didn't start until after the Pulitzer Prize & the publication of the *Invocation To The Social Muse*. But most of the critics — Conrad at least — knew all about me long before that. Did Conrad just turn against my vast fortune recently? Or did he just discover recently that it would be a popular move if he did? Well its a dull & stupid inquiry & one hardly

worth answering. Let it go. Do come again. And never mind the at-
tackers. I don't — unless I'm obliged to think about them — which I
rarely do.   yrs affly   A.

ALS: DLC

1. *Union Pacific,* a ballet with story by M, music by Nicholas Nabokoff, and chore-
ography by Léonide Massine, first performed by the Ballet Russe de Monte Carlo in
New York City on 25 April 1934.

To Bernard De Voto[1]

Dear Benny: [*c.* June 1934]   [Conway]

I feel a little like the young man who asked for the elephant and
got it. If I had had the slightest idea that my eager interest in American
history would put you through three pages of type and titles I should
have kept it to myself. As it is I am grateful and overwhelmed. And
only the fact that I have been preparing a commencement address to
the young Hotchkissers and have thus come to loathe this bloody
machine has kept me from telling you so long before this. The address
passed off or over or whatever on Monday. It was a memorable occasion. I got up and told them why I felt as bitterly as I did about the
school and what they could still do to take the curse off. Mr. Oswald
Garrison Villard who was there to see a son graduate remarked afterward that it was brave speech. He didn't know the half of it. It took
all the courage I had and a hell of a lot more. I'm still afraid of that
goddam place. It massacred me for four years. It was brave all right.
But it wasn't much good. In fact it was no good at all. Bravery without
matter. You know. The giddy whirl in front of the fire engine when you
are just drunk enough not to fall down.

Almost two months gone and so little done. Gives me the Willies.
See you at Bread Loaf.[2] My regards to your wife and my thanks added
to Ada's for the Bach which is already well grooved. It was grand of
you to come up. Please do it again.   yrn   Archie

TLS: SUL

1. American historian and critic (1897–1955). 2. De Voto, like M, was a frequent
participant in the Bread Loaf Writers' Conference in Vermont.

To H. Phelps Putnam

Dear Phelps: [*c.* June 1934?]   [Conway]

Great guy. I needed the good word. You probably don't keep in touch
with the journals of literary opinion being safe from boredom of that
kind whatever other kinds of boredom the wops may inflict upon you.[1]

If you had you would have seen as pretty a campaign of denigration as was ever successfully carried to a successful (but not yet) conclusion. The boys have me all finished and done for. Somehow or other those Frescoes seem to have gotten way under the Marxian hide and since everyone who is not now a Marxian tries hard to be mistaken for one or spends his waking moments like Mr. Chamberlain of the Times[2] trying to show the Marxians what a thoroughly nice feller he is my attentive friends are both numerous and enthusiastic. I am not only a Fascist. I am also a bloody rotten poet. In fact I got it all from Eliot. Which either makes Eliot a bloody rotten poet too or makes me something worse. Anyway and in spite of the fact that I am now fairly well used to the whole business the kind word from you was not only a new start but also something I could really believe in you being what you are. I have been finding out recently what it is that you are. I spent a few weeks up here alone and a lot of that time I spent reading back over the books I have — largely such books as yours and Pounds and Eliots etc.. I am far enough away from you now so that the personal thing doesn't get in between and I got them all clean and new. What used to worry me as I used to tell you in the rhythm of some of the lines came out as an accent of the poet's voice — very real and a little harsh the way it ought to be. Its real poetry. The actual thing. You don't need to be told that but its true.

Gerald is over there cruising now. He ought to be at Antibes (Villa America) in July. He talks about you a lot. I'm sure he'd like to see you. He's a pretty lonely guy you know. He knows it now.

I am up here with six months off trying to do a verse play.[3] If I can pull it off it will be good. A play in which the verse carries the action as it should — a kind of long lyric play — but for acting. I won't print it unless I can get it acted. The trouble is it goes so slowly and I only have six months and two are gone already. It isn't like writing a poem where each line can carry you into the next. You have to feel the whole thing to feel any part of it and I keep losing it. The time business is the worst. I feel trapped. Frost who has been up to see me a couple of times asks me why I don't just get my standard of living down to nothing and take the time I need. He's right of course. But I'm trapped. Its a trap. Its a one way street. Kenny goes to College next year and there are two more to educate and I love this farm. And there you have it. With no other income it takes every cent I have and a lot more just [to] buy food and clothes and educate those three and keep this place the way it ought to be. Rotten business. I feel the juice running out a little every year too. The poetry gets better. More honest. Less fake. But then the stuff that makes the fake is the singing in your ears and I don't hear that any more — or only rarely. I hear the sober rhythms that make sense. Trap. But we're all trapped one way or the other. I suppose the whole thing is to keep on throwing yourself against the bars. Sorry Asolo turned out lousy. Sorry as hell about all the illness. Come back and see me. Our lives go along together.

affectionately   Archie

TLS: YCAL

1. Putnam had gone to live in Italy the previous summer. 2. John Chamberlain, daily book critic of *The New York Times;* later a colleague of M's at *Fortune.* 3. *Panic: A Play in Verse,* published by Houghton Mifflin Company on 9 March 1935.

To the Editors of The Modern Monthly

Gentlemen: [*c.* 18 June 1934]   [Conway]

I am told by affectionate friends that a recent number of your publication contains an unusually virulent example of the politico-literary attack upon myself which has recently achieved some popularity — this one by a gentleman named Humphries.[1] (Presumably not Joe though they seem to have something in common.)[2] With Mr. Humphries' politerary opinions of my work, whatever they may be — and I am told they are quite crushing — I have no quarrel. Doubtless it gives him a pleasure to express them which is as comprehensible as it is harmless. But when Mr. Humphries permits himself an allegation of fact I must beg leave briefly to reply. I have been accused of fascism by members of the Lost Regeneration before this — but always in the large mystic sense in which members of the ancient church spoke of heresy. Mr. Humphries is the first of whom I have knowledge to come out flatly with the statement that I am A Fascist. Since my statement on that point is entitled to at least as much weight as Mr. Humphries' I ask you to print it with equal prominence. I am not a Fascist and have never been one. I am as strongly opposed to a dictatorship of the Right as of the Left — more strongly in fact since a dictatorship of the Right is an actual possibility in America. So far as my affirmative political beliefs are concerned Mr. Humphries will discover them where presumably he did discover and suppress them — in the FORUM for (I believe) April under the title *Preface to an American Manifesto.*[3] Suffice it here to say that I believe in the classic American tradition of democracy as the only form of government which offers intellectual and personal freedom and responsibility to an adult human being. It is an unorthodox and doubtless ridiculous opinion which cannot be substantiated in any text-book.

I do not wish however to give the impression that Mr. Humphries erred in attacking me or that he would not have attacked me had he known (i.e. stated) the facts. On the contrary he was quite right. My warm distaste for fascism does not in the least cancel my equally warm distaste for those spiritually insufficient members of our society who join (or do not quite join) The Party as their prototypes joined (or did not quite join) the Masons or the Elks or the Church. And for the same reasons.[4]   yours truly   Archibald MacLeish

TL-Dr: DLC

1. Rolfe Humphries, "Archibald MacLeish," *The Modern Monthly* 8 (May 1934), 264–270. 2. Joe Humphries was a boxing announcer. 3. *The Forum* 91 (April 1934), 195–198. 4. M's letter did not appear in *The Modern Monthly*, and may not even have been sent.

To Ernest Hemingway

Dear Pappy: [*c.* 20 July 1934] [Conway]
   This relic of the days when we bought this kind of letter paper is not so much to impress you as to take the place of toilet paper or whatever else I should have had to use if I hadn't found it, the old yellow sheets formerly supplied gratis by Fortune having run out and New York thank God being no nearer than next 7 November. You'll be in Cuba by now. I might as well be but wont. The goddam poem[1] crawls. I get up at six and work until five and still the goddam poem crawls.

> As well by thinking of it
> Erect the colossus of love
> To an unloved woman
> As make this poem come
> By thinking of it — thumbing
> A tool that was good lumber
> Till threaded with bad le[a]d
> Or chafing the delicate nape
> Of so much pulp-wood paper

However I go right on doing it. I keep thinking how near Nov. 7 is and how long the next eighteen months will be. Its good news that you have the 201 pages[2] behind you. With the help of the absence of a few Marlin you ought to have double that by fall which is good news for the lot of us. Except for President Strater of the Maine Tuna Club who can't do anything *and* fish. Or so he says. Being no Labrador Setter. President Strater, in case he doesn't send you the photographs himself due to pique at not being the first recipient of bad news, has recently caught a GIGantic twohundredandfiftyormorepoundTuna. I'm going down to see the great man after they get through with their fogs. We'll talk of your Atlantic Sail-fish record and President Strater will be very sporting about it and I'll explain why I didn't catch it now that you have given me a sound explanation [*MacLeish wrote in the margin*: Which incidentally gives me a taste of that Gulf Stream Book which ought to be grand. God what a thing that Stream is. And how much you have gotten about it.] which restores the sense of manly sufficiency as well as having the additional virtue of seriously deflating my father-in-law [*MacLeish wrote in the margin*: First time the old boy has ever deflated for anything. But I didn't tell him. I just deflated him myself] w. Hank (Hemingway not Strater) and I had better go after them in the old man's season when gents without roe catch fish with it. Or visa versa.

Henry Dolphin Canby the baouhy with the changeable tints wants me to do a piece on you for a series they are running on Great American Artists or something — the man and his work. I want very much to do it. Not for the fee of twenty dollars which the Sat Rev unlike magazines (but to Hell with magazines) offers. But because I have long wanted to do a piece on you and because I have so far restrained myself due to your express and expressed wishes — having to do I believe with considerations of nepotism or whatever the word is when a guy admires another guy not only for his work. I repeat that I want to do it. But I leave you the decision. I can imagine a number of reasons why you might prefer silence on my part — not all of them reasons of friendship. One for example might well be the extent of the politerary attack on me which has now reached such proportions that Houghton Mifflin wish someone else were publishing me. An introduction by me is now said to be sufficient to kill any budding poet.[3] But since you are a poet in the full and laureled leaf I don't think I'd really finish you for good even if I let myself go with every applicable superlative. I wish you'd let me. I have a lot to say. Quite a good bit that no one has yet said. The generation that has come up since your fame and has had to listen to the envious yawp of those who, before you blanketed them, spent all their hot breath praising you, should be allowed to listen to a few basic facts. But decide it as you see fit. Don't bother to explain if you decide No. Just the word will be enough and understood.[4] Love to Pauline   yrn affly   A.

I think the check I gave Charles for the reel has never been cleared by the bank. There must be some mistake. I know you wouldn't tell him not to clear it and pay yourself because you wouldn't do that to me so there is some mistake. Will you ask him? I have read again tonight to Ada the Clean Well-lighted Place. It moves me always in the same way. I think of once when I first knew you driving over to Nice. I have great respect and admiration for you — more than for any other living writer.

What does Bra [Saunders] think of Key West the American Bermuda? Can I use Bra's "men dying who never died before" in my poem?[5] It makes one entire page.

TLS: JFK

1. *Panic.* 2. Of Hemingway's *Green Hills of Africa* (1935). 3. M had contributed a preface to *An Anthology of the Younger Poets*, edited by Oliver Wells (Philadelphia: The Centaur Press, 1932), and written another, for James Agee's *Permit Me Voyage* (New Haven: Yale University Press), published in October 1934. 4. Hemingway, in a letter dated August 13, told M he could go ahead with the essay, which he hoped would concentrate on his work and his adult life. M wrote the piece and submitted it to Canby, who decided not to publish it. The manuscript seems not to have survived. 5. M did use a version of the phrase Hemingway attributed to his Key West friend in McGafferty's second speech in *Panic;* he made use of it again in *Actfive* (1948).

To Bernard De Voto

Dear Benny: [*c.* September 1934?]   [Conway?]

Would have written you but then you said you'd [come and][1] where were you? The 4th came and went and no deVoteaux [and we] had the guest room all aired and the sheets ironed.

Well — the novel.[2] You know as well as I do and as Mr. John Chamberlain would if he could stop for one moment trying to make himself popular on the New Masses and the New York Times by one and the same gesture thus preparing for any eventuality that its good. Its damn good. The chief criticism to be made of it is that its too good. There's stuff enough for at least five novels. [Charlie] Curtis was saying last night (we spent most of the week end talking about you if you'll forgive us) that from the point of view of sheer wit it backed Mr. Huxley counter one point[3] right off the table. Myself having no great estimate of wit I prefer to praise the architecture of the book which is as seeming simple as it is in truth complicated and the taste of alkali which your work always has and which blows dust over so much of the too often turned earth the New York boys go right on turning and returning. There is a fair gail of asceptic laughter which I love. And by God Benny — think what you may — you are mature. As for your people — Hester's death really made me cry: Jonothan was a shape — I know the Boston bar from the outside and I know that kind of Bostonian from the outside and from my outside I don't know Jonothan: Libby/Avis[4] is a duck — by all odds the realest of them all — made me wonder how you *could* write her final bed scene — you must have truly suffered thinking of it: Loring is magnificent satire but Loring-Bee is one of those relations I am just too goddam well married or unintelligent to understand. I could go on like Aunt Sally. I'd love to talk to you about the book. Its one of the few books I ever did want to talk about. But [it's d]amn presumptuous of me to try for I know nothing at all about [nove]ls. What I do think I know a little about is the thing inside a [book] which is to a book what balls are to a man. And unless I have [lost] all my eye for such things this book has them. I am getting a bit hysterical. The way to leave it perhaps is that your existence on the American scene is one of the very few things which makes it seem to me worth while to try to run my little show. And I feel so even more strongly now than I did before.

God bless you   A MacL

TLS: SUL

1. The bracketed phrases in this letter were supplied by the editor to replace words entirely or partly cut off the original document, apparently when a stamp was removed from the envelope. 2. De Voto's *We Accept with Pleasure* (1934). 3. A reference to Aldous Huxley's *Point Counter Point* (1928). 4. Avis was (and is) Mrs. De Voto.

To Ernest Hemingway

Dear Pappy: [14 January 1935] [New York]

I write letters with whole days & I haven't had a whole day since last May & I have never felt since last May that three or four sentences would suffice or that all ambiguities would be resolved in my favor but rather as though I had to be as careful as I would have to be if I wrote a letter to the New Masses which I haven't I hasten to add done.[1] I mean not at all that I haven't trusted you but that I knew you had not trusted me — which comes to the same thing when you are writing letters. I suppose I am wrong to have felt that way so long but I am a sullen resentful Scot & a bastard at heart. I don't resent insults very long because they don't penetrate. But I resent the rejection of affection because I rarely offer it & have therefore come to a sort of perverted idea that it must have value.

That is really why I have not been able to write letters but then you knew that anyway. So far as I am concerned it is my conception of the relationship between two people who are fond of each other that full faith & credit is allowed & attached regardless of surface appearances & I intend to practice it from now on. In other words you will have to terminate all communication to make me believe that you do not repose the deepest confidence in the poor Scotchman.

272

I wrote the piece about Hemingway last summer.[2] Canby hasn't printed it yet. I don't know when he will though I mean to find out. It isn't much of a piece but within its limits I think its all right. Anyway it gives the egg-experts something to shoot at.

The Zebra skin is superb. It makes our bed look like a scene in Persia. Ada is in a jitter about it. I like it even better. I know you don't approve of Zebras but we do. My love to my Paulinos & to the children — particularly to Patrick in the hope that his 6th year is not proving as hard as he thought.   always yrs   Archie

ALS: JFK

1. M had quarreled with Hemingway in May 1934 during a fishing trip in Florida.
2. *See* M to Hemingway, *c.* 20 July 1934, note 4.

To Ernest Hemingway

Dear Pappy: [23 January 1935] [New York]

Well I could weep about that letter — about my making you feel you had to write it & about your being willing to write it & about what is in it. I will drop it all. I'll never speak of it again. Only now I want to say that I wasn't trying to bring it all up again. I was trying to apologize for the way I had acted in not writing & to excuse myself to you for being sullen & holding grudges but all I seem to have done is to sound self righteous & Christ knows I don't feel it. I am more to blame than you if there is any blame which there isn't any more or even because I went on remembering a thing you forgot long ago & a thing which happened to us both by us both. And I'll never speak of it again. And I have forgotten it. And I'm ashamed to have made you write that letter & so damn grateful for it at the same time that there is nothing more I can write now. I'll write you soon
                         always yours affly   Archie
ALS: JFK

To F. Scott Fitzgerald

Dear Scott: 27 February 1935 [New York]

I have been thinking about you a great deal and very frequently since we had lunch together in Washington. It was the greatest pleasure to see you and it is the greatest delight to me to hear from Max Perkins that you are working hard with great projects in mind for the future.

I wish it might be possible for you to come up to New York on the

15th of March when my play [*Panic*] is to be produced. Any man who is foolish enough to put on a verse play in the present theatre needs the unreasoned and unreasoning support of his friends. But, in any event, whether you can come then or not, I hope that we shall be able to meet each other in the near future. I hear grand things of the work you are doing and I want to talk to you about it.

Yours always, affectionately,   Archie

TLS: NjP

To John Houseman

Dear Jack: [*c.* 18 March 1935]   [New York?]

Its hard to say it — easy to write it. My gratitude to you & Jimmy & to Zatkin.[1] I don't think you will ever regret what you have done however you may feel about it now. You have created one of the most beautiful productions of the modern theatre — a production incredibly more beautiful than the verse which occasioned it — & you have thrown that verse & that production uncompromisingly into the teeth of the commercial critics. If you have gotten back affected boredom instead of anger the compliment is all the greater. The returns aren't in yet.

Saturday night's audience was the true measure of what you have done. They did not come to like that play. They went away liking it — more than liking it.[2]

Personally I have long since decided that the test of the success of any art is not the praise it wins but the enemies it creates. Could we ask more of God than to have the commercial critics & Mrs. Askew[3] against us?

I wish to God I could feel you were as completely happy about it all as I am.

And don't have the money on your mind. As I told you the only vital thing is the money to repay Bob [Lovett] & that we have. Whether I get mine back or only a fraction of it doesn't matter. It was worth it a million times over.

I have written Adele [Lovett] a list of the people for the party Thursday night. Will you add *all* the names you want to & call her up — she is waiting to hear. Bu 8: ----.

Can you have the chair sent back to 129E10? The carpenter has the two missing casters. They might drop a cloth over it to keep it as clean as possible.

I'm in bed with that same fever I can't shake. I'll be down Wednesday & we can clean everything up then & forget all the stuff that has worried you so much. Poor Jack.

274

Wasn't that Sat. night audience superb? What more could any of us ask?

With all my thanks for more than all I can say.

Affectionately   Archie

ALS: CLU

1. Houseman and Nathan Zatkin were cofounders of the Phoenix Theatre, whose first production was M's *Panic.* James Light directed the play, which was performed at New York's Imperial Theatre on March 14, 15, and 16. 2. The play's third — and final — performance was attended mostly by communists and other leftists brought in by *New Theatre* and *New Masses* magazines, which had underwritten the performance on the condition that M afterwards participate in a "symposium" on the play's ideological merits. M agreed to do so and, though running a fever at the time, he took part in a lively discussion with three intellectuals of the American Left, Stanley Burnshaw, John Howard Lawson, and V. J. Jerome. 3. Constance Askew, who — with her husband, Kirk — was the organizer of the fashionable "Askew Salon," frequented by many leading writers, musicians, photographers, critics, dancers, and others.

To John and Katharine Smith Dos Passos

Dear Dos & Katy: [20 March 1935]   Farmington

Well *we* came & *they* saw & *Mr. John Mason Brown* of the Post conquered but it was a great fight.[1] You can't imagine a more beautiful or exciting performance & when, after the opening Friday night, & after the assassin reviews Saturday morning, the New Theatre New Masses gang turned up Saturday night, it was superb. A better audience I have never seen & the symposium afterwards, with Lawson & Burnshaw & V. J. Jerome & myself (with the grippe), was exciting as hell. I have never had such a sense of *audience* before. Don't be sad because your play was a flop.[2] It wasn't really a flop. Some of the people you care about liked it. Take care of yourself & yourself & God bless you. I'll be back from England in a month. About Baoth I can't write.[3] That was *fancy. Fancy.* There's no other word for it. They could have thought & thought for a million years & they wouldn't have been able to think of one like that. Sara is all of a heap. Gerald has been superb but he is really heart-broken. It is a heart-breaking thing. Poor kid — tortured with knives — wracked with agony. Sara kept him alive for four hours sitting beside him saying Breathe Baoth! Breathe Baoth. He didn't know her but the will came through & he went on. Sara could not believe he was dead. She fights all her enemies in the gate. Once they break into the house she has no doors to close. She would like to lie in the gate facing them.

my love to you both   Archie

275

1. Brown had reviewed the Phoenix Theatre production of *Panic* in the New York *Post,* 16 March 1935, page 10. 2. Possibly referring to an abortive production of Dos Passos's *Fortune Heights* (1933). 3. The Murphys' elder son, Baoth, had died of spinal meningitis on March 17.

To Gerald and Sara Murphy

My dears: [*c.* 29 March 1935]   [Aboard S.S. *Majestic*]

For some things in this world one must give words to one's admiration — for courage & grace & nobility such as yours. It is hard that people must suffer so to raise these memorials to the greatness of the human spirit. It is hard: but also just. Because the human spirit is not often great — because the greatness of the human spirit is the only enduring beauty — because it would not be fitting to achieve greatness without pain. All this is of no comfort to you. You did not wish for that cruel marble tearing the palms of your hands. You wished for your son. But for the rest of us, who have not suffered as you have suffered, a new justification of *all* suffering, a new explanation of the eternal mystery of pain, has been created. It is the heart of the irony of our lives that this justification — this explanation — should be apparent not to you who need it but to us. For the symbol of the irony of our lives is the phoenix which must die to live.

No one can give you comfort — only time whose comfort (until, like unwanted sleep, it is given) we reject. Those who love you can only ask you to believe that you have not suffered in vain. It is true.

I love you both   Archie.

To Ernest Hemingway

Dear Pappy: [15 April 1935]   [London]

I can't think of any more appropriate place to write you from than the reading room of the British Museum[1] with Englishmen as thick as Englishmen & a draft on the back of my neck which I can feel in my balls. (I think its my balls). I'm writing about the King of England. You remember him. For two weeks I've been getting the run around in the London Clubs & the Lord Chancellors back pantry and the servants' entrance at Windsor & I know all about him now. He is a great and good man who loves his people & whom everyone loves & respects & thinks is just wonderful & so are you Mr. Hemingway I am sure & Mrs. Hemingway would be the first to say so because you are so goooood to Your Peepul & occasionally go out on a balcony & bow to them. Well I'm enjoying it. Ada won't go out with me anymore because I laugh out loud. Yesterday I saw them training the horses for the Jubilee. They had forty horses in a line & a man with a trombone in front of every horse blowing at it to get it accustomed to bands, and then they waved flags at the horses. I thought I should fall over. The horses looked exactly like Englishmen. Then too I've been getting plastered at night & asking people named Fitzhenry & Fitzclarence about their royal bastardry & that makes Ada nervous. I'm not a success. Jane Mason[2] was here & the Prince of Wales had her in for dinner & she tried to fix it up for me to meet the Prince to ask him about his father which he would have liked & she tried & he said he wouldn't meet me socially. That was bad because I don't know how else he can meet me as I'm not keeping office hours here. Jane was just back from Africa having gone out on Safari with 14 men & there were signs up asking them please to shout before shooting but why exactly I couldn't tell unless it was because they were so many & the lions so few. There is a fine article in the Spectator here saying you are the best writer since Hell was a match-fire, which is a fine thing to read. It is by Bunny Garnett. I call him Bunny because that is Edmund Wilson's name but his real name is David & he is one swell gent & very bright as you may agree. I think I remember that you do. Well I must go out & get my letters. I miss you like Hell kid. When do we meet? My love to Mrs H. my favorite brunette. Shall I remember you to George? When is the book coming out?[3] I won't read instalments. Could I see a proof? Did you like my play or did you think it was lousy? I had a fine evening with the Communists the last night we played it. I'll tell you about it one day as we say here in London. Be back May 1. You coming up?

Aff'ly always yours   A.

ALS: JFK

1. M was in England to prepare a *Fortune* story on King George V. 2. Mrs. George Grant Mason, the wife of a Pan American Airways executive who lived and worked in Havana. 3. Hemingway's *Green Hills of Africa*, published in October 1935.

To James B. Conant

Dear President Conant: 14 May 1935 [New York]

I have put in a long and soul-searching week-end terminating in a conference here late last night and the conclusion of the whole matter is that I think I should continue to dig in this particular garden. Let me say first of all that I am very proud indeed that the opportunity should have come to me and I feel very deeply the presumption of declining a position of such possibilities and particularly such associations.[1]

What it comes to in my mind is this: first, that I am under considerable obligations here which I cannot easily rid my mind of, and secondly, that the nature of the work at Harvard would, I am afraid, fit into my purposes as a writer no better — and perhaps actually less well — than the nature of the work here.

As to the first point, the new position as a member of the Editorial Committee of FORTUNE which has been offered me here is a position which grows out of some six years of work and which I cannot refuse without a very troublesome sense of avoiding responsibilities which I have really already accepted. As to the second point, the difficulty arises more in my own mind than in the external circumstances of the position at the Harvard University Press. I am completely aware that no pressure would be brought upon me to produce immediate results as a publisher and I am also aware that every sympathy and every help would be offered me. At the same time, I know myself well enough to know that I would have no sense of freedom to write or even a freedom to think about writing until I had more or less mastered the job and until the press was proceeding in a satisfactory manner. In other words, even though every effort were made to relieve the pressure, I am very sure that I should create my own pressure and should for some years at least have less freedom than I am able to have here.

This all sounds very glib and easy as I dictate it, but I think you will know that the conclusion was not at all glib or easy to arrive at. Many things were involved of which the chief — I hope you will permit me to say so — was the possibility of working under you in the kind of university you are going to make. Had I been a publisher by profession I don't think I should have hesitated. As it is, I cannot feel that I ought to decide otherwise than as I have. I shall always remember as one of the greatest satisfactions of my life the fact that you wanted me to come to Cambridge.

Always faithfully yours,   [Archibald MacLeish]

TL-C: DLC

1. Conant, who had become president of Harvard University in 1933, had offered M a position with Harvard University Press.

To Ernest and Pauline Hemingway

Dear Pappy and Paulinos: [c. April 1936]   [Tokyo]

You had ought to see the beautiful islands of Japan.[1] It is indeed a wonderful sight. The pee-pul are quite small and mostly covered with babies. They fold up into very small spaces and can be inserted where you wouldn't think. In this country it is impolite to blow your nose or wear shoes but quite general to hawk, spit, belch and appear in your socks. We smell of butter to the inhabitants but they do not smell of anything to us: they are in fact remarkably clean which is attributed by learned travellers to the fact that they bathe. I myself attribute it to the fact that they do not smell. All the trains in this country are uncomfortable and on time. It is an interesting combination. There is a bird in this country who sits in bamboo groves and makes a certain sound. He is known as the Japanese nightingale. The reason why he is known as the Japanese nightingale is that he sings in the day-time. Many things are similarly turned about with these interesting and artistic people who are naturally different from ourselves since it is Wednesday here when it is Yesterday morning where you are. For example the countryside in spring smells of earth and rain in your country but here with us it doesn't smell of earth and rain. It smells of crap. This odor is valued by the people as a sign of good rice both past and to come. In some remote areas where I have been the smell of crap is very expensive indeed and most impressive. I could go on at some length to tell you more of the habits and customs of this nation but it would hardly be worth while because you would not reply. I know because I sent you a post card from Salt Lake Utah USA and you never replied. It is improbable that you are dead because I have seen in the local prints a picture of Mr. Hemingstein the famous author and bitters taster upright between two objects one of which was said to be a Sales Fish and the other a Movie Queen. The one that had its tail up was the fish. This picture was said to have appeared originally in the New York Times and though it did not flatter either the fish or Mr. Hemingway who remains in my opinion one of the most beautiful of Anglo-Saxon males nevertheless I was able by certain stigmata to identify the aforesaid bitters bugler and there was and is no doubt but that you are not dead. If you prefer to appear so for reasons of polity I can only object that goddam it you aint. My wife Mrs. MacLeish who knows the Japanese word for can* sends you her neatly folded love.

yrn affly and as ever   Archie

*She learned it on a train. If you shd ever need to know it is benjo. It is very well known here.

TLS: JFK

1. M was in Japan to prepare a major *Fortune* series on that country. His five articles, all of which appeared in the September 1936 issue, were: "The Rising Sun of Japan," "The History of Japan," "The Farmer Does Without," "The Citizens — Subjects," and "Who Runs the Empire?"

To John Farrar

Dear John: 29 May 1936 [New York]

I have a note from Miss Sherer saying that Boriswood is going to take *Public Speech*.¹ I wonder if this is a good idea. My English history to date, as I think you know, is this: *Conquistador* was published by Gollancz.² They were unable to move the book at all. Then after some fishing around on the part of Houghton Mifflin, somebody hooked Boriswood. My English friends were very dubious, but Houghton Mifflin were not and arrangements were made for them to bring out the *Selected Poems*, followed by *Panic*.³ Before we give them *Public Speech*, would it or would it not be a good idea to find out what they have done with the others? I suppose the answer to the question depends upon what alternatives we have and upon your estimate of the quality of Boriswood.

While we are talking business, perhaps I'd better go on with a few ideas of mine relating to *Public Speech* in this country. I don't expect very much from sales of my books, as you know, but I was and am discouraged by the performance of *Public Speech* because of the fact that the total sale to date, after three months, is only about two-thirds of the advance sale on my last book [*Panic*] — this in spite of the fact that *Public Speech* sells at a dollar and is a much more attractive book in appearance as it is, I think, a considerably better book in content. Also in spite of the fact that, as you tell me, the reviews were excellent.

I am wondering precisely where this leaves us. You warned me in advance that you proposed doing nothing like the advertising of *Public Speech* that you proposed to do for Steve's book.⁴ This seemed to me reasonable in view of the fact that you may properly anticipate selling many more copies of Steve's book. Nevertheless I should hate to see you accept our present defeat without a struggle of some kind. I dare say you have already exhausted the small appropriation for advertising you spoke of, but if you have not and if you think of any step which could properly be taken, I wish you would consider it.

This all adds up to something that sounds like a complaint. It is not so intended. I do not, as I know you believe, publish verse with the idea of making money out of it. I am happier about *Public Speech* than I have been about work I have done before. What disturbs me is the apparent falling off of sales when the book has been well received critically, and when the price has intentionally been lowered in order to extend the reading of the book among those whom I particularly wish to reach. Please understand, therefore, that I have no blame for anyone, but am merely deeply concerned with the implications of the situation. I wish you would let me know what you think you can do, if anything at all.

I am sending this by hand with the manuscript of Guenther Stein's new book,[5] which I hope you will read as soon as you can, letting me have it back when you are through with it. I cannot too strongly urge it upon your attention. I found I was unable to hold up the British manuscript with its photographs, because the Normandie was sailing Tuesday night.   Affectionately yours,   [Archie]

TL-C: DLC

1. Having helped to place two books by Ezra Pound with Farrar & Rinehart, M had decided to give his own *Public Speech* to them as well. It was published on 16 March 1936. 2. The first British edition of *Conquistador* had been published by Victor Gollancz Ltd., of London, in May 1933. 3. The Boriswood editions of M's *Poems* and *Panic* had been published, respectively, in October 1935 and April 1936. 4. Benét's *Burning City* (New York: Farrar & Rinehart, 1936). 5. *Far East in Ferment* (London: Methuen, 1936).

To Carl Sandburg[1]

Dear Carl: [*c.* July 1936] [Conway]

I kept these because I wanted to look them over under my own trees.[2] You have distilled in your poem[3] all the rich irony of these decisions which require that the right of a man to work be property before it can be protected. Harry needed that letter.[4] Did he ever answer it? He worked himself up into a fury the other day over Ickes[5] 'who treats business success as though it were criminal'. It is through the rust spots of bunkum phrases like that that the Hearst works into a publisher.

I have a letter this morning from the New Masses. They would "make reservations" but they will publish the review as is.[6] The sad part of it is that only you and I of all the people who read it will understand what that review means. It is the full answer to Bill Benet who accuses you of getting nowhere. You get somewhere. You get where it is good to be. You pull out of the big double drawer of the old statesman's desk the wax-coloring foolscap that has the real issue written on it. You are the one to see that the real issue is whether or not we believe in the people. We made a revolution to believe in the people and the Scotch bastard from St. Kitts[7] took it away from us and the honorable money-lenders buried it in the world's greatest document. What I wanted to say to the Comrades who know very little about America but are honorable and brave men and disinterested men was this: that no revolution will succeed in America which proposes to take the government away from the people and create the kind of cabinet tyranny which we see now in its intrigues and its jealousies in Russia in this fantastic trial.[8] Only one kind of revolution can succeed in America — the revolution which will return the government to the people as the Revolution of 1776 did NOT return the government to the people. You are the man who has shown them that. And the sad thing I say is this: that they cannot profit by it. And yet someone must profit by it. Let me speak candidly and as I think. I think this: You and I have a considerable responsibility. We are poets but we are also men able to live in the world. We cannot escape our duty as political animals. You have fulfilled that duty in your Lincoln and in this book. This book is a basis for political action. It is not a program. It was not intended to be a program. But it makes clear an issue — it makes clear the issue. You cannot escape its consequences and neither can I, as a man who has perceived its meaning, escape its consequences. We must act now politically to drive this issue into the forefront of the sensitive minds of all men, both those who think and those who do not think. We must now become pamphleteers, propogandists — you by your own right, I as one who can aid you somewhat.[9] Well?   Archie

TLS: IU

1. American poet and biographer (1878–1967), with whom M had a cordial but largely epistolary relationship over many years. 2. M probably refers to a letter and a memorandum written by George E. Q. Johnson, a former federal judge and U.S. district attorney, which letter and memorandum were enclosed in a letter of Sandburg's to M dated 30 June 1936 and published in Herbert Mitgang, ed., *The Letters of Carl Sandburg* (New York: Harcourt, Brace & World, 1968), pages 341–342. 3. Possibly a reference to Sandburg's *The People, Yes*, published in August 1936 by Harcourt, Brace & World. 4. Probably the letter to Henry R. Luce dated 3 July 1936 and published in *The Letters of Carl Sandburg*, pages 343–344. 5. Harold L. Ickes, secretary of the interior and head of the Public Works Administration under President Roosevelt. 6. M's review of *The People, Yes*, entitled "The Tradition and the People," appeared in *New Masses* 20 (1 September 1936), pages 25–27. 7. A reference to Alexander Hamilton, secretary of the treasury under George Washington. 8. Joseph Stalin had recently launched a purge that included highly publicized show trials of his opponents in the Soviet Communist Party. 9. Partly in response to this letter, Sandburg wrote, in 1940, a poem entitled "Open Letter to the Poet Archibald MacLeish Who Has Forsaken His Massachusetts Farm to Make Propaganda for Freedom." It was collected in *The Complete Poems of Carl Sandburg* (New York: Harcourt, Brace, 1950).

To Ernest Hemingway

Dear Pappy: [c. 24 September 1936] [Conway?]

    And that would have been a fine thing to do too.[1] Only the dates are the wrong way to. I'm about half way or better through the three months I have off and a long job left to do. I don't know really why I keep on at it. I go on turning up stones in the hope, so far fanciful, of finding my own picture underneath in the worm cast. Its never really mine. You can make it out more or less the way you can make an elephant out of a cloud. What is the necessity? I no longer suffer from the delusion if I ever did which I doubt that I have anything to add to the sum total of man's knowledge of the universe. As for giving pleasure I can give more with a case of good Scotch and be thanked for it. Besides which I have no particular desire to give pleasure. Besides which the equation of pleasure given against pain spent won't work out. The personal anguish in bringing out a book so far as I am concerned is simply unspeakable: the praise because I know it unearned is as bad as the blame which I think earned whether it is or not. If it weren't for that I could imagine that I wrote books for the same reason that they put scaffolding around a rotten peace [sic] of stone work — to support a self-confidence which won't stand by itself. But the actual repeated pain of the performance knocks that theory into a cocked hat. I'm left at the end of the row with nothing more philosophic than this — that I keep at it because nothing on earth makes me as happy as I am for about twenty minutes after I've finished a poem — and that I wouldn't be as happy as that (for some inexplicable reason) unless I knew that I would go ahead and smash the happiness by publishing the thing. It isn't just having something to do. I can work my hair out twelve hours a day at Fortune and have no happiness — only the kind of jag which comes from using up time in a necessary duty. My own work is the precise opposite. There's no fun in doing it as there is fun in doing a piece of journalism but there does come briefly at the end and soon lost something that the greatest piece of journalism ever attempted is incapable of giving. The world is really lousy isn't it? It ought to be possible to make the things you want to in a kind of innocence of labor and have them remain what they are when you make them — not what they are when they become "literature" — or don't.

None of this ever happens to you and therefore it will sound idiotic to you. You will wonder why, if it is as bad as that, I don't simply stay drunk. Which is the question.

I am glad you are at work on a novel.[2] I do wish you luck. Not because you ask for it and not because you need it but because your success is curiously essential to me — as though the unarguable reality and invention of your work made up for the dough-tasting inadequacy I find in most of mine. I wish I were a believing Baptist and knew for certain that everything would be made clear in the end.

Have you looked at Mr. Huxley's I-less in Gaza?[3] It reads the way a thumbed plumb tastes — all fingered over with the pale cast of thought.

Mr. Huxley's world is a prick on which the Bertillion system has been demonstrated by a penitentiary full of British intellectuals. Wherein it resembles Tom-boy Anthony Eden.[4]

My love to Pauline and her men

yrs always and forgive the gloom   Archie

TLS: JFK

1. Hemingway had invited M to visit him in Montana. 2. Hemingway's *To Have and Have Not* (1937). 3. Aldous Huxley's *Eyeless in Gaza* (1936). 4. The British foreign minister.

To Ernest Hemingway

Dear Pappy: [14 October 1936]   [Conway]

Jeez Kid it seems like not only a number of days but a couple of lives since I wrote you. Now for ten days I feel swell and I am working like CKGBillins horse Lou Dillon on a fly day with the sweat in a lather and two minutes flat just around the corner where all good things always are if only Mr Hoover hadn't found it out. The trouble is moving into and moving out of being a journalist. Not that I have anything against being a journalist. It pays good and keeps the boys in school and teaches the old man a lot about such places as Japan about which he also forgets just as much almost at once and leads to the forming of many delightful associations in our national capital where it is still advisable not to know how to play Rummy and has the great advantage of being practised anonymous with no more monicker than a Ford tourer with blue body and black wheels the way they used to be. Its the moving in and out that raises hell. Mostly the moving out. You and N. Hawthorne are the birds who discovered that a man could only work well with his ass on a board seat and his hands at some other business. That's what's so hard to recover after a couple of years of turning out ten to twenty to forty thousand words a month on something you get through the ears and never really do know anything at all about. It takes me a couple of months after I stop journalizing to dissolve the tension in sunlight and get the weight off the gravel so the water can come up through again. Well that's enough about my Lifeasawriter for now and for a hell of a long time to come. I'm sorry I ever bored you with it in the first place but I was so damn miserable I had to write it down and I had been thinking all day long for no reason at all about the winter afternoon we boxed at some kind of an American club or ymca or something and then walked toward the Blvd St Germain and stopped and had a beer at a funny bum cafe and then walked on to the place you were not living anymore. Some funny way it all came back with most of the words and I had to drop the whole cart load of kelp in your lap. Excuse it.

Mimi will always have that bear rug she says which is better than if she had it because it would get moth eaten after a while. But first she had to think how it looked exactly.[1]

Where do you go from where you are and when? Key West next? I have no news of anybody. Sara was very unhappy when we saw her a month ago and it is the kind of unhappiness you can't reach because it is not only about Patrick but about another winter at Saranac[2] and about the headaches she has so much of the time and about a lot of other things she won't talk about. Gerald is better and better all the time — more and more solid and more and more made of himself. Dos and Katy were here for a night and very fine they were too. I haven't seen anyone now for many weeks. Most of the time I am alone in the house which I like: a girl comes up in the morning and gets some food ready and the rest of the time there isn't a live breath drawn but Finn's[3] and mine and the mice's for a mile and a half in any direction and for ten miles in all but one. Ada and I too send you all the love of Ada and   yrn   Archie

TLS: JFK

1. In a letter to M dated September 26, Hemingway had sent his love to M's daughter and instructed M to tell her to pretend he had sent her the most wonderful silver-tipped grizzly hide in the world. 2. Patrick Murphy was hospitalized in Saranac Lake, New York. 3. Finn MacCool, the MacLeish family dog, so christened by the Irish-American writer Padraic Colum.

To Robert N. Linscott

Dear Bob: 15 December 1936 [New York]

I talked to J. Farrar yesterday and ran into the kind of attitude of mind you might anticipate. So far as practical details were concerned, what the conversation came down to was this: that J. Farrar is at present very much occupied along the frontier where radio and letters meet and apparently has negotiations going forward and a program in mind into which my project might fit. Also, Farrar & Rinehart would be willing to bring the play out at 50¢.[1]

What is your reaction to this as a purely practical matter? My general attitude is one of wanting to work with you again, but I am now wondering whether this little experimental venture is really the thing with which to resume relations. Will you let me know as soon as you have a chance to think about it? Please believe that no question of shopping around is involved. The only question is whether, with a new dramatic form to handle in a very tricky medium, it might not be better to use the experience of a man who apparently has been working actively in the field. There is also, of course, the question of price — I am very anxious to get the thing out as cheaply as possible, provided it is also decent looking.   Hurriedly and faithfully yours,   Archie

This is a letter to RL — not to HM&Co.. I.e. I am wondering what your advice would be. I am torn two ways — ① to have R.L. for a publisher again ② to make this radio-verse play experiment work.   Archie

TLS: MH

1. M's *The Fall of the City: A Verse Play for Radio* was published by Farrar & Rinehart on 26 April 1937.

To Laird S. Goldsborough[1]

Dear Goldie,   16 January 1937 [New York]

I'm sorry to be so late in answering your memorandum of the eighth but I have been out with 'flu.

The facts stated in John Gunther's review of Langdon-Davies' book[2] in the Herald Tribune "Books" of January 10, more or less accord with my information. That is to say, it is my understanding of the situation that a Popular Front government with neither Socialists nor Communists in its membership took power in February, 1936; that it was a liberal government of the Left; that army officers backed by landowners and the Church attempted to overthrow this government by arms; that that revolt would have been crushed except for German and Italian intervention; that fascist intervention preceded Russian intervention — i.e. that German and Italian munitions were appearing in Spain last August, whereas the Russians were only able to provide material assistance along in November; that the present complexion of the government leadership in Madrid is very definitely the result and not the cause of the armed rebellion.

What I object to is the attitude that objectivity requires the presentation of the Spanish civil war as though it were some sort of spontaneous cockfight between Whites and Reds in which both sides are equally guilty. I may be wrong and I express myself thus only because you asked me to, but it is my feeling that entirely objective journalism would have presented the facts in such a way as to indicate that the fascists, backed by landowners and church[,] were the aggressors against a popular government lawfully elected, and must bear the responsibility for the consequences.

More specifically, I have continually objected to the use of the phrase "Red militia" in TIME. I wrote Harry some time ago that I thought TIME should be able to justify its use of that phrase with actual, factual proof that the majority or even a large proportion of the government's forces were Communists. The facts as I understand them are very definitely to the contrary. I am interested to see in the New York Times this morning in a dispatch from Matthews[3] a statement which you also will have seen, to the effect that the phrase Red Army as "a designation for the Spanish government forces has always been a misnomer. The troops on the loyalist side represent a wide variety of Left political organizations." The rest of the statement, which you will find on page 3, second column of the Times today, will also interest you.

Briefly, I feel that TIME has never presented the war in Spain for what it was — an inexcusable and unjustifiable act of aggression by reactionary forces against a popular government. This to my mind is of infinitely greater historical importance than the attempt, however laudable (and it is laudable), to present the atrocity stories objectively and with equal-handed blame. Blame there is in the Spanish civil war and it falls definitely upon the aggressor forces. Not to make that clear seems to me to be a failure in objective news reporting.

Let me repeat again that I make these statements in response to your invitation to do so. I realize that your sources of information are doubtless more authoritative than mine and your means of communication more direct. If the statements I have made are incorrect in fact, I should be very glad to know what the actual facts are. I should also be glad to have authority for the actual facts.

Yours faithfully,   [Archie]

TL-C: TIME

1. Foreign news editor of *Time*. 2. John Langdon-Davies's *Behind the Spanish Barricades* (1937). 3. Herbert L. Matthews, "Leftists on Offensive," *The New York Times*, 16 January 1937, page 3.

To Henry R. Luce

Dear Harry: 5 May 1937   Conway

This is a letter to Eric & Mitch[1] as well as to you: not to save my pencil & your yellow paper but because I want to speak to all three of you together.

I have been alone up here on this hill for three days lying around in the sun and chopping brush and reading as little Armament research as my conscience will permit.[2] Result is I've gotten through quite a bit of sleep and quite a bit of thinking. And my thinking has at last brought me out on firm ground as regards A.MacL. and Fortune Mag. Ever since last January as you will recall I have been trying (unsuccessfully) to get a flat answer to the question whether I have gotten as far as I can

287

get on Time Inc's payroll. This question was motivated by the fact that practically everyone else on Fortune had been given a raise and that several of them, younger than I in years & in service, had gone on up in the corporate hierarchy. What I was really asking was whether Fortune was going to be able to provide for a contingency it had never foreseen with its young founder & its young staff: was it going to be able to make provision for a writer who, for whatever reason, wished to remain a writer but who, malgré tout, was getting older & facing heavier expenses & who, malgré tout, had a certain personal competetive sense?

From the point of view of New York it seemed obvious to me that it should make such provision. The notion that a man doing the actual productive work of writing the magazine was less valuable to the corporation than the same man doing something *about* the production of the magazine struck me as just plain silly. Mitch & Eric will agree that if Fortune had eight competent & responsible writers the managing editor's job, instead of being the toughest, would be the most delightful in American journalism. The result was that I worked up a pretty good head of steam thinking of all this on the 52nd floor of the Chrysler Building.

But all that was in New York. Up here the picture looks very different & the pieces all go together. The disillusionment of the past few months fits in perfectly with my dearest hopes. I now see where the whole weakness of my Fortune position lies. I also see why and wherein it is a weakness. I may disapprove the bureaucratic system but I am bound to admit that once a magazine turns into a corporation you are going to get a business hierarchy. I may believe a good writer more valuable than twenty "executives" but that won't change the fact that the corporate pyramid will be a pyramid capped by people with official titles. And all that being so, my position is very obviously untenable. I can't sit half-way up the pyramid & refuse to admit that it is a pyramid. Or, better, I can't sit half-way up the pyramid & demand that a special lift be built to hoist me straight up into space by my boot straps. I have either got to climb by the pyramid like anyone else. Or I have got to get off. Since I can't climb by the pyramid & do my own work as a poet I have only one alternative — to get off.

I propose to get off in a very simple way & one I know you & Mitch & Eric will approve. I propose to resign as an editor of Fortune & take up my position outside as a contributor. This arrangement will solve most of my difficulties & most of those I have created for you. For one thing I shall be hors de concours so far as the promotions & assumptions of the pyramid are concerned. For another I shall give up my flat in New York, pull in my horns, live in the country with my family & save, I estimate, about a quarter of my income — for it costs me about a quarter of what I get to keep the separate establishment in New York. Again, I shall be relieved of my personal editorial burdens which are all the heavier for being informal & irregular (— and are much heavier than you, Harry, have ever realized). With this saving & this release I should consider my present rate of pay — which seems to me at present inadequate *in relation to the Fortune scale* — adequate, & should cease to send you bitter memoranda on the subject.

I think — & I think you will agree with me — that this is the solution of the problem of the Fortune writer who wanted to stay a writer & had no yearning to compete with R. MacA. Ingersoll for titles & the concomitant stock-holdings & salary checks.[3] If you do agree I suggest we make the change at the end of this year when my present arrangement, which is on a yearly basis, comes to its next end-and-beginning.

yours always   Archie

ALS: TIME

1. Eric Hodgins and Russell "Mitch" Davenport, who had recently been named publisher and managing editor, respectively, of *Fortune*. 2. M was writing a six-part *Fortune* series called "Background of War," which ran from March through August 1937; the armaments story, entitled "Who Dares to Fight," was part five. 3. The recently named publisher of *Time*, Ingersoll had previously been managing editor of *Fortune* and general manager of Time Inc.

To Ernest Hemingway[1]

Dear Pappy: 8 August [1937]   Conway

I was glad to get your letter. I don't think there is much point my writing about the film anymore because so far as I am concerned there never has been any misunderstanding. My whole concern when we talked about the California trip was what I as president of the corporation ought to do when there was no money in the sock. There was no question that the publicity would be valuable, the only question was whether we could afford it with several thousands in unpaid bills. Also my only suggestion was that the Ambulance Committee might share the expense since the Ambulance Committee would get the subscriptions. There was never any suggestion that you should carry it yourself. You have already put in much more than you should have and your name has done more for the film than anything else except the actual picture itself. What I was trying to talk about was a very simple business question as to what I ought to do as the responsible party. And the thing that has troubled me was that we weren't able to talk about it as a simple business question. Probably, for some reason or other which I don't understand, that is still true. So I would rather not talk about it at all. If you don't believe I have worked like a nigger at this thing for seven months simply in order to do what little I could for the film and for things we both believe in then nothing I can say now will convince you. I have never questioned your motives or your integrity. I know you take the Spanish war seriously. I do too.

Well to hell with it. I told you years ago in a car riding around back of Key West how I feel about you and always will. But its a long long time since we've met — how many years?

Take care of yourself in Spain. Ada & Mimi send you their love. Kenny is in Arizona working for an Archaeological Expedition

Archie

Eaton[2] will give you (if she hasn't already) notes for your last money which was an absolute godsend: we were [through?]   A.

TLS: JFK

1. This letter and another to Hemingway dated 6 August [1938] have to do with the making of a documentary film, called *The Spanish Earth*, that tells the story of the Spanish civil war from the loyalist point of view. M was a founder and some-time president of the corporation called Contemporary Historians, Inc., which raised money for the making and distribution of *The Spanish Earth;* Hemingway was a principal contributor and fund raiser, went to Spain to assist film maker Joris Ivens, and wrote the narration. The immediate sources of friction in these two letters to Hemingway are too complicated to summarize here, nor are they especially significant in themselves. 2. Louise Eaton, who worked for M at *Fortune* and who was also assisting him in his work for Contemporary Historians.

To Dudley Fitts [1]

Dear Dudley: 14 January 1938   [New York]

Let me begin at the true beginning. In spite of the fact that I have been wildly attempting to put my affairs, my family, a new poem, a moving picture corporation and a dozen other things, not to mention visas and income taxes, in order for an imminent departure, I read your translations with a delight which I hesitate to attempt to describe to you. Not only I but others in this office who had an opportunity to look at the book[2] have been simply overwhelmed with admiration. Gerald Murphy was talking to me about it at breakfast this morning, remarking that these poems which seem so quiet when you read them, go on living and working in your viscera afterwards until you wonder why you ever read anything else.

The exhibition at Yale embarrassed me so that I was unable to look at it, and this in spite of the fact that Mr. Mizener showed the very greatest tact and consideration.[3] I am most grateful to him for what he did, but I think you can understand how it feels to walk into that room full of ghosts. There is a point beyond which mediocrity cannot be inflated to look like the real thing, and I think that point has been well reached at Yale in the Rare Book Room.

As for your specific questions, I think I can get you a couple of copies of Kenneth's letters when I get back in the spring. "The Pot of Earth" I have no other copy of. If I ever do turn one up you shall have it. Kreymborg[4] has vanished, and I fear the worst. He apparently is out of a job, licked and defeated. I did everything I could to keep him on the WPA rolls, but it was no use. You will have a scenic postalcard from every town in South America named Santa Minerva de la Cucaracha.

Affectionately   [Archie]

TL-C: DLC

1. American poet and translator (1903–1968) whose work on a Spanish translation of M's *Conquistador* had been aborted by the Spanish civil war.   2. Probably Fitts's *One Hundred Poems from the Palatine Anthology in English Paraphrase* (Norfolk, Conn.: New Directions, 1938).   3. M refers to an exhibition of his works at Yale University Library that had been arranged by Yale English professor Arthur Mizener with help from various persons including Fitts. The exhibition coincided with M's delivery of the first Francis Bergen Memorial Lecture at Yale on 7 January 1938. Mizener also prepared *A Catalogue of the First Editions of Archibald MacLeish* ([New Haven]: Yale University Library, 1938) for distribution at the exhibition. 4. Alfred Kreymborg (1883–1966), American playwright, poet, and critic.

To Henry R. Luce[1]

Dear Harry: [*c.* 20 July 1938]   [Conway]

I've taken God's time — I assume it is God's time? — to an answer partly because your letter asked no questions and partly because I wanted a good haunch of an evening to write you in.

I say your letter asks no questions. There are nevertheless questions implicit in it. For one the New School. I'm delighted you've done that.[2] I had always hoped you would. And it would have given me greater pleasure than you can imagine to bring your consent in to the good Doctor. I say Bravo. Go to meetings when you can. And get to know Alvin. There are few better men — few as good.

For another Fortune and my work on it. There I think I can say something to you which will truly be to your advantage as they say in the personals in the *Times*. I refer to your courteous and kindly remark that you do not need to tell me of your appreciation of my work on Fortune. Well, my lad, you do. And I'll tell you why — and it applies to many other than myself. The last story of mine about which you had anything encouraging to say to me was the story last before the *Grass Lands*.[3] And the *Grass Lands* was a long time ago. I will admit (with resentment) that Fortune is not the association of mutually assisting

291

journalists it was for five or six very exciting years. I will admit (without enthusiasm) that it is now a part of a publishing enterprise in which not more than a dozen or so people know each other's names and not more than half that many wish each other well enough to stand by each other in the only work that finally counts — the writing of the journal. But I will still reply that you *do* need to tell your associates when their work is good. Because if you don't the last element of personal humanity will drain out of that organization and you will be left with nothing on your hands but a business which earns money. I can speak of this freely first because I am no longer a part of that organization and secondly because your silence has never seriously hurt me — the reason being that I have always counted on a solid and substantial friendship between us and have always known that when the work *was* good (and a man knows) you recognized its value. But there are a lot of others who haven't that solid basis and that mutual faith. And you owe them more than they get in the way of appreciation. They work for you — or for your magazine — harder than any comparable group in the country. And they value your praise more than you could believe possible. It isn't necessarily that they think you the ultimate judge though most or many of them know you to be the best editor around the shop by a big jugfull. Its rather that you represent humanly and in person the invisible entity for which they work. Well — you know all this.

So. Then there's Fortune itself and its organization and its direction. I too think Fortune is in good shape organization-wise though understaffed as always good-writer-wise. I think perhaps too enthusiastically that it has a future commensurate with its past. But then I am not sure you would agree with me about its past. I won't go over all that again. You know what I think. I think when they take the final inventory on Time Inc Fortune will stand out as by far the most important single item because Fortune will stand out as the one great journalistic innovation of our time. I don't know whether you are aware of the extent to which the jury of intelligent and disciplined minds has already come to that conclusion. I hear it everywhere. If there were some possible means to get rid of that vast and ritzy bulk and to put the price within possible reach of the educated American public Fortune would become an even greater influence than it now is. And it is now an influence of much greater persuasion than any survey or any possible statistic will ever show. Because it provides the basis upon which are made and shaped the judgments which form opinion — *effective* opinion — in this country. All right — laugh your head off. Some day you'll find out its true. Its a very great magazine. Its a very great magazine because it is a true and honest and efficient journalistic technique. And God help the editor who ever meddles with that technique. . . . . who ever puts the editorial wish above the research girl's yes-say or nay-say. Because there is no better way to kill an egg than to murder its mother the goose.

And then there's you. I don't know you very well these days. I probably never will know you very well again. I think you're all right. I don't think the kind of people you are going mostly to see from now on will be able to shake your apprenticeship in loyal journalism. They'll try to. But then you know they'll try to and you are therefore forearmed. I wish some things had gone differently with you — though I'd find it hard to say just which. Maybe what I mean is that I wish you hadn't been so successful. Because its very hard to be as successful as you have been and still keep your belief in the desperate necessity for fundamental change. I think what you have done amazing and I give you all credit and all honor for it. It would have been very easy for you to forget everything you believed true when you were twenty. Other men have found it almost unmentionably easy. That you haven't done that is admirable. I admire you for it. But I don't know — you were meant to be a progressive — a pusher-over — a pryer-up. You were meant to make common cause with the people — all the people. You would have been very happy I think if you could have felt that the New Deal was your affair. Because it was your affair. You would have been very happy inside yourself as one of the leaders in a democratic revolution in this country — a revolution which would have brought to pass everything that Alexander H. and his friends brought to failure. Maybe I'm wrong. Its presumptuous to guess about another man's happiness but I think you would have been. I think you hate being rich. I think you hate being a pal of the people who want you to be their pal. I think you would have liked to write *The People Yes*.

Don't misunderstand me. I don't think you've gone the other way. I don't think you've pared the nails of your youth. I think you have been an honorable journalist. You would have been happier in a fight though — and Jesus there are things to fight for. I'm not telling you either. You're telling me. Please tell Clare[4] I like her and wish her very well. It won't matter to her but please tell her anyway.

Did you see Nicolson?[5] Let me know sometime.

yrs affly   Archie

TLS: TIME

1. M had resigned from the staff of *Fortune* on 30 June 1938 to accept a position at Harvard University as curator of the recently endowed Nieman Foundation. 2. M had urged Luce to meet Dr. Alvin Johnson, president of the New School for Social Research in New York. Luce reported that he had not only met Johnson but had agreed to serve on the school's board of directors. 3. "The Grasslands" had appeared

in *Fortune* in November 1935. It had been preceded, in August 1935, by a story on the Chrysler Corporation.   **4.** Clare Boothe Luce, the playwright and former *Vanity Fair* editor, whom Luce had married in 1935.   **5.** Probably Harold Nicolson (1886–1968), the English biographer, historian, and diplomat.

To Ernest Hemingway [1]

Dear Pappy: 6 August [1938]   Conway

Thanks for writing to me. I wanted to write you. You and me communicating through Mac Ingersoll struck me odd.

I'm horribly sorry that what I said offended you. When I saw the copy of your letter to Mac which he sent me I went down to New York to talk to him to try to get the thing straight in my head.

I don't know whether you understand the situation altogether. Mac's first letter to me seemed to me to mean (I was wrong about it) that you had accused me to some people in New York of dishonesty. If you'll imagine the situation reversed you'll imagine how I felt. I knew you did not think very well of me — or as well as you had. But it seemed to me absolutely incredible you should think me dishonest. I guess I don't need to tell you how I felt about it. So I said what I did — that the accusation, in addition to every thing else, was ridiculous because it couldn't make any difference to me or anyone else whether the note was preferred or not because the money was already allocated if there should be any. This didn't have any bearing, I said, on your absolute right to have a preferred note but it did have a bearing on the possibility that anyone had tried to cheat you by not giving you one. [*MacLeish wrote in the margin:* What you have to understand is that I thought I was] I was defending myself against a very cruel and injurious charge of dishonesty. So I went down to see Mac and try to find out what in hell it was all about. I found out that I was wrong in my understanding of his first letter, that you had never made the charge about me or even the charge as I understood it at all. I am now writing you to say that I am very very sorry that what I said offended you in any way. You know without my saying it again how much I together with everyone else connected with the picture appreciates what you did for the picture. You put much more money into it than any other individual and you did much more about it than any one except Joris himself. The fact that there should ever have been any difficulty for you as a consequence is a reproach to me who am absolutely responsible for the error however it may have come about. I am going to make it my business to see that it is corrected.

As things are there wouldn't be much point in my keeping your check. I should only send it on [to] the corporation (I don't want the capital stock repaid *to me* and never have) and the corporation is already in your debt and would send it back to you in some form. So there's no point in my keeping it. The other check I don't need to write to you about. I think from what you say it was a check to cover my share of that party we all gave for Sara and Gerald. However you may feel about me now you can hardly ask me to take it back. Please as a personal favor to me — if you'll let me put it that way — have it cashed.

Ada and Mimi want me to send their love to you all. I wish you did know Peter and he you.   yours   Archie

TLS: JFK

1. *See* M to Hemingway, 8 August 1937, note 1.

To Martha Hillard MacLeish

Dearest Mother: [*c.* 17 August 1938]   [Conway]

Its one thing to get to be eighty-two. And its another thing to be Martha Hillard getting to be eighty-two. The first is just a date. The second is proof of the fundamental logic of life. We assume — at least we did assume once upon a time — that the universe was — is — organized in such a way as to secure the ultimate triumph of virtue — of goodness — of truth — of selflessness — of honesty — of belief. But whatever proofs of that divine dispensation may have been available to spectators in other generations very few are available to spectators in ours. The only one of which I have personal and certain knowledge is your life. Your life has all the elements of irrefutable proof. It has all the inner logic, all the patient endurance, all the eventual realization of its own inward meaning which one expects only in a great poem or a great work of art. And it is, I say, the one proof of which I have first hand knowledge or even good second hand knowledge that the great Christian virtues do win in the end or can win in the end a reward worthy of themselves and commensurate with themselves. Its a curious thing that it should be so difficult to talk of this. One finds no difficulty in talking about the excellence of a work of art — even to the artist who may suffer exquisitely in the discussion. But to discuss the triumphs of the world of morality requires evidently a thick skin or a letter such as this written on an occasion which makes all things possible and from a distance which makes all answer remote. If I were praising you — and this is not praise, not even filial recognition but only scientific observation — if I were praising you I should say what is most certainly true and most truly beautiful — that you alone of all human beings I have known except only Ada — and you in some ways even more than Ada — believe in life, trust in life and are certain of the goodness of life. To me there is nothing humanly possible which can be compared for a moment with that victory. I am very proud to be your son.   Archie

TLS: M

To the Editor of Poetry

Dear Sir: [*c*. September 1938]   [Conway?]

Sorry I can't oblige with a reply to Mr. Rosenberg's piece.[1] Very busy at the moment and besides it pretty well replies to itself. When you run into a blast like this you look for the animus. The animus is stated. It is insolence in me to suggest that the poets of this country must give form and shape to the imagination of the people because this has already been done. What Mr. Rosenberg means is that this has already been done by the Marxists. He may be right but the trouble is, as a lot of very wise Marxists can tell him, that the people of this country don't know it.

The rest is all pretty obvious. The straw man antithesis between "faith" and scientific economic determinism at the beginning won't fool anyone who has ever seen a straw man. Economic determinism is of course a "faith" itself — one of the most powerful faiths of our time. As for Hitler and Mussolini — it is comforting to know that they are really on the rocks. Someone ought to tell them. It would save the lives of a lot of American and English and other anti-fascists who are fighting them in Spain, to say nothing of the Spaniards themselves. All any of us need to do apparently is to sit back and wait for the collapse foretold in the books. If this were the general Communist position liberals who are making common cause with Communists against fascism would do better to stand alone. Fortunately it isn't. Communists know as well as other anti-fascists that fascism is a very real and terrible danger and precisely for the reason I state in the article Mr. Rosenberg attacks. There remains one last word of heartfelt thanks however. I am an unconscious fascist again. And I crib my ideas from Herbert Hoover. That really tickles me.   A. MacL.

P: ICU

1. Harold Rosenberg, "The God in the Car," *Poetry* 52 (September 1938), 334–342, immediately following which the present letter appeared as "A Letter from Archibald MacLeish." Rosenberg's piece was directed against M's "In Challenge Not Defense," *Poetry* 52 (July–September 1938), 212–219.

To Henry R. Luce

Dear Harry: [*c*. 8 September 1938] [Conway]

You will forgive me for being so long in the answering of your letter. I have had the pleasure of marrying a son combined with the burden of marrying a daughter — for the son's bride, having no means whatever, was married from the son's house — the son having of course enormous means.[1] But it was something to go through particularly as the weather, having tempted Ada into weeks of work in her garden for a garden wedding, went thoroughly sour on the day itself. I have composed a poem in your native idiom for the event. It reads:

> Tuesday was a beautiful day
> Thursday was also brilliant
> The wedding was Wednesday

But there are compensations even for bad weather. Our friends turned out rain or no rain in a way to warm the most cynical heart. Mac [Ingersoll] coming all the way up for the little wedding party was something never to forget. I could have cried when I saw him coming over the lawn.

I am grateful to you for writing me as you did.[2] It is heart-warming also to know that you had plans for me at Fortune even if they never did materialize. It is good to know also that you still look forward perhaps to such a future. If as and when you come to the sill of the door I'd be happy to talk to you about it. Meantime I shall of course say nothing whatever to Mitch or Eric. I said nothing to Mac though I assume he knows what you wrote me since you say you discussed it with him.

Good luck to you. . . . . . Have you recently seen a pair of incredibly beautiful children of twenty one and twenty with not a cent between them and tomorrow married? Its a tremendous thing to see in these times. I was crying like a — well what DOES cry that way?

yours   Archie

TLS: TIME

1. The son was Kenneth MacLeish, who on September 7 had married Carolyn de Chadenèdes. 2. Luce had written on September 1 to say that the year before he had considered making M the editor of a *Fortune* editorial page similar to that in *The New York Times*, and that he continued to regard such an assignment as a possibility.

To Ernest Hemingway

Dear Pappy: [30 January 1939] [Farmington]

Its sleeting like hell from the northeast with two inches or less of slush just freezing on the ground and the house leaks air like a loose intestine and I either have a cold or haven't and so I think about Key West which makes me happy or think about the weather which produces this — [1]

> As one on whom
> The Triple Stinker publicly hath stunk
> I claim the usual convenience. Room!
> Room at the horse trough! Blankets from the bunk-house bunk!
>
> Move over Hemingway. Your Spanish pants
> Are stained but there's no Wilson on your coat.
> The noise was pompous as an elephant's:
> The nuisance though — it looks like — is it only goat?
>
> The load you got was envy. Bad enough!
> The wounded ego of a man gone rotten
> Sticks to the pant-leg and will stain the stuff.
> But what you got was nothing to the load I've gotten.
>
> I took the whole frustration on the nose.
> The wish to be a poet: the ambition
> To Think of Daisy in immortal prose:
> The hope to publish in a limited edition:
>
> The strong intelligence that should have won
> A Princeton Aristotle's decent fame
> But quibbled when the fascists pulled a gun:
> I got it all with all the shamelessness of shame.
>
> Move over Ernest till I rinse my shirt
> And see for what they spend *New Yorker* money:
> The blast was like a mule's that feels the quirt.
> The nuisance. . . . .
> Look!
> It isn't even goat.
> Its bunny!

Well — hardly worth the trouble but still I like the last line. Did you read the Vogue pieces you and I were side by side in?[2] Probably not but if you did do you remember your telling me that about the kings? Its quite true that I remember it that way. You certainly make that Wyoming-Montana country jump out of the print and come real.

Cheerist what weather. Wish I'd seen you in New York that evening you and Sadie and Quintanilla[3] and Ada put in together. Ada had a fine time. Said you were in wonderful form. Love to Pauline

as always Archie

TLS: JFK

1. The heretofore unpublished poem that follows was written in retaliation against Edmund Wilson's verse parody "The Omelet of A. MacLeish," in *The New Yorker* 14 (14 January 1939), 23–24. 2. M's essay "Dry Tortugas" had appeared with Hemingway's "The Clark's Fork Valley, Wyoming" as well as essays by Irwin Edman and by James Vincent Sheean in "America, We Love You," *Vogue* 93 (1 February 1939), 68–69, 157–160. 3. Spanish painter Luis Quintanilla, in New York to execute a large fresco for the Spanish pavilion at the 1939 World's Fair.

To Felix Frankfurter[1]

Dear Felix: 15 May 1939 [Cambridge]

If I were the distinguished person to whom your memorandum of May eleventh was addressed, I should immediately and without more [ado] pull down my flag and appoint your candidate: a more persuasive brief I have never read. Being merely your candidate I can only tell you, first, how proud I am of the golden opinions you hold and how troubled I am that I cannot feel as you do about the end result. Friday at the request of Mr. Kent Keller, the Chairman of the House Committee on the Library of Congress, I dashed down to New York for a two-hour talk with him between trains. Coming back to Boston that evening I thought as long and hard as I can — which is very long but perhaps not quite hard enough — about the face of fate.

This, as I think you will understand, is the most critical of my many crises, but it is none the less characteristic of them all. From the beginning of my more or less adult life I have been plagued by the fact that I seem to be able to do more or less well things which don't commonly go together. Being on the Yale football team and the *Yale Lit* presented the characteristic pattern. When I first decided on leaving the school not to go into practice, and when later I left practice to write verse, the decision in each case was made difficult by the fact that many of my friends thought I was leaving an active life in which I could do well for a life as an artist in which I was not apt to do well because I was not the kind of person with whom the word artist is commonly associated. I think I was made to suffer as acutely over my decision to quit the law for poetry as it is possible to make a man suffer over any decision in his own life. As you may perhaps know, people like Bob Proctor[2] still tell the ladies of Boston what a disaster it is that I gave up a career as a first-rate lawyer to become a third-rate poet. The most recent of the many crises of this type presented itself about a year ago when, as I think I told you, Harry Luce wanted to make me Editor of *Fortune* in complete charge of the editorial content of the magazine.

When I decided instead to go to Harvard on a half-time job, he expressed himself in words which I still vividly recall.

I tell you all this not because you don't know it but because you do. I know very well what the direction of your interest in my life is. Being yourself a man of very much broader interests and more diverse talents than I, you will understand as few other men could possibly understand that an ability to get along in the world does not argue an inability to practice an art. Furthermore, being a man who loves art as he loves life, you will understand why the practice of my art seems to me to be the thing I must do. What you will perhaps not understand — because it is so easy for you to do many things together — is that the practice of my art requires, in my practice of it at least, long periods of completely free time. I can practice journalism in the afternoons while doing something else in the morning, but I can only write the poems I must write when I can count on months together in which nothing but the poem need have present reality in my mind.

This, it seems to me, the directorship of the Congressional Library could not give. I do not refer merely to the fact that the place is a place of great honor and distinction with the corresponding obligations. I understand I think and most enthusiastically agree with your enthusiasm for a non-technical librarian as head of that great library, but even such a man would have to give a close and almost day-by-day attention to the library, first, because it is an enormous institution with a budget close to $3,000,000 a year, secondly, because it has close to a thousand employees whose appointment at the present time involves the whole problem of political patronage, and, finally, because of its many problems as a library. As a matter of fact, I think any man who undertook the job, even though he were appointed as a non-librarian, would sooner or later be obliged to learn the librarian's profession in order to support the heavy responsibilities of his office. Over and above all this are the tremendous opportunities for a new and useful work of cultural dissemination to which you refer so persuasively and so movingly in your memorandum.

It may be that I have now come to the place in my life where I should stop writing poetry and turn to the public service. But if I thought so, I am afraid I should not be of much use to the public service, because the one thing I have ever wanted to do with all my heart was to write poetry and the one thing I have ever wanted to be was a poet. As it is, I have never wanted to write as much as I do at the moment and have never had so many things which demanded to be written. I am afraid they would never be written in the Library of Congress or with the Library of Congress as the principal interest in my life.

Forgive this inordinately long letter which I write you only because

I want to be sure that you understand what is in my mind when I tell you that I offer you all my affectionate thanks and my profoundest regret that I should not be able to accompany those thanks with the acceptance of the very great honor you have done me and the great opportunity for public service you have attempted to make available.

Yours,

Archie

P. S. I have just had a telephone call from the White House saying that the President would like me to come down to lunch with him Tuesday of next week. I am left in something of a quandary. It would be a delight to me to go, and I shall, of course, do whatever the President wishes me to do in that regard. Nevertheless I suppose I may assume that the purpose of the luncheon has to do with the subject of this letter and that being so, I am reluctant to take the President's time when I feel so clear about the matter. What do you think I should do? I have wired the White House that I can come on Tuesday, but if you feel I should spare the President an hour which he could certainly devote to much better uses, I shall be glad to have your advice.

Regards,

Archie

TLS: DLC

1. In a letter dated 3 May 1939, President Roosevelt had written to Frankfurter asking what the associate justice of the U.S. Supreme Court thought of M as a possible successor to the retiring Librarian of Congress, seventy-eight-year-old Herbert Putnam. "He is not a professional Librarian nor is he a special student of incunabula or ancient manuscripts," the President wrote. "Nevertheless, he has lots of qualifications that said specialists have not." Frankfurter, in a letter dated 11 May 1939, heartily endorsed the nomination of M, describing what he regarded as the qualifications the Librarian should possess, and averring that M possessed these qualifications in abundance. Frankfurter sent M a copy of his letter to the President; this is M's reply. 2. A member of Choate, Hall & Stewart.

To Franklin D. Roosevelt

Dear Mr. President: 28 May [1939] [Farmington]

I must apologize for my delay in writing this letter. It is not, I assure you, a delay caused by carelessness or neglect. For four days — ever since I left your office last Tuesday — nothing else has been in my mind, waking or sleeping, but the question of the words which this letter ought to contain. The difficulty of answering that question has made me as miserable as the necessity of answering it has made me proud.

You will perhaps recall what the difficulty was when you first suggested to me that you had considered me for the post of Librarian of

Congress. It was a difficulty of time. My trade is poetry and poetry, though it is a non-continuous operation, is nevertheless a time-consuming operation. My fear, when you first spoke of a possible appointment, was the fear that a job of such responsibility and importance would leave no time for my own work. Later, because I believe so deeply in the possibilities of the job, I attempted to argue myself into a contrary opinion. I argued so successfully that I wrote you two letters, each of which I later destroyed. When it came down to it I could not believe that the job of Librarian of Congress was a job a man with an art to practice could fairly undertake. Either the art or the library would suffer, and either result would be disastrous to the man. I have been round and round the apple tree for four days but I end up every day at the same place. I have therefore sadly and regretfully concluded that there is nothing to be gained by going round again. I can only thank you with all my heart for thinking of me and for the great honor you have done me and tell you with what regret I feel I must decline.

I should like also to add this, if you will permit me to do so. One reason why the job of librarian of Congress frightens me is the fact that the job is pretty much a permanent job. A man would hardly be much good at it for three or four years and it would be unfair of him to leave until he had passed his apprenticeship and served for many years thereafter. I should therefore feel, in taking it, that I have given up my own work pretty much for the rest of my life. I should not feel the same way about work which did not have this character. I should also be proud to be of service to you. If therefore the occasion should arise when you felt I could be of service to you I hope you will not think that my inability to accept the office you have now in mind implies that I intend to crawl into an ivory tower. I do intend to put in the next year writing a long poem, if the world doesn't blow up under us. And I am not, as I think you know, a job-hunter in any sense of the word. But I admire you and your work, as you may realize. And I should be proud indeed to be useful to you in any capacity which did not deprive me of the trade I follow.

very respectfully yours,
Archibald MacLeish

ALS: NHpR

To Franklin D. Roosevelt

Dear Mr. President: 1 June 1939 [Farmington]

I must apologize for my delay in writing you about the matter you asked me last week to consider. The question which troubled me when you first told me what you had in mind — the question, that is, of time in which to continue my own writing — touched me even more as I realized more clearly the great responsibility of the position of which you spoke & the great importance of the work which might be done in it. I am assured, however, by those in whose judgment I trust that time undoubtedly could be found. I am therefore writing you now to say that I should be very proud indeed to serve as director of the Congressional Library should you wish to name me. The place is, of course, one any man might be proud to have. And it would be a great delight to me to feel that I could be of service to you: a very great delight.

The question of the time when I should be expected to undertake my duties was not, I think, discussed last week. I should perhaps have told you at that time that I have work in hand to which I am deeply committed which will require some months to clear up. It is hard to foresee the precise time required. I should probably be out of deep water by the end of the summer — say October first. But I should deeply appreciate any further time I might be allowed as I am quite certain I should have to devote myself entirely to the Library for a considerable period after taking over.

I trust this fact will not seem an inconvenience. I should perhaps add — in case my situation has any relevance — that there is no reason, so far as I am concerned, why the appointment should not be made, or announced, at any time you see fit, either now or later.[1]

Will you permit me to say again in closing how much I appreciate the honor you have done me, & how much I value your thought of me in this connection.

very respectfully yours
Archibald MacLeish

ALS: NHpR

1. M's nomination for the position of Librarian of Congress was announced by President Roosevelt on June 6. He took office on 2 October 1939, and served until 19 December 1944.

To Carl Sandburg

Dear Carl: 13 June 1940 [Washington]

I have been hoping we might run into each other so that I could say face to face what I must now say in writing. Raney[1] told me at Cincinnati that you were in the offing down in Kentucky somewhere, but I was obliged to leave before you got to town.

What I have in mind this time is not the Lincoln job which I hoped you might be willing to undertake for the Library when we last talked here, but something much simpler though no less important and no less near your heart. The Library of Congress has, as you may or may not know, a group of Consultantships in various fields — one of which is the field of English poetry, or rather, more correctly, Poetry in the English Language. I want you to accept that Consultantship in the Library of Congress for a year beginning in July 1941. I have two reasons: one the personal but not selfish reason of wishing to bring you to the Library of Congress as frequently as possible; the other, the professional reason of wishing to make the Consultantship in Poetry in the Library of Congress a position of the greatest possible distinction and prestige. In other words, I want you to set the job up on a pinnacle for me and at the same time I want to have you around.

Neither the duties nor the emoluments need trouble you. Attendance at the Library would be extremely part-time, and the duties of the post at the Library could be handled by an assistant who already exists. The emolument, which is $2500 or $3000 a year, can go into your private account for goat feed. The gains, however, to the Library and to the country would be very considerable indeed. Your presence from time to time, your talk with members of the Library staff — particularly with Alan Lomax and the boys working with folksong and music — your educational influence upon the people's representatives in Congress, to say nothing of the Librarian of the people's representatives in Congress — all the by-products, that is[,] of your presence and your talk and your writing and your thinking, would be invaluable. And the job, once you had held it, would be a job any man thereafter would be proud to hold.

You probably know that the present incumbent is Joe Auslander. I have already told Joe that I am going to replace him at the end of this next fiscal year, i.e., on July 1, 1941. I won't go into the details of all that: you can certainly supply them for yourself.

Please think about it and think about it in as sympathetic a way as you can, because I do tremendously want you to do it. It would be grand for us all and I can't help but think it would be pretty good fun for you too.[2]

Always with my affection,   Faithfully yours,   [Archie]

p. s. Do you mind keeping this all very much under your hat, since there are lots of sensitive personalities involved as you can well understand?

TL-C: DLC

1. M. Llewellyn Raney, director of the University of Chicago Libraries and a principal defender of M's nomination as Librarian of Congress. M had seen him at the Ameri-

can Library Association's annual meeting in Cincinnati. **2.** Sandburg declined the appointment, as did several others to whom M offered it, and William Carlos Williams was later named Auslander's successor as poetry consultant at the Library of Congress.

To Van Wyck Brooks[1]

Dear Van Wyck: 20 August 1941   Washington

I think you once said of an article that it might change a little the contemporary climate. But yours is *surely* such a piece.[2] It blows in through the little leaves like the East wind that changes weather. It blows in, and you can hear the poplars pattering and splashing — all the little leaves that grow on the little brief-lived trees. Reading it, I thought how truly *real* time is. There was a time when your words could not have been heard because of the loud rattling of the little leaves. But now, because time is real and the changes of time are real, they roar like a great gale and the leaves, for all their rattling, are inaudible. Worse than inaudible. Their rattling & splashing is suddenly silly and incredibly flimsy & false so that one wonders how one ever listened to them. This is true in part because of you & in part because of the changes of time. It is true because of you because you speak well & clearly & with great patience & understanding. It is true because of the changes of time because the terrible changes & menace of our time make true things true again the way the flat white light before a storm shows all the shapes & contours of the earth. It was conceivable — it was almost comprehensible — that men should have written, in the hurricane-center void & emptiness & calm of the 20s, as these people you speak of, or their masters, then wrote. It is not conceivable — indeed it is inconceivable & almost indecent — that they should write in that way now. And not because there are wars & armies. Not at all. But because the armies & the wars, the murders & the lies, have made suddenly real & visible & true the moral beauty against which all this violence is worked.

To speak of people, I should make this distinction about Eliot & Pound — that whatever the essential frivolity & sterility of their *critical* writing, their *poetry itself* was a great and creative power. Their *poetry itself* — whatever they said of it or whatever their critic-imitators now say of it — cleared away mountains of rhetoric & restored to words their meaning in the human mouth & made possible a living poetry. All of us now writing verse owe them much — more perhaps than any poets of our age except Yeats & perhaps Alexis Leger. Besides which they, each in his way, have written poetry of great &, I believe, lasting beauty. But the edifice built by their "criticism" on their work, &, worse still, the filagree committed on that edifice by the "coterie critics", is neither generative nor regenerative but academic, sterile, frivolous — and as false as criticism can well be. As critics they were both enemies of poetry, & enemies of poetry — doubly enemies of poetry — are the ringers of the tiny bells, the rustlers of the little leaves.

I salute you with hommage   Archie

ALS: PU

1. American writer and critic (1886–1963). 2. Brooks's then-forthcoming book, *The Opinions of Oliver Allston* (1941), had been excerpted in *The New Republic* 104 (23 June 1941), 853–855, and 105 (11 August 1941), 185–187, the latter of which presumably prompted M's letter.

To Grace Tully[1]

Dear Grace: 4 December 1941   [Washington]

I seem to be bothering you a lot these days, but I want to clear one name for OFF.[2] I want very much to borrow Allen Grover, who is a Vice President of Time, Inc., for six months to help me organize and staff the Office of Facts and Figures. I think I can persuade Luce to make it possible for Grover to come, and I hope to be able to persuade Grover also. Under all the circumstances, however, I thought the President might like a chance to say "no" if he would rather I didn't proceed along this line.

The point is that I desperately need some help. The Office of Facts and Figures is still without office space and apparently will have none until a new temporary building is completed (I am going to try to tuck it into a corner of the Library of Congress for a while). Secondly, I am finding the job of keeping an eye on the Library of Congress and organizing and running OFF a pretty considerable job and I'd like the help of a man who has had a good deal of organizational experience. Grover is, I think, a very good man.

                          Faithfully yours,   Archibald MacLeish

TL-C: DLC

1. Secretary to President Roosevelt. 2. On 24 October 1941 President Roosevelt had created the Office of Facts and Figures and had named M its director. The OFF's mandate was to act as a clearinghouse of information about the status and progress of the national defense effort. M served without pay and reported directly to the President, while continuing to serve as Librarian of Congress.

To Robert Sherwood[1]

Dear Bob: 9 December 1941   [Washington]

I don't know if this could be of use to you or not, but on the chance that it may be, here it is:

The American people at the moment are fighting mad. That temper requires action to endure or to create positive political and military strength. Let's assume that offensive action on our part is now unlikely in the near future. A combination of rage and inability to hit back is one of the notorious combinations which produce frustration and defeatism.

What we have to do then is to give the country a substitute for offensive action. The country has lost its cake (the belief that it could push Japan over in two weeks) and we are unable to give it bread in the form of a counter stroke. Therefore we have to give it something to bite on and bite hard.

One of the things the American people believe in is the ability of Americans, once they are aroused, to fight like hell. Let's remind them that our navy, whatever may have happened at Pearl Harbor, is manned by American youngsters — maybe the best American youngsters, by and large. Let's assure them — and let's give them the President's assurance in explicit terms — that the American navy, if it was caught napping once, won't be caught napping again: that isn't the way with Americans. Let's suggest to them that if the American people fighting mad can lick the world, then the American navy is part of the American people and the personification of the American people.

Second, let's point out to them that what happened at Pearl Harbor was obviously a carefully prepared attack, engineered by all the brains, all the audacity, and all the treachery of the Axis combination *and that its purpose was to knock us out of the war at one blow.* That was its clear purpose and the only possible explanation of the tremendous risk taken and the vast and complicated paraphernalia of diplomatic conversations and wholesale lies which prepared for it.

Then let's say — Bang! — that the attempt miscarried and that we were not knocked out of the war: far from it.

Then let's make this point.

The Loss we suffered at Pearl Harbor was a heavy loss. For any other country it might have been a disaster. But for this country, with its tremendous productive capacity, it was not a disastrous loss. It was a loss which this country at its present rate of production can make good in a period of time which no other nation in the world could begin to approach — a period of time so short that it can have no real effect upon the outcome of the war. But let's add — and this is perhaps the affirmative usefulness of the presentation — that if we will really put our powers into production we will provide such an answer to the Japanese at Pearl Harbor as will astonish and confound them.

Let's make the point also that with a coastline like ours and with outposts as remote as ours no navy, nor any possible combination of conceivable navies[,] can protect every point. We must expect more such attacks. We must expect raids and destruction and loss of life. But against these risks we have our unshaken confidence in ourselves as a great fighting nation. We have, to support that confidence in ourselves, the greatest and most rapidly available productive capacity in the world.

The Japanese expected to knock us out of the war with one treacherous blow. Instead they have aroused and awakened us as a people. They have enabled us to muster all our resources of heart and body for the greatest productive effort ever made by any nation. And they have written in letters of treachery their own final and inescapable doom.

Obviously, the order of these suggestions is not carefully worked out. The warning of further American losses should undoubtedly come early in any such arrangement. However some of these suggestions may be useful to you. God strengthen you!

Faithfully yours,   [Archie]

TL-C: DLC

1. Sherwood (1896–1955), the Pulitzer Prize–winning playwright, was a principal speech writer for President Roosevelt and director of the Foreign Information Service. M's letter was probably intended to assist Sherwood with his work on the President's fireside chat broadcast of the evening of December 9, two days after the Japanese attack on Pearl Harbor and one day after the American declaration of war.

To Henry R. Luce

PERSONAL

Dear Harry: 13 February 1942 [Washington]

This is not a letter to the Editor: it is a letter to a personal friend. But it breathes a good deal of the same indignation which may be frequently found in letters to the Editor.

The February sixteen issue of *Time* carries a story about Malcolm Cowley which seems to me about as outrageous a piece of journalism, given the magazine in which it appears and the obvious purpose for which it was published, as I have ever seen.[1] The obvious purpose — indeed the only possible purpose — is to add fuel to the fire of an attack made on Malcolm Cowley as an employee of OFF by Westbrook Pegler and Martin Dies,[2] and his friends. One expects such attacks from Pegler and Dies. One — or at least I personally — does not expect them from *Time*.

Evidence: *The Dry Season* is not "the most inopportune book of the month". It is not a book of the month at all. It is not even a book of the year. It was published on December 10, 1941. That is one plain, and obviously calculated, misstatement of fact.

Second. The magazine used to have, and I dare say still has, a rule against reviewing books more than a week old. This rule, if it still exists, was disregarded in this instance for an unstated purpose, but a purpose which, I submit, is all too plain.

Again. *Time Magazine*, like all honest magazines, has generally required of its reviewers that they should not take matter — particularly poetry — out of context in order to make a case. The article here in question does precisely that. Lines are taken out of context in two poems in such a way as to make both poems mean what they do not mean when read as a whole. "The Last Internationale" is a poem about the millions who died in the unsuccessful revolutions following the first world war. It describes, as any man intelligent enough to write verse criticism for *Time* must have known, a nightmare — a fantastic parade of the dead. "Tomorrow Morning" is a poem, as anyone reading it could see at once, about the Civil War in Spain — which explains the "Central Committee" and the "labor unions". The poem is not even a political poem, let alone being a revolutionary poem. It is a lament from men who died in vain in consequence of the frantic and fanatical preoccupation with the future which has cost so many thousands of lives.

Again, Mr. Cowley is called a "chief information analyst" — a phrase obviously picked up from Pegler. "Chief information analyst", as your research people here could have told your writers in New York, is a civil service classification. As your researchers could have also told you, Cowley is one of a number of writers, including that good G.B., Charlie Poore, that highly conservative editor Marty Sommers, Associate Editor of the *Saturday Evening Post*, and that distinguished biographer, Henry Pringle, and a number of others of almost equal distinction. His job is the job he has followed all his life, i.e., writing.

In fact, speaking of researchers, my great admiration for the *Time* and *Fortune* research system makes me wonder very seriously whether the piece about Cowley was based on research at all. And that suspicion leads me to suggest to you that you might find it interesting to call for the research on the subject and contrast it with the piece finally written. You are probably not aware — neither was I until this piece of pure poison appeared — that some of your editors (my good friend, Bob

Cantrell for one) have long been feuding with Cowley. I don't say that *Time* has been used by one of its editors as a vehicle for the settling of an old grudge no matter at what cost to the agency of government in which Cowley is employed, but I do say that I can't think of any other good reason for taking a book review of a two months old volume of verse, mis-naming it a book of the month, misrepresenting its contents, and publishing it in the front of the magazine.

I go into all this at such great length partly because I think an injury has been done to Cowley, partly because I think an injury has been done to *Time Magazine,* and partly because I think an injury has been done to an agency of government — OFF — which is already working under pretty heavy handicaps of manufactured prejudice. On reviewing the whole case, I think you may feel that it would serve the interest of general understanding and specific truth if *Time* would publish the actual facts about the staff of OFF and about the job OFF undertakes to do. These facts have been made available to Felix Belair[3] and any information he lacks will be willingly supplied.

I close with one direct appeal. Will you, as a personal favor to me, take time to get to the bottom of this very distressing business? I am not saying that you will find serpents at the bottom of the cesspool, but I do think you may make some interesting discoveries.[4]

Always,   Faithfully yours,   Archie

TLS: TIME

1. "Inopportune," *Time* 39 (16 February 1942), 13–14. 2. Pegler was a journalist with the Chicago *Daily News;* Dies was chairman of the House Committee on Un-American Activities. 3. Washington bureau chief of *Time.* 4. As a result of the pressure brought to bear against his serving with the OFF, Cowley shortly resigned and returned to private life.

To Samuel I. Rosenman[1]

Dear Sam: 24 March 1942 [Washington]

I don't know whether I made myself altogether clear to you the other evening or not. I thought you looked a little puzzled when I got through trying to tell you my position. I'd like to try again, therefore, in black and white.

The shortest way I can say it is this: that the centralized organization of the government's information service is so vitally important that nothing, and least of all any question of personalities, ought to stand in its way. If it can be brought about more easily or more effectively by leaving me personally out, that is the way it should be done. If, on the other hand, it needs me, then I am available. In other words, I don't think my personal preference is important. But since you asked for it the best way I can put it is that I have put in six hard months at OFF, that I have become intensely interested in the broad information job, as a man always becomes interested in anything he puts his full self into, and that I should like to go on with it simply because I think I have now learned a good deal about it and because I have some pretty clearly defined plans which I should like to carry out.

You also asked me whether I thought I could do the job. The answer to that is that I do think I could do the policy-making job, the intra-governmental coordinating job, but that I don't think I would be much good at the job of actually running the production end of a central government propaganda agency — the press releasing, promotional job which, once the policy is set, needs to be carried out. In other words, if we centralize domestic control of radio, movies, press, advertising relations, etc. etc. in one place, the man to run that should be an experienced, hard-boiled, totally extrovert, highly energetic operator. And I am certainly not that man.

Finally, let me say again in black and white what I said by word of mouth — that though, being human and having worked hard at this end, I should be disappointed to be dropped out, I should certainly have no bitterness whatever but, on the contrary, should cheer as loud as any man if a real centralizing job were done.

I think that about says it. Incidentally, your ears would have burned if you had heard Felix and Francis Biddle[2] talking last night about the kind of job you are doing. Two victories in a row on housing and the antitrust laws are pretty spectacular. If you can make it three in a row with this one, we will build a statue to you in front of the Library of Congress.

Faithfully yours,   [Archie]

TL-C: DLC

1. President Roosevelt's chief speech writer and one of his principal advisers. 2. U.S. attorney general.

To Felix Frankfurter

Personal and Confidential

Dear Felix: 9 April 1942 [Washington]

This is what is on my mind, not to say heavily upon my heart.

I think I should ask to see the President to tell him what has happened in connection with OFF's statement of government information policy issued about a month ago, and the effect of what has happened on OFF and on myself.

As a preliminary, I should like to say this:

That OFF was set up to work through other departments of the government. Which meant necessarily that OFF was assigned to do an essential but nevertheless ungrateful job. If things went well, OFF would get no credit. If things went badly, OFF, as the over-all information agency, would necessarily be charged with the blame. In neither case would OFF be able to speak for itself, since its real success in doing its job would be directly proportionate to its anonymity.

I realized this, more or less, when I took the job, and most of my people have come to realize it. Indeed, I have impressed it upon them repeatedly at Board meetings. None of us complains about the task. None of us wants to see our names on brass plaques, and none of us cares very much about taking unmerited cracks on the chin. We all realize perfectly well that a government information service is the natural prey of the press and that a press hostile to the Administration will reek its spleen first and most passionately upon the information services, and, among them, first and most viciously upon the over-all information agency.

What has now happened, however, goes considerably beyond anything I had anticipated and, I think, considerably beyond what I ought in justice to be asked to abide. The story is this: After months of debate in the Committee on War Information, and solely as the result of the efforts — the planning, the thinking, the negotiating — of the staff of OFF, the Committee on War Information adopted a statement of information policy, a copy of which is enclosed. The essential elements of the statement are: First, that there will be a regularly issued production communique; second, that there will be regularly issued casualty lists under certain restrictions; third, that there will be a regularly issued over-all explanatory communique by the joint Chiefs of Staff. This statement of policy was unanimously approved by all the departments involved, including War and Navy. The statement was released to the press on March 18. Since that time practically none of the things agreed to there, specifically not the three things listed above, have been effectuated. Casualty lists are not yet appearing as the statement said they would appear. Ship sinkings are not being announced, as it was said they would be announced. (For your private and highly confidential information, the Navy is about fifty ships behind in announcing sinkings of freighters). The last of several deadlines for the joint Chiefs of Staff communique has been passed and Army and Navy representatives, after an incredible comedy of errors, have not yet been able to get together. And, finally, the production communique, agreed to by the War Department, has been blocked by the War Department's G-2.

The certain and easily foreseeable result of all this is that a blast will shortly issue against the government information activities, and that blast will be aimed at us. Now, as I have stated above, I am in no way averse to taking cracks on the chin which really ought to be aimed at the Army and Navy when it is proper for us to interpose our collective chin between the fist and the target. When, however, OFF is attacked for what can only be described as a breach of faith, and when the cause of the breach of faith is the failure of the Armed Services to make good on the solemn commitments of a Committee on which they are represented, I think the limits of Christian tolerance have been well passed.

The question then arises as to what I can do. Clearly, I cannot, in answers to criticisms, state that the blame belongs to the Army and the Navy. What I can do is, now, and in advance of the storm which will inevitably break, to resign in protest against the failure of the departments to fulfill the undertakings passed by the Committee on War Information with their approval.

In other words, I am willing to give everything I possess to this cause except my reputation for basic honesty. That I will not sacrifice to anyone for any purpose, and least of all for the purpose of covering the failure of the Armed Services to make good on their commitments. Down to now, I have been quite willing to see the Army and the Navy praised for a magnificent information effort, while we have been charged with every failure in the government information policy. When, however, the integrity of the statement of information policy put out over my signature comes into question, I am unwilling to go on playing that game.

I want very much to have your advice on what, after all, is a fairly important matter, since my resignation for the purpose and on the grounds mentioned would inevitably have considerable repercussions. Forgive me for loading this all on you, but I particularly need advice and yours is the best advice there is. I might add that there isn't very much time. In fact, there isn't any time left.[1]   Yours,   Archie

TLS: DLC

1. M did not resign as director of the OFF. On 13 June 1942 the Office of War Information was created by executive order, with the journalist, author, and popular radio commentator Elmer Davis as its head. M served under Davis as an assistant director (as did playwright-turned-propagandist Robert E. Sherwood), resigning in January 1943 over policy differences and to devote more time to his work as Librarian of Congress.

To McGeorge Bundy[1]

Dear Mac: 25 June 1942 [Washington]

I have been carrying your letter around with me, hoping that I might have half an hour sometime to answer it personally even at the risk of subjecting you to the task of deciphering my wholly illegible scrawl. However, I am off for Milwaukee this afternoon and back God knows when, and I don't want to let another sun go down without telling you what it meant to me to have this particular letter from your particular hand. Or rather to tell you that I can't put into words my feeling. It may sound a little excessive to you, but it is nevertheless quite strictly and literally true that I would rather have had that letter from you than from anyone in this country — and I include the gentleman on Pennsylvania Avenue.

It is a curious thing, but the end of OFF has turned out to be one of the deepest satisfactions of my life instead of being, as I had feared it might, one of the bitterest disappointments. The reason is simply that OFF, whatever its inadequacies in other directions, had a human warmth and reality which have somehow or other come to light more clearly over these last few days than they would ever have done in any other dispensation. Whatever else OFF was, it was a group of devoted people who felt about each other as members of an organization rarely feel. Now that we are breaking up and going through all the transformations, the truth comes out and you will understand what I mean when I say that it has given me more satisfaction than anything that could possibly have happened either to the office or to me.

I won't go on about it. But you are one of the two or three people to whom I can say it, because you are one of the two or three people who will really understand what I mean. You turned in a magnificent job here. You have the unforgetting admiration of everyone who worked with you, and you have in addition, as you know, the old and long-lasting affection of   Your ex Herr Direktor   [Archie]

TL-C: DLC

1. Bundy, son of M's Boston (and Washington) friends Katharine and Harvey Hollister Bundy, had served on the staff of the OFF before enlisting in the Army Signal Corps.

To Paul Engle[1]

Dear Paul: 8 July 1943 [Washington]

It was good to hear from you. It is water over the dam, of course, but I do wish you had been able to come with me in OFF. I think the whole British thing would have worked itself out very simply and naturally.

I thought of you when I heard of Steve's death.² I knew what it would mean to you. I think you know what it meant to me.

I am delighted to have the copy of the Army test. I will take a look at it, as soon as I can.

The poem I like a very great deal.³ I quite agree with you that those who think of Robert as a rural bard quite miss the point. What I will never understand, however, is why a man of his stature should permit himself to be eaten by hatred and even, I think, by jealousy. I know few human beings who need to suffer from jealousy as little as he. I don't, as I think you know, share the more enthusiastic view about his poetry. In fact, his poetry has meant little or nothing to me since *North of Boston*, and even *North of Boston* didn't really get under my hide. However, no living writer has had, I think, more universal respect and few have had as much general praise. A mysterious thing is that Robert desires fame* [*MacLeish wrote in the margin:* *And nobly too. With real nobility.] and lives for fame and has fame and yet eats his heart out. Perhaps because he has an inkling what the final verdict will be. Perhaps for some other reason. I don't know.

Anyway, your poem is grand, and I am delighted to have it. Thank you for sending it to me.   Faithfully yours,   Archie

TLS: IaU

1. A poet and professor of English at the University of Iowa (b. 1908).   2. Stephen Vincent Benét had died on 13 March 1943.   3. Engle had presumably sent M his poem "Cuban Voyage," which recorded a trip Engle had made to Cuba with Robert Frost in 1939. The poem was first published in *The Kenyon Review* 6 (Spring 1944), pages 196–197, and was collected in Engle's *Poems in Praise* (New York: Random House, 1944).

To Ernest Hemingway

Dear Ernest: 27 July 1943   [Washington]

I am sending you, under separate cover, a set of negative photostats of transcripts of Ezra Pound's broadcasts. Monday they indict him for treason, Tuesday I send you the evidence. Prompt service I call it.¹

I haven't been able to read them all, but it is pretty clear that poor old Ezra is quite, quite balmy. What motivates him primarily is apparently the fact that he just plain doesn't like Jews. Also, there is that Major Douglas bug he swallowed.² Plus his conviction that he has read American history — which the facts don't seem to support.

Anyway, it is a very sad business. What will save him, if anything

315

does, is the fact that no jury on earth could think this kind of drivel would influence anybody to do anything, anywhere, at any time.

I can find only one reference to you. He says you once told him he was the only American who ever got out of England alive. I can't find any references to myself in this batch, though there were plenty about a year ago. However, in one or two broadcasts, he is quite eloquent about the fact that America was promises.[3]

I will reply to your fine epistle from *Pilar* in a day or two, but I wanted to get this batch of stuff off to you.

Poor old Ezra! Treason is a little too serious and a little too dignified a crime for a man who has made such an incredible ass of himself, and accomplished so little in the process.

Faithfully yours,   Archie

TLS: JFK

1. The Federal Communications Commission had been monitoring Pound's broadcasts over Radio Rome since 7 December 1941; Pound had been indicted in U.S. District Court, District of Columbia, on July 26. 2. C. H. Douglas (1879–1952), English economist who devised the theory of Social Credit. 3. A reference to M's poem *America Was Promises*, first published in *The New Republic* 101 (8 November 1939), 46–48.

To Henry R. Luce

Dear Harry: 8 September 1943 [Washington]

Sorry that my plans went cockeyed. I had hoped to stop off in New York on the way down, but the manuscript of my Annual Report completed itself a day early, and I was obliged to come straight through.

I don't need to tell you how earnestly and how appreciatively I thought, and talked to Ada, about your very flattering invitation.[1] The outstanding fact in my mind is this: that when, as, and if I can free myself from the administrative responsibility I am now carrying, I want to get back, for a while at least, to my own writing. It is five years now since I went out to Harvard, which means that most of my life for the last five years has been administrative. During that period I have written one poem, and a couple of books of speeches,[2] but the real work I want to do has been backing up behind the dam. At least I hope it has been backing up — all I know is that the dam is there, and that I feel a pressure which is sometimes almost unendurable.

What this all comes down to, then, is a regretful statement that I can't do what you want — at least now — and it is now, as I understand it, that you want it. If things work out for me, however, as I suggested to you they may, I hope very much we can reestablish, in one way or another, the arrangement we had some ten years ago. Per-

haps you will recall that you were understanding enough, and generous enough, to make it possible for me to put in the months necessary to pay my bills at Fortune and then to disappear until my own
work was done. It is all in the future, of course, but I do hope we can
arrange something which will have the wonderful elasticity and mutual
confidence that that arrangement had. You are a pretty understanding
guy, but I don't believe you have the remotest idea of the depth of
my gratitude for that arrangement and for what it did for me for
seven or eight of the most important years of my life.

My best to you and to Al [Grover].   Faithfully yours,   Archie
TLS: TIME

1. Luce had presumably invited M to rejoin Time Inc., perhaps as editor of *Fortune*.
2. The two books of speeches were *A Time to Speak: The Selected Prose of Archibald
MacLeish*, published in March 1941, and *A Time to Act: Selected Addresses*, published in April 1943, both by Houghton Mifflin Company. M wrote and published
at least eight poems from October 1939 through September 1943.

To Harvey Hollister Bundy[1]

Dear Harvey: 10 September 1943   [Washington]
You have certainly had no time these very busy days to think about
an American poet, who has been living in Italy for the last ten years
or so, named Ezra Pound. My excuse for writing you about him is this:

Pound has been broadcasting for the Fascists over the last year and
has been indicted for treason by a grand jury in, I think, the District.
Since there is no question whatever but that he was engaged in propaganda for the Fascist government, the indictment was understandable
enough. In any case, it is not the fact of the indictment which worries
me or any of the other writers who have been disturbed about the
problem. What bothers us is the possibility that summary action might
be taken by Allied military quarters in Italy as we occupy the country
and that the result might be to create a situation of considerable
potential unhappiness. The result, that is to say, might be to confer
the paraphernalia of martyrdom upon a half-cracked and extremely
foolish individual and to bring down upon this government the kind
of criticism this government should not have to face.

Both Ernest Hemingway and I have gone through the monitorings
of the Pound broadcasts. We agree entirely that they are the product of
a completely distracted mind. I won't ask you to undergo the boredom
of reading them, but you can take it from me that they are obscene,
rambling, spiteful, and altogether foolish. Pound, who has written as
good poetry as has appeared in his lifetime, seems to have gone completely to pieces under the pressure of a swollen and dropsical ego.

317

Briefly, he feels he has not been appreciated at home and he has taken it out in babbling correspondence with people at home which has now turned into babbling broadcasting which, in form at least, comes awfully close to treason.

I am not asking you, however, to think of the problem in terms of Pound, or Pound's reputation. The real question seems to me to be a question of the way in which this government should treat as tragicomic a figure. You undoubtedly recall the case of Clement C. Vallandingham of Ohio, who, having started out as opposed to the Civil War, ended up as an active propagandist for the south and a violent and vicious opponent of the President. It has always seemed to me that Lincoln's handling of that situation was a model of justice as well as of taste. Vallandingham, as you recall, was sent across the lines to the Confederates. The Confederates, considering him a traitor to the north, would have none of him, and he finally ended up in Canada, where he died obscurely just before the end of the war.

If you agree with me that the Pound case has potential elements of importance in terms of government policy, I wonder if you won't feel like suggesting to the Secretary that orders be given to prevent any summary disposition of the case by the military authorities in Italy. If time is allowed to pass and Pound is brought to civil trial, or if his case is handled as the Vallandingham case was handled, there is, I think, no question but that his punishment will very precisely fit his crime.

Always,   Faithfully yours, [Archie]

TL-C: DLC

1. Bundy was serving as assistant secretary of war under Henry L. Stimson.

To James Allen [1]

Dear Jay: 12 October 1943 [Washington]

I have been unpardonably remiss about the two paragraphs. My remissness is inexcusable also, because I am most anxious to have those two paragraphs written. OFF has been booted around by a lot of extremely ill-informed — and intensely ill-informed — people to such a point that I am beginning to get pretty sick of it. The actual record is one of which I am very proud and one which, I believe, since I have faith in the processes of history, will some day receive its due.

What OFF was trying to do throughout its brief eight months life was to put the facts, meaning all the facts, meaning the profound facts of belief, as well as the superficial facts of statistics, before the people of this country, on the theory that the people could stand hearing them and had a right to hear them, and would know what to do about them when they did hear them. The theory was, in other words, that the people had a right to know precisely why they were at war, and what their enemy was like, and what they were up against. The Arthur Krocks[2] and the Patterson presses[3] believed, or pretended to believe, that the only facts the people of the country had a right to hear were the facts of so-called "military news" and the statistical facts about production — the facts, generally speaking, which would enable a Washington correspondent to build himself up a reputation. And the thing wasn't limited to the Krocks, big and little. Papers as good as the *Washington Post* sneered at us for concerning ourselves with the "morale" of the people — as though the morale of a great nation in time of war were a matter of no concern — or as though the only people entitled to concern themselves with questions of that kind were the boys who made a living out of selling papers.

What the people believed seemed to us tremendously important. It seemed to us important, therefore, that they should have before them all the facts relevant to belief. Since belief is not a question of communiques or of production statistics but of an understanding of what you are fighting against and why, it seemed to us important to provide the materials for that understanding. I thought we were right then, and every day that passes convinces me anew that we were right. Indeed, if I may interject the observation, the reason we have a disintegrating situation in this country today is that all the believers have been replaced by the fixers and that the fixers are fixing not only each other, but themselves and us.

But you wanted me to talk about *This is War.*[4] *This is War* was an attempt to put the fundamental facts before the country, meaning by the fundamental facts the facts as they truly presented themselves to living men in terms of observation and feeling and perception. In other words, we were trying to do the same thing with *This is War* which we did with our publications. The history of those publications proves, I think, pretty well that we were right in our feeling as to what the people of the country wanted, and right in our confidence that if the people were given the kind of information they wanted, they would know how to deal with it. All the important publications of the government information service of this character were ours, though some of them appeared under the name of OWI. *Divide and Conquer, The Four Freedoms,* and *The Thousand Million* reached circulations, directly and indirectly[,] up to thirty and forty and fifty millions. At the time when OWI decided, under the Congressional whip, that all publications must stop and destroyed the remnants of these publications, requests for them were coming in by four to six to eight thousand a week.

The same thing was true with *This is War*. The newspaper critics for the most part sneered at it, but there is no question of the public reaction to it. You will remember what the series was. It too presented the nature of the enemy, and the nature of the issues, and the sort of thing we were up against. There was a program about the frantic, heartbreaking, but nevertheless heartening efforts of the civil government to prepare itself for war — a program about the White House. There was another about the tremendous production task we had undertaken and what it meant humanly. There were others about the Air Forces and the Army and the Navy. There was one about Axis propaganda — what it was like, and what it meant to face it. There was another about the sort of thing the families in the small towns and the cities would have to face and how they were facing it. There was one called "To the Young", there was another called "Smith Against the Axis". There was one on the United Nations which none of us who heard it will ever forget — though we may forget the title and who was in it, and who wrote it.

The newspapers said this was all tripe. They said our job was to help them get news for last editions. I don't think it was tripe. I think it was an absolutely necessary job which was certainly not done as well as it could have been done — which could have been done much better by better men — but which had to be done, notwithstanding — which somebody had to do. We were there and we tried to do it. I am not ashamed that we tried — only ashamed that we weren't allowed to keep on doing it.

Has it ever occurred to you that if you listen very carefully in the middle of any conversation or on the streets of any town in this country today, there is a huge and terrible silence within and beyond the words and sounds that fill your ears? Have you ever thought that that silence is as dangerous and inwardly explosive as a vacuum in the world of physical things? The American press won its fight against OFF, which was a good deal like a railroad train winning its fight with a snail on the right of way. Only the real battle was won not over a little government agency of two or three hundred overworked, devoted, and bloody-headed human beings, but over the American people and their future. For the real victory was a victory for the proposition that all the people are entitled to is "news" over the proposition that the people are entitled to know and to understand.

You take it: I'm sick of it.   Yours always,   [Archie]

TL-C: DLC

1. Assistant director, Domestic Branch, Office of War Information. 2. Washington correspondent of *The New York Times*. 3. Joseph Medill Patterson and his family controlled various newspapers including the *Chicago Tribune* and the New York

Daily News. **4.** A series of factual radio programs designed to dramatize and interpret the government's wartime activities. The series was proposed by the four major radio networks and was produced, in cooperation with the Office of Facts and Figures, beginning in February 1942.

To William Meredith

Dear Lieutenant Meredith: 23 November 1943   [Washington]

It gives me a great deal of pleasure to inform you that I have accepted your manuscript for publication in the *Yale Series of Younger Poets.*[1] I think my news will come as no surprise to you, for you must have felt my admiration for your work and particularly for your latest poems. My one question had to do with the size of the book, but the size of a book of verse has never seemed to me a very important consideration, and it should be no consideration at all in the case of a book written under the shadow of a war, and in the war itself by a man engaged in the fighting. Moreover, there is enough in your manuscript even for the most academic of the "literature people." There is enough to show what the beginnings were, and what the undergraduate influences were and how you dealt with them. For myself, lacking the interest I undoubtedly should have in such puzzles, that aspect of the book is relatively unimportant. It interests me to see how you have shaken off the sterilizing and numbing influence of Auden and the Audenists. But what really matters is the work itself, and I have no hesitancy in telling you that the best of the work itself is good on any basis of judgment and will continue to be good no matter how much time goes by. I am grateful to Allen Tate for letting me see the poems of yours which persuaded me that I ought to hold up the award until I could see the whole body of your work.

With my congratulations on a very distinguished book and with all good wishes,   Faithfully yours,   [Archibald MacLeish]

TL-C: DLC

1. M edited the series for three years beginning in 1943, when he succeeded the late Stephen Vincent Benét. Meredith's *Love Letter from an Impossible Land* (New Haven: Yale University Press, 1944) was the first year's choice, followed by Charles E. Butler's *Cut Is the Branch* (1945) and Eve Merriam's *Family Circle* (1946), to each of which M contributed a foreword. At the time of his selection Meredith was a navy flier.

To Martha Hillard MacLeish

Mother my darling: [6 February 1944]   [Washington?]

What a woman you are! When I saw the young firm handwriting on the envelope of your letter to Ada I could hardly believe my eyes: when

I read the letter itself I was flabbergasted. Here it is the sixth of February and barely two months ago you couldn't have held a pen in your hand, poor dear. You *did* look so — well, not sick, or ill, but *elsewhere*. And yet even then you spoke to me across those millions of miles between with a voice that could have carried any distance. (Odd phrase you used. You leaned up on your elbow and looked me square in the eye & said, You're a good-looking fellow yourself, and nodded & lay back. Which was welcome news but entirely irrelevant, if I may say so, besides being inaccurate to a high degree). But what miraculous source of strength you draw on, I can't think or understand. Ishbel said, when she sent me the first good news after I came back, that the spirit had refilled you. I'm sure that was it — nothing less. I suppose it is that experience of the presentness of the spirit — of its power to go & to come — which has persuaded so many human beings of its existence &, more than that, of its existence *apart* from the body. But you have to learn these things of your own observation seeing them. At least I do & I suppose most others. Sometimes I think the whole process of education, which life is — or ought to be — consists in *learning* what you already "know" — making true for yourself what is not true unless it is made so.

I sound like The Preacher. Which reminds me that I seem to be coming around backwards by a kind of literary & political circle to the pulpit! Not literally, of course, but in a sense. Many of my recent speeches, if you come to think of it, are more like sermons than anything else. And they seem to take people so — I mean that people react to them as though they were. It would be a strange thing surely if I ended my life in the way I might well have begun it. I'm not very serious of course. A "change of souls" is hardly a responsibility I could assume at this time of night. I'd murder them all. And I think the things I want to say are actually more effective said outside the church — any church — than in it. But nevertheless ——

The thing is in my mind because of an extraordinary remark of the younger Whitehead which Lady Sansom[1] quoted to Ada — that the world, spiritually speaking, had been living on its capital for two generations. Its wonderfully true isn't it? And I suppose you could go on to say that in the world of the spirit as well as in the other world — if there *is* another — capital is accumulated by any society by the self-discipline which permits you to do without immediately desired things in order to secure a longer object. And that the moment, in the life of the spirit, you begin to "spend", as it were, your accumulation of moral and spiritual strength by relaxing here & easing up there & cutting corners somewhere else you go the spend-thrift way: you are suddenly rich & easy & opulent — but at a price which no miracle can help you pay. There is only one recovery from those spices. And it is very hard & long. I suppose us children, if you come to think of it, had a tremendous capital, which you & father had earned for us, to spend. I'm afraid we did too — at least I did. I don't know about Norman. Ishbel has earned her own. She's a saint.

I must stop. I got in from the first American Story Broadcast in N.Y.[2] at three this morning after no sleep at all the night before & I'm dead. As well as having the next broadcast to write?

Sit in the sun & be easy. You have a right to all the sun & peace there is.   dearest love   Archie

ALS: M

1. Wife of Sir George Bailey Sansom, a British diplomat and expert on Japan then serving in Washington, D.C.   2. M's "American Story" series consisted of ten radio programs broadcast on NBC's *University of the Air* in February, March, and April 1944. In December 1944, M's scripts were issued in book form as *The American Story: Ten Broadcasts* by Duell, Sloan & Pearce.

To Allen Grover[1]

Personal and Confidential

Dear Allen: 3 November 1944   [Washington]

Your letter of the 18th increased my affection (which was already great enough, as you very well know) but has decreased my respect for your judgment (which had previously been excessively high). I can think of no one I should be less inclined to turn to for the answer to the question you put before me than A. MacL.

For myself, I have no difficulty in coming to a conclusion — nor would I have, I think, even if I had never set eyes on the President and never worked for him. Dewey[2] is simply too much — or rather too little — to ask the American people to swallow at this particular moment in their history. The job ahead in the making of the peace, if we are really going to tackle that job, will be the hardest job any American government has ever walked up to. We are going to try to do what men have never yet succeeded in doing and what generations of men have longed for. We are going to try to make a real peace. You can't make a real peace if you approach the problems of the peace with the shyster lawyer mentality which Dewey has disclosed in his lamentable campaign. One can have — and I have, as you have guessed — all manner of reservations about the warmth and fervor of the President's commitments to a people's peace — a peace between peoples. But whatever the reservations as to fervor and emphasis, no one can doubt that that is the *kind* of peace he proposes to make if he is given a chance. And regardless of all reservations, there can be no question, I think, in the mind of any observant man, that the President's experience, and his whole approach to the problem, give him an infinitely better chance of arriving at or near the desired result than Dewey's cold, inexperienced, District Attorney, club politician mentality and approach.

So much for the men. Even more important, perhaps, is the baggage they carry with them. The vital weakness in Dewey's campaign — a weakness which the Democrats are much to blame for not pointing out — is the fact that he carries with him the isolationist bloc and the high-tariff-free-loan bloc, which was largely responsible for the international economic situation in the 20's. Dewey may think he can check this baggage at the White House door but, if so, he is even more callow than I think he is. And as long as that baggage is in the house and under the bed, he can no more make a peace than Harding could have made a peace even if Harding had really wanted to. As for the President, he has his unpleasant baggage too, but it will embarrass him at home rather than abroad. He can still make a peace with the Southern reactionaries and the Kellies and the Hagues bundled in his attic.[3]

Anyway, that is how I come out. This letter, needless to say, is for your eyes only. The Librarian of Congress has no more politics in him than a shark's egg has egg. If you know what I mean.

Best.   Yours,   Archie

ALS: TIME

1. *See* M to Grace Tully, 4 December 1941. Grover had assisted M in organizing and running the Office of Facts and Figures; he had served in Washington for several months before returning to his duties as a vice president of Time Inc. 2. Thomas E. Dewey, the Republican presidential nominee. 3. David C. Kelly and Frank Hague, members of the Democratic National Committee.

To Franklin D. Roosevelt

Dear Mr. President: 8 November 1944   [Washington]

I submit herewith my resignation as Librarian of Congress.

When you did me the honor to appoint me to this position five years ago, I left work of my own unfinished to which I should now like to return.

The reorganization of the Library of Congress which I undertook shortly after my appointment is now completed.

The war-time measures planned for the security of the Library's collections have been carried out: its evacuated materials are now restored, with the approval of the Joint Chiefs of Staff, to the Library's shelves.

I feel deeply the honor you did me in entrusting the administration of the Library to my care. I have tried to administer it as I think you would have wished — as a Library for the people as well as for the people's Government in Washington.[1]

Very respectfully yours,   [Archibald MacLeish]

TL-C: DLC

1. On December 4, M's nomination to serve as assistant secretary of state for public and cultural relations was announced by President Roosevelt; M took office late that month.

To Edward R. Stettinius, Jr.[1]

Personal and Private

Dear Ed: 15 December 1944 [Washington]

First of all, let me thank you again with all my heart for your loyal and friendly support, and for everything you have tried to do on my behalf. Believe me, I shall never forget it.[2]

Second, as regards the report you gave me over the phone as to the President's intention in case I am not confirmed, I think we ought to talk that over very carefully. I think I ought to tell you also that my first-hand reaction is that it would be a great mistake to send my name up again. I can quite see why the President should feel that it would be unfortunate to have the member of the team who has been characterized as a "liberal" picked out for defeat. At the same time, I think it is quite clear that the man who is to do the information job in the Department must have support and confidence outside the Department. To put in that position a man who had been forced through the Senate on a personal fight would be unfair to the Department and, perhaps you will let me add, unfair to the man.

If you see Arthur Krock, I hope you will congratulate him for me on his attempt at assassination this morning.[3] He has been trying for five years, ever since I caught him out on a limb in his fight against the transfer of the 50 destroyers to Great Britain. This is the first time he has put himself around behind me in the dark where he could really stick the knife in. I think it is an adroit and wonderful job, for which he deserves high public acclaim. I have no doubt he will receive it.

Always, with my affectionate regards,   [Archie]

TL-C: DLC

1. U.S. secretary of state from November 1944 to June 1945, when he became the first U.S. representative to the United Nations. 2. Stettinius had testified at M's confirmation hearings before the Senate Committee on Foreign Relations. 3. Krock's "In the Nation" column in *The New York Times* of December 15 had impugned M's motives in seeking public office, his performance in such office, his politics, and even his poetry.

To Adlai E. Stevenson[1]

Personal and Strictly Confidential

Dear Adlai: 16 January 1945   [Washington]

Let me begin with the sentiments and end with the facts. The sentiments in this case won't wait. You will forgive me if what I say has a barefaced and shameless look. I can't help that.

I have felt since the days of the Committee on War Information that you were one of the most valuable men in this Government. I have felt that, not on the basis of personal affection — though the personal affection exists — but on the basis of observation and experience. In that difficult, confused, and rather desperate first year of the war, there were about a dozen men in Washington who seemed to me to be irreplaceable. You were one of them. I felt at the time that your resignation from the Government was a disaster. I feel the same thing now.

As a matter of fact, I feel it more strongly now, because the job which now needs to be done is a job tailored to measure for you. The job is, first, to give the people of this country the information about foreign affairs they need to have in order to form a foreign policy which will produce the peace which alone will justify this war — and which alone will preserve us from another war to follow; second, to create, in a world in which communication has been interrupted and suppressed and blanketed by the war and by the conquests of our enemies, the kind of communication between peoples which is essential to the understanding on which, and on which alone, a true peace can be built.

Both of these jobs head up in the Department of State. The President has recognized that fact by creating a new Assistant Secretaryship to deal with them. It is clearly the responsibility of the Department of State to see that the information necessary to the making of the peace is provided to the American people. It is equally clearly the responsibility of the Department of State, working through OWI and CIAA,[2] and working out plans for carrying on certain functions of those agencies as they withdraw at the war's end, to set up the essential communication between the peoples of the world which alone can make a world organization operable.

Both these functions in the Department, as I think you know, are my responsibility. Quite frankly, it is a responsibility far too great for my unaided capacities. I have in certain of the Divisions under my jurisdiction a number of competent and able people. I have in the Director of the Office of Public Affairs a first-class public servant — John Dickey. But I need far more assistance than I have, and, above all, I need the assistance and the counsel and the collaboration and the advice of a man who believes what you believe, who sees the problems as you see them, and who has had your experience, both of this country and of this Government.

That is the problem in its essential terms. So far as the job is concerned, it can be set up in almost any way you want. That is, it can be the job of Special Assistant to me, or it can be the job of head of the Division of International Information which will direct OWI and CIAA on policy, and which, working with them, will develop the continuing information apparatus of this country for the years after the war — or it can be set up in any other kind of association with the responsibilities added to my job. So far as salary goes, we could, of course, get the top of the classification scale which is, as you know, a mere $8,000. But all this — the title — the details — are things I'd like to talk over with you and work out with you, if you feel, as I most profoundly hope you will, that the essential work to be done relates directly to your beliefs about the world and your hopes for it.[3]

Faithfully yours,　　Archie

TLS: NjP

1. Stevenson (1900–1965) had been special counsel to the Agricultural Adjustment Administration, assistant general counsel to the Federal Alcohol Bureau, and (1941–1944) assistant to Secretary of the Navy Frank Knox, whom he represented on the Committee on War Information. 2. The coordinator of inter-American affairs, a position held by Nelson A. Rockefeller from 1940 to 1944. 3. Stevenson's appointment as special assistant to Assistant Secretary MacLeish was announced on February 23.

To Martha Hillard MacLeish

Dearest Mother:　　　　　　　7 March 1945　[Hot Springs, Virginia]

You'd never believe it but we've taken a week off. However everything else is just as you would expect it to be. My conscience hurts like a stone bruise on the heel. I lie here in bed of a late rainy morning and think of poor Joe Grew and poor Dean[1] pounding away at the regulation State Department fifteen hours a day and I feel guilty as a discovered thief. What a thing is a Scotch forebear! To say nothing of having Elder Brewster looking over your biological shoulder twenty-four hours a day every day of the year. Because actually I suppose there is no occasion for guilt. I was as nearly done when I left Washington as I have ever been in my life. One never realizes what an experience like the Senate hearings takes out of you until afterward. And the Department has a pressure about it, particularly for a new hand, which is formidable. There is always more to do than can be done & it is always urgent. The old hands learn to take it easy the way a steam boiler takes a head of steam but I've never really learned to take anything easy & I'm afraid I never shall now. The only way to think of it is as a job of soldiering which has to be done. And generally I think things are going well — as well at least as any of us have the right to hope in a world as torn & tangled as this.

Do you hear any of our broadcasts — 7 to 7:30 (E.S.T.) over NBC?[2] Please listen if you can & tell me what you think.

What a tower of strength & of faith you are to all of us — to more of us than you would ever dream!

Our dearest love & all mine   always   Archie

ALS: M

1. Joseph C. Grew and Dean Acheson were, respectively, undersecretary of state and assistant secretary of state for congressional relations and international conferences. 2. Weekly radio broadcasts by M and others explaining the activities and foreign policy objectives of the State Department.

To John Sloan Dickey[1]

Dear John: 29 April 1945   Conway

I suppose the news will be out by the time this letter comes to you. But whether it is or not, and whether or not this is one of many similar letters, it carries a very particular message. I can't think of anything which can be accomplished by the process of appointment and selection which could possibly have given me more pleasure than your election as President of Dartmouth. It is precisely and in every way right. It is right for you because it is the thing you were always intended to do. It is right — even more right — for Dartmouth and through Dartmouth for the country. Dean and I, who have talked about you more frequently than you might believe possible, have always come out with the conclusion that you ought to be the President of a university or a college, and if we had been free to choose the university or college, we would, of course, have chosen your own college of Dartmouth. As for Dartmouth — the trustees presumably know now how lucky they are. The College will know later. I hope you will know, without my trying to tell you in words which must inevitably sound banal by now, that if I can ever in any way be of any use or service to you, you have only to tell me. I owe you a very great deal, and I shall not forget.

As for the Department, I don't know what will happen to your Office and to the whole undertaking you and I had so near our hearts. I don't know who will or can carry it forward. I don't believe — and I have so written Ben Cohen[2] today — that it will have much support from the Secretary's Office. With you gone and with me gone,[3] it will have little support, for the time being at least, down below in the boiler room where we worked. But I don't feel too sad about that, because I think the battle has to be fought now outside government, and that the best place to fight it is in the great forum of the free mind — a forum in which college presidents and poets can be heard as well perhaps over a long period of time [as] even a Secretary of State — perhaps better, who knows.

I should consider it an uncommon pleasure if I might be in Hanover when you take office. If it is going to be this fall while I am still in the country, won't you tell me the day and hour so that I can drive up? Don't have me on your mind because I can find an inn somewhere in the country roundabout, but I would like to be there and cheer a little for one of the few great appointments which ever made me wholly and completely happy.   Yours,   [Archie]

TL-C: DLC

1. Director of the State Department's Office of Public Affairs, in which capacity he reported to M. As M indicates, he had just been elected to the presidency of Dartmouth College. 2. Benjamin V. Cohen, counselor to the State Department. 3. M refers to his planned resignation at the end of the war. He did resign, along with several other State Department officials, in August 1945.

To T. S. Eliot

My dear Eliot: 18 May 1945 [Washington?]

Your cable has just come in. There is nothing I can think of now which can be done about Ezra Pound — at least at the moment.[1] He is under indictment for treason here in the District of Columbia, and it is my understanding of a newspaper account published here that he will be returned to the United States for trial. According to the same newspaper account, Pound admits having broadcast for the Fascists and the Nazis for pay. If he takes that position on trial here, I assume the only defensive position will be a defense based upon some mitigating circumstance. I should be very happy to keep you informed of Pound's return and of the probable date of the action. Prior to that time, and in view of the indictment now outstanding, I doubt if there is anything that can be done.   Faithfully yours,   [Archibald MacLeish]

TL-C: DLC

1. In late April or early May 1945 Pound had been captured by Italian partisans and turned over to the American army in Genoa, Italy.

To Adlai E. Stevenson

Dear Adlai: 30 July 1945 [Washington]

That letter of yours of the 26th I shall keep in a small folder of papers I don't want to be separated from.[1] Your description of AES makes me think of one of those travel books about America written by distinguished British men of letters which enlivened the literary history of the last century. The features of the landscape were always recognizable and the natives were always picturesquely presented. The only trouble was that the distinguished authors had never seen the things they looked at. I suspect your acquaintance with AES is of the same character. You make him a charming and lovable figure, which indeed he is, but you have never really penetrated the depth or the height of his soul. Some day I shall enlighten you. For the moment I accept, with gratitude, your guidance to the Assistant Secretary of State as I accept with far more than gratitude your personal message to,

Yours always,   Archie

TLS: NjP

1. The letter to which M refers appears in Walter Johnson, ed., *The Papers of Adlai E. Stevenson, Volume II, Washington to Springfield, 1941–1948* (Boston: Little, Brown, 1972–1978), pages 253–254.

To T. S. Eliot

My dear Eliot: 13 August 1945   [Washington]

I am replying to your cable of August 7 asking when it will be possible to communicate with Pound on the question of the choice of American counsel to defend him. I have communicated with the Department of Justice which informs me that Pound is still in Italy and in the hands of the Army. For your private and personal information, I should add that I am further informed that Pound's conduct since his arrest has suggested the desirability of psychiatric examination. No report has been received by the Department of Justice as to the results of the examinations believed to have taken place.

I think you will also be interested to know that Pound has written the Attorney General admitting in effect the substance of the charges against him and contending that the Constitutional guarantee of freedom of speech justifies his actions.

Pound can be addressed as follows: Disciplinary Training Center, Caserta, Italy.

If I can be of any further assistance to you, I hope you won't hesitate to call upon me.

Always,   Faithfully yours,   [Archibald MacLeish]

TL-C: DLC

To Dean Acheson

Personal and Private

Dear Dean: 30 August 1945   Conway

Never lend the keys to your house, because if you do, your friends will pick letters up off the floor and carry them around in their brief cases. The attached must serve as an example. I wish you would tell the Belgian Ambassador that I am heartbroken to have been the innocent cause of his failure to polish the first segment of the Under Secretary's newest, reddest apple.

Speaking of which, I recommend to your attention, should you be interested in the ancient art of apple polishing, the recent success of our former colleague, The Honorable, James Clement Dunn.[1] I gather from the public press that Mr. James Clement Dunn is to represent the United States permanently on the continuing Council of Foreign Ministers, which — as the American people have not yet been informed — will determine the shape of the new peace. As one who has sat across the table of Mr. James Clement Dunn off and on for eight not-too-memorable months, I can only say that it is not the American people who are to be complimented on this extraordinary choice. I cannot help but wonder what the American press would say if they realized what decisions the permanent Deputy of the Secretary of State will be making in their name and on their behalf. Personally and privately, and for your secret ear, I think it stinks.

All this by way of backing gracefully into a combined declaration of affectionate regard for the person of the new Under Secretary of State, pride in the unselfishness of the decision which made him what he is today, and deep sympathy for him in the all-too obvious trials which lie ahead. It would be unkind — I dare say it would be unpatriotic — to tell you how I spent this day and how I plan to spend a very considerable number of days from this time on forward. Knowing how you had planned to spend these same weeks, I can hardly rub my private saltpeter in your public wounds.[2] Nevertheless, I would like to tell you that you are never very far out of my thoughts, such as they are, and that, knowing more than anyone else of the various considerations which made your decision so difficult, I have only admiration for the final choice you made. I hope to God you won't have to eat too many pecks of dirt over the next twelve months and that the serried legions of the apple polishers won't too completely and too profoundly disgust you.

May I say again in cold print what I told you in very living words — that if there is anything I can do, either with what I own or with what I am, to help you, you have only to pick up the movable portion of

331

that black gutta-percha gadget on your desk and ask for Conway 26. And tell Eddie Miller,[3] when you think of it and while you think of it, that his note was one of the nicest things that has happened to me.

Affectionately,   [Archie]

TL-C: DLC

1. Dunn had served as the State Department's director of the Office of European Affairs and, contemporaneously with M, as assistant secretary of state for European, Near Eastern, African, and Far Eastern affairs. 2. M's resignation had been accepted by President Harry S Truman on August 17, one day after Acheson was appointed to succeed Joseph C. Grew as undersecretary of state. 3. Edward G. Miller, Jr., an Acheson associate in the State Department.

To Julian P. Boyd[1]

Dear Julian: 30 August 1945   Conway

Forgive a typewritten answer to a letter which deserves an answer written in the heart's blood. Forgive also the formal acknowledgment of my Executive Assistant who wanted to be sure that letters were not left too long unacknowledged.

For what you say about my years in the Government I am profoundly grateful. There is no man whose judgment I more value or whose judgment I would rather have.

As for what you say of yourself — I think, if I have the right to say so, that you are quite wrong. I think the President's choice of you to be Librarian of Congress was the wisest choice he could possibly have made. I think it would have been a wonderful thing for the country if you could have taken the job. But I am sure that you were moved by instincts which you ought to continue to respect. You have made, and you continue to make, and you will always make, a tremendous contribution to your country and to your time. You felt last winter that you could make it better with the relative independence of Princeton than you could in Washington. You thought it through very carefully then. I think you must now remember that your decision was taken on reflection and in all sincerity. I think you must do yourself the credit of believing that the conclusion you then reached was sound for you.

This letter brings you as always my deep affection, my admiration, and my enduring regard.   Yours,   Archie

TLS: NjP

1. The Librarian of Princeton University, Boyd had been M's first choice as his successor at the Library of Congress. Boyd had declined the appointment on the ground that it would conflict with his work as editor of the Thomas Jefferson papers.

To Ralph McA. Ingersoll

Dear Mac: 15 October 1945 [Washington?]

I sent you a despairing telegram yesterday, telling you that I hadn't been able to reach you by phone. I'd love to talk to you about your letter — which moved me very deeply. It now looks as though I were going to have to go to England next week, to be gone for anything up to six weeks.[1] That being so, I am afraid we will have to postpone our conversation until I get back.[2]

The terms of my problem are simple enough to be extremely difficult. That is to say, I want an editorial connection with an organ of opinion which will let me continue the fight, but I also want enough free time — by which I mean really free time — to get some of my own work under way. You and I have always been able to work together with complete understanding and confidence, which is one reason for thinking that my problem might be solved in terms of your work, if you continue to want me. On the other hand, your work will be tremendously urgent and exciting and pressing for many months and perhaps years to come, and I have a deep instinctive feeling — which I think you will probably share — that no one could participate in it actively without getting in all the way up to the neck, and maybe deeper. So that, as I think about it now, I am inclined to think it won't work, my temperament being what it is, and your job and your energy being what they are. That, however, is only the way I feel about it now and without having had a chance to talk to you. I suspect, however, that you will feel I am right.

Best regards to you, and I will be seeing you as soon as I get back.

Faithfully yours,   [Archie]

TL-C: DLC

1. M was about to be appointed chairman of the U.S. delegation to the organizing conference of the United Nations Educational, Scientific, and Cultural Organization (UNESCO), set to begin in London on November 1. 2. Ingersoll, who had left Time Inc. in 1939 to start the New York newspaper *PM*, had invited M to join the paper's editorial staff.

To Felix Frankfurter

Dear Felix: 19 October 1945 [Washington]

I have an extremely kind letter from Professor Griswold from Kansas City, Missouri, in which he tells me that you have written him and that he is at my disposition. His letter is the occasion for this, but not altogether the explanation. It was unlike anyone else, but like you, to take the trouble to try to arrange things so that Griswold and I should meet to talk about Carolyn and what lies ahead of her.[1] Meantime, I have the blessed assurance, through Ada, that Carolyn will walk again, and that she will, as the doctors put it, altogether recover. That doesn't mean that what Griswold has to tell me would be irrelevant but only that things won't be as difficult for Ken as they were for him — *if* the doctors are right. I won't be able to see Griswold before I go to London, but I shall certainly see him afterwards.

But the real significance of Griswold's letter to me is its reference to you and the opportunity it offers to tell you, in so far as it will ever be possible for me to tell you, what your letter about my six years in the Government of the United States has meant to me. You received my telegram, I know. There is much more that I could say, if I could only achieve the other personality — the absence from myself — necessary to say it. Whenever I think of those six years which seem now so important in my life, my mind goes back to a breakfast you and Tommy[2] and I had in a house curiously unlike you, which you were renting in the spring of 1939 on Prospect Street, or whatever the street is that looks out over the river in Georgetown. What you and Tommy and I talked about during the breakfast was the Republic and the obligation to serve it. Never after that hour, except from you, did I ever hear from anyone talk of the obligation to serve the Republic. I heard only the opposite — talk colored by the universally accepted assumption that it was not for that reason but for other reasons that men were in Government in Washington. I am not thinking of the columns in which Krock informed his wise-guy readers that I was in Washington to keep my nose in the public trough. I am talking about the assumption of better men that it was in some way naive or unsophisticated or uninformed to attribute to the wish to serve the Republic what could conceivably be attributed to other impulses. You and you alone — and this is not the least of my reasons for loving you — have dared to believe that men do enter Government — do actually enter Government — because they believe in the Republic and wish to serve it. The greater part of Washington seems now to be made up of men who accept, without question, the weary, decayed sophistication of Mr. Krock's view of the public service, with only a few, the greater part of them too young to matter, who believe, as you believe, that the public service is what you and Tommy and I thought it was something better than six years ago. And yet the paradox is that we were right, and that the rest are as wrong as Krock and as dead as he is, which is very dead indeed.

Last night I talked to Phil Graham[3] about many things. I told him I had a letter of yours for which I would decline 40,000 smackers in cold cash. I don't know, Jedge, if the evidence is relevant, but I offer it.

Yours,   Archie

TLS: DLC

1. Carolyn MacLeish, Kenneth's wife, had suffered a mild case of polio. 2. Thomas W. Lamont (1870–1948), the American banker, public servant, and philanthropist. 3. Philip L. Graham, a Washington attorney who had served in the Office for Emergency Management and in the Office of Lend-Lease Administration.

To Julien Cornell[1]

Dear Mr. Cornell: 6 December 1945 New York

My day and a half in Washington turned out to be so crowded with Departmental engagements that I couldn't get out to see Pound.[2]

As regards Psychologists, the few people I know here who are familiar with the membership of the profession in New York seem to agree on Gregory Zilbourg as a disinterested and highly competent man. I am, however, probably the worst adviser on earth on this subject, since I know nothing about it myself.

I hope you will keep me informed of developments. As I told you when we first met, I find myself pulled in opposite directions by the whole Pound business. I have long admired him, and admired him deeply, as a poet. I have never thought his economics made any sense — and I mean precisely that. As for his broadcasts, if the excerpts I have seen published are typical, then I have only the most complete contempt for what seems to have been a toadying attempt to please the Fascist government by beastly personal attacks on President Roosevelt, by a recurrent anti-Semitism, and by a misinterpretation of the American people which could only be justified on the ground that Pound knows nothing about them.

I don't know whether it is proper for me to ask you, as Pound's lawyer, to tell me more about the content of the broadcasts as you learn more about it. I recall you saying, when we met, that you had not yet begun your study of that aspect of the case. If you could give me some conception of the accuracy or inaccuracy of the published newspaper reports of what Pound said, I should appreciate it.

I am not sure whether I told you that I have met Pound only once, though we have conducted a desultory correspondence over a considerable period of years. Clippings sent to me within the last few days suggest that Pound told the Court when he first appeared that he wished to call Henry Wallace[3] and me as witnesses apparently on the ground that he had talked to us in 1939 about matters which were later the subjects of his broadcasts. I can't speak for Henry Wallace. For myself, I can only say that if Pound said this, his memory was at fault. I met him after a lecture at Harvard and accompanied him to the house of

Theodore Spencer, a Professor of English, where we talked about Pound's lecture, the subject of which was poetry.

All this, however, has nothing to do with the question of Pound's health while he is awaiting trial. Like everyone else who knows and appreciates the poetry written in our time, I feel a deep obligation to Pound as a poet, and I shall be glad to help in any way I can to see that he has books, etc., and that his health improves.

I am returning to Washington again on December 18, and I shall take your letter with me and make another attempt at that time to see him. Meantime, may I repeat, I should welcome any further word from you as to the way in which things develop.

Faithfully yours,   [Archibald MacLeish]

TL-C: DLC

1. A Washington attorney who represented Ezra Pound at his 1945 hearings in District of Columbia Court and for several years thereafter. 2. Pound had been brought from Italy to Washington, D.C., on November 18; when this letter was written he was undergoing psychiatric examination at Gallinger Hospital in Washington, though M may have planned to see him at the District of Columbia jail, where he had been held from his arrival until December 4. Later in December Pound was judged unfit to stand trial and remanded to St. Elizabeths Hospital in Washington. 3. Vice President of the United States, 1941–1945.

To T. S. Eliot

My dear Eliot: [c. 6 December 1945]   New York

I took your letter of the 17th, with the enclosed copy of a letter from Pound, to London with me in the expectation that we would be able to talk there. As things turned out, the United Nations Conference took all my time. And even the best efforts of Lady Colfax[1] to bring us together came to nothing. I am sorry for that for more reasons than one.

Since I got back to this country, I have talked to young Julien Cornell, who has been asked by Mrs. Pound's lawyers to represent Pound. When I saw him he had talked to Pound twice and was convinced that Pound could not even be arraigned because he was in no mental condition to enter a plea. This does not accord with your impression of Pound's letter which was apparently written on the 5th of October, but what Cornell told me about his conversations with Pound and of Pound's experience in Italy seem to me to support his conclusion.

Cornell's hope — I have not yet learned what luck he had with it — was that the Court would release Pound on bail for necessary psychiatric treatment. Beyond that, his plans for the case are not fully developed. I gather that there is little question but that Pound said a number of things which were at best extremely stupid and at worst far worse than that. There is some question, however, whether he had a contract with the Italian Government in the usual sense. He was apparently paid a weekly sum which just about covered his travel expenses to Rome and back — but he was paid it.

I think I should say, quite frankly, that my feelings about this whole thing are increasingly mixed as I learn more about it. I shall be glad to do what I can, if anything is necessary, to see to it that Pound gets a fair trial. I shall be glad also to help as I can in getting him books and the things he needs — I plan to go to see him when I am next in Washington. But beyond that, I must reserve judgment until I know more about the facts than I now know. If the broadcasts as a whole were of the character of the excerpts printed here, then it would be very difficult indeed to justify Pound's behavior on any theory of the freedom of the intellectual to speak his mind. A calculated campaign of anti-Semitism, for one example, is hardly an expression of the right of the intellectual to tell the truth as he sees it.

I shall be glad to keep you informed of events as they develop, and, if you are interested, in my own reactions to the story as I learn more of it. I shall also be glad, of course, to carry out for you any commissions which you wish to entrust to me and which I feel I can accomplish for you.

Again with my regret that we did not meet in London, I am

Faithfully yours,   [Archibald MacLeish]

TL-Dr: DLC

1. Lady Sibil Colfax, a well-known London society hostess.

To Dean Acheson

Personal

Dear Dean: 30 December 1945   New York

I badly need some official as well as personal advice on the Department's position with reference to UNESCO. You will remember my memorandum on UNESCO and the Moscow Conference — the question whether exchanges of scientific information are to be conducted through UNESCO, which has been set up for the purpose, or whether a new and duplicating channel is to be set up for exchanges in the field of nuclear physics. The Moscow communique leaves that question unsettled, although it can be interpreted to mean that UNESCO might be used. I enclose a clipping from the *Times* on the views of the American Association of Scientific Workers on that subject which indicates that the scientists are as much concerned about the ambiguity of the Department's position as the American Delegation is.[1]

What troubles me now is that if the Associated Press is right, the Department is apparently equally dubious about its support of UNESCO in another and equally important field. UNESCO's first function as stated in Article I is to "collaborate in the work of advancing the mutual knowledge and understandings of peoples through all means of mass communication and to that end recommend such international agreements as may be necessary to promote the free flow of ideas by word and image".[2] The Associated Press in a Washington dispatch dated December 29, says that American Delegates to the Assembly meeting have been instructed by the Department to push for a prompt international study aimed at promoting freedom of the press and that "the Delegation will urge that a Commission under the Economic and Social Council" should tackle the question. The dispatch goes on to say, quoting "government officials[,]" that the American Delegates will advocate "that the Commission for the Promotion of Human Rights take up the study".[3]

The Commission on Human Rights is hardly likely to be a body which can maintain the kind of active, continuing and affirmative concern with the international problems of the press, positive as well as negative, which will be necessary. It was my understanding, when I was in the Department, that this was the Department's view, and it was my understanding of my job in London, as it was the understanding of the United States Delegation as a whole, that we were to see to it that UNESCO included in its field of jurisdiction the international activities of the mass media. Indeed, it could hardly expect to work at its principal task of promoting international understanding rapidly and broadly unless the mass media were included.

You can see my difficulty. If the Department, having sent a Delegation to London to set up UNESCO, is now in doubt as to whether UNESCO should be entrusted with two of its most important functions, it would seem to follow that the Department's confidence, or, at any rate, interest, in UNESCO was fairly slight. If that is the case, my personal plans — to say nothing of the public plans of nations represented at London — would seem to require some tinkering. If UNESCO is to be the Organization its Constitution describes, then I am willing to put in any amount of time on the various jobs the Department has asked me to perform. The Organization described by the UNESCO Constitution is, I should say, one of the principal United Nations agencies and as important, granted the present state of the world, if not, indeed, more important than any. If, however, the Department feels that the principal functions of the UNESCO Constitution should be performed by other agencies, then I should say that the sooner we deflated, or forgot, the whole thing, the better.

I am writing you about this, first, because I know that you will see, and will care about, my personal problem, and, second, because the question of departmental position is a question which can only be answered at the highest level. I'd appreciate it very much if you could let me have some kind of word by telephone, or in any other form, at your fairly early convenience, as I am getting deeper and deeper into the work the Department has asked me to undertake. To put it briefly and bluntly, I don't like to be made a fool of, and I don't like to make a fool of myself. Going around to talk at public meetings about the importance of UNESCO when the newspapers indicate that the Department thinks very little of the reasons I advance at these meetings for the importance of UNESCO, makes me look like what I perhaps am but would rather not be in public.

Best to you. Yours, [Archie]

TL-C: DLC

1. "Science Workers Back Big Three for Control of Atomic Energy," *The New York Times*, 30 December 1945, page 5. 2. From Article I, "Purposes and Functions," of the UNESCO Constitution, adopted in London on 16 November 1945. 3. "U.S. Groups to Push Free Press in UNO," *The New York Times*, 30 December 1945, pages 1 and 5.

To Gerald Murphy

Dear Dow: 12 October 1946 Conway

It suddenly came over me today — I don't know why today more than any other day except that there is a warm rainy autumn wind like the presence of memory driving the leaves down and the summer visibly with them — it suddenly came over me that I haven't seen you since the summer was first full and the elms full and green as you said like bunches of young parsley and the maples green and full and round and the grass under it all like time's reflection of eternity — which is surely blue in itself but green in the earth's reflection because green is brief. But "came over me" is wrong for it was like a blow. I count on your being in the world and not only in *the* world but in mine. So I write you this letter to tell you and to say that I miss you. Quite simply and truly that. Yours, Archie

ALS: DONNELLY

To Alexis Saint-Léger Léger

My Alexis: 6 July 1947   [Conway]

A man's life might well be full to overflowing for no cause whatever but that he found such generous & loyal & affectionate words on the blank pages at the beginning of *such* poems.[1] You have given me a great gift & one I shall never be able in smallest part to repay for I have neither your mastery of this most difficult of all arts nor your burning perfectness of soul. All I can do — all I shall ever be able to do — is to try to make you understand what richness you conferred upon me when you made me your friend.

I think often of that day so many years ago when you came into my room in the Library of Congress.[2] Walking lately in your own Paris I thought often of it. You have many friends there — many who love you & wish you well — but none more grateful for your affection than
                                                           yours   Archie

ALS: FSJP

1. Probably Léger's *Vents* (Paris, 1946). 2. A prominent French diplomat before the fall of France in 1940, Léger had gone into self-imposed exile in that year and had taken up residence in Washington, D.C. M, long an admirer of Léger's poetry, had willingly arranged a position for Léger at the Library of Congress that permitted him to resume his life as a poet.

To Robert N. Linscott[1]

Dear Bob: 18 March 1948   [New York]

You are a good friend and I am grateful to you. It was a hell of a question for me to ask. You have answered it honestly and simply.

What I wanted, as of course you understood, was a clarification of our conversation at the Century. Your statement that you would be glad to publish the long poem[2] but that I must expect to be massacred by the critics, was open to the interpretation that though Random House would be willing to bring the book out for publisher's reasons I, as a poet and having regard to my reputation as a poet, would be well advised not to offer it. And what troubled me about this possible interpretation was that it seemed to involve *your* opinion. I have never put out a book, as you know, which the poet-critics you have in mind haven't attacked with more or less fury. You would not, therefore, have made so strong a point of this unless you yourself shared their view. And that, for me, would be very serious. I can discount attacks by these gentlemen because I know that they are not, and are not intended to be, judgments of my work. Your opinion of a poem is a very different thing. And, to me, a very serious thing indeed.

I asked you therefore to reread the poems with the stiffest comparisons of our time in mind and to tell me on the basis of those comparisons whether you believed they should be published — whether, in your opinion, I should want them published. If, as I feel certain you did, you understood my question, your reply is Yes. It is not a very loud Yes. You find yourself looking for something in poetry which my poems do not give you: something which Eliot does. But though you feel no personal enthusiasm for the book you want to publish it which means, I take it, that, in your opinion, I should want it published.

That is all I have a right, even as a friend, to ask of you — though I confess I had allowed myself to hope for more, remembering as I do what your words in the past have meant. Let's go ahead then. I accept, of course, your decisions on the poems I left with you Monday.

And again my thanks for a difficult act of true friendship.

yours as ever   Archie

TLS: NNC

1. Linscott had left Houghton Mifflin Company to join Random House in March 1944.
2. "Actfive," which first appeared in M's *Actfive and Other Poems*, published by Random House in August 1948.

To Robert N. Linscott

Dear Bob: 22 September [1948] [Conway]

It was generous of you, and like you, to write me at this particular moment. I'm relieved to know that orders at least come in and that Random House isn't left with a wholly glass egg.

What a prophet you were! And with honor. And in your own hills. I enclose a curious document from Bob Fitzgerald about the review in *Time*.[1] I didn't even know he had written it — though I should have guessed that wounded Catholic sensibilities lay behind. I have replied gently and affectionately that we do indeed live in the new babel when a man who writes in all truth out of the pain of his heart can only be understood even by the most understanding if he says what his listeners already believe. So you can toss his letter away when you have remarked its generosity.

All this is very bewildering — as bewildering as it was, you may remember, when the prophet first prophesied these things. I should understand them but I don't. And whenever I get near an understanding along comes a letter like this from Walter Lippmann which I'd like back. Its personal of course and can't be seen beyond you and me but it adds to my confusion. If he and Harry Levin and Allen Tate aren't liars......[2] But the imagination boggles.

Turn over for refreshment. (I mean turn this page over, you dope!)[3]

yours   Archie

TLS: NNC

1. Robert Fitzgerald, the poet, translator, and book reviewer for *Time,* had presumably written to M in connection with the scathing review of *Actfive and Other Poems* in *Time* 52 (20 September 1948), 104, 106. 2. All had written to praise *Actfive.* 3. M enclosed an early, untitled version of the poem first published as "What Riddle Asked the Sphinx" in *The Atlantic Monthly* 190 (October 1952), 69.

To Henry R. Luce

Dear Harry: 26 November [1948]   [Conway]

That astonishing contradiction in the last paragraph of your excellent series on western culture[1] is so significant in every way that you ought to acknowledge it as what it is — the central weakness of our position. The great lesson of 1848, according to the author of your series, is that freedom "like man's other possessions" must be "defended". As witness to this conclusion you quote Goethe as saying that only that man deserves his life and his freedom who daily "conquers them anew".[2] Goethe is of course saying the precise opposite of the proposition in support of which your author quotes him. And Goethe of course is right. Freedom is not a "possession" to be "defended". Those who think it is are led down the paths which run to Thomas Committees[3] with their doctrine that "freedom" must be "defended" even at the cost of the destruction of freedom. The truth is that freedom is not something you *have*: it is something you *do*. The only way you can defend it is to exercise it. And that is a daily task and a task daily new. Unless, as Goethe says, you daily conquer your freedom anew, you not only don't deserve it — you haven't "got" it. If instead of thinking of freedom as a possession and trying to defend it with extra-legal police and extra-judicial committees we would think of it the way the founders of the Republic thought of it — as something to be created, something to be used: if instead of trying to build a wall around our freedom to keep others out we would increase our freedom until it overflowed the world, we would have less to fear. And we would be better and more admirable human beings. Forgive so long a letter. But I think your author hit his thumb with the hammer so brilliantly that he durn near made a nail of it.

always with my affectionate regards
Archie MacLeish
and forgive a bad typer who
never gets better

TLS: TIME

1. The anonymous ten-part series "The History of Western Culture" ran in *Life* magazine between March 1947 and November 1948. The statement to which M refers occurred in the last installment, "1848," in *Life* 25 (22 November 1948), 84–111. **2.** From Faust's final speech in Part Two (1832) of Goethe's play. **3.** J. Parnell Thomas was chairman of the House Committee on Un-American Activities.

To Ernest Hemingway

Dear Pappy: 1 December [1948]   [New York]

I thought I had a letter on that ship for you to read on the way to France. Instead it came back to me with more Cuban post-marks on it than I've ever seen on one envelope. Probably got caught in the Big Send-off I read about in the Havana papers Dos sent back. If you could hold the ship up three hours while they drained your friends and well-wishers over the sides or down the scuppers you probably had the mail clerk so boiled he forwarded everything aboard to Cienfuegas.

The news it contained is all old now except the main item which was that I was so goddam glad to hear from you in the old voice with the old kick in it that I filed yr epistle inside the Copy of In Our Time which is inscribed to Ada and me from an old cork-screw thief. Referring to the first time you came to rue du Bac and walked off with our corkscrew in your trowsers pocket which is very dangerous and don't do it any more. You sound fine, you old maquis. Also you sound damn well married[1] and no horrors the way you used to have them in all that empty sun at Antibes that summer. What pleases me most, being an addict of old standing, is the news that its the sea you are after. You used to talk about a book on the Stream that would make it really move. I've kept hoping for it. You and sea water have a natural relation and I don't mean brine. The war will keep. It will keep fine in the back of your head where so much stuff lies waiting like the walnut drying in that carpenter's loft.

With me things are so-and-so. The main things are good. The things that aren't so good have to do with what makes Archie tick. Ada is fine — in wonderful form and as pretty as ever which, as you justly observe, is damn pretty. Ken has the best wife next to Ada in the North-East States with two children, a girl and a boy, and another on the way. He's Science Editor at Life and doing well that way but he wants to hunt and fish and you can't do either in the Time and Life Bldg. Mimi is married to an ex-Ensign[2] and is working his way through the graduate school at Chicago by doing jobs in the University Library. He's a nice kid but very severe with me. Pete is a Junior at Yale and very good looking but shorter than he meant to be — about five-nine which he regards as runtish and has some reason to along side these forty foot females they are turning out these days. As for living — we put in part of last winter here and I'm against it. New York makes no sense to me at all. Conway is still wonderful but I never see the water and its water I want. Somehow I seem to have buggered my life up that way and I don't see what I can do about it. Finances are all right. I'm going to lecture for six weeks this winter to try to get caught up with my check book and I hate the idea but its said to be the quickest way to make money there is. Somehow I doubt it. I'll report in full when its all over.

If you feel in the mood and if the Calvados works some afternoon write me a post card from whatever jernt you now hang out at on whatever boulevard. And give my best pls to Mary. I wish we could all meet up somewhere.   love from Ada and   yrs   Archie

[handwritten below the typed portion of the letter, MacLeish added:]
That was a grand letter, Ernest, — I feel fine about a lot of the best years of my life now. Formerly I didn't. I'm obleeged to you — more than that   A.

TLS: JFK

1. Hemingway had married his fourth wife, the former Mary Welsh, in March 1946.
2. Karl Grimm, whom Mary Hillard MacLeish had married in July 1945.

To Harrison Smith[1]

Dear Mr. Smith: 27 May 1949   [New York?]

You have sent me proofs of two articles by Mr. Robert Hillyer[2] and asked me to comment on them. I am glad to do so on the understanding that you will have room to publish what I say in full. I shall be as brief as I can.

Fundamentally, my comment comes to this — that it is discouraging to see contemporary literary journalism imitating the worst feature of contemporary political journalism. In contemporary political journalism you dispose of anything you don't like and cannot understand by discovering a conspiracy — usually Communist. Mr. Hillyer doesn't like and cannot explain the preference of some of his most distinguished contemporaries for "modern poetry" and, specifically, for a recent book of poetry by Mr. Ezra Pound. The question he is concerned with — or ought to be concerned with — is something well worth the serious effort at understanding and explanation of a scholar of his training. The problem of "modern poetry" is an integral part of the problem of "modern art" which, in turn, is intimately related to the whole problem of the condition of man in our epoch.

If Mr. Hillyer had undertaken seriously to find out why the kind of poetry he disapproves of expresses for a number of his contemporaries a sensibility they recognize as belonging to their world and themselves he might well have told us something about our time we should have been interested to read.

Instead he discovers a Fascist conspiracy by Mr. T. S. Eliot with Mr. Theodore Spencer as agent and operative and the entire group of fellows in American literature in the Library of Congress — a group which includes men and women of the stature of Carl Sandburg, Allen Tate, Katherine Anne Porter and Wystan Auden — as stooges and fellow travelers. The "evidence" offered in support of this damaging and insulting attack upon the integrity and reputations of a group of the most distinguished living writers is as follows:

The existence of the conspiracy. This is "proved" by the allegation that Pound's *Pisan Cantos* is so contemptible as poetry that no reasonable man could have selected it for honor under honorable conditions. I agree that the *Pisan Cantos* is Mr. Pound's weakest work, that its selection was a mistake and that the decision reflects glory neither on Mr. Pound nor on the committee. Had I been a Fellow at the time I should have voted against it. Nevertheless the book is certainly not beneath Mr. Hillyer's contempt or any other man's — if only for the reason that it contains one passage any living poet might have been proud to write.

Mr. Eliot's leadership of the conspiracy. The "proof" here is that the award given to Mr. Pound was established in the Library of Congress after Mr. Eliot became a Fellow and that therefore he must have inspired it. No supporting facts are offered.

Mr. Spencer's participation as Mr. Eliot's agent. The "evidence" here is admitted to be hearsay — supported by the fact that Mr. Spencer, who was Mr. Hillyer's former colleague,[3] and a man of unquestioned probity[,] is now dead and cannot defend himself.

The Fascist nature of the conspiracy. The "evidence" here is that the award was established by a gift from Mr. Paul Mellon who — or whose wife — admires Jung; that Mr. Eliot also admires Jung; that Jung is anti-Semitic; that Mr. Pound is anti-Semitic; that Mr. Eliot some 15 or 20 years ago attacked the influence of "free thinking Jews" in a speech.

This, as I read the articles, is the sum and substance of the "evidence" offered in support of a serious aspersion on the integrity and decency of a number of the principal writers of our time. I have searched my mind in vain to discover a reason which would lead a responsible and intelligent writer like Mr. Hillyer to compose articles like these. Mr. Hillyer has much to say about "the new criticism". I suppose I have suffered far more at the hands of the "new criticism" than Mr. Hillyer. I know well their stale addiction to the dry crottes of intellectual song. I cannot believe that Mr. Hillyer was moved to produce these pieces solely by a desire to confound the critics. There are more intelligent ways of doing that.

But neither can I understand how a responsible publisher can offer his pages to personal aspersions as little supported by evidence as those Mr. Hillyer has committed to paper. In sending me the proof, you wrote me, Mr. Hillyer's articles might at least, "clear the air". The air, particularly the high air of poetry[,] is not cleared by personal affront.

Yours truly,   [Archibald MacLeish]

TL-C: DLC

1. Publisher of *The Saturday Review of Literature*. 2. "Treason's Strange Fruit: The Case of Ezra Pound and the Bollingen Award," *The Saturday Review of Literature* 32 (11 June 1949), 9–11, 28; "Poetry's New Priesthood," *Saturday Review* 32 (18 June 1949), 7–9, 38. In 1950, M published *Poetry and Opinion: The Pisan Cantos of Ezra Pound* (Urbana: University of Illinois Press), an imaginary dialogue between "Mr. Bollingen" and "Mr. Saturday" over the merits of the Bollingen award to Pound and over the role of poetry generally. Though M's letter was set in type (*see* M to Allen Tate, 15 October 1949), it was never published. 3. Both men had been members of the English department at Harvard University.

To F. O. Matthiessen[1]

Dear Matty: 27 June [1949]   [Conway]

It was good of you to think of me. I was loathe is the word — the precise word — to impinge with my troubles which must seem very footling to you. You well foresaw what they would be when the question first came up. To teach WHAT is still the question. But ideas boil and roil and the excitement grows and I look forward with a kind of anticipation which may very well be that of the fool rushing in though I don't wholly think so. In any event when you come back East you may well find me in a saner mind. *Would* you by any happy chance come this far to talk to me? Ada keeps a fine clean house and the wines are really good as long as they last which ought to be about ten weeks as the winds blow. We'd love it if you would. Think of it and pray on it.

I heard fine things about you down below. The lads loved what you told them and my Peter thought you an understanding lad.

What in hell are you doing in Santa foo?   yours ever   Archie

TLS: YCAL

1. Matthiessen (1902–1950), a member of the Harvard English department, had written in response to M's appointment as Boylston Professor of Rhetoric and Oratory at Harvard, announced on May 10 and effective July 1.

To Alexis Saint-Léger Léger

My dear Alexis: 8 July [1949] [Conway]

It is not for lack of thinking of you that your beautiful letter has not been answered long since. Indeed I have thought of little else. As you will see from the enclosed, the Saturday Review sent me the Bollingen *Exil* to review (the copy from the publisher did not reach me — must have gone astray).[1] First they offered me space for four hundred words. I wrote them twice that. Then, seeing in what estimation I held the book, they called up and said they were making it their "cover" article and asking me to double its length. I did — in a surgical operation which is only too painfully evident in the finished product as you will see. Then, when that had been sent off they called up in a frenzy to say they had just learned I was a personal friend of yours and that one of the poems in Exil was dedicated to me. I told them that if they hadn't known that before sending me the book to review they were even more ignorant than I thought them. I then offered to withdraw the review. That however created a situation they didn't relish and the upshot — silly upshot — was that they inserted (or said they would insert) a note explaining that they had really known all along that Exil was dedicated to me but that they had asked me to review it anyway. Its all enfuriating and but for the fact that I want a warm review of Exil in a widely read American magazine I'd tell them to go to the devil.

The worst of it is, however, that the mauling the piece has taken has pretty well destroyed any claims it might have to literary merit and I'm ashamed to have you see it as it is. I hope the enthusiasm will make up for the clumsiness. And please forgive me for quoting the half sentence from the end of your letter to me. Its too fine to leave out.

Meantime I've had a letter from Paulhan and have written him "trois ou quatre pages de" moi as he requested.[2] I've used a few sentences from this review where I couldn't improve on them.

So you will see that I've had you in mind!

Your letter is so beautiful and so moving. But so are they all. I plan to give them to the L of C when I die. For surely they will be my most valuable literary property.

My love to K and F.[3] I wish you'd all come up here and drink my Niersteiner and my Gewurtztraminer and throw eggs over the hill at

Bullitt and talk about the world. You can't be too far away. AND
WE'D LOVE TO HAVE YOU. Tell K, I understand she is the one
real authentic vote against the Pisan Fiasco.[4]

yours ever   Archie

TLS: FSJP

1. M's review of St.-John Perse's (Léger's) *Exile and Other Poems* (New York: Pantheon, 1949) appeared in *The Saturday Review of Literature* 32 (16 July 1949), 8–9.
The book itself (a bilingual edition with English translation by Denis Devlin, published as part of the Bollingen Series) contained an essay by M entitled "The Personality of St.-John Perse." 2. Jean Paulhan, editor in chief of the French periodical
Les Cahiers de la Pléiade, was preparing a special St.-John Perse issue (Été–Automne
1950); for it M had produced an essay entitled "Le Temp de la Louange." His text,
in English but accompanied by a French translation by Dominique Aury, appeared
on pages 116–119. 3. Katherine and Francis Biddle, close friends of Léger's. 4. Mrs.
Biddle — Katherine Garrison Chapin — had been one of the Fellows in American
Letters of the Library of Congress who had voted to award Pound the Bollingen Prize.

To Henry R. Luce

Dear Harry: 24 August [1949] [Conway]

The first thing to say about your letter is Thank you.[1] And most
seriously and gravely. For when one man writes another out of his
naked candor and truth he has earned thankfulness. It is a rare thing
— rare even between those who have had the kind of friendship we
had for many years, and have still in the measure in which our altered
lives permit.

The second thing to say is that I accept the premise though not the
over-generous phrase with which you modify it. We have, it is true, a
common crusading instinct and a common pre-occupation with the
spiritual and moral life of this republic as (potentially) the great
saving force of our difficult time. It is not true however that I have
been luckier in giving this instinct flesh and bones. What I *say* is a
whisper in an empty well. What you *think* is a vast voice which a
quarter of the country hears in some measure or is at least aware of.
I will agree with you, however, to this extent — that I think you have
not been lucky in making your real concern and purpose clear to your
intellectual equals. There are perhaps two reasons for this. One is that
many of these people judge by externals and attribute to you the
opinions, views and intentions which they regard as appropriate to a
man of great wealth and power who has made a thunderous success
of a new and inventive enterprise in journalism. The other is that you
yourself have made it relatively easy for the malevolent and even for
the well-wishing to misunderstand you. *I* know, because I know *you*[,]

that you have a strong positive belief: your readers know what you are against — particularly the readers of *Time* but to some extent the other papers also. I know also, or think I know, what that positive belief is — again because I know *you*. I know, or think I know, that you believe in the old American dream of a society of free and responsible men and women who will make up their own minds and govern their own lives and who will become by this labor as whole and complete as it is possible for human beings to be. But what your readers see is that your papers have been largely silent on the great critical issues within the United States affecting the realization of this dream of responsible individual freedom — the issues of freedom of the mind and freedom of the press and freedom of education which are now not only urgent but dangerous — dangerous to speak out about: dangerous also to be silent about. What your readers see further is that your papers either oppose or are indifferent to efforts to deal with certain of the difficulties which modern industrialization has put in the way of the realization of the American dream: efforts by government action in various ways and degrees. Here of course we disagree politically and I am not now urging that you are wrong and I am right. I am saying only that your position on these matters creates some confusion as to what you believe *positively* about the realization of the American proposition in a world of potential mass unemployment and metropolitan living. I said in my Atlantic article that the great task this nation should be performing is the task Henry Stimson set — the task of demonstrating how and under what conditions an individualistic and responsible democracy, individualistic and responsible for ALL, might be made to work. I for one regret that you and your papers have not hammered out a positive proposal in this direction for public debate. Perhaps it is too much to ask. But the point here is that, if you had, your position would be clearer to the country.

But all this — which is far too much already — has to do with your premise and your premise is simply foreword to what you have to say about God and His absence from the article I wrote and you read. Here I am not as certain that I understand you. Let me say what I think the position is. More and more as these evil times move toward their utterance — whatever it is to be — I find the spirit and the tongues of the Ministers of the Kirk and Congregational preachers, my ancestors, moving in me. I have always believed in God: Yes. But I have not always believed in protestantism because I saw only its narrowness and not its necessity. Now, in this great conflict between the dream of a free society on the one side and the rival authoritarianisms of political Moscow and political Rome on the other I suddenly see and feel as John Knox (to compare small things with great) might have felt

it, the direct and logical and essential relationship between Protestantism and individualism, Protestantism and individual freedom, Protestantism and freedom. If this is what you mean — and I dare say it is —
dare say because, again, I know your own beliefs — then I say Amen.
But Amen as a Protestant — as a man who believes in a God Who
expects much from US — who demands that we should be ourselves
and bear our responsibilities first. That there must be a new world
built, and that it must be the world God wants built — Yes — a thousand times Yes. But that it must be the world a Church, a priesthood,
tells us to build — well, that you cannot mean. For you too hold to the
hard and burdensome faith that calls upon a man to decide in his soul.

Have I wholly misunderstood? Please tell me. I hope not. For I am
truly and wholly grateful for your letter and I send you my affectionate
friendship   Archie

TLS: TIME

1. Luce had written M to praise and comment upon his article "The Conquest of
America," in *The Atlantic Monthly* 184 (August 1949), 17–22.

To Alexander Campbell[1]

Dear Alec: 9 October 1949   [Conway]

At last the spasm in the solar plexus relaxes. I don't need to tell you
— though one needs apparently to tell everyone else — what the first
two weeks of teaching are like. I am reliably told that one begins
slowly to recover after the third week or the fourth. Would you agree,
doctor?

But what is important is not my pedagogical virginity but the book.[2]
I think its heavenly — the page, the print, the cover — the whole
physical object. AND Ishbel's last words. And the illustrations. And
the apparatus. If Mother knows anything of all this she must be particularly pleased that you had this essential part in it. As for the rest
of us — there is no end to our gratitude and no word for it.

You must have had the bill — if one can apply so brief a word to it —
by now. Be prompt to send me a note of my share in it. And if Bruce
does not respond with his usual alacrity let me know about that too.
I am quite shameless in pounding on the thin door of his ear. Ada and
I will try to have a list soon. It won't be long for we have lived away
from most of Mother's friends. We count on Ishbel and Elizabeth[3]
to put together the definitive codex.

You should both be here this moment — a damp and breathless day
with no sun but a suffusion of light and a great clamor of crows and
the continuous trembling of leaves about to fall and falling. The Levins[4]

are here and Harry and Elena and I walked down past the pool to the
pond and back along the wood road to Mr. Harris's[5] meadow blue green
under yellow maple leaves and through your birch bars and up across
your down dale meadow to the gate again.[6] What a miracle it is to live
(when one can) in the one place in which it is a miracle to live!

my love to you both and my thanks
Archie

TLS: CAMPBELL

1. Ishbel MacLeish's husband and a professor of English at Hobart and William
Smith Colleges. 2. *Martha Hillard MacLeish (1856–1947)* (Geneva, N.Y.: privately
printed, 1949), the autobiography of M's mother, who had died, at the age of ninety-
one, on 19 December 1947. The book included a foreword by M and chapters by
Ishbel MacLeish Campbell and Norman Hillard MacLeish. 3. Bruce MacLeish's wife.
4. Harry Levin, a professor of comparative literature at Harvard, and his wife. 5.
Warren Harris, a Conway neighbor and friend of the MacLeishes. 6. The Campbells
had (and have) a farm, "Downdale," adjacent to the MacLeishes' "Uphill Farm."

To Allen Tate

Dear Allen: 15 October [1949] Conway

The proof[1] came this morning and goes back this afternoon. "Crottes"
had become "grottoes" for Mr. Freud's sake but all else was more or
less in order. I made the change you wrote me about. As I am sure I
don't need to tell you, my quarrel is not with "modern poetry" as your
last letter would imply. I regard myself as a humble practitioner in that
orchard. My quarrel is with the arid intellectualist mess which certain
critics have compounded out of the elements of what was once a great
and promising *poetic* movement. And with the betrayal of that movement by some of its former champions like — particularly like —
Pound of the Pisans. I don't know how often you have read that book.
I have now read it with minute care three times, searched (as the lawyers
say) its references including the Chinese (with the help of a great Chinese scholar here — i.e. Harvard)[2] and though I can only be sure even
now that I understand forty or fifty percent of the references I understand enough to be satisfied in my own mind that it is sterile where it
isn't ugly, intellectually and morally speaking, and that it is childish
to a degree almost never before encountered in a serious work — or
one which has been taken seriously. I'd like to go over it with you some
time. The fascist and anti-semitic stuff is far more prevalent than the
Fellows, in their statement, contend. In fact it is pervasive throughout.
It is this I have in mind when I say that Hillyer's adolescent attack
and the resultant controversy about that attack haven't touched the
real problem. The real problem goes to the living root of the question

whether the one great movement in poetry in our time hasn't been betrayed from within and from behind. I think you rather agree that it has. But I'm not sure because we've never talked about it. As for the next step in the controversy — the publication of your pamphlet — I'm not sure how much good it will do. I have had my class — a very good one too — go through the whole documentation as a preparation for the definition of the issue we are working on. Their reaction, *before* I put *my* position to them, was about as follows: that the Pisan Cantos, in spite of their intellectual and moral corruption, are certainly not to be dismissed as contemptible (several of the boys admired them intensely and would, I think, reject my judgment as spelled out above); that Hillyer's attack, though it raises a substantial question, is hardly worth serious consideration as a critical statement; but that the Fellows' defense is largely irrelevant and in some ways quite footling (indeed it provoked mirth in some quarters) because it is too much taken up with personalities and literary politics (in response to Hillyer's literary politics) and because it accepts battle on the phoney field Hillyer has mapped out. This may not be the reaction of others but it is, I assure you, the unguided reaction of a number of very intelligent young men and women. It may be too late to do anything about it. But it raises, in my mind at least, the question whether the pamphlet will achieve a positive purpose — whether it will not rather confound the confusion and open the way to a second round in which the Fellows' position will be less, rather than more, strong. I tell you all this because I am sure you would want to know how the documentation struck one cross section of interested opinion and because, if there is still freedom to reconsider tactics, you may wish to do so. My warm and devoted regards to you both   as ever   Archie

TLS: NjP

1. Of M's letter of 27 May 1949 to Harrison Smith of *The Saturday Review of Literature*. 2. James R. Hightower, a professor of Chinese languages and literature at Harvard.

To Ilona Karmel[1]

Dear Ilona: "July something" [1951]   [Conway]

Wonderful long letter. Wish I could answer it in kind. Instead of in kind of. Mountain of mail as high as your hand, or rather as high as mine. And no more chance of a secretary on this hill than of measles. Which would be equally welcome.

But there are a few things I must, however inadequately, respond to. First about your work. You know, of course, what happened. You can't go off into new things and take yourself with you. Yourself follows along after in her own sweet time. She'll make use of Brown County when *she* gets ready to. Meantime you can only wait. And not worry. Or try not to. Its hard — nothing harder — but you must. My guess is that you'll find yourself waiting for you in Cambridge on a step somewhere sitting and looking. One thing you can't worry about is the book. The book is *there*. Like a head of Diana in the Aegean sand.

Secondly about writing and people who take the technique of writing off into a class-room as you might take a girl's gesture without the girl. Of course you're right. It can't be done. And those who try to do it die terribly in the mirror. There is no such thing as "writing". There is only THE writing. And THE writing is not a way of writing but a thing written, not to be known without the thing. What is Rilke's way of writing except what Rilke has written? And what is it Rilke has written except Rilke? Does any one believe a student could borrow Rilke's *way* without Rilke's *thing* and possess anything at the end? Why is it that those who imitate Hemingway imitate his world as well as his rhythm and those who imitate Faulkner go down into Faulkner?

No you are a thousand times right. Poetry is a way of entering the world. Which means that poetry is an action by which one man enters the world which is his world. Do they think you can take the door down and hang it on nothing and make it swing? Art is man's highest possibility but it is nevertheless *man*'s highest possibility and without the man the work of art is a vocable. You cannot take them apart. And any critic who undertakes to do so inflicts, not on the work of art but on himself, the self-defeating wound.

Forgive a lecture you never asked for. My love to you all three. S with the gift of tongues will be more than ever marvel. Tell Judy not to take the golden apple until she is sure it can be eaten also.

AMacL

TLS: KARMEL

1. A student at Radcliffe College (Class of 1952), Ilona Karmel had taken M's English S writing course, where she had begun to write *Stephania*, her widely praised first novel. Based on her experiences as a Polish Jew during and after World War II, the novel, dedicated to M, was published by Houghton Mifflin Company in 1953.

To Alexis Saint-Léger Léger[1]

29 February [1952]

Dear Alexis: [Antigua, British West Indies]

Your letter will go with the others I so treasure. But, of course, the truth — as we both know — is quite the opposite. Whatever small service I have been able to perform for you over the past twelve years has been but the abstract, miniscule and meaningless shadow of the inadequate interest on the debt I have owed you since the year 1922 when your first poem came to my hands — first to me, not to you. Your *existence* as poet and artist is, to me, the fundamental obligation. Which I gladly acknowledge. If I am proud of anything it is of the blunt historic fact that you came to Washington saying you would never write again and that you *have* written — written as no man alive can write — and that you speak now, in this last letter, of your oeuvre poetique *en cours*. For that miracle I accept — not too humbly — some small part of the *practical* causation. But with rejoicing and gratitude, not satisfaction.

I never thought you would accept the Norton Chair unless you were driven by necessity and I am heartily glad you have refused it. But I wanted you to be *able* to take it if you needed to.[2] That was all. Now we are both satisfied.

You see from the head of this paper that your choice of a name has become a reality. They have told us — those from Guadaloupe — that La Désirade is now a leper colony. The metaphor is complete. For la désirade is still La Désirade.

We both send you our love. Truly. Archie

TLS: FSJP

1. The MacLeishes had recently purchased a property at the Mill Reef Club, Antigua, British West Indies, and had had a house constructed on it. As the letterhead indicated, they had named their new winter residence "La Désirade," the derivation of which M explains in this and the two following letters. 2. M was chairman of the Charles Eliot Norton lecture committee at Harvard.

To Paul H. Buck[1]

Dear Paul: 14 March [1952] [Antigua]

Thought you might like a brief word from your wandering boy. Though wandering is scarcely the word. You can't go far on an island seventeen miles across. Particularly when everything you want is at home. Columbus's La Desirade may be a leper colony but ours isn't. Cinder block house with a living room and two bedrooms on top of lime rock fifteen feet above and fifteen feet back from the clearest water a man could hope to find — shallow green-blue over coral reefs that run out a hundred yards to a deep blue channel with a little parched olive-green island beyond and the whole Atlantic over its shoulder. I work in a one room shack back up the hill. People complain about the tropics. I find this piece of them perfect for work. Hot, yes, but I start early in the morning and knock off when I begin to smell myself broiling. So far I've rewritten a short verse play which the BBC broadcast last Jany in its earlier form and which Houghton Mifflin are wonderfully pleased with in its new.[2] Also started a new verse play which persists in staying alive in spite of my every-other-day depression about it. Also the usual between shots harvest of short pieces which may or may not turn out to be worth working on. I bless you with my morning banana. And hope I'll come up with something which will convince you your generosity was justified.

Schorer writes me he's enjoying my writing course.[3] Which means, certainly, that the lads are. They are luckier than they probably know.

President Fred of the University of Wisconsin invites me to be Knapp Visiting Professor during the first semester of '52–3. I have regretted with thanks. And I do feel gratified. I'm still dubious enough about my qualifications as a teacher to relish any such expression of confidence.

I hope you are not too worn and weary — though I feel sure you are. Its the season of the great fatigue isn't it?

My very best to Jim [Conant] if you happen to think of it when next you see him.

And please give my love to Harry and Elena [Levin].

yours ever   Archie

TLS: MH (ARCHIVES)

1. Provost of Harvard University. 2. *The Trojan Horse*, first published by Houghton Mifflin in a limited paperbound edition (1952) and also included in M's *Collected Poems, 1917–1952*. 3. Mark Schorer, then a visiting professor of English at Harvard.

To Ilona Karmel

Dear Ilona: 14 April [1952] [Antigua]

There's a letter-head to paste in your ear. Its the name Columbus gave to his land-fall on the Second Voyage — a little coffin-shaped island east of Guadaloupe. Which is now a leper colony for the French West Indies. But Apollinaire had already saved it. "Quand bleuirat sur l'horizon la Desirade?"[1] A Spanish word turned French by the reverse magic of A into E. And supplying a mythological need we all know. Western poetry had El Dorado — which came from the same journeys into the ocean and the isles. But La Desirade is *another* journey, for la desirade is not only longed-for but raised at last, blue on the horizon. Hence. . . .

Except that no island ever was as lovely as the bloom of its shadow on the edge of the world. Which is just as well for all of us. Where would poetry be if the realization were more beautiful than the guess?

I'm happy about all your news — or almost all. As well as some of your news that came from elsewhere. Gay says the short story is a miracle

355

and I trust Gay.[2] That the leg works is wonderful.[3] That you went to see the Rockefeller people and that it turned out — or didn't turn out — whichever — as it did is a tribute to your objectivity, sense of humor, detachment and all the rest of the irreplaceable qualities we ask you to share with the world. I don't know what will come of it. Its a long shot. But they haven't heard the last of me. As for this summer — the plan is, of course, definite. That is, it is definite if you want it to be. Smith-Petersen has said he will operate. Radcliffe is ready to do its part. I think you said the Window-Shop was ready too. In any case, if your mind still holds, as I am sure it does, do please write Dr. S-P and begin to plan dates. I'll be back in the States May 2 and in Cambridge a week or ten days later. We must work out everything at once.

Everyone has written me all in a wonderful flurry of letters. I'm not going to answer them all. I wish you'd tell Charles Flood[4] my plans and that I'm most eager to see the ms — will he keep in touch with Widener W. And give Sy my best and tell him I must see him before he goes off to basic training. I'll hope also to see a finished novel. Same to Jim Chace except that I know he doesn't plan to finish the book this spring. My love of course to Bill Alfred. Tell him we'll do a reading party on the Agamemnon ourselves if the Poicks won't — though I can't believe they wouldn't have (forgive the dangle in my participle). Do you suppose we could have that evening together, the lot of us, I missed last January? I'd love it. Peter too of course. And David. And all of us. Ask Gay what she thinks. I'll supply the Bourbon and a handsome West Indian tan which makes me look like an advanced case of jaundice now that its all lemoned out. And thank that dear Judy for her fine letter.

my love to you   AMacL

TLS: KARMEL

1. From Apollinaire's "Le Brasier," in *Alcools* (1913). 2. Gay Luce, an English S classmate of Karmel's. 3. Shortly before the Nazi collapse, Karmel had been run over deliberately by a German tank. During a long recuperation in Germany, Sweden, and the United States — which included the surgery to which M indirectly refers in his letter to Karmel dated 26 July 1952 — Karmel recovered from her injuries. 4. Another English S classmate of Karmel's. Others referred to in this paragraph include English S students Sy Heifetz, James Chace, and William Alfred; Humanities 130 (M's poetry lecture course) student Judith Illsley (now Judith Gleason); and Humanities 130 graduate-student "section man" David Aivaz.

To Ilona Karmel

Ilona dear: 15 June 1952 [Conway]

Only you of all human creatures would have taken *that* time to write comfortingly to some one else. And such a letter! I am still tasting it

356

sentence by sentence. It leaves a kind of fragrance in the mind. As you yourself do, also.

It is about that I want to write to you now, though, caught in the web of pain as you are, this may be quite the wrong time. I have to begin with myself. I have been thinking a great deal about this art of ours these last months — thinking very gravely and almost desperately as I count out years and strength, and think of all I have to do — the many poems pressing to be conceived. And as I have thought of it more and more in that urgent, insistent, painful way, struggling always and at every moment to be honest with myself — to think only what in truth I do think — a kind of deep certainty has been rising in me as the deepest under-black rises through the blue and the shine if you look down long, long, in unfathomable water. That certainty is this: it is truly to testify we are here — to bear witness — those of us who are artists. But not to testify to the angel. No. To testify to ourselves and to the others. To testify about life to those who have to live life and who cannot see what they live because it is their lives. Our labor is the inconceivably difficult labor of putting away from us, where we can look at it and recognize it, what is too close to us to see because it is ourselves. Not to "order" the experiences of our lives so much as to *know* them, to *recognize* them. This is the labor and everything else is incidental to it. The skill is incidental to it — tool not labor. The theories are incidental to it — scaffoldings to be kicked down when they do not serve. The "knowledge", the books read, the languages spoken, the things seen and done, are all incidental to it — materials to serve perhaps or not to serve, depending always on our capacity to use them in the labor we must perform. Even the beliefs, the deepest convictions, the faith, are incidental — commitments to be suspected until *their* recognition becomes that other recognition we, as workmen, must — MUST — accomplish for ourselves in our own way. There can be no such thing as a Christian poet. There can be only a poet whose witness lies, in his measure, beside the witness of Christ. This is the distance — the immeasurable distance — which separates a Crashaw from Dante. We cannot begin, in this labor, half way to the goal. We must begin with what we are — which is what we touch and sense and see and guess and dream — which is what we mean by "life" — "this life".

Much of this I have said to you before for whatever truth it may seem to you to have. I repeat it now because there is this to add to it:

In this labor — this long, difficult and often heart-breaking labor — of constant and creative attentiveness — this labor truly of God's spies — everything depends, I now see, on the heart. We can only truly see, even the best of us, even the greatest, what we love. Those whose lives disgust them may make brilliant play of their hate, and touching pathos of their despair, but they are shrunken witnesses. Eliot, for all his brilliance, is not a great poet for this reason. Yeats, for the same reason, is. And this is Shakespeare's reason. And Keats'. And Dante's for all his cruel darkness — for the tart, sweet savor of life is there even in those supurating pools of hatred — those who are hateful are those who have sinned against life, call it by what name you will. The great Greeks too. Homer above all. Those loved Chinese. Heart alone has never made an artist as the sugary wrecks of millions upon millions of poems and paintings and works of music testify. But without heart, without the love of life, the hunger for life, was never anything that lived.

It is this, I now see, I have always, though sometimes shame-facedly, looked for in the beginning work which is to make the art of this next generation here. The fashionable models held before the young are models of a skillful and withering heartlessness. We are proud now that we have rediscovered evil and that we are big with contempt. But this pride leads nowhere but to death. And I am sick of that death.

You will understand then why, when I found Bill [Alfred] with that great gift of love in him and the gayety which can make misery homely and hopeful, I was full of excitement. Before I knew, as I do now, that he is worthy of that noblest name, I knew there was a poet somewhere, and not far.

It is so, my dear, with you. This is your great gift — and it is the greatest gift. You will not like to be told so in these blunt words. You will think back to that unkindness of which you are ashamed and to many other cruelties of which I know nothing. All this is meaningless. You have the gift of heart. The proofs are all around you in your work and in your friends. Do not think the two have no relation to each other. They have every relation. Only those artists who never come to human birth live like foetuses in the alcohol of work-alone.

It is for this reason, I now see, I was impatient with you a year ago when you told me you were going to devote yourself to philosophy for some years in order to become wise enough to write. It is for this reason I am delighted you reacted so violently to a course in deterministic psychology that you failed it — you! (If poor Professor [B. F.] Skinner — whoever he is — only knew!) Read all the philosophy you please. Soak yourself in the guesses, inspired or not, of the psychologists. But don't comfort yourself with the hope that all this will in some way deliver you from your labor of loving and seeing and bringing to recognition. Testifying. To yourseif and to the others. Every book of poems I write will be called Praise. Though not all may be happy. What else is there? To praise.

What you plan now is right. These people. Caught in the net of compulsion. Their lives a tissue of accidents to them. Your labor is the labor of the skillful surgeon, separating nerve and splinter and flesh to re-create the human. You say the problem is the problem of freedom and necessity. Does it help to say so? The problem is the problem of art. Of which the stuff is life and the means is love and the solution is the most difficult and the most rewarding labor of which men are capable.

If I preach to you when you are helpless you will forgive me because you know I love you. And if this has come at the wrong time you will forget it and think of other things. yours ever A.MacL.

TLS: KARMEL

To Ilona Karmel

Dear Ilona: 26 July [1952] [Conway]

I loved your tall ladies of great years and limber tongues. I can hear them. I hope by now you are off in the silence of the Cape — its Wood's Hole, dear, not Wood's Hall. I don't wonder you took it the other way. Why Wood's Hole! Well, I suppose the harbor — deepish. But whether it was a Mister Wood or the foliage round about I don't dare guess. Also it isn't wood's: its Woods. Which makes the mystery darker.

First, your story of the deaf old lady is going to be marvellous. I can feel it working in me. How much more powerfully must it stir in you. It belongs truly to you — of your blood and kind — regardless of a hundred Flauberts.

Secondly, what you say about understanding and judging is, to me, quite true and most truly said. The obligation a man takes on who really commits himself to the great art is precisely the obligation *not* to judge but to understand — which means necessarily to love in the deep meaning of love — instead. It is very difficult. Judgment is, as you say, easier. And, as you say again, it will be made anyway. But the obligation of those who are able to serve the great art is to be what Lear conceived of as God's spies.[1] Which means, as the blind man says to him later, not only to "see how this world goes" but to "see it feel-ingly." Gloucester's blindness becomes, in that phrase, a kind of meta-phor for people like you and me. We are not able to see with those eyes that judge so quickly and dismiss. We must see otherwise and more deeply: feelingly in both senses. It does not mean that one is not to be-lieve, not to know right from wrong, merely to record like a sensitive plate in a camera. It means only, that as with the blind man, recogni-tion comes *afterward* — after the tentative and touching fingers — not before.

Write me after you return to M.G..[2] I want so much to know what they tell you. I am off to Nashville in the blazing South for four lectures but I'll be back Thursday. The doctor thinks I can make it.[3] I hope he's right. But I have to go anyway.   I send you my love

AMacL

TLS: KARMEL

1. See *King Lear* V, iii, 8–19.   2. Massachusetts General Hospital.   3. M had recently suffered an attack of stomach ulcers.

To Adlai E. Stevenson

Dear Adlai: 8 August [1952]   [Conway]

I will. With great happiness.[1]

But to be any real use to you I need a steer. Could you find time to read this letter and to write, or better, wire me Yes or No?

I'll be as brief as I can even at the risk of being a bit obscure.

Your Aug. 27 speech is to be "non-political" but because it is your first speech as a candidate it will be one of the most important political speeches you make, whatever you say.

The subject, as I see it, is dictated in part by that fact and in part by the occasion — the audience. The two facts together add up, in my mind, to a speech, the central concern of which will be with the concept of *Patriotism*.

The ideal of patriotism is the ideal which holds the Legion together. But it is also the mask behind which some of the most dangerous and evil influences of our day conceal themselves — in the Legion and outside it. The McCarthys and the Jenners: the blacklisters and the subverters of free education.

Nothing would more effectively further your purpose to illuminate the issues and educate the people than such a discussion of the true nature of patriotism as you above all others can give.

What is patriotism? Love of country — yes: of the physical, visible beloved land. But only of the land? No, of the people — the past of the people — their accomplishments, their endurance, their hopes. Their hopes. The whole tradition of people and land together. And what is that tradition with us?

You would move in some such direction. You would attribute to the Legion that true patriotism which a great part of its membership must indeed feel — but which a few have betrayed.

I think the point is clear. And the foundation it would give you for the positive campaign you mean to lead on the great central, critical issue of individual freedom in a frightened world.

Shall I go ahead or not? I *hate* truly to bother you but I need *your* word if I'm to be of any use to you. Bless you! You're doing fine.

yours ever Archie

TLS: NjP

1. Stevenson, the Democratic presidential nominee, had invited M to help draft the first speech of his campaign, to be delivered on August 27 to the American Legion convention in New York.

To Ernest Hemingway

Dear Pappy: [*c.* 2 October 1952] [Conway]

Everything about it[1] is like old times except no bicycles and no butler. That butler! I can see him looking at the two of us in from the Bois and smelling. But it is. The same shock of excitement I had when I saw *In Our Time* and ran into you at the Closerie. The butler, though, was later. That was a brief moment of glory which would never have lifted you and me to the level of the rez de chausee if Marise Hamilton hadn't slept — or lain awake — with that Canadian ace and if Peter Hamilton hadn't met her on the stairs and grabbed her by the fat on the backs of her upper arms and if she hadn't kicked him as high up as she could which was plenty. On such improbabilities does the social elevation of the modest depend. Maybe Peter wouldn't even have gotten the Medal of Honor if we hadn't kept a bicycle in the front hall.[2] And the same mail that brought The Old Man brought a book about Hemingway the writer[3] — remember Nora saying James Joyce the writer!? — and I read it the way I read all such books by looking myself up in the index and there was that line about whittling a style for his time from Years of the Dog if you remember that poem.[4] It all tied itself together and I was homesick as a puppy. For the past. Which who is it has found his way back to? Its a masterpiece: that's all that matters. But it would have been. So there's no astonishment in that. Only in the way it slips back into the memories.

I wonder sometimes will we ever meet again? I doubt it. Though we might find ourselves face to face somewhere. The language we could have talked in would have to be translated out of the present and whose [*sic*] to do that? Not me. Not, I think, even you. Its sad because, as you used to put it quoting Bra [Saunders] who was probably quoting you, men are dying who never died before. Some know it and lie down. Some go walking around and run cattle farms. We might be the only two live ones left who knew all that. Well, I'm no prophet. It might happen. I only know this — that its true, the old slogan we used to

361

twist one way and then the other. All DOES pass. And art DOES alone endure. And its worth it. Don't ask me why. It is. As you know also. You've proved it on your nerves.   yours as once   Archie

TLS: JFK

1. Hemingway's *The Old Man and the Sea*, published in September 1952. 2. Pierpont Morgan Hamilton, who rose to the rank of major general in the U.S. Air Force, had won the Congressional Medal of Honor for his service in North Africa during World War II. 3. Carlos Baker, *Hemingway: The Writer as Artist* (Princeton, N.J.: Princeton University Press, 1952). 4. The poem had appeared in *Actfive and Other Poems* (1948).

To Adlai E. Stevenson

Dear Adlai: 27 December [1952]   [Conway]

My spies and operatives tell me — if I may so characterize John Cowles[1] — that you and Bill Blair[2] are heading for Ronnie Tree's[3] marble mausoleum on Barbadoes to do a stint of work in peace and quiet. Now this information violently excites Ada and myself. To get to Barbadoes you will have to fly over, and most likely put down on, that island Paradise, Antigua. Where Ada and I have a small but beautiful house — not as beautiful as Ronnie's but beautiful enough for the likes of you and me what with the big seas from Africa whispering away to a white froth of silence over the coral reefs at the front door and the big palms overhead telling the Trade winds what the Trade winds never seem to have time to wait to hear. In addition to which you have under that roof, as you well know, two hearts that beat as true as any you'll ever find. All of which boils down — or up — I think its up — to this:

Why don't you and Bill stop off for a bit going or coming?

Our schedule is simple. We fly down with John and Betty Cowles on the 15 Jan and get the house opened. (A terrific labor! You open the door, whistle for the nearest cook and sit down to dinner! Well — practically.) Dean and Alice come down about the 25 Jan and stay for two weeks with us, moving thereafter to a house about two miles further along the coast where they plan to stay for maybe six weeks more. From the end of the first week in February until our boy Ken and his wife come down along in early March we are alone* [*MacLeish wrote in the margin*: *Also between, say, Jan 18 & Jan 25]. Which means that the guest room complete with two beds and a bath and quite often water, will be sitting waiting, waiting.

Why not?

And don't think this is something dreamed up on the spur of a letter from Cowles. Ada and I have been pondering this for months.

Young Arthur Schlesinger[4] put us off it a few weeks ago when he told us you were headed off around the world: otherwise you would have heard from us in peremptory tones of urgent invitation three weeks ago. Now that we know you'll be over our roof we simply won't take no for an answer. We'll be strident and unmannerly. And why? Because we love you, long to see you and can think of no place on earth where seeing you would be pleasanter. Bill would be the most welcome possible addition. I'd like very much to get to know him.

Do you mind my closing by saying we're still so proud of you we walk like fire horses?   yrs   Archie

TLS: NjP

1. President of the *Minneapolis Star and Tribune*, chairman of the board of Cowles Magazines, Inc., and one of the MacLeishes' neighbors in Antigua. 2. William McCormick Blair, Jr., one of Stevenson's top aides in his unsuccessful presidential campaign in 1952. 3. Ronald Tree, husband of Stevenson's close friend Marietta Tree; they had a winter estate in Barbados. 4. Arthur M. Schlesinger, Jr., a professor of history at Harvard and one of Stevenson's principal speech writers.

To Paul H. Buck

Dear Paul: 1 January 1953   [Conway]

I don't know whether this letter will serve a useful purpose or not. If not, your waste-paper basket is at hand.

My radio reports that various Congressional Committees plan to investigate colleges and universities to determine whether they are riddled with Communists. Senator McCarthy is reported as including "Communist thinkers". Since he has already told us that he regards Benny de Voto and young Arthur Schlesinger as "Communist thinkers" we have some notion of what that means.

You will recall that I am to be away the second half year. You will recall also that Senator McCarthy has already attacked me as belonging to more Communist front organizations than any man he has ever mentioned.[1] He — or one of the other committees — can be expected to attack me again when he or they get around to Harvard — which should be early in the campaign. If I am away in the British West Indies at the time I should like you to have the facts.

But before I set them down I should like to ask a question which must be in your mind and in the minds of many others. Has not the time come for the believers in the American tradition of intellectual liberty — above all the believers in positions of responsibility on the faculties of the free universities — to take a firm stand on the fundamental issue? There is no disagreement, I take it, on the issue of Communists in teaching. No man who accepts a prior loyalty to any authority other than his own conscience, his own judgment of the truth, should be permitted to teach in a free society. That view, I take it, is held by those responsible for the selection of teachers in all colleges and universities in this country. It is also applied in the case of Communists at least — though it is notoriously not applied in certain cases at the other extreme. Now, this standard is a professional standard to be applied, under the American system, by the profession itself and by the institutions of education in which the profession is practised. To permit Congressional Committees to apply such standards, or to replace them with standards of their own, is, quite literally, to permit governmental regulation and control of matters which the American system regards as beyond governmental competence. This is true in theory. It is even more true in practise, for the whole record of such investigations proves that it is not only members of the Communist Party the investigators aim to reach but all those whose opinions the investigators find distasteful. Government supervision of education through investigative committees means, in effect, government thought control. And once established in educational institutions, governmental control of opinion could readily be extended to newspapers, publishing houses and all the rest of the institutions of freedom of opinion. If Harvard can be "investigated" for "Communist thinking" by a Congressional Committee headed by Senator McCarthy, so can the New York *Times* which has openly opposed McCarthy and which Senator McCarthy must therefore regard as infected by "Communist thinking" since anything is pro-Communist which is anti-him.

The issue is manifestly serious — nothing could be more serious so far as the preservation of liberty of thought in this country is concerned. The question, which you must have considered at length, is what to do about it. For myself, I don't believe defiance of the Committee on the ground that it was exceeding its powers in undertaking to police the opinions of teachers, would be wise or effective. But I do believe a solemn protest setting forth the vivid reality of the danger to the critical American liberty should be made by the heads of the great universities and colleges. The party newly in control of the government should be faced with the meaning of an act for which it will have to take a major part of the responsibility. Do the Republicans in Congress and in the new Administration believe that government can or should supervise the selection of teachers or determine what opinions are permissible in institutions of learning? Are they ready to say that the governing bodies of American institutions of learning are incapable of applying professional standards and that government must take over? Are they prepared to face the consequences of such a decision as regards newspapers and radio stations? Do they, in short, believe that the only way to rid the Republic of propaganda for Communism is to apply to the Republic such controls as Communism advocates?

So much for my initial question. I hope such a statement is under consideration. I hope it can be made in the most impressive possible way before the New Congress acts on such proposals as Senator McCarthy and the new Republican head of the Committee on Un-American Activities have made. Now as to myself.

The interesting fact, as I said to the press when McCarthy attacked me during the campaign, is that not even in his most reckless and irresponsible attacks on members of the State Department, past or present, had he mentioned my name — until I made a country-wide appeal for funds for the campaign of his opponent in Wisconsin, Fairchild. Neither, so far as I am informed, did the Committee on UnAmerican Activities mention me.

I have not been told what Communist-front organizations the Senator has in mind but I assume they include the League of American Writers and various other organizations of an anti-fascist character to which I belonged at the time of the Spanish War and during the rise of the Nazi danger and from which I removed myself when I entered the Government as Librarian of Congress in 1939. After leaving the Government and during the period when I was working to secure backing for UNESCO among artists and writers I was a director of the National Council of Arts Sciences and Professions but resigned after attending one directors' meeting because it was quite apparent the Council did not represent either Artists or Scientists or Professional people. I had some trouble getting my name off the letter-head but my activity, as I recall it, was limited to that one directors' meeting. If there were other meetings they were not numerous. I heard nothing, I should add, to suggest that the organization had an improper or subversive purpose. Its principal weakness seemed to be that it didn't have *any*.

My own personal position on the issue of Communism has been clear throughout, and the record is a matter of public knowledge. I was, I think I can say without immodesty, one of the first American writers to attack the Marxists. This was, of course, on the literary front since it was on the literary front I met them. In the early Thirties the Marxist position was, as you know, a fashionable position among the critics. Attacks on Communism were not the pleasant and profitable exercises they are now when all politicians and most publicists fall all over themselves and each other to demonstrate their detestation of everything Communism is or stands for. In the early Thirties, to attack the Communists was to bring the hornets out and the stings could hurt. You will find mine, if you have occasion to look, in my new *Collected Poems*[2] on page 76 (*Background with Revolutionaries* 1933) and page 93 (*Invocation to the Social Muse*, 1932)[.] Also on page 186 of my *Poems 1924–1933* you will find my Harvard Phi Beta Kappa Poem, *1933*. (This appears in an abbreviated form and without the Tiresias sections in my *Collected Poems* under the title Elpenor[.]) Of these, the first — *Background With Revolutionaries* — a satire on the New York Communist poets — was made the text of a major blast at me delivered by John Strachey[3] and the second, the *Invocation To The Social Muse*, a satire on the critical doctrine of social consciousness, earned me a flaying in the *New Masses*

Later my verse play *Panic*, which ran on Broadway for three nights (!) was followed by a Marxist inquest in which my presentation of the Radicals as led by a blind man uttering sententious views on fate and destiny was much complained of. A lot of Marxists had turned up the last night because the play was about the depression and the bank panic and had been grievously disappointed.

Subsequently, when the Spanish War started I thought I saw (rightly enough) the unfolding fascist pattern and threw myself passionately into the work of arousing the country, or as much of it as I could reach by my small whistle, to the nature of the danger. It was at this time that I joined the League of American Writers to which most of the writers of the period belonged. I spoke at a meeting of the League in Carnegie Hall, speaking as a Liberal and stating my position on the issue of the relation of Liberals to Communists in the face of the fascist danger. My position was, in brief, that a man who would not declare his convictions for fear of declaring them in the wrong company had no convictions. The speech was published in the New Masses and is printed in my *A Time To Speak* under the title, *The Communists, The Writers and The Spanish War*. I was not, however, a believer in the popular front as another article, reprinted in *A Time to Speak*[,] demonstrates.

I undoubtedly underestimated the potentialities for evil of the USSR at that time: Hitler's potentialities were too terrifying to leave room for much else. But Communism in the United States was as offensive to me at the end of the decade as it had been at the beginning. As *Speech To Those Who Say Comrade* on page 101 of the *Collected* will indicate. As for other organizations, I have no present memory of association with any except a little corporation Hemingway and Dos Passos and I formed to make a film of the Spanish War — script by Hemingway — photography by Joris Ivens. Corporation called, I think, Contemporary Historians or something like that. That my name was used by other organizations of this character I have no doubt — very possibly with my permission in certain cases. But I was active only in the League and the little corporation and my activity in the League was pretty well limited to the Carnegie Hall meeting.

The rest is brief. I was in Government from 1939 to 1945. My position in that period is set forth in speeches collected in *A Time To Act* — support of the war etc. Thereafter questions of foreign policy and of the Soviet imperialism occupied my mind. The position is stated in articles published in my *Freedom Is The Right To Choose*.[4] The central theme is the theme which has held me [from] the beginning — the theme of individual freedom — of the "right to choose". The articles speak for themselves. It is perhaps relevant to the present concern to add that one of them published in the Atlantic under the title *The Conquest of America* produced an angry reaction from *Pravda* which charged me with slandering the Soviet Union. I don't think I had, but that didn't prevent *Pravda* from hoping for my early demise.

I'm sorry this is so long. It may be of no use to you at all. But just on the chance that it might be I'd like you to have it in your files. I know I can count on your confidence. But I know also what Senator McCarthy is capable of and I should feel happier if I felt certain that the facts were there to lay along side the libels.

faithfully   Archie MacLeish

TLS: MH (ARCHIVES)

1. Senator Joseph McCarthy had made the charge in October 1952, shortly after M, Arthur M. Schlesinger, Jr., and Mark A. DeWolfe Howe, all of Harvard, circulated letters calling for McCarthy's defeat in the coming election. 2. M's *Collected Poems, 1917–1952*, published by Houghton Mifflin Company in November 1952, and later winner of the Pulitzer Prize (M's second), the National Book Award, and the Bollingen Prize. 3. English left-wing economist, a cousin of Lytton Strachey's. 4. *Freedom Is the Right to Choose: An Inquiry into the Battle for the American Future* (Boston: Beacon Press, 1951), M's first collection of essays since *A Time to Act* (1943).

To Harry Levin

Dear Harry: 4 July [1953]   [Conway]

A suitable day to reply to your letter. One looks at the blue clean sky and the green pure hills and thinks of the great Declaration which gives meaning to this occasion and then winces with almost physical pain to remember that for many Americans this year McCarthy is spokesman for the Republic. It must hurt more with you in Europe than with me here. It isn't McCarthy who matters now, obscene as he is: it is the millions upon millions of people who think America is what he thinks it is. How shall they be answered? How shall they ever be answered?

There was a letter in the Times two days ago from an American who has been abroad for a year and a half and who concludes his observations with the remark that McCarthy has been worth five crack divisions to the Communists. McCarthy, however, has his answer to that. He has discovered a Communist plot to murder him. (His personal Reichstag Fire). One might as probably discover a plot by the children to murder Santa Claus.

What a year you and I chose to be away from Cambridge. I know nothing of Pusey[1] but his public record and the fact that Pick[2] was moved by his face. But I am encouraged by those who have deplored his choice. If there is nothing more to say against him than they have found to say he must be invulnerable. What is missing thus far is the case pro. All we know is that he is the right age, had the right education and comes from (how far back?) the right field. But it is not to be forgotten that he also took the field openly against the shame of Wisconsin. I suspect he may do very well after the inevitable ructions of the first year or so.

My little verse play (This Music Crept By Me . . .) was done by the BBC ten days or so ago and Geoffrey Bridson writes me that it had a "considerable success" — which the clippings enclosed would seem to confirm. I am not going to try to get it a radio production here: the networks have been too contemptible about *The Trojan Horse*. Lillian[3] thinks it might make an evening in the theatre by itself. I don't quite see how since it runs under an hour and since I won't stretch it for any reason. When she gets back perhaps she'll tell me. The time thing is the only difficulty I see. I feel very sure after the London reaction that it will play — really play. Wouldn't it be fun to have a play well done and have it go? Our dear love to you both. We think of you very often   Archie

TLS: LEVIN

1. Nathan Marsh Pusey, who had recently been elected James B. Conant's successor as president of Harvard University. 2. Edward Motley Pickman, a Harvard alumnus and scholar-gentleman who, with his wife, Hester, had long known the MacLeishes. 3. Lillian Hellman (b. 1905), American playwright, whose friendship with M began when they worked together in Contemporary Historians, Inc., during the Spanish civil war.

To Ilona Karmel

Ilona my dear: 29 July [1953]   [Conway]

Your letter closes the odd circle of one of those paradoxes with which life enriches us all. You are writing me (and I do indeed understand) about your feeling that you had betrayed my faith in you. But your letter itself would renew that faith had it ever lapsed (which it never has) or create and beget it had it never existed. What you say about the false promises of agony is as true an insight as even Rilke, that most subtle of in-see-ers, ever achieved. And what you say about the presumptions of the art of the novel is one of those hard and just sayings which only the artist born imposes upon himself. But the truth is, my dear, that you have never written a page which did not convince me that you are what I know you are. When you wonder whether you are a writer I smile at you. Try to escape being one and you will see. Do you remember that Sonnet to Orpheus in which it is the god's departure (the silence after the singing) that proves what music is? Just try. You will see then.

And you don't need me to tell you that the task imposed on you by the hard rule of art you have accepted for yourself is a task of unspeakable difficulty. To write of the dullness of the soul without dullness — that is the supreme test. Anyone, aided by the excitement of expectation, can carry a reader along. But to persuade a reader to WAIT — only a few can do that: those who can make their people so alive and so present that to wait with them is to wait for life itself. Your people in Stephania were sometimes almost as alive as that, but still more is required of you. You are not to use the word "fail" of this labor even if you have not succeeded. One does not say of a rocket that it failed to reach the moon — only that it went very high. Write me what has happened. And let me see a copy of the ms when you feel you want to.

If I understand the meaning of "commitment" I am very happy for you. When there is time — the right kind of time — you will tell me about that too.

my love to you
A.MacL.

My wife sends many messages.

Did you know Judy was graduated from her graduate school year at Columbia with highest honors? They wrote me to tell me. Since I don't know her address I can't write her. I think she'd rather I didn't. Why? God knows but I respect all silences.

TLS: KARMEL

To Ilona Karmel

Darling Ilona: 31 July [1953]   Conway

I read it aloud to Ada last night.[1] She was absolutely still when I had finished and for a long time after — only the wind in those elms.

Then she said she knew what you meant when you said you had written it not so much with your heart as with your stomach. Then she said — tell her how deeply I am moved: it doesn't mean much to her perhaps but tell her. I said it would mean everything to you. As it will. And should. She rarely praises but when she does it is true.

Ilona, it is good. Truly good. The old miracle of the understanding heart is there as miraculous as ever. But you yourself as artist have grown. As you had to grow and should have. You are surer of yourself and therefore surer of your story. And the English idiom of course is much more natural. I should change very little if I were blue-pencilling now. But that is of less importance than the other. The thing is alive as only art is alive.

I have only two suggestions now. The scene in the camp in the early morning when the Americans were to have come and instead the march begins doesn't come into focus as it should at a single reading. There is perhaps too much movement — pulling back and forth — and too little feeling in the movement. The feeling is there — the horror is almost unbearable — but the outlines are too near nightmare for the mind to perceive. Only the mind in nightmare itself can accept nightmare. Your difficult problem here — superbly resolved in the march itself — is to reduce nightmare to art which at once is and is not.

The other is the very end — the "accidents" — are there two? You have scamped these sentences a little. The rest — the milk — Mrs. Davidov under her dry leaf — are seen — held in the mind. The action blurs more than it can. Its the same problem over again. The action here must blur because it is so sensed by Mina. But it must not blur for the reader. That is to say, it must not blur in the art.

I don't wonder that Peter would be willing to recommend it to the Princess.[2] But don't let him send it. I have just learned to my astonishment (I should have known having been, as Librarian of Congress, the head of the Copyright Office) that both Bill and I may very well have lost copyright in our plays[3] by publishing them in *Boteghe Oscure* which doesn't carry a valid US copyright notice. I have been trying for a month to save Bill's rights and incidentally my own (which matter less because I have no immediate plans to publish This Music). So don't send your novel off till the Princess can protect her contributors. My advice would be to ask Paul Brooks[4] before doing anything with any part of the novel.

But this is all very dull and technical. Its the novel that counts. I am more proud of you than ever. Now aim for the sky-star and sail!

yours ever   AMacL

TLS: KARMEL

1. Karmel had sent M the manuscript of a novel in progress that she did not subsequently complete. 2. Peter was Peter Seng, a graduate-student "section man" in M's Humanities 130 lecture course at Harvard; the princess was Princess Bassiano (Marguerite Caetani), publisher of *Botteghe Oscure*. 3. M's *This Music Crept by Me on the Water* (subsequently published as *This Music Crept by Me upon the Waters*) and William Alfred's *Agamemnon* — undertaken when Alfred was a student in M's English S course — had been published in *Botteghe Oscure* 11 (April 1953), pages 172–225 and 249–353, respectively. 4. Editor in chief of the trade department at Houghton Mifflin Company.

To McGeorge Bundy[1]

Dear Mac: 30 December 1953   [Antigua]

Yours of seven days ago.

The answer is, of course, Yes.[2] And with a very real sense of the honor done me. And not only for reasons of friendship — which are real enough, also, as you know. I am very much moved by the sense of the President's confidence as you tell me of it.[3] And I have — as I know you have also — a feeling of profound obligation and loyalty to Harvard which has become, with time, one of the compelling influences in my life.

I should like to defer, as you say I may, the question of sleeping in the master's house. I know you would much prefer it if we did and I understand why. I know, also, that you appreciate the considerations which make me loth to ask it. Ada will gladly do whatever appears to be necessary if it is also physically and psychologically possible. We should be able, during this next term, to work our way through that problem. I will report progress.

You put the problem of teaching responsibilities generously and understandingly. I am sure, at this point, of one thing only — that I can't do the Poetry course and also undertake the duties of Master. A better and better-prepared man could. Probably — although the mere mechanics of the "notebook" method I use which requires a kind of colloquy between lecturer and note-takers, demands a full working day per lecture — at least the way I work. Maybe I could give a series of readings and comments — six or eight a term — for anybody in the House who wanted to come. That plus my writing course. Or maybe I could take on as tutor a number of students particularly interested in poetry. Again plus my writing course. You leave all this to me and I shall try to make as wise and well-advised a decision as I can.

I have been thinking a little about what I should like to do in the House. Not, I think, altogether what John does. Partly because I couldn't emulate him if I wished. Partly because my interests run in slightly different directions. I am not so anxious to know all the lads by name — though I realize the importance of that kind of relationship in a place as big and as impersonal as Harvard. Rather, I should like to engineer that kind of informal contact between student and scholar or student and artist in which so much of the real communication of education takes place. Something might happen between Yaeger,[4] say, and a dozen students in an evening over a few beers which wouldn't happen in a class-room. Or Piston[5] with someone to make a little of the music — Ada if she would. Has Wolfinsohn[6] ever played at Eliot House? I know I have never been asked to read there. Formal seminars with Richards and Bush[7] and me talking about poetry and science are all very well — but they are class-rooms all over. The thing really happens otherwise in most men's lives. How would you do it? I don't know. Probably its impossible or it would be happening in all the Houses all the time. But I'd like to find out. And I mean to. I don't suppose I can destroy the House in one year even if I fail. John has built it too well.

Would it be well, while we are settling this, to settle also the other half of the question of A.MacL.? I can put it in chronological terms. I am going to be 62 in May. I have a whole new world of poems to deal with. There is not time enough. Above all there is not time enough if I am to teach a full year because the two things won't go together. What I should like to do — beginning year after next — would be to teach in the Fall Term only. When we talked you did not preclude the possibility. Do you think it could be accepted?

I suppose what I should do is to pull out of teaching altogether. Something opened up for me in the new poems in my *Collected* and in the verse plays which promises to lead farther. I have always been a late starter in everything and now I feel as though I were a young man, just beginning. I have a sense of *possibility* such as I have never had before. But I can't conceive, now, of cutting myself off from Harvard unless I have to. It is a rich and creative source for me. If I could combine it with *time* I should feel I had arrived at such a solution as few writers in our day are lucky enough to achieve.

Meantime — and on this same theme of Harvard — let me use two of your minutes to tell you how the perspective shapes itself from this distance in time and space. I have been talking to Ted Pickman about it on the sand. I feel in my bones a new age — a new era. It is not only the President's youth and yours. Not only the vitality you both have and the complementary intelligences which so patently create a new kind of thinking. Not only the courage and candor which make the air good to breathe. It is more than all those things and the many others I can think of. It is the fact that this Harvard cares about values. "The process is the reality" — yes. But the real is not merely a process. Keats is right in the great Ode — the human equation combines, with the order imposed by nature, the order imposed by the imagination. When one can say, understanding what he is saying, that Beauty is Truth, Truth Beauty, one has spoken as a man.

Love to Mary.   yrs   Archie

TLS: MH (ARCHIVES)

1. M's friend and former OFF colleague was now dean of the Faculty of Arts and Sciences at Harvard University. **2.** M was agreeing to serve as acting master of Eliot House for the academic year 1954–1955, temporarily replacing Professor John H. Finley while Finley spent a year at Oxford. **3.** Nathan M. Pusey, who had recently been installed as president of Harvard. **4.** Werner Yaeger, the Harvard classicist. **5.** Walter Piston, the composer, a member of the Music Department at Harvard. **6.** Wolf Wolfinsohn, first violinist of the Stradivarius String Quartet. **7.** I. A. Richards and Douglas Bush, Harvard English professors.

To Ernest Hemingway[1]

Dear Pappy,   17 February 1954   [Cambridge]

Your letter just came in. Wonderful news! The Academy will be delighted. It will be particularly wonderful if you and Mary can come.

Also, it is wonderful to have direct news about the result of the smash-up. When we walked in the front door getting back from Antigua, the telephone was ringing with a newspaper reporter announcing that you were dead. I am proud to say that I never did believe it. I'll give everybody your messages.

This is just to say thanks and tell you how truly delighted I am that you can make it. I'll *write* later.   Yours,   Archie

TLS: JFK

1. Ernest and Mary Hemingway had survived two airplane crashes in Africa in January 1954, in the second of which Hemingway had been injured more seriously than he initially realized. As the next letter indicates, his injuries forced him to cancel his plan to accept personally the Gold Medal of the American Academy of Arts and Letters, of which M had become president in December 1953.

To Ernest Hemingway

Dear Pappy,   5 May 1954   [Cambridge]

I hope you got my cable telling you we all understand perfectly why you can't be in New York on the 26th of May and that, although we shall miss you, we will carry through with the little ceremony as well as we can in your absence.

I had a pretty good idea from the piece in Look[1] that things were a lot worse than you had allowed them to appear to be but I had no idea

373

that they were as bad as they are. I have no doubt a few months of the Spanish treatment will put all right but Ada and I were sad indeed to realize how much you must have suffered. This isn't a letter — which I will write as soon as the mountain of paper work here blows away. This is just a note to send you our love and to tell you not to bother about a statement for the Academy business unless it comes easily to you to shoot one off but don't forget to tell me where you want the check sent.　　　　　　　　　　　　　　Faithfully,

　　　　　　　　　　　　　　　　　　Yours　Archie

TLS: JFK

1. "The Christmas Gift," Parts I and II, *Look* 18 (20 April and 4 May 1954), Hemingway's account of his recent misfortunes.

To J. Robert Oppenheimer[1]

Dear Robert:　　　　　　　　　　　　　　7 July 1954　[Conway]

　　Those several unanswered letters of mine to you left me feeling that maybe you'd just as soon not have to read another — after all, a man has a right to choose his correspondents — but I can't wholly restrain the push of my own feelings and certainly not the push of Ada's. Like so many others we suffered personally through the whole ordeal[2] as though something intimately valuable to us was being hurt — as indeed it was — and we came out at the end feeling, as every decent human being must feel, that a terrible wrong had been perpetrated but that a very great spirit had been revealed also — a spirit, the presence of which we had guessed in those days, so unbelievably far back now, at Antigua. We send you, both of us, if we may, our love.

　　And whatever was true of the earlier letters this one needs no answer.

　　　　　　　　　　　　　　　　　yours　Archie

TLS: DLC

1. American physicist (1904–1967), leader of the group that designed and built the first atomic bombs and, from 1947, director of the Institute for Advanced Study. M had met and befriended him at Antigua in the winter of 1953. 2. After a highly publicized hearing, the Atomic Energy Commission had voted, on June 29, not to reinstate Oppenheimer's revoked security clearance because of alleged character defects and communist associations.

To J. Robert Oppenheimer

Dear Bob:　　　　　　　　　　　　　13 September 1954　[Cambridge]

　　Are you and Kitty going to be at or near Cambridge on any foreseeable Thursday and Friday this next autumn, winter or spring and if so will you stay with us and, particularly, will you dine with us on the Thursday evening?

It is, I agree, a rather large invitation but it has its reasons, the first of which is that we want to see you and the second of which is that we want a few of the members of the Harvard faculty and the boys at Eliot House to see you too. We are going to be running the House, or trying to, in the absence at Oxford of the Master and we want to use the opportunity to do something which has been very much on our minds for some time: to create a situation in which certain Harvard undergraduates may see men they admire not on the other side of a reading stand but in the same room and in the living breathing flesh. Most of us know in our own experience that education is a matter of personal inoculation but we do very little about it in practice. Ada and I, with your help and the help of others of our friends, would like to do what we can.

What would happen, as we imagine it, is something like this: you would give us a date or several dates when it might be convenient for you to come, together with the names of people at Harvard, members of the faculty, whom you would like to dine with. We would put together the most agreeable party of eight or ten we could conceive of and dinner would take the usual course except that I would try to keep the conversation as general as possible and as close to your concerns of that particular moment. Meantime some twenty boys would have been gathering in the Master's study with beer or something else to keep them occupied and, when dinner was well over, we would take our brandies with us and join them. I would attempt to give a resumé of the talk at table and we would go forward from there, still by way of conversation, in the hope that some of the lads might eventually join us but with no insistence that they do unless so moved. It would all, in other words, be as easy and civilized as we could make it, and as pleasant for all concerned.

It does, however, demand a good deal of our friends, for Cambridge is not a place all of them are near or are apt to visit, and we are well aware that there may be other inconveniences. We hope very much, in other words, that you will want to do it but we will wholly understand if you can't. So far Dean Acheson and Felix Frankfurter have agreed to come; Lefty Lewis[1] has accepted in principle; and Scotty Reston[2] says he is sure it can be arranged — these all being people I have happened to run into during the summer.

What we hope in your case is that you will be able to come on Thursday, October 21st, but if that date is impossible for you or if others are preferable, I wish you would name your choice. I will then try to put the Chinese puzzle together.

Please do it if you can, and please write me soon in any case.

Yours,   Archie (MacLeish)

TLS: DLC

1. Wilmarth S. Lewis, biographer and editor of the correspondence of Horace Walpole. 2. James Reston, the *New York Times* columnist.

To Ferris Greenslet

Dear Greenslet: 28 September 1954   [Cambridge?]

You know because you are wise in these things, how very much your letter meant to me.[1] I am not sure that you do know, or can know, what your encouragement counted for during those years in the 'twenties and 'thirties. Bless you for what you say now. One is always a bad judge of a new book because one is so much involved personally, but I do feel myself that, if I know anything about the art of poetry, this is the farthest I have yet gone.

And thank you for your good wishes in the House. It's a rather frightening assignment to try to follow John even for a year, as you will well understand.   Faithfully yours,   [Archibald MacLeish]

TL-C: DLC

1. Greenslet had written M on September 22 to praise his new book, *Songs for Eve*, which had just been published by Houghton Mifflin Company.

To Edward Hoagland[1]

Dear Ted: 10 March 1955   [Cambridge]

That letter of yours made me happier than almost anything that has come my way in years. Coming from you and coming after our long association it means a very great deal.

I think you are right in your suggestion about the course — that I should be harder on my people from the point of view of output. This year's class is intelligent and alert and some of them are really talented, but the output is low and laggard. I keep longing for the days when I had you and Elizabeth [Marshall Thomas] and Jean [Higgins] and the rest of the writers who really wrote.

This brings you my very best wishes for the trip you so well deserve. Keep me informed about the book.[2] I will be in touch with Houghton Mifflin myself, but I want to know what happens at your end.

Faithfully yours,   AMacLeish

TLS: HOAGLAND

1. American novelist and essayist (b. 1932). Hoagland, as an undergraduate at Harvard (Class of 1954), had taken M's advanced writing course, English S. 2. *Cat Man*, Hoagland's first book (a novel), published by Houghton Mifflin Company in January 1956.

To Ezra Pound

Dear Ezra: [*c.* August 1955] [Conway]

Yours of the 4 Aug.. I haven't been in Washington since that winter day when I got snowed in at a female seminary outside of Baltimore and was unable to make the rest of the trip. Next time I'm down you'll see me if you'll let me come.

If there's a service to the arts which *you* think is a service to the arts I'd like to know about it. No man alive has served them more faithfully than you. Can you tell me what it is?

But the service to the arts I should most like to see performed is the service which would give you some peace and quiet in which to work. You and I differ politically, and I regard your views about the late war about as you regard mine, but I have always been and still am, as you know, of one mind with those who HAVE minds about your work.

I have been told by personal friends of yours that nothing is to be done — that no solution would be acceptable to you which did not involve vilification of President Roosevelt and those who served the Republic under him. If that is so its so — but I'd like to hear it from you before I accept it as the truth.

If all this is none of my business you can and will tell me to go to Hell as you have done in the past. But if the report I have heard is untrue and if there is a feasible solution of the whole problem I'd like to know it.   yours faithfully   Archie

TLS: YCAL

To Ezra Pound

Dear Ez: 18 August [1955] [Conway]

Thank you for a friendly and highly informative letter. I hope to get to Washington in the middle of the fall sometime. I'll let you know in advance in the hope that you will let me come out to see you.

Meantime I am going to assume — please tell me at once if I am wrong — that you would agree to what would be called, I suppose, a medical disposition of the problem: meaning by that, a disposition based on medical opinion, as distinguished from a legal or political (whatever that would be) disposition.

377

I don't know what I can do. Even in a medical disposition the Administration would have to act and I am not exactly grata in this Administration. But at least, if my assumption is correct, I will do what I can and try to instigate others who can do more. I don't mean by this, organization or, least of all, publicity. I mean the only kind of action that ever really counts — individual action in individual terms.

About the painter whom you do not name (I suppose I can get his name from — by — a glance at the Hudson Review) I'd like to help if I can.[1] What needs to be done? I know nobody in Va who can roll a log over. I enclose the color print which is fine too.

faithfully   Archie

TLS: YCAL

1. The unnamed artist was Sheri Martinelli, a frequent visitor of Pound's at St. Elizabeths, whose painting entitled *Leucothoe* had appeared as a frontispiece in *The Hudson Review* 8 (Spring 1955), immediately preceding Pound's *Cantos 86* and *87*.

To Ezra Pound

Dear Ez: [*c*. September 1955?]   [Conway]

On the contrary — I'm proud to be seen writing you and don't give a gd gd dm who reports it. Wrote you at the other address because Achilles, golden hero, so advised.[1] Said he did it himself.

Your reply is as clear as an oracle. Precisely. Selloi oak has nothing on old Ez.

When you say I am overlooking the simple and direct solution WHAT do you mean? I have heard talk of a "presidential pardon". But surely you don't mean that. A man can't be pardoned for something he has never been convicted of. You aint been convicted of nothing.

WHAT is simpler and more obvious than what I suggested? Please be specific. I don't want to undertake something you don't want me to undertake. I therefore wait upon your word. But please, Oh Lord, send it in unmistakable form. I may not be able to accomplish anything at all (a Republican would be better) but the one thing I want to avoid is making things worse for you by attempting what you don't want attempted.   yrs   AMacL

TLS: YCAL

1. Achilles Fang, a research fellow in Far Eastern languages at Harvard.

To Ezra Pound

Dear Ezra: 3 March [1956] [Antigua]

A batch of yr letters got forwarded to me on this Leeward — place makes me think of yr Second Canto — the Mediterranean has more behind it in the way of human bones but the water here is finer in color and clarity than anything you ever saw off Rapallo and the sun is more violent and also — honesty compels — the drought is dryer. No one is allowed to flush a toilet on this coast unless the contents will (forgive the specificity) no longer stir. You brush yr teeth in rum (which taste awful with Colgates) and stay in the water as long as possible which keeps you from knowing how you smell yourself. Nothing can keep you from knowing how the rest smell. Food is out of cans — British mostly! — and though the sea is full of fish its a festival when the fishermen catch as much as one grouper or snapper. Otherwise its heavenly if heaven is still what they used to say it was. We live in three cinder block rooms, keep peering around for clouds, play Mozart, who goes well with the blue, on the victrola and read like wood lice. I'm trying to finish a verse play[1] but that won't interest you! (Even I can learn.)

I won't try to answer your letter about why did we let the Russians into the war. If you have read anything you've been reading McCarthy. Unless its MacArthur. Why don't you read the sources? Why don't you read Stimson who was a Republican and no admirer of FDR? Why don't you read anything except what you do read? You have founded a whole position on an almost complete ignorance of your own country and its too late to do anything about it. Whenever I talk about your poetry which I do (for my own pleasure) a lot, youngsters jump down my throat with questions about your History. I reply that you haven't got any and that it doesn't matter but they won't let it go at that. Incidentally, your theory about the Russians getting into Berlin is — as you have probably forgotten — precisely Mr. Churchill's. You haven't had a decent word to say for him for thirty years if ever. Well, to Hell with it. I'm not going to argue McCarthyisms with a poet of your stature. I'm not even going to admit to myself that you are full of them.

Library of Congress bothers me. Plenty. I had a solemn promise that you would get books as requested. Since the shadowy business about Sprague Coolidge[2] I wonder if there's anybody IN there anymore. As for the bindery — I agree. Its dreadful. So dreadful I didn't even try to tackle it in the reorganization of the Institution. I was saving that for when I had some boards under my feet. Next thing I knew I was in the State Department and treading water.

Harvard. Another example of the indictment based on no evidence. I am not much of a teacher having been at it not over six years but if I know what a university ought to be that place is a university. You remember that crack in the Cantos — Teach? At Harvard, teach?[3] — well it damn well can be done and is. The gents you propose have long been used as you propose they shd. Only improvement I would like to see of major variety would be to get you into the teaching there yourself. The lads would learn. So would you.   yrs   Archie

TLS: YCAL

1. *J.B.: A Play in Verse*, published by Houghton Mifflin Company in March 1958, first performed at the Yale Drama School the following month, and successfully produced on Broadway beginning in December 1958. 2. Albert Sprague Coolidge had been denied a $250-a-year position as adviser to the Coolidge Foundation his mother had endowed at the Library of Congress after an FBI check had turned up "derogatory information" about him — presumed to be his past membership on the "subversive" North American Committee to Aid Spanish Democracy. 3. From *Canto 74*, the first of Pound's *Pisan Cantos*.

To Ezra Pound

Dear Ez: 17 April [1956]   Conway

Got back here couple of days ago to find eight foot drift where the yard ought to be. T'wuz a relief after that island which got baked to a cookie the last few weeks but still I'd like to see ground. Stopped off for a sight of Ernest in Habana on the way up — first view of the precipice in more than twenty yrs. He was off to Peru to catch gigantic marlin for forthcoming film of Old Man and Sea and was consequently totally surrounded by doctors taking his blood pressure and pricking his ear lobe but seemed otherwise in fine shape as did his wife Mary who is his finest wife with only possible exception of Pauline who was as fine a wife as anybody has a right to have. Wonderful dinner with ortolans and other rarities. No literary conversation which was a great relief — a relief which can always be counted on with Pappy. Learned for the first time of death of that great prosateur and agriculturist Mr. L. Bromfield, once of Paris, later of the Republican Party.[1] Seems Mr. Bromfield died (first in radio, then in pictures) of hepatitis. Which occasioned pleasant song on primitive model. Otherwise no news except what won't be news to you — that the consensus of opinion gathered from my Republican friends and political acquaintances is that it would be unwise as well as useless to approach Dept of Justice before the election. Number of reasons — among others that Brownell[2] is getting out regardless of election outcome. My notion therefore is to prepare for a serious approach to Department in November — not by me, naturally, but by someone who might be grata if, as I suspect, the Reps return. Unless you tell me not to I'm going to prepare to that end. When I go down to Cambridge wh. will have to be soon I'll inquire at the Press about the missing ms. yrn as usual Archie

TLS: YCAL

1. Louis Bromfield had died on March 18. 2. Attorney General Herbert Brownell, Jr.

To Gerald Murphy

Dear Daouw: 3 June [1956] [Conway]

Your card.[1] You are (as always) so right about those countries. One does not know how to figure them — whether as a kind of vast out-back of pain surrounding an island of not-pain as the darkness surrounds the not-dark, or, the other way around, as the intensely feeling center which, in the thoughtlessness of unpain, we circle and into which, from time to time, and always at the end, we fall. The one certainty is the one you name — that it is intensely personal — that there is only room within it for one's self alone — that no matter how one craves sympathy one resents too the intrusion of those who are not part of it — are only trespassers however generous. But it is in part for all these reasons that one feels at the end he would not for anything give up the journey through that place. Malraux says in that weak novel, *La Voie Royale*, that it is only in the presence of death one learns what one really loves. Pain, I suppose[,] is that presence, and it does sort out the meanings. I am no wiser than I was and certainly no better but I have seen something which I can go back to and see again even though I can't bring it forward with me. And when I see it again, as I shall, I shall recognize it. Which, for one who has been as ignorant of pain as I have been all my life, is a gift. I think you have always known more about it because you sense more than I do. Also you have been there more often.

I am sad about the 21st of June. Not that these returning dates mean anything in themselves but because they make a kind of structure on which one can hang the continuances of one's life — of which our long love for S and G is one of the dearest. I know you feel that that continuance is broken — broken by me — and I am sure you have good reason to think so, but it is not true. I wish you had felt you could come. But your instinct in these things is, as I have long known, truer than mine. You have made an art of what I have only blundered at. Perhaps the time will come when you will find it possible again. But we shall be thinking most of you. yours as always Archie

TLS: DONNELLY

1. Murphy had presumably sent a get-well card occasioned by M's hospitalization for removal of a nonmalignant tumor. Murphy had also informed M that he and his wife would be unable to attend the celebration in Conway, on June 21, of the Mac-Leishes' fortieth wedding anniversary.

To Ezra Pound

Dear Ez: 5 June [1956]   [Conway]

I am back in more or less circulation. . . . . . I think my wife, Ada, wrote you that they had opened me like Tut-Ankh's tomb and removed a foot of my Colon together with a little stranger who had no business there. No ill effects except a great lassitude and a belly like a portrait by Klee. From the size of the scar, you'd think they had removed J. Caesar. Maybe, as you suggest, it was Malcolm Cowley. Anyway I'll be fit as a . . . (why are fiddles fit? who knows that they are?) in a matter of weeks or so. While I was still in the horsepuddle Tom Eliot called me and we talked about the plan for next fall which he seemed to approve. Anyway he was going to think about it and write me. As soon as I can tuck myself together I am going to begin correspondence with a few assorted Senators in the hope of building up a little quiet support in that quarter. Nothing gives an attorney general courage like a friendly Senator. If I could only budge Lehman![1] Have you ever had dealings with him? I know him a bit and at least he is a Democrat and therefore may conceivably have read a poem somewhere. No Republican ever has. My notion is three or four interested Senators and a small, *very* small, group of people whose presence will impress an Attorney General and some one bird who will take the lead. If the Republicans are back it will have to be a Republican and who? Who? That's what keeps me awake. I don't know one who has the mind, the spirit and above all the heart. Do you?

One thing you might be thinking about if you will. Do you know a youngster who has judgment as well as brains and who could be counted on to produce a fair and objective (as they say) resumé of those broadcasts and who would be willing to take it on this summer as a service to the Muses and the cause of reason and truth? I assume [Julien] Cornell must have a copy of the monitorings. Am I right?   yrs   Archie

TLS: YCAL

1. Herbert H. Lehman, an influential liberal senator from New York who, as a Jew, was a potentially forceful opponent of Pound's continued incarceration.

To Alexis Saint-Léger Léger

Dear Alexis- 9 June [1956] [Conway]

I have reread your letter many times since I first and most ineffectually tried to answer it. Each time it renews the warmth about my heart — warmth I badly need these days. Why does the process of recuperation take place in such darkness of the spirit — as though, to "recover" one's self one had first to lose the taste for one's self, even the belief in one's self? In the illness itself one insists on one's self — one believes in one's self voraciously — but afterwards. . . . . I am physically almost well but spiritually I have such distaste for everything I have done that I cannot bear to think of it. It is there that your affection strengthens me. What you love must have value.

And how perceptively you see Ada's part.

Char. What do you make of it?[1] I am sure that the inadequacy of my French accounts for a great part of my difficulty. But not all of it. The tone is wrong for me. There is something voulu about those paradoxes, those contradictions. "Moderate as stone, I remain a mother with far-away cradles". So Jackson Mathews' translation. To me the juxtaposition does not let the light in as it does in Chinese poems sometimes — the collision of the unexpected. There is merely the collision of the unexpected. I hear the crash and am startled — a little — but not enlightened. To Marguerite [Caetani] he is the wonder of the world. I am blind to this wonder. I am sure, as I say, that the blindness is in my own eyes. But is it only there?

Pound. I am fighting feathers and losing my way. Ever since I went to see him at St. Elizabeth's last fall I have been determined to do something to get him out of that horror. When, after many months of thinking and of talking to the wise, I write him what I have in mind to attempt he replies with two pages of irrelevancies — personal attacks on those whose help I had thought of enlisting — that sort of thing. What can one do? One cannot leave him there to rot. But whoever offers him a hand will have his fingers broken.

Could you come to us for a weekend or something of the kind on your way to Mina's?[2] We would love so to have you. We will try to arrange the grandchildren so that they won't be here then if you will suggest a time. Will you? yours ever Archie

TLS: FSJP

1. René Char, *Hypnos Waking: Poems and Prose,* selected and translated by Jackson Matthews et al. (New York: Random House, 1956). 2. Mina Curtiss, a friend of Léger's and a neighbor of the MacLeishes'.

To Ezra Pound

Dear Ez: 5 July [1956]   [Conway]

Yours of the 27th was a great help. I'm beginning to see if not the light at least the direction of the light. I don't mean the substance of your argument but its tendency. At least its relevance to the decision we have to make — or you have to make, for my wish in this matter is to follow your wish.

A word first about substance. When you say that FDR and others would murder any man who suggests taking Article One, Section 3 Para 3 seriously you are talking I suppose in parables. I:3:3 provides, of course, that you can't be a Senator until you are 30 and have been 9 years in the country and, further, that you must reside in the state from wh. you are elected. Which, equally of course, doesn't quite add up to reason for murder even if FDR had been what your fairy tale makes him out to be. I am equally bebaffled and bebuggered by your dark suggestion that the Supreme Court pays no mind to I:9:2 which provides that the privilege of habeas corpus shall not be suspended except when in invasion or rebellion the public safety requires. When? In what case? You will have to be a hell of a lot more specific to persuade me that FDR did not uphold the Constitution. Have you fallen for the Republican line on that? So far as I know no Republican above the level of McCormick[1] ever believed in it. Or maybe you now accept the bankers' doctrine that FDR let the Constitution down when we went off gold? And the same thing goes for your theory that Mussolini was the lad to stop Hitler and that we should have sat back and let him do it. We'd be sitting back still only the place would be Buchenwald. Why and how a man with your passion for truth and independence of mind and the art of poetry which you so superbly practise can fail to believe — to have believed and to believe still — in the supreme necessity of the war against Hitler beats me. Does your case against FDR really come down to anything else but the fact that he saw what Hitler was and dared to fight him and won? Until you can provide EVIDENCE other than dark hints and dirty adjectives I shall continue to believe that he was a very great president of the United States.

But this is by the way because the real significance of your letter to me is not its argument, which I don't accept, but the light it throws on the real issue between us. Let me be as specific as I can because this is important — and the time, as I have been saying, is running out.

I have been assuming that the objective is to get you out of St. Elizabeths.

I have further been assuming, on the basis of the best advice I can get (and I have talked to a lot of informed people) that the best —

indeed the only — way of accomplishing that objective rapidly is to persuade the new Attorney General[2] to nol pros the indictment.

My suggestions, and particularly the suggestion that I try to build up support among a few influential senators, have been directed to that end.

NOW

If I read your letter correctly you are saying that I am wrong not only in my suggestion as to method but in the objective itself: that what you want is as you put it "for a few people to learn the FACTS" — meaning, I take it, the facts about your position over the past many years of your life as a writer including the Rome broadcasts.

This is, of course, a perfectly reasonable thing to want — something any man might well want in your place or out of it.

But what it involves, as of course you realize, is a renewal of the trial — or a second trial if that is the proper procedure.

If that is what you want, then clearly I am way off base and should desist and withdraw.

BUT IS IT?

On that point I have to be absolutely clear. My position in all this is simple. I want to do what I can to get you out because it hurts me personally and seems to me a disgrace to the country that you are held there still after all these years. But obviously I am not going to do what *you* don't want done in order to end this pain and remove this disgrace.

Will you do one thing for me? Will you write me your answer to that specific question leaving all the arguments out for the moment? We can pick them up later any time you want — though I think there is very little chance we'll come out in agreement about anything except your integrity which I will never doubt: your information may be horse-crackers but your heart is sound.   yrn   Archie

TLS: YCAL

1. Colonel Robert R. McCormick, editor and publisher of the *Chicago Tribune* and a vocal opponent of President Roosevelt and the New Deal. 2. Attorney General Herbert Brownell, Jr., had announced his intention to resign, but did not do so until November 1957. M hoped for (and got) better results from his successor, William P. Rogers.

To Adlai E. Stevenson[1]

Dear Adlai: "July 10 et seq et seq" [1956]   Conway

I'm pretty sure you won't want to read all this but I'm going to write it out anyway. In order to get down the "words" you want its going to be necessary, first, to know what the words are for. Which means not only for *whom* they are to be spoken but *AGAINST whom*. Particularly — this campaign being what it is — *against* whom.

The obvious answer is President Eisenhower, but that answer is also obviously wrong — and the obvious source of a great part of our difficulty in planning what to say and do. It is not President Eisenhower who is the adversary to be overcome, but President Eisenhower's popularity, and they are not at all the same thing. President Eisenhower is not strong. You have to go back to Coolidge to find a president who has exerted as little leadership either in his administration or in the country. He is not an intellectual force or a moral force or, indeed, any kind of force. And his subordinates are as unimpressive as he. His Secretary of State [John Foster Dulles] is as close to a figure of fun as a man can get without arriving there. His Attorney General is a politician without principles. And so on down. If President Eisenhower and the Eisenhower administration were the adversary it would be difficult to lose. President Eisenhower's popularity, however, is something else again. It would be my guess, subject to correction by the eminent historians by whom you are surrounded, that no president in the history of the Republic has been as popular at the end of four years in the White House as the present incumbent — more universally and genuinely liked.

Our first problem, then, if we want to know precisely what we are up against, is to decide what this extraordinary popularity, so wholly out of proportion to its object, actually IS. If it is clear (as it is) that it does not reflect any particular achievement or quality of the man who is thus admired it must reflect a peculiar state of mind among the admirers. What state of mind?

Infantilism? Do we revere the President because he is a nice guy — one of the nicest — or because he has an elastic smile? I shouldn't think so. We have our share of infantilism — perhaps more than our share — but not enough to account for the phenomenon to be explained.

Militarism? The love of generals? Undoubtedly President Eisenhower's accomplishments in the War play their part, but the President is not popular BECAUSE he was a general. How often does the country think of [Omar] Bradley who deserves at least as much credit and who was a fighting general in addition?

What then?

The answer, I submit, is to be found precisely in the discrepancy between admiration and object: in the fact that President Eisenhower is very evidently admired not for what he is but for what he isn't: not for what he does but for what he doesn't. He doesn't have ideas. He doesn't say anything you have to think about. He doesn't act. He doesn't lead. But at the same time he is not a nonentity, not a Harding. He is a Somebody — very much of a Somebody: a Somebody who fills the seat but doesn't use it.

The state of mind which makes President Eisenhower popular, in other words, is the state of mind which wants a president in the White House who will look like a president and make like a president but who will not talk like one or think like one or act like one.* [*MacLeish wrote in the margin:* *a hard-won popularity — won at the cost of never fighting anyone or anything]

Now, that state of mind is doubtless compounded of many elements not excluding that curious longing to return to the womb of history which is mis-called Isolationism. But whatever elements it may or may not include the dominant sentiment is complacency. It is only when you believe or can persuade yourself that things are about right as they are that you can indulge in the luxury of not trying to go anywhere else. A Coolidge would not have been popular or possible in 1916 or 1932. He was both in the middle Twenties. Eisenhower's kind of presidenting is acceptable and, indeed, admired because the country has gotten it into its head today that nothing else is needed. In Liebling's² judgment, what the country as a whole wants is for everything to stay the way it is. To which I should add — only more so.

But if all this is true then the conclusion is fairly plain. If our real adversary is not President Eisenhower but his popularity, and if his popularity is an expression not of the man but of the public attitude toward the man, and if the public attitude toward the man is a reflection of a general public complacency with regard to the national situation, then it is that complacency we must attack. Pounding away at Eisenhower's failure to lead will come to nothing unless we can drive home the realization that a failure to lead may well be disastrous. The putter is Mr. Eisenhower's symbol as the umbrella was Neville Chamberlain's³ but there is nothing wrong with a putter unless something more effective is demonstrably required.

If we reach this conclusion then we should admit, I think, that the situation is not without its irony. We Democrats may not be directly responsible for the national complacency but we are responsible for the assumptions on which it rests. It was we who led the country to believe that our national mission was merely to *resist* Communism, and that the menace of Communism was merely military and con-spiratorial, and that once we had enough planes and enough police-men we would be "safe". That doctrine made inevitable the defensive psychology which has dominated American thinking for ten years past and prepared the way, as anyone could have foreseen it would, for the mood of complacency which followed, once the merely military danger subsided and the Red scare petered out.

But though we Democrats are guilty (and God knows we have paid for our guilt) we are not the only ones who will suffer. It is the country, not the party, which is endangered by the public mood. What is at stake is not our immediate safety from military attack or conspiratorial subversion. Military attack is increasingly unlikely and the danger of any considerable part of the American people turning Communist is so small that even McCarthy and Walters[4] can't see it with the naked eye. What is at stake is our greatness as a people. We have before us in France and Britain two examples of what can happen to nations which become complacent in the face of historic change; which go on preparing for the last war, or living in the last generation; — which lose control of their destiny.

If we go on much longer in our present state of mind; if we persist in believing that the one problem with which we are faced in our generation is Communism — that the whole stir and ferment of our time is in some way or other merely an aspect of the Communist Revolution; if we continue to act on the assumption that Communism can be overcome by planes and policemen and to determine our relations with other peoples on the basis of their willingness or unwillingness to line up on our side of a future war against Communism, we may very well wake up a generation from now to find that history has passed us by, that the great social and political revolution of our time has taken place without us and that we are no longer a dynamic and creative force in the world, a great nation.

It is here that the national interest and the Democratic interest coincide. It is *actually* (not merely politically) true that a continuation of the state of mind of the past four years (and more) and a continuation of the kind of unthinking, unacting, unleading leadership which that state of mind has accepted, and by which, in turn, that state of mind is nurtured, might well be disastrous to the United States.

How then is this complacency to be attacked? In part, quite clearly, by scaring the country into a realization that "things the way they are" are NOT right. This involves a re-education of the people but political campaigns and popular education have long been synonymous — at least in theory. What is needed is a reexamination of the Time and particularly of the revolutionary forces in the Time and of our relation to them and theirs to us. Is Communism, as the French intellectuals believe, the great revolutionary dynamic of the Time? Is it still a revolutionary force at all? Is it not rather an established form of government in a considerable part of the world — a form of government which is not only established but which, as the Communists themselves have been forced to admit, is already rotten with the diseases from which all established police states suffer? Have we perhaps permitted the Communist Revolution to obsess our minds too long? Should we begin to think in terms of the great world revolution which is sweeping across Asia and will inevitably reach every "backward" area of the world in every continent? Should we think of this revolution as a force — an enormous force — in its own right rather than as a mere consequence or extension of the Communist Revolution? Should we try to realize that this great new revolution, though it has infinite possibilities for human good[,] has also infinite possibilities for human hurt — our own included? Should we try to see that the form it takes in country after country is of vital importance to us, not merely in terms of our present struggle with the Communists but in terms of our ultimate survival as a great nation? Communism is as evil as it ever was, and Russia is enormously powerful, but is it in Moscow, as so many Americans now think, that our future will be decided? Is it not in America and in the world? And if it is in the world — this rapidly changing, new, revolutionary world — can we afford to drift, putter in hand, putting our trust in policemen and in planes? To survive in the future must we not have a hand in shaping it, and to shape the future must we not *act?*

These things are difficult for a Democrat to talk about — difficult for anyone to talk about. We are paralyzed by our horror and hatred of Communism like a man confronted by a cobra. But some time we are going to have to free ourselves in order to act and the time is short. It is possible now, in my opinion, to state the essentials: that though we must be prepared to defend ourselves against the Communists we cannot live defensively; that the time is a time of enormous change and that, in a time of enormous change, a great nation cannot stand still, cannot content itself with "things the way they are", must shape the change, must foresee, must think, above all must act.

That is one side of the attack on complacency: to talk turkey to the American people.

The other side is equally important: not to scare the country into action but to inspire it to action — and I mean quite literally inspire. The fact is, and I think we all know it, that the American mind and spirit have been on dead center for the better part of the past ten years. One reason is the lack of spiritual leadership during that period. Another is the success of the Communists and the Anti-Communists, between them, in making the old American ideals — love of mankind, love of peace, hope for a better future — suspect. It would take a Jonathan Swift to make us see what we have become but some day the portrait will be painted. It is time that the Democratic party, the traditional party of these ideals, should reclaim them: should dare to say that a nation which, like India, wants peace and a better life is a nation Americans admire; that the aspiration of the peoples of Asia for a decent human life is an aspiration the United States can understand and will support. To make honest citizens of our hearts — nothing would restore us to self-respect more effectively. And the way to make honest citizens of our hearts is to unite them again to the great causes in which they have always believed. The greatest triumph of Communism has been its triumph in turning us from ourselves. . . . . and that triumph was assured by men who think of themselves as the implacable enemies of Communism.

* * *

I think your acceptance speech at Chicago should go to the heart of this problem if you see it at all as I do. I think it should state that the adversary in this campaign is the complacency of a great part of the American people — and should state, with a decent respect, why it is *not* Eisenhower or his Administration. I think it should state the case against that complacency. I think it should recall us to ourselves.

You may very well wholly disagree: I realize that this is, much of it, dangerous footing and that it may seem to you footling footing as well. But if you want me to try my hand at any part of it I'll gladly do so. Only, in that case, please return this. I have no copy.

And again forgive me for taking so much time and space.

Ada sends her love   yours ever   Archie

TLS: NjP

1. Well on his way to securing a second Democratic presidential nomination, Stevenson, as he had done in 1952, invited M to contribute ideas and words to his campaign. This letter was offered as a preliminary draft for possible use in Stevenson's acceptance speech at the nominating convention in Chicago on August 17. 2. A. J. Liebling, the *New Yorker* writer. 3. The British prime minister (1937–1940) whose policy of appeasement toward Hitler and Nazi Germany culminated in the Munich Pact. 4. Francis E. Walter, chairman of the House Committee on Un-American Activities.

To Ezra Pound

Dear Ezry: 16 November [1956] [Cambridge]

The unhappy election is now ten days down wind and tide and the time has come to proceed proceedingly. I am therefore at work on a letter which four or five of your most distinguished contemporaries might sign, to be presented to the Attorney General with a view to requesting — or, better, I suppose, *suggesting* since they will have no standing to represent you — a Nol Pros of the indictment. I shall clear the draft first with the psychiatrists at St. Elizabeth's since their opinion will eventually be asked, and thereafter with the wisest lawyers I know, and shall hope to have it ready for presentation within a month's time. Who should present it is, of course, the question. Certainly I, as a Democrat who worked with that dreadful creature FDR, would scarcely be the right man. If Tom [Eliot] is to be in this country he would be. If not we will have to take counsel. I shall also begin again my attempt to find support in the Senate — among Republican Senators. Of whom I know very few but still. . . . . How are you?   best   Archie

TLS: YCAL

To Adlai E. Stevenson

Dear Adlai: 18 November [1956]   [Cambridge]

I know how high the mountain of mail on your desk must be and I have not wanted to add to it but I can't let the days go by without telling you how proud of you Ada and I are and how much we think the country owes you and how certain we are that time will let the light through. If ever a man deserved well of his fellow men you do. I wasn't happy about the campaign all the way through but neither, I am sure, were you. What is important is that you defined the crucial issue which all the flatulent fat-headedness in Washington has done its best to obscure and that it can never be undefined again. I have raged to see how the papers which, with that wonderful Republican unanimity, derided your estimates of the situation before the election now adopt them. Don't answer this.   our love to you   Archie

TLS: NjP

To Ezra Pound

Dear Ez: 7 December [1956]   Cambridge

All I can say — if Harvard ISn't a university then there is something very wrong with you because you do a lot of teaching in it. You and HSM had them in the aisles a month ago.[1]

I'll send Chao's cur. vit. around to the Far Eastern boys. Whether they need anybody I haven't the foggiest. It would have helped if he had put his address on it.

Had a run in with a student — one of your great admirers — who told me with tears in his eyes he understood you were tied up with some juvenile delinquent who has been preaching hate down in Tennessee.[2] I told him he ought to be ashamed of himself: that the one thing you hated worse than stupidity was bigotry and the one thing you hated worse than either was nastiness. He wasn't convinced. He said he KNEW. Went off nearly sobbing.

I have put together a rough draft of the letter to the Atty Genl and sent it to Tom [Eliot] to put it in such shape as would merit his sig.. He doesn't care to sign other men's words and why should he! Have also talked to Robert [Frost] who agrees to sign sight unseen. As soon as I get the draft back I'll send it to Ernest. Problem then will be to find the right man to present it. Maybe I can persuade Robert himself. Robert thinks we ought to add Louis Unterm[e]yer for tactical reasons: believes he would do it. Any views?

I am strongly advised to take two bites of the cherry — i.e. to apply first for action by the Dept of Justice nol-prossing the indictment — i.e. to get rid of the charges first. It sounds sensible to me and I have prepared the draft accordingly. Once the charges are out of the way the other problems can be approached sensibly and in an orderly way. Hope you approve. faithfully Archie

TLS: YCAL

1. Pound's *Hugh Selwyn Mauberley* was a regular feature of M's Harvard lecture course, Humanities 130, "An Approach to Poetry." 2. John Kasper, a young book-seller-publisher who, under Pound's influence, had toured parts of the South de-nouncing racial integration, Jews, and the Supreme Court. His activities in Tennessee had recently resulted in his arrest, and the attendant publicity, in which Pound's name figured prominently, complicated the efforts to secure Pound's release.

To Ernest Hemingway

Dear Pappy: 15 December [1956] Cambridge

Have at last lined up an effort to help Ezra which sounds as though it might make sense. With the backing of the head of St. Elizabeth's[1] we propose to approach the Attorney General to ask for a Nol Pros which will dispose of the charges thus putting the question of release on a medical basis etc. etc.. I have drafted the letter and have sent it off to Eliot who has agreed to sign. Frost will join him. I have been hoping I could get you to be the third. (I am not well liked in the Brownell office and my name had better be omitted). We don't want a big list. Three of that caliber is plenty. And there will be no publicity — I mean no publication of the letter. Would you do it? And if you would where can I send the document to reach you? Best to Miss Mary and much love to you both Archie

TLS: JFK

1. Dr. Winfred Overholser.

To Ernest Hemingway

Dear Pappy: 8 January 1957   [Conway]

Would you write Chris Herter[1] about Ezra making again the point you made so well in your letter to the Atty Gen — that it is the US which will suffer if Pound is allowed to rot in St. Elizabeth's?

Chris is much impressed by the fact that you are interested and a page from you would help a lot.

I went around to see him because it became very clear that [William P.] Rogers, the new [Deputy] Atty Gen'l, wasn't going to do anything positive. Chris heard me out but was obviously worried by the possibility that, once released, Ezra might embarrass the government by shooting his face off in his usual way. The answer, in theory, is that the government has no right to keep him in an insane asylum for *that* reason — but the theoretical answer needs bolstering and you can bolster it powerfully.

Don't know what Chris can accomplish. Dulles[2] is apparently doing everything he can to wall Chris in and discourage him into quitting. But he would be listened to in Justice.

Are you better? Do they let you drink anything? I wish I could hop in there this afternoon and look at you and that svelt Miss Mary who takes all hearts.   our love to you both   Archie

TLS: JFK

1. Christian A. Herter, U.S. undersecretary of state.   2. Secretary of State John Foster Dulles.

To Ernest Hemingway

Dear Pappy: [*c.* 14 January 1957]   Cambridge

Enclosed is the letter I wrote you about. It seemed wise and now seems even wiser to have three signers only — you and Frost and Eliot. I don't know much about Brownell but I should guess he would be more apt to respond to the suggestion of three highly meaningful names than to a column of signatures.

The text is Tom Eliot's based on a draft of mine. It has been kept as unexcited as possible on the theory that what we want to do is to persuade. One thing, however, needs explanation. Just before I started drafting this thing Dr. Overholzer, the head doc at St. Elizabeths, reversed his field and intimated that we ought not to talk about the "release" of Ezra at this point but only about quashing the charges. Apparently the doc thinks Ezra has slipped back a bit. I don't believe it. His letters to me are more coherent than they have ever been. But, in any case, since success depends on keeping the doc with us, the letter is drafted to raise the question of nol prossing the charges only. Once the charges are quashed I feel quite certain the medical aspect of the case can be handled. In any event we will be that much nearer a solution

I know the text won't be all that you would have wished but I hope you will sign notwithstanding. Its pretty hard to get you three together on one piece of paper and if there are any shortcomings charge them to me.

Since I am going back to Antigua on the 25th I'd be grateful if you would send the letter to J. Laughlin[1] at. . . . . . Hell, I haven't his address. . . . . . Send it to Miss Geffen, American Academy of Arts and Letters, 633 West 155th St. New York City. She will send it along through Laughlin to the Attorney General.

Love to Mary and to thineself   Archie

TLS: JFK

1. James Laughlin of New Directions, Pound's principal American publisher.

To McGeorge Bundy

Dear Mac: 21 February [1957]   Antigua

You know how to measure time down here. Multiply that by mornings spent on my play and afternoons getting ready for Rome and you will understand why I have let a month go by without writing you about Nate's and your most heartening suggestion that I stay on after my to-me-still-incredible retirement. (Stay on — as of course I understand — on a year by year basis until you repent of your bargain or senility catches up with me).

As you know, there is no question, so far as I am concerned, on the merits. Harvard has given me far more than I could ever give Harvard, I am deeply devoted to the university and I can't imagine living without it. The problem has been Ada — who has never once peeped herself. I witnessed the consequences of trying to move into, live in briefly, and leave 4 Willard Street last fall and I wouldn't put her through that again without servants for anything — even my own dearest happiness. It was that question we had to work out and we have, I think, done it. We will sell Willard Street, distribute the furniture and work out a hotel arrangement somewhere during the falls. It isn't ideal but it will work.

All this is of minor interest to you as Dean but of considerable interest to you as friend. Let me now address the Dean. You suggested to me, when we talked in December, that I give English S (my advanced writing course) and a series of public lectures: four or five or six. It is a fascinating but scary proposal. English S, yes — obviously. But wouldn't it look presumptuous for a member of the faculty to announce a half dozen public lectures? When I asked Harry [Levin], who is a sure barometer on these things, he replied in effect: "Certainly not. That is what I am doing this spring in California". But its one thing to come to Berkeley from Cambridge and offer a series of public lectures: its another thing to lift one's pipes in Cambridge when one belongs in Cambridge. All this is a way of saying that I'd like to do just that if it doesn't seem presumptuous and bumptious. For I don't want to go on with my Humanities 130 "Approach to Poetry". That course devours my tripes. It takes about forty hours a week in preparation and haunts my dreams besides.

When you have had a chance to talk this all over with Nate and with anyone else who could bear to listen will you drop me a line in care of the American Academy in Rome? We should get there, via Guadeloupe and Lisbon, about the sixth.

The financial arrangements are distinctly secondary though I should hope for enough to cover my hotel rooms during the fall! Schedule also is secondary though I should like to feel I could get away during the reading period *if* I wanted to. So too is title — though I *hope* I may hang onto the chair of which I am so proud. The real question is what you want me to do.

My best to Nate. My love to Mary.   yours as ever
TLS: MH (ARCHIVES)   Archie

To Ernest Hemingway

Dear Pappy: 3 June [1957]   [Conway]
    How be you?
    Thought much of you as I surveyed the scene of the great liberation first from outside and then, with the aid of a brace of Martinis, from inside.[1] Matter of fact, all over Europe I kept thinking of you and our youth. Which was younger youth mit dich but still youth even mit me. (I never learned German grammar)
    Mountain of mail waiting and a copy of your cable on top. So happens both Frost and Eliot were in London last week and I had a chance to talk to them both. Also with Pound's daughter, Mary, at Sermione.
    What it boils down to is that Frost would be willing to go to Washington when he gets back in a couple of weeks to call on the bird in the Dept of Justice who wrote that he would like to talk to youse.[2] Could you be there at some date convenient to you both? If not would

you spell out your ideas for Frost to present? Or how would you like to do it?

I know Dr. Overholzer's views and I also know — or did know — Ezra's and I would be glad to go down though I don't think my presence at the interview itself would help much since Brownell and I are not exactly pals. Would you like me to write you at length about the correspondence and events of the past year along the lines of your cable or is there any chance of our meeting to talk about it? I'd like to do it the best way for you. Will you write me? Love to Miss Mary

yrs ever   Archie

TLS: JFK

1. M had been traveling in Italy, Greece, and possibly elsewhere in Europe and the Mediterranean. The "scene" to which he refers is unidentified.   2. William P. Rogers, deputy attorney general, who had written to Frost, Eliot, and Hemingway to that effect on April 10.

To Kathleen Morrison[1]

Dear Kay: 17 June [1957]   [Conway]

I am writing you because I don't know how to reach Robert who must, I suppose, be back by now. Please forgive the trouble.

Robert told me in London he would be willing to talk to the Assistant Attorney General who wrote him about the Pound case. I said I would go down with him if he went. Its a lot to ask of him in the heat of summer. However, if we let this chance go by it may go by for good.

I should like to suggest two things:

First, that Robert should reply to the Assistant Attorney General — actually Deputy Attorney General — whose name is William P. Rogers — if he has not already done so. In his letter of April 10 Mr. Rogers said the Attorney General would like to meet with Frost, Eliot and Hemingway and that he, Rogers, would be writing again soon to arrange a conference. Probably Robert has already replied but if he hasn't it might be helpful to write now suggesting a time when Robert could come. Hemingway MIGHT be willing to come up too. I've written him. Eliot is, of course, in England.

Second, I'd be grateful if you or Robert would let me know whether he feels he can go and if so when so that I can make my plans since I have to do a bit of running around this summer for lectures. I'm bankrupt what with Europe and all.

Love to you both   Archie

TLS: NhD

1. Robert Frost's long-time secretary-manager and friend.

To Ernest Hemingway

Dear Pappy: 19 June 1957 [Conway]

What a bloody goddam business! After everything you have had to take in the last few years to have to take that too! Of course I understand. I wouldn't let you come up even if you wanted to risk it because you shouldn't risk it and it isn't necessary.[1]

Let me answer your various questions about Ezra first.

(1) Ezra's attitude. I went down to see him in December of 55. Second time I'd ever seen him. What I saw made me sick and I made up my mind I wouldn't rest till he got out. Not only for his sake but for the good name of the country: after ten years it was beginning to look like persecution and if he died there we'd never wash the stain out. So I began writing him. Told him I had been informed by some alleged friend of his that he wouldn't accept out without a presidential pardon which would include an indictment of FDR. Told him he couldn't have a pardon because he had never been convicted of anything and as for FDR if FDR wasn't right in opposing Adolph and old Musso then I was the crazy boy and I ought to be in there too. We carried on along those lines for some reams of the usual kind of blather and finally I told him I had been talking to the lawyers all of whom agreed there was only one way out — to try to persuade the Atty Gen to nol pros the indictment. Would he accept that solution. More correspondence. Finally, yes — he would. He has stuck to that ever since and his solicitor in London whom Tom Eliot got me to write agrees also.

(2) Medical opinion. When I went down in winter of 55 I went to see Dr. Overholzer who is the head of St. Elizabeths. Good psycho (Harvard) and good man. He told me he would let Ez out in eighteen minutes if the Dept of Justice would nol pros the indictment. Said he had never thought Ez's "treason" amounted to much anyway. That, however[,] was '55. Last fall when I had gotten Ez to agree (or, more accurately, when *he* had agreed) to the nol pros I wrote Overholzer again. This time he was much more cautious: told me I ought not to talk about Ez's "release" but only about the nol prossing of the indictment. Said he was not at all sure Ez could be released at once but was still certain the indictment ought to be dropped so that the problem would become medical merely. I interpreted this to mean — and I may be wrong — that Ez has gone off a bit but that, with the indictment out of the way, and the pressure off, it might be possible to ease him out into more bearable surroundings and, in any case, to get the U. S. and A. out from under. I therefore told Tom Eliot, who has been a bit nervous about the whole thing, that this was a two-bites-to-the-cherry case and that we had best take the first bite first. Frost, who doesn't like Ezra from

397

London days (and with pretty good reason) never boggled at all. He may not like Ez but he wants to get him out and bit by bit is as good as all in one swallow. Anyway we went ahead on that basis and I hope you will agree it was wise.

(3) Department of Justice reaction. The Department of Justice has been brushing off inquirers for years. They responded to your letter by saying they would review the whole case and they now want to talk to you. That may not be hopeful but it is at least less hopeless. The great obstacle for them and for us is of course this bird Kasper. Mary de Rachlewiltz, Pound's daughter, told me at Sermiento last month that she had seen him hanging around her father a couple of years ago and had warned Ezra that he was no good. Ez was flattered by him and told her not to get flustered. Turns out Mary was right. He has given the opposition, which hates Ezra for his anti-Semitism, just the handle they need. Brownell is a politician first last and all the time and he wont do anything impolitic. If we are to get anywhere we must get there in spite of Kasper. But we wont have Ezra's help. He hasn't replied to the letter I wrote him three months ago telling him what I thought of K..

(4) Family situation. Before I met Mary de Rachlewiltz I was pretty desperate. Dorothy [Mrs. Ezra] Pound has apparently no influence and though she has a little money of her own she couldn't carry Ezra if he were let out and unloaded on her. But Mary is an intelligent woman and a good one and she wants to take her father over. If the indictment could be dropped and if Dulles could be persuaded to give him a passport (an unlikely eventuality given Dulles's mental and moral parts) Mary would take care of him and he could die in peace up there in that Merano country you know and love so well.

I think that covers the facts. If it doesn't wire me and I'll try to fill in.

Now about procedure. Frost is now back from England and is probably up in Vermont. At least I think he is back. I had written him, before I got your letter, asking him to reply to the Deputy Attorney General (Rogers) and say he was available for an interview. I told him I would be glad to go to Washington with him but that I wasn't a good bet to interview the Atty Genl not being a Republican — which is very important to Atty Genl. I haven't heard from Frost but I make the following suggestion:

Why don't you write Frost (BUT SEND THE LETTER TO ME HERE) telling him your doctor thinks you had better not fly up to Washington just now but spelling out your feelings about the argument to be made: that Ezra has been in there for eleven years; that you understand the psychos say he can never be brought to trial; that his continued incarceration under those circumstances has already done us considerable damage abroad and may do us more — particularly if he should die in St. Elizabeths; that he is a very great poet and although that may not entitle him to special treatment it raises considerations which you as an American think should be kept in mind since one of the great pastimes abroad is nailing our asses to the barn door as bloody materialists who care nothing for art or artists (you might quote your remarks about Pound when you got the Nobel Prize — they were very impressive); that you are particularly concerned with the hook the U. S. and A. has got itself caught on in this affair but that you are also concerned for Pound and that you believe that, if the indictment were nol prossed[,] it might well be possible to turn him over to his daughter at Merano who can and would take care of him.

Forgive me for seeming to suggest what you should say. You know I am not doing that but merely suggesting what I would say myself. You can do it far far better.

What I have in mind then is this: with your letter and one I will try to get from Eliot[,] Frost and I will go down to Washington and Frost will talk to Rogers or Healey[2] or whoever and will leave your letters with him and we will hope.

I can't see anything better to do. It would be wonderful to come down and talk it all out and prepare a statement or, better still, get hold of the legal attache at the Embassy. Maybe we should do that. But I know Frost couldn't make it just now and I know I shouldn't because I have been away for five months and I have got to catch up on myself. But thank you for wanting me to come. I wish I could not for Pound reasons but for my own.

Anyway think about it and let me know what more I can tell you and how you feel about this suggestion and anything else you want to say. We love Miss Mary and we send you our love and we are very much worried but will be quiet if you will tell us what happens and how things go and how you really feel   yours   Archie

TLS: JFK

1. Hemingway had written of health problems, the lingering effects of his airplane accidents in 1954, that would prevent him from participating in the approaching meeting with Rogers in Washington. 2. Harold H. Healy, Jr., executive assistant to Attorney General Brownell.

To Robert Frost[1]

Dear Robert: 28 June [1957] [Conway]

Bless you. I won't forget the promise and I know you won't. I don't suppose we could tease you down here? Would you come if I drove up and got you?

About Ezra — I agree. And I don't feel too sure of my judgment but I can't bear to have him rot. That's about all I am wholly sure of.

I have asked Miss Geffen at the Academy to write the Deputy Attorney General asking whether July 19 (late in the PM) or the 20th would do. Of course I would go along if you want me. I have also written Ernest asking him to send you a full statement of his views and I shall ask Tom to do the same so that you will go fully armed. Maybe it would be easier if their letters came to me so that I could turn the whole file over to you.

More when I know more. It was GOOD to see you in London.

yours aye   Archie

TLS: NhD

1. The June 24 letter from Frost to which this letter replies appears in Lawrance Thompson, ed., *Selected Letters of Robert Frost* (New York: Holt, Rinehart & Winston, 1964), page 569.

To Robert Frost

Dear Robert: 9 July [1957]   Conway

Kay called up to ask if we had heard from the Depy Atty Gen'l & to talk plans.

We have heard: his Secy writes that he is out of town but implies that he will be back before our date. She will write again.

As for plans, Kay says you will be in Fairfield Conn. on Thursday the 17th of July & could start for Washington the next morning. What would you think of our meeting in Washington that afternoon if Rogers can see you? I *believe* (don't know) there are trains from Boston to Washington which stop at Stamford. If you could get in by 3 PM (the hour you fixed & which we communicated to Rogers) I could meet you at the train. We could then come back here on Saturday & I'd get you home. Let me know how it strikes you. I have to be in Louisville the 17th & I could go directly to Wash. & wait for you.

I enclose the letter from Hemingway which seems to me very fine & which I was holding for you.[1] I am sending this registered to protect the enclosure. Be sure to bring it along won't you? I'll hope to have Eliot's by that time

Ada sends her love   yours ever   Archie

Forgive this handwriting. I've been chopping wood & my fingers knot up. Can you make it out?

ALS: NhD

1. Hemingway's letter to Frost, dated June 28, appears in Carlos Baker, ed., *Ernest Hemingway: Selected Letters, 1917–1961* (New York: Charles Scribner's Sons, 1981), pages 878–880.

To Ernest Hemingway

Dear Pappy: 21 July 1957 [Conway]

Just a line by way of report.

Your letter was fine and Robert thought it was fine too. We went down day before yesterday. Hot as hell. Robert came all the way down from Ripton Vermont.

General report is, I think, hopeful. What it boils down to is (a) Department of Justice realizes the case is tough (b) Department would apparently be willing to drop the indictment if somebody could come forward with a sound plan for taking care of Pound outside St. Elizabeths; (c) sending him to Italy to live with his natural daughter is not considered a sound plan because it would provide a "story" for the papers and because it is feared that there may be — are — people in Italy who would like to make use of him, get him talking; (d) nothing can be done while the Kasper case is active and the relation between Pound and that bastard is under discussion: this may mean delay for as much as a year.

Robert and I were, on balance, encouraged. We incline to agree about Italy, much as Pound wants to go there and pleasant as it would be to have him there. I think you will agree too because you were troubled by the possibility that he might get into bad trouble by working his jaw. What he says here, once he is out of the hatch, won't matter much. In Italy he would be very audible. As to an alternative plan, we may have something to suggest later. Any ideas you may have would be welcome. We also think the less said about all this at the moment the better. The Dept people agree.

                    love to Miss Mary   yours ever   Archie

Do you mind if I send a copy of yr letter to RF to Chris Herter in the State Department? Might help later.

TLS: JFK

To Ezra Pound

Dear Ezra: 22 July 1957 Conway

Robert Frost and I went to see the boys at the Department of Justice last Friday. Hot as it was, Robert came all the way down from Ripton, Vermont.

We had with us letters from Tom Eliot and Ernest.

What the conversations boiled down to was about what we expected: though maybe a little more hopeful than we feared.

For the immediate future and so long as the Kasper mess is boiling

and stewing the Department will not move. I have never understood —
and neither, incidentally, has your daughter Mary — how you got mixed
up with that character.

Beyond that, though there are no commitments, the Department does
not close the door provided somebody can come forward with a sensible
plan for your future. The impression we got was that that future would
have to be in the United States.

Robert has some ideas about a sensible plan which he would be glad
to explore if you approve and which seem promising to me: a sound
professional arrangement with your publishers which might work for
you as it has for him over many years.

All this, you understand, is hypothetical as Hell. No commitments
or near commitments were made. But the door wasn't closed and we
were left with the impression that once the Kasper stink has blown
over they would be willing to consider proposals.

We ran into one thing you ought to know about. Somebody has
spread the rumor at the Department of Justice (I heard it also in
Italy) that you and your wife would really prefer to stay on at St.
Elizabeths. If it is false, as I assume, your wife ought to make that clear
to the Department. But if she does, ask her please not to quote me.

Did you ever get my note about our visit with that lovely Mary?

yours faithfully   Archie

TLS: YCAL

To Robert Frost

Dear Robert: 22 August [1957] [Conway]

As I understand it, J. Laughlin is going to drive up to see you (IF
you'll have him) when he gets back from the West which ought to be
about now. Then, if you work out a "sensible plan" with him we are
to submit it to Rogers at the Department of Justice. I'll gladly do that
if you'll give me the necessary information.

I have at last had some replies from Pound. He doesn't seem disturbed
about not being able to go to Italy but the rumor about his not wanting
to leave St. Elizabeths infuriates him. He says someone has been ped-
dling this for some time. Maybe its Merrill Moore![1] Who knows? He's
very much touched that you made the trip on his account.

Hemingway is pleased by developments and anxious to know what
more must be done and when. Eliot is disturbed at the thought that the
doctors might let Ezra go off and live somewhere down south with nobody but his wife etc. to look out for him. He apparently thinks Ezra

is nuttier than he is. I've told him that decision will be for the docs to make. Does Eliot strike you as a bit timid?

Will you let me know if Laughlin shows up? Or if he doesn't? We oughtn't to let Rogers get the idea that we aren't interested any longer. I'd like to get our "sensible plan" down to him before too long. And I'm sure you would too.

And may I ask a great favor — another? Would you let me have *The Most of It* mimeographed for my class at Harvard? They can't afford to buy many books, most of them, but the way to get them started is by poems, not by talk from me. I'd be deeply grateful. That poem means a lot to me. Not necessarily more than others of yours but a lot.

yrs   A.

TLS: NhD

1. American psychiatrist and poet (1903–1957).

To Robert Frost

Dear Robert: 16 October [1957] [Cambridge]

J. Laughlin called me up at the farm last weekend to ask me to arrange an interview for you with Dr. Overholzer at St. Elizabeths.

I'd be delighted to call him if you want me to but I'd like to spare you the long drive out there — particularly since I know pretty well what he would say since he has already said it to me twice. He would say that Ezra can't stand trial without going right off his rocker and therefore, as long as the indictment hangs over his head, there is nothing to do but hold him in the hospital. If, however, the indictment were dropped so that that risk to his sanity were removed there would be no reason to continue to hold him provided sensible arrangements for his care could be made.

The first part of this, which is the part now pertinent, Overholzer has reported to the Dept of Justice. The second part, which is "iffy" and lies in the future, he has not reported and he is very emphatic that he does not wish to be quoted. I have therefore not quoted him to anyone but you and Tom and Ernest. I am sure you will agree that we should not repeat his views.

If you decide you do want to drive over to St. Elizabeths and if you want me to call Overholzer give me a ring at Conway, Mass (Emerson 4: - - - - — I think that's it — new number) and I'll call him at once. However I am sure he would be simply delighted to see you. He's a civilized man and a graduate of this college. So that really all you need do is ask Richman to give him a buzz. I think he's back from Europe but I'm not sure.

Best to you — and bless you for going to see Rogers again. Do let me know what happens.   yours ever   Archie

TLS: NhD

To Ezra Pound

Dear Ez: 11 December [1957]   [Cambridge]

I've been damn remiss but for two reasons, one of them good — that I hoped to have some news to report. Other reason was just that the damn [*sic*] broke and I got swep away.[1]

As for the news. Robert (Frost) went down again about a month ago and saw the Atty Gen, Rogers. Rogers is the lad Robert and I saw last summer at which time he was deputy atty gen.. He was at that time definitely aware of the fact that this can't go on *in*definitely, but wanted a (as I wrote you) "sensible plan" (not to include Italy) and didn't want to act at all as long as Mr. K was in the prints. Robert felt down-right hopeful. I was less so but was heartened, nevertheless, by the recognition that something was going to have to be done fairly soon.

Well — as I say, Robert came back about a month ago with new and fresh hope having had a real heart-to-heart and we both waited for the postman. Nothing has, however, happened since. I am going to go see Robert tomorrow (he is hot for consequences — all stirred up) at which time we will try to agree on what to do next. In all probability I'll have to go to Washington again — though I have no assurance Rogers will see me. He regards Robert as a fellow Republican which he very nearly is, being a [Grover] Cleveland Democrat as he puts it.

I have been, as you justly say, a quietist on the theory that no amount of yelping is going to move the Department of Justice but it looks now as though nothing else will move them either. If we can't get action or a definite promise of action soon I'll stop trying to sit on lids. But I want one more real crack at it.

You read a lot more than I do and many of your references are blind to me. What has the Nation been up to? I never see it.

About Mary — we thought she was wonderful. But I can quite see your point about the grandchildren. Though I can see hers too. She wants them to get to know you — and why not.

If I have anything at all to report after tomorrow I'll write again at once. Sorry to have been so dumbdumbdumb   Archie

I haven't heard from Carl [Sandburg?] but will try to get in touch.

TLS: YCAL

1. M had suffered another attack of stomach ulcers.

To Ezra Pound

Dear Ezrie: 18 February 1958   Antigua

Yours of the third. I hope a letter of mine along early January hasn't miscarried misfired or mistook.

What I have to report is not very enlivening — rather like a report of a conversation between a man and an empty well.

You are aware of the high hopes following Frost's and my visit to the now Attorney General last summer.

You are aware of the higher hopes in Frost's mind following his repeat visit to same in November.

What happened then was that I wrote the Atty Gen to ask for specific confirmation of Frost's understanding of his conversation with Rogers (Atty Gen). I received an answer two months later suggesting I drop in when next in Washington!! But meantime, interpreting the protracted silence to mean no soap (which seems to be the correct interpretation), I had called on Chris Herter, Under Secretary of State and an old friend and former colleague of mine in that dreadful Roosevelt Administration. I told Herter that whereas the decision had, obviously, to be made by Justice, it was State that was suffering, because your continued incarceration was hurting our prestige abroad and undoing a lot of the things his Department is or ought to be trying to do. He was interested and impressed, being a decent human being, and said he would make inquiries — which I assume to mean inquiries at Justice and at St. Elizabeths.

I then wrote to Eliot and Hemingway, asking them to support my appeal to Herter. Eliot said he would. I haven't heard from Ernest who may be abroad somewhere but I am sure he will when he can. However I have relatively little hope for this demarche because Herter has been walled off by Dulles and has relatively little power. Since the Administration as a whole seems to fear to possess power or to use it this means that Herter is not likely to burst from his cell with a hell of a yell. A week ago or so I wrote him again making as strong an appeal as I am capable of making. If I receive a reply I'll let you know.

Where does this leave us? I'm afraid the answer is: just about where we were. We now know that the Administration is aware of l'affaire Pound and would like to resolve it. But we also know that it is afraid of Walter Winchell et al as it is afraid of almost everything else. I doubt if a more wholly impotent and timid administration ever held office in Washington. If Roosevelt had had the same kidney Hitler would be master of the world today. What should be done? I don't know. Perhaps we should all take to our typewriters. However I am not ready to say, for my own part, that there is no hope of progress on this front. At least I shall go on pushing.

yours as ever   Archie

TLS: YCAL

To Ezra Pound

Dear Ezra: 16 March 1958 [Antigua]

I have at last (after how many months and years?) a firm and understandable statement from a responsible member of the present Administration who is also a good and responsible man. I would rather not name him at this juncture unless you very much want me to.[1]

In brief the position is this: a legal way can be found to release you to live as a kind of out-patient of some private sanitarium which means that you would be visited from time to time by a recognized physician, but would live in your own quarters like any body else and would have — I quote — "a maximum degree of freedom".

The Government is willing to make use of this legal way if your friends can find a suitable "inconspicuous place" within reach of the medical attentions described and can raise the necessary money if your own means won't suffice. The locus would have to be in the US.

But all this of course depends on your own willingness to accept such an arrangement.

Will you think it over and let me have word as soon as you conveniently can? The above address will reach me until April fifth or so. Only air-mail reaches here. The rate is ten cents a half ounce.

I hope very much you will agree with me that this suggestion should be treated as confidential for the present. There are, as you know, plenty of people who would do their best by yammer and yelp to make any solution impossible and word gets around very fast where you are concerned. Some of your young friends seem to be wired for sound. I am always hearing things attributed to you which I am dead certain you never said and I suspect that they originate in the chorus.

Rereading the above, that word "quarters" seems to me unfortunate. Let me be specific about that. The idea is that you and, I assume, D.P., would live in a house of your own in some quiet town with the kind of climate you like where you could be visited from time to time by a recognized medic and where you would have "a maximum degree of freedom".

If you have any questions and will shoot them along to me I'll try

to get them answered. I have told no one about this so far except J. Laughlin who will have to go to work on the money end if you approve the project.   yours faithfully   Archie
TLS: YCAL

1. M refers to Christian A. Herter, whose letter to M dated March 5 (DLC) had contained the information M herein relates.

To Ezra Pound

This replies to yours of no date but post-marked March 25
Dear Ezra: 30 March 1958 [Antigua]
   Anyway, thanks for supposing I mean well. First kind word I've had from you since I started butting my head against this stone wall two years ago.
   I'll try to sort the questions out from the insults and answer the questions. God knows you have a right to all the answers anybody can give. Its your decision. If you say No, that's final and irrevocable. All the rest of us are trying to do is to see whether there is a solution which the government and courts would accept and then to submit it to you. If you decide you don't want to accept it that's the end of it.
   You describe the solution I described to you as "an illegal arrangement with an anonymity". I told you I would supply names if you wanted but that I hoped they would not be publicized for the time being as that would mean the end of the conversations. The official I have been talking to and writing to is Christian Herter, the Under Secretary of State, who is a friend of mine and in whose good faith I have complete trust. Herter has been in conversation with the Attorney General and with Dr. Overholser. Nothing about the proposed arrangement is "illegal" in any sense. If you decide to accept it it will have court approval. Any one who tells you it is "illegal" is either uninformed or incompetent.
   You ask about your control of your earnings. No one has made any suggestion to the contrary. Your publishers will, as I understand it, propose to you an arrangement by which you would be guaranteed a definite *minimum* amount per month plus, of course, anything over that figure which your books might earn in a particular year. But this they will discuss with you directly. The purpose is to give you every possible cent of royalties plus a guaranteed minimum on which you could always count. In addition, if you will permit us to do so, some of us would like to raise funds to defray medical costs.
   The question of the nature of these medical services you might wish

to discuss with Dr. Overholser. You can be sure that what he has in mind is a physician, not a quack.

These seem to be the principal questions put by your letter. If you have more, please ask them. I'll be back in Conway, Mass., in two weeks and can be reached there. If I don't know the answers myself I'll try to get them.

And please let me say once more that the decision is, of course, wholly yours. If you are against it that's the end of it. I think myself that this is the best solution we can now hope for but what I think is of no importance. Its up to you. Let me know.   A.

TLS: YCAL

To McGeorge Bundy

Dear Mac: 6 May 1958   [Conway]

If this letter should be written at all it should be written now. Meaning at the first possible moment.

The news on JB is good — so good that it scares me — but also troubling. [Alfred] DeLiagre[, Jr.,] is producing it in November on Broadway. Elia Kazan wants to direct it and co-produce it and the probability is that he will — though I want to find out first how he sees it: he is a man of such force that once he starts rolling no mere author is going to hold him.

All of this is, of course, unbelievably good news. But it means that I will be under the frenzied pressures of a production in September and October. And I will be sixty÷six (that divider got in by subconscious thrust!) tomorrow. And though I feel like a squirrel there is no question but that the attempt to start a new year's teaching with an experimental course at the same time that I am working seven days a week on the play would shrivel my larder.

So you see what I'm coming to. I couldn't put it to anybody but you but I can to you. Would it be possible to postpone my 1958 fall term to 1959 if the Corporation would still want me in 1959?

I know, or can guess, at the difficulties involved. Its only because the difficulties the other way are even more menacing that I can get up the gall to ask. And it may be that the question I ought to ask is not this one but another — would you like me just to resign as of June 1958 when I reach the age Nate has gallantly wished to overlook? I don't want to do that: my Harvard professorship means to me what maybe only you can guess. But I will if you think that is the best way out. Otherwise I'd like to be the Boylston still and to pick up again in the fall of '59. One reason, in addition to the reasons of necessity, is that I'd like to wind up with that experimental course. And another relevant consideration is that maybe by 1959 we could find a place in Cambridge to live. But the real one is that I don't want to stop being a member of your faculty.

If this is feasible I should wish to go on — but much more actively — with the theater committee and with the Norton Committee if you want me to (I do think we should revive the Pasternak possibility for consideration for '59–60).[1]

And of course what I am talking about is leave without pay. There would be problems on that front also — how to keep my retirement arrangement solvent while subsisting without salary etc. etc. — but these are minor in comparison with the basic question.

Forgive me for adding to your cares in a careful season.

Oh — add to the good news on JB a letter just received from Reinhold[2] who, I had expected, would blast me off the earth. He calls it a masterpiece (from Reinhold!!!) and says it provides an answer he can accept. Tie that!

Give Mary my dear thanks for calling Ada to tell her about poor Don. And add to the thanks my love.   yours Archie

TLS: MH (ARCHIVES)

1. Boris Pasternak (1890–1960), the Russian poet and novelist whose novel *Doctor Zhivago* had just appeared in an English translation. 2. Reinhold Niebuhr (1892–1971), the American theologian.

To David C. Mearns[1]

Dear David: 4 August [1958] Conway

Thanks. Glad you got the dossier.[2] Glad you share my feeling that it will be a fallen apple to some literary historian — if the plankton still writes history after Dulles and Crewshove[3] get through with our future.

By way of gratitude I am, as usual, asking a new favor. I ask it of you instead of asking it of the Reference people because you will understand what I want and will interpret for me. I am doing an hour show on the crisis of democracy for NBC to be produced sometime this fall.[4] My general theme is the old one I have always been twanging at which just gets newer with every disaster — the theme of affirmation — that you don't fight Communism by being AGAINST IT but by being FOR something immeasurably better — Pericles theme when he told the Athenians to fix their eyes on Athens every day — not what she was but what she had the power to become, until they became her lovers:

Whit Griswold's[5] theme when he told the Yalis that what has been challenged is our courage and our will: Reuther's theme when he told that British journalist that our tragedy was we weren't *trying* — "we're still only fighting against something".[6] Well, you see what I'm coming to. I want a few sayings — very few — from the Founding Fathers which look forward — which affirm. You remember Turgot's letter just after Saratoga which has the sentence: "This people is the hope of the world".[7] That sort of thing but with purpose and intention behind it. Jefferson will be easy, of course. But what about Franklin. What about John Adams. What about old wooden teeth himself the noblest Roman of all Romans.[8]

Let me try again. What's wrong with this country now — and plenty is — is the fact that we have the highest standard of living in the world and that it isn't a high standard of living but just a high standard of having and that our attitude toward the Russians is like the attitude of the peasant with a sock full of gold toward the tramp on the street — we're afraid we're going to lose what we HAVE. We aren't going anywhere ourselves — just hanging on to what we have. That's why our souls are rotting. Well, the old boys whether they blew penny whistles the way I do or not, weren't just hanging on. They had will. They had courage. They fixed their eyes on what Athens might become . . .

See? I don't say it very well but you know what I'm TRYING to say because you've figgered it out before. Will you translate into English and pass on? Not a lot of stuff. I probably won't be able to use more than four sentences or brief sayings.

I'd be, as always, profoundly grateful. God 'ield thee

Archie

TLS: DLC

1. Chief of the Manuscript Division of the Library of Congress, Mearns had worked closely with M during M's tenure as Librarian of Congress, when Mearns was director of the reference department. 2. M had sent Mearns a group of letters from, and concerning, Ezra Pound, for inclusion among M's papers at the Library of Congress. 3. A phonetic spelling — and deliberate misspelling — of Khrushchev, the Soviet premier. 4. The program, a one-hour dramatization of M's first television script, was entitled "The Secret of Freedom." With a cast that included Tony Randall, Kim Hunter, and Thomas Mitchell, it was first aired over NBC on 28 February 1960. 5. A. Whitney Griswold, president of Yale University. 6. Walter P. Reuther, president of the AFL-CIO. 7. Anne Robert Jacques Turgot (1727–1781), French economist and contributor to the *Encyclopédie* (1751–1772). 8. George Washington.

To Ernest Hemingway

Dear Pappy: [30 September 1958]   Conway

George Plimpton, admirable character, handsome boss, has sent me
his interview with you in the Paris Review.[1] Velly nice. But his quotation of A.MacL., which you kindly and correctly corrected[,] gave me
a crise. Neither he nor anyone else ever heard me say "A writer should"
let alone all the rest of that stuff of conscious and subconscious. What
I remembered was the sailing glove and I told him about it one day to
get him thinking about what he felt when he thought he was feeling.
Nobody ever quotes anybody else correctly I suppose but the poor
teacher doesn't have a chance because nobody even *hears* what he says.

Same thing probably applies to your remarks about Paris. George has
you saying the only writers you knew were Joyce and Ezra and Stein.
I won't believe you are ashamed of the poor relations until you tell me
so yourself. Anyway I remember you. Never more clearly than now.
Probably means I am getting to be an old, old whatdoyoucall *it* and the
past is flooding in on me. But I can see you as clear as gin in a glass
the first time I ever layed eyes on you. Not that I'm given to laying
eyes but you know.

Important question is how you are. Last report you were down to one
glass of wine a day and then off that. That was when we were twisting
the Atty Gen's arm about EZ — must be almost a year ago. I hope
you're back up to a quart of something — not Cuban — and, whatever
you are drinking or not drinking, feeling better. I tried to discourage
George from going down because I didn't think you'd feel much like
being interviewed but he wrote me I was all wrong — you were feeling
wonderful. Implication was that I'd do better to mind my own.

Someday we ought to catch up on the Ez business. It still has me
puzzled. Last January I shifted from the Atty Gen to the State Department and talked to Chris Herter who agreed to intervene (which
he did) but who told me that one thing was certain: Ez couldn't go
back to Italy. So he did.[2] I think Frost gets a large part of the credit.
The old boy despises Ez for personal reasons but once he got started
nothing could stop him and I think Rogers finally gave up out of sheer
exhaustion. I haven't seen Frost since. Will try to get his story this fall.
Anyway, as you know, Ez hasn't changed none. If anything his letters
more abusive than previous which was plenty.

Went to Dick Myers funeral[3] and sat between Gerald and Sarah whom
haven't seen for maybe two years, Gerald having written me off. And
for good reason. I didn't behave well. Numerous occasions, as you know,
I haven't. Anyway I felt very sad and far off somehow sitting between
them with no relationship anymore except of Sarah's warmth and

generosity and thinking about the years when I knew Dick and everything off at the back of those years. The only friends you make really
are the ones you make when you are young — or so, anyway, of my
life — and you keep them but don't keep them. I mean they are always
anyway your friends because they once were but only in memory. When
you see them again you go back there where they were. Well — I sound
old.

Funny year for me. I have a verse play being produced in New York
— opening Washington in November — New York in December. Result Ada and I will be living in New York those months and I'll be
commuting up here teaching one course which has come to seem pretty
unreal with all that turmoil down at the Music Box theater. Probably
ought to give up teaching but I love some things about it — the kids
particularly — and it's a steady source of. But probably I ought to. At
sixty-six with a new play boiling around in my head and a new life in
the theater to learn I probably ought to stop. To hell with it — why
do I bore you with all this. Getting sentimental and running on at the
mouth — to quote a bird with a beard I used to know at Gstaad with
a crossbow. Love to Mary. Ada and I talk about you both more than
you'd guess.   my love to you   Archie

TLS: JFK

1. The interview had appeared in *The Paris Review* 5 (Spring 1958), 60–89. 2. In
Washington District Court, on 18 April 1958, the treason indictment against Pound
had been dismissed by Judge Bolitha Laws, presiding judge in the 1945 hearing that
had sent Pound to St. Elizabeths. On June 30 Pound had sailed for Italy. 3. Richard
E. Myers, M's friend from his days in Paris, had died on August 8.

To Elia Kazan[1]

Gadgabout: 12 December [1958]   [New York]

Molly[2] says you *did* hear the love song of J. Alfred McGillicuddy on
Dave Garroway's show this morning. I called you up the minute I got
back to the hotel and no answer. So I thought to myself, *Poor Gadg
is asleep and ought to be and I wish I was;* but I was sad because those
remarks were for *you.* I thought I was going to weep under the television lights when Frank Blair read the Atkinson review.[3] Of course I
knew it was good because I heard people talking about it at that Chinese joint the night before — I knew from the shouting that *all* the
reviews were good, unbelievably good — but I had no idea Atkinson
said what he *did* say. Tears on television would have been fine! But it
wasn't only fatigue. It was, I'm afraid, joy. Plain, old-fashioned joy.
After all that . . . all those struggles . . . searchings of the soul . . .

labors into the night . . . despair in Washington[4] . . . to meet with such a generous welcome, such general evidence that the problems *were* solved! Of course there are troubles ahead. If the newspaper strike goes on we may drown, in spite of everything, with land in sight and the palm trees waving. Also there are bound to be loud dissenting voices: I can't imagine that Bright Young Britisher *The New Yorker* has hired liking the play.[5] Nevertheless and notwithstanding, I had and have a vast feeling of — well, I guess the word is reward.

And still, when I try to define the "reward" it isn't this morning I think of. It's the line rehearsal yesterday afternoon when suddenly the whole cast became absorbed in the words of the play. Or it's the moment in Washington when we looked at each other in the back row of that gloomy cavern of a theatre and said to each other in the same breath that the second act was better than the first.

What was the moment of change — the hinge of fate? Was it that cold bright morning just before Thanksgiving when we walked round and round Jackson Park in front of the White House and realized that we had simply failed to *accomplish* dramatically that moment of recognition I had been talking about so glibly — that moment when J.B. understands what the Distant Voice has said to him and what it means and where he is? You said it was your fault — that you had left him there at that crucial moment with his back to the audience. But the truth is that it was mine. I had put that moment into the mouths of Mr. Zuss and Nickles, leaving J.B. dumb. It worked on the printed page but on that obstinate *fact*, the stage, it didn't work.

Curious that the fault was there all the time, unseen by all of us. Molly was right about the Comforters: they were mocking themselves and the moment they spoke *as* comforters (which is what these "comforts" want to be) that scene became a true part of the play. But the destructive fault was not in the Comforters. The destructive fault was in my failure as a dramatist. The moment you showed it to me — claiming it, in the immeasurable generosity of your heart, as your own — the whole scheme fell into place. J.B.'s recognition is a recognition not only of the insignificance of his human place in the vast scale of the universe, but of the *significance* of that insignificance. He is at least *a man*. It is his "integrity" as a man (Job's word) that he has been struggling for: first, by trying to take upon himself the vast load of guilt for the world's injustice; second, by rejecting those deterministic "comforts" which give comfort only by destroying the self; now, in the struggle with the huge Voice of God, the vast majesty and beauty and power of the Universe with its majestic indifference to the suffering of a man alone. Ahead lies the final struggle, the struggle with himself, the struggle to accept life again, which means — for there is no other way to accept life — the struggle to accept love, to risk himself again in love.

Thinking back over these feverish but wonderful months which have given me, as greatest reward of all, our collaboration and friendship, it suddenly strikes me as marvelous and strange that this final resolution of our common labor is a resolution we had been discussing from the very beginning. It's rather like life itself; all we ever learn in life is the true truth of what we had surmised at the beginning — and it's enough.

But our whole journey has been something of a circle. We end by putting back into the final scene those lines about Sarah's attempted suicide which were almost the first things we took out — and their return has given the final scene new meaning. So that the published poem which has been so often cut and reorganized has also it's moment of justification and still stands in its own — may I borrow Job's word again? — integrity.

It is agreed between us that there are no words for the thanks. Nevertheless you hear them. Yrs. Archie

P: M

1. American stage and screen director, novelist, and actor (b. 1909). Kazan directed the ANTA Theatre (New York) production of M's *J.B.*, the fate of which was initially cast in doubt by a citywide newspaper strike. After local television and radio stations broadcast reviews of the play by various drama critics of the struck newspapers, it quickly became a major success. 2. Mrs. Kazan. 3. Brooks Atkinson, drama critic of *The New York Times*. 4. *J.B.* had been plagued by major dramatic problems during its tryouts in Washington, D.C. 5. Kenneth Tynan reviewed *J.B.* — unfavorably — in *The New Yorker* 34 (20 December 1958), 70–72.

To Lester Markel[1]

Dear Markel: 5 January [1959] [Antigua]

I am very much touched and pleased that you should want to write me about my play. You could not pay it or me a more meaningful compliment.

I'd rather reply to your letter than to the author of the review in the New Yorker[2] and for a very simple reason — that he writes and apparently thinks and may, for all I know, live in terms which make discussion of the play impossible. His difficulty in understanding it is a difficulty inside himself and one fairly common among Englishmen of his literary generation.

Your first question is whether it is conceivable that a modern man should be concerned with the justice of God. I can't think of any question which concerns modern men more. Even those who have dropped the word God from their vocabulary (see *Dr. Zhivago*) are haunted with the problem of making sense, making "justice", of a world in which men and women and children suffer and die by the millions in holocausts which seemingly take no account of humanity. What is the modern philosophy, existentialism, but precisely an attempt to make sense of senselessness? You and I may reject the existentialists but we understand what they are struggling with for we struggle with it too. *You* distinguish the God of the Creation from the God of Justice. Can you? The fundamental question is *whether the creation is just* or can be understood in terms of justice. For if it cannot we are indeed "mad men all".

Implicit in this first question of yours is another — whether a hero like mine would believe (at least in the beginnings of his troubles) in the justice of God. I think he would. Indeed, as I said in that same *Times* piece, I think he *does*.[3] It is part of the essential naivete of the successful American business man to believe that something in the order of things justifies his having what he has. Rich men in my father's generation were candid about this to the point of embarrassment. There are fewer since 1929 but they still exist. Do you know Chicago?

I am puzzled by your remark that I seem to feel that Job and everybody else including you should accept whatever happens in the world. Something is really dreadfully wrong here. It is precisely Job's inability to accept whatever happens which is the spring and source of his agony. He cannot believe that God is just, seeing his own sufferings around him, but neither can he live UNLESS he can believe in the justice of God. It is the ancient human quandary: the heart of the human agony. The whole play is an attempt to resolve it. And the play's resolution is the only one humanity has ever found which I can accept for myself: the resolution in and through love. We cannot, as JB says to Sarah at the end, "know". That is, we cannot resolve the insupportable dilemma by reason and logic. No religion ever has or, I fear, ever can. We can resolve it only by loving life in spite of life. And I do not mean by this to say in other terms that the resolution is the Christian resolution for it seems to me much wider and much more fundamental — though certainly the teachings of Christ have their footing in this great affirmation also. But the wisest of the Greeks had been there long before. And it is precisely because the Biblical poem, Job, carries this same meaning in that curious chapter at the end that Job is one of the great and certainly immortal poems.

Forgive me if I seem to lecture. I know I don't need to with you.

With a man who does not understand what love is, the argument would be a waste of time. With you, who do, I can only hope you won't think it an argument.

Incidentally, the affirmation does not come only from Sarah. Ask Delly to show you the acting version.[4]

The same mail which brought your letter brought one from a German girl (Eliot's translator and now mine)[5] who says that JB's decision to take up life again is a "true choice" and "as such a critical reflection upon God and the universe" and she then goes on with words you will forgive me for quoting because they not only praise the play but speak of it meaningfully — that is, in terms of the kind of meaning I hope it conveys: "Like all truly great poetry of the world JB represents (to me) the drama and tragedy of man's coming to consciousness". That touched me deeply. I sometimes dare to hope that the play may be remembered at least as a small step in the coming to consciousness of the American mind, in our time.

Thank you again for taking the trouble to write me. I hope you are now fully recovered.   faithfully   Archie MacLeish

TLS: de LIAGRE

1. Editor of the Sunday edition of *The New York Times*. 2. *See* previous letter, note 5. 3. *See* "About a Trespass on a Monument," M's discussion of his thematic intentions in *J.B.*, in *The New York Times*, 7 December 1958, Section II, pages 5 and 7. 4. Alfred de Liagre, Jr. Certain of the speeches assigned to J.B. in the Houghton Mifflin edition of the play were shifted to Sarah in the Broadway version. 5. Eva Hesse, also the German translator of Pound, Cummings, and others.

To Adlai E. Stevenson

Dear Adlai: 7 January [1959]   Antigua

There have been a lot of letters these last few weeks but none that touched me as yours did. Not only because You are who but because you are also goddam busy. That you took time to go and see the play (my scouts had reported that fact before you did) and that you also sat down to write me about having seen it went straight to my heart.

I don't like the way time goes by. Not that I fear coming to the end of my allotment but that I hate like hell not seeing the people I want to see in the time left. You and I haven't really had so much as an hour together for years past and, to be quite frank about it, I miss you. Your letter helps — but it also aggravates the complaint because it makes me realize again how *much* I am missing.

God keep you. Ada sends her love.   thine   Archie

TCO: DLC

To Ezra Pound

Dear Ezra: 11 July 1959 [Conway]

It isn't I who am mumping. The silence started from your end just
about the time you said good-bye to dear St. Elizabeth and it has been
constant and persistent ever since. I didn't think I deserved it and I
gather from the overtones of your letter that you don't think so either.
How about a few informative words free of political and economic
abstractions?

Eva writes me that those Trachis women of yours were a tremendous
success in Berlin.[1] What lovely people the Germans are!

I send you my affectionate regards and to hell with you if you won't
accept them.   Archie

TLS: YCAL

1. Eva Hesse had accompanied Pound and his daughter to the Berlin production of
Pound's translation of Sophocles' *Women of Trachis.*

To Ezra Pound

Dear Ezra: 17 August 1959 [Conway]

That letter warmed my heart. Of course, it doesn't wholly state the
case because, as you know and as I know, you don't really want answers
to those questions: you want *your* answer. Since my answer means
nothing to you, and since I can't accept your answer, there just hasn't
seemed to me to be much point in continuing the discussion. But
nevertheless and notwithstanding, this letter has made me very happy
indeed because for the first time in a long time I can hear a human
voice. Since it is the human voice of one of the men I most admire in
our time, the event has significance.

The above isn't butter or rhetoric. I have been re-reading your
translation of The Woman [*sic*] of Trachis for the 10th or 11th time,
lost in admiration for the way in which you bring that usually inert
play — that is, inert in the usual translation — to vivid life. Eva has
written me of the enormous and very real success you had in Berlin
and of the depth of Mary's reaction to the performance. I have no
difficulty in believing it. Your melange of dialects which sometimes
bothers me on the printed page wouldn't bother on the stage for one
moment — I am sure of that. You have, in addition to everything else,
a formidable dramatic instinct.

I wish you would do two things for me. First, I wish you would give
my love to Mary when you next see her. I met her only once but at a
dark time for her, for you, and if I may say so, for me, but I shall never

forget that evening. Second, I wish you would let me have two words about the practicality of your present situation and plans. Have you settled in Rapallo for good or will you go up to the mountains later? In general, how are things going? You will do me the credit to acknowledge that I haven't bothered you with questions of this kind before, but the fact is that I am, as I always have been, very concerned.

Archie

TLS: YCAL

To Ezra Pound

Dear Ez: [c. December 1959] Cambridge

Your letter frightened the living bejeezzzz out of me.[1] Gentleness — even affection — out of Old Ez, says I: he's sick! Not that I didn't relish it. I do. But I feel like the ship's cook who looked in on the skipper and didn't have to dodge a shoe. Matter of fact I had just written the glorious Eva to beg her intervention on my behalf to get word to Mary to get word to you around backwards that the reason you hadn't heard from me was that I put the problem of your income tax and your income to your lawyer down in Norfolk[2] asking him to explain the trouble to me so that I could translate it into English for you and the so-and-so has never answered and never sent me your letter back which I had asked him to do. He doesn't behave like a lawyer. Is he one? Well I suppose he is and the best no doubt but he has bad manners. Down in the old south, Suh, they used to answer letters.

Don't have your abuse of my friends on your conscience. FDR was abused by experts all his latter life and it didn't sour him none. I think he'd have liked some of your expletives. What I want to know is where you are and if you're warm enough and what you plan to do next and how lovely Mary is and those children and all and all. Write me informatively. I'm just out of hospital[3] and I need information and kindness. Everything seems to be all right except my brains. I think I must have left them hanging in the closet beside that hospital Johnny that ties with strings up the back. Merry Christmas you Old Buzzard and God keep you yours Archie

TLS: YCAL

1. In a letter to M dated December 16, Pound had written, in part, "Forgive me for about 80% of the violent things I have said about some of your friends" (DLC). 2. Robert M. Furniss, Jr. 3. M had suffered another attack of stomach ulcers.

To Donald Hall[1]

Dear Don: 29 September 1961   [Conway]

I am glad you finally got my letter and I am sorry for the delay. The news at this end is better from day to day and I am simply delighted with the news from your end. I have just come back from Cambridge where I got my last English S class started and where I found your book[2] which has the look, feel, and taste of a lovely thing. I am greedy to get at it. But what pleases me even more than the new book is your decision to stop ravelling yourself out in journalism and criticism. You are quite right when you remember that this was one of the things that worried me 12 years ago but you have so completely disproved all the dismal things I used to tell you that I now believe the truly golden future is on its way. Do please send me the manuscript of the collection of poems. Let's agree that "no comment is required or expected" — but not leave it at that.   Yours ever,   A.

TLS: HALL

1. A poet, essayist, teacher, and editor, Hall had taken M's advanced writing course as an undergraduate at Harvard, Class of 1951. 2. Hall's *String Too Short to Be Saved* (1961), a prose book of New Hampshire reminiscences.

To Robert Frost

Dear Robert: 12 June 1962   Cambridge

Crossing the Square this morning something made me remember that it's more than a year since I've seen you & therefore more than a year since I've had a chance to tell you with what delight & pride all of us who follow you so far behind watch your tremendous progress through time and place. Also to tell you with what gratitude I think of your unfailing generosity and friendship to me. A good part of whatever confidence I have rests on that. This needs, of course, no answer.

                                            yours ever   Archie

Ada & I (just back from Italy) will be in Conway all summer beginning this blessed afternoon. If you come to Amherst would you let us know? Emerson 4- - - - -

ALS: NhD

To Gerald Murphy[1]

It occurred to me this morning that this age in which we have lived, you and I, is actually, if one looks through the trash, plastic containers, paper cups, half-used words and soiled hypocrisies which float on its surface like the steamer-leavings on the precipitous deep blue of Lake Como — is actually a heroic age and that that is its tragedy. The heroic ages in the myths — those only true rememberers — were the ages in which men, some men, perhaps only one, dared to believe that it might be possible — that it WAS possible — with nothing but human head and hands to slaughter the great beasts, to overcome the monsters, to go down into the dark, into death itself, and drag the dog up howling and so, as Herakles was assured by the oracle, to live thereafter like gods.

I have known for a long time that that myth was our myth. That is why I have been struggling for five years with a play about Herakles.[2] But not until this morning did I see what I must have known all along — that it is because our age like his life is heroic in that highest and most daring sense that we take our meaning from him. For our age is tragic as his life was and as all the heroic ages must be. The deeds are performed, the miracles accomplished, the wonders visited — and there is still the world as it was — the dog as it was . . . except that the dog is now tied up in the cook's slops in Eurystheus' kitchen. Le prince d'Acquitaine a la tour abolie.[3] It is true tragedy — tragedy to wring the heart: all these tremendous intelligences daring to take space and time and matter apart and to dig deep down under into the eternal dark and returning in triumph to what? Night as usual. Dust as usual. Someone sprinkling water on the dust as usual — the old sad smell. But then one reminds one's self that in the myth Herakles DOES become a god at the end. So that the oracle comes true in the myth. So what should we think of ourselves — of our destiny? The myths are always right — but right in another language. Are we also gods, we victims of ourselves — but in some sense we do not understand?

Certainly not in the sense of your beloved friend Hopkins to whom the just man

> Acts in God's eye what in god's eye he is —
> Christ — for Christ plays in ten thousand places,
> lovely in limbs, and lovely in eyes not his
> to the Father through the features of men's faces.[4]

Not in that sense but in some other?

Let the last word be his too — Hopkins: "How to keep — is there any, is there none such, nowhere known some, bow or brooch or braid or brace, lace, latch, catch or key to keep

["]Back beauty, keep it, beauty, beauty, beauty . . . from vanishing away?["]⁵   our dear and always love to you both   Archie

TLS: DONNELLY

1. Murphy was terminally ill with cancer when M wrote this and the following letters. He died on October 17. **2.** *See* M to Richard Burton, 7 August 1965, note 4. **3.** A phrase from Gérard de Nerval's poem "El Desdichado." **4.** From Gerard Manley Hopkins's untitled poem beginning "As kingfishers catch fire, dragonflies draw flame." M had introduced Murphy to the poetry of Hopkins. **5.** From Hopkins's "The Leaden Echo and the Golden Echo."

To Gerald Murphy

Dear Gerald: 19 September [1964] [Conway]

I was still wondering whether a letter would be an intrusion when yours came. Featureless horizon — yes. That is precisely what one sees from the uninhabited bare hills old men climb to, though only you would think of the just word. But the point is — or at least I think the point is — the horizon, not the featurelessness. When one expects to go on "forever" as one does in one's youth or even in middle age, horizons are merely limits, not yet ends. It is when one first sees the horizon as an end that one first begins to *see*. And it is then that the featurelessness, which one would not have noticed, or would have taken for granted, before, becomes the feature. Ends are the hardest things in the world to see — and precisely because they aren't *things*, they are the end of things. And yet they are wonderful. What would life be without them! Or art — imagine a work of art without ends: it would be worse than a novel by Thomas Wolfe. So that this featureless sky is as far as it is possible to be from negation. It is affirmation. It says the world is possible to man because to man there are horizons, there are beginnings and ends, there are things known and things unknown. Frost said (I don't believe he thought so) that the world was God's joke on him.¹ Meaning, I suppose, that because we die, because everything dies, vanishes, blows away, our lives are nonsense and our works worse. But it isn't true. Because if we didn't die there would be no works — not works of art certainly, the only ones that count. There would be no painter's line to include and exclude and so create. Death is the perspective of every great picture ever painted and the underbeat of every measurable poem and the enviable men are the ripe men who can sit as you do and look at a featureless sky above an endless sea that does, nevertheless, and at that point, *end*. I like to think of you there looking. Or at the rose, that other inward horizon of horizon on horizon. We have time to think of all this, you and I — much time — summers and winters. And time, I hope, trust and pray, to talk about it. Because *now* there is so much to talk about. No richer gift to any of us than a glimpse of death and then time after — even to one who has had to live with death as much as you — or one whose glimpse was brief as mine. Think of you? You would not believe how much or with what love. We will see each other soon. Meantime a great hug to that darling ever young Sadie.   yours   Archie

TLS: DONNELLY

1. M refers to the couplet appearing under the title "[Forgive, O Lord . . .]" in Edward Connery Lathem, ed., *The Poetry of Robert Frost* (New York: Holt, Rinehart & Winston, 1969), page 428.

To Gerald Murphy

Dear Gerald: 29 September [1964]   [Conway]

When I got back from Chicago yesterday I found a letter from Alfred Barr, the Director of Acquisitions at the Museum of Modern Art, asking me to tell you that the Museum of Modern Art is proud to have a work by you in its permanent collection. He is referring to the Pear and the Wasp. When you told me a few weeks ago about the loss of the picture Vladimir had,[1] I wrote the Museum telling them that, if I could keep it in my house as long as I live, I should like to give the painting to the Museum.[2] They accepted at once and with the greatest eagerness and Alfred now sends this word to you by me. I don't need to tell you how happy I am that the picture is to go where it belongs and where it will long represent your great work. Ada and I send our dear love to you and Sarah as always.

                                        hurriedly   Archie

TLS: DONNELLY

1. Murphy had given his last painting, *Portrait* (1929–1930), to his friend Vladimir Orloff in 1933. The painting was destroyed by the Nazis in 1944.   2. *Wasp and Pear* (1927) is now in the permanent collection of the Museum of Modern Art, New York.

To May Sarton[1]

Dearest May: 13 November 1964   [Antigua]

You are not only a good friend but a forgiving one. I have had two letters under the brick which marks letters most to be answered for months and never have because I never could. Never could because I should have said too much and suffered and lain awake. So that yours of the first which came in this noon is a god send.

I wanted to thank you for taking me into that house in Belgium where you most love to be. I wish I could see it.

Now you give me other things to be thankful for — the news about those bloody cigarettes and about the novel-near-its-end . . .

and the news about Agnes Scott. I do so completely agree. For one thing I've never seen so many truly pretty girls together — and not a Southernbelle in the bunch. Nor so sophisticated and courageous a faculty. I gather they don't get paid much to be brave. They just are.

Explain those girls. How can they all be the right size? And listen with such good heart?

And that faculty. I thought perhaps they had been taken in by Robert[2] whose smallness lived under his greatness like a crab under palm. But no — not for a minute. They knew where the one ended and the other began. Marvellous journey.

I send you my dear love. Bird of ash thou never wert: bird of flame   Archie

TLS: NN

1. Sarton (b. 1912), the American novelist and poet, had first known M at Harvard when, from 1949 to 1952, she was Briggs-Copeland Instructor in English Composition there. 2. Frost, who had died in 1963, had been a regular visitor to Agnes Scott College for many years.

To Richard Burton

My dear Burton: 7 August 1965 [Conway]

You and your wife have been much in our minds since Governor Stevenson's death[1] because we always think of the evening the five of us had together as one of the best evenings we ever spent with him.[2] I know his death must have hurt you, too — and very deeply.

I have been under pressure from friends of mine in the Island of Antigua in the British West Indies, where we spend our winters, to approach you with an inquiry as to whether you would be willing and/or able to record the script of a son et lumiere show which Christopher Ede is preparing in London for English Harbor on Antigua. English Harbor is one of the great monuments of British sea power; a pure and unspoiled 18th Century naval depot on a small and magical harbor which was Nelson's base during his service in the West Indies and, in general, one of the most memorable of all British strong points.

I know of nothing about the Ede production — don't know who is writing it or who the actors will be. All I know is that the subject is a great one worthy of any actor and that you are the perfect person to do the narration if you would and could.

I still play over and over the recording of your Hamlet, which your wife sent us after that memorable evening.

Ede, who has written me about all this, tells me that the script could be recorded in London at your convenience, provided something brought you to London during the fall. He thinks the recording would take less than a day. I, myself, on the basis of experience in doing a son et lumiere show at Independence Hall in Philadelphia,[3] would guess that it would take a few hours at the most. Needless to say, I know nothing about the business arrangements or, indeed, about any other practical aspect of the matter. If, however, you were in any way attracted by what seems to me a noble and exciting project (if Ede's people handle it right) I would be most grateful if you would drop me a line here.

All of which brings me to the urgent and important thing which is the countryside here is rocking with rumors that you two are coming to Smith College in connection with Albee's film.[4] If this turns out to be true I wish you would make a special point of remembering that we are here only about 20 miles from Northampton and would like nothing better than giving you a quiet dinner a quatre any evening when you are free. I am starting rehearsals of a new play in New York[5] but I am spending as much time up here as I possibly can. In any case, do let me know if there is any possibility of our seeing you. And my homage and regards please to your wife.

Yours most faithfully,   [Archie MacLeish]

TL-C: M

1. Adlai Stevenson had died on July 14. 2. Burton and Elizabeth Taylor, the acting couple, Stevenson, and the MacLeishes had dined together at Stevenson's New York apartment in 1961. 3. "The American Bell," a sound-and-light show with text by M, music by David Amram (who had written the music for M's *J.B.*), and narrated by Fredric March, was first produced in Philadelphia on 4 July 1962. 4. *Who's Afraid of Virginia Woolf?* 5. M's play *Herakles*, starring Rosemary Harris as Megara, was coproduced by the University of Michigan Professional Theatre Program and the APA Repertory Company of New York. Casting and rehearsals took place at the APA-Phoenix Theatre in New York; the play opened at the University of Michigan's Mendelssohn Theatre on 27 October 1965 and ran through November 7. *Herakles: A Play in Verse* was published by Houghton Mifflin Company in June 1967.

To John Dos Passos

Dear Dos: 29 March [1968] Conway

What have we come to — writing on wrapping paper![1] But at least we're back from the Land of Aloha which is a good land to be back from, and in the mountains of old mail and Christmas cards was yours to remind us. How this life goes *BY!* Here I am going on for 76 and feeling not much different from the way I've always felt and yet the companions — where are they? Gerald and Ernest and Cummings and Scott and poor Sadie in a troubled dream and all the rest. You & we should somehow make our way to each other while there's someone left to find. The way I know I'm really old is the world — it's an old man's world to me — far worse than the one I knew forty years ago. (But what bothers me is that the young think so too: *NO* one loves *this* world.) Uxmal was a comfort. Time is so old there I felt somehow like a child — falsely like a child. Every now & then I read in the 42nd Parallel and savor the words. Love to you all — & to *you,* old friend

Archie

ALS: ViU

1. M's letter was written on a large brown sheet of personalized stationery, a Christmas gift from his friends Robert and Adèle Lovett.

To Dean Acheson

Dear Dean: 6 April 1968 [Conway?]

Forgive me for writing you on wrapping paper. It somehow suits the time — not *you,* dear lad.

I was glad to read your views of Vietnam as of III/26. I don't see how anyone who reads the papers could disagree with you. It's a war we never meant to get into and don't know how to get out of and the country has been increasingly sick of it for months. Not only the country either: a great part of the world — the whole world perhaps except China which is the only nation to gain by it. *How* we disengage is another question. I'd love to hear your views of that.

But your letter & your memorandum have different tones.

Johnson's $\begin{cases} \text{withdrawal} \\ \text{resignation} \\ \text{what do you call it} \end{cases}$ which you deplore in your letter may

help in the disengagement which you so persuasively recommend in your memorandum. And *will* it hand the country to Nixon? May it not have an equally unpalatable political consequence in a different direction? I don't know — don't even trust my hopes. Another weekend like this & we'll elect Wallace!

Ada has written Alice to ask if we can come down for May 3 & 4. I am speaking at Johns Hopkins (the first Milton Eisenhower Lecture) on the afternoon of the 3rd & I'll get a drive-yourself in Baltimore and come down after dinner at Linc Gordon's.[1]* [*MacLeish wrote in the margin:* *that is, if you can have us at Sandy Spring.] Don't let them twist your arm into coming to the lecture. The last thing you want to

425

hear is my views on the giant's heart or the duck's egg or the church
well!!   My love to the two of yez   Archie

ALS: CtY

1. Lincoln Gordon, president of The Johns Hopkins University.

To Eliza Howe Keith[1]

Darling Lidy: 25 June 1968 [Conway]

A beautiful and loving and true letter — true for those who can test
its truth where Keats tested his: on the pulses — true for you. To me,
and increasingly as I approach it, death is a reason to love life — and
the more so the more death it is. Which doesn't mean that death to me
is obliteration: we are all living proofs, existing as we do in the echo
of other lives, that it isn't. *Life* continues — and not only continues
but intends something, moves toward something. Not merely a brief
green fire — a spontaneous combustion on a whirling planet in a vast
night — but a journey *toward*. Toward what, I don't pretend to know
but, touching occasionally great souls — yours, I guess. I guess! As for
Baskin: I wrote that foreword to tell him he *didn't* believe what I think
he did. He has since written words in the Massachusetts Review which
seem to say he agrees.[2] I go to Hollywood (!) Thursday for five days.
Back July 2. We must meet soon after.

                         dear love to you always   Archie

ALS: KEITH

1. A neighbor and friend of the MacLeishes', Mrs. Keith had recently written to
acknowledge M's gift to her of a copy of the sculptor Leonard Baskin's *Figures of
Dead Men* ([Amherst?]: University of Massachusetts Press, 1968), to which M had
contributed a preface. 2. Baskin's comments had appeared in *The Massachusetts
Review* 9 (Winter 1968).

To Richard M. Nixon

Dear Mr. President: [26 June 1969] [Conway?]

Mr. William Safire[1] has told me of the honor you propose to do me
in requesting that I write a poem on the occasion of the July moon-
landing. I am most grateful for your thought of me in such a connection and at such a time.

I am also, as I am sure you will understand, somewhat aghast. To be
asked by the President of the United States to compose a poem on a
great public event is to be asked, in a sense, to speak for the Republic
and the burden of such a responsibility would be very heavy indeed.
I should be happy to undertake the task — particularly happy to under-

take it at your suggestion — but I would find it almost impossible to perform if I undertook it as a public burden. Poems are unpredictable enough when approached in private.

I am therefore writing you this note — I hope you will forgive the intrusion on your time — to ask if I may regard your letter when it comes as a personal and confidential communication to me for my private encouragement in this difficult labor. Should a poem result — doubtful in the brief time remaining — and should you wish to see it I will happily send you a copy.[2]

May I also thank you for the very great honor you did me in quoting from my *Reflections* on the Apollo Eight mission in your Inaugural address.[3] It did not seem fitting for me to write you at the time but I was very much moved & I should like to say so.

faithfully and respectfully yours,
Archibald MacLeish

FDr: M

1. Special assistant to the President. 2. M's poem "Voyage to the Moon" appeared on page one of *The New York Times* of 21 July 1969, which page also carried the historic headline MEN WALK ON MOON. 3. M's essay "A Reflection: Riders on Earth Together, Brothers in Eternal Cold" had appeared on page one of *The New York Times* of 25 December 1968, which page also reported the circumlunar flight of *Apollo 8*. President Nixon had quoted from it in his inaugural address of 20 January 1969.

To Dean Acheson

Dear Dean: 5 May 1970 [Conway]

As Western Union told you — that makes it unanimous. The National Book Award doesn't count. It is a publishers' racket and the plaque I believe to be brass: I haven't had it assayed.[1] But the important thing remains, of course, the book itself.[2] That *lasts* — and will. You have raised your own monument.

Kingman[3] is regarded in these parts as having had something very close to a triumph: certainly Yale is at the top of all the leagues in all categories. Bill (Peter) says the University has never been as substantially unified as it is this week — something Harvard has yet to achieve. But, as everyone is agreed, Kingman had more than his just share of luck. Who could have foreseen that the preposterous Spirochete[4] would call for his ouster? [. . .]

So much to talk about. I wish we were within talking range. The President's twenty-two minutes on television the other night were the most embarrassing I have ever lived through. The total inadequacy of the man as man, to say nothing of President, was so nakedly obvious that I kept wanting to turn the thing off out of shame. And at that time I didn't know the half of it. I believed him when he said there was a great and dangerous enemy build-up in the sanctuaries! Now, of course, it appears there is simply no enemy there worth body-counting.

From the top of this hill the whole thing looks like a fraud — and not even a new fraud — the same old fraud we have been buying for how many years. I'm scared. Not of the Viet-cong or the stockmarket or the Ohio National Guard or the Black Panthers but of Mr. Nixon. Have you any comfort?

I'm hammering out a second draft of the play.[5] The first one pleased the producer & director[6] more than I had dared hope & the reworking is largely for my own satisfaction. Which is a lovely mood in which to rework!   Yours ever   Archie

ALS: CtY

1. M had won the award in 1953 for his *Collected Poems, 1917–1952*. 2. Acheson's *Present at the Creation* (New York: W. W. Norton, 1969) had just been awarded a Pulitzer Prize for history. 3. Kingman Brewster, president of Yale University. 4. A scornful reference to Vice President Spiro Agnew, who had recently attacked Brewster for expressing skepticism that black radicals could get a fair trial anywhere in the United States. 5. *Scratch*, a prose play suggested by, and based on, Stephen Vincent Benét's short story "The Devil and Daniel Webster," was produced in Boston and on Broadway in May 1971 and published in November 1971 by Houghton Mifflin Company. 6. Stuart Ostrow and Peter Hunt, respectively.

To Julian P. Boyd

Dear Julian: 21 May 1970   Conway

As though we had been writing each other every day — though it's true there are few days when, in one way or another, I *don't* think of you. (Do you ever wish you'd said Yes to FDR?)

But I mustn't start that. I have a problem you, & perhaps you alone, might find interesting. Suppose you were looking for damned men among the American dead — and suppose you wanted damned men whose damnation would have meaningful modern significance as, e.g. Charles Lynch of Virginia whose passion for LawandOrder was equal to Mr. Mitchel's[1] and whose disregard for legal *procedure* and for *other* men's ideas of order were almost as great. Whom would you think of and where would you turn for nominations? Would you include Burr — not for his undoubted treason, or for his apparently cold-blooded execution of Hamilton, but for that so-modern combination of viciousness and charm? I am hopelessly lost among questions such as these. I keep thinking of the man (men?) responsible for the hanging of the three Quaker women on the Common of a little Massachusetts town named Boston. But, apparently, we know nothing about that hanging but the fact that it took place.

As you have guessed by now I am at work on a new play. What I need, as you see, is to be headed toward lines and channels of research — or, more simply, of reading. Two months of thrashing around on my own have produced nothing but a clutter of obvious* [*MacLeish* wrote in the margin: *e.g. "Damaged Souls" by Gamaliel Bradford. !!!!] (and useless) titles. Write me a post card with *a* title on it: By This Gate Enter. Love to you both.   Archie

ALS: NjP

1. John N. Mitchell, President Nixon's attorney general and political adviser.

To Dorothy de Santillana[1]

Dear Dorothy: 7 October 1970 [Conway]

Apparently you didn't get a letter I sent you last week as your last letter is dated October 5th. However, that letter did not cover the questions you ask. It did say that I think of the selection of poems as a book which Houghton Mifflin could very well do although I have no way of knowing whether it would be commercially viable. I should think it would have a brief foreword in which the basis of selection was stated: the poems I find myself reading to audiences as I go about the country, etc. etc. Precisely how many there would be I don't know but I could readily hazard a guess on paper if that would be useful. Let me know and I will do what you ask as quickly as I can.[2]

As for *Scratch*, there has been a completely new draft since the draft you now have and that completely new draft is now in process of alteration — mostly minor alterations but important notwithstanding. There will then be the changes made during rehearsal as we begin to see how the thing actually sounds when spoken by actors. Rehearsals start November 2, we move onto a stage early in December and we begin preview performances (we are going to stay in New York and not go on the road) about the 21st of December, opening on January 7th.

Translating these various dates and plans into script terms, I should say I would have finished major rewriting by the date you name — by the end of November. However, there will certainly be some changes when we first face audiences and the question is whether they will be important enough so that we should postpone publication. Since I am quite happy about the play as it stands and fairly adamant about responding to the whims and whams of every actor, I do think we would be fairly safe to count on the end of November date, but the real decision will have to be yours on the basis of the above facts. And the above facts may not turn out to be final facts, as you know. For one thing, we have not yet cast Webster.

Now as to Bob Dylan. He proved to be simply incapable of producing new songs, and things looked desperate until Ostrow decided about a month ago to use old songs of Dylan's in spite of the fact that songs on Broadway are all supposed to be new. For one thing the old songs are more to our purpose since Dylan has now entered advanced middle age, being almost 30 and no longer fiery: for another, they are far better than anything he is now doing. The published form of the play should, of course, include reference to the Dylan songs but this reference is going to be fairly hard to draft. The play is not a "musical": it is *a* play *with* songs by Dylan.[3] Actually the songs will be sung by a balladeer — a more or less hippy type — and will be heard between scenes. That is to say, there will be no singing in the play itself.

I have already written you about the question of the terms of the contract between Ostrow and the Benet estate. As I understand a letter from Ostrow's lawyer, I am not at liberty even to sign a contract for publication until after the play has run a number of nights on Broadway. But your legal people will know far better than I do about all that.

Dear Love from us both.   Archie

TLS: HMCO

1. M's editor at Houghton Mifflin Company. **2.** The book under discussion was published by Houghton Mifflin Company in November 1972 under the title *The Human Season: Selected Poems, 1926–1972.* **3.** Dylan eventually withdrew from the production, and the idea of using songs in the play was dropped. Some of the songs Dylan had written for the play, including "New Morning" and "Father of Night," appeared on his recording entitled *New Morning* (1970).

To the Editor of The New York Times

Sir: 10 May 1971   Conway

There has been some discussion in your columns and elsewhere of the procedures by which new plays are certified for public consumption in the United States. A recent case history may be relevant.

On May 6 a new play of mine opened in New York. The New York Times of the following morning carried an announcement by its drama critic, Mr. Clive Barnes, that the play had failed (his word).[1] Thereupon, and without waiting for other reviews, Mr. Stuart Ostrow, producer of the play, decided he had no choice but to close. Not out of respect for Mr. Barnes' authority as a critic but out of respect for his employment by The Times. Mr. Ostrow is a brave man but he is also a veteran of the New York theater. He had no doubt that it would be quixotic to attempt to continue in the face of a damning review in the most influential newspaper in the city, to say nothing of the country. And Mr. Barnes' review was damning: as damning as a man of his talents could make it.

All this raises a question of greater importance than the fate of my play. If it is the authority of the New York Times which confers on a single individual the power of life or death in the American theater is not the Times itself involved in the exercise of that power? To put it bluntly, does not that individual under those circumstances speak *for* the Times? A man who has established his own position as critic is one thing: his opinions need not involve his paper. He speaks for himself as Brooks Atkinson spoke for himself. But a critic without position of his own is something else. He speaks for his paper whether his paper likes it or not because there is nothing else he can speak for.

And the result, whether or not his paper likes it, can be confusing to readers. Take the present instance. The issue with which my play concerned itself was the issue which divided New England in the decade before the Civil War and which divides the country again today. On the one side the Boston Abolitionists who were ready to tear the Union apart in the name of freedom; on the other, Webster and his Whigs who were determined to preserve the Union even though it meant the preservation of slavery as well. On the one side the young protesters in Washington a few days ago; on the other the brutal rhetoric of the Attorney General of the United States. To Emerson — see his Journal for May 1851 — this was a great moral issue. To me and to many others it still is. Not so to Mr. Barnes: his awkward word for it was "pseudo-moral" — not up to Broadway standards.

The Times is a great liberal newspaper with a deep sense of the American past. Does it relish the taste of Mr. Barnes' cynicism in its mouth? For this word, believe me, is spoken *by* the Times. There is no other speaker.   truly yours   Archibald MacLeish

TL-C: M

1. Clive Barnes, "Theater: 'Scratch' Opens," *The New York Times*, 7 May 1971, page 50.

To Ranald H. Macdonald, Jr.

Dear Ranald: [c. March 1972] [Antigua]

   I am a Hell of a correspondent and I apologize. I too read the piece about Pound in the Sunday Times a month ago.[1] [. . .] Pound is an historical curiosity. He is, unquestionably, the greatest single influence on modern poetry in English in this century but there is considerable question about his own status as a poet. Leaving aside his translations it is hard to name a single poem of his which will stand up as a poem. Maybe *Hugh Selwyn Mauberley* — but only maybe. There are wonderful passages in the *Cantos* but the *Cantos*, as a work, don't make it. Which sends us back to the translations — particularly the Chinese. Some of these are really good (though not as good as Waley's) and there are even a few which may be said to owe more to Pound than to the original poet. Add that all up and what do you get? A man of letters who is certain of a place in history. But a poet? As poet he is simply not in the same class as Yeats. After all, the work of a poet is to make *poems*.

Our other subject is Dean[2] and there I must beg your understanding. The project to use Dean's death as the occasion for a money-raising drive bothers me in principle. I know it is the kind of thing which is done — and not only at Yale. But is it a good thing to do? A right thing? And that — with me — is not the only question. If such a campaign is to be run I should be one of the principal contributors. But I am at that point in my professional life at which I can do less and less in the direction of gifts and contributions. We live on my income from royalties and readings and articles (the entire income from my investments goes to pay income tax) and royalties, readings etc yield less and less as I grow older. (The murder of *Scratch*, my last years play, was a financial disaster which will affect my earning power for a long time.) So I simply can't contribute a large amount to the fund in Dean's name. Not even what would look like a moderate gift to people in the money world. All I can say is that I will do what I can but that I shall be embarrassed by the check. Please do try to understand.

But I know you will. Anyway, to get back to your letter — I am in great shape. People at Mill Reef fall off with prostate and aneurism and what not, but me — I still weigh 165 and swim a four-beat fifty and though my eyes are dim my heart is bold. I'll pray as you suggest but vote for Nixon!?!?!? Can you really mean it after the disasters of the year just past? (Answer: you can!) Milton Eisenhower, who left a few weeks ago, told me that if "we" (the Dimmikrats) nominated a half-way decent man he'd go to work for him himself. Let that be your text for the day. Love to Anne   yours ever   Archie

TLS: MACDONALD

1. Alan Levy, "Ezra Pound's Voice of Silence," *The New York Times Magazine*, 9 January 1972, page 14.   2. Dean Acheson had died on 12 October 1971.

To Ranald H. Macdonald, Jr.

Christmas Day [1973]   [Antigua]

Dear Ranald (Clan Ranald) the jury impanelled . . .

> what's the matter with Ranald as a name?
> did you like it when they called you Mac?
> and have you ever thought of Archibald? as a *name?*

What I like about your letter of December 5, received December 25, is the way you are softening. Not in the head, the heart. You are realizing as your life ripens that you are shot with luck, and its good for you. But what is all this gloom about the future? By the future do you mean the future of the stock market? The stock market no longer means anything. If you had a thermometer that went up and down like that you'd put a match to the bulb. I think the prospects for the Republic are hopeful. The wave of indignation which has swept the country with the revelation of Nixon's lies and frauds and nasty indecencies proves that we still respect the truth. Which means that we may well become a great people again. And as for the oil shortage — that has been imminent for years: now we are going to have to face up to it and the result can only be good. The lousy "age of affluence" which produced Los Angeles and Las Vegas and the crowded highways and all those billion acres of cement is over — to say nothing of the suburb civilization which went with it. We are going to begin to live like human beings again — to save the planet — to restore our souls — to build beautiful cities and to keep the earth for living. I think for myself we are well past the worst — the vulgarities and dishonesties of the last ten years: the future has to be better & it will

affly yrs as ever & always   A.

ALS: MACDONALD

To Richard B. McAdoo[1]

Dear Dick: 16 June 1974   Conway

Thank you for your nice letter. I am delighted by the suggestion that you might feel like heading west when the wind from the hills tempts you. We'd love to provide lunch under the apple tree for you and the companion of the voyage. Also, although I have nothing urgent on my mind there is a great deal to talk *about* — I mean, a great deal you & I ought some day to talk about at leisure. I am now, as I have been all spring, deep in a "play for voices" about the Bicentennial which will be done live at Pittsburgh next winter and then, I hope, put on the radio channels.[2] I won't try to describe it here but I want to some time. Also I have the beginning of a new book of poems, a dozen of which I read, at the New York Historical [Society], for the Academy of American Poets a month ago. They went well enough to make me wish the play was done. But it will be — should be — in three or four weeks. And finally there is the prose book Austin & I talked about. I wanted to make it out of the Op-Ed pieces and other articles of the years since [A] *Continuing Journey*[3] — a sort of private history of a critical decade. Evan Thomas's idea might give it its "slant" but I'm dubious about an attempt to deal with values only: that might end up as something too close to a sermon. I'd like to be personal — even, to some extent, autobiographical — not a Voice.[4] Try to come west some time in July or August if you can.   Until then   Archie

ALS: HMCO

1. Dorothy de Santillana's successor as M's editor at Houghton Mifflin. Austin (Olney) and Evan Thomas, also mentioned in this letter, were, respectively, editors at Houghton Mifflin Company and at W. W. Norton & Company, Inc. 2. *The Great American Fourth of July Parade*, a play M had been invited to write in 1973 by Samuel Hazo, president and director of the Pittsburgh-based International Poetry Forum. It was first presented, under Forum auspices, in April 1975 at Pittsburgh's Carnegie Hall and was published that month by the University of Pittsburgh Press. 3. A collection of essays published by Houghton Mifflin Company in November 1967. 4. The book that eventually emerged was published in April 1978 as *Riders on the Earth: Essays and Recollections*.

To Edward Hoagland

Dear Ted: 7 September 1974   Conway

I was delighted with your letter — above all, delighted to get it. George [Plimpton]'s guess (what a considerate man he is!) was right and wrong. My feelings *were* bruised but not by what you wrote, by what you didn't write. By your silence in answer to my long letter about your book.[1] And even that is now healed: I gather from your last that my letter never reached you. It was mailed, as I recall it, to you in care of your publisher and publishers are most public-relations bastards: they regard letters to their authors as potential quotes or nothing. In which latter case they treat them accordingly.

I think I can remember what I said. The main theme, developed at length, was that I liked the book immensely — above all the style which seemed to me the first real advance in English style since *In Our Time*. Minor observations related to two matters of minor importance, about which I had some personal knowledge, where your powers of "seeing" had, I thought, failed you. One was your attribution of certain mannerisms of mine which you didn't like to the fact that I had spent some years in Washington.[2] I reminded you that there are more ways than one to keep yourself to yourself. When you are young it is possible to hide. When you get older and are caught up in life — particularly if you love life and want to live it — you have to be out on the street: and your only safeguard there is the persona — what Yeats was always writing about. A lot of academic critics who spend their lives in the stacks at Widener or elsewhere regard Yeats's concern with the mask as something peculiar to him, or to Ireland, or to the Troubles or God knows what else. They simply don't understand what he was talking about. Remember "Among School Children"? Read it again. You were talking (writing) more or less in those terms and I told you I thought it was bad observation. As a matter of fact I know it was — and so will you as the world closes around Ted Hoagland — as I believe and hope it will. Life has to come first — should come first. But you now know who you are and you'll find yourself protecting that Who. Perhaps not in the way I have over the past thirty or forty years, but protecting it notwithstanding.

The other minor matter was de Gaul[l]e. There you were simply ignorant. He was a pompous self-imposing fraud whose contribution to the liberation of France was to put obstacles of amour propre and naked vanity in the way of our people and the British. Believe me I know what I am talking about: I heard Churchill and FDR talking about him more than once and Harry Hopkins on that subject was eloquent as a silver trumpet. I have also the unwilling witness of Malraux, an old friend and an honest man, who ended fed to the cars. E.H., six years younger than I, once volunteered the advice (when I attempted a poem about skiing) "Never write about anything you don't know about *yourself!*". It's still good advice. I hand it on to a beloved young friend.   yours   Archie

Flaubert, in Flaubert's way, said the same thing in wholly different terms in a letter to George Sand sometime in December 1867. "What form should one take to express occasionally one's opinion on the things of the world without the risk of passing later for an imbecile? It is a tough problem. It seems to me that the best thing is simply to depict the things which exasperate one . . .". He was writing about Thiers. Characteristic escape isn't it? Simply depict. Let the depiction stand for itself — speak for itself. Don't judge. But that's precisely why Flaubert is a great writer but not a great artist. Tolstoy judges from one end of War and Peace to the other. Dante judges. Shakespeare who is supposed never to judge judges life itself — all of it. *You* set Flaubert to one side and judged. Which was right. The trouble was you didn't *know*. Didn't know *yourself*. God keep you looking and looking.

A

TLS: HOAGLAND

1. Hoagland's *Walking the Dead Diamond River* (New York: Random House, 1973). 2. See "The Assassination Impulse" in *Walking the Dead Diamond River*, pages 109–110.

To Julian P. Boyd

Dear old Julian: 20 September [1974] Conway

If I have been in your mind you have dominated mine. I have just finished, after almost ten months without interruption, an hour's play for radio (verse play) on the paradox of the bicentennial of self-government in the slough of Nixon which ends with John Adams' last words.[1] At every page I have asked myself, dear friend, if you would nod your head or no. When I have a fair copy I'll send it on the chance you would have a free half-hour to read it. I think your American Philosophical project admirable. The belief in man (for what else is the Declaration?) is the nightmare of knowledge. Another superstition to be outgrown? Or an old dream coming painfully true? Knowing what we now think we know of the inevitable end of the earth — of the sun — how can man any longer matter? And if not man, then how his liberty (is his liberty conceivable?) — how his happiness? In brief: Who dares to hope? And the answer, of course, is *Man*. Up the continuing revolution ("in some parts sooner, in others later").[2] I obey your command of silence and await your word. And I send you both my love

Archie

ALS: NjP

1. "Thomas Jefferson still lives." 2. An approximation of a phrase occurring in Jefferson's letter of 24 June 1826 to Roger C. Weightman.

To Anthony Piccione[1]

Dear Tony: 22 November [1974] Conway

That is a beautiful letter: a work of heart and hence of art: "tenderness, link to the race and to the planet". You have a tone, a resonance, like that of Georges Sand whose letters to Flaubert I had been reading when we met. You trust yourself — which is the great achievement — particularly for a poet. There is a school (academy rather) of criticism which asserts what it calls the "autonomy of the poem". Which means, if it means anything, that a poem writes itself — bubbles up out of the subconscious. But this, of course, is a delusion. Poems are written by poets as paintings are painted by painters. There is a man — a woman — involved in the process. If the man is Keats you get a poem *by* Keats. If the man is a Freudian critic you get a poem *by* a Freudian critic. Which means that this tone of yours is important to your work. Your confidence in yourself is important to your work. *You* are important to your work. Don't be afraid to take charge of your life — of your work: you are capable of it. Don't be afraid to BE poet — a maker. The subconscious will play its part (which is negative — a veto — a sudden surge of consent — consent to *you*)[.] You have earned the right. You have the power of love. God keep you — yrs ever

Archie MacLeish

ALS: PICCIONE

1. A poet and professor of English at the State University of New York College at Brockport, where M had recently given a talk and reading

To William Heyen[1]

Dear Bill: 11 March 1975 [Antigua]

I am *indeed* interested. It's really good news — consecutive publications are like consecutive rains in a dry year: they start the springs. You have the kind of nature which will produce and go on producing. Yeats said that what matters is to survive and for once he used the wrong word. Survival doesn't mean a thing: what does is *making* life, not keeping alive. You can see it with all the marked men: the voice isn't there at the start; it develops as the work piles up. Yeats's voice is only an occasional hint before Responsibilities. Pound's is as unsure as the cracked voice of an adolescent boy before Hugh Selwyn Mauberley. It takes Frost half a lifetime to lose the New England twang he wasn't born to. You will wake one morning after a half dozen books with a cadence the ear catches before it catches the sense and people will say: Listen! I'd know Bill Heyen's voice anywhere. And when that happens you'll begin listening yourself — you'll know yourself as maybe you don't yet. It's terribly important all this. The art of poetry has somehow fallen among the deaf, which means it is only half an art. The deaf read it on the page and think they have the meaning: all they have is the translation of a meaning they can never hear. Your generation is going to have to undo the mischief — your generation and you, I would guess, among the first. I am overrunning with good wishes for you but they are also good wishes for the art which needs whole poets again — men who know that "to capture Heaven and Earth in the

437

cage of form"[2] you have to weave the house of sight and sense with sound to catch the wonder. Forgive a lecture not asked for. [. . .] Love to Han[3] and the kids and you and Tony. I have a hurting heart: I need your friendship — all of you   Archie

TLS: HEYEN

1. A poet and professor of English at the State University of New York College at Brockport. 2. M discusses this phrase by the ancient Chinese poet Lu Chi in *Poetry and Experience* (Boston: Houghton Mifflin Company, 1961), pages 3–20. 3. Hannelore (Mrs. William) Heyen.

To Helen E. Ellis[1]

Dear Helen: 2 May 1975   Conway

Tossing notions in my sleep I've come more or less to the conclusion that the trouble lies in the relation between your proposal and me. I am the subject, not to say the object, and the consequence could be embarrassment to me and irritation to the bureaucrats, all of which, or most of which, would disappear if I were made the means and if the object were learning, broadly defined. Meaning not "research" into *me* but into certain aspects of human experience over the past fifty years with which I have been involved and which *my* experience might illuminate.

Why *me*? For two reasons: because I happened to be caught up one way or another in several critical aspects of those years, and because I am still alive. To which I should perhaps add a third consideration: that I have, throughout this period, and regardless of whatever else I undertook, labored at the art of poetry which is the art of attempting to make sense of human experience. I have left, in other words, a record of sorts behind me — a record which might, occasionally, have something to say.

Let me be specific as to these aspects of experience. I was born into an entirely different America from the one we live in, and I began writing in an awareness of that America. I knew the First World War at first hand: a year in France in the field artillery — and I wrote some very bad and a few still readable poems that belong peculiarly to that war. Thereafter I was a spy in the camps of the Egyptians — a teacher of law and a practising lawyer and therefore a small and insignificant figure on the frontier where the new American system and the beginnings of "modern poetry" met each other: there are lines about that — quite a lot of them. Then I dropped everything, took my small family and my non-income to Paris and lived there for five or six years in a world which seems for some reason to excite the insatiable curiosity of the contemporary young. What was important about all that was not the "expatriates" (I never met one) or the "lost" generation (we were no more lost than any other) but the extraordinary burst of creative energy in Paris with young artists and composers and poets and writers from all over the world, some of whom I knew. After that when the economic collapse hit us all I had almost a decade as an "editor" of *Fortune* spending most of my time on trips all over the country and abroad to Asia and Europe and South America — an unusual graduate course in the Depression, in the beginnings of fascism, in Marxist economics — most of all in the Republic itself, its kind, its true quality, its underlying nature — all of which left its record not only in Fortune but in verse — a rather lengthy record.

That ended with seven or eight years of public service beginning with the Library of Congress of which I was director (Librarian of Congress) for five years during which the entire library was reorganized. This involved a war of words with the professional librarians who were, at first, violently opposed to my appointment for very understandable reasons, and then a continuing struggle, with the professional librarians on my side, to reshape the institution and, to some degree, the profession. There is, needless to say, no record of this in poems but there is an extended record in speeches, articles etc. etc. (*Champion of a Cause*)[2] which raises a great many issues which are still unfinished business in our, if you will pardon the expression, civilization.

Early in this period we entered the Second World War and I was instructed by the President to take on additional duties (work on speeches in the White House, beginnings of a ministry of information (Office of Facts and Figures)) which produced, again, a body of speeches and articles and involved me in ructions with the America Firsters, the Chicago Tribune, the Fulton Lewises and so on down the line. There is, however, a long poem at the end, when FDR died and I resigned as Assistant Secretary of State, which tries to put all this into a perspective of sorts. Also, during this period (no, before Pearl Harbor) I published *The Irresponsibles*[3] which took the academic community and many of my friends among the writers, to task for their failure to see that the Second World War was not the First all over again and that Fascism *had* to be stopped. This precipitated a real verbal war of which the record is scattered over the next many years. The issue, in fact, is still very much alive.

After that, and after the war ended, I was appointed Chairman of the American Delegation to the London U.N. Conference which established UNESCO and wrote the preamble to the Constitution of Unesco. Here too there is a body of prose pieces dealing with issues which are still very much with us.

Then comes my appointment as Boylston Professor at Harvard and the work which took me into literary criticism — specifically *Poetry and Experience* etc.

What this all comes down to is that there is a considerable body of material in prose and, more importantly, in verse dealing with aspects of poetic and political and economic and moral issues which are by no means of merely historic interest, and that there is, still alive and in really good shape, an old character over here on a hill, who might well be willing to discuss points of difficulty with scholars young or old who had mastered the written materials and wanted to push the discussion farther. How much time he could give would depend on how busy he was (and he plans to be good and busy) but something could certainly be worked out.

Now all this seems to me to make sense. You collect the materials, the materials attract the interested, and the interested have an opportunity (within reason) to consult the old codger when they know enough about the record to put the right questions.

But how this translates into a project to be *funded* I simply don't know. There would be materials to buy or secure copies of and there would perhaps be some recording to do but beyond that I have no inklings. Certainly I wouldn't want recompense for occasional conversations: all I would demand would be the intervention of some person or persons who would see to it that my work wasn't interfered with — because I plan to go on working full time as long as I can keep it up. Too much to DO! best AMacL

TLS: GCC

1. Professor Ellis, of Greenfield (Massachusetts) Community College, had been exploring with M ideas for grant funding for a series of taped interviews to be done by GCC students. The project, later refined and funded by the National Endowment for the Humanities, was completed with Professor Ellis and Professor Bernard Drabeck, also of GCC, as the interviewers. 2. M's *Champion of a Cause: Essays and Addresses on Librarianship* (Chicago: American Library Association, 1971). 3. *The Irresponsibles: A Declaration* (New York: Duell, Sloan & Pearce, 1940).

To Dorothy Van Doren[1]

Darling Dorothy: 23 November [1975]   Conway

What a lovely, lovely letter — like a touch of warm hands: ". . . to have pleased you in this tender way". Oh, Dorothy, my dear! my dear! Since you can say *that* you must know what it meant to us to find you — late — in the middle of our lives — but to find you. Mark was dearer to me than any brother — than any man I have ever known. I grieve for him still. I always shall until I come to the end too. And you have been and are and always will be a part of us. We love you.

Archie

ALS: VAN DOREN

1. The widow of the poet, critic, and teacher Mark Van Doren, who had died in December 1972. The Van Dorens had been regular visitors to the MacLeish home in Conway, Massachusetts, as the MacLeishes were to the Van Doren home in Falls Village, Connecticut.

To Richard Wilbur[1]

Dear Dick: 30 June 1976   Conway

"Crumple"! Good God, diamonds *can't* crumple. The heel that tried to step on *you* would make a hole of itself — and doubtless did in this case — I didn't see the event.[2] But I know, of course, what you mean. When my Selected Poems appeared — a critical moment in any man's life — a Harvard Square pundit who had declared a private war on me when I became the Boylston (God knows why: I'd never met him) put me firmly in my place in a New York Times review which drove Dorothy di Santillana out of publishing, or so she said.[3] It would have crumpled me but for the obvious malice. I dare say that's what you find bracing in your bugger — the malice. But whatever the explanation it's the bracing that will last. There are never more than a dozen poets — usually less — in any time. You are one of them and you know it. And this little event will end by serving to remind you.

The summer with us is like yours. Ken is in a trap of extreme pain from which there is no escape by drugs.[4] We think of little else. But we must meet sometime before fall, Charlee[5] and Ada and you and I. If we see a light under a door we'll call you. Try to come. Love to you both

Archie

ALS: WILBUR

1. American poet and translator (b. 1921). 2. Wilbur's verse collection *The Mind-Reader* had been unfavorably reviewed by Herbert Leibowitz in *The New York Times Book Review* of 13 June 1976. 3. M's *The Human Season: Selected Poems, 1926–1972* had been reviewed by John Malcolm Brinnin of Boston University in *The New York Times Book Review* of 19 November 1972. 4. M's elder son had been battling cancer for three years. He died in August 1977. 5. Mrs. Wilbur.

To Harry Levin

Dear Harry: 25 January 1978   [Bermuda]

Thirty years ago when I was trying to find my way into my new life as Boylston Professor you taught me, among other useful (essential) lessons, that if I wanted to know who ran Harvard, I should keep an eye on the face I shaved in the morning. It is a difficult lesson to remember now that I am sixteen years emeritus and wholly — totally — out of touch, but it has stood by me even so — as this letter proves. (Though I should never write it, even so, to anyone but you.)

Three or four years ago a young (to me) novelist moved in to the other end of our road. He was a Harvard graduate of the great (Bill Alfred) years after the Second War, an interesting novelist (*Dog Tags* etc.) who wrote not only well but with verve and life, a remarkable and civilized conversationalist, a truly well-read reader and a heroic sufferer, but never *victim*, of muscular dystrophe, which had floored him in his thirties. His name was (and is) Steve Becker. And he and his wife, Mary, became great friends of ours as those years went by.

I tell you about him not only because you would like him but because it gives me pleasure to think of you knowing each other and because recent events have proved him a remarkable teacher. He began, two years ago, teaching a course at Bennington which was an extraordinary success (Malamud can tell you all about it) and he has now been asked to join the Bennington faculty.

It is my increasing conviction that he belongs at Harvard and I enclose a document, received yesterday, as supporting evidence. It is in effect, though never so intended, a self-portrait. By which I mean that what has most impressed me about him is simply and naturally and gracefully *there*. It needn't come back to me: shouldn't — I have never talked to him about its subject.

I don't know what the situation of the writing courses at Harvard now is — only that if Steve had crossed my ken in the fifties I would have wanted him not only as a teacher of writing but (far more important) as a demonstration of what writing *is* — the one lesson undergraduates [. . .] never seem to learn. All this is what you know and care about and you will know, therefore, why Steve's letter about Montaigne–Hazlitt made me think of you.

My dear love to Elena. We are, as you see, in Bermuda — out of the winter but . . . where? But that's the trouble with growing old and living by the climate: what you *get* is the climate.

my love to you, dear and admired friend,   Archie

ALS: LEVIN

442

To Robert Fitzgerald[1]

Dear Robert   28 January 1978   Bermuda

A basket of posies for you. Two or three months ago Red [Robert Penn] Warren's lovely wife, Elinor, wrote me, as she may well have written you, that it was your *Odyssey* which helped her through those terrible months when she was losing her sight. When we got to Bermuda three weeks ago and found ourselves in a pleasant room cupped, like an ear, toward the Homeric surge, I began to read it aloud to Ada. I believe Elinor entirely. You have established a pure expectation in the ear like the expectation Pound too established but wholly different, wholly your own. It is not a "*trans*-lation" but something far better — a re-saying: the true get and heir of those wonderful plays you and Dudley [Fitts] remade a long generation ago. Admirable! Ada finally made me turn Kirkê back to Circe for her ear's sake and I understand why: Kirkê is indeed as beastly a sound as could be well imagined. I didn't myself mind it so much: After all, a Kelt myself, I have been subjected for years to a reverse indignity by a basket-ball team and I have put up with it.

I have one question if you ever have a moment free. In Book Eleven, line 330-odd, you have the King saying:

You told the Argive troubles and your own troubles
as a poet would — a man who knows the world.

This implies a definition of that often mis-read word which should be more remembered than it is — "a man who knows the world". If I call you to witness will you draw your unstained blade and respond?

a heart light with admiration   Archie (MacLeish)

ALS: FITZGERALD

1. Poet, translator, journalist (with *Time*, 1936–1949), and since 1965 Boylston Professor of Rhetoric and Oratory at Harvard.

To William Heyen

Dear Bill: 3 March [1978]   Conway

What I owe you! What a father owes a son for being young! I, eighty-six, wondering when the tragic year which left the golden boulder in Pine Hill Cemetary will finally end leaving me to myself and the work I think of as me — and you, barely a third of that, writing so easily, so hungrily, you worry about it. You're the elixir I need, my lad. Keep telling me.

Oh, I remember the feeling of too fast, too soon. I used to deal with it by never finishing anything until *it* had finished with *me*. I'd identify it somehow or other and put it away in a drawer and leave it there for months until I could read it as though for the first time and if, then, I had nothing to say to it I'd type it out, and if it could take *that*, I'd mail it off to Hither or Yon and wait for the proof with my heart in my mouth. That was always the great test — the temptation to rewrite it in proof. If I could master that it was indeed finished

I am enchanted by your account of Lord Dragonfly but I'm confused by the black dwarf image — specifically by the word "escapes". "But here . . ." (marvellous, homing phrase) "light escapes/even the blackberries". Escapes *them?* Escapes *from* them? I can't see. Probably neither, for nothing is as full of light as a blackberry. But what then "escapes"? It's far too good a glimpse to leave in doubt.

I read Robert Fitzgerald's Ulysses to Ada under the hum of the reef off the south shore of Bermuda. Elinor Warren wrote me that she had listened to it when she knew she was going blind. I can see why. It lacks the marvellous "said" quality of the plays Robert and Dudley Fitts wrote together — the absolute rhythmic rightness — but it is better than any other verse translation I know and it gave me a great gift. In Book Eleven after Odysseus has taken over as the poet of his own voyage and has told the tale of the landing on the foreshore of the dead and all that followed, Alkinoos, king of the Phaiakians, reassures him:

> "You speak with art, but your intent is honest.
> The Argive troubles, and your own troubles,
> you told as a poet would, a man who knows the world . . ."

That last line was like the bursting of a sun. "As a poet would, a man who knows the world". Of course, I said. What else is a great poet! A man who knows the world. Who else knows the world? Who else but Shakespeare, Dante, Homer himself. So I wrote Robert. Was this truly what Homer wrote? He replied that what Homer said "might simply be taken to mean 'a man knowing in the art of song'[.]" Whether he did not understand or did not want to I can't make out so I have written him again. What made him use the magnificent phrase he did? If he answers I will tell you, but whether he answers or not nothing will be quite the same again for I have now the word for it — a man who knows the world.

I breathe the breath of the new long poem. It is true that our lives have lost their dignity now they are released from those pools of manure under the old barns, those winters stained with yellow like an old man's beard. The subways have liberated us from the freezing cold and we carry the smell of them in our souls. That's why we rage at ourselves —

because we broke our nails for two hundred years to free our children and their mothers and at last ourselves from demeaning, unendurable[,] unending labor and now we are free and our freedom is unworthy of us. It is freedom *from* our selves, not *for* ourselves, and we can taste it in our mouths like rot in food. The whole "energy" business has been poisoned by it. It was by the use of machines that we "freed" our bodies and by buried coal and oil that we fed our machines and now we are told we must save our oil and our coal or find new forms of energy or go back to the old human burden — bondage — and we have the taste of ashes as we think about it — and refuse to think. Somehow we must reinvent a freedom which will be *truly* freedom and which we can earn. Somehow we must raise the body of the buried farmer. But we won't, you say — can't? — and you're right.

Typewriter tells me its time to stop.　　　love to you　　Archie

TLS: HEYEN

To Anthony Piccione

Dear Tony:　　　　　　　　　　　8 March 1978　Conway

Your true and singing letter of the 5th came in this morning and I answer it at once to assure you about the Depression of the Thirties. It will not come back. There are innumerable signs. For one, the squirrels have sewed their pockets up and moved out onto their front porches. For another the trout have found holes in the brook ice and are blowing bubbles. Also the sun has promised to appear between the shadows for a billion years. So all is well and will remain so until our bones are ground up by the glaciers which have not yet even begun to freeze. Only one thing troubles me about your plans for the future. You speak of dismantling your old personae. It is much better, as your poem is trying to tell you, to hang them out like old worksocks to dry. They will then be ready for you tomorrow when your new personae have unravelled. Al[1] tells me the good news of dragging anchors all sold and people digging around in the sand looking for their chains. Love to you all　　　　　　　　　　　　　　　Archie

ALS: PICCIONE

1. Alfred A. Poulin, Jr., a professor of English at Brockport and proprietor of a small press, BOA Editions, in that town. BOA Editions had recently published Piccione's first book, a verse collection called *Anchor Dragging*, to which M had contributed a foreword.

To Donald Hall

Dear Don: 12 March 1978   Conway

You have not only written a good book, you have invented a new kind, and the kind isn't "gossip".[1] It is direct, one-to-one observation reported with complete personal involvement and a candor which scares the living be-Jesus out of a projected subject as he reflects on his appearance, habits, conversation and general inadequacy![2] You have also devised a tone and a prose style which fit the task perfectly and read like pure delight. Where I know the tale of my own knowledge your accuracy astonishes. I wonder how many times that evening Dylan [Thomas] told the story of fucking all the girls up the street and back having fucked their mothers beforehand. He told me *before* his reading. By the way, speaking of fucking, I do *not* believe, for the best of all possible reasons, the story of Yeats's use of the word in News. It would have been rhythmically impossible for him at that stage, regardless of anything else.

Its a grand book & we thank you. I have nothing I can send you by way of gratitude — nothing to weigh as it weighs — but I want you to have the big sheet of *Night Watch*.[3] It is on its way. It was grand to meet Jane[4] and a wonderful renewal to see you again. My love to you both.   Archie

ALS: HALL

1. Hall's *Remembering Poets: Reminiscences and Opinions* (New York: Harper & Row, 1978).   2. An article by Hall entitled "Visiting the MacLeishes" appeared in *The New York Times Book Review* of 9 July 1978.   3. "Night Watch in the City of Boston," a poem commissioned by the City of Boston on the occasion of the U.S. Bicentennial and first read by M at the Boston Public Library on 16 April 1975. It appears in M's *New & Collected Poems, 1917–1976*, published by Houghton Mifflin Company in September 1976.   4. Jane Kenyon, wife of Donald Hall.

To Dorothy Van Doren

Dearest Dorothy: 12 December [1978]   [Conway?]

For a while I tried to get used to a world without Mark in it and then discovered what you, of course, would have known — that for those who loved him (and how many they were and are) there is no such world and never will be. I can't perhaps say to myself as I used to: "I know what Mark would think of *that*". But then I don't need to, because I know what he *would* have. No one in our time left as sure a print on the world as he. Which is one reason why I loved "Oh World, my friend, my foe . . ." There is, for me, a beautiful irony in that "impossible to know", for the world, as I feel it, is in great part available to me precisely *through* his knowing. But my part in all this is so small and yours is so great that I am embarrassed to speak of what I feel. And yet I have to if only to say that what I felt at first — an agonizing personal bereavement — is gone now, leaving me almost ashamed. For I know as surely as if he had told me himself, that I still have, and always will, that arc of friendship — true arc — which you and Mark and Ada and I made together over those long October years. It exists now, of itself and in itself, and will continue to exist somewhere, somehow, even when the last of us is gone. We know, Ada and I, what we owe and to whom and we send you our gratitude. Our sympathy too. Our sorrow in your sorrow and in our own. But most of all our gratitude. For the enrichment of our lives. We love you.

Archie

TLS: VAN DOREN

To Alice Acheson

Dearest Alice: 29 April 1980 [Conway?]

You are a wise and lovely lady. I resorted to the truth as you tactfully suggested and told the Social Secretary that our trouble was, and will continue to be, advancing age.[1] *You* will never grow old but you have to agree that others do. A trip on Allegheny can reduce Ada to total exhaustion and me to total rage and if you multiply the trip by two to get you home again and add a White House reception standing on one foot and then the other, the consequences can last a week. I'm sure somebody meant to be kind but kindness can kill. Particularly when you are eighty-eight which I will shortly be.

Not that we haven't been lucky — Ada and I. I am still working which is the key to everything and neither Ada nor I has been seriously ill. But Ada did have long periods of exhaustion last summer when she couldn't see even her dearest friends, including sometimes me. But her friends understood and I learned to and this year things are better. I think we have come out on the other side in a way. Meaning that we love each other more than we ever did when we loved each other most. We know what you know too but in a deeper way — what it is to have each other. You have learned the hardest way: we the other. It is you that knows. We talk of it often when we talk of you — which is often. I wish you knew how much we love you. How we long to see you.

Give David and Pat our love. We had wonderful hours with them a year ago. And our dear love to you. Archie

TLS: ACHESON

1. The MacLeishes had been invited to a reception for writers to be given at the White House by President and Mrs. Carter.

To Barbara Tuchman[1]

Dear Barbara: 28 July [1980] Conway

The affection was (& is) real and the hug was intended: thank you for permitting it! Also the question is and long has been (to me) fascinating — "Is that a conscious change?" There is some very impressive evidence that it is:

Paul Valéry: "Of two words, always choose the lesser".[2]

Pascal: "When we see a natural style we are surprised and delighted, for we thought to see an author and found a man".[3]

But are these lessons learned in old age? Arthur Waley writing of that marvelous poet, Po Chü-I, says "there is a story that he was in the habit of reading his poems to an old peasant woman and altering any expression she could not understand . . ."[4] This was when Po Chü-I was old and living in the Hsiang-shan monastery "collecting his complete works". But Keats was very young when he wrote his famous axiom "That if Poetry comes not as naturally as the Leaves to a tree it had better not come at all". And it was in the same letter (to John Taylor) he wrote: "I think Poetry should surprise by a fine excess and not by Singularity".[5]

It takes most servants of the art a long time to learn that last. Yeats was an Irish bard until *Responsibilities* changed him and he did not become a great poet until *Crazy Jane*. I myself think old age is the teacher and Keats the immortal exception — but Shakespeare is of course an exception to all exceptions and the whole ancient world thought Homer was old.

What you say about your own work is very fine but you must agree that you had, in *The Proud Tower*, a superb theme superbly handled. And even so I'm not sure you will always feel as you do now about the others. Wait till *you* are old!

How and when are we to see the Jefferson Lecture? I long to read that burst of enthusiasm for the experience of being human. You have W.S. with you there and most of the great Chinese, and Jefferson himself and John Adams in spite of the growling. I read your letter to Ada. We send you our love Archie

ALS: TUCHMAN

1. American historian (b. 1912). 2. From Paul Valéry's *Littérature* (Paris, 1929). 3. From Article One of Pascal's *Pensées* (1670). 4. From Arthur Waley's *A Hundred and Seventy Chinese Poems* (New York: Knopf, 1925). 5. From Keats's letter to Taylor of 27 February 1818.

To William Heyen

Dear Bill: 26 October [1981]   Conway

You are a good friend — about the best I can claim. At 89, the greater part of the world is unreal but not you — never you. I think Han must have a great deal to do with it. I've watched her watching you. (And you her). I like to think of it. Yours in the fog and the chill as well as the other days.   Archie

ALS: HEYEN

To William Heyen, Anthony Piccione, and Alfred A. Poulin, Jr.[1]

14 March 1982   Conway

To the three young poets of Brockport who appear with their magical works among these hills leaving no tracks except the tracks of their flowers, always too early for the sun. This was a supreme work: it was defined by its silence. Neither Ada nor I will ever forget that evening — feet through the crust on four-foot snow and a knock on the door and that luminous whiteness: whiteness everywhere [—] whiteness of snow — of flowers — of love. Love to the three of you.   Archie

ALS: HEYEN

1. In the winter of 1982, M had slipped on a patch of ice at his home in Conway and broken an elbow. Learning of the mishap, his three Brockport friends had arranged to have delivered to him at Conway, by messenger, a gift of flowers. A week after this letter was written M entered Massachusetts General Hospital in Boston for exploratory surgery unrelated to the ice mishap. There, on 20 April 1982, two and a half weeks before his ninetieth birthday, Archibald MacLeish died.

Index

NOTE: Boldface numerals indicate the page on which a letter to or by the person (or publication) cited begins. References to books, plays, poems, essays, and other works by Archibald MacLeish are cited under the heading *MacLeish, Archibald*.

About the type

The text of *Letters of Archibald MacLeish* has been set in linotype Baskerville, originally designed by the English printer, John Baskerville (1706–1775). The display type is foundry Palatino, designed in the 1950s by Herman Zapf.